# The Wikipedia Legends of the
# CIVIL WAR

## The Incredible Stories of the
## 75 Most Fascinating Figures
## from the War Between the States

Skyhorse Publishing

First Skyhorse Publishing edition 2019. All rights to any and all materials in copyright owned by the publisher are strictly reserved by the publisher. All inquiries should be addressed to Skyhorse Publishing, 307 West 36th Street, 11th Floor, New York, NY 10018.

Skyhorse Publishing books may be purchased in bulk at special discounts for sales promotion, corporate gifts, fund-raising, or educational purposes. Special editions can also be created to specifications. For details, contact the Special Sales Department, Skyhorse Publishing, 307 West 36th Street, 11th Floor, New York, NY 10018 or info@skyhorsepublishing.com.

Skyhorse® and Skyhorse Publishing® are registered trademarks of Skyhorse Publishing, Inc.®, a Delaware corporation.

Visit our website at www.skyhorsepublishing.com.

10 9 8 7 6 5 4 3 2 1

Library of Congress Cataloging-in-Publication Data is available on file.

ISBN: 978-1-5107-5540-6
eBook: 978-1-5107-5541-3

Cover design by Kai Texel

Printed in the United States of America

# Table of Contents

# Notes from The Editors

All content is used under the terms of the Creative Commons Attribution Share-Alike license (CC-BY-SA). The license is available for review at the following URL: https://creativecommons.org/licenses/by-sa/3.0/

Some articles have been modified; not every article includes the complete Wikipedia text. Articles have been edited to include the most Civil War-relevant information only.

All images are in the public domain unless otherwise noted. More information about each image can be found at the article URLs listed on page 520.

All citations, references, and footnotes for each article, including bibliographies and suggestions for further reading, are available online at the URLs listed on page 520.

# The Wikipedia Legends of the
# CIVIL WAR

# William T. Anderson

*Anderson, c. summer 1864*

**William T. Anderson**[a] (1840–October 26, 1864), known by the nickname "Bloody Bill" Anderson, was one of the deadliest and most notorious pro-Confederate guerrilla leaders in the American Civil War. Anderson led a band of volunteer partisan rangers who targeted Union loyalists and federal soldiers in the states of Missouri and Kansas.

Raised by a family of Southerners in Kansas, Anderson began supporting himself by stealing and selling horses in 1862. After his father was killed by a Union loyalist judge, Anderson fled to Missouri. There he robbed travelers and killed several Union soldiers. In early 1863 he joined Quantrill's Raiders, a group of pro-Confederate guerrillas which operated along the Kansas–Missouri border. He became a skilled bushwhacker, earning the trust of the group's leaders, William Quantrill and George M. Todd. Anderson's bushwhacking marked him as a dangerous man and eventually led the Union to imprison his sisters. When there was a building collapse in the makeshift jail and one of them died in custody and another permanently maimed, Anderson devoted himself to revenge. He took a leading role in the Lawrence Massacre and later participated in the Battle of Baxter Springs, both in 1863.

In late 1863, while Quantrill's Raiders spent the winter in Sherman, Texas, animosity developed between Anderson and Quantrill. Anderson, perhaps falsely, implicated Quantrill in a murder, leading to the latter's arrest by Confederate authorities. Anderson subsequently returned to Missouri as the leader of his own group of raiders and became the most feared guerrilla in the state, killing and robbing dozens of Union soldiers and civilian sympathizers. Although Union supporters viewed him as incorrigibly evil, Confederate supporters in Missouri saw his actions as justified, possibly owing to their mistreatment by Union forces. In September 1864, Anderson led a raid on the town of Centralia, Missouri. Unexpectedly, his men were able to capture a passenger train, the first time Confederate guerrillas had done so. In what became known as the Centralia Massacre, Anderson's bushwhackers executed 24 unarmed Union soldiers on the train and set an ambush later that day which killed more than a hundred Union militiamen. Anderson himself was killed in battle a month later. Historians have made disparate appraisals of Anderson: some see him as a sadistic, psychopathic killer, but for others his actions cannot be separated from the general desperation and lawlessness of the time.

## Quantrill's Raiders

*A photograph of William Quantrill, under whom Anderson served in 1863*

Missouri had a large Union presence throughout the Civil War, but was also inhabited by many civilians whose sympathies lay with the Confederacy. From July 1861 until the end of the war, the state suffered up to 25,000 deaths from guerrilla warfare, more than any other state.[24] Confederate General Sterling Price failed to gain control of Missouri in his 1861 offensive and retreated into Arkansas, leaving only partisan rangers and local guerrillas known as "bushwhackers" to challenge Union dominance.[25] Quantrill was at the time the most prominent guerrilla leader in the Kansas–Missouri area.[26] In early 1863, William and Jim Anderson traveled to Jackson County, Missouri, to join him. William Anderson was initially given a chilly reception from other raiders, who perceived him to be brash and overconfident.[27]

In May 1863, Anderson joined members of Quantrill's Raiders on a foray near Council Grove, Kansas,[27] in which they robbed a store 15 miles (24 km) west of the town. After the robbery, the group was intercepted by a United States Marshal accompanied by a large posse,[28] about 150 miles (240 km) from the Kansas–Missouri border.[29] In the resulting skirmish, several raiders were captured or killed and the rest of the guerrillas, including Anderson, split into small groups to return to Missouri.[28] Castel and Goodrich speculated that this raid may have given Quantrill the idea of launching an attack deep in Kansas, as it demonstrated that the state's border was poorly defended and that guerrillas could travel deep into the state's interior before Union forces were alerted.[29]

In early summer 1863, Anderson was made a lieutenant, serving in a unit led by George M. Todd. In June and July, Anderson took part in several raids that killed Union soldiers, in Westport, Kansas City and Lafayette County, Missouri.[30] The first reference to Anderson in *Official Records of the American Civil War* concerns his activities at this time, describing him as the captain of a band of guerrillas. He commanded 30–40 men, one of whom was Archie Clement, an 18-year-old with a predilection for torture and mutilation who was loyal only to Anderson.[31] By late July, Anderson led groups of guerrillas on raids and was often pursued by Union volunteer cavalry. Anderson was under Quantrill's command, but independently organized some attacks.[32]

Quantrill's Raiders had an extensive support network in Missouri that provided them with numerous hiding places. Anderson's sisters aided the guerrillas by gathering information inside Union-controlled territory.[33] In August 1863, however, Union General Thomas Ewing, Jr. attempted to thwart the guerrillas by arresting their female relatives,[34] and Anderson's sisters were confined in a three-story building on Grand Avenue in Kansas

City with a number of other girls. While they were confined, the building collapsed, killing one of Anderson's sisters.[35] In the aftermath, rumors that the building had been intentionally sabotaged by Union soldiers spread quickly;[36] Anderson was convinced that it had been a deliberate act. Biographer Larry Wood wrote that Anderson's motivation shifted after the death of his sister, arguing that killing then became his focus, and an enjoyable act.[37] Castel and Goodrich maintain that by then killing had become more than a means to an end for Anderson: it became an end in itself.[38]

## Lawrence Massacre

Although Quantrill had considered the idea of a raid on the pro-Union stronghold that was the town of Lawrence, Kansas before the building collapsed in Kansas City, the deaths convinced the guerrillas to make a bold strike. Quantrill attained near-unanimous consent to travel 40 miles (64 km) into Union territory to strike Lawrence. The guerrillas gathered at the Blackwater River in Johnson County, Missouri.[39] Anderson was placed in charge of 40 men, of which he was perhaps the angriest and most motivated—his fellow guerrillas considered him one of the deadliest fighters there.[40] On August 19, the group, which proved to be the most guerrillas under one commander in the war, began the trip to Lawrence. En route, some guerrillas robbed a Union supporter, but Anderson knew the man and reimbursed him.[41]

Arriving in Lawrence on August 21, the guerrillas immediately killed a number of Union Army recruits and one of Anderson's men took their flag.[42] The Provost Marshal of Kansas, a Union captain who commanded military police, surrendered to the guerrillas and Anderson took his uniform[43] (guerrillas often wore uniforms stolen from Union soldiers).[44] They proceeded to pillage and burn many buildings, killing almost every man they found, but taking care not to shoot women.[43] Anderson personally killed 14 people. Although some men begged him to spare them, he persisted, only relenting when a woman pleaded with him not to torch her house.[45] The guerrillas under Anderson's command, notably including Archie Clement and Frank James, killed more than any of the other group.[46] They left town at 9 a.m. after a company of Union soldiers approached the town.[47] The raiding party was pursued by Union forces but eventually managed to break contact with the soldiers and scatter into the Missouri woods.[48] After a dead raider was scalped by a Union-allied Lenape Indian during the pursuit, one guerrilla leader pledged to adopt the practice of scalping.[49]

## Texas

Four days after the Lawrence Massacre, on August 25, 1863, General Ewing retaliated against the Confederate guerrillas by issuing General Order No. 11, an evacuation order that evicted almost 20,000 people from four counties in rural western Missouri and burned many of their homes. The order was intended to undermine the guerrillas' support network in Missouri. On October 2, a group of 450 guerrillas under Quantrill's leadership met at Blackwater River in Jackson County and left for Texas.[50]

*Anderson around the time of his wedding in Sherman, Texas*

They departed earlier in the year than they had planned, owing to increased Union pressure. En route, they entered Baxter Springs, Kansas, the site of Fort Blair. They attacked the fort on October 6, but the 90 Union troops there quickly took refuge inside, suffering minimal losses.[50] Shortly after the initial assault, a larger group of Union troops approached Fort Blair, unaware that the fort had been attacked and that the men they saw outside the fort dressed in Union uniforms were actually disguised guerrillas.[51] The guerrillas charged the Union forces, killing about 100. Anderson and his men were in the rear of the charge, but gathered a large amount of plunder from the dead soldiers, irritating some guerrillas from the front line of the charge.[52] Not satisfied with the number killed, Anderson and Todd wished to attack the fort again, but Quantrill considered another attack too risky. He angered Anderson by ordering his forces to withdraw.[53]

On October 12, Quantrill and his men met General Samuel Cooper at the Canadian River and proceeded to Mineral Springs, Texas to rest for the winter.[54] During the winter, Anderson married Bush Smith, a woman from Sherman, Texas.[55] Anderson ignored Quantrill's request to wait until after the war and a dispute erupted, which resulted in Anderson separating his men from Quantrill's band. The tension between the two groups markedly increased—some feared that open warfare would result—but by the time of the wedding, relations had improved.[56] In March 1864, at the behest of General Sterling Price, Quantrill reassembled his men, sending most of them into active duty with the regular Confederate Army. He retained 84 men and reunited with Anderson.[57] Quantrill appointed him a first lieutenant, subordinate only to himself and to Todd.[58]

A short time later, one of Anderson's men was accused of stealing from one of Quantrill's men. Quantrill expelled him and warned him not to come back, and the man was fatally shot by some of Quantrill's men when he attempted to return.[59] It is likely that this incident angered Anderson, who then took 20 men to visit the town of Sherman.[60][61] [62] They told General Cooper that Quantrill was responsible for the death of a Confederate officer; the general had Quantrill arrested.[60] Sutherland described Anderson's betrayal of Quantrill as a "Judas" turn.[62][g] Quantrill was taken into custody but soon escaped. Anderson was told to recapture him and gave chase, but he was unable to locate his former commander and stopped at a creek. There, his men briefly engaged a group of guerrillas loyal to Quantrill, but no one was injured in the confrontation. Upon returning to the Confederate leadership, Anderson was commissioned as a captain by General Price.[63]

## Return to Missouri

Anderson and his men rested in Texas for several months before returning to Missouri.

Although he learned that Union General Egbert B. Brown had devoted significant attention to the border area, Anderson led raids in Cooper County and Johnson County, Missouri, robbing local residents. On June 12, 1864, Anderson and 50 of his men engaged 15 members of the Missouri State Militia, killing and robbing 12. After the attack, one of Anderson's guerrillas scalped a dead militiaman.[64] The next day, in southeast Jackson County, Anderson's group ambushed a wagon train carrying members of the Union 1st Northeast Missouri Cavalry, killing nine. The attacks prompted the *Kansas City Daily Journal of Commerce* to declare that rebels had taken over the area. Anderson and his men dressed as Union soldiers, wearing uniforms taken from those they killed. In response, Union militias developed hand signals to verify that approaching men in Union uniforms were not guerrillas. The guerrillas, however, quickly learned the signals, and local citizens became wary of Union troops, fearing that they were disguised guerrillas.[65]

On July 6, a Confederate sympathizer brought Anderson newspapers containing articles about him. Anderson was upset by the critical tone of the coverage and sent letters to the publications.[66][67] In the letters, Anderson took an arrogant and threatening yet playful tone, boasting of his attacks. He protested the execution of guerrillas and their sympathizers, and threatened to attack Lexington, Missouri. He concluded the letters by describing himself as the commander of "Kansas First Guerrillas" and requesting that local newspapers publish his replies.[68] The letters were given to Union generals and were not published for 20 years.[69]

In early July, Anderson's group robbed and killed several Union sympathizers in Carroll and Randolph counties.[70] On July 15, Anderson and his men entered Huntsville, Missouri and occupied the town's business district.[71] Anderson killed one hotel guest whom he suspected was a U.S. Marshal, but spoke amicably with an acquaintance he found there. [72] Anderson's men robbed the town's depository, gaining about $40,000 (equivalent to $641,000 in 2018) in the robbery, although Anderson returned some money to the friend he had met at the hotel.[73]

## Growing infamy

In June 1864, George M. Todd usurped Quantrill's leadership of their group and forced him to leave the area. Todd rested his men in July to allow them to prepare for a Confederate invasion of Missouri. As Quantrill and Todd became less active, "Bloody Bill" Anderson emerged as the best-known, and most feared, Confederate guerrilla in Missouri.[74] By August, the *St. Joseph Herald*, a Missouri newspaper, was describing him as "the Devil."[75] As Anderson's profile increased, he was able to recruit more guerrillas.[76] Anderson was selective, turning away all but the fiercest applicants, as he sought fighters similar to himself.[77][78] His fearsome reputation gave a fillip to his recruiting efforts. Jesse James and his brother Frank were among the Missourians who joined Anderson; both of them later became notorious outlaws.[79] General Clinton B. Fisk ordered his men to find and kill Anderson, but they were thwarted by Anderson's support network and his forces' superior training and arms.[75] Many militia members had been conscripted and lacked the guerrillas' boldness and resolve.[80] In 1863, most Union troops left Missouri and only four regiments remained there. These regiments were composed of troops from out of state, who sometimes mistreated local residents, further motivating the guerrillas and their supporters. The Union militias sometimes rode slower horses and may have been intimidated by Anderson's reputation.[81]

On July 23, 1864, Anderson led 65 men to Renick, Missouri, robbing stores and tearing down telegraph wires on the way. They had hoped to attack a train, but its conductor learned of their presence and turned back before reaching the town. The guerrillas then attacked Allen, Missouri. At least 40 members of the 17th Illinois Cavalry and the Missouri State Militia were in town and took shelter in a fort. The guerrillas were only able to shoot the Union horses before reinforcements arrived; three of Anderson's men were killed in the confrontation.[82] In late July, the Union military sent a force of 100 well-equipped soldiers and 650 other men after Anderson. On July 30, Anderson and his men kidnapped the elderly father of the local Union militia's commanding officer. They tortured him until he was near death and sent word to the man's son in an unsuccessful attempt to lure him into an ambush, before releasing the father with instructions to spread word of his mistreatment.[83] On August 1, while searching for militia members, Anderson and some of his men stopped at a house full of women and requested food. While they rested at the house, a group of local men attacked.[84] The guerrillas quickly forced the attackers to flee, and Anderson shot and injured one woman as she fled the house. This action angered his men, who saw themselves as the protectors of women, but Anderson dismissed their concerns, stating that such things were inevitable. They chased the men who had attacked them, killing one and mutilating his body. By August 1864, they were regularly scalping the men that they killed.[85]

In early August, Anderson and his men traveled to Clay County. Around that time, he received further media coverage: the *St. Joseph Morning Herald* deemed him a "heartless scoundrel," publishing an account of his torture of a captured Union soldier. On August 10, while traveling through Clay County, Anderson and his men engaged 25 militia members, killing five of them and forcing the rest to flee. After hearing of the engagement, General Fisk commanded a colonel to lead a party with the sole aim of killing Anderson.[86]

## Missouri River and Fayette

On August 13, Anderson and his men traveled through Ray County, Missouri to the Missouri River, where they engaged Union militia.[87] Although they forced the Union soldiers to flee, Anderson and Jesse James were injured in the encounter and the guerrillas retired to Boone County to rest.[88] On August 27, Union soldiers killed at least three of Anderson's men in an engagement near Rocheport. The next day, the 4th Missouri Volunteer Cavalry pursued them, but Anderson launched an ambush that killed seven Union soldiers. Anderson's men mutilated the bodies, earning the guerrillas the description of "incarnate fiends" from the *Columbia Missouri Statesman*. On August 30, Anderson and his men attacked a steamboat on the Missouri River, killing the captain and gaining control of the boat. They used it to attack other boats, bringing river traffic to a virtual halt.[89] In mid-September, Union soldiers ambushed two of Anderson's parties traveling through Howard County, killing five men in one day. They found the guerrillas' horses decorated with the scalps of Union soldiers. A short time later, another six of Anderson's men were ambushed and killed by Union troops;[90] after learning of these events, Anderson was outraged and left the area to seek revenge.[91]

Anderson met Todd and Quantrill on September 24, 1864; although they had clashed in the past, they agreed to work together again. Anderson suggested that they attack Fayette, Missouri, targeting the 9th Missouri Cavalry, which was based at the town. Quantrill disliked the idea because the town was fortified, but Anderson and Todd prevailed. Clad in Union uniforms, the guerrillas generated little suspicion as they approached the town,[92] even though it had received warning of nearby guerrillas.[93] However, a guerrilla fired his weapon before they reached the town, and the cavalry garrisoned in the town quickly withdrew into their fort while civilians hid. Anderson and Todd launched an unsuccessful attack against the fort, leading charge after futile charge without injury. The defeat resulted in the deaths of five guerrillas but only two Union soldiers, further maddening Anderson.[94]

On September 26, Anderson and his men reached Monroe County, Missouri[95] and traveled towards Paris, but learned of other nearby guerrillas and rendezvoused with them near Audrain County. Anderson and his men camped with at least 300 men, including Todd.[96] Although a large group of guerrillas was assembled, their leaders felt that there were no promising targets to attack because all of the large towns nearby were heavily guarded.[97]

## Raid on Centralia

On the morning of September 27, 1864, Anderson left his camp with about 75 men to scout for Union forces. They soon arrived at the small town of Centralia and proceeded to loot it, robbing people and searching the town for valuables.[98] They found a large supply of whiskey and all began drinking. Anderson retreated into the lobby of the town hotel to drink and rest. A stagecoach soon arrived, and Anderson's men robbed the passengers, including Congressman James S. Rollins and a plainclothes sheriff. The two were prominent Unionists and hid their identities from the guerrillas.[99][100] As the guerrillas robbed the stagecoach passengers, a train arrived. The guerrillas blocked the railroad, forcing the train to stop.[101] Anderson's men quickly took control of the train, which included 23 off-duty, unarmed Union soldiers as passengers.[102] This was the first capture of a Union passenger train in the war.[103]

Anderson ordered his men not to harass the women on the train, but the guerrillas robbed all of the men, finding over $9,000 (equivalent to $144,000 in 2018) and taking the soldiers' uniforms.[104] Anderson forced the captured Union soldiers to form a line and announced that he would keep one for a prisoner exchange but would execute the rest. He addressed the prisoners, castigating them for the treatment of guerrillas by Union troops.

After selecting a sergeant for a potential prisoner swap, Anderson's men shot the rest.[105] Anderson gave the civilian hostages permission to leave but warned them not to put out fires or move bodies.[106] Although he was alerted to the congressman's presence in the town, he opted not to search for him.[107] The guerrillas set the passenger train on fire and derailed an approaching freight train.[108] Anderson's band then rode back to their camp, taking a large amount of looted goods.[109]

## Battle with Union soldiers

Anderson arrived at the guerrilla camp and described the day's events, the brutality of which unsettled Todd.[110] By mid-afternoon, the 39th Missouri Volunteer Infantry had arrived in Centralia. From the town, they saw a group of about 120 guerrillas and pursued them. The guerrillas heard that the cavalry was approaching,[110] and Anderson sent a party to set an ambush. They drew the Union troops to the top of a hill; a group of guerrillas led by Anderson had been stationed at the bottom and other guerrillas hid nearby.[111] Anderson then led a charge up the hill.[112] Although five guerrillas were killed by the first volley of Union fire, the Union soldiers were quickly overwhelmed by the well-armed guerrillas, and those who fled were pursued.[113] One Union officer reached Centralia and gave word of the ambush, allowing a few Union soldiers who had remained there to escape. However, most were hunted down and killed.[114] Anderson's men mutilated the bodies of the dead soldiers and tortured some survivors.[115]

By the end of the day, Anderson's men had killed 22 soldiers from the train and 125 soldiers in the ensuing battle in one of the most decisive guerrilla victories of the entire war. It was Anderson's greatest victory, surpassing Lawrence and Baxter Springs in brutality and the number of casualties.[115] The attack led to a near-complete halt in rail traffic in the area and a dramatic increase in Union rail security.[116] Anderson achieved the same notoriety that Quantrill had previously enjoyed, and he began to refer to himself as "Colonel Anderson," partly in an effort to supplant Quantrill.[117][118] Sutherland saw the massacre as the last battle in the worst phase of the war in Missouri,[119] and Castel and Goodrich described the slaughter as the Civil War's "epitome of savagery."[117] However, Frank James, who participated in the attack, later defended the guerrillas' actions, arguing that the federal troops were marching under a black flag, indicating that they intended to show no mercy.[119]

## Aftermath

Anderson left the Centralia area on September 27, pursued for the first time by Union forces equipped with artillery.[120][121] Anderson evaded the pursuit, leading his men into ravines that the Union troops would not enter for fear of ambush.[122] In the aftermath of the massacre, Union soldiers committed several revenge killings of Confederate-sympathizing civilians.[123] They burned Rocheport to the ground on October 2; the town was under close scrutiny by Union forces, owing to the number of Confederate sympathizers there, but General Fisk maintained that the fire was accidental.[124] Anderson watched the fire from nearby bluffs.[125]

Anderson visited Confederate sympathizers as he traveled, some of whom viewed him as a hero for fighting the Union, whom they deeply hated. Many of Anderson's men also despised the Union, and he was adept at tapping into this emotion.[126] The Union soldier held captive at Centralia was impressed with the control that Anderson exercised over his men.[127] Although many of them wished to execute this Union hostage, Anderson refused to allow it.[128] On October 6, Anderson and his men traveled to meet General Price in Boonville, Missouri.[124][129] Price was disgusted that Anderson used scalps to decorate his horse, and would not speak with him until he removed them. He was, however, impressed by the effectiveness of Anderson's attacks.[129] Anderson presented him with a gift of fine Union pistols, likely captured at Centralia.[130] Price instructed Anderson to travel to the Missouri railroad and disrupt rail traffic,[129] making Anderson a *de facto* Confederate captain.[131]

Anderson traveled 70 miles (110 km) east with 80 men to New Florence, Missouri.[132] The group then traveled west, disregarding the mission assigned by General Price[133] in favor of looting. Anderson reached a Confederate Army camp; although he hoped to kill some injured Union prisoners there, he was prevented from doing so by camp doctors.[134] After Confederate forces under General Joseph O. Shelby conquered Glasgow, Anderson traveled to the city to loot. He visited the house of a well-known Union sympathizer, the wealthiest resident of the town, brutally beat him, and raped his 12- or 13-year-old black servant.[135][136] Anderson indicated that he was particularly angry that the man had freed his slaves, then trampled him with a specially trained horse.[137] Local residents gathered $5,000, which they gave to Anderson; he then released the man, who died of his injuries in 1866.[138][139] Anderson killed several other Union loyalists and some of his men returned to the wealthy resident's house to rape more of his female servants.[139][138] He left the area with 150 men.[138]

## Death

Union military leaders assigned Lieutenant Colonel Samuel P. Cox to kill Anderson, providing him with a group of experienced soldiers. Soon after Anderson left Glasgow, a local woman saw him and told Cox of his presence.[140] On October 26, 1864, he pursued Anderson's group with 150 men and engaged them in battle.[141] Anderson and his men charged the Union forces, killing five or six of them, but turned back under heavy fire.[142] Only Anderson and one other man, the son of a Confederate general, continued to charge after the others had retreated. Anderson was hit by a bullet behind an ear, likely killing him instantly.[143] Four other guerrillas were killed in the attack.[142] The victory made a hero of Cox and led to his promotion.[144]

Union soldiers identified Anderson by a letter found in his pocket and paraded his body through the streets of Richmond, Missouri.[145] The corpse was photographed and displayed at a local courthouse for public viewing, along with Anderson's possessions.[146] Union soldiers claimed that Anderson was found with a string that had 53 knots, symbolizing each person he had killed.[147] Union soldiers buried Anderson's body in a field near

Richmond in a fairly well-built coffin.[148] Some of them cut off one of his fingers to steal a ring.[149] Flowers were placed at his grave, to the chagrin of Union soldiers.[150] In 1908, Cole Younger, a former guerrilla who served under Quantrill, reburied Anderson's body in the Old Pioneer Cemetery in Richmond, Missouri.[151] In 1967, a memorial stone was placed at the grave.[152]

Archie Clement led the guerrillas after Anderson's death, but the group splintered by mid-November.[153] Most Confederate guerrillas had lost heart by then, owing to a cold winter and the simultaneous failure of General Price's 1864 invasion of Missouri, which ensured that the state would remain securely under Union control for the rest of the war. [154] As the Confederacy collapsed, most of Anderson's men joined Quantrill's forces or traveled to Texas.[155] Jim Anderson moved to Sherman, Texas, with his two sisters.[156]

## Legacy

After the war, information about Anderson initially spread through memoirs of Civil War combatants and works by amateur historians.[157] He was later discussed in biographies of Quantrill, which typically cast Anderson as an inveterate murderer.[158] Three biographies of Anderson were written after 1975.[159] Asa Earl Carter's novel *The Rebel Outlaw: Josey Wales* (1972) features Anderson as a main character. In 1976, the book was adapted into a film, *The Outlaw Josey Wales*, which portrays a man who joins Anderson's gang after his wife is killed by Union-backed raiders.[160] James Carlos Blake's novel *Wildwood Boys* (2000) is a fictional biography of Anderson.[161] He also appears as a character in several films about Jesse James.[162]

Historians have been mixed in their appraisal of Anderson. Wood describes him as the "bloodiest man in America's deadliest war"[163] and characterizes him as the clearest example of the war's "dehumanizing influence."[164] Castel and Goodrich view Anderson as one of the war's most savage and bitter combatants, but they also argue that the war made savages of many others.[165] According to journalist T.J. Stiles, Anderson was not necessarily a "sadistic fiend,"[166] but illustrated how young men became part of a "culture of atrocity" during the war.[166] He maintains that Anderson's acts were seen as particularly shocking in part because his cruelty was directed towards white Americans of equivalent social standing, rather than targets deemed acceptable by American society, such as Native Americans or foreigners.[166]

In a study of 19th-century warfare, historian James Reid posited that Anderson suffered from delusional paranoia, which exacerbated his aggressive, sadistic personality. He sees Anderson as obsessed with, and greatly enjoying, the ability to inflict fear and suffering in his victims, and suggests he suffered from the most severe type of sadistic personality disorder. Reid draws a parallel between the bashi-bazouks of the Ottoman Army and Anderson's guerrillas, arguing that they behaved similarly.[167]

# Clara Barton

**Clarissa Harlowe Barton** (December 25, 1821–April 12, 1912) was a pioneering American nurse who founded the American Red Cross. She was a hospital nurse in the American Civil War, a teacher, and patent clerk. Nursing education was not very formalized at that time and she did not attend nursing school, so she provided self-taught nursing care.[1] Barton is noteworthy for doing humanitarian work and civil rights advocacy at a time before women had the right to vote.[2] She was inducted into the National Women's Hall of Fame in 1973.[3]

*Photo by James E. Purdy (1904)*

## American Civil War

On April 19, 1861, the Baltimore Riot resulted in the first bloodshed of the American Civil War. Victims within the Massachusetts regiment were transported to Washington D.C., after the violence, which happened to be Barton's home at the time. Wanting to serve her country, Barton went to the railroad station when the victims arrived and nursed 40 men.[12] Barton provided crucial, personal assistance to the men in uniform, many of whom were wounded, hungry and without any supplies other than what they carried on their backs. She began helping them by personally taking supplies to the unfinished Capitol Building where the young men of the 6th Massachusetts Militia, who had been attacked in Baltimore, Maryland,

*Clara Barton circa 1866.*

were housed.

Barton quickly recognized them, as she had grown up with some of them, and some she had even taught. Barton, along with several other women, personally provided clothing, food, and supplies for the sick and wounded soldiers. She learned how to store and distribute medical supplies and offered emotional support to the soldiers by keeping their spirits high. She would read books to them, write letters to their families for them, talk to them, and support them.[13]

It was on that day that she identified herself with army work and began her efforts towards collecting medical supplies for the Union soldiers. Prior to distributing provisions directly onto the battlefield and gaining further support, Barton used her own living quarters as a storeroom and distributed supplies with the help of a few friends in early 1862, despite opposition in the War Department and among field surgeons.[2] Ladies' Aid societies helped in sending bandages, food, and clothing that would later be distributed during the

Civil War. In August 1862, Barton finally gained permission from Quartermaster Daniel Rucker to work on the front lines. She gained support from other people who believed in her cause. These people became her patrons, her most supportive being Senator Henry Wilson of Massachusetts.[14]

After the First Battle of Bull Run, Barton placed an ad in a Massachusetts newspaper for supplies; the response was a profound influx of supplies.[15] She worked to distribute stores, clean field hospitals, apply dressings, and serve food to wounded soldiers in close proximity to several battles, including Cedar Mountain, Second Bull Run, Antietam, and Fredericksburg.[16] Barton helped both Union and Confederate soldiers.[15] Supplies were not always readily available though. At the battle of Antietam, for example, Barton used corn-husks in place of bandages.[17]

In 1863 she began a romantic relationship with an officer, Colonel John J. Elwell.[18]

In 1864, she was appointed by Union General Benjamin Butler as the "lady in charge" of the hospitals at the front of the Army of the James. Among her more harrowing experiences was an incident in which a bullet tore through the sleeve of her dress without striking her and killed a man to whom she was tending. She was known as the "Florence Nightingale of America."[19] She was also known as the "Angel of the Battlefield"[13] after she came to the aid of the overwhelmed surgeon on duty following the battle of Cedar Mountain in Northern Virginia in August 1862. She arrived at a field hospital at midnight with a large amount of supplies to help the severely wounded soldiers. This naming came from her frequent timely assistance as she served troops at the battles of Fairfax Station, Chantilly, Harpers Ferry, South Mountain, Antietam, Fredericksburg, Charleston, Petersburg and Cold Harbor.[9][20]

## Post American Civil War

After the end of the American Civil War, Barton discovered that thousands of letters from distraught relatives to the War Department were going unanswered because the soldiers they were questioning about were buried in unmarked graves. Many of these soldiers were labeled just as "missing." Motivated to do more about the situation, Miss Barton contacted President Lincoln in hopes that she would be allowed to respond officially to these unanswered inquiries. She was given permission, and "The Search for the Missing Men" commenced.[21]

After the war, she ran the Office of Missing Soldiers, at 437½ Seventh Street, Northwest, Washington, D.C., in the Gallery Place neighborhood.[22] The office's purpose was to find or identify soldiers killed or missing in action.[23] Barton and her assistants wrote 41,855 replies to inquiries and helped locate more than twenty-two thousand missing men. Barton spent the summer of 1865 helping find, identify, and properly bury 13,000 individuals who died in Andersonville prison camp, a Confederate prisoner-of-war camp in Georgia.[24] She continued this task over the next four years, burying 20,000 more Union soldiers and marking their graves.[21] Congress eventually appropriated $15,000 toward her project.[25]

## Final years

She continued to live in her Glen Echo, Maryland home which also served as the Red Cross Headquarters upon her arrival to the house in 1897. Barton published her autobiography in 1907, titled *The Story of My Childhood*.[20] On April 12, 1912, at the age of 90, she died in her home. The cause of death was pneumonia.

# P. G. T. Beauregard

**Pierre Gustave Toutant-Beauregard** (May 28, 1818–February 20, 1893) was an American military officer who was the first prominent general of the Confederate States Army during the American Civil War. Today, he is commonly referred to as P. G. T. Beauregard, but he rarely used his first name as an adult. He signed correspondence as G. T. Beauregard.

Trained as a civil engineer at the United States Military Academy, Beauregard served with distinction as an engineer in the Mexican–American War. Following a brief appointment as superintendent at West Point in 1861, and after the South seceded, he resigned from the United States Army and became the first brigadier general in the Confederate States Army. He commanded the defenses of Charleston, South Carolina, at the start of the Civil War at Fort Sumter on April 12, 1861. Three months later he won the First Battle of Bull Run near Manassas, Virginia.

Beauregard commanded armies in the Western Theater, including at the Battle of Shiloh in Tennessee, and the Siege of Corinth in northern Mississippi. He returned to Charleston and defended it in 1863 from repeated naval and land attacks by Union forces. His greatest achievement was saving the important industrial city of Petersburg, Virginia, in June 1864, and thus the nearby Confederate capital of Richmond, from assaults by overwhelmingly superior Union Army forces.

His influence over Confederate strategy was lessened by his poor professional relationships with President Jefferson Davis and other senior generals and officials. In April 1865, Beauregard and his commander, General Joseph E. Johnston, convinced Davis and the remaining cabinet members that the war needed to end. Johnston surrendered most of the remaining armies of the Confederacy, including Beauregard and his men, to Major General William Tecumseh Sherman.

Following his military career, Beauregard returned to Louisiana, where he advocated black civil rights and black suffrage, served as a railroad executive, and became wealthy as a promoter of the Louisiana Lottery.

## Civil War
### Charleston

On first meeting, most people were struck by [Beauregard's] "foreign" appearance. His skin was smooth and olive-complexioned. His eyes, half-lidded, were dark, with a trace of Gallic melancholy about them. His hair was black (though by 1860 he maintained this hue with dye). He was strikingly handsome and enjoyed the attentions of women, but probably not excessively or illicitly. He sported a dark mustache and goatee, and he rather resembled Napoleon III, then ruler of France—although he often saw himself in the mold of the more celebrated Napoleon Bonaparte.

—David Detzer, *Allegiance.*[18]

Beauregard traveled by steamship from New York to New Orleans and immediately began giving military advice to the local authorities, which included further strengthening Forts St. Philip and Jackson, which guarded the Mississippi approaches to New Orleans. He hoped to be named commander of the state army, but was disappointed that the state legislature appointed Braxton Bragg. Aware that Beauregard might resent him, Bragg offered him the rank of colonel. Instead Beauregard enrolled as a private in the "Orleans Guards," a battalion of French Creole aristocrats. At the same time, he communicated with Slidell and the newly chosen President Davis, angling for a senior position in the new Confederate States Army. Rumors that Beauregard would be placed in charge of the entire Army infuriated Bragg. Concerned about the political situation regarding the Federal presence at Fort Sumter in Charleston Harbor, Davis selected Beauregard to take command of Charleston's defenses. Beauregard seemed the perfect combination of military engineer and charismatic Southern leader needed at that time and place.[19]

Beauregard became one of the most frequently described generals in Confederate chronicles, and almost every observer noted his foreign French visage.[20] His comportment was "courteous, grave, sometimes reserved and severe, sometimes abrupt with people who displeased him." Associates would see him go months without smiling.[21] "Many who saw him thought he looked like a French marshal or like Napoleon in a gray uniform—which was what he wanted them to think.[22]

"Because he was French and seemed different, he was the victim of all kind of rumors, most of them baseless. The charge of immorality was, of course, inevitable. Some soldiers believed that he was accompanied by a train of concubines and wagons loaded with cases of champagne. Even in Louisiana it was said, by non-Creoles, that he was unfaithful to his wife, infidelity being allegedly a Creole characteristic."[23]

Beauregard's "military retinue was a wonderful collection in itself to inspire rumor. His staff glittered with former governors and senators serving as voluntary aides."[24] "A prominent member of" Beauregard's "entourage was Frederick Marinnis," a slave whom Beauregard hired from a South Carolinian woman whom he personally described as being a very intelligent fellow.[25] Marinnis would comport himself with an air of importance and would talk liberally about General Beauregard's future plans and was his confidant.[25] "Another eminent camp follower was a young Spaniard who served as Beauregard's barber and valet."[25]

Beauregard became the first Confederate general officer, appointed a brigadier general in the Provisional Army of the Confederate States on March 1, 1861.[8] (On July 21, he was promoted to full general in the Confederate Army, one of only seven appointed to that rank; his date of rank made him the fifth most senior general, behind Samuel Cooper, Albert Sidney Johnston, Robert E. Lee, and Joseph E. Johnston.)[26]

Arriving in Charleston on March 3, 1861, Beauregard met with Governor Francis Wilkinson Pickens and inspected the defenses of the harbor, which he found to be in disarray. He was said to display "a great deal in the way of zeal and energy . . . but little professional knowledge and experience."[27] Major Robert Anderson at Fort Sumter wrote to Washington, D.C., that Beauregard, who had been his student at West Point in 1837,[28] would guarantee that South Carolina's actions be exercised with "skill and sound judgment." Beauregard wrote to the first Confederate capital of Montgomery, Alabama, that Anderson was a "most gallant officer." He sent several cases of fine brandy and whiskey and boxes of cigars to Anderson and his officers at Sumter, but Anderson ordered that the gifts be returned.[29]

By early April, political tensions were mounting and Beauregard demanded that Sumter surrender before a planned Union expedition to re-provision the fort could arrive. Early on the morning of April 12, negotiations with Anderson had failed and aides of Beauregard, sent to deal personally with Anderson, ordered the first shots of the American Civil War to be fired from nearby Fort Johnson. The bombardment of Fort Sumter lasted for 34 hours. Subjected to thousands of rounds fired from batteries ringing the harbor, Anderson surrendered Fort Sumter on April 14. Biographer T. Harry Williams described the extravagant praise from throughout the Confederacy that "The Hero of Fort Sumter" received for his victory: "He was the South's first paladin."[30]

## First Bull Run (First Manassas)

Summoned to the new Confederate capital of Richmond, Virginia, Beauregard received a hero's welcome at the railroad stations along the route. He was given command of the "Alexandria Line"[31] of defenses against an impending Federal offensive that was being organized by Brig. Gen. Irvin McDowell (one of Beauregard's West Point classmates) against the Confederate railroad junction at Manassas. Beauregard devised strategies to concentrate the forces of (full) General Joseph E. Johnston from the Shenandoah Valley with his own, aiming not only to defend his position, but to initiate an offensive against McDowell and Washington. Despite his seniority in rank, Johnston lacked familiarity with the terrain and ceded tactical planning of the impending battle to Beauregard as a professional courtesy. President Davis considered many of Beauregard's plans to be impractical for an army as inexperienced as the Confederates could field in 1861; throughout the war, Davis and Beauregard would argue about Beauregard's tendencies to devise grand strategies based on formal military principles. Davis believed he lacked a pragmatic grasp of logistics, intelligence, relative military strengths, and politics.[32]

The First Battle of Bull Run (First Manassas) began early on July 21, 1861, with an element of surprise for both armies—both McDowell and Beauregard planned to envelop their opponent with an attack from their right flank.[33] McDowell struck first, crossing Bull Run and threatening Beauregard's left flank. For a while, Beauregard persisted in moving his troops for an attack on his right flank (McDowell's left, toward Centreville), but Johnston urged him to travel with him to the threatened flank at Henry House Hill, which was weakly defended. Seeing the strength of the Union attack at that point, Beauregard insisted that Johnston leave the area of immediate action and coordinate the overall battle from a position 1.5 miles (2.4 km) to the rear. Beauregard rallied the troops, riding among the men, brandishing regimental colors, and giving inspirational speeches. The Confederate line held.[34]

As Johnston's final troops arrived from the Shenandoah Valley, the Confederates launched a counterattack that routed the Union Army, sending it streaming in disorder back toward Washington. William C. Davis credits Johnston with the majority of the tactical decisions that led to the victory, judging that "Beauregard acted chiefly as a dime novel general, leading the charge of an individual regiment, riding along the line to cheer the troops, accepting the huzzas of the soldiers and complementing them in turn. The closest he came to a major tactical decision was his fleeting intention to withdraw from the Henry Hill line when he briefly mistook the advance of Johnston's reinforcements for the arrival of fresh Union troops."[35] Nonetheless, Beauregard received the bulk of the acclaim from the press and general public. On July 23, Johnston recommended to President Davis that Beauregard be promoted to full general. Davis approved, and Beauregard's date of rank was established as the date of his victory, July 21.[36]

*Confederate soldier in front of official Confederate battle flag*

After Bull Run, Beauregard advocated the use of a standardized battle flag other than the "Stars and Bars" Confederate national flag to avoid visual confusion with the U.S. flag.[37] He worked with Johnston and William Porcher Miles to create the Confederate Battle Flag. Confederate women visiting Beauregard's army contributed silk material from their dresses to create the first three flags, for Beauregard, Johnston, and Earl Van Dorn; thus, the first flags contained more feminine pink than martial red.[38] However, the official battle flag had a red background with white stars.[39] Throughout his career, Beauregard worked to have the flag adopted, and he helped to make it the most popular symbol of the Confederacy.[40]

As the Army went into winter quarters, Beauregard caused considerable friction with the Confederate high command. He strongly advocated an invasion of Maryland to threaten the flank and rear of Washington. With his plan rebuffed as impractical, he requested reassignment to New Orleans, which he assumed would be under Union attack in the near future, but his request was denied. He quarreled with Commissary General Lucius B. Northrop (a personal friend of Davis) about the inadequate supplies available to his army. He issued public statements challenging the ability of the Confederate Secretary of War to give commands to a full general. And he enraged President Davis when his report about Bull Run was printed in the newspaper, which suggested that Davis's interference with Beauregard's plans prevented the pursuit and full destruction of McDowell's army and the capture of Washington.[41]

## Shiloh and Corinth

Having become a political liability in Virginia, Beauregard was transferred to Tennessee to become second-in-command to General Albert Sidney Johnston (no relation to Joseph E. Johnston) in his Army of Mississippi, effective March 14, 1862. The two generals planned the concentration of Confederate forces to oppose the advance of Maj. Gen. Ulysses S. Grant before he could combine his army with that of Maj. Gen. Don Carlos Buell in a thrust up the Tennessee River toward Corinth, Mississippi. The march from Corinth was plagued by bad weather, which delayed the army's arrival by several days, and during that time, several contacts were made with Union scouts. Because of this, Beauregard felt the element of surprise had been lost and recommended calling off the attack, but Johnston decided to proceed with the plan. In the Battle of Shiloh, which began April 6, 1862, the Confederates launched a surprise attack against Grant's Army of the Tennessee, which despite days of prior reports of Confederate troop movements, were completely unaware that the entire Army of Mississippi was coming right at them. Once again a more senior general named Johnston deferred to the junior Beauregard in planning the attack. The massive frontal assault was marred by Beauregard's improper organization of forces—successive attacks by corps in lines 3 miles (4.8 km) long, rather than assigning each corps a discrete portion of the line for a side-by-side assault. This arrangement caused intermingling of units and confusion of command; it failed to concentrate mass at the appropriate place on the line to affect the overall objectives of the attack. In midafternoon, Johnston, who was near the front of the battle action, was mortally wounded. Beauregard, positioned in the rear of the army to send reinforcements forward, assumed command of the army and Johnston's overall Western department (officially designated "Department Number Two"). As darkness fell, he chose to call off the attack against Grant's final defensive line, which had contracted into a tight semicircle backed up to the Tennessee River at Pittsburg Landing.[42]

Beauregard's decision was one of the most controversial of the Civil War. Numerous veterans and historians have wondered what might have happened if the assault had gone forward into the night. Beauregard believed that the battle was essentially won and his men could finish off Grant in the morning. He knew the terrain to be crossed (a steep ravine containing a creek named Dill Branch) was extremely difficult and Grant's defensive line was heavy with massed artillery and supported by gunboats in the river. Unbeknownst to Beauregard, Buell's Army of the Ohio began arriving that afternoon, and he and Grant launched a massive counterattack on April 7. Overwhelmed, the Confederates retreated to Corinth.[43]

Grant was temporarily disgraced by the surprise attack and near defeat, causing his superior, Maj. Gen. Henry W. Halleck, to assume field command of the combined armies. Halleck cautiously and slowly approached Beauregard's fortifications at Corinth; his action became derisively called the Siege of Corinth. Beauregard withdrew from Corinth on May 29 to Tupelo, Mississippi. He was able to deceive Halleck into thinking the Confederates were about to attack; he ran empty trains back and forth through the town while whistles blew and troops cheered as if massive reinforcements were arriving. Beauregard retreated because of the overwhelming Union force and because of contaminated water supplies in Corinth. In April and May, the Confederates lost almost as many men to death by disease in Corinth as had been killed in battle at Shiloh. Nevertheless, his leaving the critical rail junction at Corinth without a fight was another controversial decision. When Beauregard went on medical leave without requesting permission in advance, President Davis relieved him of command and replaced him with Gen. Braxton Bragg.[44]

## Return to Charleston

At Beauregard's request, his allies in the Confederate Congress petitioned Davis to restore his command in the West. Davis remained angry at Beauregard's absence and told him he should have stayed at his post even if he had to be carried around in a litter. He wrote, "If the whole world were to ask me to restore General Beauregard to the command which I have already given to General Bragg, I would refuse it."[45] Beauregard was ordered to Charleston and took command of coastal defenses in South Carolina, Georgia, and Florida,[46] replacing Maj. Gen. John C. Pemberton. The latter was promoted to lieutenant general and transferred to command the defenses of Vicksburg, Mississippi.[47]

Beauregard was unhappy with his new assignment, believing that he deserved command of one of the great Confederate field armies. He performed successfully, however, preventing the capture of Charleston by Union naval and land attacks in 1863. On April 7, 1863, Rear Admiral Samuel Francis Du Pont, commander of the South Atlantic Blockading Squadron, led a union ironclad attack against Fort Sumter that was repulsed by highly accurate artillery fire from Beauregard's forces. In July through September 1863, union land forces under Brig. Gen. Quincy A. Gillmore launched a series of attacks on Fort Wagner on Morris Island and other fortifications at the mouth of the harbor, while Rear Adm. John A. Dahlgren attempted to destroy Fort Sumter. Because the latter operation failed, the successful seizure of Morris Island was not effective in threatening Charleston.[48]

During this period, Beauregard promoted innovative naval defense strategies, such as early experimentation with submarines, naval mines (called "torpedoes" in the Civil War), and with a small vessel called a torpedo-ram. A swift boat fitted with a torpedo on a pole projecting from its bow under water, it could be used to surprise an enemy vessel and impale it underneath the water line. He was also busy devising strategies for other generals in the Confederacy. He proposed that some of the state governors meet with Union governors of the Western states (what are called the Midwest states today) for a peace conference. The Davis administration rejected the idea, but it caused considerable political maneuvering by Davis's enemies in the Congress. Beauregard also proposed a grand strategy—submitted anonymously through his political allies so that it was not tainted by his reputation—to reinforce the Western armies at the expense of Robert E. Lee's army in Virginia, destroy the Federal army in Tennessee, which would induce Ulysses S. Grant to relieve pressure on Vicksburg and maneuver his army into a place where it could be destroyed. The Confederate Army would continue to Ohio, and induce the Western states to ally with the Confederacy. Meanwhile, a fleet of torpedo-rams built in England could be used to recapture New Orleans, ending the war. There is no record that his plan was ever officially presented to the government.[49]

While visiting his forces in Florida, which had just repelled a Union advance at Jacksonville, Beauregard received a telegram that his wife had died on March 2, 1864. Living in Union-occupied New Orleans, she had been seriously ill for two years. A Northern-leaning local newspaper printed an opinion that her condition had been exacerbated by the actions of her husband. This so fanned negative popular opinion that 6,000 people attended her funeral. Union Maj. Gen. Nathaniel P. Banks provided a steamer to carry her body upriver for burial in her native parish. Beauregard wrote that he would like to rescue "her hallowed grave" at the head of an army.[50]

## Richmond

In April 1864, Beauregard saw little opportunity for military glory because he foresaw that there would be no more significant assaults against Charleston, and prospects for a major field command were unlikely. He requested a leave to recover from fatigue and a chronic throat ailment, but he instead received an order to report to Weldon, North Carolina, near the Virginia border, to play a key role in the defense of Virginia. His new assignment, the Department of North Carolina and Cape Fear, also included Virginia south of the James River. When he took command on April 18, he renamed it, on his own initiative, the Department of North Carolina and Southern Virginia. The Confederates were preparing for the spring offensive of Union Lt. Gen. Ulysses S. Grant and were concerned that attacks south of Richmond could interrupt the critical supply lines to Richmond and the army of Robert E. Lee.[51]

Nothing illustrates better the fundamental weakness of the Confederate command system than the weary series of telegrams exchanged in May and early June between

Davis, Bragg, Beauregard, and Lee. Beauregard evaded his responsibility for determining what help he could give Lee; Davis and Bragg shirked their responsibility to decide, when he refused. The strangest feature of the whole affair was that, in the face of Lee's repeated requests, nobody in the high command thought to *order* Beauregard to join Lee.

—T. Harry Williams, *Napoleon in Gray*[52]

As Grant moved south against Lee in the Overland Campaign, Union Maj. Gen. Benjamin Butler launched the surprise Bermuda Hundred Campaign with landings up the James River. Beauregard successfully lobbied with Jefferson Davis's military adviser, Braxton Bragg, to prevent significant units of his small force from being transferred north of Richmond to the aid of Lee. His timely action, coupled with the military incompetence of Butler, bottled up the Union army, nullifying its threat to Petersburg and Lee's supply line. Now that this sector was stable, pressure began to rise to transfer troops from Beauregard's front to Lee's. Beauregard did send a division (Maj. Gen. Robert Hoke's) to Lee for the Battle of Cold Harbor, but Lee urgently wanted more and took the step of offering Beauregard command of the right wing of the Army of Northern Virginia for his cooperation. Beauregard replied in a passive–aggressive manner, "I am willing to do anything for our success, but cannot leave my Department without orders of War Department."[53]

After Cold Harbor, Lee and the Confederate high command were unable to anticipate Grant's next move, but Beauregard's strategic sense allowed him to make a prophetic prediction: Grant would cross the James River and attempt to seize Petersburg, which was lightly defended, but contained critical rail junctions supporting Richmond and Lee. Despite persistent pleas to reinforce this sector, Beauregard could not convince his colleagues of the danger. On June 15, his weak 5,400-man force—including boys, old men, and patients from military hospitals—resisted an assault by 16,000 Federals, known as the Second Battle of Petersburg. He gambled by withdrawing his Bermuda Hundred defenses to reinforce the city, assuming correctly that Butler would not capitalize on the opening. His gamble succeeded, and he held Petersburg long enough for Lee's army to arrive. It was arguably his finest combat performance of the war.[54]

Beauregard continued commanding the defenses of Petersburg in the early days of the siege, but with the loss of the Weldon Railroad in the Battle of Globe Tavern (August 18–21), he was criticized for not attacking more forcefully and he became dissatisfied with the command arrangements under Lee. He hoped for an independent command, but his desires were thwarted in two instances: Lee chose Lt. Gen. Jubal Early to lead an expedition north through the Shenandoah Valley and threaten Washington, and Davis chose Lt. Gen. John Bell Hood to replace the faltering Joseph E. Johnston in the Atlanta Campaign.[55]

## Return to the West
After the fall of Atlanta in September 1864, President Davis considered replacing John

Bell Hood in command of the Army of Tennessee and he asked Robert E. Lee to find out if Beauregard would be interested. Beauregard was indeed interested, but it is unclear whether Davis seriously considered the appointment, and in the end decided to retain Hood. Davis met with Beauregard in Augusta, Georgia, on October 2 and offered him command of the newly created Department of the West, responsible for the five Southern states from Georgia to the Mississippi River, with the armies of Hood and Richard Taylor under his ostensible command. However, it was a thankless job that was limited to logistical and advisory responsibilities, without true operational control of the armies unless he should join them in person during an emergency. Nevertheless, anxious to return to the field, he accepted the assignment.[56]

The major field operation of the fall was Hood's Franklin-Nashville Campaign, an invasion of Tennessee, which he undertook under Beauregard and Davis' orders. Beauregard always kept in touch with Hood, despite all the obstacles facing the latter General's way. The two would later develop a friendship lasting until Hood's death in 1879, after which Beauregard became chairman of the Hood Relief Committee; he arranged for the publication of Hood's memoirs, *Advance and Retreat*, in order to care for the orphaned Hood children.[57]

While Hood traveled through Alabama and into Tennessee, Union Maj. Gen. William Tecumseh Sherman began his March to the Sea from Atlanta to Savannah, which focused Beauregard's attention back to Georgia. He was ineffective in stopping, or even delaying, Sherman's advance. He had inadequate local forces and was reluctant to strip defenses from other locations to concentrate them against Sherman. Furthermore, Sherman did an excellent job of deceiving the Confederates as to the intermediate and final targets of his march. Savannah fell on December 21 and Sherman's army began to march north into South Carolina in January. Also in late December, Beauregard found out that Hood's army had been severely damaged in its defeat at the Battle of Nashville; there were very few men in fighting condition who could oppose Sherman's advance.[58]

Beauregard attempted to concentrate his small forces before Sherman could reach Columbia, South Carolina, the state capital. His urgent dispatches to Richmond were treated with disbelief—Davis and Robert E. Lee (now the general in chief of all the Confederate armies) could not believe that Sherman was advancing without a supply line as quickly as Beauregard was observing him do. Also concerned about what he considered Beauregard's "feeble health," Lee recommended to Davis that he be replaced by Joseph E. Johnston. The change of command came on February 22 and Beauregard, although outwardly cooperative and courteous to Johnston, was bitterly disappointed at his replacement. For the remainder of the war, Beauregard was Johnston's subordinate, assigned to routine matters without combat responsibilities. Johnston and Beauregard met with President Davis on April 13 and their assessment of the Confederate situation helped convince Davis that Johnston should meet with Sherman to negotiate a surrender of his army. The two surrendered to Sherman near Durham, North Carolina, on April 26, 1865, and were paroled in Greensboro on May 2. Beauregard traveled to Mobile and then took a U.S. naval transport to his hometown of New Orleans.[59] In August that year Beauregard's house was surrounded by troops who suspected he was harbouring Edmund Kirby Smith. All the inhabitants were locked in a cotton press overnight. Beauregard complained to General Philip Sheridan who expressed his annoyance at his erstwhile enemy's treatment.[60]

## Postbellum life

After the war, Beauregard was reluctant to seek amnesty as a former Confederate officer by publicly swearing an oath of loyalty, but both Lee and Johnston counseled him to do so, which he did before the mayor of New Orleans on September 16, 1865. He was one of many Confederate officers issued a mass pardon by President Andrew Johnson on July 4, 1868. His final privilege as an American citizen, the right to run for public office, was restored when he petitioned the Congress for relief and the bill on his behalf was signed by President Grant on July 24, 1876.[61]

Beauregard pursued a position in the Brazilian Army in 1865, but declined the Brazilians' offer. He claimed that the positive attitude of President Johnson toward the South swayed his decision. "I prefer to live here, poor and forgotten, than to be endowed with honor and riches in a foreign country." He also declined offers to take command of the armies of Romania and Egypt.[62]

As a lifelong Democrat, Beauregard worked to end Republican rule during Reconstruction. His outrage over the perceived excesses of Reconstruction, such as heavy property taxation, was a principal source for his indecision about remaining in the United States and his flirtation with foreign armies, which lasted until 1875. He was active in the Reform Party, an association of conservative New Orleans businessmen, which spoke in favor of civil rights and voting for former slaves, hoping to form alliances between African-Americans and Democrats to vote out the Radical Republicans in the state legislature.[63]

Beauregard's first employment following the war was in October 1865 as chief engineer and general superintendent of the New Orleans, Jackson and Great Northern Railroad. In 1866 he was promoted to president, a position he retained until 1870, when he was ousted in a hostile takeover. This job overlapped with that of president of the New Orleans and Carrollton Street Railway (1866–1876), where he invented a system of cable-powered street railway cars. Once again, Beauregard made a financial success of the company, but was fired by stockholders who wished to take direct management of the company.[64]

In 1869 he demonstrated a cable car[65][66][67] and was issued U.S. Patent 97,343.

After the loss of these two railway executive positions, Beauregard spent time briefly at a variety of companies and civil engineering pursuits, but his personal wealth became assured when he was recruited as a supervisor of the Louisiana State Lottery Company in 1877. He and former Confederate general Jubal Early presided over lottery drawings and made numerous public appearances, lending the effort some respectability. For 15 years the two generals served in these positions, but the public became opposed to government-sponsored gambling and the lottery was closed down by the legislature.[68]

Beauregard's military writings include *Principles and Maxims of the Art of War* (1863), *Report on the Defense of Charleston*, and *A Commentary on the Campaign and Battle of Manassas* (1891). He was the uncredited co-author of his friend Alfred Roman's *The Military Operations of General Beauregard in the War Between the States* (1884). He contributed the article "The Battle of Bull Run" to *Century Illustrated Monthly Magazine* in November 1884. During these years, Beauregard and Davis published a series of bitter accusations and counter-accusations retrospectively blaming each other for the Confederate defeat.[69]

Beauregard served as adjutant general for the Louisiana state militia, 1879–88. In 1888, he was elected as commissioner of public works in New Orleans. When John Bell Hood and his wife died in 1879, leaving ten destitute orphans, Beauregard used his influence to get Hood's memoirs published, with all proceeds going to the children. He was appointed by the governor of Virginia to be the grand marshal of the festivities associated with the laying of the cornerstone of Robert E. Lee's statue in Richmond. But when Jefferson Davis died in 1889, Beauregard refused the honor of heading the funeral procession, saying "We have always been enemies. I cannot pretend I am sorry he is gone. I am no hypocrite."[70]

Beauregard died in his sleep in New Orleans. The cause of death was recorded as "heart disease, aortic insufficiency, and probably myocarditis."[71] Edmund Kirby Smith, the last surviving full general of the Confederacy, served as the "chief mourner" as Beauregard was interred in the vault of the Army of Tennessee in historic Metairie Cemetery.[72]

## Civil Rights

Immediately after the Civil War, after being insulted and ridiculed in his own community, losing the right to vote, and becoming outraged in learning that properties he owned before the war just outside of the city limits of Memphis had been confiscated by the Freedman's bureau and developed into houses for blacks and a schoolhouse, he wrote letters to his friend John Slidell about his opinion on the emancipated black population. He wrote that the colored people were inferior, ignorant, and indolent. He gave a fantastical prediction "that in seventy-five years the colored race would disappear from America along with the Indians and the buffalo" and a more historically-accurate one in which blacks would be controlled by the whites politically; blacks had not yet voted in the South, and it did not appear to him that they would.[73]

In the following years, Beauregard's inflamed opinion of blacks changed; in March 1867 Radical Republicans enforced black suffrage, as many Southerners became excited and resistant, and Beauregard wrote a widely-published public letter that advised Southerners to accept the new situation. He said that the South could either submit or resist and that sensibly resistance is futile. He saw that through the colored right to vote and cooperation, the excesses of Radical Republican reconstruction like the burden of heavy taxation could be overcome and create a better future for the South. His pragmatic change in opinion is illustrated when he wrote that "the Negro is Southern born; with a little education and some property qualifications he can be made to take sufficient interest in the affairs and prosperity of the South to insure an intelligent vote."[74]

In 1868, while Beauregard was vacationing at White Sulphur Springs, West Virginia, he was invited by Robert E. Lee to a resort along with other famous Confederates as well as William S. Rosecrans, a former Union general and politician. The purpose of the meeting was to combat the charge by the Republicans that the mostly-Democratic Southerners could not be trusted to deal justly with blacks. The result of the meeting was documentation signed by the parties present, including Beauregard, stating that the South would accept the results of the war and emancipation and that they felt kindly towards blacks but that there was opposition to their exercising of political power.[75]

Rosecrans gave an interview upon returning to the north and described Lee's efforts as somewhat weak but that Lee was a sincere man. When asked if Beauregard were weak, Rosecrans responded, "By the side of Lee, certainly. Take him alone, however, and he strikes you as quick, ready and incisive—well, a man of the world, a good business character, a smart active Frenchman. But with Lee he dwindles. Lee says shut the door, and Beauregard shuts the door." The interviewer asked if the Southern generals would really allow blacks to vote. Rosecrans responded by saying, "Lee will not, probably, but Beauregard will. He is in favor of it and so expressed himself to me." [76]

In 1872, the Reform Party formed in Louisiana and was made up of conservative New Orleans businessmen, advocating an economical state government and recognition of black civil and political rights, and held the position that black political power was a reality and should be accepted. Beauregard was one of the leading members of the group. The Reform party attempted to coordinate its efforts on a state level with the Democratic party in order to elect a non-Republican governor. Beauregard, however, had different preferences for presidential candidates. He endorsed in a public letter the Liberal Republican nominee Horace Greeley, who at the time was running against Ulysses S. Grant. Beauregard "called for peace, reconciliation, a forgetting of old issues, and a union of conservative-minded people to remove corruption and extravagance from the government."[79]

In 1873, the Reform Party created a detailed and specific plan to induce cooperation between the races in a political union. The plan called for the creation of the Louisiana Unification Movement. Approving letters and interviews about the movement came flooding into the newspapers. The majority of the communications came from businessmen who declared that they were willing to work with blacks and recognize their political and civil equality if they would agree to cooperate to lower the high Republican taxes. The chant of the Unification movement was "Equal Rights! One Flag! One Country! One People!"[80][78]

Beauregard approached Lieutenant Governor C.C. Antoine, who was a black Republican and invited fifty leading white and fifty black families to join together for a meeting on June 16, 1873. The fifty white sponsors were leaders of the community in business, legal, and journalistic affairs and the presidents of almost every corporation and bank in the city attended. The black sponsors were the wealthy, cultured Creoles of color who were well-off and had been free before the war. Beauregard was the chairman of the resolutions committee. Beauregard spoke at the meeting:

> I am persuaded that the natural relation between the white and colored people is that of friendship, I am persuaded that their interests are identical; that their destinies in this state, where the two races are equally divided are linked together, and that there is no prosperity in Louisiana that must not be the result of their cooperation. I am equally convinced that the evils anticipated by some men from the practical enforcement of equal rights are mostly imaginary, and that the relation of the races in the exercise of these rights will speedily adjust themselves to the satisfaction of all.

The result of the meeting was a report that "advocated complete political equality for blacks, an equal division of state offices between the races, and a plan where blacks would become land owners. It denounced discrimination because of color in hiring laborers or in selecting directors of corporations, and called for the abandonment of segregation in public conveyances, public places, railroads, steams, and public schools." Beauregard argued that blacks "already had equality and the whites had to accept that hard fact." [80][78]

Beauregard lived a paradoxical life; instead of what he seemed to be and the cause of the South for which he fought, unlike many ex-Confederates, he did not look back on "the planting South and the mellow glories of the ancient regime" but looked toward the future of the international house of Louisiana, to the industrial district of New Orleans, and a bustling delta of a better tomorrow.[81]

Beauregard was admired by many because of his work after the war, and when he went to a meeting Waukesha, Wisconsin in 1889, he was given the title by a local reporter of "the Sir Galahad of Southern Chivalry." A Northerner at the meeting welcomed Beauregard, commenting on the fact that 25 years ago, the North "did not feel very kindly toward him; but the past was dead and now they admired him." Beauregard responded by saying "As to my past life, I have always endeavored to do my duty under all circumstances, from the point I entered West Point, a boy of seventeen, up to the present." He was then loudly applauded.[82]

At Beauregard's death and funeral in 1893, Victor E. Rillieux, a Creole of color and poet who wrote poems for many famous contemporary civil rights activists, including Ida B. Wells, was moved by Beauregard's passing to create a poem, titled "Dernier Tribut" English: Last Tribute.

*Dernier Tribut* (English: Last Tribute) by Victor E. Rillieux (1893)

French:

Oh! chez lui l'on peut dire avec toute franchise,
Qu'en tout temps l'on trouvait un [vrai]ment beau regard
Pour l'humble vétéran, pour la veuve soumise
Aux coups du dur destin, frappant sans nul égard!
Noble, grand, généreux; durant sa longue vie
Jamais le noir soupçon par son fatal venin
Ne put même effleurer sa gloire, son génie,
Lui donnant l'une et l'autre un prestige divin!
Tendre époux, bon soldat et chevalier créole,
Son nom, dictame saint aux cœurs louisianais,
Resplendira toujours, ainsi que l'auréole
Qui partant d'un ciel pur brille et ne meurt jamais!
Sur la tombe où repose un guerrier magnanime,
Près de ses compagnons morts en braves soldats,
Je viens y déposer pour tout gage d'estime
Une modeste palme à leur noble trépas![77]

English:

Oh! Of him we can say with all frankness,
At all times we found him a truly beautiful judgment
For the humble veteran, for the widow subjected
To the blows of hard destiny, striking without regard!
Noble, great, generous: during his long life
Never the fatal venom of any dark suspicion
Could even caress his glory, his genius,
That gave him a divine prestige.
Tender husband, good soldier, and Creole knight,
His name, saintly balm to the hearts of Louisianans,
Will always shine, like the sun's halo
That leaving from a pure sky shines and never dies.
In the grave where rests a magnanimous warrior,
Near his dead companions the brave soldiers,
I come here to deposit for all a pledge of esteem
A modest laurel to your noble passing![78]

# Judah P. Benjamin

**Judah Philip Benjamin, QC** (August 11, 1811–May 6, 1884) was a lawyer and politician who was a United States Senator from Louisiana, a Cabinet officer of the Confederate States and, after his escape to the United Kingdom at the end of the American Civil War, an English barrister. Benjamin was the first Jew to hold a Cabinet position in North America, and the first to be elected to the United States Senate who had not renounced that faith. (He was preceded by David Levy Yulee.) He successively held the Cabinet positions of Attorney General, Secretary of War, and Secretary of State of the Confederate States of America.

Benjamin was born to Sephardic Jewish parents from London, who had moved to St. Croix in the Danish West Indies when it was occupied by Britain during the Napoleonic Wars. Seeking greater opportunities, his family immigrated to the United States, eventually settling in Charleston, South Carolina. Judah Benjamin attended Yale College but left without graduating. He moved to New Orleans, where he read law and passed the bar.

Benjamin rose rapidly both at the bar and in politics. He became a wealthy planter and slaveowner and was elected to and served in both houses of the Louisiana legislature prior to his election by the legislature to the US Senate in 1852. There, he was an eloquent supporter of slavery. After Louisiana seceded in 1861, Benjamin resigned as senator and returned to New Orleans.

He soon moved to Richmond after Confederate President Jefferson Davis appointed him as Attorney General. Benjamin had little to do in that position, but Davis was impressed by his competence and appointed him as Secretary of War. Benjamin firmly supported Davis, and the President reciprocated the loyalty by promoting him to Secretary of State in March 1862, while Benjamin was being criticized for the rebel defeat at the Battle of Roanoke Island.

As Secretary of State, Benjamin attempted to gain official recognition for the Confederacy by France and the United Kingdom, but his efforts were ultimately unsuccessful. To preserve the Confederacy as military defeats made its situation increasingly desperate, he advocated freeing and arming the slaves late in the war, but his proposals were only partially accepted in the closing month of the war. When Davis fled the Confederate capital of Richmond in early 1865, Benjamin went with him. He left the presidential party and was successful in escaping from the mainland United States, but Davis was captured by Union troops. Benjamin sailed to Great Britain, where he settled and became a barrister, again rising to the top of his profession before retiring in 1883. He died in Paris the following year.

## Electoral career

### *Spokesman for slavery*

Benjamin's view that slavery should continue was based in his belief that citizens had a right to their property as guaranteed by the Constitution. As Butler put it, "he could no more see that it was right for Northern people to rob him of his slave than it would be for him to connive at horse stealing."[36] He avoided the arguments of some that the slaves were inferior beings, and that their position was ordained by God: Evans ascribes this to Benjamin not being raised as a slaveowner, but coming to it later in life.[37] Benjamin joined in a widespread view of white Southerners that the African American would not be ready for emancipation for many years, if ever. They feared that freeing the slaves would ruin many and lead to murders and rapes by the newly liberated of their former masters and mistresses. Such a massacre had been feared by Southerners since the Haitian Revolution, the violent revolt known as "Santo Domingo" in the South, in which the slaves of what became Haiti killed many whites and mulattoes in 1804 while gaining independence from French control.[38] When the anti-slavery book *Uncle Tom's Cabin* was published in 1852, Benjamin spoke out against Harriet Beecher Stowe's portrayal. He said that slaves were for the most part well treated, and plantation punishments, such as whipping or branding, were more merciful than sentences of imprisonment that a white man might receive in the North for similar conduct.[39]

In early 1854, Senator Douglas introduced his Kansas–Nebraska Bill, calling for popular sovereignty to determine whether the Kansas and Nebraska territories should enter the Union as slave or free states. Depending on the outcome of such elections, slavery might spread to territories closed to it under the Missouri Compromise of 1820. In the debate over the bill, Benjamin defended this change as returning to "the traditions of the fathers," that the federal government not legislate on the subject of slavery. He said that the South merely wished to be left alone. The bill passed,[40] but its passage had drastic political effects, as the differences between North and South that had been settled by both the 1820 and 1850 compromises were reopened.[41] The Whig Party was torn apart North from South, with many Northern Whigs joining the new Republican Party, a group pledged to oppose the spread of slavery. Benjamin continued to caucus with the remains of the Whig Party through 1854 and 1855,[42] but as a member of a legislative minority, he had little influence on legislation, and received no important committee assignments.[43]

In May 1856, Benjamin joined the Democrats, stating they had the principles of the old-time Whig Party.[44] He indicated, in a letter to constituents, that as Northern Whigs had failed to vote to uphold the rights granted to Southern states in the Constitution, the Whigs, as a national party, were no more.[45]

At a state dinner given by Pierce, Benjamin first met Secretary of War Jefferson Davis, whose wife Varina described the Louisiana senator as having "rather the air of a witty bon vivant than of a great senator."[46] The two men, both ambitious for leadership in the South and the nation, formed a relationship that Evans describes as "respectful but wary."[32] The two had occasional differences; when in 1858, Davis, by then a Mississippi senator, was irritated by Benjamin's questioning him on a military bill and suggested that Benjamin was acting as a paid attorney, the Louisianan challenged him to a duel. Davis apologized.[47]

Benjamin, in his speeches in the Senate, took the position that the Union was a compact by the states from which any of them could secede. Nevertheless, he understood that any dissolution would not be peaceful, stating in 1856 that "dreadful will be the internecine war that must ensue."[48] In 1859, Benjamin was elected to a second term, but allegations of involvement in land scandals and the fact that upstate legislators objected to both of Louisiana's senators being from New Orleans stretched the contest to 42 ballots before he prevailed.[49]

## Secession crisis

*Benjamin, c. (1860–1865)*

Benjamin worked to deny Douglas the 1860 Democratic presidential nomination, feeling he had turned against the South. Douglas contended that although the Supreme Court, in *Dred Scott v. Sandford*, had stated Congress could not restrict slavery in the territories, the people of each territory could pass legislation to bar it. This position was anathema to the South. Benjamin praised Douglas's opponent in his re-election bid, former congressman Abraham Lincoln, for at least being true to his principles as an opponent of the expansion of slavery, whereas the senator considered Douglas to be a hypocrite. Benjamin was joined in his opposition to Douglas by Senator Davis; the two were so successful that the 1860 convention was not able to nominate anyone and split into Northern and Southern factions. The Northerners backed Douglas while Southern delegates chose Vice President John C. Breckinridge of Kentucky. Despite their agreement in opposing Douglas, Benjamin and Davis differed on some race issues: in May, Benjamin voted for a bill to aid Africans liberated by U.S. naval vessels from illegal slave ships, in order to return them to their native continent from Key West. Davis and many other Southerners opposed the bill.[50][51]

Between June and December 1860, Benjamin was almost entirely absorbed in the case of *United States v. Castillero*, that was tried in San Francisco during the latter part of that period.[52] The case concerned a land grant by the former Mexican government of California. Castillero had leased part of his land to British mining companies, and when American authorities ruled the grant invalid, they hired Benjamin; he spent four months in San Francisco working on the case.[53][54] The trial began in October, and Benjamin gave an address lasting six days. The local correspondent for *The New York Times* wrote that Benjamin, "a distinguished stranger," drew the largest crowds to the courtroom and "the Senator is making this terribly tedious case interesting."[55] Benjamin sailed for New York once the case was submitted for decision in early November. The court's ruling, rendered in January 1861, was substantially for the company but, not satisfied, it appealed. It lost the case entirely to an adverse decision by the U.S. Supreme Court, three justices dissenting, the following year. Benjamin was by then a Confederate Cabinet officer, and could not argue the case. His co-counsel filed his brief with the court.[56]

By the time Benjamin returned to the East Coast, the Republican candidate, Lincoln, had been elected president, and there was talk, in Louisiana and elsewhere, of secession from the Union. The *New Orleans Picayune* reported that Benjamin favored secession only in the last resort. On December 23, 1860, another Louisiana periodical, the *Delta*, printed a letter from Benjamin dated the eighth stating that, as the people of the North were of unalterable hostility to their Southern brethren, the latter should depart from the government common to them. He also signed a joint letter from Southern congressmen to their constituents, urging the formation of a confederation of the seceding states.[57] According to a letter reportedly written by Benjamin during the crisis, he saw secession as a means of obtaining more favorable terms in a reformed Union.[58]

With Southern opinion turning in favor of secession, Benjamin made a farewell speech in the Senate on December 31, 1860, to a packed gallery, desirous of hearing one of the South's most eloquent voices. They were not disappointed; Evans writes that "historians consider Benjamin's farewell . . . one of the great speeches in American history."[59] Benjamin foresaw that the South's departure would lead to civil war:

> What may be the fate of this horrible contest none can foretell; but this much I will say: the fortunes of war may be adverse to our arms; you may carry desolation into our peaceful land, and with torch and firebrand may set our cities in flames . . . you may do all this, and more, but you never can subjugate us; you never can convert the free sons of the soil into vassals, paying tribute to your power; you never can degrade them to a servile and inferior race. Never! Never![59]

According to Geoffrey D. Cunningham in his article on Benjamin's role in secession, "Swept up in the popular cries for independence, Benjamin willingly went out with the Southern tide."[60] He and his Louisiana colleague, John Slidell, resigned from the U.S. Senate on February 4, 1861, nine days after their state voted to secede from the Union.[61]

## Confederate statesman
### *Attorney General*
Fearful of arrest as a rebel once he left the Senate, Benjamin quickly departed Washington for New Orleans. On the day of Benjamin's resignation, the Provisional Confederate States Congress gathered in Montgomery, Alabama, and soon chose Davis as president.

Davis was sworn in as provisional Confederate States President on February 18, 1861. At home in New Orleans for, it would prove, the last time, Benjamin addressed a rally on Washington's Birthday, February 22, 1861.[62] On February 25, Davis appointed Benjamin, still in New Orleans, as attorney general; the Louisianan was approved immediately and unanimously by the provisional Congress.[63] Davis thus became the first chief executive in North America to appoint a Jew to his Cabinet.[64]

Davis, in his memoirs, remarked that he chose Benjamin because he "had a very high reputation as a lawyer, and my acquaintance with him in the Senate had impressed me with the lucidity of his intellect, his systematic habits, and capacity for labor."[65] Meade suggested that Davis wanted to have a Louisianan in his Cabinet, but that a smarter course of action would have been to send Benjamin abroad to win over the European governments.[66] Butler called Benjamin's appointment "a waste of good material."[67] Historian William C. Davis, in his volume on the formation of the Confederate government, notes, "For some there was next to nothing to do, none more so than Benjamin."[68] The role of the attorney general in a Confederacy that did not yet have federal courts or marshals was so minimal that initial layouts for the building housing the government in Montgomery allotted no space to the Justice Department.[68]

Meade found the time that Benjamin spent as attorney general to be fruitful, as it allowed him the opportunity to judge Davis's character and to ingratiate himself with the president.[66] Benjamin served as a host, entertaining dignitaries and others Davis had no time to see.[68] At the first Cabinet meeting, Benjamin counseled Davis to have the government buy 150,000 bales of cotton for shipment to the United Kingdom, with the proceeds used to buy arms and for future needs. His advice was not taken, as the Cabinet believed the war would be short and successful.[65] Benjamin was called upon from time to time to render legal opinions, writing on April 1 to assure Treasury Secretary Christopher Memminger that lemons and oranges could enter the Confederacy duty-free, but walnuts could not.[69]

Once Virginia joined the Confederacy, the capital was moved to Richmond, though against Benjamin's advice—he believed that the city was too close to the North. Nevertheless, he traveled there with his brother-in-law, Jules St. Martin; the two lived in the same house throughout the war, and Benjamin probably procured the young man's job at the War Department. Although Alabama's Leroy Walker was Secretary of War, Davis—a war hero and former U.S. War Secretary—considered himself more qualified and gave many orders himself. When the Confederates were unable to follow up their victory at the First Battle of Manassas by threatening Washington, Walker was criticized in the press.[70] In September, Walker resigned to join the army as a brigadier general, and Davis appointed Benjamin in his place.[71] Butler wrote that Davis had found the cheerfully competent Benjamin "a most useful member of the official family, and thought him suited for almost any post in it."[72] In addition to his appointment as War Secretary, Benjamin continued to act as Attorney General until November 15, 1861.[73]

## Secretary of War

As War Secretary, Benjamin was responsible for a territory stretching from Virginia to Texas. It was his job, with Davis looking over his shoulder, to supervise the Confederate Army and to feed, supply, and arm it—in a nascent country with almost no arms manufacturers. Accordingly, Benjamin saw his job as closely tied to foreign affairs, as the Confederacy was dependent on imports to supply its troops. Davis had chosen a "defensive war" strategy— the Confederacy would await invasion by the North, then seek to defeat its armies until Lincoln tired of sending them. Davis and Benjamin worked together closely, and as Davis came to realize that his subordinate was loyal both to the Confederacy and to Davis personally, he returned complete trust in Benjamin. Varina Davis wrote, "It was to me a curious spectacle, the steady approximation to a thorough friendliness of the President and his War Minister. It was a very gradual rapprochement, but all the more solid for that reason."[74]

In his months as War Secretary, Benjamin sent thousands of communications. [75] According to Evans, Benjamin initially "turn[ed] prejudice to his favor and play[ed] on the Southerner's instinctive respect for the Jewish mind with a brilliant performance." Nevertheless, Benjamin faced difficulties that he could do little about. The Confederacy lacked sufficient soldiers, trained officers to command them, naval and civilian ships, manufacturing capacity to make ships and many weapons, and powder for guns and cannon. The Union had these things, and moved to block the South's access to European supplies, both by blockade and by buying up supplies the South might have secured. Other problems included drunkenness among the men—and their officers—and uncertainty as to when and where the expected Northern invasion would begin.[76] Further, Benjamin had no experience of the military, or of the executive branch of the government, placing him in a poor position to contradict President Davis.[77]

> Judah P. Benjamin, the dapper Jew,
> Seal-sleek, black-eyed, lawyer and epicure,
> Able, well-hated, face alive with life,
> Looked round the council-chamber with the slight
> Perpetual smile he held before himself
> Continually like a silk-ribbed fan.
> Behind the fan, his quick, shrewd, fluid mind,
> Weighed Gentiles in an old balance.
> —Stephen Vincent Benét, "John Brown's Body" (1928)[78]

An insurgency against the Confederacy developed in staunchly pro-Union East Tennessee in late 1861, and at Davis's order, Benjamin sent troops to crush it. Once it was put down, Benjamin and Davis were in a quandary about what to do about its leader, William "Parson" Brownlow, who had been captured, and eventually allowed him to cross to Union-controlled territory in the hope that it would cause Lincoln to release Confederate prisoners.[79] While Brownlow was in Southern custody, he stated that he expected "no more mercy from Benjamin than was shown by his illustrious predecessors towards Jesus Christ."[77]

Benjamin had difficulty in managing the Confederacy's generals. He quarreled with General P. G. T. Beauregard, a war hero since his victory at First Manassas. Beauregard sought to add a rocket battery to his command, an action Benjamin stated was not authorized by law. He was most likely relaying Davis's views, and when challenged by Beauregard, the president backed Benjamin, advising the general to "dismiss this small matter from your mind. In the hostile masses before you, you have a subject more worthy of your contemplation."[80] In January 1862, Thomas J. "Stonewall" Jackson's forces had advanced in western Virginia, leaving troops under William W. Loring at the small town of Romney. Distant from Jackson's other forces and ill-supplied, Loring and other officers petitioned the War Department to be recalled, and Benjamin, after consulting Davis, so ordered, using the pretext of rumored Union troop movements in the area. Jackson complied, but in a letter to Benjamin asked to be removed from the front, or to resign. High-ranking Confederates soothed Jackson into withdrawing his request.[81]

The power of state governments was another flaw in the Confederacy and a problem for Benjamin. Georgia Governor Joseph E. Brown repeatedly demanded arms and the return of Georgian troops to defend their state. North Carolina's governor, Henry T. Clark, also wanted troops returned to him to defend his coastline.[82] After Cape Hatteras, on North Carolina's coast, was captured, Confederate forces fell back to Roanoke Island. If that fell, a number of ports in that area of the coast would be at risk, and Norfolk, Virginia, might be threatened by land.[83]

General Henry A. Wise, commanding Roanoke, also demanded troops and supplies. He received little from Benjamin's War Department that had no arms to send, as the Union blockade was preventing supplies from being imported. That Confederate armories were empty was a fact not publicly known at the time. Benjamin and Davis hoped the island's defenses could hold off the Union forces, but an overwhelming number of troops were landed in February 1862 at an undefended point, and the Confederates were quickly defeated.[84] Combined with Union General Ulysses S. Grant's capture of Fort Henry and Fort Donelson in Tennessee, this was the most severe military blow yet to the Confederacy, and there was a public outcry against Benjamin, led by General Wise.[85]

It was revealed, a quarter century after the war, that Benjamin and Davis had agreed for the secretary to act as scapegoat rather than reveal the shortage of arms.[86] Not knowing this, the Richmond *Examiner* accused Benjamin of "stupid complacency."[87] Diarist Mary Chestnut recorded, "the mob calls him Mr. Davis's pet Jew."[88] The Wise family never forgave Benjamin, to the detriment of his memory in Southern eyes. The general's son, Captain Jennings Wise, fell at Roanoke Island, and Henry's grandson John Wise, interviewed in 1936, told Meade that "the fat Jew sitting at his desk" was to blame.[86] Another of the general's sons, also named John Wise, wrote a highly popular book about the South in the Civil War, *The End of an Era* (1899), in which he said that Benjamin "had more brains and less heart than any other civic leader in the South ... The Confederacy and its collapse were no more to Judah P. Benjamin than last year's birds nest."[86]

The Confederate Congress established a special committee to investigate the military losses; Benjamin testified before it.[89] The Secretary of State, Virginia's Robert M. T. Hunter, had quarreled with Davis and resigned and in March 1862, Benjamin was appointed as his replacement. Varina Davis noted that some in Congress had sought Benjamin's ouster "because of reverses which no one could have averted, [so] the President promoted him to the State Department with a personal and aggrieved sense of injustice done to the man who had now become his friend and right hand."[90] Richmond diarist Sallie Ann Brock Putnam wrote, "Mr. Benjamin was not forgiven ... this act on the part of the President [in promoting Benjamin], in defiance of public opinion, was considered as unwise, arbitrary, and a reckless risking of his reputation and popularity ... [Benjamin] was ever afterwards unpopular in the Confederacy, and particularly in Virginia."[91] Despite the promotion, the committee reported that any blame for the defeat at Roanoke Island should attach to Wise's superior, Major General Benjamin Huger, "and the late secretary of war, J.P. Benjamin."[92]

## Confederate Secretary of State

Throughout his time as Secretary of State, Benjamin tried to induce Britain and France to recognize the Confederacy—no other nation was likely to do so unless these powerful states led the way. The protection this would bring to the Confederacy and its foreign trade was hoped to be enough to save it.[93]

## Basis of Confederate foreign policy

By the 1850s, cheap Southern cotton fueled the industries of Europe. The mills of Britain, developed during the first half of the 19th century, by 1860 used more cotton than the rest of the industrialized world combined. Cotton imports to Britain came almost entirely from the American South. According to an article in *The Economist* in 1853, "let any great social or physical convulsion visit the United States, and England would feel the shock from Land's End to John O'Groat's. The lives of nearly two million of our countrymen ... hang upon a thread."[94]

In 1855, an Ohioan, David Christy, published *Cotton Is King: or Slavery in the Light of Political Economy*. Christy argued that the flow of cotton was so important to the industrialized world that cutting it off would be devastating—not least to the Northern United States, as cotton was by far the largest U.S. export. This became known as the "King Cotton" theory, to which Davis was an enthusiastic subscriber.[95] Benjamin also spoke in favor of the theory, though Butler suspected he may have "known better," based on his firsthand knowledge of Europe.[92]

When war came, Davis, against Benjamin's advice, imposed an embargo on exports of cotton to nations that had not recognized the Confederate government, hoping to force such relations, especially with Britain and France.[96] As the Union was attempting to prevent cotton from being exported from Confederate ports by a blockade and other means, this played to a certain extent into the hands of Lincoln and his Secretary of State, William H. Seward.[97] Additionally, when the war began, Britain had a large surplus of cotton in warehouses, enough to keep the mills running at least part-time for a year or so. Although many prominent Britons believed the South would prevail, there was a reluctance to recognize Richmond until it had gained the military victories to put its foe at bay. Much of this was due to hatred of slavery, though part of it stemmed from a desire to remain on good terms with the U.S. government—due to a drought in 1862, Britain was forced to import large quantities of wheat and flour from the United States.[98] Also, Britain feared the expansionist Americans might invade the vulnerable Canadian colonies, as Seward hinted they might.[99]

## Appointment

Davis appointed Benjamin as Secretary of State on March 17, 1862. He was promptly confirmed by the Confederate Senate. A motion to reconsider the confirmation was lost, 13–8.[100] According to Butler, the appointment of Benjamin brought Davis little political support, as the average white Southerner did not understand Benjamin and somewhat disliked him.[101] As there was not much open opposition to Davis in the South at the time, Benjamin's appointment was not criticized, but was not given much praise either. Meade noted, "the silence of many influential newspapers was ominous. [Benjamin's] promotion in the face of such bitter criticism of his conduct in the war office caused the first serious lack of confidence in the Davis government."[102]

Meade wrote that, since the Secretary of State would have to work closely with Jefferson Davis, Benjamin was likely the person best suited to the position.[102] In addition to his relationship with the President, Benjamin was very close to the Confederate First Lady, Varina Davis, with whom he exchanged confidences regarding war events and the President's health. "Together, and by turns, they could help him over the most difficult days."[103]

For recreation, Benjamin frequented Richmond's gambling dens, playing poker and faro. He was incensed when British correspondent William Howard Russell publicized his gambling, feeling that it was an invasion of his private affairs. He was also displeased that Russell depicted him as a losing gambler, when his reputation was the opposite.[104]

## Early days (1862–1863)

The *Trent* Affair had taken place before Benjamin took office as Secretary of State: a U.S. warship had in October 1861 removed Confederate diplomats James Mason and James Slidell (Benjamin's former Louisiana colleague in the U.S. Senate) and their private secretaries from a British-flagged vessel. The crisis brought the U.S. and Britain near war, and was resolved by their release.[105] By the time of Benjamin's appointment, Mason and Slidell were at their posts in London and Paris as putative ministers from the Confederacy, seeking recognition by the governments of Britain and France. With difficult communications between the South and Europe (dispatches were often lost or intercepted), Benjamin was initially reluctant to change the instructions given the agents by Secretary Hunter. Communications improved by 1863, with Benjamin ordering that dispatches be sent to Bermuda or the Bahamas, from where they reached the Confederacy by blockade runner.[106]

As a practical matter, Benjamin's chances of gaining European recognition rose and fell with the military fortunes of the Confederacy. When, at the end of June 1862, Confederate General Robert E. Lee turned back Union General George B. McClellan's Peninsula Campaign in the Seven Days Battles, ending the immediate threat to Richmond, Emperor Napoleon III of France favorably received proposals from Benjamin, through Slidell, for the French to intervene on the Confederacy's behalf in exchange for trade concessions. Nevertheless, the Emperor proved unwilling to act without Britain.[107] In August 1862, Mason, angered by the refusal of British government ministers to meet with him, threatened to resign his post. Benjamin soothed him, stating that while Mason should not submit to insulting treatment, resignation should not take place without discussion.[108]

The bloody standoff at Antietam in September 1862 that ended Lee's first major incursion into the North gave Lincoln the confidence in Union arms he needed to announce the Emancipation Proclamation.[109] British newspapers mocked Lincoln for hypocrisy in freeing slaves only in Confederate-held areas, where he could exercise no authority. British officials had been shocked by the outcome of Antietam—they had expected Lee to deliver another brilliant victory—and now considered an additional reason for intervening in the conflict. Antietam, the bloodiest day of the war, had been a stalemate; they read this as presaging an overall deadlock in the war, with North and South at each other's throats for years as Britain's mills sat empty and its people starved. France agreed with this assessment.[110]

The final few months of 1862 saw a high water mark for Benjamin's diplomacy.[111] In October, the British Chancellor of the Exchequer, William Gladstone, expressed confidence in Confederate victory, stating in Newcastle, "There is no doubt that Jefferson Davis and other leaders of the South have made an army. They are making, it appears, a navy, and they have made what is more than either—they have made a nation."[112] Later that month, Napoleon proposed to the British and Russians (a U.S. ally) that they combine to require a six months' armistice for mediation, and an end to the blockade; if they did so, it would likely lead to Southern independence.[113] The proposal divided the British Cabinet. In mid-November, at the urgings of Palmerston and War Secretary George Cornewall Lewis, members decided to continue to wait for the South to defeat Lincoln's forces before recognizing it.[114] Although proponents of intervention were prepared to await another opportunity, growing realization among the British public that the Emancipation Proclamation meant that Union victory would be slavery's end made succoring the South politically infeasible.[115]

Benjamin had not been allowed to offer the inducement for intervention that might have succeeded—abolition of slavery in the Confederacy, and because of that, Meade deemed his diplomacy "seriously, perhaps fatally handicapped."[116] The Secretary of State blamed Napoleon for the failure, believing the Emperor had betrayed the Confederacy to get the ruler the French had installed in Mexico, Maximilian, accepted by the United States.[117]

In Paris, Slidell had been approached by the banking firm Erlanger et Cie. The company offered to float a loan to benefit the Confederacy.[c] The proposed terms provided a large commission to Erlanger and would entitle the bondholder to cotton at a discounted price once the South won the war.[118] Baron Frederic Emile d'Erlanger, head of the firm, journeyed to Richmond in early 1863, and negotiated with Benjamin, although the transaction properly fell within the jurisdiction of Treasury Secretary Memminger. The banker softened the terms somewhat, though they were still lucrative for his firm. Benjamin felt the deal was worth it, as it would provide the Confederacy with badly needed funds to pay its agents in Europe.[119]

## Increasing desperation (1863–1865)

The twin rebel defeats at Gettysburg and Vicksburg in early July 1863 made it unlikely that Britain, or any other nation, would recognize a slaveholding Confederacy staggering towards oblivion.[120] Accordingly, in August, Benjamin wrote to Mason telling him that as Davis believed the British unwilling to recognize the South, he was free to leave the country.[121] In October, with Davis absent on a trip to Tennessee, Benjamin heard that the British consul in Savannah had forbidden British subjects in the Confederate Army from being used against the United States. The Secretary of State convened a Cabinet meeting, that expelled the remaining British consuls in Confederate-controlled territory, then notified Davis by letter. Evans suggests that Benjamin's actions made him the Confederacy's acting president[122]—the first Jewish president.[123]

Benjamin supervised the Confederate Secret Service, responsible for covert operations in the North, and financed former federal Interior Secretary Jacob Thompson to work behind the scenes financing operations that might undermine Lincoln politically. Although efforts were made to boost Peace Democrats, the most prominent actions proved to be the St. Albans Raid (an attack on a Vermont town from Canada) and an unsuccessful attempt to burn New York City.[124] In the aftermath of the war, these activities led to accusations that Benjamin and Davis were involved in the assassination of Abraham Lincoln, as one Confederate courier, John H. Surratt, who had received money from Benjamin, was tried for involvement in the conspiracy, though Surratt was acquitted.[125]

As the Confederacy's military fortunes flagged, there was increasing consideration of what would have been unthinkable in 1861—enlisting male slaves in the army and emancipating them for their service. In August 1863, B. H. Micou, a relative of a former law partner, wrote to Benjamin proposing the use of black soldiers. Benjamin responded that this was not feasible, principally for legal and financial reasons, and that the slaves were performing valuable services for the Confederacy where they were.[126] According to Meade, "Benjamin did not offer any objections to Micou's plan except on practical grounds—he was not repelled by the radical nature of the proposal."[127] A British financial agent for the Confederacy, James Spence, also urged emancipation as a means of gaining British recognition. Benjamin allowed Spence to remain in his position for almost a year despite the differences with Confederate policy, before finally dismissing him in late 1863.

[128] Despite official neutrality, tens of thousands from British-ruled Ireland were enlisting in the Union cause; Benjamin sent an agent to Ireland hoping to impede those efforts and Dudley Mann to Rome to urge Pope Pius IX to forbid Catholic Irish from enlisting. The Pope did not do so, though he responded sympathetically.[129]

In January 1864, Confederate General Patrick Cleburne, of the Army of Tennessee, proposed emancipating and arming the slaves. Davis, when he heard of it, turned it down and ordered it kept secret. Evans notes that Benjamin "had been thinking in similar terms for much longer, and perhaps the recommendation of so respected an officer was just the impetus he needed."[130] The year 1864 was a disastrous one for the Confederacy, with Lee forced within siege lines at Petersburg and Union General William T. Sherman sacking Atlanta and devastating Georgia on his march to the sea.[131][132] Benjamin urged Davis to send the secretary's fellow Louisianan, Duncan Kenner, to Paris and London, with an offer of emancipation in exchange for recognition. Davis was only willing to offer gradual emancipation, and both Napoleon and Palmerston rejected the proposal.[133] Benjamin continued to press the matter, addressing a mass meeting in Richmond in February 1865 in support of arming the slaves and emancipating them. A bill eventually emerged from the Confederate Congress in March, but it had many restrictions, and it was too late to affect the outcome of the war.[134]

In January 1865, Lincoln, who had been re-elected the previous November, sent Francis Blair as an emissary to Richmond, hoping to secure reunion without further bloodshed. Both sides agreed to a meeting at Fort Monroe, Virginia. Benjamin drafted vague instructions for the Southern delegation, led by Vice President Alexander Stephens, but Davis insisted on modifying them to refer to North and South as "two nations." This was the point that scuttled the Hampton Roads Conference; Lincoln would not consider the South a separate entity, insisting on union and emancipation.[135]

## Escape

By March 1865, the Confederate military situation was desperate. Most major population centers had fallen, and General Lee's defense of Richmond was faltering against massive Union forces. Nevertheless, Benjamin retained his usual good humor; on the evening of April 1, with evacuation likely, he was at the State Department offices, singing a silly ballad of his own composition, "The Exit from Shocko Hill," a graveyard district located in Richmond.[136] On April 2, Lee sent word that he could only keep Union troops away from the line of the Richmond and Danville Railroad for a short time. Those who did not leave Richmond would be trapped.[137] At 11:00 p.m. that night, the Confederate President and Cabinet left aboard a Danville-bound train. Navy Secretary Stephen R. Mallory recorded that Benjamin's "hope and good humor [was] inexhaustible . . . with a 'never-give-up-the-ship' sort of air, referred to other great national causes which had been redeemed from far gloomier reverses than ours."[138]

In Danville, Benjamin shared a room with another refugee, in the home of a banker. [139] For a week, Danville served as capital of the Confederacy, until word came of Lee's surrender at Appomattox Court House. With no army to shield the Confederate government, it would be captured by Union forces within days, so Davis and his Cabinet, including Benjamin, fled south to Greensboro, North Carolina. Five minutes after the train passed over the Haw River, Union cavalry raiders burned the bridge, trapping the trains that followed Davis's.[140]

Greensboro, fearing wrathful reprisal from the Union, gave the fugitives little hospitality, forcing Benjamin and the other Cabinet members to bunk in a railroad boxcar. Davis hoped to reach Texas, where rumor had it large Confederate forces remained active.[141] The Cabinet met in Greensboro, and Generals Beauregard and Joseph E. Johnston sketched the bleak military situation. Davis, backed as usual by Benjamin, was determined to continue to fight. The refugee government moved south on April 15. With the train tracks cut, most Cabinet members rode on horseback, but the heavyset Benjamin declared he would not ride on one until he had to, and shared an ambulance with Jules St. Martin and others. For the entertainment of his companions, Benjamin recited Tennyson's "Ode on the Death of the Duke of Wellington."[142]

In Charlotte, Benjamin stayed in the home of a Jewish merchant as surrender negotiations dragged. Here, Benjamin abandoned Davis's plan to fight on, telling him and the Cabinet that the cause was hopeless. When negotiations failed, Benjamin was part of the shrunken remnant of associates that moved on with Davis. The party reached Abbeville, South Carolina on May 2, and Benjamin told Davis that he wanted to separate from the presidential party temporarily, and go to the Bahamas to be able to send instructions to foreign agents before rejoining Davis in Texas.[143] According to historian William C. Davis, "the pragmatic Secretary of State almost certainly never had any intention of returning to the South once gone."[144] When he bade John Reagan goodbye, the postmaster general asked where Benjamin was going. "To the farthest place from the United States, if it takes me to the middle of China."[145]

With one companion, Benjamin travelled south in a poor carriage, pretending to be a Frenchman who spoke no English. He had some gold with him, and left much of it for the support of relatives. He was traveling in the same general direction as the Davis party, but evaded capture whereas Davis was taken by Union troops. Benjamin reached Monticello, Florida, on May 13 to learn Union troops were in nearby Madison. Benjamin decided to continue alone on horseback, east and south along Florida's Gulf Coast, pretending to be a South Carolina farmer.[146] John T. Lesley, James McKay, and C. J. Munnerlyn assisted in hiding Benjamin in a swamp,[147][148] before eventually transporting him to Gamble Mansion in Ellenton, on the southwest coast of Florida.[d][150] From there, assisted by the blockade runner Captain Archibald McNeill, he reached Bimini in the Bahamas. His escape from Florida to England was not without hardship: at one point he pretended to be a Jewish cook on McNeill's vessel, to deceive American soldiers who inspected it—one of whom stated it was the first time he had seen a Jew do menial labor. The small sponge-carrying vessel on which he left Bimini bound for Nassau exploded on the way, and he and the three black crewmen eventually managed to return to Bimini. McNeill's ship was still there, and he chartered it to take him to Nassau. From there, he took a ship for Havana, and on August 6, 1865, left there for Britain. He was not yet done with disaster; his ship caught fire after departing St. Thomas, and the crew put out the flames only with difficulty. On August 30, 1865, Judah Benjamin arrived at Southampton, in Britain.[151]

## Exile

Benjamin spent a week in London assisting Mason in winding up Confederate affairs. He then went to Paris to visit his wife and daughter for the first time since before the war. Friends in Paris urged him to join a mercantile firm there, but Benjamin felt that such a career would be subject to interference by Seward and the United States. Accordingly, Benjamin sought to shape his old course in a new country, resuming his legal career as an English barrister. [152] Most of Benjamin's property had been destroyed or confiscated, and he needed to make a living for himself and his relatives.[153] He had money in the United Kingdom as he had, during the war, purchased cotton for transport to Liverpool by blockade runner.[154]

On January 13, 1866, Benjamin enrolled at Lincoln's Inn, and soon thereafter was admitted to read law under Charles Pollock, son of Chief Baron Charles Edward Pollock, who took him as a pupil at his father's direction.[155] Benjamin, despite his age of 54, was initially required, like his thirty-years-younger peers, to attend for twelve terms, that is, three years. According to Benjamin's obituary in *The Times*, though, "the secretary of the Confederacy was dispensed from the regular three years of unprofitable dining, and called to the bar" on June 6, 1866.[156]

Once qualified as a barrister, Benjamin chose to join the Northern Circuit, as it included Liverpool, where his connections in New Orleans and knowledge of mercantile affairs would do him the most good. In an early case, he defended two former Confederate agents against a suit by the United States to gain assets said to belong to that nation. [154] Although he lost that case (*United States v Wagner*) on appeal, he was successful against his former enemies in *United States v McRae* (1869).[157] He had need of rapid success, as most of his remaining assets were lost in the collapse of the firm of Overend, Gurney and Company. He was reduced to penning columns on international affairs for *The Daily Telegraph*.[154]

According to Justice Ruth Bader Ginsburg, "repeating his Louisiana progress, Benjamin made his reputation among his new peers by publication."[153] In an early representation, he wrote a complex governing document for an insurance firm that other counsel had declined despite the substantial fee, due to the early deadline. After brief study, Benjamin wrote out the document, never making a correction or erasure.[154] In 1868, Benjamin published *A Treatise on the Law of Sale of Personal Property, With Reference to the American Decisions, to the French Code, and Civil Law*. This work, known for short as *Benjamin on Sales*, became a classic in both Britain and America, and launched his career as a barrister.[156] It went through three editions prior to Benjamin's death in 1884;[158] an eighth edition was published in 2010.[159] Today *Benjamin's Sale of Goods* forms part of the "common law library" of key practitioner texts on English civil law.[160]

In 1867, Benjamin had been indicted in Richmond, along with Davis, Lee, and others, for waging war against the United States. The indictment was soon quashed. Davis visited London in 1868, free on bail, and Benjamin advised him not to take legal action against the author of a book that had angered Davis, as it would only give the book publicity.[161] Benjamin corresponded with Davis, and met with him on the former rebel president's visits to Europe during Benjamin's lifetime, though the two were never as close as they had been during the war.[162]

Benjamin was created a "Palatine silk," entitled to the precedence of a Queen's Counsel within Lancashire, in July 1869.[154] There was a large creation of Queen's Counsel in early 1872, but Benjamin was not included; it was stated in his *Times* obituary that he had put his name forward. Later that year, he argued the case of *Potter v Rankin* before the House of Lords and so impressed Lord Hatherley that a patent of precedence was soon made out, giving Benjamin the privileges of a Queen's Counsel. As he became prominent as a barrister, he discontinued practice before juries (at which he was less successful) in favor of trials or appeals before judges. In his last years in practice, he demanded an additional fee of 100 guineas (£105) to appear in any court besides the House of Lords and the Privy Council.[156] In 1875, he was made a bencher of Lincoln's Inn.[163]

In 1881, Benjamin represented Arthur Orton, the Tichborne claimant, before the House of Lords. Orton, a butcher from Wagga Wagga, New South Wales, had claimed to be Sir Roger Tichborne, a baronet who had vanished some years previously, and Orton had perjured himself in the course of defending his claim. Benjamin sought to overturn the sentence of 14 years passed on Orton, but was not successful.[164]

In his final years, Benjamin suffered from health issues. In 1880, he was badly injured in a fall from a tram in Paris. He also developed diabetes. He suffered a heart attack in Paris at the end of 1882, and his doctor ordered him to retire.[163] His health improved enough to allow him to travel to London in June 1883 for a dinner in his honor attended by the English bench and bar. He returned to Paris and suffered a relapse of his heart trouble in early 1884.[165] Natalie Benjamin had the last rites of the Catholic Church administered to her Jewish husband before his death in Paris on May 6, 1884, and funeral services were held in a church prior to Judah Benjamin's interment at Père Lachaise Cemetery in the St. Martin family crypt. His grave did not bear his name until 1938, when a plaque was placed by the Paris chapter of the United Daughters of the Confederacy.[166]

# Ambrose Bierce

*Bierce around* 1866

**Ambrose Gwinnett Bierce** (June 24, 1842[2]–circa 1914[3]) was an American short story writer, journalist, poet, and Civil War veteran.

Bierce's book *The Devil's Dictionary* was named as one of "The 100 Greatest Masterpieces of American Literature" by the American Revolution Bicentennial Administration.[4] His story "An Occurrence at Owl Creek Bridge" has been described as "one of the most famous and frequently anthologized stories in American literature";[5] and his book *Tales of Soldiers and Civilians* (also published as *In the Midst of Life*) was named by the Grolier Club as one of the 100 most influential American books printed before 1900.[6]

A prolific and versatile writer, Bierce was regarded as one of the most influential journalists in the United States,[7][8] and as a pioneering writer of realist fiction.[9] For his horror writing, Michael Dirda ranked him alongside Edgar Allan Poe and H. P. Lovecraft.[10] His war stories influenced Stephen Crane, Ernest Hemingway, and others,[11] and he was considered an influential and feared literary critic.[12] In recent decades Bierce has gained wider respect as a fabulist and for his poetry.[13][14]

In December 1913, Bierce traveled to Chihuahua, Mexico, to gain first-hand experience of the Mexican Revolution.[15] He disappeared, and was rumored to be traveling with rebel troops. He was never seen again.

## Military career

At the outset of the American Civil War, Bierce enlisted in the Union Army's 9th Indiana Infantry. He participated in the operations in Western Virginia (1861), was present at the Battle of Philippi (the first organized land action of the war), and received newspaper attention for his daring rescue, under fire, of a gravely wounded comrade at the Battle of Rich Mountain. Bierce fought at the Battle of Shiloh (April 1862), a terrifying experience that became a source for several short stories and the memoir "What I Saw of Shiloh."

In April 1863 he was commissioned a first lieutenant, and served on the staff of General William Babcock Hazen as a topographical engineer, making maps of likely battlefields.[20] As a staff officer, Bierce became known to leading generals such as George H. Thomas and Oliver O. Howard, both of whom supported his application for admission to West Point in May 1864. General Hazen believed Bierce would graduate from the military academy "with distinction" and William T. Sherman also endorsed the application for admission even though stating he had no personal acquaintance with Bierce.[21] In June

1864, Bierce sustained a serious head wound (since diagnosed as a traumatic brain injury)[22] at the Battle of Kennesaw Mountain,[23] and spent the rest of the summer on furlough, returning to active duty in September. He was discharged from the army in January 1865.

His military career resumed, however, in mid-1866, when he joined General Hazen as part of an expedition to inspect military outposts across the Great Plains. The expedition traveled by horseback and wagon from Omaha, Nebraska, arriving toward year's end in San Francisco, California.

## Literary works

*Bierce,* 1892

During his lifetime, Bierce was better known as a journalist than as a fiction writer. His most popular stories were written in rapid succession between 1888 and 1891, in what was characterized as "a tremendous burst of consummate art."[35] Bierce's works often highlight the inscrutability of the universe and the absurdity of death.[36][37]

Bierce wrote realistically of the terrible things he had seen in the war[38] in such stories as "An Occurrence at Owl Creek Bridge," "A Horseman in the Sky," "One of the Missing," and "Chickamauga." His grimly realistic cycle of 25 war stories has been called "the greatest anti-war document in American literature."[39]

According to Milton Subotsky, Bierce helped pioneer the psychological horror story.[40] In addition to his ghost and war stories, he also published several volumes of poetry. His *Fantastic Fables* anticipated the ironic style of grotesquerie that became a more common genre in the 20th century.

One of Bierce's most famous works is his much-quoted *The Devil's Dictionary*, originally an occasional newspaper item, first published in book form in 1906 as *The Cynic's Word Book*. Described as "howlingly funny,"[41] it consists of satirical definitions of English words which lampoon cant and political double-talk. Bierce edited the twelve volumes of *The Collected Works of Ambrose Bierce*, which were published from 1909 to 1912. The seventh volume consists solely of *The Devil's Dictionary*.

Bierce has been criticized by his contemporaries and later scholars for deliberately pursuing improbability and for his penchant toward "trick endings."[36] In his later stories, apparently under the influence of Maupassant, Bierce "dedicated himself to shocking the audience," as if his purpose was "to attack the reader's smug intellectual security."[42]

Bierce's bias towards Naturalism has also been noted:[43] "The biting, deriding quality of his satire, unbalanced by any compassion for his targets, was often taken as petty meanness, showing contempt for humanity and an intolerance to the point of merciless cruelty."[44]

Stephen Crane was of the minority of Bierce's contemporaries who valued Bierce's experimental short stories.[45] In his essay "Supernatural Horror in Literature," H. P. Lovecraft characterized Bierce's fictional work as "grim and savage." Lovecraft goes on to say that nearly all of Bierce's stories are of the horror genre and some shine as great examples of weird fiction.[46]

Critic William Dean Howells said, "Mr. Bierce is among our three greatest writers." When told this, Bierce responded, "I am sure Mr. Howells is the other two."[47]

## Disappearance

In October 1913, Bierce, then age 71, departed from Washington, D.C., for a tour of his old Civil War battlefields. By December he had passed through Louisiana and Texas, crossing by way of El Paso into Mexico, which was in the throes of revolution. In Ciudad Juárez he joined Pancho Villa's army as an observer, and in that role he witnessed the Battle of Tierra Blanca.[48]

Bierce is known to have accompanied Villa's army as far as the city of Chihuahua. His last known communication with the world was a letter he wrote there to Blanche Partington, a close friend, dated December 26, 1913.[49][50][51] After closing this letter by saying, "As to me, I leave here tomorrow for an unknown destination," he vanished without a trace, his disappearance becoming one of the most famous in American literary history. Skeptic Joe Nickell argued that no letter had ever been found;[52] all that existed was a notebook belonging to his secretary and companion, Carrie Christiansen, containing a rough summary of a purported letter and her statement that the originals had been destroyed.

There was an official investigation by U.S. consular officials of the disappearance of one of its citizens. Some of Villa's men were questioned at the time of his disappearance and afterwards, with contradictory accounts. Pancho Villa's representative in the U.S., Felix A. Sommerfeld, was contacted by U.S. chief of staff Hugh L. Scott and Sommerfeld investigated the disappearance. Bierce was said to have been last seen in the city of Chihuahua in January.[53]

Oral tradition in Sierra Mojada, Coahuila, documented by a priest named James Lienert, states that Bierce was executed by firing squad in the town cemetery there.[54] However, Nickell[52] finds this story to be unreliable. He quotes Bierce's friend and biographer Walter Neale as saying that Bierce had not ridden for quite some time, was suffering from serious asthma, and had been severely critical of Pancho Villa. Neale concludes that it would have been highly unlikely for Bierce to have gone to Mexico and joined Villa.

All investigations into his fate have proven fruitless, and Nickell concedes[52] that despite a lack of hard evidence that Bierce had gone to Mexico, there is also none that he had not. Therefore, despite an abundance of theories (including death by suicide), his ultimate fate remains shrouded in mystery.

# Malinda Blalock

*Sarah M Pritchard Blalock. She is holding a picture of her husband Keith.*

**Sarah Malinda Pritchard Blalock** (March 10, 1839 or 1842–March 9, 1901 or 1903) was a female soldier during the American Civil War. Despite originally being a sympathizer for the right of secession, she fought bravely on both sides. She followed her husband and joined the CSA's 26th North Carolina Regiment, disguising herself as a young man and calling herself Samuel Blalock. The couple eventually escaped by crossing Confederate lines and joining the Union partisans in the mountains of western North Carolina. During the last years of the war, she was a pro-Union marauder raiding the Appalachia region. Today she is one of the most remembered female combatants of the Civil War.

## Early life and marriage

Sarah Pritchard was born March 10, 1839, in Caldwell County, North Carolina[1] (now part of Avery County) which is located in the steep region of Grandfather Mountain.[2] Sarah Pritchard was the daughter of John and Elizabeth Pritchard, and the sixth of nine children.[1]

When she was a child, Sarah Pritchard resided in Watauga County (also now Avery County) which was her main residence until her death. There, she attended a single-room schoolhouse.

She became a close friend of William McKesson Blalock, nicknamed "Keith" after a contemporary boxer, due to his skill at boxing.[3] Despite their families having been rivals for many years, she married William in 1861, aged 19.[1]

## Civil War

After the Civil War began, the western North Carolina communities in the Appalachian Mountains were divided over their political adherences. Neighbors and families argued with each other. Originally Malinda expressed her sympathy for the right of secession, but Keith and his stepfather Austin Coffey were ardent unionists, although Keith was opposed to President Lincoln, and they had planned to desert toward the Union someday. The Blalocks' opposing views did not affect their marriage.

When the Confederate 26th North Carolina Infantry, commanded by Colonel Zebulon Vance, showed up in the region to recruit, Keith began to plan an escape across the frontier from his local political enemies. He was hesitant about whether to flee directly toward Kentucky or enroll temporarily with the Confederate Army to desert across the enemy lines later.

Keith also considered the consequences of an untimely escape on Malinda, fearful that local distaste of his actions would cause her to be scapegoated in his absence. Spurred by the good pay in serving the "Grays," Keith trusted that he would receive a light military commission, possibly to northern Virginia for example, from where it would be easy to desert to the nearest "Yankee" regiment. He accompanied his neighbors to the recruitment office, signing up with the Confederate infantry.

## Samuel Blalock

Fearing for Malinda, Keith had made sure that all local secessionists would see him leaving with the Confederates. However, when arriving at the enlistment gathering at the town's railroad depot, someone began to walk by his side, a mysterious recruit who was wearing a forage cap and had a particularly little physique and delicate features. Surprisingly, "he" turned out to be Malinda, his own wife.[1]

Malinda was officially registered on March 20 of 1862 at Lenoir, North Carolina,[4] as "Samuel 'Sammy' Blalock," Keith's 20-year-old brother.[1] This document and her discharge papers survive as one of the few existing records of a female soldier from North Carolina, from the many ones who may have actually served.

## Confederate military life

Their plan to defect proved unworkable because, already before their arrival, the 26th had fought its biggest battle, which was the loss to the Union of the town of New Bern in eastern North Carolina. Instead of moving to Virginia's battlefront, they remained stationed far from the northern frontier at Kinston, North Carolina, on the Neuse River.

While maintaining her hidden identity, Malinda was a good soldier. One of their assistant surgeons, named Underwood, pointed out that "her disguise was never penetrated. She drilled and did the duties of a soldier as any other member of the Company, and was very adept at learning the manual and drill."[5]

Later Keith became a respected brevet sergeant, ordering Malinda then to "stay close to him." They fought in three battles together, but "Samuel's" true identity remained still unknown.

## The desertion

In April 1862, Keith's squad received the order to range the Neuse River's region by fording it during the night, to detect any enemy guarding-posts. Their ultimate objective was to track down the location of a particular Union regiment commanded by US General Ambrose Burnside.

At one point of the mission, a hard skirmish began. Most of Keith's squad retreated to safety, crossing back over the Neuse River. However, after regrouping, it was found that "Samuel" was missing. Keith promptly returned to the battlefield. He found Malinda clinging to a pine and bleeding profusely, with a bullet lodged in her left shoulder.[1]

As quickly as he could, Keith carried Malinda back to the 26th. He brought her to the infirmary tent where she was attended by its surgeon, Dr. Thomas J. Boykin. The bullet was successfully removed, but the truth about "Samuel" was discovered during the medical examination.

After obtaining a promise from Boykin that he would spare them some time before reporting, Keith went to a nearby field of poison ivy. He stripped his clothes and flailed through the underbrush for about half an hour.

The next morning, he suffered a persistent fever while his affected skin was inflamed and covered by blisters. Keith told the doctors that he had a serious recurrent illness which was highly contagious, adding the ailment of a hernia also. Fearing an outbreak of smallpox, the doctors discharged Keith expeditiously from the regiment and confined him to his tent.

Malinda would remain stranded in the camp because her recent wound didn't yet merit a discharge. She decided to confront Colonel Vance once and for all. She offered herself as a volunteer to aid the sick Sergeant Keith on his return to Watauga. Vance's response was a clear "no," communicating to "Samuel" that instead "he" would be his new personal orderly.

At that point Malinda decided to tell Vance the truth. Vance's first reaction was of disbelief while calling the surgeon and commenting to him: "Oh Surgeon, have I a case for you!" However, the physician corroborated Malinda's statement. Immediately, Vance discharged "Samuel" and demanded the restitution of "his" original enlisting reward of 50 dollars.

## Marauders

Malinda and her husband could return to Watauga then. Once there, though, Keith was soon required by the local Confederate forces, which demanded that he enlist again—after noting his healthy status—and return to the front. Otherwise, he would be judged by the new Confederate laws of military draft.

Therefore, Malinda and Keith fled again, toward Grandfather Mountain. There, they found more local deserters in the same condition. They stayed with them until the Confederate Army intercepted the group, injuring Keith in his arm.

Malinda and Keith moved then to Tennessee, where they joined the US-10th Michigan Cavalry of Colonel George Washington Kirk, who was later succeeded by General George Stoneman. For some time, Keith accomplished some administrative chores as a recruitment agent.

However, the couple decided to enter in action again, this time for the Union, by joining Colonel Kirk's voluntary guerrilla squadrons on scouting and raiding missions throughout the Appalachia region of North Carolina.

With Malinda next to him, Keith began in Blowing Rock, North Carolina, as one of the leaders of the guides for the Watauga Underground Railroad. This was a way of escape from the Confederate jail at Salisbury, North Carolina, which was the largest facility of the state. Keith had to guide the escaped Union soldiers to safety in Tennessee.

However, from 1863 on, the skirmishes against the patrolling enemy forces in the region were increasingly tougher.

Keith's pro-union guerrilla forces began to raid Watauga County. Because once they had been harshly humbled by the southern loyalists, the outlaws pitilessly raided their farms, stole and killed. Marauding throughout North Carolina's Appalachia region, they were soon feared by the entire state.

In 1863 Malinda realised she was pregnant, so she travelled to Tennessee to stay with another of the marauders' wives. Giving birth to a son on April 8, 1864, she spent some time with relatives in the area before leaving her young son with them and returning to military activities.[6]

Confederate vigilantes then murdered Keith's stepfather, Austin Coffey, and one of Austin's four brothers (William), while the other two survived the attack. The Coffeys had been betrayed by some local folks who were found and killed by Keith after the war.[7]

During the war, some of the most ill-fated actions of Malinda and Keith were their two pillaging incursions to the Moore family's farm in Caldwell County, late in 1863. One of Moore's sons, James Daniel, was the 26th's officer who recruited them originally. In the first incursion, Malinda was injured in her shoulder. During the second one, Moore's son was at home, recovering after the Battle of Gettysburg, while Keith got a shot in his eye and lost it.

During the war, Keith lost the use of a hand. He also murdered one of his uncles who had turned to the Confederacy.

## Later life

After the war, Malinda and Keith returned to Watauga, to live the rest of their lives as farmers, with their four children. For some time, they had troubles getting Keith's government pension. Afterward, they joined the Republican Party where, in 1870, Keith ran unsuccessfully for a place in the Congress of the United States.

Sarah Malinda Pritchard Blalock died in 1901, at age 59, due to natural causes while she was sleeping. She was buried in the Montezuma Cemetery of Avery County. Very affected, Keith moved to Hickory, North Carolina, taking his son Columbus with him.

On April 11, 1913, Keith died in a railroad accident. He lost control of his handcar on a curve, and was crushed to death.[1] Some versions attribute his death to a local payback for his past years with Malinda. He was buried beside her at Montezuma Cemetery. His stone badge reads: "Keith Blalock, Soldier, 26th N.C Inf., CSA."

# John Wilkes Booth

*Booth c. 1865*

**John Wilkes Booth** (May 10, 1838–April 26, 1865) was an American actor who assassinated President Abraham Lincoln at Ford's Theatre in Washington, D.C. on April 14, 1865. He was a member of the prominent 19th-century Booth theatrical family from Maryland and a well-known actor in his own right.[1] He was also a Confederate sympathizer, vehement in his denunciation of Lincoln, and strongly opposed to the abolition of slavery in the United States.[2]

Booth and a group of co-conspirators originally plotted to kidnap Lincoln but later planned to kill him, Vice President Andrew Johnson, and Secretary of State William H. Seward in a bid to help the Confederacy's cause.[3] Robert E. Lee's Army of Northern Virginia had surrendered four days earlier, but Booth believed that the American Civil War was not yet over because Confederate General Joseph E. Johnston's army was still fighting the Union Army.

Booth was completely successful in carrying out his part of the plot. He shot Lincoln once in the back of the head, and the President died the next morning. Seward was severely wounded but recovered, and Vice President Johnson was never attacked.

After the assassination, Booth fled on horseback to southern Maryland and, 12 days later, arrived at a farm in rural northern Virginia where he was tracked down. Booth's companion gave himself up, but Booth refused and was shot by Union soldier Boston Corbett after the barn in which he was hiding was set ablaze. Eight other conspirators were tried and convicted, and four were hanged shortly after.

## Civil War years

Booth was strongly opposed to the abolitionists who sought to end slavery in the U.S. He attended the hanging of abolitionist leader John Brown on December 2, 1859, who was executed for leading a raid on the Federal armory at Harpers Ferry in present-day West Virginia.[65] Booth had been rehearsing at the Richmond Theatre when he abruptly decided to join the Richmond Grays, a volunteer militia of 1,500 men traveling to Charles Town for Brown's hanging, to guard against an attempt by abolitionists to rescue Brown from the gallows by force.[65][66] When Brown was hanged without incident, Booth stood in uniform near the scaffold and afterwards expressed great satisfaction with Brown's fate, although he admired the condemned man's bravery in facing death stoically.[43][67]

Lincoln was elected president on November 6, 1860, and the following month Booth drafted a long speech, apparently undelivered, that decried Northern abolitionism and made clear his strong support of the South and the institution of slavery.[68] On April 12, 1861, the Civil War began, and eventually 11 Southern states seceded from the Union. In Booth's native Maryland, some of the slaveholding portion of the population favored joining the Confederate States of America. Although the Maryland legislature voted decisively (53–13) against secession on April 28, 1861,[69][70] it also voted not to allow federal troops to pass south through the state by rail, and it requested that Lincoln remove the growing numbers of federal troops in Maryland.[71] The legislature seems to have wanted to remain in the Union while also wanting to avoid involvement in a war against Southern neighbors.[71] Adhering to Maryland's demand that its infrastructure not be used to wage war on seceding neighbors would have left the federal capital of Washington, D.C., exposed, and would have made the prosecution of war against the South impossible, which was no doubt the legislature's intention. Lincoln suspended the writ of *habeas corpus* and imposed martial law in Baltimore and other portions of the state, ordering the imprisonment of many Maryland political leaders at Ft. McHenry and the stationing of Federal troops in Baltimore.[72] Many Marylanders, including Booth, agreed with the ruling of Marylander and U.S. Supreme Court Chief Justice Roger B. Taney, in *Ex parte Merryman*, that Lincoln's suspension of *habeas corpus* in Maryland was unconstitutional.[73]

As a popular actor in the 1860s, Booth continued to travel extensively to perform in the North and South, and as far west as New Orleans. According to his sister Asia, Booth confided to her that he also used his position to smuggle the anti-malarial drug quinine, which was crucial to the lives of residents of the Gulf coast, to the South during his travels there, since it was in short supply due to the Northern blockade.[62]

*Lucy Lambert Hale, Booth's fiancée in 1865*

Booth was pro-Confederate, but his family was divided, like many Marylanders. He was outspoken in his love of the South, and equally outspoken in his hatred of Lincoln.[56][74] As the Civil War went on, Booth increasingly quarreled with his brother Edwin, who declined to make stage appearances in the South and refused to listen to John Wilkes' fiercely partisan denunciations of the North and Lincoln.[62] In early 1863, Booth was arrested in St. Louis while on a theatre tour, when he was heard saying that he "wished the President and the whole damned government would go to hell."[75][76] He was charged with making "treasonous" remarks against the government, but was released when he took an oath of allegiance to the Union and paid a substantial fine.

In February 1865, Booth became infatuated with Lucy Lambert Hale, the daughter of U.S. Senator John P. Hale of New Hampshire, and they became secretly engaged when

Booth received his mother's blessing for their marriage plans. "You have so often been dead in love," his mother counseled Booth in a letter, "be well assured she is really and truly devoted to you."[77] Booth composed a handwritten Valentine card for his fiancée on February 13, expressing his "adoration." She was unaware of Booth's deep antipathy towards Lincoln.[77]

## Plot to kidnap Lincoln

As the 1864 presidential election drew near, the Confederacy's prospects for victory were ebbing, and the tide of war increasingly favored the North. The likelihood of Lincoln's re-election filled Booth with rage towards the President, whom Booth blamed for the war and all of the South's troubles. Booth had promised his mother at the outbreak of war that he would not enlist as a soldier, but he increasingly chafed at not fighting for the South, writing in a letter to her, "I have begun to deem myself a coward and to despise my own existence."[78] He began to formulate plans to kidnap Lincoln from his summer residence at the Old Soldiers Home, three miles (4.8 km) from the White House, and to smuggle him across the Potomac River and into Richmond, Virginia. Once in Confederate hands, Lincoln would be exchanged for Confederate Army prisoners of war held in Northern prisons and, Booth reasoned, bring the war to an end by emboldening opposition to the war in the North or forcing Union recognition of the Confederate government.[78][79][80][81]

Throughout the Civil War, the Confederacy maintained a network of underground operators in southern Maryland, particularly Charles and St. Mary's Counties, smuggling recruits across the Potomac River into Virginia and relaying messages for Confederate agents as far north as Canada.[82] Booth recruited his friends Samuel Arnold and Michael O'Laughlen as accomplices.[83] They met often at the house of Confederate sympathizer Maggie Branson at 16 North Eutaw Street in Baltimore.[29] He also met with several well-known Confederate sympathizers at The Parker House in Boston.

In October, Booth made an unexplained trip to Montreal, which was a center of clandestine Confederate activity. He spent ten days in the city, staying for a time at St. Lawrence Hall, a rendezvous for the Confederate Secret Service, and meeting several Confederate agents there.[84][85] No conclusive proof has linked Booth's kidnapping or assassination plots to a conspiracy involving the leadership of the Confederate government, but historian David Herbert Donald states that "at least at the lower levels of the Southern secret service, the abduction of the Union President was under consideration."[86] Historian Thomas Goodrich concludes that Booth entered the Confederate Secret Service as a spy and courier.[87]

Lincoln won a landslide re-election in early November 1864, on a platform that advocated abolishing slavery altogether, by Constitutional Amendment.[88] Booth, meanwhile, devoted increased energy and money to his kidnapping plot.[89][90] He assembled a loose-knit band of Southern sympathizers, including David Herold, George Atzerodt, Lewis

Powell (also known as Lewis Payne or Paine), and rebel agent John Surratt.[82][91] They began to meet routinely at the boarding house of Surratt's mother Mary Surratt.[91]

By this time, Booth was arguing vehemently with his older, pro-Union brother Edwin about Lincoln and the war, and Edwin finally told him that he was no longer welcome at his New York home. Booth also railed against Lincoln in conversations with his sister Asia. "That man's appearance, his pedigree, his coarse low jokes and anecdotes, his vulgar similes, and his policy are a disgrace to the seat he holds. He is made the tool of the North, to crush out slavery."[92] Asia recalled that he decried Lincoln's re-election, "making himself a king," and that he went on "wild tirades" in 1865, as the Confederacy's defeat became more certain.[93]

Booth attended Lincoln's second inauguration on March 4 as the guest of his secret fiancée Lucy Hale. In the crowd below were Powell, Atzerodt, and Herold. There was no attempt to assassinate Lincoln during the inauguration. Later, Booth remarked about his "excellent chance . . . to kill the President, if I had wished."[78] On March 17, he learned that Lincoln would be attending a performance of the play *Still Waters Run Deep* at a hospital near the Soldier's Home. He assembled his team on a stretch of road near the Soldier's Home in hope of kidnapping Lincoln en route to the hospital, but the President did not appear.[94] Booth later learned that Lincoln had changed his plans at the last moment to attend a reception at the National Hotel in Washington — where Booth was staying.[78]

## Assassination of Lincoln

On April 12, 1865, Booth heard the news that Robert E. Lee had surrendered at Appomattox Court House. He told Louis J. Weichmann, a friend of John Surratt and a boarder at Mary Surratt's house, that he was done with the stage and that the only play he wanted to present henceforth was *Venice Preserv'd*. Weichmann did not understand the reference; *Venice Preserv'd* is about an assassination plot. Booth's scheme to kidnap Lincoln was no longer feasible with the Union Army's capture of Richmond and Lee's surrender, and he changed his goal to assassination.[95]

The previous day, Booth was in the crowd outside the White House when Lincoln gave an impromptu speech from his window. Lincoln stated that he was in favor of granting suffrage to the former slaves, and Booth declared that it would be the last speech that Lincoln would ever make.[94][96][97]

On the morning of Good Friday, April 14, 1865, Booth went to Ford's Theatre to get his mail. While there, he was told by John Ford's brother that President and Mrs. Lincoln would be attending the play *Our American Cousin* at Ford's Theatre that evening, accompanied by Gen. and Mrs. Ulysses S. Grant.[98] He immediately set about making plans for the assassination, which included making arrangements with livery stable owner James W. Pumphrey for a getaway horse and an escape route. Booth informed Powell, Herold, and Atzerodt of his intention to kill Lincoln. He assigned Powell to assassinate Secretary of State William H. Seward and Atzerodt to do so to Vice President Andrew Johnson. Herold would assist in their escape into Virginia.[99]

By targeting Lincoln and his two immediate successors to the presidency, Booth seems to have intended to decapitate the Union government and throw it into a state of panic and confusion.[100] The possibility of assassinating the Union Army's commanding general as well was foiled when Grant declined the theatre invitation at his wife's insistence. Instead, the Grants departed Washington by train that evening for a visit to relatives in New Jersey.[29] Booth had hoped that the assassinations would create sufficient chaos within the Union that the Confederate government could reorganize and continue the war if one Confederate army remained in the field or, that failing, to avenge the South's defeat.[101]

Booth had free access to all parts of the theater as a famous and popular actor who had frequently performed at Ford's Theatre and who was well known to its owner John T. Ford, even having his mail sent there.[102] He bored a spyhole into the door of the presidential box earlier that day, so that he could observe the box's occupants and verify that the President had made it to the play.

Booth slipped into Lincoln's box that evening at around 10 p.m. as the play progressed and shot the President in the back of the head with a .41 caliber Deringer pistol.[103] Booth's escape was almost thwarted by Major Henry Rathbone, who was in the presidential box with Mary Todd Lincoln.[104] Booth stabbed Rathbone when the startled officer lunged at him.[82] Rathbone's fiancée Clara Harris was also in the box but was not harmed.

Booth then jumped from the President's box to the stage, where he raised his knife and shouted "*Sic semper tyrannis*." (Latin for "Thus always to tyrants," attributed to Brutus at Caesar's assassination; state motto of Virginia and mentioned in the new "Maryland, My Maryland," future anthem of Booth's Maryland.) According to some accounts, Booth added, "I have done it, the South is avenged!"[36][105][106] Some witnesses reported that Booth fractured or otherwise injured his leg when his spur snagged a decorative U.S. Treasury Guard flag while leaping to the stage.[107] Historian Michael W. Kauffman questioned this legend in his book *American Brutus: John Wilkes Booth and the Lincoln Conspiracies*, writing that eyewitness accounts of Booth's hurried stage exit made it unlikely that his leg was broken then. Kauffman contends that Booth was injured later that night during his flight to escape when his horse tripped and fell on him, calling Booth's claim to the contrary an exaggeration to portray his own actions as heroic.[108]

Booth was the only one of the assassins to succeed. Powell was able to stab Seward, who was bedridden as a result of an earlier carriage accident. Seward was badly wounded but he survived. Atzerodt lost his nerve and spent the evening drinking alcohol; he never made an attempt to kill Johnson.

## Reaction and pursuit

In the ensuing pandemonium inside Ford's Theatre, Booth fled by a stage door to the alley, where his getaway horse was held for him by Joseph "Peanuts" Burroughs.[109] The owner of the horse had warned Booth that the horse was high spirited and would break halter if left unattended. Booth left the horse with Edmund Spangler and Spangler arranged for Burroughs to hold it.

The fleeing assassin galloped into southern Maryland, accompanied by David Herold, having planned his escape route to take advantage of the sparsely settled area's lack of telegraphs and railroads, along with its predominantly Confederate sympathies.[99][110] He thought that the area's dense forests and the swampy terrain of Zekiah Swamp made it ideal for an escape route into rural Virginia.[89][99][111] At midnight, Booth and Herold arrived at Surratt's Tavern on the Brandywine Pike, 9 miles (14 km) from Washington, where they had stored guns and equipment earlier in the year as part of the kidnap plot.[112]

The fugitives then continued southward, stopping before dawn on April 15 for treatment of Booth's injured leg at the home of Dr. Samuel Mudd in St. Catharine, 25 miles (40 km) from Washington.[112] Mudd later said that Booth told him the injury occurred when his horse fell.[113] The next day, Booth and Herold arrived at the home of Samuel Cox around 4 a.m. As the two fugitives hid in the woods nearby, Cox contacted Thomas A. Jones, his foster brother and a Confederate agent in charge of spy operations in the southern Maryland area since 1862.[82][114] The War Department advertised a $100,000 reward ($1.64 million in 2019 USD) by order of Secretary of War Edwin M. Stanton for information leading to the arrest of Booth and his accomplices, and Federal troops were dispatched to search southern Maryland extensively, following tips reported by Federal intelligence agents to Col. Lafayette Baker.[115]

Federal troops combed the rural area's woods and swamps for Booth in the days following the assassination, as the nation experienced an outpouring of grief. On April 18, mourners waited seven abreast in a mile-long line outside the White House for the public viewing of the slain president, reposing in his open walnut casket in the black-draped East Room. [116] A cross of lilies was at the head and roses covered the coffin's lower half.[117] Thousands of mourners arriving on special trains jammed Washington for the next day's funeral, sleeping on hotel floors and even resorting to blankets spread outdoors on the Capitol's lawn. [118] Prominent African-American abolitionist leader and orator Frederick Douglass called the assassination an "unspeakable calamity."[119] Great indignation was directed towards Booth as the assassin's identity was telegraphed across the nation. Newspapers called him an "accursed devil," "monster," "madman," and a "wretched fiend."[120] Historian Dorothy Kunhardt writes: "Almost every family who kept a photograph album on the parlor table owned a likeness of John Wilkes Booth of the famous Booth family of actors. After the assassination Northerners slid the Booth card out of their albums: some threw it away, some burned it, some crumpled it angrily."[121] Even in the South, sorrow was expressed in some quarters. In Savannah, Georgia, the mayor and city council addressed a vast throng at an outdoor gathering to express their indignation, and many in the crowd wept.[122] Confederate general Joseph E. Johnston called Booth's act "a disgrace to the age."[123] Robert E. Lee also expressed regret at Lincoln's death by Booth's hand.[119]

Not all were grief-stricken. In New York City, a man was attacked by an enraged crowd when he shouted, "It served Old Abe right!" after hearing the news of Lincoln's death.

[122] Elsewhere in the South, Lincoln was hated in death as in life, and Booth was viewed as a hero as many rejoiced at news of his deed.[119] Other Southerners feared that a vengeful North would exact a terrible retribution upon the defeated former Confederate states. "Instead of being a great Southern hero, his deed was considered the worst possible tragedy that could have befallen the South as well as the North," writes Kunhardt.[124]

Booth lay in hiding in the Maryland woods, waiting for an opportunity to cross the Potomac River into Virginia. He read the accounts of national mourning reported in the newspapers brought to him by Jones each day.[124] By April 20, he was aware that some of his co-conspirators had already been arrested: Mary Surratt, Powell (or Paine), Arnold, and O'Laughlen.[125] Booth was surprised to find little public sympathy for his action, especially from those anti-Lincoln newspapers that had previously excoriated the President in life. News of the assassination reached the far corners of the nation, and indignation was aroused against Lincoln's critics, whom many blamed for encouraging Booth to act. The *San Francisco Chronicle* editorialized:

> Booth has simply carried out what . . . secession politicians and journalists have been for years expressing in words . . . who have denounced the President as a "tyrant," a "despot," a "usurper," hinted at, and virtually recommended.[126]

Booth wrote of his dismay in a journal entry on April 21, as he awaited nightfall before crossing the Potomac River into Virginia (*see map*):

> For six months we had worked to capture. But our cause being almost lost, something decisive and great must be done. I struck boldly, and not as the papers say. I can never repent it, though we hated to kill.[127][128]

That same day, the nine-car funeral train bearing Lincoln's body departed Washington on the Baltimore and Ohio Railroad, arriving at Baltimore's Camden Station at 10 a.m., the first stop on a 13-day journey to Springfield, Illinois, its final destination.[82][129][130] The funeral train slowly made its way westward through seven states, stopping en route at Harrisburg, Philadelphia, Trenton, New York, Albany, Buffalo, Cleveland, Columbus, Cincinnati, and Indianapolis during the following days. About 7 million people[131] lined the railroad tracks along the 1,662-mile (2,675 km) route, holding aloft signs with legends such as "We mourn our loss," "He lives in the hearts of his people," and "The darkest hour in history."[132][133]

In the cities where the train stopped, 1.5 million people viewed Lincoln in his coffin.[119] [130][132] Aboard the train was Clarence Depew, president of the New York Central Railroad, who said, "As we sped over the rails at night, the scene was the most pathetic ever witnessed. At every crossroads the glare of innumerable torches illuminated the whole population, kneeling on the ground."[130] Dorothy Kunhardt called the funeral train's journey "the mightiest outpouring of national grief the world had yet seen."[134]

Mourners were viewing Lincoln's remains when the funeral train steamed into Harrisburg at 8:20 p.m., while Booth and Herold were provided with a boat and compass by Jones to cross the Potomac at night on April 21.[82] Instead of reaching Virginia, they mistakenly navigated upriver to a bend in the broad Potomac River, coming ashore again in Maryland on April 22.[135] The 23-year-old Herold knew the area well, having frequently hunted there, and recognized a nearby farm as belonging to a Confederate sympathizer. The farmer led them to his son-in-law, Col. John J. Hughes, who provided the fugitives with food and a hideout until nightfall, for a second attempt to row across the river to Virginia.[136] Booth wrote in his diary:

> With every man's hand against me, I am here in despair. And why; For doing what Brutus was honored for . . . And yet I for striking down a greater tyrant than they ever knew am looked upon as a common cutthroat.[136]

The pair finally reached the Virginia shore near Machodoc Creek before dawn on April 23.[137] There, they made contact with Thomas Harbin, whom Booth had previously brought into his erstwhile kidnapping plot. Harbin took Booth and Herold to another Confederate agent in the area named William Bryant who supplied them with horses.[136][138]

While Lincoln's funeral train was in New York City on April 24, Lieutenant Edward P. Doherty was dispatched from Washington at 2 p.m. with a detachment of 26 Union soldiers from the 16th New York Cavalry Regiment to capture Booth in Virginia,[139] accompanied by Lieutenant Colonel Everton Conger, an intelligence officer assigned by Lafayette Baker. The detachment steamed 70 miles (113 km) down the Potomac River on the boat *John S. Ide*, landing at Belle Plain, Virginia, at 10 p.m.[139][140] The pursuers crossed the Rappahannock River and tracked Booth and Herold to Richard H. Garrett's farm, about 2 miles (3 km) south of Port Royal, Virginia. Booth and Herold had been led to the farm on April 24 by William S. Jett, a former private in the 9th Virginia Cavalry, whom they had met before crossing the Rappahannock.[135] The Garretts were unaware of Lincoln's assassination; Booth was introduced to them as "James W. Boyd," a Confederate soldier, they were told, who had been wounded in the battle of Petersburg and was returning home.[141]

Garrett's 11-year-old son Richard was an eyewitness. In later years, he became a Baptist minister and widely lectured on the events of Booth's demise at his family's farm.[141] In 1921, Garrett's lecture was published in the *Confederate Veteran* as the "True Story of the Capture of John Wilkes Booth."[142] According to his account, Booth and Herold arrived at the Garretts' farm, located on the road to Bowling Green, around 3 p.m. on Monday afternoon. Confederate mail delivery had ceased with the collapse of the Confederate government, he explained, so the Garretts were unaware of Lincoln's assassination.[142] After having dinner with the Garretts that evening, Booth learned of the surrender of Johnston's army, the last Confederate armed force of any size. Its capitulation meant that the Civil War was unquestionably over and Booth's attempt to save the Confederacy by Lincoln's assassination had failed.[143] The Garretts also finally learned of

Lincoln's death and the substantial reward for Booth's capture. Booth, said Garrett, displayed no reaction other than to ask if the family would turn in the fugitive should they have the opportunity. Still not aware of their guest's true identity, one of the older Garrett sons averred that they might, if only because they needed the money. The next day, Booth told the Garretts that he intended to reach Mexico, drawing a route on a map of theirs. [142] Biographer Theodore Roscoe said of Garrett's account, "Almost nothing written or testified in respect to the doings of the fugitives at Garrett's farm can be taken at face value. Nobody knows exactly what Booth said to the Garretts, or they to him."[144]

## Death

Conger tracked down Jett and interrogated him, learning of Booth's location at the Garrett farm. Before dawn on April 26, the soldiers caught up with the fugitives, who were hiding in Garrett's tobacco barn. David Herold surrendered, but Booth refused Conger's demand to surrender, saying, "I prefer to come out and fight." The soldiers then set the barn on fire.[145][146] As Booth moved about inside the blazing barn, Sergeant Boston Corbett shot him. According to Corbett's later account, he fired at Booth because the fugitive "raised his pistol to shoot" at them.[146] Conger's report to Stanton stated that Corbett shot Booth "without order, pretext or excuse," and recommended that Corbett be punished for disobeying orders to take Booth alive.[146] Booth, fatally wounded in the neck, was dragged from the barn to the porch of Garrett's farmhouse, where he died three hours later, aged 26.[141] The bullet had pierced three vertebrae and partially severed his spinal cord, paralyzing him.[21][145] In his dying moments, he reportedly whispered, "Tell my mother I died for my country."[141][145] Asking that his hands be raised to his face so that he could see them, Booth uttered his last words, "Useless, useless," and died as dawn was breaking.[145][147] In Booth's pockets were found a compass, a candle, pictures of five women (actresses Alice Grey, Helen Western, Effie Germon, Fannie Brown, and Booth's fiancée Lucy Hale), and his diary, where he had written of Lincoln's death, "Our country owed all her troubles to him, and God simply made me the instrument of his punishment."[148]

Shortly after Booth's death, his brother Edwin wrote to his sister Asia, "Think no more of him as your brother; he is dead to us now, as he soon must be to all the world, but imagine the boy you loved to be in that better part of his spirit, in another world."[149] Asia also had in her possession a sealed letter that Booth had given her in January 1865 for safekeeping, only to be opened upon his death.[150] In the letter, Booth had written:

> I know how foolish I shall be deemed for undertaking such a step as this, where, on one side, I have many friends and everything to make me happy . . . to give up all . . . seems insane; but God is my judge. I love justice more than I do a country that disowns it, more than fame or wealth.[83]

Booth's letter was seized by Federal troops, along with other family papers at Asia's house, and published by the *New York Times* while the manhunt was still underway. It explained his reasons for plotting against Lincoln. In it he decried Lincoln's war policy as one of "total annihilation," and said:

> I have ever held the South was right. The very nomination of Abraham Lincoln, four years ago, spoke plainly war upon Southern rights and institutions. . . . And looking upon African Slavery from the same stand-point held by the noble framers of our constitution, I for one, have ever considered it one of the greatest blessings (both for themselves and us,) that God has ever bestowed upon a favored nation. . . . I have also studied hard to discover upon what grounds the right of a State to secede has been denied, when our very name, United States, and the Declaration of Independence, both provide for secession.[2]

## Aftermath

Booth's body was shrouded in a blanket and tied to the side of an old farm wagon for the trip back to Belle Plain.[151] There, his corpse was taken aboard the iron-clad USS *Montauk* and brought to the Washington Navy Yard for identification and an autopsy. The body was identified there as Booth's by more than ten people who knew him.[152] Among the identifying features used to make sure that the man that was killed was Booth was a tattoo on his left hand with his initials J.W.B., and a distinct scar on the back of his neck.[153] The third, fourth, and fifth vertebrae were removed during the autopsy to allow access to the bullet. These bones are still on display at the National Museum of Health and Medicine in Washington, D.C.[154] The body was then buried in a storage room at the Old Penitentiary, later moved to a warehouse at the Washington Arsenal on October 1, 1867.[155] In 1869, the remains were once again identified before being released to the Booth family, where they were buried in the family plot at Green Mount Cemetery in Baltimore, after a burial ceremony conducted by Fleming James, minister of Christ Episcopal Church, in the presence of more than 40 people.[155][156][157] [158] Russell Conwell visited homes in the vanquished former Confederate states during this time, and he found that hatred of Lincoln still smoldered. "Photographs of Wilkes Booth, with the last words of great martyrs printed upon its borders . . . adorn their drawing rooms."[119]

Eight others implicated in Lincoln's assassination were tried by a military tribunal in Washington, D.C., and found guilty on June 30, 1865.[159] Mary Surratt,[160] Lewis Powell, David Herold, and George Atzerodt were hanged in the Old Arsenal Penitentiary on July 7, 1865.[161] Samuel Mudd, Samuel Arnold, and Michael O'Laughlen were sentenced to life imprisonment at Fort Jefferson in Florida's isolated Dry Tortugas. Edmund Spangler was given a six-year term in prison.[77] O'Laughlen died in a yellow fever epidemic there in 1867. The others were eventually pardoned in February 1869 by President Andrew Johnson.[162]

Forty years later, when the centenary of Lincoln's birth was celebrated in 1909, a border state official reflected on Booth's assassination of Lincoln: "Confederate veterans held public services and gave public expression to the sentiment, that 'had Lincoln lived' the days of Reconstruction might have been softened and the era of good feeling ushered in earlier."[119] The majority of Northerners viewed Booth as a madman or monster who murdered the savior of the Union, while in the South, many cursed Booth for bringing upon them the harsh revenge of an incensed North instead of the reconciliation promised by Lincoln.[163] A century later, Goodrich concluded in 2005, "For millions of people, particularly in the South, it would be decades before the impact of the Lincoln assassination began to release its terrible hold on their lives."[164]

## Theories of Booth's motivation

Author Francis Wilson was 11 years old at the time of Lincoln's assassination. He wrote an epitaph of Booth in his 1929 book *John Wilkes Booth*: "In the terrible deed he committed, he was actuated by no thought of monetary gain, but by a self-sacrificing, albeit wholly fanatical devotion to a cause he thought supreme."[165] Others have seen less unselfish motives, such as shame, ambition, and sibling rivalry for achievement and fame.[9]

## Theories of Booth's escape

In 1907, Finis L. Bates wrote *Escape and Suicide of John Wilkes Booth*, contending that a Booth look-alike was mistakenly killed at the Garrett farm while Booth eluded his pursuers.[166] Booth, said Bates, assumed the pseudonym "John St. Helen" and settled on the Paluxy River near Glen Rose, Texas, and later moved to Granbury, Texas. He fell gravely ill and made a deathbed confession that he was the fugitive assassin, but he then recovered and fled, eventually committing suicide in 1903 in Enid, Oklahoma, under the alias "David E. George."[11][166][167] By 1913, more than 70,000 copies of the book had been sold, and Bates exhibited St. Helen's mummified body in carnival sideshows.[11]

In response, the Maryland Historical Society published an account in 1913 by Baltimore mayor William M. Pegram, who had viewed Booth's remains upon the casket's arrival at the Weaver funeral home in Baltimore on February 18, 1869, for burial at Green Mount Cemetery. Pegram had known Booth well as a young man; he submitted a sworn statement that the body which he had seen in 1869 was Booth's.[168] Others positively identified this body as Booth at the funeral home, including Booth's mother, brother, and sister, along with his dentist and other Baltimore acquaintances.[11] In 1911, the *New York Times* had published an account by their reporter detailing the burial of Booth's body at the cemetery and those who were witnesses.[156] The rumor periodically revived, as in the 1920s when a corpse was exhibited on a national tour by a carnival promoter and advertised as the "Man Who Shot Lincoln." According to a 1938 article in the *Saturday Evening Post*, the exhibitor said that he obtained St. Helen's corpse from Bates' widow.[169]

*The Lincoln Conspiracy* (1977) contended that there was a government plot to conceal Booth's escape, reviving interest in the story and prompting the display of St. Helen's mummified body in Chicago that year.[170] The book sold more than one million copies and was made into a feature film called *The Lincoln Conspiracy* which was theatrically released later that year.[171] The 1998 book *The Curse of Cain: The Untold Story of John Wilkes Booth* contended that Booth had escaped, sought refuge in Japan, and eventually returned to the United States.[172] In 1994 two historians together with several descendants sought a court order for the exhumation of Booth's body at Green Mount Cemetery which was, according to their lawyer, "intended to prove or disprove longstanding theories on Booth's escape" by conducting a photo-superimposition analysis.[173][174] The application was blocked by Baltimore Circuit Court Judge Joseph H. H. Kaplan, who cited, among other things, "the unreliability of petitioners' less-than-convincing escape/cover-up theory" as a major factor in his decision. The Maryland Court of Special Appeals upheld the ruling.[153][175]

In December 2010, descendants of Edwin Booth reported that they obtained permission to exhume the Shakespearean actor's body to obtain DNA samples to compare with a sample of his brother John's DNA to refute the rumor that John had escaped after the assassination. Bree Harvey, a spokesman from the Mount Auburn Cemetery in Cambridge, Massachusetts, where Edwin Booth is buried, denied reports that the family had contacted them and requested to exhume Edwin's body.[176] The family hoped to obtain samples of John Wilkes's DNA from remains such as vertebrae stored at the National Museum of Health and Medicine in Maryland.[177] On March 30, 2013, museum spokeswoman Carol Johnson announced that the family's request to extract DNA from the vertebrae had been rejected.[178]

# Mary Bowser

**Mary Jane Richards Denman** was a Union spy during the Civil War.[1] She was an American former slave and worked in connection with Elizabeth "Bet" Van Lew.[2] She is often referred to as Mary Bowser although there are no records of her using this name.[3] According to historian and author Lois Leveen, much of what is claimed about this figure is actually untrue, and focusing only on her Civil War espionage ignores larger issues about race in America.[1][2][3][4]

## Early years

Mary Jane was born near Richmond, Virginia, and was enslaved from birth by Eliza Baker Van Lew and John Van Lew (parents of Bet) or their extended family.[5][6][7]

The first record directly related to her is her baptism, as "Mary Jane" at St. John's Church in Richmond, on May 17, 1846.[2] Mary Jane's baptism at the Van Lew family church, rather than at Richmond's First African Baptist Church, where the other Van Lew slaves were baptized, indicates that someone in the Van Lew family took special notice of Richards.[1] Sometime after this baptism, Bet Van Lew, soon sent Richards north to school in Princeton, New Jersey, or Philadelphia, Pennsylvania.[1][2]

In 1855, Richards went to Liberia, West Africa, to join a missionary community, as arranged by Elizabeth Van Lew. By spring of 1860, Richards had returned to Richmond.[1][2][8][9]

## The American Civil War

> When I open my eyes in the morning, I say to the servant, "What news, Mary?" and my caterer never fails! Most generally our reliable news is gathered from negroes, and they certainly show wisdom, discretion and prudence, which is wonderful.
> —Elizabeth Van Lew, diary entry dated May 14, 1864

On April 16, 1861, Mary wed Wilson Bowser. The ceremony took place in St. John's Church, just four days after Confederate troops opened fire on Fort Sumter, the first battle of the Civil War.[2] The marriage was relatively short lived, and by the time the war ended, she was once again using the surname Richards.[3]

Throughout the war, Mary participated in the pro-Union underground espionage ring organized by Elizabeth Van Lew.[1] Although many sources focus solely on her daring infiltration of the Confederate White House, which she undertook by posing as a slave to "serve" Jefferson Davis's family, this was only one of the many pro-Union activities in which she and other African Americans participated.[8][3] It is possible that Union military leaders such as Alfred Terry, Edward Ord, and Colonel S. H. Roberts benefited from her work.[6] Although exactly what intelligence she collected is unknown, the value of this espionage ring was noted by Generals Benjamin Butler, Ulysses S. Grant, and George H. Sharpe.[2]

## Postwar life

Even just a few days after the fall of Richmond, Mary Jane Richards worked as teacher to former slaves in the city.[1]

Richards gave at least two lectures in the North in 1865 about her education, travel to Liberia, and wartime exploits.[1] In September, a reporter claimed that she and the famed white political orator Anna Dickinson "might, indeed, easily be mistaken for twin sisters," likely referring to the strangeness of a woman speaking about political issues to a group.[4] While speaking in New York, Richards protected her identity by using pseudonyms at both lectures, calling herself Richmonia Richards at Abyssinian Baptist Church in Manhattan on September 11 and Richmonia R. St. Pierre a week or two later at the African Methodist Episcopal Church on Bridge Street in Brooklyn.[1] It is possible that more information about Richards may be found by searching 19th-century Northern black papers for mention of more of her lectures.[6]

Again using the name Mary J. Richards, she founded a freedmen's school in Saint Marys, Georgia, in early 1867.[1][10] Her school served day students, adult night students, and Sunday school students, all taught by herself.[2]

In a June 1867 letter to the superintendent of education for the Georgia Freedmen's Bureau, she requested that he now refer to her as Mary J. R. Garvin.[1] Though a later letter may imply that she intended to join her new husband in the West Indies after St. Mary's school closed, it has not yet been confirmed.[6] After that date, there is no further record of her use of the name Garvin, and until 2019, historians had not been able to trace anything about her later life.[4]

In November 2018, Emily Payne "a specialist in American history at Cowan's Auctions in Cincinnati, Ohio," contacted historian Lois Leveen regarding a letter dated 1870 and signed "M J Denman," which she believed might have been written by Mary Jane to Bet Van Lew. Leveen recognized the handwriting as belonging to the former slave and spy, but only after months of archival research was she able to confirm that M J Denman was the same person as Mary Jane Richards.[10] Based on information learned from this letter and from other documents she located as a result of the letter, Leveen, who is the author of the critically acclaimed novel *The Secrets of Mary Bowser*, says she is now writing a nonfiction book about the real Mary Jane Richards Denman.[3][10]

# Belle Boyd

**Isabella Maria Boyd** (May 9, 1844[1]—June 11, 1900[2]), best known as Belle Boyd (or as Cleopatra of the Secession or Siren of the Shenandoah), was a Confederate spy in the American Civil War. She operated from her father's hotel in Front Royal, Virginia, and provided valuable information to Confederate General Stonewall Jackson in 1862.

*Belle Boyd, Confederate spy, circa 1865*

## Southern spy

Boyd's espionage career began by chance. According to her highly fictionalized 1866 account, a band of Union army soldiers heard that she had Confederate flags in her room on July 4, 1861, and they came to investigate. They hung a Union flag outside her home. Then one of the men cursed at her mother, which enraged Boyd. She pulled out a pistol and shot the man, who died some hours later. A board of inquiry exonerated her of murder, but sentries were posted around the house and officers kept close track of her activities. She profited from this enforced familiarity, charming at least one of the officers whom she named in her memoir as Captain Daniel Keily.[7] She wrote in her memoir that she was indebted to Keily "for some very remarkable effusions, some withered flowers, and a great deal of important information."[8] She conveyed those secrets to Confederate officers via her slave Eliza Hopewell, who carried them in a hollowed-out watch case. Boyd was caught on her first attempt at spying and told that she could be sentenced to death, and she realized that she needed to find a better way to communicate.

General James Shields and his staff gathered in the parlor of the local hotel in mid-May 1862. Boyd hid in the closet in the room, eavesdropping through a knothole that she enlarged in the door. She learned that Shields had been ordered east from Front Royal, Virginia. That night, she rode through Union lines, using false papers to bluff her way past the sentries, and reported the news to Colonel Turner Ashby, who was scouting for the Confederates. She then returned to town. When the Confederates advanced on Front Royal on May 23, Boyd ran to greet Stonewall Jackson's men, avoiding enemy fire that put bullet holes in her skirt. She urged an officer to inform Jackson that "the Yankee force is very small [ . . . ] Tell him to charge right down and he will catch them all."[9] Jackson did and wrote a note of gratitude to her: "I thank you, for myself and for the army, for the immense service that you have rendered your country today."[10][11] For her contributions, she was awarded the Southern Cross of Honor. Jackson also gave her captain and honorary aide-de-camp positions.[12]

Boyd was arrested at least six times but somehow evaded incarceration.[13] By late July 1862, detective Allan Pinkerton had assigned three men to work on her case.[14] She was finally captured by Union officials on July 29, 1862, after her lover gave her up, and they brought her to the Old Capitol Prison in Washington, D.C., the next day.[15][16] An inquiry was held[*by whom?*] on August 7, 1862, concerning violations of orders that Boyd be kept in close custody.[17] She was held for a month before being released on August 29, 1862, when she was exchanged at Fort Monroe.[18] She was arrested again in June 1863, but was released after contracting typhoid fever.[19]

In March 1864, Boyd attempted to travel to England, but she was intercepted by a Union blockade and sent to Canada,[19] where she met Union naval officer Samuel Wylde Hardinge. The two later married in England[19] and had a daughter named Grace.[20] Boyd became an actress in England after her husband's death to support her daughter. Following the death of her husband in 1866, she and her daughter returned to the United States. [20] Boyd assumed the stage name Nina Benjamin to perform in several cities, eventually ending up in New Orleans where she married John Swainston Hammond in March 1869, a former British Army officer who fought for the Union Army during the Civil War. [21] They had two sons and two daughters; their first son died as an infant. Boyd divorced Hammond in 1884 and married Nathaniel Rue High in 1885. She subsequently began touring the country giving dramatic lectures of her life as a Civil War spy.[21]

## Post-War years and death

Boyd published a highly fictionalized narrative of her war experiences in the two-volume *Bell Boyd in Camp and Prison*.[22] She died of a heart attack in Kilbourn City, Wisconsin (Wisconsin Dells) on June 11, 1900, at age 56. She was buried in the Spring Grove Cemetery in Wisconsin Dells, with members of the Grand Army of the Republic as her pallbearers.[23] For years, her grave simply read:

BELLE BOYD
CONFEDERATE SPY
BORN IN VIRGINIA
DIED IN WISCONSIN
ERECTED BY A COMRADE[24]

# Mathew Brady

**Mathew B. Brady** (c. 1822–January 15, 1896) was one of the earliest photographers in American history, best known for his scenes of the Civil War. He studied under inventor Samuel F. B. Morse, who pioneered the daguerreotype technique in America. Brady opened his own studio in New York in 1844, and photographed Andrew Jackson, John Quincy Adams, and Abraham Lincoln, among other public figures.

When the Civil War started, his use of a mobile studio and darkroom enabled vivid battlefield photographs that brought home the reality of war to the public. Thousands of war scenes were captured, as well as portraits of generals and politicians on both sides of the conflict, though most of these were taken by his assistants, rather than by Brady himself.

After the war, these pictures went out of fashion, and the government did not purchase the master-copies as he had anticipated. Brady's fortunes declined sharply, and he died in debt.

## Civil War documentation

*Ulysses S. Grant*

At first, the effect of the Civil War on Brady's business was a brisk increase in sales of *cartes de visite* to departing soldiers. Brady readily marketed to parents the idea of capturing their young soldiers' images before they might be lost to war by running an ad in *The New York Daily Tribune* that warned, "You cannot tell how soon it may be too late."[4] However, he was soon taken with the idea of documenting the war itself. He first applied to an old friend, General Winfield Scott, for permission to travel to the battle sites, and eventually, he made his application to President Lincoln himself. Lincoln granted permission in 1861, with the proviso that Brady finance the project himself.[1]

His efforts to document the American Civil War on a grand scale by bringing his photographic studio onto the battlefields earned Brady his place in history. Despite the dangers, financial risk, and discouragement by his friends, Brady was later quoted as saying "I had to go. A spirit in my feet said 'Go,' and I went." His first popular photographs of the conflict were at the First Battle of Bull Run, in which he got so close to the action that he barely avoided capture. While most of the time the battle had ceased before

*Soldier guarding arsenal Washington, D.C., 1862*

pictures were taken, Brady came under direct fire at the First Battle of Bull Run, Petersburg, and Fredericksburg.

He also employed Alexander Gardner,[12] James Gardner, Timothy H. O'Sullivan, William Pywell, George N. Barnard, Thomas C. Roche, and seventeen other men, each of whom was given a traveling darkroom, to go out and photograph scenes from the Civil War. Brady generally stayed in Washington, D.C., organizing his assistants and rarely visited battlefields personally. However, as author Roy Meredith points out, "He [Brady] was essentially the director. The actual operation of the camera though mechanical is important, but the selection of the scene to be photographed is as important, if not more so than just 'snapping the shutter.'"[13]

This may have been due, at least in part, to the fact that Brady's eyesight had begun to deteriorate in the 1850s. Many of the images in Brady's collection are, in reality, thought to be the work of his assistants. Brady was criticized for failing to document the work, though it is unclear whether it was intentional or due simply to a lack of inclination to document the photographer of a specific image. Because so much of Brady's photography is missing information, it is difficult to know not only who took the picture, but also exactly when or where it was taken.

In October 1862 Brady opened an exhibition of photographs from the Battle of Antietam in his New York gallery, titled *The Dead of Antietam*. Many images in this presentation were graphic photographs of corpses, a presentation new to America. This was the first time that many Americans saw the realities of war in photographs, as distinct from previous "artists' impressions."

Mathew Brady, through his many paid assistants, took thousands of photos of American Civil War scenes. Much of the popular understanding of the Civil War comes from these photos. There are thousands of photos in the US National Archives and the Library of Congress taken by Brady and his associates, Alexander Gardner, George Barnard and Timothy O'Sullivan.[12] The photographs include Lincoln, Grant, and soldiers in camps and battlefields. The images provide a pictorial cross reference of American Civil War history. Brady was not able to photograph actual battle scenes, as the photographic equipment in those days was still in the infancy of its technical development and required that a subject be still in order for a clear photo to be produced.[14]

Following the conflict, a war-weary public lost interest in seeing photos of the war, and Brady's popularity and practice declined drastically.

## Later years and death

*Photograph of Brady, c. 1889*

During the war, Brady spent over $100,000 to create over 10,000 plates. He expected the US government to buy the photographs when the war ended. When the government refused to do so he was forced to sell his New York City studio and go into bankruptcy. Congress granted Brady $25,000 in 1875, but he remained deeply in debt. The public was unwilling to dwell on the gruesomeness of the war after it had ended, and so private collectors were scarce. Depressed by his financial situation and loss of eyesight, and devastated by the death of his wife in 1887, he died penniless in the charity ward of Presbyterian Hospital in New York City on January 15, 1896, from complications following a streetcar accident.

Brady's funeral was financed by veterans of the 7th New York Infantry. He was buried in the Congressional Cemetery in Washington, D.C.

Levin Corbin Handy, Brady's nephew by marriage, took over Brady's photography business after his death.

*Photograph of Abraham Lincoln taken by Brady on the day of Lincoln's Cooper Union speech*

## Legacy

Brady photographed 18 of the 19 American Presidents from John Quincy Adams to William McKinley. The exception was the 9th President, William Henry Harrison, who died in office three years before Brady started his photographic collection. Brady photographed Abraham Lincoln on many occasions. His Lincoln photographs have been used for the $5 bill and the Lincoln penny. One of his Lincoln photos was used by the National Bank Note Company as a model for the engraving on the 90c Lincoln Postage issue of 1869.[15]

The thousands of photographs which Mathew Brady's photographers (such as Alexander Gardner and Timothy O'Sullivan) took have become the most important visual documentation of the Civil War, and have helped historians and the public better understand the era.

Brady photographed and made portraits of many senior Union officers in the war, including:

- Ulysses S. Grant
- Nathaniel Banks
- Don Carlos Buell
- Ambrose Burnside
- Benjamin Butler
- Joshua Chamberlain
- George Custer
- David Farragut
- John Gibbon
- Winfield Hancock
- Samuel P. Heintzelman
- Joseph Hooker
- Oliver Otis Howard
- David Hunter
- John A. Logan
- Irvin McDowell

- George McClellan
- James McPherson
- George Meade
- Montgomery C. Meigs
- David Dixon Porter
- William Rosecrans
- John Schofield
- William Sherman
- Daniel Sickles
- Henry Warner Slocum
- George Stoneman
- Edwin V. Sumner
- George Thomas
- Emory Upton
- James Wadsworth
- Lew Wallace

On the Confederate side, Brady photographed: Jefferson Davis, P. G. T. Beauregard, Stonewall Jackson, Albert Pike, James Longstreet, James Henry Hammond, and Robert E. Lee.[16] Brady also photographed Lord Lyons, the British ambassador to Washington during the Civil War.

## Photojournalism and honors

Brady is credited with being the father of photojournalism.[17] He can also be considered a pioneer in the orchestration of a "corporate credit line." In this practice, every image produced in his gallery was labeled "Photo by Brady"; however, Brady dealt directly with only the most distinguished subjects and most portrait sessions were carried out by others.[18]

As perhaps the best-known US photographer in the 19th century, it was Brady's name that came to be attached to the era's heavy specialized end tables which were factory-made specifically for use by portrait photographers. Such a "Brady stand" of the mid-19th century typically had a weighty cast iron base for stability, plus an adjustable-height single-column pipe leg for dual use as either a portrait model's armrest or (when fully extended and fitted with a brace attachment rather than the usual tabletop) as a neck rest. The latter was often needed to keep models steady during the longer exposure times of early photography. While *Brady stand* is a convenient term for these trade-specific articles of studio equipment, there is no proven connection between Brady himself and the Brady stand's invention circa 1855.[19]

# Braxton Bragg

**Braxton Bragg** (March 22, 1817–September 27, 1876) was a senior officer of the Confederate States Army who was assigned to duty at Richmond, under direction of the President of the Confederate States of America, Jefferson Davis, and charged with the conduct of military operations of the armies of the Confederate States from February 24, 1864, until January 13, 1865, when he was charged with command and defense of Wilmington, North Carolina. He previously had command of an army in the Western Theater.

Bragg, a native of Warrenton, North Carolina, was educated at West Point and became an artillery officer. He served in Florida and then received three brevet promotions for distinguished service in the Mexican–American War, most notably the Battle of Buena Vista.

He established a reputation as a strict disciplinarian, but also as a junior officer willing to publicly argue with and criticize his superior officers, including those at the highest levels of the Army. After a series of posts in the Indian Territory, he resigned from the U.S. Army in 1856 to become a sugar plantation slave owner in Louisiana.

During the Civil War, Bragg trained soldiers in the Gulf Coast region. He was a corps commander at the Battle of Shiloh and subsequently was named to command the Army of Mississippi (later known as the Army of Tennessee).

He and Edmund Kirby Smith attempted an invasion of Kentucky in 1862, but Bragg retreated following the inconclusive Battle of Perryville, Kentucky, in October. In December, he fought another inconclusive battle at Murfreesboro, Tennessee, the Battle of Stones River, but once again withdrew his army. In 1863, he fought a series of battles against Maj. Gen. William S. Rosecrans and the Union Army of the Cumberland.

In June, he was outmaneuvered in the Tullahoma Campaign and retreated into Chattanooga. In September, he was forced to evacuate Chattanooga, but counterattacked Rosecrans and defeated him at the Battle of Chickamauga, the bloodiest battle in the Western Theater, and the only major Confederate victory therein. In November, Bragg's army was routed in turn by Maj. Gen. Ulysses S. Grant in the Battles for Chattanooga.

Throughout these campaigns, Bragg fought almost as bitterly against some of his uncooperative subordinates as he did against the enemy, and they made multiple attempts to have him replaced as army commander. The defeat at Chattanooga was the last straw, and Bragg was recalled in early 1864 to Richmond, where he became the military adviser to Confederate President Jefferson Davis.

Near the end of the war, he defended the region surrounding Fort Fisher near

Wilmington, North Carolina, and served as a corps commander in the Carolinas Campaign. After the war, Bragg worked as the superintendent of the New Orleans waterworks, a supervisor of harbor improvements at Mobile, Alabama, and as a railroad engineer and inspector in Texas.

Bragg is generally considered among the worst generals of the Civil War. Although his commands often outnumbered those he fought against, most of the battles in which he engaged ended in defeats. The only exception was Chickamauga, which was largely due to the timely arrival of Lieutenant General James Longstreet's corps.

Some historians fault Bragg as a commander for impatience and poor treatment of others. Some, however, point towards the failures of Bragg's subordinates, especially Leonidas Polk, a close ally of Davis and known enemy of Bragg, as the more significant factors in the many Confederate defeats at which Bragg commanded.

## American Civil War

On December 31, 1855, Bragg submitted his resignation from the Army, which became effective on January 3, 1856. He and his wife purchased a sugar plantation of 1,600 acres (6.5 km²) 3 miles (4.8 km) north of Thibodaux. Never one to oppose slavery in concept— both his father and his wife were slaveowners—he used 105 enslaved Africans on his property. There is no evidence that he was a cruel slaveowner, but he continued to uphold his reputation as being a stern disciplinarian and an advocate of military efficiency. His

*Braxton Bragg, CSA*[16]

*"[Bragg] was the only General in command of an Army who has shown himself equal to the management of volunteers and at the same time commanded their love and respect."*

*Confederate President Jefferson Davis*[17]

methods resulted in almost immediate profitability, despite a large mortgage on the property. He became active in local politics and was elected to the Board of Public Works in 1860. Throughout the 1850s, Bragg had been disturbed by the accelerating sectional crisis. He opposed the concept of secession, believing that in a republic no majority could set aside a written constitution, but this belief would soon be tested.[15]

Before the start of the Civil War, Bragg was a colonel in the Louisiana Militia. On December 12, 1860, Governor Thomas O. Moore appointed him to the state military board, an organization charged with creating a 5,000-man army. He took the assignment, even though he had been opposed to secession. On January 11, 1861, Bragg led a group of 500 volunteers to Baton Rouge, where they persuaded the commander of the federal arsenal there to surrender. The state convention on secession also established a state army and Moore appointed Bragg its commander, with the rank of major general, on February 20, 1861. He commanded the forces around New Orleans until April 16, but his commission was transferred to be a brigadier general of the Confederate States Army on March 7, 1861. He commanded forces in Pensacola, Florida, Alabama, and the Department of West Florida and was promoted to major general on September 12, 1861. His tenure was successful and he trained his men to be some of the best disciplined troops in the Confederate Army, such as the 5th Georgia and the 6th Florida Regiments.[18][19][20][21]

In December, President Davis asked Bragg to take command of the Trans-Mississippi Department, but Bragg declined. He was concerned for the prospects of victory west of the Mississippi River and about the poorly supplied and ill-disciplined troops there. He was also experiencing one of his periodic episodes of ill health that would plague him throughout the war. For years he had suffered from rheumatism, dyspepsia, nerves, and severe migraine headaches, ailments that undoubtedly contributed to his disagreeable personal style. The command went to Earl Van Dorn. Bragg proposed to Davis that he change his strategy of attempting to defend every square mile of Confederate territory, recommending that his troops were of less value on the Gulf Coast than they would be farther to the north, concentrated with other forces for an attack against the Union Army in Tennessee. Bragg transported about 10,000 men to Corinth, Mississippi, in February 1862 and was charged with improving the poor discipline of the Confederate troops already assembled under General Albert Sidney Johnston.[22]

## Battle of Shiloh

Bragg commanded a corps (and was also chief of staff) under Johnston at the Battle of Shiloh, April 6–7, 1862. In the initial surprise Confederate advance, Bragg's corps was ordered to attack in a line that was almost 3 miles (4.8 km) long, but he soon began directing activities of the units that found themselves around the center of the battlefield. His men became bogged down against a Union salient called the Hornet's Nest, which he attacked for hours with piecemeal frontal assaults. After Johnston was killed in the battle, General P. G. T. Beauregard assumed command, and appointed Bragg his second in command. Bragg was dismayed when Beauregard called off a late afternoon assault against the Union's final position, which was strongly defended, calling it their last opportunity for victory. On the second day of battle, the Union army counterattacked and the Confederates retreated back to Corinth.[23]

Bragg received public praise for his conduct in the battle and on April 12, 1862, Jefferson Davis appointed Bragg a full general, the sixth man to achieve that rank and one of only seven in the history of the Confederacy.[24] His date of rank was April 6, 1862, coinciding with the first day at Shiloh. After the Siege of Corinth, Beauregard departed on sick leave, leaving Bragg in temporary command of the army in Tupelo, Mississippi, but Beauregard failed to inform President Davis of his departure and spent two weeks absent without leave. Davis was looking for someone to replace Beauregard because of his perceived poor performance at Corinth, and the opportunity presented itself when Beauregard left without permission. Bragg was then appointed his successor as commander of the

Western Department (known formally as Department Number Two), including the Army of Mississippi, on June 17, 1862.[25]

## Battle of Perryville

In August 1862, Confederate Maj. Gen. Edmund Kirby Smith decided to invade Kentucky from Eastern Tennessee, hoping that he could arouse supporters of the Confederate cause in the border state and draw the Union forces under Maj. Gen. Don Carlos Buell, beyond the Ohio River. Bragg considered various options, including an attempt to retake Corinth, or to advance against Buell's army through Middle Tennessee. He eventually heeded Kirby Smith's calls for reinforcement and decided to relocate his Army of Mississippi to join with him. He moved 30,000 infantrymen in a tortuous railroad journey from Tupelo through Mobile and Montgomery to Chattanooga, while his cavalry and artillery moved by road. Although Bragg was the senior general in the theater, President Davis had established Kirby Smith's Department of East Tennessee as an independent command, reporting directly to Richmond. This decision caused Bragg difficulty during the campaign.[26]

Smith and Bragg met in Chattanooga on July 31, 1862, and devised a plan for the campaign: Kirby Smith's Army of Kentucky would first march into Kentucky to dispose of the Union defenders of Cumberland Gap. (Bragg's army was too exhausted from its long journey to begin immediate offensive operations.) Smith would return to join Bragg, and their combined forces would attempt to maneuver into Buell's rear and force a battle to protect his supply lines. Once the armies were combined, Bragg's seniority would apply and Smith would be under his direct command. Assuming that Buell's army could be destroyed, Bragg and Smith would march farther north into Kentucky, a movement they assumed would be welcomed by the local populace. Any remaining Federal force would be defeated in a grand battle in Kentucky, establishing the Confederate frontier at the Ohio River.[27]

On August 9, Smith informed Bragg that he was breaking the agreement and intended to bypass Cumberland Gap, leaving a small holding force to neutralize the Union garrison, and to move north. Unable to command Smith to honor their plan, Bragg focused on a movement to Lexington instead of Nashville. He cautioned Smith that Buell could pursue and defeat his smaller army before Bragg's army could join up with them.[28]

Bragg departed from Chattanooga on August 27, just before Smith reached Lexington. On the way, he was distracted by the capture of a Union fort at Munfordville. He had to decide whether to continue toward a fight with Buell (over Louisville) or rejoin Smith, who had gained control of the center of the state by capturing Richmond and Lexington, and threatened to move on Cincinnati. Bragg chose to rejoin Smith. He left his army and met Smith in Frankfort, where they attended the inauguration of Confederate Governor Richard Hawes on October 4. The inauguration ceremony was disrupted by the sound of approaching Union cannon fire and the organizers canceled the inaugural ball scheduled for that evening.[29]

On October 8, the armies met unexpectedly at the Battle of Perryville; they had skirmished the previous day as they were searching for water sources in the vicinity. Bragg ordered the wing of his army under Maj. Gen. Leonidas Polk to attack what he thought was an isolated portion of Buell's command, but had difficulty motivating Polk to begin the fight until Bragg arrived in person. Eventually Polk attacked the corps of Maj. Gen. Alexander M. McCook on the Union army's left flank and forced it to fall back. By the end of the day, McCook had been driven back about a mile, but reinforcements had arrived to stabilize the line, and Bragg only then began to realize that his limited tactical victory in the bloody battle had been against less than half of Buell's army and the remainder was arriving quickly.[30]

Kirby Smith pleaded with Bragg to follow up on his success: "For God's sake, General, let us fight Buell here." Bragg replied, "I will do it, sir," but then displaying what one observer called "a perplexity and vacillation which had now become simply appalling to Smith, to Hardee, and to Polk,"[31] he ordered his army to retreat through the Cumberland Gap to Knoxville. Bragg referred to his retreat as a withdrawal, the successful culmination of a giant raid. He had multiple reasons for withdrawing. Disheartening news had arrived from northern Mississippi that Earl Van Dorn and Sterling Price had been defeated at Corinth, just as Robert E. Lee had failed in his Maryland Campaign. He saw that his army had not much to gain from a further, isolated victory, whereas a defeat might cost not only the bountiful food and supplies yet collected, but also his army. He wrote to his wife, "With the whole southwest thus in the enemy's possession, my crime would have been unpardonable had I kept my noble little army to be ice-bound in the northern clime, without tents or shoes, and obliged to forage daily for bread, etc."[32] He was quickly called to Richmond to explain to Jefferson Davis the charges brought by his officers about how he had conducted his campaign, demanding that he be replaced as head of the army. Although Davis decided to leave the general in command, Bragg's relationship with his subordinates would be severely damaged. Upon rejoining the army, he ordered a movement to Murfreesboro, Tennessee.[33]

## Battle of Stones River

Bragg renamed his force as the Army of Tennessee on November 20. On November 24 Don Carlos Buell was replaced in command of the Union Army of the Ohio by Maj. Gen. William S. Rosecrans, who immediately renamed it the Army of the Cumberland. In late December, Rosecrans advanced from Nashville against Bragg's position at Murfreesboro. Before Rosecrans could attack, Bragg launched a strong surprise attack against Rosecrans's right flank on December 31, 1862, the start of the Battle of Stones River. The Confederates succeeded in driving the Union army back to a small defensive position, but could not destroy it, nor could they break its supply line to Nashville, as Bragg intended. Despite this, Bragg considered the first day of battle to be a victory and assumed that Rosecrans would soon retreat. By January 2, 1863, however, the Union troops remained in place and the battle resumed as Bragg launched an unsuccessful attack by the troops of Maj. Gen. John C. Breckinridge against the well-defended Union left flank. Recognizing his lack of progress, the severe winter weather, the arrival of supplies and reinforcements for Rosecrans, and heeding the recommendations of corps commanders Hardee and Polk, Bragg withdrew his army from the field to Tullahoma, Tennessee.[34]

> While Washington breathed a sigh of relief after Stones River, dissension came to a head in the Army of Tennessee. All of Bragg's corps and division commanders expressed a lack of confidence in their chief. Senior Generals William J. Hardee and Leonidas Polk asked Davis to put Johnston in command of the army. Division commander B. Franklin Cheatham vowed he would never again serve under Bragg. Breckinridge wanted to challenge Bragg to a duel. Bragg struck back, court-martialing one division commander (McCown) for disobeying orders, accusing another (Cheatham) of drunkenness during the battle, and blaming Breckinridge for inept leadership. This internecine donnybrook threatened to do more damage to the army than the Yankees had done. Disheartened, Bragg told a friend that it might "be better for the President to send someone to relieve me," and wrote Davis to the same effect.
>
> James M. McPherson, *Battle Cry of Freedom: The Civil War Era*[35]

Bragg's generals were vocal in their dissatisfaction with his command during the Kentucky campaign and Stones River. He reacted to the rumors of criticism by circulating a letter to his corps and division commanders that asked them to confirm in writing that they had recommended withdrawing after the latter battle, stating that if he had misunderstood them and withdrawn mistakenly, he would willingly step down. Unfortunately, he wrote the letter at a time that a number of his most faithful supporters were on leave for illness or wounds.[36] Bragg's critics, including William J. Hardee, interpreted the letter as having an implied secondary question—had Bragg lost the confidence of his senior commanders? Leonidas Polk did not reply to the implied question, but he wrote directly to his friend, Jefferson Davis, recommending that Bragg be replaced.[37]

Davis responded to the complaints by dispatching Gen. Joseph E. Johnston to investigate the condition of the army. Davis assumed that Johnston, Bragg's superior, would find the situation wanting and take command of the army in the field, easing Bragg aside. However, Johnston arrived on the scene and found the men of the Army of Tennessee in relatively good condition. He told Bragg that he had "the best organized, armed, equipped, and disciplined army in the Confederacy."[38] Johnston explicitly refused any suggestion that he take command, concerned that people would think he had taken advantage of the situation for his own personal gain. When Davis ordered Johnston to send Bragg to Richmond, Johnston delayed because of Elise Bragg's illness; when her health improved Johnston was unable to assume command because of lingering medical problems from his wound at the Battle of Seven Pines in 1862.[39]

## Tullahoma Campaign

As Bragg's army fortified Tullahoma, Rosecrans spent the next six months in Murfreesboro, resupplying and retraining his army to resume its advance. Rosecrans's initial movements on June 23 took Bragg by surprise. While keeping Polk's corps occupied with small actions in the center of the Confederate line, Rosecrans sent the majority of his army around Bragg's right flank. Bragg was slow to react and his subordinates were typically uncooperative: the mistrust among the general officers of the Army of Tennessee for the past months led to little direct communication about strategy, and neither Polk nor Hardee had a firm understanding of Bragg's plans. As the Union army outmaneuvered the Confederates, Bragg was forced to abandon Tullahoma and on July 4 retreated behind the Tennessee River. Tullahoma is recognized as a "brilliant" campaign for Rosecrans, achieving with minimal losses his goal of driving Bragg from Middle Tennessee. Judith Hallock wrote that Bragg was "outfoxed" and that his ill health may have been partially to blame for his performance, but her overall assessment was that he performed credibly during the retreat from Tullahoma, keeping his army intact under difficult circumstances.[40]

Although the Army of Tennessee had about 52,000 men at the end of July, the Confederate government merged the Department of East Tennessee, under Maj. Gen. Simon B. Buckner, into Bragg's Department of Tennessee, which added 17,800 men to Bragg's army, but also extended his command responsibilities northward to the Knoxville area. This brought a third subordinate into Bragg's command who had little or no respect for him.[41] Buckner's attitude was colored by Bragg's unsuccessful invasion of Buckner's native Kentucky in 1862, as well as by the loss of his command through the merger.[42] A positive aspect for Bragg was Hardee's request to be transferred to Mississippi in July, but he was replaced by Lt. Gen. D. H. Hill, a general who had not gotten along with Robert E. Lee in Virginia.[43]

The Confederate War Department asked Bragg in early August if he could assume the offensive against Rosecrans if he were given reinforcements from Mississippi. He demurred, concerned about the daunting geographical obstacles and logistical challenges, preferring to wait for Rosecrans to solve those same problems and attack him.[44] An opposed crossing of the Tennessee River was not feasible, so Rosecrans devised a deception to distract Bragg above Chattanooga while the army crossed downstream. Bragg was rightfully concerned about a sizable Union force under Maj. Gen. Ambrose E. Burnside that was threatening Knoxville to the northeast, and Rosecrans reinforced this concern by feinting to his left and shelling the city of Chattanooga from the heights north of the river. The bulk of the Union army crossed the Tennessee southeast of Chattanooga by September 4 and Bragg realized that his position there was no longer tenable. He evacuated the city on September 8.[45]

## Battle of Chickamauga

After Rosecrans had consolidated his gains and secured his hold on Chattanooga, he began moving his army into northern Georgia in pursuit of Bragg. Bragg continued to suffer from the conduct of his subordinates, who were not attentive to his orders. On September 10, Maj. Gens. Thomas C. Hindman and D. H. Hill refused to attack, as ordered, an outnumbered Federal column at McLemore's Cove (the Battle of Davis's Cross Roads). On September 13, Bragg ordered Leonidas Polk to attack Maj. Gen. Thomas L. Crittenden's corps, but Polk ignored the orders and demanded more troops, insisting that it was he who was about to be attacked. Rosecrans used the time lost in these delays to concentrate his scattered forces. Finally, on September 19–20, 1863, Bragg, reinforced by two divisions from Mississippi, one division and several brigades from the Department of East Tennessee, and two divisions under Lt. Gen. James Longstreet from Robert E. Lee's Army of Northern Virginia, turned on the pursuing Rosecrans in northeastern Georgia and at high cost defeated him at the Battle of Chickamauga, the greatest Confederate victory in the Western Theater during the war. It was not a complete victory, however. Bragg's objective was to cut off Rosecrans from Chattanooga and destroy his army. Instead, following a partial rout of the Union army by Longstreet's wing, a stout defense by Maj. Gen. George H. Thomas allowed Rosecrans and almost all of his army to escape.[46]

After the battle, Rosecrans's Army of the Cumberland retreated to Chattanooga, where Bragg laid siege to the city. He began to wage a battle against the subordinates he resented for failing him in the campaign—Hindman for his lack of action in McLemore's Cove, and Polk for delaying the morning attack Bragg ordered on September 20. On September 29, Bragg suspended both officers from their commands. In early October, an attempted mutiny of Bragg's subordinates resulted in D. H. Hill being relieved from his command. Longstreet was dispatched with his corps to the Knoxville Campaign against Ambrose Burnside, seriously weakening Bragg's army at Chattanooga.[47]

Some of Bragg's subordinate generals were frustrated at what they perceived to be his lack of willingness to exploit the victory by pursuing the Union army toward Chattanooga and destroying it. Polk in particular was outraged at being relieved of command. The dissidents, including many of the division and corps commanders, met in secret and prepared a petition to President Jefferson Davis. Although the author of the petition is not known, historians suspect it was Simon Buckner, whose signature was first on the list.[48] Lt. Gen. James Longstreet wrote to the Secretary of War with the prediction that "nothing but the hand of God can save us or help us as long as we have our present commander." With the Army of Tennessee literally on the verge of mutiny, Jefferson Davis reluctantly traveled to Chattanooga to personally assess the situation and to try to stem the tide of dissent in the army. Although Bragg offered to resign to resolve the crisis,[49] Davis eventually decided to leave Bragg in command, denounced the other generals, and termed their complaints "shafts of malice."[50]

## Battles for Chattanooga

While Bragg fought with his subordinates and reduced his force by dispatching Longstreet to Knoxville, the besieged Union army received a new commander—Maj. Gen. Ulysses S. Grant—and significant reinforcements from Mississippi and Virginia. The Battles for

Chattanooga marked Bragg's final days as an army commander. His weakened left flank (previously manned by Longstreet's troops) fell on November 24 during the Battle of Lookout Mountain. The following day in the Battle of Missionary Ridge, his primary defensive line successfully resisted an attack on its right flank, but the center was overwhelmed in a frontal assault by George Thomas's army. The Army of Tennessee was routed and retreated to Dalton, Georgia. Bragg offered his resignation on November 29 and was chagrined when Pres. Davis accepted it immediately. He turned over temporary command to Hardee on December 2 and was replaced with Joseph E. Johnston, who commanded the army in the 1864 Atlanta Campaign against William T. Sherman.[51]

## Advisor to the President

Davis relied heavily upon Bragg's understanding of military affairs and institutions. Although he did not always agree with Bragg, Davis consistently sought his expertise and opinion on a variety of matters. By untiringly assuming many of the duties and much of the criticism that had burdened and perplexed Davis, Bragg eased some of the president's vexations. In the process he maintained old enmities and created many new ones.

—Judith Lee Hallock, *Braxton Bragg and Confederate Defeat, Volume II*[52]

In February 1864, Bragg was summoned to Richmond for consultation with Davis. The orders for his new assignment on February 24 read that he was "charged with the conduct of military operations of the Confederate States," but he was essentially Davis's military adviser or chief of staff without a direct command, a post once held by Robert E. Lee. Bragg used his organizational abilities to reduce corruption and improve the supply system. He took over responsibility for administration of the military prison system and its hospitals. He reshaped the Confederacy's conscription process by streamlining the chain of command and reducing conscripts' avenues of appeal. During his tenure in Richmond, he had numerous quarrels with significant figures, including the Secretary of War, the Commissary General, members of Congress, the press, and many of his fellow generals; the exception to the latter was Robert E. Lee, who treated Bragg politely and with deference and who had, Bragg knew, an exceptionally close relationship with the president.[53]

In May, while Lee was occupied defending against Ulysses S. Grant's Overland Campaign in Virginia, Bragg focused on the defense of areas south and west of Richmond. He convinced Jefferson Davis to appoint P.G.T. Beauregard to an important role in the defense of Richmond and Petersburg. Meanwhile, Davis was concerned that Joseph Johnston, Bragg's successor at the Army of Tennessee, was defending too timidly against Sherman's Atlanta Campaign. He sent Bragg to Georgia on July 9, charged with investigating the tactical situation, but also evaluating the replacement of Johnston in command. Bragg harbored the hope that he might be chosen to return to command of the army, but was willing to support Davis's choice. Davis had hinted to Bragg that he thought Hardee would be an appropriate successor, but Bragg was reluctant to promote an old enemy and reported back that Hardee would provide no change in strategy from Johnston's. Bragg had extensive conversations with a more junior corps commander, Lt. Gen. John Bell Hood, and was impressed with his plans for taking offensive action, about which Hood had also been confidentially corresponding to Richmond for weeks behind Johnston's back. Davis chose Hood to replace Johnston.[54]

## Operations in North Carolina

In October 1864, President Davis sent Bragg to assume temporary command of the defenses of Wilmington, North Carolina, and his responsibility was soon increased at the recommendation of Robert E. Lee to include all of the Department of North Carolina and Southern Virginia. In November, with William T. Sherman's March to the Sea under way, Davis ordered him to the defenses of Augusta, Georgia, and then to Savannah, Georgia, Charleston, South Carolina, and in January 1865, the defenses of Wilmington again. The Confederates were able to successfully repulse the first Union attempt to capture Fort Fisher, which dominated the seaborne supply line to Wilmington. However, when the Union returned in January, Bragg's performance in the Second Battle of Fort Fisher was poor. He assumed that the first failed siege meant that the fort was invulnerable, when in fact bad weather had played a large role. Thus, he did not come to the fort's assistance in a timely fashion after it was attacked the second time. The Confederates were forced to evacuate Wilmington, their last remaining seaport on the Atlantic coast.[55]

Bragg's now-fragile military career began to crumble around him. To his disgust, Joseph E. Johnston was returned to service to command the remnants of the Army of Tennessee and other forces defending against Sherman in North Carolina. At about the same time, Bragg lost his position as military adviser to Davis when Robert E. Lee was promoted to be general in chief of all the Confederate armies in February, and John C. Breckinridge, who had hated Bragg since the debacle at Perryville, was named Secretary of War. Davis was sympathetic to Bragg's discomfort and discussed transferring him to command the Trans-Mississippi Department, replacing Edmund Kirby Smith, but the politicians from that region were strongly opposed. Bragg became in effect a corps commander (although his command was less than a division in size) under Johnston for the remainder of the Carolinas Campaign. His men were able to win a minor victory at the Second Battle of Kinston, March 7–10, and fought unsuccessfully at the Battle of Bentonville, March 19–21. After the fall of Richmond on April 2, Jefferson Davis and remnants of the Confederate government fled to the southwest. Bragg, who had been headquartered at Raleigh, North Carolina, caught up with Davis near Abbeville, South Carolina, on May 1. He attended the final cabinet meeting and was instrumental in convincing Davis that the cause was lost. Bragg and a small party of his staff rode to the west and were captured and paroled in Monticello, Georgia, on May 9.[56]

## Later life and death

Bragg and Eliza had lost their home in late 1862 when the plantation in Thibodaux was confiscated by the Federal Army. It briefly served as a shelter, the Bragg Home Colony, for freed people under the control of the Freedmen's Bureau. The couple moved in with his brother, a plantation owner in Lowndesboro, Alabama, but they found the life of seclusion there to be intolerable. In 1867 Bragg became the superintendent of the New Orleans waterworks, but he was soon replaced by a former slave as the Reconstructionists came to power. In late 1869 Jefferson Davis offered Bragg a job as an agent for the Carolina Life Insurance Company. He worked there for four months before becoming dissatisfied with the profession and its low pay. He considered but rejected a position in the Egyptian Army. In August 1871 he was employed by the city of Mobile, Alabama, to improve the river, harbor, and bay, leaving after quarreling with a "combination of capitalists." Moving to Texas, he was appointed the chief engineer of the Gulf, Colorado, and Santa Fe Railway in July 1874, but within a year disagreements with the board of directors over his compensation caused him to resign. He remained in Texas as inspector of railroads.[57]

On September 27, 1876, at the age of 59, Bragg was walking down a street with a friend in Galveston, Texas, when he suddenly fell over unconscious. Dragged into a drugstore, he was dead within 10 to 15 minutes. A physician familiar with his history believed that he "died by the brain" (or of "paralysis of the brain"), suffering from the degeneration of cerebral blood vessels. An inquest ruled that his death was due to "fatal syncope," possibly induced by organic disease of the heart. He is buried in Magnolia Cemetery, Mobile, Alabama.[58]

# John Brown

*Photo by Augustus Washington, circa 1846–1847*

**John Brown** (May 9, 1800–December 2, 1859) was an American abolitionist. Brown advocated the use of armed insurrection to overthrow the institution of slavery in the United States. He first gained national attention when he led small groups of volunteers during the Bleeding Kansas crisis of 1856. He was dissatisfied with the pacifism of the organized abolitionist movement: "These men are all talk. What we need is action—action!" In May 1856, Brown and his supporters killed five supporters of slavery in the Pottawatomie massacre, which responded to the sacking of Lawrence by pro-slavery forces. Brown then commanded anti-slavery forces at the Battle of Black Jack (June 2) and the Battle of Osawatomie (August 30, 1856).

In October 1859, Brown led a raid on the federal armory at Harpers Ferry, Virginia (today West Virginia), intending to start a slave liberation movement that would spread south through the mountainous regions of Virginia and North Carolina; there was a draft constitution for the state he hoped to establish. He seized the armory, but seven people were killed, and ten or more were injured. He intended to arm slaves with weapons from the arsenal, but only a small number of local slaves joined his revolt. Within 36 hours, those of Brown's men who had not fled were killed or captured by local farmers, militiamen, and US Marines, the latter led by Robert E. Lee. He was hastily tried for treason against the Commonwealth of Virginia, the murder of five men (including three blacks), and inciting a slave insurrection; he was found guilty on all counts and was hanged. He was the first person convicted of treason in the history of the country.[1]:179

Historians agree that the Harpers Ferry raid and Brown's trial, both covered extensively by the national press, escalated tensions that led to the South's secession a year later and the American Civil War. Brown's raid captured the nation's attention; Southerners feared that it was just the first of many Northern plots to cause a slave rebellion that might endanger their lives, while Republicans dismissed the notion and claimed that they would not interfere with slavery in the South. "John Brown's Body" was a popular Union marching song that portrayed him as a martyr.

Brown's actions as an abolitionist and the tactics he used still make him a controversial figure today. He is both memorialized as a heroic martyr and visionary, and vilified as a madman and a terrorist.[2] Historian James Loewen surveyed American history textbooks and noted that historians considered Brown perfectly sane until about 1890, but generally portrayed him as insane from about 1890 until 1970, when new interpretations began to gain ground.[1]:173–203

## Early life

John Brown was born May 9, 1800, in Torrington, Connecticut.[3] He was the fourth of the eight children of Owen Brown (1771–1856) and Ruth Mills (1772–1808) and grandson of Capt. John Brown (1728–1776).[4] Brown could trace his ancestry back to 17th-century English Puritans.[5]

In 1805, the family moved to Hudson, Ohio, where Owen Brown opened a tannery; there is a historical marker at the site of their house. Hudson was a center of anti-slavery activity and debate, and Owen participated fully, offering a safe house to Underground Railroad fugitives. There not being a high school in Hudson at that time, John studied at the school of the abolitionist Elizur Wright, father of the famous Elizur Wright, in nearby Tallmadge.

In 1820, Brown married Dianthe Lusk. Their first child, John Jr., was born 13 months later. In 1825, seeking a safer location (for fugitive slaves), Brown and his family moved to New Richmond, Pennsylvania, where he bought 200 acres (81 hectares) of land. He cleared an eighth of it and built a cabin, a barn, and a tannery, the latter with a secret room to hide escaping slaves.[8] The John Brown Tannery Site was listed on the National Register of Historic Places in 1978.[9] It "was a major stop on the [Underground] Railroad, marking its place in history from 1825 to 1835." During that period, "Brown aided in the passing of an estimated 2,500 slaves."[10] Presumably, Brown was also helping a smaller number of fugitive slaves when he lived in the village of Hudson.

In 1831, one of his sons died. Brown fell ill, and his businesses began to suffer, leaving him in terrible debt. In the summer of 1832, shortly after the death of a newborn son, his wife Dianthe died, leaving him with the children John Jr., Jason, Owen, and Ruth. (Another three of their children did not survive to adulthood.) On June 14, 1833, Brown married 16-year-old Mary Ann Day (April 15, 1817–May 1, 1884), originally from Washington County, New York.[11] They eventually had 13 children; those alive at John Brown's death were Salmon, Annie, Sarah, and Ellen.[12]

In 1837, in response to the murder of Elijah P. Lovejoy, Brown publicly vowed: "Here, before God, in the presence of these witnesses, from this time, I consecrate my life to the destruction of slavery!"[14] Brown was declared bankrupt by a federal court on September 28, 1842. In 1843, four of his children died of dysentery. As Louis DeCaro Jr. shows in his biographical sketch (2007), from the mid-1840s Brown had built a reputation as an expert in fine sheep and wool, and entered into a partnership with Col. Simon Perkins of Akron, Ohio, whose flocks and farms were managed by Brown and sons. Brown eventually moved into a home with his family across the street from the Perkins Stone Mansion on Perkins Hill. The John Brown House (Akron, Ohio) still stands and is owned and operated by The Summit County Historical Society of Akron, Ohio.

## Transformative years in Springfield, Massachusetts

In 1846, Brown and his business partner Simon Perkins moved to the ideologically progressive city of Springfield, Massachusetts. There Brown found a community whose white leadership—from the community's most prominent churches, to its wealthiest business-men, to its most popular politicians, to its local jurists, and even to the publisher of one of the nation's most influential newspapers—were deeply involved and emotionally invested in the anti-slavery movement.[16] Brown and Perkins' intent was to represent the interests of the Ohio's wool growers as opposed to those of New England's wool manufacturers—thus Brown and Perkins set up a wool commission operation. While in Springfield, Brown lived in a house at 51 Franklin Street.[17]

Two years before Brown's arrival in Springfield, in 1844, the city's African-American abolitionists had founded the Sanford Street Free Church—now known as St. John's Congregational Church—which went on to become one of the United States most prom-inent platforms for abolitionist speeches. From 1846 until he left Springfield in 1850, Brown was a parishioner at the Free Church, where he witnessed abolitionist lectures by the likes of Frederick Douglass and Sojourner Truth.[18] In 1847, after speaking at the Free Church, Douglass spent a night speaking with Brown, after which he wrote, "From this night spent with John Brown in Springfield, Mass. 1847 while I continued to write and speak against slavery, I became all the same less hopeful for its peaceful abolition. My utterances became more and more tinged by the color of this man's strong impres-sions."[16] During Brown's time in Springfield, he became deeply involved in transforming the city into a major center of abolitionism, and one of the safest and most significant stops on the Underground Railroad.[19]

Brown also learned much about Massachusetts' mercantile elite; while he initially con-sidered this knowledge a curse, it proved to be a boon to his later activities in Kansas and at Harpers Ferry. The business community had reacted with hesitation when Brown asked them to change their highly profitable practice of selling low-quality wool *en masse* at low prices. Initially, Brown naively trusted them, but he soon realized they were deter-mined to maintain their control of price-setting. Also, on the outskirts of Springfield, the Connecticut River Valley's sheep farmers were largely unorganized and hesitant to change their methods of production to meet higher standards. In the *Ohio Cultivator*, Brown and other wool growers complained that the Connecticut River Valley's farmers' tendencies were lowering all U.S. wool prices abroad. In reaction, Brown made a last-ditch effort to overcome the wool mercantile elite by seeking an alliance with European manufacturers. Ultimately, Brown was disappointed to learn that Europe preferred to buy Western Massachusetts wools *en masse* at the cheap prices they had been getting. Brown then traveled to England to seek a higher price for Springfield's wool. The trip was a dis-aster, as the firm incurred a loss of $40,000, of which Perkins bore the brunt. With this misfortune, the Perkins and Brown wool commission operation closed in Springfield in late 1849. Subsequent lawsuits tied up the partners for several more years.

Before Brown left Springfield in 1850, the United States passed the Fugitive Slave Act, a law mandating that authorities in free states aid in the return of escaped slaves and impos-ing penalties on those who aided in their escape. In response Brown founded a militant group to prevent slaves' capture, the League of Gileadites. In the Bible, Mount Gilead was the place where only the bravest of Israelites gathered to face an invading enemy. Brown founded the League with the words, "Nothing so charms the American people as personal bravery. [Blacks] would have ten times the number [of white friends than] they now have were they but half as much in earnest to secure their dearest rights as they are to ape the follies and extravagances of their white neighbors, and to indulge in idle show, in ease, and in luxury."[20] Upon leaving Springfield in 1850, he instructed the League to act "quickly, quietly, and efficiently" to protect slaves that escaped to Springfield—words that would foreshadow Brown's later actions preceding Harpers Ferry.[20] From Brown's founding of the League of Gileadites onward, not one person was ever taken back into slavery from Springfield. Brown gave his rocking chair to the mother of his beloved black porter, Thomas Thomas, as a gesture of affection.[16]

Brown's time in Springfield sowed the seeds for the future financial support he received from New England's great merchants, introduced him to nationally famous abolitionists like Douglass and Truth, and included the foundation of the League of Gileadites.[16][17] During this time, Brown also helped publicize David Walker's speech *Appeal*.[21] Brown's personal attitudes evolved in Springfield, as he observed the success of the city's Underground Railroad and made his first venture into militant, anti-slavery community organizing. In speeches, he pointed to the martyrs Elijah Lovejoy and Charles Turner Torrey as whites "ready to help blacks challenge slave-catchers."[22] In Springfield, Brown found a city that shared his own anti-slavery passions, and each seemed to educate the other. Certainly, with both successes and failures, Brown's Springfield years were a transformative period of his life that catalyzed many of his later actions.[16]

## Homestead in New York

In 1848, Brown heard of Gerrit Smith's Adirondack land grants to poor black men, called Timbuctoo, and decided to move his family there to establish a farm where he could provide guidance and assistance to the blacks who were attempting to establish communities in the area.[23] He bought from Smith land in the town of North Elba, New York (near Lake Placid), for $1 an acre ($2/ha), and spent two years there.[24] After he was executed, his wife took his body there for burial; 12 of his collaborators were later buried in a mass grave there. Since 1895, the John Brown Farm and Gravesite has been owned by New York State and it is now a National Historic Landmark.[23]

## Actions in Kansas

In 1855, Brown learned from his adult sons in the Kansas territory that their families were completely unprepared to face attack, and that pro-slavery forces there were militant. Determined to protect his family and oppose the advances of slavery supporters, Brown left for Kansas, enlisting a son-in-law and making several stops just to collect funds and weapons. As reported by the New York *Tribune*, Brown stopped en route to participate in an anti-slavery convention that took place in June 1855 in Albany, New York. Despite the controversy that ensued on the convention floor regarding the support of violent efforts on behalf of the free state cause, several people gave Brown financial support. As he went westward, Brown found more militant support in his home state of Ohio, particularly in the strongly anti-slavery Western Reserve section where he had been reared.

## Pottawatomie

*John Brown, 1856*

Brown and the free settlers were optimistic that they could bring Kansas into the union as a slavery-free state. [25] After the winter snows thawed in 1856, the pro-slavery activists began a campaign to seize Kansas on their own terms. Brown was particularly affected by the sacking of Lawrence in May 1856, in which a sheriff-led posse destroyed newspaper offices and a hotel. Only one man, a Border Ruffian, was killed. Preston Brooks's caning of anti-slavery Senator Charles Sumner in the United States Senate also fueled Brown's anger. A pro-slavery writer, Benjamin Franklin Stringfellow, of the *Squatter Sovereign*, wrote that "[pro-slavery forces] are determined to repel this Northern invasion, and make Kansas a Slave State; though our rivers should be covered with the blood of their victims, and the carcasses of the Abolitionists should be so numerous in the territory as to breed disease and sickness, we will not be deterred from our purpose."[26] Brown was outraged by both the violence of the pro-slavery forces and what he saw as a weak and cowardly response by the antislavery partisans and the Free State settlers, whom he described as "cowards, or worse."[27]

The Pottawatomie massacre occurred during the night of May 24 and the morning of May 25, 1856. Using swords, Brown and a band of abolitionist settlers took from their residences and killed five "professional slave hunters and militant pro-slavery"[28] settlers north of Pottawatomie Creek in Franklin County, Kansas.

Speaking of the threats that were supposedly the justification for the massacre, Free State leader Charles L. Robinson stated:

> When it is known that such threats were as plenty as blue-berries in June, on both sides, all over the Territory, and were regarded as of no more importance than the idle wind, this indictment will hardly justify midnight assassination of all pro-slavery men, whether making threats or not . . . Had all men been killed in Kansas who indulged in such threats, there would have been none left to bury the dead.[29]

In the two years prior to the Pottawatomie Creek massacre, there had been eight killings in Kansas Territory attributable to slavery politics, but none in the vicinity of the massacre. The massacre was the match in the powderkeg that precipitated the bloodiest period in "Bleeding Kansas" history, a three-month period of retaliatory raids and battles in which 29 people died.[30]

## Palmyra and Osawatomie

A force of Missourians, led by Captain Henry Pate, captured John Jr. and Jason, and destroyed the Brown family homestead, and later participated in the Sack of Lawrence. On June 2, John Brown, nine of his followers, and 20 local men successfully defended a Free State settlement at Palmyra, Kansas against an attack by Pate (see Battle of Black Jack). Pate and 22 of his men were taken prisoner.[31] After capture, they were taken to Brown's camp, and received all the food Brown could find. Brown forced Pate to sign a treaty, exchanging the freedom of Pate and his men for the promised release of Brown's two captured sons. Brown released Pate to Colonel Edwin Sumner, but was furious to discover that the release of his sons was delayed until September.

In August, a company of over 300 Missourians under the command of General John W. Reid crossed into Kansas and headed towards Osawatomie, intending to destroy the Free State settlements there, and then march on Topeka and Lawrence.[32]

On the morning of August 30, 1856, they shot and killed Brown's son Frederick and his neighbor David Garrison on the outskirts of Osawatomie. Brown, outnumbered more than seven to one, arranged his 38 men behind natural defenses along the road. Firing from cover, they managed to kill at least 20 of Reid's men and wounded 40 more.[33] Reid regrouped, ordering his men to dismount and charge into the woods. Brown's small group scattered and fled across the Marais des Cygnes River. One of Brown's men was killed during the retreat and four were captured. While Brown and his surviving men hid in the woods nearby, the Missourians plundered and burned Osawatomie. Despite his defeat, Brown's bravery and military shrewdness in the face of overwhelming odds brought him national attention and made him a hero to many Northern abolitionists.[34]

On September 7, Brown entered Lawrence to meet with Free State leaders and help fortify against a feared assault. At least 2,700 pro-slavery Missourians were once again invading Kansas. On September 14, they skirmished near Lawrence. Brown prepared for battle, but serious violence was averted when the new governor of Kansas, John W. Geary, ordered the warring parties to disarm and disband, and offered clemency to former fighters on both sides.[35] Brown, taking advantage of the fragile peace, left Kansas with three of his sons to raise money from supporters in the North.

## Later years

### Gathering forces

Brown returned to the East by November 1856, and spent the next two years in New England raising funds. Initially he returned to Springfield, where he received contributions, and also a letter of recommendation from a prominent and wealthy merchant, George Walker. Walker was the brother-in-law of Franklin Benjamin Sanborn, the secretary for the Massachusetts State Kansas Committee, who introduced Brown to several influential abolitionists in the Boston area in January 1857.[17][36] Amos Adams Lawrence, a prominent Boston merchant, secretly gave a large amount of cash. William Lloyd Garrison, Thomas Wentworth Higginson, Theodore Parker and George Luther Stearns, and Samuel Gridley

*John Brown in 1859*

Howe also supported Brown. A group of six wealthy abolitionists—Sanborn, Higginson, Parker, Stearns, Howe, and Gerrit Smith—agreed to offer Brown financial support for his antislavery activities; they eventually provided most of the financial backing for the raid on Harpers Ferry, and came to be known as the Secret Six[37] or the Committee of Six. Brown often requested help from them with "no questions asked" and it remains unclear how much of Brown's scheme the Secret Six were aware of.

On January 7, 1858, the Massachusetts Committee pledged to provide 200 Sharps Rifles and ammunition, which were being stored at Tabor, Iowa. In March, Brown contracted Charles Blair of Collinsville, Connecticut for 1,000 pikes.

In the following months, Brown continued to raise funds, visiting Worcester, Springfield, New Haven, Syracuse and Boston. In Boston, he met Henry David Thoreau and Ralph Waldo Emerson. He received many pledges but little cash. In March, while in New York City, he was introduced to Hugh Forbes, an English mercenary, who had experience as a military tactician fighting with Giuseppe Garibaldi in Italy in 1848. Brown hired him as his men's drillmaster and to write their tactical handbook. They agreed to meet in Tabor that summer. Using the alias Nelson Hawkins, Brown traveled through the Northeast and then visited his family in Hudson, Ohio. On August 7, he arrived in Tabor. Forbes arrived two days later. Over several weeks, the two men put together a "Well-Matured Plan" for fighting slavery in the South. The men quarreled over many of the details. In November, their troops left for Kansas. Forbes had not received his salary and was still feuding with Brown, so he returned to the East instead of venturing into Kansas. He soon threatened to expose the plot to the government.

As the October elections saw a free-state victory, Kansas was quiet. Brown made his men return to Iowa, where he told them tidbits of his Virginia scheme.[38] In January 1858, Brown left his men in Springdale, Iowa, and set off to visit Frederick Douglass in Rochester, New York. There he discussed his plans with Douglass, and reconsidered Forbes' criticisms.[39] Brown wrote a Provisional Constitution that would create a government for a new state in the region of his invasion. He then traveled to Peterboro, New York, and Boston to discuss matters with the Secret Six. In letters to them, he indicated that, along with recruits, he would go into the South equipped with weapons to do "Kansas work."

Brown and 12 of his followers, including his son Owen, traveled to Chatham, Ontario, where he convened on May 10 a Constitutional Convention.[40] The convention, with several dozen delegates including his friend James Madison Bell, was put together with the help of Dr. Martin Delany.[41] One-third of Chatham's 6,000 residents were fugitive slaves, and it was here that Brown was introduced to Harriet Tubman. The convention assembled 34 blacks and 12 whites to adopt Brown's Provisional Constitution. According to Delany, during the convention, Brown illuminated his plans to make Kansas rather than Canada the end of the Underground Railroad. This would be the Subterranean Pass Way. Delany's reflections are not entirely trustworthy. Brown was no longer looking toward Kansas and was entirely focused on Virginia. Other testimony from the Chatham meeting suggests Brown did speak of going south. Brown had long used the terminology of the Subterranean Pass Way from the late 1840s, so it is possible that Delany conflated Brown's statements over the years. Regardless, Brown was elected commander-in-chief and named John Henrie Kagi his "Secretary of War." Richard Realf was named "Secretary of State." Elder Monroe, a black minister, was to act as president until another was chosen. A. M. Chapman was the acting vice president; Delany, the corresponding secretary. In 1859, "A Declaration of Liberty by the Representatives of the Slave Population of the United States of America" was written.

Although nearly all of the delegates signed the constitution, very few volunteered to join Brown's forces, although it will never be clear how many Canadian expatriates actually intended to join Brown because of a subsequent "security leak" that threw off plans for the raid, creating a hiatus in which Brown lost contact with many of the Canadian leaders. This crisis occurred when Hugh Forbes, Brown's mercenary, tried to expose the plans to Massachusetts Senator Henry Wilson and others. The Secret Six feared their names would be made public. Howe and Higginson wanted no delays in Brown's progress, while Parker, Stearns, Smith and Sanborn insisted on postponement. Stearns and Smith were the major sources of funds, and their words carried more weight. To throw Forbes off the trail and invalidate his assertions, Brown returned to Kansas in June, and remained in that vicinity for six months. There he joined forces with James Montgomery, who was leading raids into Missouri.

On December 20, Brown led his own raid, in which he liberated 11 slaves, took captive two white men, and looted horses and wagons. (See Battle of the Spurs.) On January 20, 1859, he embarked on a lengthy journey to take the liberated slaves to Detroit and then on a ferry to Canada. While passing through Chicago, Brown met with abolitionists Allan Pinkerton, John Jones, and Henry O. Wagoner who arranged and raised the fare for the passage to Detroit[42] and purchase clothes and supplies for Brown. Jones's wife, Mary, guessed that the supplies included the suit Brown was later hanged in.[43] On March 12, 1859, Brown met with Frederick Douglass and Detroit abolitionists George DeBaptiste, William Lambert, and others at William Webb's house in Detroit to discuss emancipation. [44] DeBaptiste proposed that conspirators blow up some of the South's largest churches. The suggestion was opposed by Brown, who felt humanity precluded such unnecessary bloodshed.[45]

Over the course of the next few months, he traveled again through Ohio, New York, Connecticut, and Massachusetts to drum up more support for the cause. On May 9, he delivered a lecture in Concord, Massachusetts, that Amos Bronson Alcott, Emerson, and

Thoreau attended. Brown reconnoitered with the Secret Six. In June he paid his last visit to his family in North Elba before departing for Harpers Ferry. He stayed one night en route in Hagerstown, Maryland at the Washington House, on West Washington Street. On June 30, 1859, the hotel had at least 25 guests, including I. Smith and Sons, Oliver Smith and Owen Smith, and Jeremiah Anderson, all from New York. From papers found in the Kennedy Farmhouse after the raid, it is known that Brown wrote to Kagi that he would sign into a hotel as I. Smith and Sons.[46]

## Raid

As he began recruiting supporters for an attack on slaveholders, Brown was joined by Harriet Tubman, "General Tubman," as he called her.[47] Her knowledge of support networks and resources in the border states of Pennsylvania, Maryland and Delaware was invaluable to Brown and his planners. Some abolitionists, including Frederick Douglass and William Lloyd Garrison, opposed his tactics, but Brown dreamed of fighting to create a new state for freed slaves and made preparations for military action. After he began the first battle, he believed, slaves would rise up and carry out a rebellion across the South.[48]

Brown asked Tubman to gather former slaves then living in present-day Southern Ontario who might be willing to join his fighting force, which she did.[49] He arrived in Harpers Ferry on July 3, 1859. A few days later, under the name Isaac Smith, he rented a farmhouse in nearby Maryland. He awaited the arrival of his recruits. They never materialized in the numbers he expected. In late August he met with Douglass in Chambersburg, Pennsylvania, where he revealed the Harpers Ferry plan. Douglass expressed severe reservations, rebuffing Brown's pleas to join the mission. Douglass had known of Brown's plans since early 1859 and had made a number of efforts to discourage blacks from enlisting.

In late September, the 950 pikes arrived from Charles Blair. Kagi's draft plan called for a brigade of 4,500 men, but Brown had only 21 men (16 white and 5 black: three free blacks, one freed slave, and a fugitive slave). They ranged in age from 21 to 49. Twelve had been with Brown in Kansas raids. On October 16, 1859, Brown (leaving three men behind as a rear guard) led 18 men in an attack on the Harpers Ferry Armory. He had received 200 Beecher's Bibles—breechloading .52 (13.2 mm) caliber Sharps rifles—and pikes from northern abolitionist societies in preparation for the raid. The armory was a large complex of buildings that contained 100,000 muskets and rifles, which Brown planned to seize and use to arm local slaves. They would then head south, drawing off more and more slaves from plantations, and fighting only in self-defense. As Douglass and Brown's family testified, his strategy was essentially to deplete Virginia of its slaves, causing the institution to collapse in one county after another, until the movement spread into the South, wreaking havoc on the economic viability of the pro-slavery states.

Initially, the raid went well, and they met no resistance entering the town. They cut the telegraph wires and easily captured the armory, which was being defended by a single watchman. They next rounded up hostages from nearby farms, including Colonel Lewis Washington, great-grandnephew of George Washington. They also spread the news to the local slaves that their liberation was at hand. Things started to go wrong when an eastbound Baltimore & Ohio train approached the town. The train's baggage master tried to warn the passengers. Brown's men yelled for him to halt and then opened fire. The baggage master, Hayward Shepherd, became the first casualty of Brown's war against slavery. Ironically, Shepherd was a free black man. Two of the hostages' slaves also died in the raid. [50] For some reason, after the shooting of Shepherd, Brown allowed the train to continue on its way.

A.J. Phelps, the Through Express passenger train conductor, sent a telegram to W.P. Smith, Master of Transportation of the B. & O. R. R., Baltimore:

Express train bound east, under my charge, was stopped this morning at Harper's Ferry by armed abolitionists. They have possession of the bridge and the arms and armory of the United States. Myself and Baggage Master have been fired at, and Hayward, the colored porter, is wounded very severely, being shot through the body, the ball entering the body below the left shoulder blade and coming out under the left side.[51]

—Monocacy, 7.05 A. M., October 17, 1859.

News of the raid reached Baltimore early that morning and Washington by late morning. In the meantime, local farmers, shopkeepers, and militia pinned down the raiders in the armory by firing from the heights behind the town. Some of the local men were shot by Brown's men. At noon, a company of militia seized the bridge, blocking the only escape route. Brown then moved his prisoners and remaining raiders into the engine house, a small brick building at the armory's entrance. He had the doors and windows barred and loopholes cut through the brick walls. The surrounding forces barraged the engine house, and the men inside fired back with occasional fury. Brown sent his son Watson and another supporter out under a white flag, but the angry crowd shot them. Intermittent shooting then broke out, and Brown's son Oliver was wounded. His son begged his father to kill him and end his suffering, but Brown said "If you must die, die like a man." A few minutes later, Oliver was dead. The exchanges lasted throughout the day.

By the morning of October 18 the engine house, later known as John Brown's Fort, was surrounded by a company of U.S. Marines under the command of First Lieutenant Israel Greene, USMC, with Colonel Robert E. Lee of the United States Army in overall command.[52] Army First Lieutenant J. E. B. Stuart approached under a white flag and told the raiders their lives would be spared if they surrendered. Brown refused, saying, "No, I prefer to die here." Stuart then gave a signal. The Marines used sledgehammers and a makeshift battering ram to break down the engine room door. Lieutenant Israel Greene cornered Brown and struck him several times, wounding his head. In three minutes Brown and the survivors were captives.

Altogether Brown's men killed four people, and wounded nine. Ten of Brown's men were killed (including his sons Watson and Oliver). Five escaped (including his son Owen), and seven were captured along with Brown. Among the raiders killed were John Henry Kagi, Lewis Sheridan Leary, and Dangerfield Newby; those hanged besides Brown included John Anthony Copeland, Jr., and Shields Green.[53]

## Imprisonment, trial, and six weeks in jail

Brown and the others captured were held in the office of the armory. On October 18, 1859, Virginia Governor Henry A. Wise, Virginia Senator James M. Mason, and Representative Clement Vallandigham of Ohio arrived in Harpers Ferry. Mason led the three-hour questioning session of Brown.

> . . . had I so interfered in behalf of the rich, the powerful, the intelligent, the so-called great, or in behalf of any of their friends, either father, mother, brother, sister, wife, or children, or any of that class, and suffered and sacrificed what I have in this interference, it would have been all right; and every man in this court would have deemed it an act worthy of reward rather than punishment. This court acknowledges, as I suppose, the validity of the law of God. I see a book kissed here which I suppose to be the Bible, or at least the New Testament. That teaches me that all things whatsoever I would that men should do to me, I should do even so to them. It teaches me, further, to "remember them that are in bonds, as bound with them." I endeavored to act up to that instruction. I say, I am yet too young to understand that God is any respecter of persons. I believe that to have interfered as I have done as I have always freely admitted I have done in behalf of His despised poor, was not wrong, but right. Now, if it is deemed necessary that I should forfeit my life for the furtherance of the ends of justice, and mingle my blood further with the blood of my children and with the blood of millions in this slave country whose rights are disregarded by wicked, cruel, and unjust enactments, I submit; so let it be done!
>
> —John Brown, in his speech following the conviction [54]

Although the attack had taken place on federal property, Wise ordered that Brown and his men be tried in Virginia in Charles Town, the nearby seat of Jefferson County just seven miles west of Harpers Ferry (perhaps to avert Northern political pressure on the Federal government, or in the unlikely event of a presidential pardon). The trial began October 27, after a doctor pronounced the still-wounded Brown fit for trial. Brown was charged with murdering four whites and a black, conspiring with slaves to rebel, and treason against Virginia. A series of lawyers were assigned to him, including Lawson Botts, Thomas C. Green, Samuel Chilton, a lawyer from Washington D.C., and George Hoyt, but it was Hiram Griswold, a lawyer from Cleveland, Ohio, who concluded the defense on October

31. In his closing statement, Griswold argued that Brown could not be found guilty of treason against a state to which he owed no loyalty and of which he was not a resident, that Brown had not killed anyone himself, and that the raid's failure indicated that Brown had not conspired with slaves. Andrew Hunter, the local district attorney, presented the closing arguments for the prosecution.

On November 2, after a week-long trial and 45 minutes of deliberation, the Charles Town jury found Brown guilty on all three counts. He was sentenced to be hanged in public on December 2. In response to the sentence, Ralph Waldo Emerson remarked that "[John Brown] will make the gallows glorious like the Cross." Cadets from the Virginia Military Institute under the leadership of General Francis H. Smith and Major Thomas J. Jackson (who earned the nickname "Stonewall" less than two years later) were called into service as a security detail in the event Brown's supporters attempted a rescue.

During the month before his execution, Brown was allowed to send and receive correspondence, and he wrote many letters. One of the letters was from Mahala Doyle, wife and mother of three of Brown's Kansas victims. She wrote "Altho' vengeance is not mine, I confess that I do feel gratified to hear that you were stopped in your fiendish career at Harper's Ferry . . . " In a postscript she added "My son John Doyle whose life I beg[g] ed of you is now grown up and is very desirous to be in Charlestown on the day of your execution."[55]

Brown refused to be rescued by Silas Soule, a friend from Kansas who somehow infiltrated the Jefferson County Jail one day and offered to break him out during the night and flee northward to New York state and possibly Canada. Brown supposedly told Silas that, aged 59, he was too old to live a life on the run from the federal authorities as a fugitive and that he was ready to die as a martyr. Silas left him behind to be executed. Many of Brown's letters exuded spirituality and conviction and, when picked up by the Northern press, won him more supporters in the North while infuriating many white people in the South. On December 1, Brown's wife arrived by train in Charles Town, where she joined him at the county jail for his last meal. She was denied permission to stay the night, prompting Brown to lose his composure and temper for the only time during the ordeal.

The Governor of Virginia was so concerned about an attempt to rescue Brown that he halted almost all transportation on the Winchester and Potomac Railroad (from Maryland south through Harpers Ferry to Charles Town) from the day before through the day after the execution.

## Death and aftermath
On the morning of December 2, 1859, Brown wrote:

> I, John Brown, am now quite certain that the crimes of this guilty land will never be purged away but with blood. I had, as I now think, vainly flattered myself that without very much bloodshed it might be done.[58]

He read his Bible and wrote a final letter to his wife, which included his will. At 11:00 a.m. he was escorted from the county jail through a crowd of 2,000 soldiers a few blocks away to a small field where the gallows were. Among the soldiers in the crowd were future Confederate general Stonewall Jackson and John Wilkes Booth (the latter borrowing a militia uniform to gain admission to the execution).[59] The poet Walt Whitman, in *Year of Meteors*, described viewing the execution.[60]

Brown was accompanied by the sheriff and his assistants, but no minister since he had consistently rejected the ministrations of pro-slavery clergy. Since the region was in the grips of virtual hysteria, most Northerners, including journalists, were run out of town, and it is unlikely any anti-slavery clergyman would have been safe, even if one were to have sought to visit Brown. He elected to receive no religious services in the jail or at the scaffold. He was hanged at 11:15 a.m. and pronounced dead at 11:50 a.m.

## Transportation of his body

*FMIB 43086 John Brown's Grave (the tombstone is now enclosed in glass)*

Brown's body was placed in a wooden coffin with the noose still around his neck. His coffin was then put on a train to take it away from Virginia to his family homestead in New York for burial. His body was supposed to be embalmed in Philadelphia, through which the train would pass. However, because of demonstrations expected from both sides—there were many Southern pro-slavery medical students in Philadelphia—Mayor Alexander Henry "made a fake casket, covered with flowers and flags which was carefully lifted from the coach and the train and sped onward in its destination . . . In reality the train carrying Brown's body never actually stopped in Philadelphia, and thus violence was averted by a 'sham coffin'." As a direct result, many Southern medical students and professors left Philadelphia *en masse* on December 21, 1859, for Southern medical schools, never to return.[61]

In the North, large memorial meetings took place, church bells rang, minute guns were fired, and famous writers such as Emerson and Thoreau joined many Northerners in praising Brown.[62]

## Senate investigation

On December 14, 1859, the U.S. Senate appointed a bipartisan committee to investigate the Harpers Ferry raid and to determine whether any citizens contributed arms, ammunition or money to John Brown's men. The Democrats attempted to implicate the Republicans in the raid; the Republicans tried to disassociate themselves from Brown and his acts.

The Senate committee heard testimony from 32 witnesses, including Liam Dodson, one of the surviving abolitionists. The report, authored by chairman James Murray Mason, a pro-slavery Democrat from Virginia, was published in June 1860. It found no direct evidence of a conspiracy, but implied that the raid was a result of Republican doctrines.[63] The two committee Republicans published a minority report, but were apparently more concerned about denying Northern culpability than clarifying the nature of Brown's efforts. Republicans such as Abraham Lincoln rejected any connection with the raid, calling Brown "insane."[64]

The investigation was performed in a tense environment in both houses of Congress. One senator wrote to his wife that "The members on both sides are mostly armed with deadly weapons and it is said that the friends of each are armed in the galleries." After a heated exchange of insults, a Mississippian attacked Thaddeus Stevens of Pennsylvania with a Bowie knife in the House of Representatives. Stevens' friends prevented a fight.[65]

The Senate committee was very cautious in its questions of two of Brown's backers, Samuel Howe and George Stearns, out of fear of stoking violence. Howe and Stearns later said that the questions were asked in a manner that permitted them to give honest answers without implicating themselves.[66] Civil War historian James M. McPherson stated that "A historian reading their testimony, however, will be convinced that they told several falsehoods."[67]

## Aftermath of the raid

The raid on Harpers Ferry is generally thought to have done much to set the nation on a course toward civil war.[68] Southern slaveowners, hearing initial reports that hundreds of abolitionists were involved, were relieved the effort was so small, but feared other abolitionists would emulate Brown and attempt to lead slave rebellions.[69] Therefore, the South reorganized the decrepit militia system. These militias, well-established by 1861, became a ready-made Confederate army, making the South better prepared for war.[70]

Southern Democrats charged that Brown's raid was an inevitable consequence of the Republican Party's political platform, which they associated with abolitionism. In light of the upcoming elections in November 1860, the Republicans tried to distance themselves as much as possible from Brown, condemning the raid and dismissing its leader as an insane fanatic. As one historian explains, Brown was successful in polarizing politics: "Brown's raid succeeded brilliantly. It drove a wedge through the already tentative and fragile Opposition-Republican coalition and helped to intensify the sectional polarization that soon tore the Democratic party and the Union apart."[70]

Many abolitionists in the North viewed Brown as a martyr, sacrificed for the sins of the nation. Immediately after the raid, William Lloyd Garrison published a column in *The Liberator*, judging Brown's raid "well-intended but sadly misguided" and "wild and futile."[71] But he defended Brown's character from detractors in the Northern and Southern press and argued that those who supported the principles of the American Revolution could not consistently oppose Brown's raid. On the day Brown was hanged, Garrison reiterated the point in Boston: "whenever commenced, I cannot but wish success to all slave insurrections."[72][73]

After the Civil War, Frederick Douglass wrote, "His zeal in the cause of my race was far greater than mine—it was as the burning sun to my taper light—mine was bounded by time, his stretched away to the boundless shores of eternity. I could live for the slave, but he could die for him."[74]

# Ambrose Burnside

*Ambrose Burnside, circa* 1880

**Ambrose Everett Burnside** (May 23, 1824–September 13, 1881) was an American soldier, railroad executive, inventor, industrialist, and politician from Rhode Island. He served as governor and as a United States Senator. As a Union Army general in the American Civil War, he conducted successful campaigns in North Carolina and East Tennessee, as well as countering the raids of Confederate General John Hunt Morgan, but suffered disastrous defeats at the Battle of Fredericksburg and the Battle of the Crater. His distinctive style of facial hair became known as sideburns, derived from his last name. He was also the first president of the National Rifle Association.

## Civil War
### First Bull Run

*General Ambrose Burnside.*

At the outbreak of the Civil War, Burnside was a colonel in the Rhode Island Militia. He raised the 1st Rhode Island Volunteer Infantry Regiment, and was appointed its colonel on May 2, 1861.[10] Two companies of this regiment were then armed with Burnside Carbines.

Within a month, he ascended to brigade command in the Department of northeast Virginia. He commanded the brigade without distinction at the First Battle of Bull Run in July, and took over division command temporarily for wounded Brig. Gen. David Hunter. His 90-day regiment was mustered out of service on August 2; he was promoted to brigadier-general of volunteers on August 6 and was assigned to train provisional brigades in the Army of the Potomac.[7]

### North Carolina

Burnside commanded the Coast Division or North Carolina Expeditionary Force from September 1861 until July 1862, three brigades assembled in Annapolis, Maryland, which formed the nucleus for his future IX Corps. He conducted a successful amphibious campaign that closed

*Burnside (seated, center) and officers of the 1st Rhode Island at Camp Sprague, Rhode Island, 1861*

more than 80 percent of the North Carolina sea coast to Confederate shipping for the remainder of the war. This included the Battle of Elizabeth City, fought on February 10, 1862, on the Pasquotank River near Elizabeth City, North Carolina.

The participants were vessels of the United States Navy's North Atlantic Blockading Squadron opposed by vessels of the Confederate Navy's Mosquito Fleet; the latter were supported by a shore-based battery of four guns at Cobb's Point (now called Cobb Point) near the southeastern border of the town. The battle was a part of the campaign in North Carolina that was led by Burnside and known as the Burnside Expedition. The result was a Union victory, with Elizabeth City and its nearby waters in their possession and the Confederate fleet captured, sunk, or dispersed.[11]

Burnside was promoted to major general of volunteers on March 18, 1862, in recognition of his successes at the battles of Roanoke Island and New Bern, the first significant Union victories in the Eastern Theater. In July, his forces were transported north to Newport News, Virginia, and became the IX Corps of the Army of the Potomac.[7]

Burnside was offered command of the Army of the Potomac following Maj. Gen. George B. McClellan's failure in the Peninsula Campaign.[12] He refused this opportunity because of his loyalty to McClellan and the fact that he understood his own lack of military experience, and detached part of his corps in support of Maj. Gen. John Pope's Army of Virginia in the Northern Virginia Campaign. He received telegrams at this time from Maj. Gen. Fitz John Porter which were extremely critical of Pope's abilities as a commander, and he forwarded on to his superiors in concurrence. This episode later played a significant role in Porter's court-martial, in which Burnside appeared as a star witness.[13]

Burnside again declined command following Pope's debacle at Second Bull Run.[14]

## Antietam

Burnside was given command of the Right Wing of the Army of the Potomac (the I Corps and his own IX Corps) at the start of the Maryland Campaign for the Battle of South Mountain, but McClellan separated the two corps at the Battle of Antietam, placing them on opposite ends of the Union battle line and returning Burnside to command of just the IX Corps. Burnside implicitly refused to give up his authority, and acted as though the corps commander was first Maj. Gen. Jesse L. Reno (killed at South Mountain) and then Brig. Gen. Jacob D. Cox, funneling orders through them to the corps. This cumbersome arrangement contributed to his slowness in attacking and crossing what is now called Burnside's Bridge on the southern flank of the Union line.[15]

Burnside did not perform an adequate reconnaissance of the area, and he did not take advantage of several easy fording sites out of range of the enemy; his troops were forced into repeated assaults across the narrow bridge, which was dominated by Confederate sharpshooters on the high ground. By noon, McClellan was losing patience. He sent a succession of couriers to motivate Burnside to move forward, ordering one aide, "Tell him if it costs 10,000 men he must go now." He further increased the pressure by sending his inspector general to confront Burnside, who reacted indignantly: "McClellan appears to think I am not trying my best to carry this bridge; you are the third or fourth one who has been to me this morning with similar orders."[16] The IX Corps eventually broke through, but the delay allowed Maj. Gen. A. P. Hill's Confederate division to come up from Harpers Ferry and repulse the Union breakthrough. McClellan refused Burnside's requests for reinforcements, and the battle ended in a tactical stalemate.[17]

## Fredericksburg

*Union General Ambrose Burnside,* 1862

McClellan was removed after failing to pursue General Robert E. Lee's retreat from Antietam, and Burnside was assigned to command the Army of the Potomac on November 7, 1862. He reluctantly obeyed this order, the third such in his brief career, in part because the courier told him that, if he refused it, the command would go instead to Maj. Gen. Joseph Hooker, whom Burnside disliked. President Abraham Lincoln pressured Burnside to take aggressive action and approved his plan on November 14 to capture the Confederate capital at Richmond, Virginia. This plan led to a humiliating and costly Union defeat at the Battle of Fredericksburg on December 13. His advance upon Fredericksburg was rapid, but the attack was delayed by his planning in marshaling pontoon bridges for crossing the Rappahannock River, as well as his own reluctance to deploy portions of his army across fording points. This allowed Gen. Lee to concentrate along Marye's Heights just west of town and easily repulse the Union attacks.

Assaults south of town were also mismanaged, which were supposed to be the main avenue of attack, and initial Union breakthroughs went unsupported. Burnside was upset by the failure of his plan and by the enormous casualties of his repeated, futile frontal assaults, and declared that he would personally lead an assault by the IX corps. His corps commanders talked him out of it, but relations were strained between the general and his subordinates. Accepting full blame, he offered to retire from the U.S. Army, but this was refused. Burnside's detractors labeled him the "Butcher of Fredericksburg."[18]

In January 1863, Burnside launched a second offensive against Lee, but it bogged down in winter rains before anything was accomplished, and has derisively been called the Mud March. In its wake, he asked that several openly insubordinate officers be relieved of duty and court-martialed; he also offered to resign. Lincoln chose the latter option, and on January 26 replaced Burnside with Maj. Gen. Joseph Hooker, one of the officers who had conspired against him.[19]

## East Tennessee

Burnside offered to resign his commission altogether but Lincoln declined, stating that there could still be a place for him in the army. Thus, he was placed back at the head of the IX Corps and sent to command the Department of the Ohio, encompassing the states of Ohio, Indiana, Kentucky, and Illinois. This was a quiet area with little activity, and the President reasoned that Burnside could not get himself into too much trouble there. However, antiwar sentiment was riding high in the Western states as they had traditionally carried on a great deal of commerce with the South, and there was little in the way of abolitionist sentiment there or a desire to fight for the purpose of ending slavery. Burnside was thoroughly disturbed by this trend and issued a series of orders forbidding "the expression of public sentiments against the war or the Administration" in his department; this finally climaxed with General Order No. 38, which declared that "any person found guilty of treason will be tried by a military tribunal and either imprisoned or banished to enemy lines."

On May 1, 1863, Ohio Congressman Clement L. Vallandigham, a prominent opponent of the war, held a large public rally in Mount Vernon, Ohio in which he denounced President Lincoln as a "tyrant" who sought to abolish the Constitution and set up a dictatorship. Burnside had dispatched several agents to the rally who took down notes and brought back their "evidence" to the general, who then declared that it was sufficient grounds to arrest Vallandigham for treason. A military court tried him and found him guilty of violating General Order No. 38, despite his protests that he was simply expressing his opinions in public. Vallandigham was sentenced to imprisonment for the duration of the war, and was turned into a martyr by antiwar Democrats. Burnside next turned his attention to Illinois, where the Chicago *Times* newspaper had been printing antiwar editorials for months. The general dispatched a squadron of troops to the paper's offices and ordered them to cease printing.

Lincoln had not been asked or informed about either Vallandigham's arrest or the closure of the Chicago *Times*. He remembered the section of General Order No. 38 which declared that offenders would be banished to enemy lines and finally decided that it was a good idea; so Vallandigham was freed from jail and sent to Confederate hands. Meanwhile, Lincoln ordered the Chicago *Times* to be reopened and announced that Burnside had exceeded his authority in both cases. The President then issued a warning that generals were not to arrest civilians or close down newspapers again without the White House's permission.[20]

Burnside also dealt with Confederate raiders such as John Hunt Morgan.

In the Knoxville Campaign, Burnside advanced to Knoxville, Tennessee, first bypassing the Confederate-held Cumberland Gap and ultimately occupying Knoxville unopposed; he then sent troops back to the Cumberland Gap. Confederate commander Brig. Gen. John W. Frazer refused to surrender in the face of two Union brigades but Burnside arrived with a third, forcing the surrender of Frazer and 2,300 Confederates.[21]

Union Maj. Gen. William S. Rosecrans was defeated at the Battle of Chickamauga, and Burnside was pursued by Lt. Gen. James Longstreet, against whose troops he had battled at Marye's Heights. Burnside skillfully outmaneuvered Longstreet at the Battle of

Campbell's Station and was able to reach his entrenchments and safety in Knoxville, where he was briefly besieged until the Confederate defeat at the Battle of Fort Sanders outside the city. Tying down Longstreet's corps at Knoxville contributed to Gen. Braxton Bragg's defeat by Maj. Gen. Ulysses S. Grant at Chattanooga. Troops under Maj. Gen. William T. Sherman marched to Burnside's aid, but the siege had already been lifted; Longstreet withdrew, eventually returning to Virginia.[19]

## Overland Campaign

Burnside was ordered to take the IX Corps back to the Eastern Theater, where he built it up to a strength of over 21,000 in Annapolis, Maryland.[22] The IX Corps fought in the Overland Campaign of May 1864 as an independent command, reporting initially to Grant; his corps was not assigned to the Army of the Potomac because Burnside out-ranked its commander Maj. Gen. George G. Meade, who had been a division commander under Burnside at Fredericksburg. This cumbersome arrangement was rectified on May 24 just before the Battle of North Anna, when Burnside agreed to waive his precedence of rank and was placed under Meade's direct command.[23]

Burnside fought at the battles of Wilderness and Spotsylvania Court House, where he did not perform in a distinguished manner,[24] attacking piecemeal and appearing reluctant to commit his troops to the frontal assaults that characterized these battles. After North Anna and Cold Harbor, he took his place in the siege lines at Petersburg.[25]

## The Crater

As the two armies faced the stalemate of trench warfare at Petersburg in July 1864, Burnside agreed to a plan suggested by a regiment of former coal miners in his corps, the 48th Pennsylvania: to dig a mine under a fort named Elliot's Salient in the Confederate entrenchments and ignite explosives there to achieve a surprise breakthrough. The fort was destroyed on July 30 in what is known as the Battle of the Crater. Because of interference from Meade, Burnside was ordered, only hours before the infantry attack, not to use his division of black troops, which had been specially trained for the assault. Instead, he was forced to use untrained white troops. He could not decide which division to choose as a replacement, so he had his three subordinate commanders draw lots.

The division chosen by chance was that commanded by Brig. Gen. James H. Ledlie, who failed to brief the men on what was expected of them and was reported during the battle to be getting drunk in a bombproof shelter well behind the lines, providing no leadership. Ledlie's men entered the huge crater instead of going around it, became trapped, and were subjected to heavy fire from Confederates around the rim, resulting in high casualties.

Burnside was relieved of command on August 14 and sent on "extended leave" by Grant. He was never recalled to duty for the remainder of the war. A court of inquiry later placed the blame for the Crater fiasco on Burnside and his subordinates. In December, Burnside met with President Lincoln and General Grant about his future. He was contemplating resignation, but Lincoln and Grant requested that he remain in the Army. At the end of the interview, Burnside wrote, "I was not informed of any duty upon which I am to be placed." He finally resigned his commission on April 15, 1865, after Lee's surrender at Appomattox.[26]

The United States Congress Joint Committee on the Conduct of the War later exonerated Burnside, and placed the blame for the Union defeat at the Crater on General Meade for requiring the specially trained USCT (United States Colored Troops) men to be withdrawn.

## Postbellum career

After his resignation, Burnside was employed in numerous railroad and industrial directorships, including the presidencies of the Cincinnati and Martinsville Railroad, the Indianapolis and Vincennes Railroad, the Cairo and Vincennes Railroad, and the Rhode Island Locomotive Works.

He was elected to three one-year terms as Governor of Rhode Island, serving from May 29, 1866, to May 25, 1869.

Burnside was a Companion of the Massachusetts Commandery of the Military Order of the Loyal Legion of the United States, a military society of Union officers and their descendants, and served as the Junior Vice Commander of the Massachusetts Commandery in 1869. He was commander-in-chief of the Grand Army of the Republic (GAR) veterans' association from 1871 to 1872, and also served as the Commander of the Department of Rhode Island of the GAR.[27] At its inception in 1871, the National Rifle Association chose him as its first president.[28][29]

During a visit to Europe in 1870, Burnside attempted to mediate between the French and the Germans in the Franco-Prussian War. He was registered at the offices of Drexel, Harjes & Co., Geneva, week ending November 5, 1870.[30] Drexel Harjes was a major lender to the new French government after the war, helping it to repay its massive war reparations.

In 1876 Burnside was elected as commander of the New England Battalion of the Centennial Legion, the title of a collection of 13 militia units from the original 13 states, which participated in the parade in Philadelphia on July 4, 1876, to mark the centennial of the signing of the Declaration of Independence.[31]

In 1874 Burnside was elected by the Rhode Island Senate as a U.S. Senator from Rhode Island, was re-elected in 1880, and served until his death in 1881. During that time, Burnside, who had been a Democrat before the war, ran as a Republican, playing a prominent role in military affairs as well as serving as chairman of the Foreign Relations Committee in 1881.[32]

Burnside died suddenly of "neuralgia of the heart" (Angina pectoris) at Bristol, Rhode Island, and is buried in Swan Point Cemetery, Providence, Rhode Island.[32] An equestrian statue in his honor was erected in the late 19th century in Burnside Park in Providence.

## Assessment and legacy

Personally, Burnside was always very popular, both in the army and in politics. He made friends easily, smiled a lot, and remembered everyone's name. His professional military reputation, however, was less positive, and he was known for being obstinate, unimaginative, and unsuited both intellectually and emotionally for high command.[33] Grant stated that he was "unfitted" for the command of an army and that no one knew this better than Burnside himself. Knowing his capabilities, he twice refused command of the Army of the Potomac, accepting only the third time when the courier told him that otherwise the command would go to Joseph Hooker. Jeffry D. Wert described Burnside's relief after Fredericksburg in a passage that sums up his military career:[34]

> He had been the most unfortunate commander of the Army, a general who had been cursed by succeeding its most popular leader and a man who believed he was unfit for the post. His tenure had been marked by bitter animosity among his subordinates and a fearful, if not needless, sacrifice of life. A firm patriot, he lacked the power of personality and will to direct recalcitrant generals. He had been willing to fight the enemy, but the terrible slope before Marye's Heights stands as his legacy.
> —Jeffry D. Wert, *The Sword of Lincoln*

Bruce Catton summarized Burnside:[35]

> . . . Burnside had repeatedly demonstrated that it had been a military tragedy to give him a rank higher than colonel. One reason might have been that, with all his deficiencies, Burnside never had any angles of his own to play; he was a simple, honest, loyal soldier, doing his best even if that best was not very good, never scheming or conniving or backbiting. Also, he was modest; in an army many of whose generals were insufferable prima donnas, Burnside never mistook himself for Napoleon. Physically he was impressive: tall, just a little stout, wearing what was probably the most artistic and awe-inspiring set of whiskers in all that bewhiskered Army. He customarily wore a high, bell-crowned felt hat with the brim turned down and a double-breasted, knee-length frock coat, belted at the waist—a costume which, unfortunately, is apt to strike the modern eye as being very much like that of a beefy city cop of the 1880s.
> —Bruce Catton, *Mr. Lincoln's Army*

## Sideburns

Burnside was noted for his unusual facial hair, joining strips of hair in front of his ears to his mustache but with the chin clean-shaven; the word *burnsides* was coined to describe this style. The syllables were later reversed to give *sideburns*.[33]

# William Harvey Carney

**William Harvey Carney** (February 29, 1840–December 9, 1908) was an African American soldier during the American Civil War. Born as a slave, he was awarded the Medal of Honor in 1900 for his gallantry in saving the regimental colors (American Flag) during the Battle of Fort Wagner in 1863. The action for which he received the Medal of Honor preceded any other African American Medal of Honor recipient; however, his medal was actually one of the very last to be awarded for Civil War service. African Americans received the Medal of Honor as early as April 1865.[1]

## Biography

William Harvey Carney was born as a slave in Norfolk, Virginia, on February 29, 1840.[2] How he made his way to freedom is not certain. According to most accounts, he escaped through the Underground Railroad, and joined his father in Massachusetts. Other members of their family were freed by purchase or by the death of their master.[2][3]

Carney joined the 54th Massachusetts Volunteer Infantry in March 1863[2] as a sergeant. He took part in the July 18, 1863, assault on Fort Wagner in Charleston, South Carolina.[4] His actions there ultimately earned him the Medal of Honor. When the color guard was killed, Carney retrieved the U.S. flag and marched forward with it, despite multiple serious wounds.[2][5] When the Union troops were forced to retreat under fire, he struggled back across the battlefield, eventually returning to his own lines and turning over the colors to another survivor of the 54th, saying, "Boys, I only did my duty; the old flag never touched the ground!"[3] He received an honorable discharge due to disability from his wounds in June 1864.[2][6]

## Post-war

After his discharge, Carney returned to New Bedford, Massachusetts, and took a job maintaining the city's streetlights. He then delivered mail for thirty-two years.[4][7] He was a founding vice president of the New Bedford Branch 18 of the National Association of Letter Carriers in 1890.[7] He married Susannah Williams, and they had a daughter, Clara Heronia.[4] He spent a few years in California, then returned again in 1869.

Carney received his Medal of Honor on May 23, 1900, nearly 37 years after the events at Fort Wagner (more than half such awards from the Civil War were presented 20 or more years after the fact).[3] Twenty African American men received the medal before him, but because his battle actions happened earlier than the others, some have incorrectly cited

*Carney after the war, wearing his Medal of Honor*

him as the first to have received the medal.[2][3][8] His citation reads,

When the color sergeant was shot down, this soldier grasped the flag, led the way to the parapet, and planted the colors thereon. When the troops fell back he brought off the flag, under a fierce fire in which he was twice severely wounded.[9]

In 1901, shortly after his medal was finally awarded, a song was published about his daring exploits. The song was entitled, "Boys the Old Flag Never Touched the Ground." It clearly tells the story of his brave and patriotic efforts to keep Old Glory flying in the midst of a fierce battle.

Carney died at the Boston City Hospital on December 9, 1908, of complications from an elevator accident at the Massachusetts State House where he worked for the Department of State. His body lay in state for one day at the undertaking rooms of Walden Banks 142 Lenox Street at the wish of his wife and daughter. He was buried in the family plot at Oak Grove Cemetery in New Bedford, Massachusetts. Engraved on his tombstone is an image of the Medal of Honor.[10]

# Albert Cashier

*November, 1864*

**Albert D. J. Cashier** (December 25, 1843–October 10, 1915), born Jennie Irene Hodgers, was an Irish-born immigrant who served in the Union Army during the American Civil War. Cashier adopted the identity of a man before enlisting, and maintained it until death. Cashier became famous as one of a number of women soldiers who served as men during the Civil War, although the consistent and long-term (at least 53 years) commitment to a male identity has prompted some contemporary scholars to suggest that Cashier was a trans man.[3][4][5][6]

## Early life

Cashier was very elderly and disoriented when interviewed about immigrating to the United States and enlisting in the army, and had always been evasive about early life; therefore, the available narratives are often contradictory. According to later investigation by the administrator of Cashier's estate, Albert Cashier was born Jennie Hodgers in Clogherhead, County Louth, Ireland on December 25, 1843,[7]:52[2] to Sallie and Patrick Hodgers.[2] Typically, the youth's uncle or stepfather was said to have dressed his charge in male clothing in order to find work in an all-male shoe factory in Illinois. Even before the advent of the war, Jenny adopted the identity of Albert Cashier in order to live independently.[7]:52 Sallie Hodgers, Cashier's mother, was known to have died prior to 1862, by which time her child had traveled as a stowaway to Belvidere, Illinois, and was working as a farmhand to a man named Avery.[8][9][10]

## Enlistment

Cashier first enlisted in July 1862 after President Lincoln's call for soldiers.[7]:52 As time passed, the need for soldiers only increased. On August 6, 1862, the eighteen-year-old enlisted in the 95th Illinois Infantry for a three-year term using the name "Albert D. J. Cashier" and was assigned to Company G.[11][12][7]:52 Cashier was listed in the company catalog as nineteen years old upon enlistment, and small in stature.[note 1]

Many Belvidere boys had been at the Battle of Shiloh as members of the Fifteenth Illinois Volunteers, where the Union had suffered heavy losses. Cashier took the train along with other boys from Belvidere to Rockford in order to enlist, in answer to the call for more soldiers.[13]:380 Along with others from Boone and McHenry counties, Cashier learned how to be a volunteer infantryman of the 95th Regiment at Camp Fuller. After being shipped out by steamer and rail to Confederate strongholds in Columbus, Kentucky, and Jackson, Tennessee, the 95th was ordered to Grand Junction where it became part of the Army of the Tennessee under General Ulysses S. Grant.[13]:380–381

## During the war

The regiment was part of the Army of the Tennessee under Ulysses S. Grant and fought in approximately forty battles,[12] including the siege at Vicksburg.[13]:381 During this campaign, Cashier was captured while performing reconnaissance,[7]:55 but managed to escape and return to the regiment. After the Battle of Vicksburg, in June 1863, Cashier contracted chronic diarrhea and entered a military hospital, somehow managing to evade detection.[7]:55–56 In the spring of 1864, the regiment was also present at the Red River Campaign under General Nathaniel Banks, and in June 1864 at the Battle of Brice's Crossroads in Guntown, Mississippi, where they suffered heavy casualties.[7]:56–57[13]:382–383

Following a period to recuperate and regroup following the debacle at Brice, the 95th, now a seasoned and battle-hardened regiment, saw additional action in the Winter of 1864 in the Franklin-Nashville Campaign, at the battles of Spring Hill and Franklin, the defense of Nashville, and the pursuit of General Hood.[13]:383

During the war, the regiment traveled a total of about 9,000 miles.[7]:52[note 2] Other soldiers thought that Cashier was small and preferred to be alone, which were not uncommon characteristics for soldiers. Cashier fought with the regiment through the war until honorably discharged on August 17, 1865, when all the soldiers were mustered out.[7]:57

Cashier was only one of at least 250 soldiers who were assigned female at birth and enlisted as men to fight in the Civil War.[14][15]

## Postwar

After the war, Cashier returned to Belvidere, Illinois, for a time, working for Samuel Pepper and continuing to live as a man.[7]:57[16] Settling in Saunemin, Illinois, in 1869, Cashier worked as a farmhand as well as performing odd jobs around the town.[7]:57 and can be found in the town payroll records.[7]:57 Cashier lived with employer Joshua Chesbro and his family in exchange for work, and had also slept for a time in the Cording Hardware store in exchange for labor. In 1885, the Chesbro family had a small house built for Cashier.[17] For over forty years, Cashier lived in Saunemin and was a church janitor, cemetery worker, and street lamplighter. Living as a man allowed Cashier to vote in elections and to later claim a veteran's pension under the same name.[7]:58 Pension payments started in 1907.[18]

In later years, Cashier ate with the neighboring Lannon family. The Lannons discovered their friend's sex when Cashier fell ill, but decided not make their discovery public.[7]:59

In 1911, Cashier, who was working for State Senator Ira Lish, was hit by the Senator's car, resulting in a broken leg.[7]:59 A physician found out the patient's secret in the hospital, but did not disclose the information. No longer able to work, Cashier was moved to the Soldiers and Sailors home in Quincy, Illinois, on May 5, 1911. Many friends and fellow soldiers from the Ninety-fifth Regiment visited.[7]:59 Cashier lived there until an obvious deterioration of mind began to take place and was moved to the Watertown State Hospital for the Insane in March 1914.[7]:60 Attendants at the Watertown State Hospital discovered Cashier's sex, at which point, the patient was made to wear women's clothes again after what we can assume would be more than fifty years.[7]:60 In 1914, Cashier was investigated for fraud by the veterans' pension board; former comrades confirmed that Cashier was in fact the person who had fought in the Civil War and the board decided in February 1915 that payments should continue for life.[19][20][21]

## Death and legacy

Albert Cashier died on October 10, 1915, and was buried in uniform. The tombstone was inscribed "Albert D. J. Cashier, Co. G, 95 Ill. Inf."[11] Cashier was given an official Grand Army of the Republic funerary service, and was buried with full military honors.[7]:60 It took W.J. Singleton (executor of Cashier's estate) nine years to track Cashier's identity back to the birth name of Jennie Hodgers. None of the would-be heirs proved convincing, and the estate of about $282 (after payment of funeral expenses)[20][21][22] was deposited in the Adams County, Illinois, treasury. The name on the original tombstone is Albert D. J. Cashier. In the 1970s, a second tombstone, inscribed with both names, was placed near the first one at Sunny Slope cemetery in Saunemin, Illinois.[11][23]

Cashier is listed on the internal wall of the Illinois memorial at Vicksburg National Military Park.[24]

A musical entitled *The Civility of Albert Cashier* has been produced based on Cashier's life; the work was described by the *Chicago Tribune* as "A timely musical about a trans soldier."[25]

*Also Known As Albert D. J. Cashier: The Jennie Hodgers Story* is a biography written by veteran Lon P. Dawson, who lived at the Illinois Veterans Home where Cashier once lived. The novel *My Last Skirt*, by Lynda Durrant, is based on Cashier's life. Cashier was mentioned in a collection of essays called *Nine Irish Lives*, in which Cashier's biography was written by Jill McDonough.[26] Cashier's house has been restored in Saunemin.[27]

Authors including Michael Bronski, James Cromwell, Kirstin Cronn-Mills, and Nicholas Teich have suggested or argued that Cashier was a trans man due to living as a man for at least 53 years.[3][4][5][6]

# Joshua Chamberlain

*Chamberlain in the 1860s*

**Joshua Lawrence Chamberlain** (born Lawrence Joshua Chamberlain, September 8, 1828–February 24, 1914)[3] was an American college professor from the State of Maine who volunteered during the American Civil War to join the Union Army. He became a highly respected and decorated Union officer, reaching the rank of brigadier general (and brevet major general). He is best known for his gallantry at the Battle of Gettysburg, for which he was awarded the Medal of Honor. Following the war, he served as Governor of Maine.

Chamberlain was commissioned a lieutenant colonel in the 20th Maine Volunteer Infantry Regiment in 1862 and fought at the Battle of Fredericksburg. He became commander of the regiment in June 1863. On July 2, during the Battle of Gettysburg, Chamberlain's regiment occupied the extreme left of the Union lines at Little Round Top. Chamberlain's men withstood repeated assaults from the 15th Regiment Alabama Infantry and finally drove the Confederates away with a downhill bayonet charge. Chamberlain was severely wounded while commanding a brigade during the Second Battle of Petersburg in June 1864, and was given what was intended to be a deathbed promotion to brigadier general. In April 1865, he fought at the Battle of Five Forks and was given the honor of commanding the Union troops at the surrender ceremony for the infantry of Robert E. Lee's Army at Appomattox Court House, Virginia.

After the war, he entered politics as a Republican and served four one-year terms of office as the 32nd Governor of Maine. He served on the faculty, and as president, of his *alma mater*, Bowdoin College. He died in 1914 at age 85 due to complications from the wound that he received at Petersburg.

## American Civil War

### Early career

At the beginning of the American Civil War, Chamberlain believed the Union needed to be supported against the Confederacy by all those willing. On several occasions, Chamberlain spoke freely of his beliefs during his class, urging students to follow their hearts in regards to the war while maintaining that the cause was just. Of his desire to serve in the War, he wrote to Maine's Governor Israel Washburn, Jr., "I fear, this war, so costly of blood and treasure, will not cease until men of the North are willing to leave good positions, and sacrifice the dearest personal interests, to rescue our country from desolation, and defend the national existence against treachery."[6] Many faculty at Bowdoin did not feel his enthusiasm for various reasons and Chamberlain was subsequently granted a leave of absence (supposedly to study languages for two years in Europe). He then promptly enlisted unbeknownst to those at Bowdoin and his family. Offered the colonelcy of the 20th Maine Regiment, he declined, according to his biographer, John J. Pullen, preferring to "start a little lower and learn the business first." He was appointed lieutenant colonel of the regiment on August 8, 1862, under the command of Col. Adelbert Ames. The 20th was assigned to the 3rd Brigade, 1st Division, V Corps in the Union Army of the Potomac. One of Chamberlain's younger brothers, Thomas Chamberlain, was also an officer of the 20th Maine, and another, John Chamberlain, visited the regiment at Gettysburg as a member of the U.S. Christian Commission until appointed as a chaplain in another Maine Volunteer regiment. The 20th Maine fought at the Battle of Fredericksburg, suffering relatively small numbers of casualties in the assaults on Marye's Heights, but were forced to spend a miserable night on the freezing battlefield among the many wounded from other regiments. Chamberlain chronicled this night well in his diary and went to great length discussing his having to use bodies of the fallen for shelter and a pillow while listening to the bullets zip into the corpses. The 20th missed the Battle of Chancellorsville in May 1863 due to an outbreak of smallpox in their ranks (which was caused by an errant smallpox vaccine), keeping them on guard duty in the rear.[7] Chamberlain was promoted to colonel of the regiment in June 1863 upon the promotion of Ames.

## Battle of Gettysburg

*Capt. Ellis Spear, Chamberlain's "right-hand man" on Little Round Top*

Chamberlain became most famous for his achievements during the Battle of Gettysburg. On July 2, the second day of the battle, Union forces were recovering from initial setbacks and hastily regrouping into defensive positions on a line of hills south of the town. Sensing the momentary vulnerability of the Union forces, the Confederates began an attack against the Union left flank. Chamberlain's brigade, commanded by Col. Strong Vincent, was sent to defend Little Round Top by the army's Chief of Engineers, Brig. Gen. Gouverneur K. Warren. Chamberlain found himself and the 20th Maine at the far left end of the entire Union line. He quickly understood the strategic significance of the small hill, and the need for the 20th Maine to hold the Union left at all costs. The men from Maine waited until troops from the 15th Regiment Alabama Infantry, commanded by Col. William C. Oates, charged up the hill, attempting to flank the Union position. Time and time again the Confederates struck, until the 20th Maine was almost doubled back upon itself. With many casualties and ammunition running low, Col. Chamberlain

*Little Round Top, western slope, photographed by Timothy H. O'Sullivan, 1863*

recognized the dire circumstances and ordered his left wing (which was now looking southeast, compared to the rest of the regiment, which was facing west) to initiate a bayonet charge. From his report of the day: "At that crisis, I ordered the bayonet. The word was enough." While battlefield conditions make it unlikely that many men heard Chamberlain's order, most historians believe he initiated the charge.

The 20th Maine charged down the hill, with the left wing wheeling continually to make the charging line swing like a hinge, thus creating a simultaneous frontal assault and flanking maneuver, capturing 101 of the Confederate soldiers and successfully saving the flank. This version of the battle was popularized by the book *The Killer Angels* and the movie *Gettysburg*, but there is debate on the historical validity of this account.[8] Chamberlain sustained two slight wounds in the battle, one when a shot hit his sword scabbard and bruised his thigh, and another when his right foot was hit by a spent bullet or piece of shrapnel. Chamberlain also personally took a Confederate prisoner with his saber during the charge. After initiating the maneuver, he came upon a Confederate officer wielding a revolver who quickly fired, narrowly missing his face. Chamberlain remained steadfast, and with his sword at the officer's throat accepted the man's arms and surrender.[9] The pistol Chamberlain captured at Gettysburg can still be seen on display in the Civil War exhibit of the Maine State Museum. For his tenacity at defending Little Round Top, he was known by the sobriquet *Lion of the Round Top*. Prior to the battle, Chamberlain was quite ill, developing malaria and dysentery. Later, due to this illness, he was taken off active duty until he recovered.

For his "daring heroism and great tenacity in holding his position on the Little Round Top against repeated assaults, and carrying the advance position on the Great Round Top," Chamberlain was awarded the Medal of Honor.

## Medal of Honor citation

The President of the United States of America, in the name of Congress, takes pleasure in presenting the Medal of Honor to Colonel Joshua Lawrence Chamberlain, United States Army, for extraordinary heroism on 2 July 1863, while serving with 20th Maine Infantry, in action at Gettysburg, Pennsylvania, for daring heroism and great tenacity in holding his position on the Little Round Top against repeated assaults, and carrying the advance position on the Great Round Top.[10]

## Siege of Petersburg

In April 1864, Chamberlain returned to the Army of the Potomac and was promoted to brigade commander shortly before the Siege of Petersburg and given command of the 1st Brigade, First Division, V Corps. In a major action on June 18, during the Second Battle of Petersburg, Chamberlain was shot through the right hip and groin, the bullet exiting his left hip. Despite the injury, Chamberlain withdrew his sword and stuck it into the ground in order to keep himself upright to dissuade the growing resolve for retreat. He stood upright for several minutes until he collapsed and lay unconscious from loss of blood. The wound was considered mortal by the division's surgeon, who predicted he would perish; Chamberlain's incorrectly recorded death in battle was reported in the Maine newspapers, and Lt. Gen. Ulysses S. Grant gave Chamberlain a battlefield promotion to the rank of brigadier general after receiving an urgent recommendation on June 19 from corps commander Maj. Gen. Gouverneur K. Warren: "He has been recommended for promotion for gallant and efficient conduct on previous occasion and yesterday led his brigade against the enemy under most destructive fire. He expresses the wish that he may receive the recognition of his services by promotion before he dies for the gratification of his family and friends." Not expected to live, Chamberlain displayed surprising will and courage, and with the support of his brother Tom, was back in command by November. Although many, including his wife Fanny, urged Chamberlain to resign, he was determined to serve through the end of the war.

In early 1865, Chamberlain regained command of the 1st Brigade of the 1st Division of V Corps, and he continued to act with courage and resolve. On March 29, 1865, his brigade participated in a major skirmish on the Quaker Road during Grant's final advance that would finish the war. Despite losses, another wound (in the left arm and chest that almost caused amputation), and nearly being captured, Chamberlain was successful and brevetted to the rank of major general by President Abraham Lincoln. Chamberlain gained the name "Bloody Chamberlain" at Quaker Road. Chamberlain kept a Bible and framed picture of his wife in his left front "chest" pocket. A Confederate shot at Chamberlain. The bullet went through his horse's neck, hit the picture frame, entered under Chamberlain's skin in the front of his chest, traveled around his body under the skin along the rib, and exited his back. To all observers Union and Confederate, it appeared that he was shot through his chest. He continued to encourage his men to attack. All sides cheered his valiant courage, and the Union assault was successful.

## Appomattox

On the morning of April 9, 1865, Chamberlain learned of the desire by General Robert E. Lee to surrender the Army of Northern Virginia when a Confederate staff officer approached him under a flag of truce. "Sir," he reported to Chamberlain, "I am from General Gordon. General Lee desires a cessation of hostilities until he can hear from General Grant as to the proposed surrender."[11] The next day, Chamberlain was summoned to Union headquarters where Maj. Gen. Charles Griffin informed him that he

*Confederate General John B. Gordon was assigned the task to surrender all arms to Gen. Chamberlain.*

had been selected to preside over the parade of the Confederate infantry as part of their formal surrender at Appomattox Court House on April 12.[12]

Thus Chamberlain was responsible for one of the most poignant scenes of the American Civil War. As the Confederate soldiers marched down the road to surrender their arms and colors, Chamberlain, on his own initiative, ordered his men to come to attention and "carry arms" as a show of respect. In memoirs written forty years after the event, Chamberlain described what happened next:

Gordon, at the head of the marching column, outdoes us in courtesy. He was riding with downcast eyes and more than pensive look; but at this clatter of arms he raises his eyes and instantly catching the significance, wheels his horse with that superb grace of which he is master, drops the point of his sword to his stirrup, gives a command, at which the great Confederate ensign following him is dipped and his decimated brigades, as they reach our right, respond to the 'carry.' All the while on our part not a sound of trumpet or drum, not a cheer, nor a word nor motion of man, but awful stillness as if it were the passing of the dead.[13]

Chamberlain stated that his salute to the Confederate soldiers was unpopular with many Unionists, but he defended his action in his memoirs, *The Passing of the Armies*. Many years later, Gordon, in his own memoirs, called Chamberlain "one of the knightliest soldiers of the Federal Army." Gordon never mentioned the anecdote until after he read Chamberlain's account, more than 40 years later.[14]

*Chamberlain as the Governor of Maine*

In all, Chamberlain served in 20 battles and numerous skirmishes, was cited for bravery four times, had six horses shot from under him, and was wounded six times.[15][16]

## Post-war service

Chamberlain left the U.S. Army soon after the war ended, going back to his home state of Maine. Due to his immense popularity, he served as Governor of Maine for four one-year terms after he won election as a Republican. His victory in 1866 set the record for the most votes and the highest percentage for any Maine governor by that time. He would break his own record in 1868. During his time in office, he was attacked by those angered by his support for capital punishment and by his refusal to create a special police force to enforce the prohibition of alcohol.

## Later life

After resigning from Bowdoin in 1883, he went to New York City to practice law.[17] [18] Chamberlain served as Surveyor of the Port of Portland, Maine, a federal appointment, and engaged in business activities, including real estate dealings in Florida (1885) and a college of art in New York, as well as hotels. He traveled to the West Coast to work

*Chamberlain later in life in Portland, wearing uniform and his medals*

on railroad building and public improvements.[17] From the time of his serious wound in 1864 until his death, he was forced to wear an early form of a catheter with a bag and underwent six operations to try to correct the original wound and stop the fevers and infections that plagued him, without success.

In 1893, 30 years after the battle that made the 20th Maine famous, Chamberlain was awarded the Medal of Honor for his actions at Gettysburg. The citation commends him for his "Daring heroism and great tenacity in holding his position on the Little Round Top against repeated assaults, and carrying the advance position on the Great Round Top." As in many other Civil War actions, controversy arose when one of his subordinate officers stated that Chamberlain never actually ordered a charge at Gettysburg. The claim never seriously affected Chamberlain's fame or notability however. This original medal was lost, and later rediscovered in 2013, and donated to the Pejepscot Historical Society in Brunswick, Maine. A second, redesigned medal issued in 1904 is currently housed at Bowdoin College.[19]

In 1898, at the age of 70, still in pain from his wounds, he volunteered for duty as an officer in the Spanish–American War. Rejected for duty, he called it one of the major disappointments of his life.

In 1905, Chamberlain became a founding member of the Maine Institution for the Blind, in Portland, now called The Iris Network. Chamberlain's wife herself was visually impaired, which led him to serve on the organization's first board of directors.[20]

Beginning with his first election as governor of Maine and continuing to the end of his life, Chamberlain was active in the Grand Army of the Republic. Despite continual pain and discomfort from his wounds of 1864, he made many return visits to Gettysburg and delivered speeches at soldiers' reunions. He made his last known visit on May 16 and 17, 1913, while involved in planning the 50th anniversary reunion. Because of deteriorating health, he was unable to attend the reunion less than two months later.[21]

## Death

Chamberlain died of his lingering wartime wounds in 1914 in Portland, Maine, at the age of eighty-five. He is interred at Pine Grove Cemetery in Brunswick, Maine.[3] Beside him as he died was Dr. Abner O. Shaw of Portland, one of the two surgeons who had operated on him in Petersburg 50 years previously. A full study of his medical history strongly suggests that it was complications from the wound suffered at Petersburg that resulted in his death.[22] He was the last Civil War veteran to die as a result of wounds from the war and considered by some the last casualty of the war.[23]

# Alonzo Cushing

**Alonzo Hereford Cushing** (January 19, 1841–July 3, 1863) was an artillery officer in the Union Army during the American Civil War. He was killed in action during the Battle of Gettysburg while defending the Union position on Cemetery Ridge against Pickett's Charge. In 2013, 150 years after Cushing's death, he was nominated for the Medal of Honor. The nomination was approved by the United States Congress, and was sent for review by the Defense Department and the President.[1][2][3]

On August 26, 2014, the White House announced he would be posthumously awarded the Medal of Honor, with President Obama presiding over the official ceremony on November 6, 2014. Helen Bird Loring Ensign, a second cousin twice removed, accepted the medal on Cushing's behalf, as Cushing left no direct descendants.[4][5]

## Civil War service

Cushing graduated from the United States Military Academy in the class of June 1861, and received commissions as second and first lieutenant on the same day. He was brevetted major following the Battle of Chancellorsville.[7] Cushing commanded Battery A, 4th U.S. Artillery at Gettysburg, and was hailed by contemporaries as heroic in his actions on the third day of the battle. He was wounded three times. First, a shell fragment went straight through his shoulder. He was then grievously wounded by a second shell fragment, which tore into his abdomen and groin. This wound exposed his intestines, which he held in place with his hand as he continued to command his battery. After these injuries, a higher-ranking officer said, "Cushing, go to the rear." Cushing, due to the limited number of men left, refused to fall back. The severity of his wounds left him unable to yell his orders above the sounds of battle. Thus, he was held aloft by his 1st Sergeant Frederick Füger, who faithfully passed on Cushing's commands. Cushing was killed when a bullet entered his mouth and exited through the back of his skull. He died on the field at the height of the assault. He was 22 years old.[8][9]

His body was returned to his family and then interred in the West Point Cemetery in Section 26, Row A, Grave 7. His headstone bears, at the behest of his mother, Mary, the inscription "Faithful unto Death."[10] His grave is next to that of Major General John Buford, another hero of Gettysburg, who had chosen the battlefield that Cushing had died defending.

Cushing was posthumously cited for gallantry with a brevet promotion to lieutenant colonel.[11]

## Medal of Honor

Cushing was nominated for a belated award of the Medal of Honor, beginning with a letter campaign in the late 1980s by a constituent of Senator William Proxmire of Wisconsin. Margaret Zerwekh began her campaign to honor Cushing in 1987 with a letter to Senator Proxmire. She lived on property once owned by Cushing's father in Delafield, Wisconsin, and spent years researching his background. For years, she received form letters in return to her letters advocating for Cushing until the early 2000s.[12] The measure was also advocated by Congressman Ron Kind of Wisconsin's 3rd congressional district.[2] In 2002, Senator Russ Feingold (D-WI) nominated Cushing for the Medal of Honor and, following a lengthy investigation, the U.S. Army approved the nomination in February 2010. In order for the medal to be awarded, it had to be approved by the United States Congress.[13] It was announced on May 20, 2010, that Cushing would receive the Medal of Honor, 147 years after his death.[14]

However, the provision granting Cushing the Medal of Honor was removed from a defense spending bill by Senator Jim Webb (D-VA) in December 2012.[15] In December 2013, the Senate passed a defense bill that included a provision granting Cushing the Medal of Honor. The nomination was sent to the Defense Department for review, before being approved by President Barack Obama.[2] On August 26, 2014, the White House announced Cushing would be posthumously awarded the Medal of Honor. On November 6, 2014, 151 years after Alonzo Cushing's death, President Obama presented the award at a ceremony at the White House, attended by two dozen relatives of the Cushing family.[16] Cushing was awarded the Medal of Honor by Department of the Army General Order (DAGO) 2014–76 dated December 19, 2014.[17]

## Medal of Honor Citation

The President of the United States of America, authorized by Act of Congress, March 3rd, 1863, has awarded in the name of Congress the Medal of Honor to First Lieutenant Alonzo H. Cushing, United States Army.

First Lieutenant Alonzo H. Cushing distinguished himself by acts of bravery above and beyond the call of duty while serving as an artillery commander in Battery A, 4th U.S. Artillery, Army of the Potomac at Gettysburg, Pennsylvania on July 3rd, 1863, during the American Civil War.

That morning, Confederate forces led by General Robert E. Lee began cannonading First Lieutenant Cushing's position on Cemetery Ridge. Using field glasses, First Lieutenant Cushing directed fire for his own artillery battery. He refused to leave the battlefield after being struck in the shoulder by a shell fragment. As he continued to direct fire, he was struck again – this time suffering grievous damage to his abdomen.

Still refusing to abandon his command, he boldly stood tall in the face of Major General George E. Pickett's charge and continued to direct devastating fire into oncoming forces. As the Confederate forces closed in, First Lieutenant Cushing was struck in the mouth by an enemy bullet and fell dead beside his gun.

His gallant stand and fearless leadership inflicted severe casualties upon Confederate forces and opened wide gaps in their lines, directly impacting the Union force's ability to repel Pickett's charge. First Lieutenant Cushing's extraordinary heroism and selflessness above and beyond the call of duty at the cost of his own life are in keeping with the highest traditions of military service and reflect great credit upon himself, Battery A, 4th U.S. Artillery, Army of the Potomac, and the United States Army.[18]

# Pauline Cushman

**Pauline Cushman** (born Harriet Wood; June 10, 1833–December 2, 1893) was an American actress and a spy for the Union Army during the American Civil War. She is considered one of the most successful Civil War spies.[1]

## Career as a spy

After a Northern performance, Cushman was paid by two local pro-Confederate men to toast Confederate President Jefferson Davis after a performance. The theatre forced her to quit, but she had other ideas.[4] She had decided to ingratiate herself with the rebels by making the toast, while offering her services to the Union as a spy.

By fraternizing with rebel military commanders, she managed to conceal battle plans and drawings in her shoes, but was caught twice in 1864[5] and brought before Confederate General Braxton Bragg, tried by a military court, and sentenced to death by hanging.[6] Though she was already ill, she acted worse off than she was. The Confederates had to postpone her execution. Cushman was spared hanging by the invasion of the area by Union troops.[7] She was also wounded twice.[8]

*Cushman in uniform in 1865*

Some reports state that she returned to the South in her role as a spy, dressed in male uniform. She was awarded the rank of brevet major by General James A. Garfield, and made an honorary major by President Abraham Lincoln for her service to the Federal cause, and became known as "Miss Major Pauline Cushman."[9] By the end of the war in 1865, she was touring the country giving lectures on her exploits as a spy.

## Later life

Because her undercover activities on behalf of the government were secret, there is a lack of corroborative information about her life at this time. After the war, however, she began a tour celebrating her experiences as a Union spy, working at one point with P. T. Barnum. In 1865, a friend, Ferdinand Sarmiento, wrote an exaggerated biography titled *The Life of Pauline Cushman: The celebrated Union Spy and Scout,* detailing her early history, her entry into the secret service notes, and memoranda.

She lost her child to sickness by 1868, and married again in 1872 in San Francisco, but was widowed within a year. Sources state that in 1879 she met Jere Fryer, and moved to Casa Grande, Arizona Territory, where they married and operated a hotel and livery stable. Jere Fryer became the sheriff of Pinal County. Their adopted daughter, Emma, died on April 17, 1888, at 6 years old of a seizure. As a result, the Fryers separated in 1890.

By 1892, she was living in poverty in El Paso, Texas. She had applied for back pension based on her first husband's military service which she received in the amount of $12 per month beginning in June 1893. Her last few years were spent in a boarding house in San Francisco, working as a seamstress and charwoman. Disabled from the effects of rheumatism and arthritis, she developed an addiction to pain medication, and on the night of December 2, 1893, she took a suicidal overdose of morphine. She was found the next morning by her landlady.

## Death and legacy

She died as Pauline Fryer at the age of sixty. The time of her Civil War fame was recalled at her funeral, which was arranged by members of the Grand Army of the Republic; Cushman was buried with full military honors.[10] "Major" Cushman's remains now rest in Officer's Circle at the Presidio's National Cemetery. Her simple gravestone recognizes her contribution to the Union's victory. It is marked, "Pauline C. Fryer, Union Spy."

# Jefferson Davis

**Jefferson Finis Davis**[a] (June 3, 1808–December 6, 1889) was an American politician who served as the president of the Confederate States from 1861 to 1865. As a member of the Democratic Party, he represented Mississippi in the United States Senate and the House of Representatives before the American Civil War. He previously served as the United States Secretary of War from 1853 to 1857 under President Franklin Pierce.

Davis was born in Fairview, Kentucky, to a moderately prosperous farmer, the youngest of ten children. He grew up in Wilkinson County, Mississippi, and also lived in Louisiana. His eldest brother Joseph Emory Davis secured the younger Davis's appointment to the United States Military Academy. After graduating, Jefferson Davis served six years as a lieutenant in the United States Army. He fought in the Mexican–American War (1846–1848), as the colonel of a volunteer regiment. Before the American Civil War, he operated a large cotton plantation in Mississippi, which his brother Joseph gave him, and owned as many as 113 slaves.[1] Although Davis argued against secession in 1858,[2] he believed that states had an unquestionable right to leave the Union.

Davis married Sarah Knox Taylor, daughter of general and future President Zachary Taylor, in 1835, when he was 27 years old. They were both stricken with malaria soon thereafter, and Sarah died after three months of marriage. Davis recovered slowly and suffered from recurring bouts of the disease throughout his life.[3] At the age of 36, Davis married again, to 18-year-old Varina Howell, a native of Natchez, Mississippi, who had been educated in Philadelphia and had some family ties in the North. They had six children. Only two survived him, and only one married and had children.

Many historians attribute some of the Confederacy's weaknesses to the poor leadership of Davis.[4] His preoccupation with detail, reluctance to delegate responsibility, lack of popular appeal, feuds with powerful state governors and generals, favoritism toward old friends, inability to get along with people who disagreed with him, neglect of civil matters in favor of military ones, and resistance to public opinion all worked against him. [5][6] Historians agree he was a much less effective war leader than his Union counterpart, President Abraham Lincoln. After Davis was captured in 1865, he was accused of treason and imprisoned at Fort Monroe in Hampton, Virginia. He was never tried and was released after two years. While not disgraced, Davis had been displaced in ex-Confederate affection after the war by his leading general, Robert E. Lee. Davis wrote a memoir entitled *The Rise and Fall of the Confederate Government*, which he completed in 1881. By the late 1880s, he began to encourage reconciliation, telling Southerners to be loyal to the Union. Ex-Confederates came to appreciate his role in the war, seeing him as a Southern patriot. He became a hero of the Lost Cause of the Confederacy in the post-Reconstruction South.[7]

## President of the Confederate States

Anticipating a call for his services since Mississippi had seceded, Davis had sent a telegraph message to Governor John J. Pettus saying, "Judge what Mississippi requires of me and place me accordingly."[81] On January 23, 1861, Pettus made Davis a major general of the Army of Mississippi.[14] On February 9, a constitutional convention met at Montgomery, Alabama, and considered Davis and Robert Toombs of Georgia as a possible president. Davis, who had widespread support from six of the seven states, easily won. He was seen as the "champion of a slave society and embodied the values of the planter class," and was elected provisional Confederate President by acclamation.[82][83] He was inaugurated on February 18, 1861.[84][85] Alexander H. Stephens was chosen as Vice President, but he and Davis feuded constantly.[86]

Davis was the first choice because of his strong political and military credentials. He wanted to serve as commander-in-chief of the Confederate armies but said he would serve wherever directed.[87] His wife Varina Davis later wrote that when he received word that he had been chosen as president, "Reading that telegram he looked so grieved that I feared some evil had befallen our family."[88]

Several forts in Confederate territory remained in Union hands. Davis sent a commission to Washington with an offer to pay for any federal property on Southern soil, as well as the Southern portion of the national debt, but Lincoln refused to meet with the commissioners. Brief informal discussions did take place with Secretary of State William Seward through Supreme Court Justice John A. Campbell, the latter of whom later resigned from the federal government, as he was from Alabama. Seward hinted that Fort Sumter would be evacuated, but gave no assurance.[89]

On March 1, 1861, Davis appointed General P. G. T. Beauregard to command all Confederate troops in the vicinity of Charleston, South Carolina, where state officials prepared to take possession of Fort Sumter. Beauregard was to prepare his forces but await orders to attack the fort. Within the fort the issue was not of the niceties of geopolitical posturing but of survival. They would be out of food on the 15th. The small Union garrison had but half a dozen officers and 127 soldiers under Major Robert Anderson. Famously, this included the baseball folk hero Captain (later major general) Abner Doubleday. More improbable yet was a Union officer who had the name of Jefferson C. Davis. He would spend the war being taunted for his name but not his loyalty to the Northern cause. The newly installed President Lincoln, not wishing to initiate hostilities, informed South Carolina Governor Pickens that he was dispatching a small fleet of ships from the navy yard in New York to resupply but not re-enforce Fort Pickens in Florida and Fort Sumter. The U.S. President did not inform CSA President Davis of this intended resupply of food and fuel. For Lincoln, Davis, as the leader of an insurrection, was without legal standing in U.S. affairs. To deal with him would be to give legitimacy to the rebellion. The fact that Sumter was the property of the sovereign United States was the reason for maintaining the garrison on the island fort. He informed Pickens that the resupply mission would not land troops or munitions unless they were fired upon. As it turned out, just as the supply ships approached Charleston harbor, the bombardment would begin and the flotilla watched the spectacle from 10 miles (16 km) at sea.

Davis faced the most important decision of his career: to prevent reinforcement at Fort Sumter or to let it take place. He and his cabinet decided to demand that the Federal garrison surrender and, if this was refused, to use military force to prevent reinforcement before the fleet arrived. Anderson did not surrender. With Davis's endorsement, Beauregard began the bombarding of the fort in the early dawn of April 12. The Confederates continued their artillery attack on Fort Sumter until it surrendered on April 14. No one was killed in the artillery duel, but the attack on the U.S. fort meant the fighting had started. President Lincoln called up 75,000 state militiamen to march south to recapture Federal property. In the North and South, massive rallies were held to demand immediate war. The Civil War had begun.[90][91][92][93]

## Overseeing the war effort

When Virginia joined the Confederacy, Davis moved his government to Richmond in May 1861. He and his family took up his residence there at the White House of the Confederacy later that month.[94] Having served since February as the provisional president, Davis was elected to a full six-year term on November 6, 1861, and was inaugurated on February 22, 1862.[95]

At the start of the war, nearly 21 million people lived in the North compared to 9 million in the South. While the North's population was almost entirely white, the South had an enormous number of black slaves and people of color. While the latter were free, becoming a soldier was seen as the prerogative of white men only. Many Southerners were terrified at the idea of a black man with a gun. Excluding old men and boys, the white males available for Confederate service were less than two million. There was also the additional burden that the near four million black slaves had to be heavily policed as there was no trust between the owner and "owned." The North had vastly greater industrial capacity; built nearly all the locomotives, steamships, and industrial machinery; and had a much larger and more integrated railroad system. Nearly all the munitions facilities were in the North, while critical ingredients for gunpowder were in very short supply in the South.

Much of the railroad track that existed in the Confederacy was of simple railway design just meant to carry the large bales of cotton to local river ports in the harvest season. These often did not connect to other rail-lines, making internal shipments of goods difficult at best. While the Union had a large navy, the new Confederate Navy had only a few captured warships or newly built vessels. These did surprisingly well but ultimately were sunk or abandoned as the Union Navy controlled more rivers and ports. Rebel "raiders" loosed on the Northern ships on the Atlantic did tremendous damage and sent Yankee ships into safe harbors as insurance rates soared. The Union blockade of the South, however, made imports via blockade runners difficult and expensive. Somewhat awkwardly, these runners didn't bring significant amounts of war materials that were so desperately needed, but rather the European luxuries sought as a relief from the war's horrifying conditions.[96][97]

In June 1862, Davis was forced to assign General Robert E. Lee to replace the wounded Joseph E. Johnston to command of the Army of Northern Virginia, the main Confederate army in the Eastern Theater. That December Davis made a tour of Confederate armies in the west of the country. He had a very small circle of military advisers. He largely made the main strategic decisions on his own, though he had special respect for Lee's views. Given the Confederacy's limited resources compared with the Union, Davis decided that the Confederacy would have to fight mostly on the strategic defensive. He maintained this outlook throughout the war, paying special attention to the defense of his national capital at Richmond. He approved Lee's strategic offensives when he felt that military success would both shake Northern self-confidence and strengthen the peace movements there. However, the several campaigns invading the North were met with defeat. A bloody battle at Antietam in Maryland as well as the ride into Kentucky, the Confederate Heartland Offensive (both in 1862)[98] drained irreplaceable men and talented officers. A final offense led to the three-day bloodletting at Gettysburg in Pennsylvania (1863),[99] crippling the South still further. The status of techniques and munitions made the defensive side much more likely to endure: an expensive lesson vindicating Davis's initial belief.

## Administration and cabinet

As provisional president in 1861, Davis formed his first cabinet. Robert Toombs of Georgia was the first Secretary of State and Christopher Memminger of South Carolina became Secretary of the Treasury. LeRoy Pope Walker of Alabama was made Secretary of War, after being recommended for this post by Clement Clay and William Yancey (both of whom declined to accept cabinet positions themselves). John Reagan of Texas became Postmaster General. Judah P. Benjamin of Louisiana became Attorney General. Although Stephen Mallory was not put forward by the delegation from his state of Florida, Davis insisted that he was the best man for the job of Secretary of the Navy, and he was eventually confirmed.[100]

Since the Confederacy was founded, among other things, on states' rights, one important factor in Davis's choice of cabinet members was representation from the various states. He depended partly upon recommendations from congressmen and other prominent people. This helped maintain good relations between the executive and legislative branches. This also led to complaints as more states joined the Confederacy, however, because there were more states than cabinet positions.[101]

As the war progressed, this dissatisfaction increased and there were frequent changes to the cabinet. Toombs, who had wished to be president himself, was frustrated as an advisor and resigned within a few months of his appointment to join the army. Robert Hunter of Virginia replaced him as Secretary of State on July 25, 1861.[102] On September 17, Walker resigned as Secretary of War due to a conflict with Davis, who had questioned his management of the War Department and had suggested he consider a different position. Walker requested, and was given, command of the troops in Alabama. Benjamin left the Attorney General position to replace him, and Thomas Bragg of North Carolina (brother of General Braxton Bragg) took Benjamin's place as Attorney General.[103]

Following the November 1861 election, Davis announced the permanent cabinet in March 1862. Benjamin moved again, to Secretary of State. George W. Randolph of Virginia had been made the Secretary of War. Mallory continued as Secretary of the Navy and Reagan as Postmaster General. Both kept their positions throughout the war. Memminger remained Secretary of the Treasury, while Thomas Hill Watts of Alabama was made Attorney General.[104]

In 1862 Randolph resigned from the War Department, and James Seddon of Virginia was appointed to replace him. In late 1863, Watts resigned as Attorney General to take office as the Governor of Alabama, and George Davis of North Carolina took his place. In 1864, Memminger withdrew from the Treasury post due to congressional opposition, and was replaced by George Trenholm of South Carolina. In 1865 congressional opposition likewise caused Seddon to withdraw, and he was replaced by John C. Breckinridge of Kentucky.[105]

Cotton was the South's primary export and the basis of its economy and the system of production the South used was dependent upon slave labor. At the outset of the Civil War, Davis realized that intervention from European powers would be vital if the Confederacy was to stand against the Union. The administration sent repeated delegations to European nations, but several factors prevented Southern success in terms of foreign diplomacy. The Union blockade of the Confederacy led European powers to remain neutral, contrary to the Southern belief that a blockade would cut off the supply of cotton to Britain and other European nations and prompt them to intervene on behalf of the South. Many European countries objected to slavery. Britain had abolished it in the 1830s, and Lincoln's Emancipation Proclamation of 1863 made support for the South even less appealing in Europe. Finally, as the war progressed and the South's military prospects dwindled, foreign powers were not convinced that the Confederacy had the strength to become independent. In the end, not a single foreign nation recognized the Confederate States of America.[106]

## Strategic failures

Most historians sharply criticize Davis for his flawed military strategy, his selection of friends for military commands, and his neglect of homefront crises.[107][108] Until late in the war, he resisted efforts to appoint a general-in-chief, essentially handling those duties himself. "Davis was loathed by much of his military, Congress and the public — even before the Confederacy died on his watch," and General Beauregard wrote in a letter: "If he were to die today, the whole country would rejoice at it."[109]

*Davis in 1859*

On January 31, 1865, Lee assumed this role, but it was far too late. Davis insisted on a strategy of trying to defend all Southern territory with ostensibly equal effort. This diluted the limited resources of the South and made it vulnerable to coordinated strategic thrusts by the Union into the vital Western Theater (e.g., the capture of New Orleans in early 1862). He made other controversial strategic choices, such as allowing Lee to invade the North in 1862 and 1863 while the Western armies were under very heavy pressure. When Lee lost at Gettysburg, Vicksburg simultaneously fell, and the Union took control of the Mississippi River, splitting the Confederacy. At Vicksburg, the failure to coordinate multiple forces on both sides of the Mississippi River rested primarily on Davis's inability to create a harmonious departmental arrangement or to force such generals as Edmund Kirby Smith, Earl Van Dorn, and Theophilus H. Holmes to work together.[110] In fact, during the late stages of the Franklin–Nashville Campaign, Davis warned Beauregard that Kirby Smith would prove uncooperative to whatever proposal the Creole general had in mind for him.[111]

Davis has been faulted for poor coordination and management of his generals. This includes his reluctance to resolve a dispute between Leonidas Polk, a personal friend, and Braxton Bragg, who was defeated in important battles and distrusted by his subordinates.[112] He was similarly reluctant to relieve the capable but overcautious Joseph E. Johnston until, after numerous frustrations which he detailed in a March 1, 1865, letter to Col. James Phelan of Mississippi, he replaced him with John Bell Hood,[113][114] a fellow Kentuckian who had shared the Confederate President's views on aggressive military policies.[115]

Davis gave speeches to soldiers and politicians but largely ignored the common people, who came to resent the favoritism shown to the rich and powerful; Davis thus failed to harness Confederate nationalism.[116] One historian speaks of "the heavy-handed intervention of the Confederate government." Economic intervention, regulation, and state control of manpower, production and transport were much greater in the Confederacy than in the Union.[117] Davis did not use his presidential pulpit to rally the people with stirring rhetoric; he called instead for people to be fatalistic and to die for their new country.[118] Apart from two month-long trips across the country where he met a few hundred people, Davis stayed in Richmond where few people saw him; newspapers had limited circulation, and most Confederates had little favorable information about him.[119]

To finance the war, the Confederate government initially issued bonds, but investment from the public never met the demands. Taxes were lower than in the Union and collected with less efficiency; European investment was also insufficient. As the war proceeded, both the Confederate government and the individual states printed more and more paper money. Inflation increased from 60 percent in 1861 to 300 percent in 1863 and 600 percent in 1864. Davis did not seem to grasp the enormity of the problem.[120][121]

In April 1863, food shortages led to rioting in Richmond, as poor people robbed and looted numerous stores for food until Davis cracked down and restored order.[122] Davis feuded bitterly with his vice president. Perhaps even more seriously, he clashed with powerful state governors who used states' rights arguments to withhold their militia units from national service and otherwise blocked mobilization plans.[123]

Davis is widely evaluated as a less effective war leader than Lincoln, even though Davis had extensive military experience and Lincoln had little. Davis would have preferred to be an army general and tended to manage military matters himself. Lincoln and Davis led in very different ways. According to one historian,

> Lincoln was flexible; Davis was rigid. Lincoln wanted to win; Davis wanted to be right. Lincoln had a broad strategic vision of Union goals; Davis could never enlarge his narrow view. Lincoln searched for the right general, then let him fight the war; Davis continuously played favorites and interfered unduly with his generals, even with Robert E. Lee. Lincoln led his nation; Davis failed to rally the South.
>
> —*William J. Cooper, Jr.*

There were many factors that led to Union victory over the Confederacy, and Davis recognized from the start that the South was at a distinct disadvantage; but in the end, Lincoln helped to achieve victory, whereas Davis contributed to defeat.[124]

## Final days of the Confederacy

In March 1865, General Order 14 provided for enlisting slaves into the army, with a promise of freedom for service. The idea had been suggested years earlier, but Davis did not act upon it until late in the war, and very few slaves were enlisted.[125]

On April 3, with Union troops under Ulysses S. Grant poised to capture Richmond, Davis escaped to Danville, Virginia, together with the Confederate Cabinet, leaving on the Richmond and Danville Railroad. Lincoln was in Davis's Richmond office just 40 hours later. William T. Sutherlin turned over his mansion, which served as Davis's temporary residence from April 3 to April 10, 1865.[126] On about April 12, Davis received Robert E. Lee's letter announcing surrender.[127] He issued his last official proclamation as president of the Confederacy, and then went south to Greensboro, North Carolina.[128]

After Lee's surrender, a public meeting was held in Shreveport, Louisiana, at which many speakers supported continuation of the war. Plans were developed for the Davis government to flee to Havana, Cuba. There, the leaders would regroup and head to the Confederate-controlled Trans-Mississippi area by way of the Rio Grande.[129] None of these plans were put into practice.

On April 14, Lincoln was shot, dying the next day. Davis expressed regret at his death. He later said that he believed Lincoln would have been less harsh with the South than his successor, Andrew Johnson.[130] In the aftermath, Johnson issued a $100,000 reward for the capture of Davis and accused him of helping to plan the assassination. As the Confederate military structure fell into disarray, the search for Davis by Union forces intensified.[131]

President Davis met with his Confederate Cabinet for the last time on May 5, 1865, in Washington, Georgia, and officially dissolved the Confederate government.[132] The meeting took place at the Heard house, the Georgia Branch Bank Building, with 14 officials present. Along with their hand-picked escort led by Given Campbell, Davis and his wife Varina Davis were captured by Union forces on May 10 at Irwinville in Irwin County, Georgia.[133] Mrs. Davis recounted the circumstances of her husband's capture as described below: "Just before day the enemy charged our camp yelling like demons . . . I pleaded with him to let me throw over him a large waterproof wrap which had often served him in sickness during the summer season for a dressing gown and which I hoped might so cover his person that in the grey of the morning he would not be recognized. As he strode off I threw over his head a little black shawl which was around my own shoulders, saying that he could not find his hat and after he started sent my colored woman after him with a bucket for water hoping that he would pass unobserved."[134]:172

It was reported in the media that Davis put his wife's overcoat over his shoulders while fleeing. This led to the persistent rumor that he attempted to flee in women's clothes, inspiring caricatures that portrayed him as such.[135] Over 40 years later, an article in the *Washington Herald* claimed that Mrs. Davis's heavy shawl had been placed on Davis who was "always extremely sensitive to cold air," to protect him from the "chilly atmosphere of the early hour of the morning" by the slave James Henry Jones, Davis's valet who served Davis and his family during and after the Civil War.[136] Meanwhile, Davis's belongings continued on the train bound for Cedar Key, Florida. They were first hidden at Senator David Levy Yulee's plantation in Florida, then placed in the care of a railroad agent in Waldo. On June 15, 1865, Union soldiers seized Davis's personal baggage from the agent, together with some of the Confederate government's records. A historical marker was erected at this site.[137][138][139] In 1939, Jefferson Davis Memorial Historic Site was opened to mark the place where Confederate President Jefferson Davis was captured.

## Imprisonment

On May 19, 1865, Davis was imprisoned in a casemate at Fortress Monroe, on the coast of Virginia. Irons were riveted to his ankles at the order of General Nelson Miles, who was in charge of the fort. Davis was allowed no visitors, and no books except the Bible. He became sicker, and the attending physician warned that his life was in danger, but this treatment continued for some months until late autumn when he was finally given better quarters. General Miles was transferred in mid-1866, and Davis's treatment continued to improve.[140] Pope Pius IX (see Pope Pius IX and the United States), after learning that Davis was a prisoner, sent him a portrait inscribed with the Latin words "*Venite ad me omnes qui laboratis,*

*The 24 members of the petit jury impaneled by the United States Circuit Court for Virginia in Richmond for Davis's trial for treason in May 1867. Contemporary composite image from two glass plate negatives.*

*et ego reficiam vos, dicit Dominus,*" which correspond to Matthew 11:28,[141][142] "Come to me, all you that labor, and are burdened, and I will refresh you, sayeth the Lord." A hand-woven crown of thorns associated with the portrait is often said to have been made by the Pope[143][144] but may have been woven by Davis's wife Varina.[145]

Varina and their young daughter Winnie were allowed to join Davis, and the family was eventually given an apartment in the officers' quarters. Davis was indicted for treason while imprisoned; one of his attorneys was ex-Governor Thomas Pratt of Maryland. [146] There was a great deal of discussion in 1865 about bringing treason trials, especially against Jefferson Davis. While there was no consensus in President Johnson's cabinet to do so, on June 11, 1866, the House of Representatives voted, 105–19, to support such a trial against Davis. Although Davis wanted such a trial for himself, there were no treason trials against anyone, as it was felt they would probably not succeed and would impede reconciliation. There was also a concern at the time that such action could result in a judicial decision that would validate the constitutionality of secession (later removed by the Supreme Court ruling in *Texas v. White* (1869) declaring secession unconstitutional).[147][148][149][150]

A jury of 12 black and 12 white men was recruited by United States Circuit Court judge John Curtiss Underwood in preparation for the trial.[151]

After two years of imprisonment, Davis was released on bail of $100,000, which was posted by prominent citizens including Horace Greeley, Cornelius Vanderbilt and Gerrit Smith.[152] (Smith was a member of the Secret Six who financially supported abolitionist John Brown.) Davis went to Montreal, Quebec to join his family which had fled there earlier, and lived in Lennoxville, Quebec until 1868,[153] also visiting Cuba and Europe in search of work.[154] At one stage he stayed as a guest of James Smith, a foundry owner in Glasgow, who had struck up a friendship with Davis when he toured the Southern

States promoting his foundry business.[155] Davis remained under indictment until Andrew Johnson issued on Christmas Day of 1868 a presidential "pardon and amnesty" for the offense of treason to "every person who directly or indirectly participated in the late insurrection or rebellion" and after a federal circuit court on February 15, 1869, dismissed the case against Davis after the government's attorney informed the court that he would no longer continue to prosecute Davis.[147][148][149]

## Later years

After his release from prison and pardon, Davis faced continued financial pressures, as well as an unsettled family life. His elder brother Joseph died in 1870, his son William Howell Davis in 1872 and Jefferson Davis Jr. in 1878. His wife Varina was often ill or abroad, and for a time refused to live with him in Memphis, Tennessee. Davis resented having to resort to charity, and would only accept jobs befitting his former positions as U.S. Senator and Confederate President; several that he accepted proved financial failures.[156]

*Jefferson Davis at his home, c. 1885*

## Death and burials

On November 6, 1889, Davis left Beauvoir to visit his Brierfield plantation. He embarked a steamboat in New Orleans during sleety rain and fell ill during the trip, so that he initially felt too sick to disembark at his stop, and spent the night upriver in Vicksburg before making his way to the plantation the next day. He refused to send for a doctor for four days before embarking on his return trip. Meanwhile, servants sent Varina a telegram, and she took a train to New Orleans, and then a steamboat upriver, finally reaching the vessel on which her husband was returning. Davis finally received medical care as two doctors came aboard further south and diagnosed acute bronchitis complicated by malaria.[195]

*Funeral procession of Jefferson Davis in New Orleans*

[196] Upon arriving in New Orleans three days later, Davis was taken to Garden District home of Charles Erasmus Fenner, a former Confederate officer who became an Associate Justice of the Louisiana Supreme Court. Fenner was the son-in-law of Davis's old friend J. M. Payne. Davis's doctor Stanford E. Chaille pronounced him too ill to travel to Beauvoir; four medical students who were sons of Confederate veterans and

a Catholic nun attended Davis in the Charity Hospital ambulance which took him to the Fenner home. Davis remained bedridden but stable for the next two weeks. He took a turn for the worse in early December. According to Fenner, just when Davis again appeared to be improving, he lost consciousness on the evening of December 5 and died at 12:45 a.m. on Friday, December 6, 1889, holding Varina's hand and in the presence of several friends. [197][198]

His funeral was one of the largest in the South, and New Orleans draped itself in mourning as his body lay in state in the City Hall for several days. An Executive Committee decided to emphasize Davis's ties to the United States, so an American national flag was placed over the Confederate flag during the viewing, and many crossed American and Confederate flags nearby. Davis wore a new suit of Confederate grey fabric Jubal Early had given him, and Varina placed a sword Davis had carried during the Black Hawk War on the bier. A common decoration during the initial funeral was a small American flag in mourning, with a portrait of Davis in the center. The Grand Army of the Republic had a prominent role, even though the Grand Marshall was John G. Glynn, head of the Louisiana National Guard, and Georgia Governor John Gordon (head of the newly organized United Confederate Veterans) was honorary Grand Marshall.[164] While the federal government officially ignored Davis's death, many church bells rang in the south, Confederate veterans held many processions, and Senators and congressmen crossed the Potomac River to join former Confederate officials and generals in eulogizing Davis in Alexandria, Virginia.[199]

Although initially laid to rest in New Orleans in the Army of Northern Virginia tomb at Metairie Cemetery, in 1893 Davis was reinterred in Richmond, Virginia at Hollywood Cemetery, per his widow's request.[200] Before his death, Davis left the location of his burial up to Varina, but within a day of his death *The New York Times* proclaimed Richmond wanted his body.[201] Varina Davis had refused to accept direct charity, but let it be known that she would accept financial help through the Davis Land Company. [202] Soon, many tourists in New Orleans visited the mausoleum. Several other locations in the South wanted Davis's remains. Louisville, Kentucky offered a site in Cave Hill cemetery, noting that two years earlier Davis had dedicated a church built on the site of his birthplace and claiming that he several times said he wanted to be buried in his native state. Memphis, Tennessee, Montgomery, Alabama, Macon and Atlanta, Georgia and both Jackson and Vicksburg, Mississippi also petitioned for Davis's remains.[203] Richmond mayor and Confederate veteran J. Taylor Ellyson established the Jefferson Davis Monument Association, and on July 12, 1891, Varina revealed in a letter to Confederate Veterans and people of the Southern States that her first choice would be Davis's plantation in Mississippi, but that because she feared flooding, she had decided to urge Richmond as the proper place for his tomb.[204]

After Davis's remains were exhumed in New Orleans, they lay in state for a day at Memorial Hall of the newly organized Louisiana Historical Association.[205] Those paying final respects included Louisiana Governor Murphy J. Foster, Sr. A continuous cortège, day and night, then accompanied Davis's remains from New Orleans to Richmond. [206] The Louisville and Nashville Railroad car traveled past Beauvoir, then proceeded northeastward toward Richmond, with ceremonies at stops in Mobile and Montgomery, Alabama, Atlanta, Georgia, then Charlotte and Greensboro, North Carolina. The train also detoured to Raleigh, North Carolina for Davis's coffin to lie in state in that capital city, having been driven by James J. Jones, a free black man who had served Davis during the war and become a local businessman and politician. After a stop in Danville, Virginia, the Confederacy's last capital, and another ceremony at the Virginia State Capital, Davis was then interred at Hollywood Cemetery in Richmond. Per the association's agreement with Varina, their children's remains were exhumed from Washington, D.C., Memphis and another plot at the Hollywood cemetery, to rest in the new family plot.[207]

A life sized statue of Davis was eventually erected as promised by the Jefferson Davis Monument Association, in cooperation with the Southern Press Davis Monument Association, the United Confederate Veterans and ultimately the United Daughters of the Confederacy. The monument's cornerstone was laid in an 1896 ceremony, and it was dedicated with great pomp and 125,000 spectators on June 3, 1907, the last day of a Confederate reunion.[208] It continues to mark his tomb.[209]

# Martin Delany

**Martin Robinson Delany** (May 6, 1812–January 24, 1885) was an African-American abolitionist, journalist, physician, soldier and writer, and arguably the first proponent of black nationalism.[1] Delany is credited with the Pan-African slogan of "Africa for Africans."[2]

Born as a free person of color in Charles Town, Virginia, now West Virginia (not Charleston, West Virginia) and raised in Chambersburg and Pittsburgh, Pennsylvania, Delany trained as a physician's assistant. During the cholera epidemics of 1833 and 1854 in Pittsburgh, Delany treated patients, even though many doctors and residents fled the city out of fear of contamination. In this period, people did not know how the disease was transmitted.

In 1850, Delany was one of the first three black men admitted to Harvard Medical School, but all were dismissed after a few weeks because of widespread protests by white students. Delany had traveled in the South in 1839 to observe slavery firsthand. Beginning in 1847, he worked alongside Frederick Douglass in Rochester, New York to publish the *North Star*.

Delany dreamed of establishing a settlement in West Africa. He visited Liberia, a United States colony founded by the American Colonization Society, and lived in Canada for several years, but when the American Civil War began, he returned to the United States. Beginning in 1863, he recruited blacks for the United States Colored Troops. Commissioned as a major in February 1865, Delany became the first African-American field grade officer in the United States Army.

After the Civil War, Delany went to the South, settling in South Carolina. There he worked for the Freedmen's Bureau and became politically active, including in the Colored Conventions Movement. Delany ran unsuccessfully for Lieutenant Governor as a Republican. He was appointed as a Trial Judge, but he was removed following a scandal. Delany later switched his party affiliation. He worked for the campaign of Democrat Wade Hampton III, who won the 1876 election for governor in a season marked by violent suppression of black Republican voters by Red Shirts and fraud in balloting.

## Union Army service

In 1863, after Abraham Lincoln had called for a military draft, the 51-year-old Delany abandoned his dream of starting a new settlement on Africa's West Coast. Instead, he began recruiting black men for the Union Army. His efforts in Rhode Island, Connecticut, and later Ohio raised thousands of enlistees, many of whom joined the newly formed

United States Colored Troops. His son Toussaint Louverture Delany (named after the major leader of the Haitian Revolution) served with the 54th Regiment.[26] The senior Delany wrote to the Secretary of War, Edwin M. Stanton, requesting that he make efforts "to command all of the effective black men as Agents of the United States," but the request was ignored. During the recruitment, 179,000 black men enlisted in the U.S. Colored Troops, almost 10 percent of all who served in the Union army.[27]

In early 1865, Delany was granted an audience with Lincoln.[28] He proposed a corps of black men led by black officers, who he believed could serve to win over Southern blacks to the Union side. Although the government had already rejected a similar appeal by Frederick Douglass, Lincoln was impressed by Delany and described him as "a most extraordinary and intelligent man."[29] Delany was commissioned as a major in February 1865, becoming the first black line field officer in the U.S. Army and achieving the highest rank an African American would reach during the Civil War.[5][30]

Delany especially wanted to lead colored troops into Charleston, South Carolina, the former secessionist hotbed. When Union forces captured the city, Major Delany was invited to the War Department ceremony in which Major General Robert Anderson would unfurl the very flag over Fort Sumter that he had been forced to lower four years earlier. Massachusetts Senator Henry Wilson and abolitionists William Lloyd Garrison and Henry Ward Beecher also participated in the ceremony. Major Delany had recruited black Charlestonians to restore the capacity of the 103rd and 104th regiments and start the 105th regiment of U.S. Colored Troops. He arrived at the ceremony with Robert Vesey, son of Denmark Vesey, who had been executed for starting a slave rebellion. The man came in the *Planter*, a ship piloted by the former slave Robert Smalls (who had taken it over during the war and driven the ship to Union lines, running the Confederate blockade outside Charleston Harbor).

The following day, the city learned that President Lincoln had been assassinated by John Wilkes Booth. Delany continued with the planned political rally for Charleston's freedmen, with Garrison and Senator Warner as speakers.[31] He soon published an open letter to African Americans asking them to contribute to a memorial for "the Father of American Liberty."[32] Two weeks later, Delany was scheduled to speak at another rally, before the visiting Chief Justice Salmon P. Chase. A journalist was surprised when Delany addressed the issue of ill-feelings between black freedmen and mulattos (or "browns," free people of color and mixed race) in Charleston. He said that two mulattos had informed authorities about Denmark Vesey's plans for a rebellion in 1822 conspiracy, rather than trying to promote racial healing and empowerment between the groups.[33]

After the war, Delany initially remained with the Army and served under General Rufus Saxton in the 52nd U.S. Colored Troops. He was later transferred to the Freedmen's Bureau, serving on Hilton Head. He shocked white officers by taking a strong position in supporting redistribution of land to freedmen. Later in 1865, Delany was mustered out of the Freedmen's Bureau and shortly afterward resigned from the Army.[5]

## Later life

Following the war, Delany continued to be politically active. He established a land and brokerage business in 1871 and worked to help black cotton farmers improve their business and negotiating skills to get a better price for their product.[34] He supported the Freedman's Bank (as did Douglass), and also traveled and spoke in support of the Colored Conventions Movement.[35] Delany also argued against carpetbaggers and black candidates for office when he saw fit. For instance, he opposed the vice presidential candidacy of Jonathan Jasper Wright and John Mercer Langston on the grounds of inexperience,[36] and he opposed the candidacy of another black man as Charleston's mayor.

Delany unsuccessfully sought various positions, such as appointment as Consul General to Liberia.[37] In 1874, Delany ran as an Independent Republican for Lieutenant Governor of South Carolina (with John T. Green as the gubernatorial candidate). Despite the corruption scandals that enveloped former Republican governor Franklin Moses, Jr. (who chose not to run for re-election), their ticket lost to Republican Attorney General Daniel H. Chamberlain and his running mate Richard Howell Gleaves.[38]

Delany was appointed as a trial justice (judge) in Charleston.[39] In 1875, charges of "defrauding a church" were brought against him. After conviction, he was forced to resign, and served time in jail. Although pardoned by Republican Governor Chamberlain, with the intervention of Wade Hampton,[40] Delany was not allowed to return to his former position.

Delany supported Democratic candidate Wade Hampton in the 1876 gubernatorial election, the only prominent black to do so.[41] Partly as a result of black swing votes encouraged by Delany, Hampton won the election by fewer than 1,100 votes. However, the election was marred by white intimidation and violence against black Republicans, in an effort to suppress the black vote. Armed men from "rifle clubs" and the Red Shirts operated openly. The latter was a paramilitary group of mostly white men who worked to suppress black voting as "the military arm of the Democratic Party."[42] By 1876, South Carolina rifle clubs had about 20,000 white men as members.[43] More than 150 blacks were killed in election-related violence.[44]

In early 1877, the federal government withdrew its troops from the South after reaching a compromise over the national election. This marked the end to Reconstruction, and Governor Chamberlain left the state. The Democrats, calling themselves Redeemers, had taken control of South Carolina's legislature. Paramilitary groups such as the Red Shirts continued to suppress black voting in the Carolinas, especially in the upland counties.

In reaction to whites regaining power and the suppression of black voting, Charleston-based blacks started planning again for emigration to Africa. In 1877, they formed the Liberia Exodus Joint Stock Steamship Company, with Delany as chairman of the finance committee. A year later, the company purchased a ship, the *Azor*, for the voyage led by Harrison N. Bouey. He served as president of the board to organize the voyage.[5]

## Last years and death

In 1880, Delany withdrew from the project to serve his family. Two of his children were students at Wilberforce College in Ohio and required money for tuition fees. His wife had been working as a seamstress to make ends meet. Delany began practicing medicine again in Charleston. On January 24, 1885, he died of tuberculosis in Wilberforce, Ohio.[5]

Delany is interred in a family plot at Massies Creek Cemetery in Cedarville, Ohio, next to his wife Catherine, who died July 11, 1894.[45] For over 120 years his family plot was only marked with a small government-issued tombstone on which his name was misspelled. Three of his children, Placido (died 1910), Faustin (died 1912) and Ethiopia (died 1920), were subsequently buried alongside their parents. Every grave except Martin's remained unmarked. In 2006, after many years of fundraising, The National Afro-American Museum and Cultural Center was able to raise $18,000 to have a monument built and placed at the grave site of Delany and his family. The monument is made of black granite from Africa and features an engraved picture of Delany in uniform during the war.[46]

# Abner Doubleday

**Abner Doubleday** (June 26, 1819–January 26, 1893)[1] was a career United States Army officer and Union major general in the American Civil War. He fired the first shot in defense of Fort Sumter, the opening battle of the war, and had a pivotal role in the early fighting at the Battle of Gettysburg. Gettysburg was his finest hour, but his relief by Maj. Gen. George G. Meade caused lasting enmity between the two men. In San Francisco, after the war, he obtained a patent on the cable car railway that still runs there. In his final years in New Jersey, he was a prominent member and later president of the Theosophical Society.

In 1908, fifteen years after his death, Doubleday was declared by the Mills Commission to have invented the game of baseball (a claim never made by Doubleday during his lifetime). This claim has been thoroughly debunked by baseball historians.[2][3]

## Early commands and Fort Sumter

Doubleday initially served in coastal garrisons and then in the Mexican–American War from 1846 to 1848 and the Seminole Wars from 1856 to 1858. In 1858 he was transferred to Fort Moultrie in Charleston Harbor serving under Colonel John L. Gardner. By the start of the Civil War, he was a captain and second in command in the garrison at Fort Sumter, under Major Robert Anderson.[4] He aimed the cannon that fired the first return shot in answer to the Confederate bombardment on April 12, 1861. He subsequently referred to himself as the "hero of Sumter" for this role.[5]

## Brigade and division command in Virginia

Doubleday was promoted to major on May 14, 1861, and commanded the Artillery Department in the Shenandoah Valley from June to August, and then the artillery for Major General Nathaniel Banks's division of the Army of the Potomac. He was appointed brigadier general of volunteers on February 3, 1862, and was assigned to duty in northern Virginia while the Army of the Potomac conducted the Peninsula Campaign. His first combat assignment was to lead the 2nd Brigade, 1st Division, III Corps of the Army of Virginia during the Northern Virginia Campaign. In the actions at Brawner's farm, just before the Second Battle of Bull Run, he took the initiative to send two of his regiments to reinforce Brigadier General John Gibbon's brigade against a larger Confederate force, fighting it to a standstill. (Personal initiative was required since his division commander, Brig. Gen. Rufus King, was incapacitated by an epileptic seizure at the time. He was replaced by Brigadier General John P. Hatch.)[8] His men were routed when they encountered Major General James Longstreet's corps, but by the following day, August 30, he took command of the division when Hatch was wounded, and he led his men to cover the retreat of the Union Army.[5]

Doubleday again led the division, now assigned to the I Corps of the Army of the Potomac, after South Mountain, where Hatch was wounded again. At Antietam, he led his men into the deadly fighting in the Cornfield and the West Woods, and one colonel described him as a "gallant officer . . . remarkably cool and at the very front of battle."[5] He was wounded when an artillery shell exploded near his horse, throwing him to the ground in a violent fall. He received a brevet promotion to lieutenant colonel in the regular army for his actions at Antietam and was promoted in March 1863 to major general of volunteers, to rank from November 29, 1862.[9] At Fredericksburg in December 1862, his division mostly sat idle. During the winter, the I Corps was reorganized and Doubleday assumed command of the 3rd Division. At Chancellorsville in May 1863, the division was kept in reserve.[5]

## Gettysburg

At the start of the Battle of Gettysburg, July 1, 1863, Doubleday's division was the second infantry division on the field to reinforce the cavalry division of Brigadier General John Buford. When his corps commander, Major General John F. Reynolds, was killed very early in the fighting, Doubleday found himself in command of the corps at 10:50 am. His men fought well in the morning, putting up a stout resistance, but as overwhelming Confederate forces massed against them, their line eventually broke and they retreated back through the town of Gettysburg to the relative safety of Cemetery Hill south of town. It was Doubleday's finest performance during the war, five hours leading 9,500 men against ten Confederate brigades that numbered more than 16,000. Seven of those brigades sustained casualties that ranged from 35 to 50 percent, indicating the ferocity of the Union defense. On Cemetery Hill, however, the I Corps could muster only a third of its men as effective for duty, and the corps was essentially destroyed as a combat force for the rest of the battle; it would be decommissioned in March 1864, its surviving units consolidated into other corps.[5]

On July 2, 1863, Army of the Potomac commander Maj. Gen. George G. Meade replaced Doubleday with Major General John Newton, a more junior officer from another corps. The ostensible reason was a false report by XI Corps commander Major General Oliver O. Howard that Doubleday's corps broke first, causing the entire Union line to collapse, but Meade also had a long history of disdain for Doubleday's combat effectiveness, dating back to South Mountain. Doubleday was humiliated by this snub and held a lasting grudge against Meade, but he returned to division command and fought well for the remainder of the battle.[5] He was wounded in the neck on the second day of Gettysburg and received a brevet promotion to colonel in the regular army for his service.[6] He formally requested reinstatement as I Corps commander, but Meade refused, and Doubleday left Gettysburg on July 7 for Washington.[10]

Doubleday's indecision as a commander in the war resulted in his uncomplimentary nickname "Forty-Eight Hours."[6]

## Washington

Doubleday assumed administrative duties in the defenses of Washington, D.C., where he was in charge of courts martial, which gave him legal experience that he used after the war. His only return to combat was directing a portion of the defenses against the attack by Confederate Lieutenant General Jubal A. Early in the Valley Campaigns of 1864. Also while in Washington, Doubleday testified against George Meade at the United States Congress Joint Committee on the Conduct of the War, criticizing him harshly over his conduct of the Battle of Gettysburg.[4] While in Washington, Doubleday remained a loyal Republican and staunch supporter of President Abraham Lincoln. Doubleday rode with Lincoln on the train to Gettysburg for the Gettysburg Address and Col. and Mrs. Doubleday attended events with Mr. and Mrs. Lincoln in Washington.

## Postbellum career

After the Civil War, Doubleday mustered out of the volunteer service on August 24, 1865, reverted to the rank of lieutenant colonel, and became the colonel of the 35th U.S. Infantry in September 1867. He was stationed in San Francisco from 1869 through 1871 and he took out a patent for the cable car railway that still runs there, receiving a charter for its operation, but signing away his rights when he was reassigned. In 1871 he commanded the 24th U.S. Infantry, an all African-American regiment with headquarters at Fort McKavett, Texas.[7] He retired in 1873.

In the 1870s, he was listed in the New York business directory as lawyer.

Doubleday spent much of his time writing. He published two important works on the Civil War: *Reminiscences of Forts Sumter and Moultrie* (1876) and *Chancellorsville and Gettysburg* (1882), the latter being a volume of the series *Campaigns of the Civil War*.[6]

## Death

Doubleday died of heart disease in 1893. Doubleday's body was laid in state in New York's City Hall and then was taken to Washington by train[5] from Mendham Township, and is buried in Arlington National Cemetery in Arlington, Virginia.[6]

# Frederick Douglass

**Frederick Douglass** (born Frederick Augustus Washington Bailey; c. February 1818[4]—February 20, 1895[5]) was an American social reformer, abolitionist, orator, writer, and statesman. After escaping from slavery in Maryland, he became a national leader of the abolitionist movement in Massachusetts and New York, gaining note for his oratory[6] and incisive antislavery writings. In his time, he was described by abolitionists as a living counter-example to slaveholders' arguments that slaves lacked the intellectual capacity to function as independent American citizens.[7][8] Northerners at the time found it hard to believe that such a great orator had once been a slave.[9]

Douglass wrote several autobiographies. He described his experiences as a slave in his 1845 autobiography, *Narrative of the Life of Frederick Douglass, an American Slave*, which became a bestseller, and was influential in promoting the cause of abolition, as was his second book, *My Bondage and My Freedom* (1855). After the Civil War, Douglass remained an active campaigner against slavery and wrote his last autobiography, *Life and Times of Frederick Douglass*. First published in 1881 and revised in 1892, three years before his death, it covered events during and after the Civil War. Douglass also actively supported women's suffrage, and held several public offices. Without his approval, Douglass became the first African American nominated for Vice President of the United States as the running mate and Vice Presidential nominee of Victoria Woodhull, on the Equal Rights Party ticket.[10]

Douglass was a firm believer in the equality of all peoples, whether white, black, female, Native American, or Chinese immigrants.[11] He was also a believer in dialogue and in making alliances across racial and ideological divides, and in the liberal values of the U.S. Constitution. When radical abolitionists, under the motto "No Union with Slaveholders," criticized Douglass' willingness to engage in dialogue with slave owners, he replied: "I would unite with anybody to do right and with nobody to do wrong."[12]

## Life as a slave

Frederick Augustus Washington Bailey was born into slavery on the Eastern Shore of the Chesapeake Bay in Talbot County, Maryland. The plantation was between Hillsboro[13] and Cordova; his birthplace was likely his grandmother's cabin[a] east of Tappers Corner, (38.8845°N 75.958°W) and west of Tuckahoe Creek.[14][15] The exact date of his birth is unknown, and he later chose to celebrate his birthday on February 14.[4] In his first autobiography, Douglass stated: "I have no accurate knowledge of my age, never having seen any authentic record containing it."[13][16]

Douglass was of mixed race, which likely included Native American and African on his mother's side, as well as European.[17] His father was "almost certainly white," as shown by historian David W. Blight in his 2018 biography of Douglass.[18] He said his mother Harriet Bailey gave him his grand name. After escaping to the North years later, he took the surname Douglass, having already dropped his two middle names.

He later wrote of his earliest times with his mother:

> The opinion was . . . whispered that my master was my father; but of the correctness of this opinion I know nothing . . . My mother and I were separated when I was but an infant . . . It [was] common custom, in the part of Maryland from which I ran away, to part children from their mothers at a very early age. . . . I do not recollect ever seeing my mother by the light of day. . . . She would lie down with me, and get me to sleep, but long before I waked she was gone.[19]

After separation from his mother during infancy, young Frederick lived with his maternal grandmother Betsy Bailey, who was a slave, and his maternal grandfather Isaac, who was free.[20] Frederick's mother Harriet Bailey remained on the plantation about 12 miles away, and only visited Frederick a few times before she died when he was seven (his grandmother Betsy Bailey would live until 1849).[21] At the age of six, Frederick was separated from his grandparents and moved to the Wye House plantation, where Aaron Anthony worked as overseer.[22] After Anthony died in 1826, Douglass was given to Lucretia Auld, wife of Thomas Auld, who sent him to serve Thomas' brother Hugh Auld in Baltimore. Lucretia Auld was essential in creating who Douglass was as she shaped his experiences. She had a special interest in Douglass from the time he was a child and wanted to give him a better life.[23] Douglass felt that he was lucky to be in the city, where he said slaves were almost freemen, compared to those on plantations.

When Douglass was about twelve, Hugh Auld's wife Sophia started teaching him the alphabet. From the day he arrived, she saw to it that Douglass was properly fed and clothed, and that he slept in a bed with sheets and a blanket.[24] Douglass described her as a kind and tender-hearted woman, who treated him "as she supposed one human being ought to treat another."[25] Hugh Auld disapproved of the tutoring, feeling that literacy would encourage slaves to desire freedom; Douglass later referred to this as the "first decidedly antislavery lecture" he had ever heard.[26] Under her husband's influence, Sophia came to believe that education and slavery were incompatible and one day snatched a newspaper away from Douglass.[27] She stopped teaching him altogether and hid all potential reading materials, including her Bible, from him.[24] In his autobiography, Douglass related how he learned to read from white children in the neighborhood, and by observing the writings of the men with whom he worked.[28]

Douglass continued, secretly, to teach himself how to read and write. He later often said, "knowledge is the pathway from slavery to freedom."[29] As Douglass began to read newspapers, pamphlets, political materials, and books of every description, this new realm of thought led him to question and condemn the institution of slavery. In later years, Douglass credited *The Columbian Orator*, an anthology that he discovered at about age twelve, with clarifying and defining his views on freedom and human rights. The book, first published in 1797, is a classroom reader, containing essays, speeches and dialogues, to assist students in learning reading and grammar.

When Douglass was hired out to William Freeland, he taught other slaves on the plantation to read the New Testament at a weekly Sunday school. As word spread, the interest among slaves in learning to read was so great that in any week, more than 40 slaves would attend lessons. For about six months, their study went relatively unnoticed. While Freeland remained complacent about their activities, other plantation owners became incensed about their slaves being educated. One Sunday they burst in on the gathering, armed with clubs and stones, to disperse the congregation permanently.

In 1833, Thomas Auld took Douglass back from Hugh ("[a]s a means of punishing Hugh," Douglass later wrote). Thomas Auld sent Douglass to work for Edward Covey, a poor farmer who had a reputation as a "slave-breaker." He whipped Douglass so regularly that his wounds had little time to heal. Douglass later said the frequent whippings broke his body, soul, and spirit.[30] The sixteen-year-old Douglass finally rebelled against the beatings, however, and fought back. After Douglass won a physical confrontation, Covey never tried to beat him again.[31] Recounting his beatings at Covey's farm in his autobiography, *Narrative of the Life of Frederick Douglass, An American Slave*, Douglass described himself as "a man transformed into a brute!"[32] But Douglass came to see his physical fight with Covey as life-transforming; he introduced the story in his autobiography with this sentence: "You have seen how a man was made a slave; you shall see how a slave was made a man."[33]

*Anna Murray-Douglass, Douglass's wife for 44 years, portrait ca. 1860.*

## From slavery to freedom

Douglass first tried to escape from Freeland, who had hired him out from his owner Colonel Lloyd, but was unsuccessful. In 1836, he tried to escape from his new master Covey, but failed again. In 1837, Douglass met and fell in love with Anna Murray, a free black woman in Baltimore about five years older than he. Her free status strengthened his belief in the possibility of gaining his own freedom. Murray encouraged him and supported his efforts by aid and money.[34]

On September 3, 1838, Douglass successfully escaped by boarding a north-bound train of the Philadelphia, Wilmington and Baltimore Railroad. The area where he boarded was a short distance east of the train depot, in a recently developed neighborhood between the modern neighborhoods of Harbor East and Little Italy. The depot was located at President and Fleet streets, east of "The Basin" of the Baltimore harbor, on the northwest branch of the Patapsco River.

Young Douglass reached Havre de Grace, Maryland, in Harford County, in the northeast corner of the state, along the southwest shore of the Susquehanna River, which flowed into the Chesapeake Bay. Although this placed him only some 20 miles (32 km) from the Maryland-Pennsylvania state line, it was easier to continue by rail through Delaware, another slave state. Dressed in a sailor's uniform provided to him by Murray, who also gave him part of her savings to cover his travel costs, he carried identification papers and protection papers that he had obtained from a free black seaman.[34][35] [36] Douglass crossed the wide Susquehanna River by the railroad's steam-ferry at Havre de Grace to Perryville on the opposite shore, in Cecil County, then continued by train across the state line to Wilmington, Delaware, a large port at the head of the Delaware Bay. From there, because the rail line was not yet completed, he went by steamboat along the Delaware River further northeast to the "Quaker City" of Philadelphia, Pennsylvania, an anti-slavery stronghold. He continued to the safe house of noted abolitionist David Ruggles in New York City. His entire journey to freedom took less than 24 hours.[37] Frederick Douglass later wrote of his arrival in New York City:

I have often been asked, how I felt when first I found myself on free soil. And my readers may share the same curiosity. There is scarcely anything in my experience about which I could not give a more satisfactory answer. A new world had opened upon me. If life is more than breath, and the 'quick round of blood,' I lived more in one day than in a year of my slave life. It was a time of joyous excitement which words can but tamely describe. In a letter written to a friend soon after reaching New York, I said: 'I felt as one might feel upon escape from a den of hungry lions.' Anguish and grief, like darkness and rain, may be depicted; but gladness and joy, like the rainbow, defy the skill of pen or pencil.[38]

Once Douglass had arrived, he sent for Murray to follow him north to New York. She brought with her the necessary basics for them to set up a home. They were married on September 15, 1838, by a black Presbyterian minister, just eleven days after Douglass had reached New York.[34][37] At first, they adopted Johnson as their married name, to divert attention.[34]

## Autobiography

Douglass's best-known work is his first autobiography, *Narrative of the Life of Frederick Douglass, an American Slave*, written during his time in Lynn, Massachusetts[51] and published in 1845. At the time, some skeptics questioned whether a black man could have produced such an eloquent piece of literature. The book received generally positive reviews and became an immediate bestseller. Within three years, it had been reprinted nine times, with 11,000 copies circulating in the United States. It was also translated into French and Dutch and published in Europe.

Douglass published three versions of his autobiography during his lifetime (and revised the third of these), each time expanding on the previous one. The 1845 *Narrative* was his biggest seller, and probably allowed him to raise the funds to gain his legal freedom the following year, as discussed below. In 1855, Douglass published *My Bondage and My Freedom*. In 1881, after the Civil War, Douglass published *Life and Times of Frederick Douglass*, which he revised in 1892.

## Civil War years
### Before the Civil War
By the time of the Civil War, Douglass was one of the most famous black men in the country, known for his orations on the condition of the black race and on other issues such as women's rights. His eloquence gathered crowds at every location. His reception by leaders in England and Ireland added to his stature.

## Fight for emancipation and suffrage
Douglass and the abolitionists argued that because the aim of the Civil War was to end slavery, African Americans should be allowed to engage in the fight for their freedom. Douglass publicized this view in his newspapers and several speeches. In August 1861, Douglass published an account of the First Battle of Bull Run that noted that there were some blacks already in the Confederate ranks.[91] A few weeks later, Douglass brought the subject up again, quoting a witness to the battle who said they saw black Confederates "with muskets on their shoulders and bullets in their pockets."[91] Douglass conferred with President Abraham Lincoln in 1863 on the treatment of black soldiers,[92] and with President Andrew Johnson on the subject of black suffrage.[93]

President Lincoln's Emancipation Proclamation, which took effect on January 1, 1863, declared the freedom of all slaves in Confederate-held territory.[94] (Slaves in Union-held areas and Northern states were freed with the adoption of the 13th Amendment on December 6, 1865.) Douglass described the spirit of those awaiting the proclamation: "We were waiting and listening as for a bolt from the sky . . . we were watching . . . by the dim light of the stars for the dawn of a new day . . . we were longing for the answer to the agonizing prayers of centuries."[95]

During the U.S. Presidential Election of 1864, Douglass supported John C. Frémont, who was the candidate of the abolitionist Radical Democracy Party. Douglass was disappointed that President Lincoln did not publicly endorse suffrage for black freedmen. Douglass believed that since African-American men were fighting for the Union in the American Civil War, they deserved the right to vote.[96]

With the North no longer obliged to return slaves to their owners in the South, Douglass fought for equality for his people. He made plans with Lincoln to move liberated slaves out of the South. During the war, Douglass also helped the Union cause by serving as a recruiter for the 54th Massachusetts Infantry Regiment. His eldest son, Charles Douglass, joined the 54th Massachusetts Regiment, but was ill for much of his service.[43] Lewis

Douglass fought at the Battle of Fort Wagner.[97] Another son, Frederick Douglass Jr., also served as a recruiter.

## After Lincoln's death

The post-war (1865) ratification of the 13th Amendment outlawed slavery. The 14th Amendment provided for citizenship and equal protection under the law. The 15th Amendment protected all citizens from being discriminated against in voting because of race.[71]

On April 14, 1876, Douglass delivered the keynote speech at the unveiling of the Emancipation Memorial in Washington's Lincoln Park. In that speech, Douglass spoke frankly about Lincoln, noting what he perceived as both positive and negative attributes of the late President. Calling Lincoln "the white man's president," Douglass criticized Lincoln's tardiness in joining the cause of emancipation, noting that Lincoln initially opposed the expansion of slavery but did not support its elimination. But Douglass also asked, "Can any colored man, or any white man friendly to the freedom of all men, ever forget the night which followed the first day of January 1863, when the world was to see if Abraham Lincoln would prove to be as good as his word?"[98] Douglass also said: "Though Mr. Lincoln shared the prejudices of his white fellow-countrymen against the Negro, it is hardly necessary to say that in his heart of hearts he loathed and hated slavery . . . "

The crowd, roused by his speech, gave Douglass a standing ovation. Lincoln's widow Mary Lincoln supposedly gave Lincoln's favorite walking-stick to Douglass in appreciation. That walking-stick still rests in Douglass's final residence, "Cedar Hill," now preserved as the Frederick Douglass National Historic Site.

*Frederick Douglass in 1876, around 58 years of age*

## Reconstruction era

After the Civil War, Douglass continued to work for equality for African-Americans and women. Due to his prominence and activism during the war, Douglass received several political appointments.

## Death

On February 20, 1895, Douglass attended a meeting of the National Council of Women in Washington, D.C. During that meeting, he was brought to the platform and received a standing ovation. Shortly after he returned home, Douglass died of a massive heart attack.[5] He was 77.

His funeral was held at the Metropolitan African Methodist Episcopal Church. Thousands of people passed by his coffin to show their respect. Although Douglass had attended several churches in the nation's capital, he had a pew here and donated two standing candelabras when this church had moved to a new building in 1886. He also gave many lectures there, including his last major speech, "The Lesson of the Hour."[44]

Douglass' coffin was transported back to Rochester, New York, where he had lived for 25 years, longer than anywhere else in his life. He was buried next to Anna in the Douglass family plot of Mount Hope Cemetery, and Helen joined them in 1903.[129]

# Lewis Henry Douglass

*Lewis Henry Douglass in his Union army uniform*

**Lewis Henry Douglass** (October 9, 1840–eptember 19, 1908) was the oldest son of Frederick Douglass and his first wife Anna Murray Douglass. He was born in New Bedford, Massachusetts. Douglass was well educated and as a boy apprenticed, in Rochester, New York, as a typesetter for his father's newspapers *The North Star* and *Douglass' Weekly*. He joined the Union Army on March 25, 1863, only two months after the Emancipation Proclamation allowed African Americans to see combat in the Union Army.[1] He fought for one of the first official African American units in the United States during the Civil War, the famed 54th Massachusetts Infantry Regiment. Shortly after joining the army, Douglass attained the rank of Sergeant Major, the highest rank a black man could reach. He took part in the Battle of James Island, the Battle of Olustee and the Second Battle of Fort Wagner.[1][2] At the Second Battle of Fort Wagner, half of his regiment was killed, but this battle turned the public's attention toward the sacrifices made by African Americans in the war.[3] Douglass addressed the bravery of the African American troops in a letter to his future wife Helen Amelia Loguen:

MORRIS ISLAND. S. C. July 20

MY DEAR AMELIA: I have been in two fights, and am unhurt. I am about to go in another I believe to-night. Our men fought well on both occasions. The last was desperate we charged that terrible battery on Morris Island known as Fort Wagoner, and were repulsed with a loss of 300 killed and wounded. I escaped unhurt from amidst that perfect hail of shot and shell. It was terrible. I need not particularize the papers will give a better than I have time to give. My thoughts are with you often, you are as dear as ever, be good enough to remember it as I no doubt you will. As I said before we are on the eve of another fight and I am very busy and have just snatched a moment to write you. I must necessarily be brief. Should I fall in the next fight killed or wounded I hope to fall with my face to the foe.

If I survive I shall write you a long letter. DeForrest of your city is wounded George Washington is missing, Jacob Carter is missing, Chas Reason wounded Chas Whiting, Chas Creamer all wounded. The above are in hospital.

This regiment has established its reputation as a fighting regiment not a man flinched, though it was a trying time. Men fell all around me. A shell would explode and clear a space of twenty feet, our men would close up again, but it was no use we had to retreat, which was a very hazardous undertaking. How I got out of that fight alive I cannot tell, but I am here. My Dear girl I hope again to see you. I must bid you farewell should I be killed. Remember if I die I die in a good cause. I wish we had a hundred thousand colored troops we would put an end to this war. Good Bye to all Write soon Your own loving LEWIS[4]

Douglass was also wounded in the Second Battle of Fort Wagner and became ill, forcing him to be medically discharged from the army in 1864.[5] After the Civil War, he worked as a teacher for the Freedman's Bureau.[5] In 1866, Lewis and his brother, Frederick Douglass Jr., went to Denver where they were hosted by Henry O. Wagoner, a friend of their father. Wagoner taught the brothers typography[6] and along with William J. Hardin, Lewis taught reading, writing, and other subjects to adult blacks in Wagoner's home.[7] Douglass married Helen Amelia Loguen in 1869 and moved to Washington D.C. where he became the first typesetter employed by the Government Printing Office.[1] Douglass's employment by the Government Printing Office as typesetter did not last long because he was unable to join the typesetters' union due to racial intimidation.

Like his father, Lewis Henry Douglass was a "valuable citizen" to Washington D.C., through his involvement with the *New National Era* and other political impact.[8] He helped establish and was the senior editor of the *New National Era* (1870–1874) with his father, a "well conducted" newspaper aimed at addressing the issues of the black community in D.C.[5][8] He had a political impact when appointed to the legislative council of the District of Columbia by Ulysses S. Grant where he pushed for racial equality by creating a bill like one that required restaurants to post their prices so they could not overcharge blacks.[5]

Douglass had a stroke in 1904 that greatly impacted his health and died four years later, at the age of 67.

# Sarah Edmonds

*Edmonds as Franklin Thompson*

**Sarah Emma Edmonds** (December 1841–September 5, 1898), was a Canadian-born woman who is known for serving as a man with the Union Army during the American Civil War. In 1992, she was inducted into the Michigan Women's Hall of Fame.[1]

## Civil War service

Sarah Emma Edmond's interest in adventure was sparked by a book she read in her youth by Maturin Murray Ballou called *Fanny Campbell, the Female Pirate Captain*,[3] telling the story of Fanny Campbell and her adventures on a pirate ship during the American Revolution while dressed as a woman[2] Fanny remained dressed as a man in order to pursue other adventures, to which Edmonds attributes her desire to cross dress. During the Civil War, on May 25, 1861, she enlisted in Company F of the 2nd Michigan Infantry, also known as the Flint Union Greys.[2] On her second try, she disguised herself as a man named "Franklin Flint Thompson," the middle name possibly after the city she volunteered in, Flint, Michigan. She felt that it was her duty to serve her country and was truly patriotic towards her new country. Extensive physical examinations were not required for enlistment at the time, and she was not discovered.[4] She at first served as a male field nurse, participating in several campaigns under General McClellan, including the First and Second Battle of Bull Run, Antietam, the Peninsula Campaign, Vicksburg, Fredericksburg, and others. However, some historians claim that these reports place her in more than one location at the same time.

Edmonds's career took a turn during the war when a Union spy in Richmond, Virginia was discovered and went before a firing squad, and a friend, James Vesey, was killed in an ambush. She took advantage of the open spot and the opportunity to avenge her friend's death. She applied for, and won, the position as Franklin Thompson. Although there is no proof in her military records that she actually served as a spy, she wrote extensively about her experiences disguised as a spy during the war.[5]

Traveling into enemy territory to gather information required Emma to come up with many disguises. One disguise required Edmonds to use silver nitrate to dye her skin black, wear a black wig, and walk into the Confederacy disguised as a black man by the name of Cuff. Another time she entered as an Irish peddler woman by the name of Bridget O'Shea, claiming that she was selling apples and soap to the soldiers. Again, she was "working for the Confederates" as a black laundress when a packet of official papers fell out of an officer's jacket. When Thompson returned to the Union with the papers, the generals were delighted. Another time, she worked as a detective in Kentucky as Charles Mayberry, uncovering a Confederacy agent.[6]

Edmonds's career as Frank Thompson came to an end when she contracted malaria. She abandoned her duty in the military, fearing that if she went to a military hospital she would be discovered. She checked herself into a private hospital, intending to return to military life once she had recuperated. Once she recovered, however, she saw posters listing Frank Thompson as a deserter. Rather than return to the army under another alias or as Frank Thompson, risking execution for desertion, she decided to serve as a female nurse at a Washington, D.C., hospital for wounded soldiers run by the United States Christian Commission. There was speculation that Edmonds may have deserted because of John Reid having been discharged months earlier. There is evidence in his diary that she had mentioned leaving before she had contracted malaria. Her fellow soldiers spoke highly of her military service, and even after her disguise was discovered, considered her a good soldier. She was referred to as a fearless soldier and was active in every battle her regiment faced.[5][7]

## Memoir

In 1864, Boston publisher DeWolfe, Fiske, & Co. published Edmonds' account of her military experiences as *The Female Spy of the Union Army*. One year later, her story was picked up by a Hartford, CT publisher who issued it with a new title, *Nurse and Spy in the Union Army*. It was a huge success, selling in excess of 175,000 copies.[8] Edmonds donated the profits from her memoir to "various soldiers' aid organization." [2]

## Personal life

In 1867, she married Linus. H. Seelye, a mechanic and a childhood friend with whom she had three children.[8] All three of their children died in their youth, leading the couple to adopt two sons.[2]

## Later life

Edmonds became a lecturer after her story became public in 1883.[2] In 1886,[8] she received a government pension of $12 a month for her military service, and after some campaigning, was able to have the charge of desertion dropped, and receive an honorable discharge. In 1897, she became the only woman admitted to the Grand Army of the Republic, the Civil War Union Army veterans' organization. Edmonds died in La Porte, Texas, and is buried in the Grand Army of the Republic (GAR) section of Washington Cemetery in Houston. Edmonds was laid to rest a second time in 1901 with full military honors.[2]

# Anna Etheridge

*Annie Etheridge Hooks, from an 1897 publication.*

*Annie Etheridge*

**Lorinda Anna "Annie" Blair Etheridge** (May 3, 1839– January 23, 1913) was a Union nurse and vivandière who served during the American Civil War. She was one of only two women to receive the Kearny Cross. She was inducted into the Michigan Women's Hall of Fame in 2010.[1]

Anna Etheridge was born Lorinda Anna Blair in 1839 in Wayne County, Michigan. In 1860, she married James Etheridge.[2] At the outbreak of the American Civil War, Etheridge enlisted in 2nd Michigan Volunteer Infantry Regiment, serving as a nurse and vivandière. Her desire to become a nurse stemmed from caring for her father before his death. Before the war, Etheridge worked in a hospital with a poor reputation for patient care, which she had attempted to improve.

## During the war

Etheridge enlisted with her husband in the Second Michigan regiment, later serving as the daughter of the Third Michigan regiment.[3] Though her husband soon deserted, Etheridge served throughout the rest of the war with the Fifth Michigan.[3] Etheridge was famous for her courageous work under fire, her skirt often being torn by bullets.[4] Armed with pistols for her protection and saddlebags filled with medical supplies, Etheridge frequently rode into the front lines on horseback to aid wounded soldiers.[3] Etheridge embodied the ideal daughter of the Union, much unlike her husband.[5] She was "brave, constant, tender possessed nerves of steel, and willing to join the fight as necessary, encourage[d] the men to greater valor, or remain[ed] in the rear treating wounds." [6] Etheridge was repeatedly exposed to the same hardships as the soldiers she treated, such as sleeping on the ground in camp.[4]The death of her father gave her the longing to save every solder.

Various accounts locate Etheridge at notable battles, such as both battles of Bull Run, Williamsburg, Antietam, Fredricksburg, and Gettysburg.[7] Etheridge was also in every battle of the Army of the Potomac except the battle of South Mountain.[8] In 1864, all women were ordered out of camp as a result of an order from General Ulysses S. Grant.[9] As a testimony to Etheridge's admirable service, numerous officers signed a petition addressed to Gen. Grant to allow Etheridge to remain in service on the field.[9] "Gentle Annie" then worked for the Hospital Transport Service, a subcommittee of the U.S. Sanitary Commission.[10] Assigned to the *Knickerbocker*, under Amy M. Bradley, she aided in the transportation of wounded men from the ports of Alexandria, Virginia, to Philadelphia, New York City, and Washington.[10] By early 1863, she had returned to vivandière duties in the Army of the Potomac.[11] For her work and courage, she received the Kearny Cross.[10]

## After the war

Etheridge's service ended with the Fifth Michigan in Detroit on July 1, 1865.[12][4] Like so many women who served, Etheridge was never paid for her service.[4] After the war, she married and worked in the United States Treasury Department, eventually receiving a monthly pension of $25 for her unpaid military service.[12] Etheridge was honored with the Kearny Cross for her bravery in service.[13] She died January 23, 1913, and was buried with veteran's honors in Arlington National Cemetery.[14][12]

# David Farragut

*Farragut as a rear admiral c.*
*1862–1864*

**David Glasgow Farragut** /ˈfærəgət/ (also spelled Glascoe;[1][2][3][4] July 5, 1801–August 14, 1870) was a flag officer of the United States Navy during the American Civil War. He was the first rear admiral, vice admiral, and admiral in the United States Navy.[5][6] He is remembered for his order at the Battle of Mobile Bay usually paraphrased as "Damn the torpedoes, full speed ahead" in U.S. Navy tradition.[7][8]

Born near Knoxville, Tennessee, Farragut was fostered by naval officer David Porter after the death of his mother. Despite his young age, Farragut served in the War of 1812 under the command of his adoptive father. He received his first command in 1824 and participated in anti-piracy operations in the Caribbean Sea. He served in the Mexican–American War under the command of Matthew C. Perry, participating in the blockade of Tuxpan. After the war, he oversaw the construction of the Mare Island Naval Shipyard, the first U.S. Navy base established on the Pacific Ocean.

Though Farragut resided in Norfolk, Virginia prior to the Civil War, he was a Southern Unionist who strongly opposed Southern secession and remained loyal to the Union after the outbreak of the Civil War. Despite some doubts about Farragut's loyalty, Farragut was assigned command of an attack on the important Confederate port city of New Orleans. After fighting past Fort St. Philip and Fort Jackson, Farragut captured New Orleans in April 1862. He was promoted to rear admiral after the battle and helped extend Union control up along the Mississippi River, participating in the Siege of Port Hudson. With the Union in control of the Mississippi, Farragut led a successful attack on Mobile Bay, home to the last major Confederate port on the Gulf of Mexico. Farragut was promoted to admiral following the end of the Civil War and remained on active duty until his death in 1870.

## Civil War service

Though living in Norfolk, Virginia prior to the American Civil War, Farragut made it clear to all who knew him that he regarded secession as treason. Just before the war's outbreak, Farragut moved with his Virginian-born wife to Hastings-on-Hudson, a small town just outside New York City.[9][23]

He offered his services to the Union, and was initially given a seat on the Naval Retirement Board. Offered a command by his foster brother, David Dixon Porter, for a special assignment, he hesitated upon learning the target might be Norfolk. As he had

*Rear Admiral David G. Farragut, c. 1863*

friends and relatives living there, he was relieved to learn the target was changed to his former childhood home of New Orleans. The navy had some doubts about Farragut's loyalty to the Union because of his Southern birth as well as that of his wife. Porter argued on his behalf, and Farragut was accepted for the major role of attacking New Orleans.[23]

Farragut was appointed under secret instructions on February 3, 1862, to command the Gulf Blockading Squadron, sailing from Hampton Roads on the screw steamer USS *Hartford*, bearing 25 guns, which he made his flagship, accompanied by a fleet of 17 ships. He reached the mouth of the Mississippi River, near Confederate forts St. Philip and Jackson, situated opposite one another along the banks of the river, with a combined armament of more than 100 heavy guns and a complement of 700 men. Now aware of Farragut's approach, the Confederates had amassed a fleet of 16 gunboats just outside New Orleans.[24]

On April 18, Farragut ordered the mortar boats, under the command of Porter, to commence bombardment on the two forts, inflicting considerable damage, but not enough to compel the Confederates to surrender. After two days of heavy bombardment, Farragut ran past forts Jackson and St. Philip and the Chalmette batteries to take the city and port of New Orleans on April 29, a decisive event in the war.[25]

Congress honored him by creating the rank of rear admiral on July 16, 1862, a rank never before used in the U.S. Navy. Before this time, the American Navy had resisted the rank of admiral, preferring the term "flag officer," to distinguish the rank from the traditions of the European navies.

Later that year, Farragut passed the batteries defending Vicksburg, Mississippi, but had no success there. A makeshift Confederate ironclad forced his flotilla of 38 ships to withdraw in July 1862.

While an aggressive commander, Farragut was not always cooperative. At the Siege of Port Hudson, the plan was that Farragut's flotilla would pass by the guns of the Confederate stronghold with the help of a diversionary land attack by the Army of the Gulf, commanded by General Nathaniel Banks, to commence at 8:00 a.m. on March 15, 1863. Farragut unilaterally decided to move the timetable up to 9:00 p.m. on March 14, and initiated his run past the guns before Union ground forces were in position. The consequently uncoordinated attack allowed

*Farragut on board* Hartford

the Confederates to concentrate on Farragut's flotilla and inflict heavy damage to his warships.

Farragut's flotilla was forced to retreat with only two ships able to pass the heavy cannon of the Confederate bastion. After surviving the gauntlet, Farragut played no further part in the battle for Port Hudson, and General Banks was left to continue the siege without the advantage of naval support. The Union Army made two major attacks on the fort; both were repulsed with heavy losses. Farragut's flotilla was splintered, yet was able to blockade the mouth of the Red River with the two remaining warships; he could not efficiently patrol the section of the Mississippi between Port Hudson and Vicksburg. Farragut's decision proved costly to the Union Navy and the Union Army, which suffered its highest casualty rate of the war at Port Hudson.

Vicksburg surrendered on July 4, 1863, leaving Port Hudson as the last remaining Confederate stronghold on the Mississippi River. General Banks accepted the surrender of the Confederate garrison at Port Hudson on July 9, ending the longest siege in U.S. military history. Control of the Mississippi River was the centerpiece of the Union strategy to win the war, and, with the surrender of Port Hudson, the Confederacy was now cut in two.

On August 5, 1864, Farragut won a great victory in the Battle of Mobile Bay. Mobile, Alabama, was then the Confederacy's last major open port on the Gulf of Mexico. The bay was heavily mined (tethered naval mines were then known as "torpedoes").[26] Farragut ordered his fleet to charge the bay. When the monitor USS *Tecumseh* struck a mine and sank, the others began to pull back.

*Rear admiral David Farragut and General Gordon Granger*

From his high perch, where he was lashed to the rigging of his flagship, USS *Hartford*, Farragut could see the ships pulling back. "What's the trouble?" he shouted through a trumpet to USS *Brooklyn*. "Torpedoes," was the shouted reply. "Damn the torpedoes.," said Farragut, "Four bells, Captain Drayton, go ahead. Jouett, full speed."[27][28] The bulk of the fleet succeeded in entering the bay. Farragut triumphed over the opposition of heavy batteries in Fort Morgan and Fort Gaines to defeat the squadron of Admiral Franklin Buchanan.

On December 21, 1864, Lincoln promoted Farragut to vice admiral.

## Post-Civil War service

After the Civil War, Farragut was elected a companion of the first class of the New York Commandery of the Military Order of the Loyal Legion of the United States on March 18, 1866, and assigned insignia number 231. He served as the commander of the Commandery of New York from May 1866 to until his death.

Farragut was promoted to full admiral on July 25, 1866, becoming the first U.S. Navy officer to hold that rank.[6]

His last active service was in command of the European Squadron, from 1867 to 1868, with the screw frigate USS *Franklin* as his flagship. Farragut remained on active duty for life, an honor accorded to only seven other U.S. Navy officers after the Civil War.[29]

## Death

Farragut died from a heart attack at the age of 69 in Portsmouth, New Hampshire, while on vacation in the late summer of 1870. He had served almost sixty years in the navy. He is interred at Woodlawn Cemetery, in The Bronx, New York City.[30] His gravesite is listed on the National Register of Historic Places, as is Woodlawn Cemetery itself.

# Nathan Bedford Forrest

**Nathan Bedford Forrest** (July 13, 1821–October 29, 1877) was a Confederate Army general during the American Civil War. Although scholars generally respect Forrest as a military strategist, he has remained a controversial figure in Southern racial history, especially for his role in the massacre of black soldiers at Fort Pillow, and his 1867–1869 leadership of the white-supremacist and terrorist organization known as the Ku Klux Klan.

Before the war, Forrest amassed substantial wealth as a cotton plantation owner, horse and cattle trader, real estate broker, and slave trader. In June 1861, he enlisted in the Confederate Army, one of the few officers during the war to enlist as a private and be promoted to general without any prior military training. An expert cavalry leader, Forrest was given command of a corps and established new doctrines for mobile forces, earning the nickname "The Wizard of the Saddle." His methods influenced future generations of military strategists, although the Confederate high command is seen by some commentators to have underutilized his talents.[3]

In April 1864, in what has been called "one of the bleakest, saddest events of American military history,"[4] troops under Forrest's command massacred Union troops who had surrendered, most of them black soldiers along with some white Southern Tennesseans fighting for the Union, at the Battle of Fort Pillow. Forrest was blamed for the massacre in the Union press and that news may have strengthened the North's resolve to win the war.

Forrest joined the Ku Klux Klan in 1867 (two years after its founding) and was elected its first Grand Wizard. The group was a loose collection of local factions throughout the former Confederacy, that used violence and the threat of violence to maintain white control over the newly-enfranchised slaves. The Klan, with Forrest at the lead, suppressed voting rights of blacks in the South through violence and intimidation during the elections of 1868. In 1869, Forrest expressed disillusionment with the lack of discipline among the various white supremacist groups across the South, and issued a letter ordering the dissolution of the Ku Klux Klan and the destruction of its costumes; he then withdrew from the organization. In the last years of his life, Forrest publicly denounced the violence and racism of the Klan, insisted he had never been a member, and made a public speech in favor of racial harmony.

## American Civil War (1861–1865)

## Early cavalry command

After the Civil War broke out, Forrest returned to Tennessee from his Mississippi ventures and enlisted in the Confederate States Army (CSA) on June 14, 1861. He reported for training at Fort Wright near Randolph, Tennessee,[33] joining Captain Josiah White's cavalry company, the Tennessee Mounted Rifles (Seventh Tennessee Cavalry), as a private along with his youngest brother and 15-year-old son. Upon seeing how badly equipped the CSA was, Forrest offered to buy horses and equipment with his own money for a regiment of Tennessee volunteer soldiers.[12][34]

His superior officers and Governor of Tennessee Isham G. Harris were surprised that someone of Forrest's wealth and prominence had enlisted as a soldier, especially since major planters were exempted from service. They commissioned him as a lieutenant colonel and authorized him to recruit and train a battalion of Confederate mounted rangers.[35] In October 1861, Forrest was given command of a regiment, the 3rd Tennessee Cavalry. Though Forrest had no prior formal military training or experience, he had exhibited leadership and soon proved he could successfully employ tactics.[22][36]

Public debate surrounded Tennessee's decision to join the Confederacy and both the Confederate and Union armies recruited soldiers from the state. More than 100,000 men from Tennessee served with the Confederacy and over 31,000 served with the Union.[37] Forrest posted advertisements to join his regiment, with the slogan, "Let's have some fun and kill some Yankees!."[38] Forrest's command included his Escort Company (his "Special Forces"), for which he selected the best soldiers available. This unit, which varied in size from 40 to 90 men, constituted the elite of his cavalry.[39]

## Sacramento and Fort Donelson

*Col. Bedford Forrest*

Forrest won praise for his performance under fire during an early victory in the Battle of Sacramento in Kentucky, the first in which he commanded troops in the field, where he routed a Union force by personally leading a cavalry charge that was later commended by his commander, Brigadier General Charles Clark.[40][41] Forrest distinguished himself further at the Battle of Fort Donelson in February 1862. After his cavalry captured a Union artillery battery, he broke out of a siege headed by Major General Ulysses S. Grant, rallying nearly 4,000 troops and leading them to escape across the Cumberland River.[42]

A few days after the Confederate surrender of Fort Donelson, with the fall of Nashville to Union forces imminent, Forrest took command of the city. All available carts and wagons were pressed into service to haul six hundred boxes of army clothing, 250,000 pounds of bacon and forty wagon-loads of ammunition to the railroad depots, to be sent off to Chattanooga and Decatur.[43][44] Forrest arranged for the heavy ordnance machinery, including a new cannon rifling machine and fourteen cannons, as well as parts from the Nashville Armory, to be sent to Atlanta for use by the Confederate Army.[45]

## Shiloh and Murfreesboro

A month later, Forrest was back in action at the Battle of Shiloh, fought April 6–7, 1862. He commanded a Confederate rear guard after the Union victory. In the battle of Fallen Timbers, he drove through the Union skirmish line. Not realizing that the rest of his men had halted their charge when they reached the full Union brigade, Forrest charged the brigade alone and soon found himself surrounded. He emptied his Colt Army revolvers into the swirling mass of Union soldiers and pulled out his saber, hacking and slashing. A Union infantryman on the ground beside Forrest fired a musket ball at him with a point-blank shot, nearly knocking him out of the saddle. The ball went through Forrest's pelvis and lodged near his spine. A surgeon removed the musket ball a week later, without anesthesia, which was unavailable.[26][46]

By early summer, Forrest commanded a new brigade of inexperienced cavalry regiments. In July, he led them into Middle Tennessee under orders to launch a cavalry raid, and on July 13, 1862, led them into the First Battle of Murfreesboro, as a result of which all of the Union units surrendered to Forrest, and the Confederates destroyed much of the Union's supplies and railroad track in the area.[47]

## West Tennessee raids

*Gen. Bedford Forrest*

Promoted on July 21, 1862, to brigadier general, Forrest was given command of a Confederate cavalry brigade.[48] In December 1862, Forrest's veteran troopers were reassigned by General Braxton Bragg to another officer, against his protest. Forrest had to recruit a new brigade, composed of about 2,000 inexperienced recruits, most of whom lacked weapons.[49] Again, Bragg ordered a series of raids, this time into west Tennessee, to disrupt the communications of the Union forces under Grant, which were threatening the city of Vicksburg, Mississippi. Forrest protested that to send such untrained men behind enemy lines was suicidal, but Bragg insisted, and Forrest obeyed his orders. In the ensuing raids he was pursued by thousands of Union soldiers trying to locate his fast-moving forces. Avoiding attack by never staying in one place long, Forrest led his troops in raids as far north as the banks of the Ohio River in southwest Kentucky.[50]

Forrest returned to his base in Mississippi with more men than he had started with. By then, all were fully armed with captured Union weapons. As a result, Grant was forced to revise and delay the strategy of his Vicksburg campaign. Newspaper correspondent Sylvanus Cadwallader, who traveled with Grant for three years during his campaigns, wrote that Forrest "was the only Confederate cavalryman of whom Grant stood in much dread."[51][52]

## Dover, Brentwood, and Chattanooga

The Union Army gained military control of Tennessee in 1862 and occupied it for the duration of the war, having taken control of strategic cities and railroads. Forrest continued to lead his men in small-scale operations, including the Battle of Dover and the Battle of Brentwood until April 1863. The Confederate army dispatched him with a small force into the backcountry of northern Alabama and western Georgia to defend against an attack of 3,000 Union cavalrymen commanded by Colonel Abel Streight. Streight had orders to cut the Confederate railroad south of Chattanooga, Tennessee to seal off Bragg's supply line and force him to retreat into Georgia.[53] Forrest chased Streight's men for 16 days, harassing them all the way. Streight's goal changed from dismantling the railroad to escaping the pursuit. On May 3, Forrest caught up with Streight's unit east of Cedar Bluff, Alabama. Forrest had fewer men than the Union side but feigned having a larger force by parading some repeatedly around a hilltop until Streight was convinced to surrender his 1,500 or so exhausted troops (historians Kevin Dougherty and Keith S. Hebert say he had about 1,700 men).[54][55][56]

## Day's Gap, Chickamauga, and Paducah

Not all of Forrest's exploits of individual combat involved enemy troops. Lieutenant Andrew Wills Gould, an artillery officer in Forrest's command, was being transferred, presumably because cannons under his command[57] were spiked (disabled) by the enemy[58] during the Battle of Day's Gap. On June 13, 1863, Gould confronted Forrest about his transfer, which escalated into a violent exchange.[59] Gould shot Forrest in the hip and Forrest mortally stabbed Gould.[60] Forrest was thought to have been fatally wounded by Gould but he recovered and was ready to fight in the Chickamauga Campaign.[6]

Forrest served with the main army at the Battle of Chickamauga on September 18–20, 1863, in which he pursued the retreating Union army and took hundreds of prisoners.[61] Like several others under Bragg's command, he urged an immediate follow-up attack to recapture Chattanooga, which had fallen a few weeks before. Bragg failed to do so, upon which Forrest was quoted as saying, "What does he fight battles for?"[62][63] The story that Forrest confronted and threatened the life of Bragg in the fall of 1863, following the battle of Chickamauga, and that Bragg transferred Forrest to command in Mississippi as a direct result, is now considered to be apocryphal.[64][65][66]

On December 4, 1863, Forrest was promoted to the rank of major general.[67] On March 25, 1864, Forrest's cavalry raided the town of Paducah, Kentucky in the Battle of Paducah, during which Forrest demanded the surrender of U.S. Colonel Stephen G. Hicks: " . . . if I have to storm your works, you may expect no quarter." Hicks refused to comply with the ultimatum, and according to his subsequent report, Forrest's troops took a position and set up a battery of guns while a flag of truce was still up. As soon as they received the Union reply, they moved forward at the command of a junior officer, and the Union forces opened fire. The Confederates tried to storm the fort, but were repulsed; they rallied and made two more attempts, both of which failed.[68][69][70]

## Fort Pillow massacre

Fort Pillow, located 40 miles (64 km) upriver from Memphis (near Henning, Tennessee), was originally constructed by Confederate general Gideon Johnson Pillow on the bluffs of the Mississippi River, and taken over by Union forces in 1862 after the Confederates had abandoned the fort.[71] The fort was manned by 557 Union troops, 295 white and 262 black, under Union commander Maj. L.F. Booth.[71]

On April 12, 1864, Forrest's men, under Brig. Gen. James Chalmers, attacked and recaptured Fort Pillow.[71] Booth and his adjutant were killed in the battle, leaving Fort Pillow under the command of Major William Bradford.[71] Forrest had reached the fort at 10:00 a.m. after a hard ride from Mississippi,[71] and his horse was soon shot out from under him, causing him to fall to the ground. He then mounted a second horse, which was shot out from under him as well, forcing him to mount a third horse.[71] By 3:30 p.m., Forrest had concluded that the Union troops could not hold the fort, thus he ordered a flag of truce raised and demanded that the fort be surrendered.[72] Bradford refused to surrender, believing his troops could escape to the Union gunboat, USS *New Era*, on the Mississippi River.[72] Forrest's men immediately took over the fort, while Union soldiers retreated to the lower bluffs of the river, but the *USS New Era* did not come to their rescue.[72] What happened next became known as the *Fort Pillow Massacre*.[73] As the Union troops surrendered, Forrest's men opened fire, slaughtering both black and white soldiers. [73][74][75] According to historians John Cimprich and Bruce Tap, although their numbers were roughly equal, two thirds of the black Union soldiers were killed, while only a third of the whites were killed.[76][77] The atrocities at Fort Pillow continued throughout the night. Conflicting accounts of what actually occurred were given later.[78][79][80]

Forrest's Confederate forces were accused of subjecting Union captured soldiers to extreme brutality, with allegations of back-shooting soldiers who fled into the river, shooting wounded soldiers, burning men alive, nailing men to barrels and igniting them, crucifixion, and hacking men to death with sabers.[81] Forrest's men were alleged to have set fire to a Union barracks with wounded Union soldiers inside[82][83] In defense of their actions, Forrest's men insisted that the Union soldiers, although fleeing, kept their weapons and frequently turned to shoot, forcing the Confederates to keep firing in self-defense.[84] The rebels said the Union flag was still flying over the fort, which indicated that the force had not formally surrendered. A contemporary newspaper account from Jackson, Tennessee stated that "General Forrest begged them to surrender" but "not the first sign of surrender was ever given." Similar accounts were reported in many Southern newspapers at the time.[85] These statements, however, were contradicted by Union survivors, as well as by the letter of a Confederate soldier who graphically recounted a massacre. Achilles Clark, a soldier with the 20th Tennessee cavalry, wrote to his sisters immediately after the battle:

> The slaughter was awful. Words cannot describe the scene. The poor deluded negroes would run up to our men fall upon their knees and with uplifted hands scream for mercy but they were ordered to their feet and then shot down. The white men fared but little better. Their fort turned out to be a great slaughter pen. Blood, human blood stood about in pools and brains could have been gathered up in any quantity.[86][87][88]

Following the cessation of hostilities, Forrest transferred the 14 most seriously wounded United States Colored Troops (USCT) to the U.S. steamer *Silver Cloud*.[89] The 226 Union troops taken prisoner at Fort Pillow were marched under guard to Holly Springs, Mississippi and then convoyed to Demopolis, Alabama. On April 21, Capt. John Goodwin, of Forrest's cavalry command, forwarded a dispatch listing the prisoners captured. The list included the names of 7 officers and 219 white enlisted soldiers. According to Richard L. Fuchs, records concerning the black prisoners are "nonexistent or unreliable."[90] President Abraham Lincoln asked his cabinet for opinions as to how the Union should respond to the massacre.[91]

At the time of the massacre, General Grant was no longer in Tennessee but had transferred to the east to command all Union troops. He wrote in his memoirs that Forrest in his report of the battle had "left out the part which shocks humanity to read."[92]

Because of the events at Fort Pillow, the Northern public and press viewed Forrest as a war criminal.[93] The *Chicago Tribune* said Forrest and his brothers were "slave drivers and woman whippers," while Forrest himself was described as "mean, vindictive, cruel, and unscrupulous."[93] The Southern press steadfastly defended Forrest's reputation.[94][95]

## Brice's Crossroads and Tupelo

Forrest's most decisive victory came on June 10, 1864, when his 3,500-man force clashed with 8,500 men commanded by Union Brig. Gen. Samuel D. Sturgis at the Battle of Brice's Crossroads in northeastern Mississippi.[96] Here, the mobility of the troops under his command and his superior tactics led to victory,[97][98] allowing him to continue harassing Union forces in southwestern Tennessee and northern Mississippi throughout the war.[99] Forrest set up a position for an attack to repulse a pursuing force commanded by Sturgis, who had been sent to impede Forrest from destroying Union supply lines and fortifications.[100] When Sturgis's Federal army came upon the crossroads, they collided with Forrest's cavalry. [101] Sturgis ordered his infantry to advance to the front line to counteract the cavalry. The infantry, tired, weary and suffering under the heat, were quickly broken and sent into mass retreat. Forrest sent a full charge after the retreating army and captured 16 artillery pieces, 176 wagons and 1,500 stands of small arms. In all, the maneuver cost Forrest 96 men killed and 396 wounded. The day was worse for Union troops, which suffered 223 killed,

394 wounded and 1,623 missing. The losses were a deep blow to the black regiment under Sturgis's command. In the hasty retreat, they stripped off commemorative badges that read "Remember Fort Pillow" to avoid goading the Confederate force pursuing them.[102]

One month later, while serving under General Stephen D. Lee, Forrest experienced tactical defeat at the Battle of Tupelo in 1864.[103] Concerned about Union supply lines, Maj. Gen. Sherman sent a force under the command of Maj. Gen. Andrew J. Smith to deal with Forrest.[104] Union forces drove the Confederates from the field and Forrest was wounded in the foot, but his forces were not wholly destroyed.[105] He continued to oppose Union efforts in the West for the remainder of the war.

## Tennessee Raids

Forrest led other raids that summer and fall, including a famous one into Union-held downtown Memphis in August 1864 (the Second Battle of Memphis)[105] and another on a major Union supply depot at Johnsonville, Tennessee. On November 4, 1864, during the Battle of Johnsonville, the Confederates shelled the city, sinking three gunboats and nearly thirty other ships and destroying many tons of supplies.[106] During Hood's Tennessee Campaign, he fought alongside General John Bell Hood, the newest commander of the Confederate Army of Tennessee, in the Second Battle of Franklin on November 30.[107] Facing a disastrous defeat, Forrest argued bitterly with Hood (his superior officer) demanding permission to cross the Harpeth River and cut off the escape route of Union Maj. Gen. John M. Schofield's army.[108] He eventually made the attempt, but it was too late.

## Murfreesboro, Nashville, and Selma

After his bloody defeat at Franklin, Hood continued on to Nashville. Hood ordered Forrest to conduct an independent raid against the Murfreesboro garrison. After success in achieving the objectives specified by Hood, Forrest engaged Union forces near Murfreesboro on December 5, 1864. In what would be known as the Third Battle of Murfreesboro, a portion of Forrest's command broke and ran.[109] When Hood's battle-hardened Army of Tennessee, consisting of 40,000 men deployed in three infantry corps plus 10,000 to 15,000 cavalry, was all but destroyed on December 15–16, at the Battle of Nashville,[110] Forrest distinguished himself by commanding the Confederate rear guard in a series of actions that allowed what was left of the army to escape. For this, he would later be promoted to the rank of lieutenant general on March 2, 1865.[111] A portion of his command, now dismounted, was surprised and captured in their camp at Verona, Mississippi on December 25, 1864, during a raid of the Mobile and Ohio Railroad by a brigade of Brig. Gen. Benjamin Grierson's cavalry division.[112]

In the spring of 1865, Forrest led an unsuccessful defense of the state of Alabama against Wilson's Raid. His opponent, Brig. Gen. James H. Wilson, defeated Forrest at the Battle of Selma on April 2, 1865.[113] A week later, General Robert E. Lee surrendered to Grant in Virginia. When he received news of Lee's surrender, Forrest surrendered as well. On May 9, 1865, at Gainesville, Forrest read his farewell address to the men under his command, enjoining them to "submit to the powers to be, and to aid in restoring peace and establishing law and order throughout the land."[114]

## Postwar years and later life
### Business ventures
As a former slave trader and slave owner, Forrest experienced the abolition of slavery at war's end as a major financial setback. He had become interested in the area around Crowley's Ridge during the war, and took up civilian life in 1865 in Memphis, Tennessee. In 1866, Forrest and C.C. McCreanor contracted to finish the Memphis & Little Rock Railroad, including a right-of-way that passed over the ridge.[115] The ridgetop commissary he built as a provisioning store for the 1,000 Irish laborers hired to lay the rails became the nucleus of a town, which most residents called "Forrest's Town" and which was incorporated as Forrest City, Arkansas in 1870.[116]

## Ku Klux Klan membership
Forrest was an early member of the Ku Klux Klan ("KKK" or simply "the Klan"), which was formed by six veterans of the Confederate Army in Pulaski, Tennessee during the spring of 1866[128][129][130] and soon expanded throughout the state and beyond. Forrest became involved sometime in late 1866 or early 1867. A common report is that Forrest arrived in Nashville in April 1867 while the Klan was meeting at the Maxwell House Hotel, probably at the encouragement of a state Klan leader, former Confederate general George Gordon.[131] The organization had grown to the point where an experienced commander was needed, and Forrest was well-suited to the role. In Room 10 of the Maxwell, Forrest was sworn in as a member by John W. Morton.[132][133] Brian Steel Wills quotes two KKK members who identified Forrest as a Klan leader.[134] James R. Crowe stated, "After the order grew to large numbers we found it necessary to have someone of large experience to command. We chose General Forrest."[135] Another member wrote, "N. B. Forest of Confederate fame was at our head, and was known as the Grand Wizard. I heard him make a speech in one of our Dens."[134] The title "Grand Wizard" was chosen because General Forrest had been known as "The Wizard of the Saddle" during the war. [136] According to Jack Hurst's 1993 biography, "Two years after Appomattox, Forrest was reincarnated as grand wizard of the Ku Klux Klan. As the Klan's first national leader, he became the Lost Cause's avenging angel, galvanizing a loose collection of boyish secret social clubs into a reactionary instrument of terror still feared today."[137] Forrest was the Klan's first and only Grand Wizard, and he was active in recruitment for the Klan from 1867 to 1868.[138][139][140][141][142][143][144]

Following the war, the United States Congress began passing the Reconstruction Acts to specify conditions for the readmission of former Confederate States to the Union,[145] [146][147] including ratification of the Fourteenth (1868) and Fifteenth (1870) Amendments to the United States Constitution. The Fourteenth addressed citizenship rights and equal protection of the laws for former slaves, while the Fifteenth specifically secured the voting rights of black men.[148] According to Wills, in the August 1867 state elections the Klan was relatively restrained in its actions. White Americans who made up the KKK hoped to persuade black voters that a return to their pre-war state of bondage was in their best interest. Forrest assisted in maintaining order. It was after these efforts failed that Klan violence and intimidation escalated and became widespread.[149] Author Andrew Ward, however, writes, "In the spring of 1867, Forrest and his dragoons launched a campaign of midnight parades; 'ghost' masquerades; and 'whipping' and even 'killing Negro voters and white Republicans, to scare blacks off voting and running for office'."[150]

In an 1868 interview by a Cincinnati newspaper, Forrest claimed that the Klan had 40,000 members in Tennessee and 550,000 total members throughout the Southern states. [151][152] He said he sympathized with them, but denied any formal connection, although he claimed he could muster thousands of men himself. He described the Klan as "a protective political military organization . . . The members are sworn to recognize the government of the United States . . . Its objects originally were protection against Loyal Leagues and the Grand Army of the Republic . . ."[153][154] After only a year as Grand Wizard, in January 1869, faced with an ungovernable membership employing methods that seemed increasingly counterproductive, Forrest dissolved the Klan, ordered their costumes destroyed,[155] and withdrew from participation. His declaration had little effect, however, and few Klansmen destroyed their robes and hoods.[156]

## Democratic convention 1868

The Klan's activity infiltrated the Democratic Party's campaign for the presidential election of 1868. Prominent ex-Confederates, including Forrest, the Grand Wizard of the Klan, and South Carolina's Wade Hampton, attended as delegates at the 1868 Democratic Convention, held at Tammany Hall headquarters at 141 East 14th Street in New York City.[157] Forrest rode to the convention on a train that stopped in a small Northern town along the way, where he faced a protester who wanted to fight the "damned butcher" of Fort Pillow.[158] Former Governor of New York Horatio Seymour was nominated as the Democratic presidential candidate, while Forrest's friend, Frank Blair, Jr. was nominated as the Democratic vice presidential candidate, Seymour's running mate. [159] The Seymour-Blair Democratic ticket's campaign slogan was: "Our Ticket, Our Motto, This Is a White Man's Country; Let White Men Rule." [159] The Democratic Party platform denounced the Reconstruction Acts as unconstitutional, void, and revolutionary.[160] The party advocated termination of the Freedman's Bureau and any government policy designed to aid blacks in the South. [160] These developments worked to the advantage of the Republicans, who focused on the Democratic Party's alleged disloyalty during and after the Civil War.[160]

## Election of 1868 and Grant

During the presidential election of 1868, the Ku Klux Klan under the leadership of Forrest, and other terrorist groups, used brutal violence and intimidation against blacks and Republican voters.[161][162] Forrest played a prominent role in the spread of the Klan in the South, meeting with racist whites in Atlanta several times between February and March 1868. Forrest probably organized a statewide Klan network in Georgia during these visits.[163] On March 31 the Klan struck, killing prominent Republican organizer George Ashburn in Columbus.[163]

The Republicans had nominated one of Forrest's battle adversaries, Union war hero Ulysses S. Grant, for the Presidency at their convention held in October. Klansmen took their orders from their former Confederate officers.[162] In Louisiana, 1,000 blacks were killed to suppress Republican voting. In Georgia, blacks and Republicans also faced a lot of violence. The Klan's violence was primarily designed to intimidate voters, targeting black and white supporters of the Republican Party.[163] The Klan's violent tactics backfired, as Grant, whose slogan was "Let us have peace," won the election and Republicans gained a majority in Congress.[161] Grant defeated Horatio Seymour, the Democratic presidential candidate, by a comfortable electoral margin, 214 to 80.[164] The popular vote was much closer: Grant received 3,013,365 (*52.7 percent*) votes, while Seymour received 2,708,744 (*47.3 percent*) votes.[164] Grant lost Georgia and Louisiana, where the violence and intimidation against blacks was most prominent.

## Klan prosecution and Congressional testimony (1871)

Many in the north, including President Grant, backed the passage of the Fifteenth Amendment, that gave voting rights to Americans regardless of "race, color, or previous condition of servitude." Congress and Grant passed the Enforcement Acts from 1870 to 1871, to protect "registration, voting, officeholding, or jury service" of African Americans. Under these laws enforced by Grant and the newly-formed Department of Justice, there were over 5,000 indictments and 1,000 convictions of Klan members across the South.[161]

Forrest testified before the Congressional investigation of Klan activities on June 27, 1871. He denied membership, but his individual role in the KKK was beyond the scope of the investigating committee, which wrote: "Our design is not to connect General Forrest with this order (the reader may form his own conclusion upon this question) . . . "[165] The committee also noted, "The natural tendency of all such organizations is to violence and crime; hence it was that General Forrest and other men of influence in the state, by the exercise of their moral power, induced them to disband."[166] George Cantor, a biographer of Confederate generals, wrote, "Forrest ducked and weaved, denying all knowledge, but admitted he knew some of the people involved. He sidestepped some questions and pleaded failure of memory on others. Afterwards, he admitted to 'gentlemanly lies.' He wanted nothing more to do with the Klan, but felt honor bound to protect former associates."[167]

## Differences with Southern White majority (1870s)

After the lynch mob murder of four blacks who had been arrested for defending themselves in a brawl at a barbecue, Forrest wrote to Tennessee Governor John C. Brown in August 1874 and "volunteered to help 'exterminate' those men responsible for the continued violence against the blacks," offering "to exterminate the white marauders who disgrace their race by this cowardly murder of Negroes."[120]

On July 5, 1875, Forrest gave a speech before the Independent Order of Pole-Bearers Association, a post-war organization of black Southerners advocating to improve the economic condition of blacks and to gain equal rights for all citizens. At this, his last public appearance, he made what *The New York Times* described as a "friendly speech"[168][169] during which, when offered a bouquet of flowers by a young black woman, he accepted them,[170] thanked her and kissed her on the cheek. Forrest spoke in encouragement of black advancement and of endeavoring to be a proponent for espousing peace and harmony between black and white Americans.[171]

In response to the Pole-Bearers speech, the Cavalry Survivors Association of Augusta, the first Confederate organization formed after the war, called a meeting in which Captain F. Edgeworth Eve gave a speech expressing strong disapproval of Forrest's remarks promoting inter-ethnic harmony, ridiculing his faculties and judgment and berating the woman who gave Forrest flowers as "a mulatto wench." The association voted unanimously to amend its constitution to expressly forbid publicly advocating for or hinting at any association of white women and girls as being in the same classes as "females of the negro race."[172][173] The *Macon Weekly Telegraph* newspaper also condemned Forrest for his speech, describing the event as "the recent disgusting exhibition of himself at the negro [*sic*] jamboree" and quoting part of a *Charlotte Observer* article, which read "We have infinitely more respect for Longstreet, who fraternizes with negro men on public occasions, with the pay for the treason to his race in his pocket, than with Forrest and [General] Pillow, who equalize with the negro women, with only 'futures' in payment."[174][175]

## Death

Forrest reportedly died from acute complications of diabetes at the Memphis home of his brother Jesse on October 29, 1877.[176] His eulogy was delivered by his recent spiritual mentor, former Confederate chaplain George Tucker Stainback, who declared in his eulogy: "Lieutenant-General Nathan Bedford Forrest, though dead, yet speaketh. His acts have photographed themselves upon the hearts of thousands, and will speak there forever."[177]

Forrest was buried at Elmwood Cemetery in Memphis.[178] In 1904, the remains of Forrest and his wife Mary were disinterred from Elmwood and moved to a Memphis city park that was originally named Forrest Park in his honor, but has since been renamed Health Sciences Park.[179]

On July 7, 2015, the Memphis City Council unanimously voted to remove the statue of Forrest from Health Sciences Park, and to return the remains of Forrest and his wife to Elmwood Cemetery.[180] However, on October 13, 2017, the Tennessee Historical Commission invoked the Tennessee Heritage Protection Act of 2013 and U.S. Public Law 85–425: Sec. 410 to overrule the city.[181] Consequently, Memphis sold the park land to a non-profit entity not subject to the Tennessee Heritage Protection Act (Memphis Greenspace), which immediately removed the monument as explained below.

## Historical reputation and legacy

### Military doctrines

Forrest is considered one of the Civil War's most brilliant tacticians by the historian Spencer C. Tucker.[205] Forrest fought by simple rules; he maintained that "war means fighting and fighting means killing" and the way to win was "to get there first with the most men."[206] Union General William Tecumseh Sherman called him "that devil Forrest" in wartime communications with Ulysses S. Grant and considered him "the most remarkable man our civil war produced on either side."[207][208][3]

Forrest became well known for his early use of maneuver tactics as applied to a mobile horse cavalry deployment.[209] He grasped the doctrines of mobile warfare[210] that would eventually become prevalent in the 20th century. Paramount in his strategy was fast movement, even if it meant pushing his horses at a killing pace, to constantly harass the enemy during raids by disrupting their supply trains and communications with the destruction of railroad tracks and the cutting of telegraph lines, as he wheeled around his opponent's flank. The Civil War scholar Bruce Catton writes:

> Forrest . . . used his horsemen as a modern general would use motorized infantry. He liked horses because he liked fast movement, and his mounted men could get from here to there much faster than any infantry could; but when they reached the field they usually tied their horses to trees and fought on foot, and they were as good as the very best infantry.[211]

Forrest is often erroneously quoted as saying his strategy was to "git thar fustest with the mostest." Now often recast as "Getting there firstest with the mostest,"[212] this misquote first appeared in a *New York Tribune* article written to provide colorful comments in reaction to European interest in Civil War generals. The aphorism was addressed and corrected as "Ma'am, I got there first with the most men" by a *New York Times* story in 1918. [213] Though it was a novel and succinct condensation of the military principles of mass and maneuver, Bruce Catton writes of the spurious quote:

> Do not, under any circumstances whatever, quote Forrest as saying 'fustest' and 'mostest'. He did not say it that way, and nobody who knows anything about him imagines that he did.[214]

## Fort Pillow

Modern historians generally believe that Forrest's attack on Fort Pillow was a massacre, noting high casualty rates, and the rebels targeting black soldiers.[215] It was the South's publicly stated position that slaves firing on whites would be killed on the spot, along with Southern whites that fought for the Union, whom the Confederacy considered traitors.[216] According to this analysis, Forrest's troops were carrying out Confederate policy. The historical record does not support his repeated denials that he knew a massacre was taking place, or that he even knew a massacre had occurred at all. Consequently his role at Fort Pillow was a stigmatizing one for him the rest of his life, both professionally and personally,[217][218] and contributed to his business problems after the war.

After Forrest's death, *The New York Times* reported that "General Bedford Forrest, the great Confederate cavalry officer, died at 7:30 o'clock this evening at the residence of his brother, Colonel Jesse Forrest," but also reported that it would not be for military victories that Forrest would pass into history, i.e., he would be most remembered for Fort Pillow.[219] Forrest's claim that the Fort Pillow massacre was an invention of Northern reporters is contradicted by letters written by Confederate soldiers to their own families, which described extreme brutality on the part of Confederate troops.[88] The New York newspaper obituary stated:

> Since the war, Forrest has lived at Memphis, and his principal occupation seems to have been to try and explain away the Fort Pillow affair. He wrote several letters about it, which were published, and always had something to say about it in any public speech he delivered. He seemed as if he were trying always to rub away the blood stains which marked him.[219]

Grant himself described Forrest as "a brave and intrepid cavalry general" while noting that Forrest sent a dispatch on the Fort Pillow Massacre "in which he left out the part which shocks humanity to read."[224]

# Ulysses S. Grant

**Ulysses S. Grant** (born **Hiram Ulysses Grant**; April 27, 1822–July 23, 1885) was an American soldier and politician who served as the 18th president of the United States from 1869 to 1877. Before his presidency, Grant led the Union Army in winning the American Civil War. As president, Grant worked with the Radical Republicans in the Reconstruction of the Union while having to deal with corruption in his administration.

Raised in Ohio, young Grant developed an exceptional ability with horses, which served him well through his military career. He was admitted to West Point and graduated from the U.S. military academy in 1843. Grant served with distinction in the Mexican–American War. In 1848, he married Julia Dent, and together they had four children. Grant abruptly resigned his army commission in 1854 and returned to his family, but lived in poverty for seven years. During the Civil War, he joined the Union Army in 1861, and led the Vicksburg campaign, which gained control of the Mississippi River in 1863. After Grant's victory at Chattanooga, President Abraham Lincoln promoted Grant to Lieutenant General. For thirteen months, Grant fought Robert E. Lee during the high casualty Overland Campaign and at Petersburg. On April 9, 1865, Lee surrendered to Grant at Appomattox. A week later, Lincoln was assassinated, and was succeeded by President Andrew Johnson, who promoted Grant to General of the Army in 1866. Later Johnson and Grant bitterly clashed over Reconstruction policies; Johnson was lenient toward former Confederates, while Grant emphasized civil rights for African freedmen.

A national war hero, Grant was unanimously nominated by the Republican Party and was elected president in 1868, but he accepted the nomination with reluctance. As president, Grant stabilized the post-war national economy, created the Department of Justice, and prosecuted the Ku Klux Klan. He appointed African-Americans and Jewish-Americans to prominent federal offices. In 1871, he created the first Civil Service Commission. The Liberal Republicans and Democrats united behind Grant's opponent in the presidential election of 1872, but Grant was handily re-elected. Grant's Native American policy had both successes and failures. In foreign affairs, the Grant administration peacefully resolved the *Alabama* claims against Great Britain, but the Senate rejected Grant's prized Caribbean Dominican Republic annexation. Grant's presidency was plagued by numerous public scandals, while the Panic of 1873 plunged the nation into a severe economic depression, that allowed the Democrats win the House majority. Grant had only one role in the intensely disputed Presidential election of 1876: he guaranteed there was a peaceful compromise approved by Congress.

In his retirement, Grant was the first president to circumnavigate the world on his tour meeting with many foreign leaders. In 1880, Grant was unsuccessful in obtaining the Republican presidential nomination for a third term. In the final year of his life, facing severe financial reversals and dying of throat cancer, he wrote his memoirs, which proved to be a major critical and financial success. At the time of his death, he was memorialized as a symbol of national unity.

Historical assessments of Grant's legacy have varied. Historians have hailed Grant's military genius, and his modern strategies of warfare are featured in military history textbooks. 20th century historical rankings of presidents of the United States, ranked Grant among the worst presidents because of his high tolerance for corruption by some of his top appointees. 21st century historians have emphasized Grant's presidential accomplishments including, protection of blacks and Indians, and the first Civil Service Commission. Grant was an embattled president who faced a difficult challenge getting the entire nation to accept Reconstruction efforts.

## Civil War

BRIGADIER-GENERAL U. S. GRANT

*Brig. Gen. U.S. Grant 1861 Published 1911*

On April 12, 1861, the American Civil War began when Confederate troops attacked Fort Sumter in Charleston, South Carolina.[101] The news came as a shock in Galena, and Grant shared his neighbors' concern about the war.[102] On April 15, Lincoln called for 75,000 volunteers.[103] The next day, Grant attended a mass meeting to assess the crisis and encourage recruitment, and a speech by his father's attorney, John Aaron Rawlins, stirred Grant's patriotism.[104][m] Ready to fight, Grant recalled with satisfaction, "I never went into our leather store again."[105][n] On April 18, Grant chaired a second recruitment meeting, but turned down a captain's position as commander of the newly formed militia company, hoping his previous experience would aid him to obtain more senior military rank.[107]

### Early commands

Grant's early efforts to be recommissioned were rejected by Major General George B. McClellan and Brigadier General Nathaniel Lyon. On April 29, supported by Congressman Elihu B. Washburne of Illinois, Grant was appointed military aide to Governor Richard Yates and mustered ten regiments into the Illinois militia. On June 14, again aided by Washburne, Grant was promoted to Colonel and put in charge of the unruly 21st Illinois Volunteer Infantry Regiment, which he soon restored to good order and discipline.[108]

Colonel Grant and his 21st Regiment were transferred to Missouri to dislodge Confederate forces.[109]

On August 5, with Washburne's aid, Grant was appointed Brigadier General of volunteers.[110] Major General John C. Frémont, Union commander of the West, passed over senior generals and appointed Grant commander of the District of Southeastern Missouri.[111][o] Grant set up his headquarters at Cairo, Illinois, to plan a campaign down the Mississippi, Tennessee, and Cumberland rivers.[113] After the Confederates moved into western Kentucky with designs on southern Illinois, Grant, after notifying Frémont, advanced on Paducah, Kentucky, taking it without a fight on September 6.[114] Having understood the importance to Lincoln about Kentucky's neutrality, Grant assured its citizens, "I have come among you not as your enemy, but as your friend."[115] On November 1, Frémont ordered Grant to "make demonstrations" against the Confederates on both sides of the Mississippi, but prohibited him from attacking the enemy.[116]

## Belmont, Forts Henry and Donelson

On November 2, 1861, Lincoln removed Frémont from command, freeing Grant to attack Confederate soldiers encamped in Cape Girardeau, Missouri.[116][p] On November 5, Grant, along with Brigadier General John A. McClernand, landed 2,500 men at Hunter's Point, and on November 7 engaged the Confederates at the Battle of Belmont.[118] The Union army took the camp, but the reinforced Confederates under Brigadier Generals Frank Cheatham and Gideon J. Pillow forced a chaotic Union retreat.[119] Grant had wanted to destroy Confederate strongholds at both Belmont, Missouri and Columbus, Kentucky, but was not given enough troops and was only able to disrupt their positions. Grant's troops fought their way back to their Union boats and escaped back to Cairo under fire from the fortified stronghold at Columbus.[120] Although Grant and his army retreated, the battle gave his volunteers much-needed confidence and experience.[121] It also showed Lincoln that Grant was a general willing to fight.[122]

Columbus blocked Union access to the lower Mississippi. Grant and General James B. McPherson planned to bypass Columbus and with a force of 25,000 troops, move against Fort Henry on the Tennessee River. They would then march ten miles east to Fort Donelson on the Cumberland River, with the aid of gunboats, opening both rivers and allowing the Union access further south. Grant presented his plan to Henry Halleck, his new commander in the newly created Department of Missouri.[123] Halleck was considering the same strategy, but rebuffed Grant, believing he needed twice the number of troops. However, after Halleck telegraphed and consulted McClellan about the plan, he finally agreed on condition that the attack be conducted in close cooperation with navy Flag Officer, Andrew H. Foote.[124] Foote's gunboats bombarded Fort Henry, leading to its surrender on February 6, 1862, before Grant's infantry even arrived.[125]

Grant then ordered an immediate assault on Fort Donelson, which dominated the Cumberland River. Unlike Fort Henry, Grant was now opposed by a force equal to his own. Unaware of the garrison's strength, Grant's forces were over-confident. Grant,

McClernand, and Smith positioned their divisions around the fort. The next day McClernand and Smith launched probing attacks on apparent weak spots in the Confederate line, only to retreat with heavy losses. On February 14, Foote's gunboats began bombarding the fort, only to be repulsed by its heavy guns. Thus far the Confederates were winning, but soon Union reinforcements arrived, giving Grant a total force of over 40,000 men. When Foote regained control of the river, Grant resumed his attack, resulting in a standoff. Grant received a dispatch from Foote, requesting that they meet. Grant mounted a horse and rode seven miles over freezing roads and trenches, reaching Smith's division, instructing him to prepare for the next assault, and rode on and met up with McClernand and Wallace. After exchanging reports, he met up with Foote. On February 16, Foote resumed his bombardment, which signaled a general attack. Confederate generals John B. Floyd and Pillow fled, leaving the fort in command of Simon Bolivar Buckner, who submitted to Grant's demand for "unconditional and immediate surrender."[126]

Grant had won the first major victory for the Union, capturing Floyd's entire rebel army of more than 12,000. Halleck was angry that Grant had acted without his authorization and complained to McClellan, accusing Grant of "neglect and inefficiency." On March 3, Halleck sent a telegram to Washington complaining that he had no communication with Grant for a week. Three days later, Halleck followed up with a postscript claiming "word has just reached me that ... Grant has resumed his bad habits (of drinking)."[127] Lincoln, regardless, promoted Grant to major general of volunteers and the Northern press treated Grant as a hero. Playing off his initials, they took to calling him "Unconditional Surrender Grant."[128]

## Shiloh and aftermath

With great armies now massing, it was widely thought in the North that another western battle might end the war.[129] Grant, reinstated by Halleck at the urging of Lincoln and Secretary of War Edwin Stanton, left Fort Henry and traveled by boat up the Tennessee River to rejoin his army with orders to advance with the Army of the Tennessee into Tennessee. Grant's main army was located at Pittsburg Landing, while 40,000 Confederate troops converged at Corinth, Mississippi.[130] Brigadier General William Tecumseh Sherman assured Grant that his green troops were ready for an attack. Grant agreed and wired Halleck with their assessment.[131] Grant wanted to attack the Confederates at Corinth, but Halleck ordered him not to attack until Major General Don Carlos Buell arrived with his division of 25,000.[132] Meanwhile, Grant prepared for an attack on the Confederate army of roughly equal strength. Instead of preparing defensive fortifications between the Tennessee River and Owl Creek,[q] and clearing fields of fire, they spent most of their time drilling the largely inexperienced troops while Sherman dismissed reports of nearby Confederates.[133]

Union inaction created the opportunity for the Confederates to attack first before Buell arrived.[134] On the morning of April 6, 1862, Grant's troops were taken by surprise when the Confederates, led by Generals Albert Sidney Johnston and P.G.T. Beauregard, struck first "like an Alpine avalanche" near Shiloh church, attacking five divisions of Grant's army and forcing a confused retreat toward the Tennessee River.[135] Johnston was killed and command fell upon Beauregard.[136] One Union line held the Confederate attack off for several hours at a place later called the "Hornet's Nest," giving Grant time to assemble artillery and 20,000 troops near Pittsburg Landing.[137] The Confederates finally broke through the Hornet's Nest to capture a Union division, but "Grant's Last Line" held the landing, while the exhausted Confederates, lacking reinforcements, halted their advance. [138] The day's fighting had been costly, with thousands of casualties. That evening, heavy rain set in. Sherman found Grant standing alone under a tree in the rain. "Well, Grant, we've had the devil's own day of it, haven't we?" Sherman said. "Yes," replied Grant. "Lick 'em tomorrow, though."[139]

Bolstered by 18,000 fresh troops from the divisions of Major Generals Buell and Lew Wallace, Grant counterattacked at dawn the next day and regained the field, forcing the disorganized and demoralized rebels to retreat back to Corinth.[140] Halleck ordered Grant not to advance more than one day's march from Pittsburg Landing, stopping the pursuit of the Confederate Army.[141] Although Grant had won the battle the situation was little changed, with the Union in possession of Pittsburg Landing and the Confederates once again holed up in Corinth.[142] Grant, now realizing that the South was determined to fight and that the war would not be won with one battle, would later write, "Then, indeed, I gave up all idea of saving the Union except by complete conquest."[143]

Shiloh was the costliest battle in American history to that point and the staggering 23,746 total casualties stunned the nation.[144] Briefly hailed a hero for routing the Confederates, Grant was soon mired in controversy.[145] The Northern press castigated Grant for shockingly high casualties, and accused him of drunkenness during the battle, contrary to the accounts of officers and others with him at the time.[146] However, Grant's victory at Shiloh ended any chance for the Confederates to prevail in the Mississippi valley or regain its strategic advantage in the West.[147]

Halleck arrived from St. Louis on April 11, took command, and assembled a combined army of about 120,000 men. On April 29, he relieved Grant of field command and replaced him with Major General George Henry Thomas. Halleck slowly marched his army to take Corinth, entrenching each night.[148] Meanwhile, Beauregard pretended to be reinforcing, sent "deserters" to the Union Army with that story, and moved his army out during the night, to Halleck's surprise when he finally arrived at Corinth on May 30.[149] Discouraged, Grant considered resigning but Sherman convinced him to stay.[150] Lincoln dismissed Grant's critics, saying "I can't spare this man; he fights."[151] Halleck divided his combined army and reinstated Grant as field commander of the Army of the Tennessee on July 11.[152]

Later that year, on September 19, Grant's army defeated Confederates at the Battle of Iuka, then successfully defended Corinth, inflicting heavy casualties.[153] On October 25, Grant assumed command of the District of the Tennessee.[154] In November, after Lincoln's preliminary Emancipation Proclamation, Grant ordered units under his command to incorporate former slaves into the Union Army, giving them clothes, shelter and wages for their services.[155]

## Vicksburg campaign

The Confederate stronghold of Vicksburg, Mississippi, blocked the way of Union control of the Mississippi River, making its capture vital.[156] While Grant held western Tennessee with almost 40,000 me, he was aggravated to learn that Lincoln authorized McClernand to raise a separate army to march on Vicksburg.[157] Halleck ordered McClernand to Memphis, and placed him and his troops under Grant's authority.[158] After Grant's army captured Holly Springs, Grant planned to attack Vicksburg's front overland while Sherman would attack the fortress from the rear on the Mississippi River.[159] However, Confederate cavalry raids on December 11 and 20, 1862, broke Union communications and recaptured Holly Springs, preventing Grant and Sherman from connecting.[160] On December 29, a Confederate army led by Lieutenant General John C. Pemberton repulsed Sherman's direct approach ascending the bluffs to Vicksburg at Chickasaw Bayou.[161] McClernand reached Sherman's army, assumed command, and independently of Grant led a campaign that captured Confederate Fort Hindman.[162]

During this time, Grant incorporated fleeing African American slaves into the Union Army giving them protection and paid employment.[163] Along with his military responsibilities in the months following Grant's return to command, he was concerned over an expanding illicit cotton trade in his district.[164] He believed the trade undermined the Union war effort, funded the Confederacy, and prolonged the war, while Union soldiers died in the fields.[165] Grant's own father, together with some Jewish partners, the Mack Brothers, attempted to gain access to this lucrative trade through Grant. On December 17, 1862, Grant issued General Order No. 11, expelling "Jews, as a class," from the district, saying that Jewish merchants were violating trade regulations.[166][s] The Northern press strongly condemned Grant's anti-semitism, while Jewish leaders complained to Lincoln.[168] Lincoln demanded the order be revoked and Grant rescinded it within three weeks.[169][t]

On January 29, 1863, Grant assumed overall command and attempted to advance his army through water-logged terrain to bypass Vicksburg's guns.[170] On April 16, Grant ordered Admiral David Dixon Porter's gunboats south under fire from the Vicksburg batteries to meet up with troops who had marched south down the west side of the Mississippi River.[171] Grant ordered diversionary battles, confusing Pemberton and allowing Grant's army to move east across the Mississippi, landing troops at Bruinsburg.[172] Grant's army captured Jackson, the state capital. Advancing west, Grant defeated Pemberton's army at the Battle of Champion Hill on May 16, forcing their retreat into Vicksburg.[173] After Grant's men assaulted the entrenchments twice, suffering severe losses, they settled in for a siege lasting seven weeks. During quiet periods of the campaign Grant would take to drinking on occasion.[174] The personal rivalry between McClernand and Grant continued until Grant removed McClernand from command when he contravened Grant by publishing an order without permission.[175] Pemberton surrendered Vicksburg to Grant on July 4, 1863.[176]

Vicksburg's fall gave Union forces control of the Mississippi River and split the Confederacy. By that time, Grant's political sympathies fully coincided with the Radical Republicans' aggressive prosecution of the war and emancipation of the slaves.[177] The success at Vicksburg was a morale boost for the Union war effort.[175] When Stanton suggested Grant be brought back east to run the Army of the Potomac, Grant demurred, writing that he knew the geography and resources of the West better and he did not want to upset the chain of command in the East.[178]

## Chattanooga and promotion

Lincoln promoted Grant to major general and assigned him command of the newly formed Division of the Mississippi on October 16, 1863, including command of the Armies of the Ohio, Tennessee, and Cumberland.[179] After the Battle of Chickamauga, the Army of the Cumberland retreated into Chattanooga where they became trapped.[180] Grant arrived in Chattanooga on horseback, assisted by Major General Joseph Hooker, with plans to resupply the city and break the siege. Union forces captured Brown's Ferry and opened a supply line to Bridgeport.[181]

On November 23, Grant organized three armies to attack at Missionary Ridge and Lookout Mountain. Two days later, Hooker's forces took Lookout Mountain.[182] Grant ordered Major General George Henry Thomas to advance when Sherman's army failed to take Missionary Ridge from the northeast.[183] The Army of the Cumberland, led by Major General Philip Sheridan and Brigadier General Thomas J. Wood, charged uphill and captured the Confederate entrenchments at the top, forcing a retreat.[184] The decisive battle gave the Union control of Tennessee and opened Georgia, the Confederate heartland, to Union invasion.[185] Grant was given an enormous thoroughbred horse, *Cincinnati*, by a thankful admirer in St. Louis.[186]

On March 2, 1864, Lincoln promoted Grant to lieutenant general, giving him command of all Union Armies.[187] Grant arrived in Washington on March 8, and he was formally commissioned by Lincoln the next day at a Cabinet meeting.[188] Grant developed a good working relationship with Lincoln, who allowed Grant to devise his own strategy.[189] Grant established his headquarters with General George Meade's Army of the Potomac in Culpeper, north-west of Richmond, and met weekly with Lincoln and Stanton in Washington.[190][u] After protest from Halleck, Grant scrapped a risky invasion plan of North Carolina, and adopted a plan of five coordinated Union offensives on five fronts, so Confederate armies could not shift troops along interior lines.[192] Grant and Meade would make a direct frontal attack on Robert E. Lee's Army of Northern Virginia, while Sherman—now chief of the western armies—was to destroy Joseph E. Johnston's Army of Tennessee and take Atlanta.[193] Major General Benjamin Butler would advance on Lee from the southeast, up the James River, while Major General Nathaniel Banks would capture Mobile.[194] Major General Franz Sigel was to capture granaries and rail lines in the fertile Shenandoah Valley.[195]

Grant now commanded in total 533,000 battle-ready troops spread out over an eighteen-mile front, while the Confederates had lost many officers in battle and had great difficulty finding replacements.[196] He was popular, and there was talk that a Union victory early in the year could lead to his candidacy for the presidency. Grant was aware of the rumors, but had ruled out a political candidacy; the possibility would soon vanish with delays on the battlefield.[197]

## Overland Campaign

The Overland Campaign was a series of brutal battles fought in Virginia for seven weeks during May and June 1864.[198] Sigel's and Butler's efforts failed, and Grant was left alone to fight Lee.[199] On the morning of Wednesday, May 4, Grant dressed in full uniform, sword at his side, led the army out from his headquarters at Culpeper towards Germanna Ford.[200] They crossed the Rapidan unopposed, while supplies were transported on four pontoon bridges.[201] On May 5, the Union army attacked Lee in the Wilderness, a three-day battle with estimated casualties of 17,666 Union and 11,125 Confederate.[202] Rather than retreat, Grant flanked Lee's army to the southeast and attempted to wedge his forces between Lee and Richmond at Spotsylvania Court House.[203] Lee's army got to Spotsylvania first and a costly battle ensued, lasting thirteen days, with heavy casualties.[204] On May 12, Grant attempted to break through Lee's *Muleshoe* salient guarded by Confederate artillery, resulting in one of the bloodiest assaults of the Civil War, known as the Bloody Angle.[205] Unable to break Lee's lines, Grant again flanked the rebels to the southeast, meeting at North Anna, where a battle lasted three days.[206]

*Commanding General Grant at the Battle of Cold Harbor. Egbert Guy Fowx June 1864*

Grant maneuvered his army to Cold Harbor, a vital road hub that linked to Richmond, but Lee's men were already entrenched there. On the third day of the thirteen-day battle, Grant led a costly assault and was soon castigated as "the Butcher" by the Northern press after taking 52,788 Union casualties; Lee's Confederate army suffered 32,907 casualties, but he was less able to replace them.[207] This battle was the second of two that Grant later said he regretted (the other being his initial assault on Vicksburg). Undetected by Lee, Grant moved his army south of the James River, freed Butler from the Bermuda Hundred, and advanced toward Petersburg, Virginia's central railroad hub.[208]

Beauregard defended Petersburg, and Lee's veteran reinforcements soon arrived, resulting in a nine-month siege. Northern resentment grew. Sheridan was assigned command of the Union Army of the Shenandoah and Grant directed him to "follow the enemy to their death" in the Shenandoah Valley. When Sheridan suffered attacks by John S. Mosby's irregular Confederate cavalry, Grant recommended rounding up their families for imprisonment at Fort McHenry.[209] After Grant's abortive attempt to capture Petersburg, Lincoln supported Grant in his decision to continue and visited Grant's headquarters at City Point on June 21 to assess the state of the army and meet with Grant and Admiral Porter. By the time Lincoln departed his appreciation for Grant had grown.[210]

At Petersburg, Grant approved a plan to blow up part of the enemy trenches from a tunnel. The explosion created a crater, into which poorly led Union troops poured. Recovering from the surprise, Confederates surrounded the crater and easily picked off Union troops within it. The Union's 3,500 casualties outnumbered the Confederates' by three-to-one; although the plan could have been successful if implemented correctly, Grant admitted the tactic had been a "stupendous failure."[211] Rather than fight Lee in a full frontal attack as he had done at Cold Harbor, Grant continued to extend Lee's defenses south and west of Petersburg to capture essential railroad links.[212]

Union forces soon captured Mobile Bay and Atlanta and now controlled the Shenandoah Valley, ensuring Lincoln's reelection in November.[213] Sherman convinced Grant and Lincoln to send his army to march on Savannah.[214] Sherman cut a 60-mile path of destruction unopposed, reached the Atlantic Ocean, and captured Savannah on December 22.[215] On December 16, after much prodding by Grant, the Union Army under Thomas smashed John Bell Hood's Confederate Army at Nashville.[216] It was the beginning of the end for the Confederacy, with Lee's forces at Petersburg being the only significant obstacle remaining.[217]

By March 1865, Grant had severely weakened Lee's strength, having extended his lines to 35 miles.[218] Lee's troops deserted by the thousands due to hunger and the strains of trench warfare.[219] Grant, Sherman, Porter, and Lincoln held a conference to discuss the surrender of Confederate armies and Reconstruction of the South on March 28.[220]

## Appomattox campaign, and victory

On April 2, Grant ordered a general assault on Lee's entrenched forces. Union troops took Petersburg and captured Richmond the next day.[221] Lee and part of his army broke free and attempted to link up with the remnants of Joseph E. Johnston's defeated army, but Sheridan's cavalry stopped the two armies from converging, cutting them off from their supply trains.[222] Grant was in communication with Lee before he entrusted his aide Orville Babcock to carry his last dispatch to Lee requesting his surrender with instructions to escort him to a meeting place of Lee's choosing.[223] Grant immediately rode west, bypassing Lee's army, to join Sheridan who had captured Appomattox Station, blocking Lee's escape route. On his way, Grant received a letter sent by Lee informing him that he was ready to surrender.[224]

On April 9, Grant and Lee met at Appomattox Court House.[225] Upon receiving Lee's dispatch about the proposed meeting Grant had been jubilant. Although Grant felt depressed at the fall of "a foe who had fought so long and valiantly," he believed the Southern cause was "one of the worst for which a people ever fought."[226] After briefly discussing their days of old in Mexico, Grant wrote out the terms of surrender. Lee expressed satisfaction and accepted Grant's terms.[227] Going beyond his military authority, Grant gave Lee and his men amnesty; Confederates would surrender their weapons and return to their homes. At Lee's request, Grant also allowed them to keep their horses, all on the condition that they would not take up arms against the United States.[228] Grant ordered his troops to stop all celebration, saying the "war is over; the rebels are our countrymen again."[229] Johnson's Tennessee army surrendered on April 26, 1865, Richard Taylor's Alabama army on May 4, and Kirby Smith's Texas army on May 26, ending the war.[230]

## Lincoln's assassination

On April 14, 1865, five days after Grant's victory at Appomattox, he attended a cabinet meeting in Washington. Lincoln invited him and his wife to Ford's Theater, but they declined as upon his wife Julia's urging, had plans to travel to Philadelphia. In a conspiracy that also targeted top cabinet members in one last effort to topple the Union, Lincoln was fatally shot by John Wilkes Booth at the theater, and died the next morning.[231] Many, including Grant himself, thought that he had been a target in the plot and during the subsequent trial, the government tried to prove that Grant had been stalked by Booth's conspirator Michael O'Laughlen.[232] Stanton notified Grant of the President's death and summoned him back to Washington. Vice President Andrew Johnson was sworn in as President on April 15. Attending Lincoln's funeral on April 19, Grant stood alone and wept openly; he later said Lincoln was "the greatest man I have ever known."[233] Grant was determined to work with Johnson, while he privately expressed "every reason to hope" in the new president's ability of running the government "in its old channel." [234]

## Commanding General

At the war's end, Grant remained commander of the army, with duties that included dealing with Maximilian and French troops in Mexico, enforcement of Reconstruction in the former Confederate states, and supervision of Indian wars on the western Plains.[235] Grant secured a house for his family in Georgetown Heights in 1865, but instructed Elihu Washburne that for political purposes his legal residence remained in Galena, Illinois. [236] That same year, Grant spoke at Cooper Union in New York in support of Johnson's presidency. Further travels that summer took the Grants to Albany, New York, back to Galena, and throughout Illinois and Ohio, with enthusiastic receptions.[237] On July 25, 1866, Congress promoted Grant to the newly created rank of General of the Army of the United States.[238]

## Reconstruction

Reconstruction was a turbulent period from 1863 to 1877 when former Confederate states were readmitted to the Union, and fierce controversy arose over the status of both the defeated Confederates and the former slaves. In November 1865, Johnson sent Grant on a fact-finding mission to the South. Grant recommended continuation of the Freedmen's Bureau, which Johnson opposed, but advised against using black troops, which he believed encouraged an alternative to farm labor.[239] Grant did not believe the people of the South were ready for self-rule, and that both whites and blacks in the South required protection by the federal government. Concerned that the war led to diminished respect for civil authorities, Grant continued using the Army to maintain order.[240] On the same day that the Thirteenth Amendment was ratified, Grant filed an unconvincing and optimistic report of his tour, expressing his faith that "the mass of thinking men of the South accept the present situation of affairs in good faith." Grant later disavowed the report.[241] In this respect, Grant's opinion on Reconstruction aligned with Johnson's policy of restoring former Confederates to their positions of power, arguing that Congress should allow representatives from the South to take their seats.[242]

## Break from Johnson

Grant was initially optimistic about Johnson, saying he was satisfied the nation had "nothing to fear" from the Johnson administration.[243] Despite differing styles, Grant got along cordially with Johnson, and attended cabinet meetings concerning Reconstruction.[243] By February 1866, the relationship began to break down.[244] Johnson opposed Grant's closure of the *Richmond Examiner* for disloyal editorials and his enforcement of the Civil Rights Act of 1866, passed over Johnson's veto.[244] Needing Grant's popularity, Johnson took Grant on his "Swing Around the Circle" tour, a failed attempt to gain national support for lenient policies toward the South. [245] Grant privately called Johnson's speeches a "national disgrace" and he left the tour early.[246] On March 2, 1867, overriding Johnson's veto, Congress passed the first of three Reconstruction Acts, using military officers to enforce policy.[247] Protecting Grant, Congress passed the Command of the Army Act, preventing his removal or relocation, and forcing Johnson to pass orders through Grant. [248]

Grant wanted to replace Edwin Stanton, a Radical Republican, as Secretary of War, but recommended against bypassing the Tenure of Office Act, prohibiting a cabinet removal without Senate approval.[249] Grant accepted the position, not wanting the Army to fall under a conservative appointee who would impede Reconstruction, and managed an uneasy partnership with Johnson.[250] In December 1867, Congress voted to keep Stanton, who was reinstated by a Senate Committee on Friday, January 10, 1868. Grant told Johnson he was going to resign office to avoid fines and imprisonment. Johnson said he would assume Grant's legal responsibility, and reminded Grant that he had promised him to delay his resignation until a suitable replacement was found.[251] The following Monday, Grant surrendered the office to Stanton.[252] Johnson accused Grant of lying at a stormy cabinet meeting. The publication of angry messages between Grant and Johnson led to a complete break between the two.[253] The controversy led to Johnson's impeachment and trial in the Senate.[254] Johnson was saved from removal from office by one vote.[255] Grant's popularity rose among the Radical Republicans and his nomination for the presidency appeared certain.[256]

## Election of 1868

When the Republican Party met at the 1868 Republican National Convention in Chicago, the delegates unanimously nominated Grant for president and Speaker of the House Schuyler Colfax for vice president.[254] Although Grant had preferred to remain in the army, he accepted the Republican nomination, believing that he was the only one who could unify the nation.[257] The Republicans advocated "equal civil and political rights to all" and African American enfranchisement.[258][259] The Democrats, having abandoned Johnson, nominated former governor Horatio Seymour of New York for president and Francis P. Blair of Missouri for vice president.[260] The Democrats advocated the immediate restoration of former Confederate states to the Union and amnesty from "all past political offenses."[261]

Grant played no overt role during the campaign and instead was joined by Sherman and Sheridan in a tour of the West that summer.[262] However, the Republicans adopted his words "Let us have peace" as their campaign slogan.[263] Grant's 1862 General Order No. 11 became an issue during the presidential campaign; he sought to distance himself from the order, saying "I have no prejudice against sect or race, but want each individual to be judged by his own merit."[264] The Democrats and their Klan supporters focused mainly on ending Reconstruction intimidating Blacks, and returning control of the South to the white Democrats and the planter class, alienating War Democrats in the North.[265] Grant won the popular vote by 300,000 votes out of 5,716,082 votes cast, receiving an Electoral College landslide of 214 votes to Seymour's 80.[266] Seymour received a majority of white votes, but Grant was aided by 500,000 votes cast by blacks,[260] winning him 52.7 percent of the popular vote.[267] At the age of 46, Grant was the youngest president yet elected, and the first president after the nation had outlawed slavery.[268]

## Memoirs, pension, and death

Throughout his career, Grant repeatedly told highly detailed stories of his military experiences, often making slight mistakes in terms of dates and locations. As a poor hardscrabble farmer in St. Louis just before the war, he kept his neighbors spellbound till midnight "listening intently to his vivid narrations of Army experiences."[524] In calm moments during the Civil War, he often spoke of his recent experiences, typically "in terse and often eloquent language."[525] Grant's interpretations changed over time—in his letters written during the Mexican War period, there is no criticism of the war. By contrast his *Memoirs* are highly critical of the political aspects, condemning the war as unwarranted aggression by the United States. Grant told and retold his war stories so many times that writing his

*Grant worked on his memoirs in June 1885, less than a month before his death. Howe June 27, 1885*

*Memoirs* was more a matter of repetition and polish rather than trying to recall his memories for the first time.[526][bh]

In the summer of 1884, Grant complained of a sore throat but put off seeing a doctor until late October, when he learned it was cancer, possibly caused by his frequent cigar smoking.[528][bi] Grant chose not to reveal the seriousness of his condition to his wife, who soon found out from Grant's doctor.[530] Before being diagnosed, Grant was invited to a Methodist service for Civil War veterans in Ocean Grove, New Jersey, on August 4, 1884, receiving a standing ovation from more than ten thousand veterans and others; it would be his last public appearance.[531] In March of the following year, *The New York Times* announced that Grant was dying of cancer, and a nationwide public concern for the former president began.[532][bj]

Grant was nearly broke and worried constantly about leaving his wife a suitable amount of money to live on. *Century* magazine offered Grant a book contract with a 10 percent royalty, but Grant's friend Mark Twain, understanding how bad Grant's financial condition was, made him an offer for his memoirs which paid an unheard-of 75 percent royalty. [534] To provide for his family, Grant worked intensely on his memoirs at his home in New York City. His former staff member Adam Badeau assisted him with much of the research, while his son Frederick located documents and did much of the fact-checking. [535] Because of the summer heat and humidity, his doctors recommended that he move upstate to a cottage at the top of Mount McGregor, offered by a family friend.[536]

Grant finished his memoir and died only a few days later.[537] Grant's memoirs treat his early life and time in the Mexican–American War briefly and are inclusive of his life up to the end of the Civil War.[538] The *Personal Memoirs of Ulysses S. Grant* was a critical and commercial success. Julia Grant received about $450,000 in royalties (equivalent to $12,500,000 in 2018).[534] Grant's successful autobiography pioneered a method for ex-presidents and veterans to earn money.[539] The memoir has been highly regarded by the public, military historians, and literary critics.[540] Grant portrayed himself in the persona of the honorable Western hero, whose strength lies in his honesty and straightforwardness. He candidly depicted his battles against both the Confederates and internal army foes.[541][bk]

After a year-long struggle with throat cancer, surrounded by his family, Grant died at 8:08 a.m. in the Mount McGregor cottage on July 23, 1885, at the age of 63.[543] Sheridan, then Commanding General of the Army, ordered a day-long tribute to Grant on all military posts, and President Grover Cleveland ordered a thirty-day nationwide period of mourning. After private services, the honor guard placed Grant's body on a special funeral train, which traveled to West Point and New York City. A quarter of a million people viewed it in the two days before the funeral. Tens of thousands of men, many of them veterans from the Grand Army of the Republic (GAR), marched with Grant's casket drawn by two dozen black stallions[544] to Riverside Park in the Morningside Heights neighborhood of Upper Manhattan. His pallbearers included Union generals Sherman and Sheridan, Confederate generals Simon Bolivar Buckner and Joseph E. Johnston, Admiral David Dixon Porter, and Senator John A. Logan, the head of the GAR.[545] Following the casket in the seven-mile-long (11 km) procession were President Cleveland, the two living former presidents Hayes and Arthur, all of the President's Cabinet, as well as the justices of the Supreme Court.[546]

Attendance at the New York funeral topped 1.5 million.[545] Ceremonies were held in other major cities around the country, while Grant was eulogized in the press and likened to George Washington and Abraham Lincoln.[547] Grant's body was laid to rest in Riverside Park, first in a temporary tomb, and then—twelve years later, on April 17, 1897—in the General Grant National Memorial, also known as "Grant's Tomb," the largest mausoleum in North America.[545]

## Historical reputation

Many historians and biographers have been intrigued and challenged by contradictions in Grant's life, and few presidential reputations have shifted as dramatically as his.[548] Grant's eulogies received tempered praise, but critics quickly castigated him a drunkard, who ran a corrupt administration, while ignoring his presidential accomplishments. [549] [548] Grant's reputation fell as post-war efforts in late-19th-century national reconciliation took hold among whites. As the popularity of the pro-Confederate Lost Cause theory and the Dunning School movement grew early in the 20th century, a more negative view of Grant became common.[550] In 1917, historian Louis Arthur Coolidge bucked the trend of negativity and said Grant's "success as President" was "hardly less significant than his success at war."[551][bl]

In 1934, historian Robert R. McCormick said Grant's military triumphs were neglected due in part to the "malicious and deliberate design" of *Lost Cause* veterans and writers. [553] In the 1950s, historians Bruce Catton and T. Harry Williams began a reassessment of Grant's military career, shifting the analysis of Grant as the victor by brute force to that of successful, skillful, modern strategist and commander.[554] Historian Jonathan D. Sarna said Grant's 1862 General Order No. 11 was "the most notorious anti-Jewish official order in American history."[555] William S. McFeely won the Pulitzer Prize for his critical 1981 biography that credited Grant's initial presidential efforts on civil rights, but lamented his failure to carry out lasting progress.[556] McFeely and later historians do note that Grant's drinking was falsely stereotyped by many of his critics.[557] However, historians debate how effective Grant was at halting corruption.[558] The scandals during the Grant administration were used to stigmatize his political reputation.[559]

In the 21st century, Grant's reputation among historians has improved markedly, start-ing with Jean Edward Smith's 2001 Grant biography.[560] Opinions of Grant's presidency demonstrate a better appreciation of Grant's personal integrity, Reconstruction efforts, and peace policy towards Indians, even when they fell short.[561][562] In 2016, Ronald C. White continued this trend with a biography that historian T. J. Stiles said, "solidifies the positive image amassed in recent decades, blotting out the caricature of a military butcher and politically incompetent, promoted by Lost Cause and Jim Crow era historians."[563] [bm] Like White's book, Ron Chernow's 2017 biography (*Grant*) continued the elevation of Grant's historical reputation.[565] In a review of Chernow's book, former U.S. President Bill Clinton offered praise for "Grant's significant achievements at the end of the war and after."[566] While historian Charles W. Calhoun noted Grant's presidential successes and his steps to modernize the presidency, he questioned whether Grant's revived reputation among scholars has been found in the "popular consciousness."[567]

# Rose O'Neal Greenhow

**Rose O'Neal Greenhow** (1813 or 1814[1]–October 1, 1864) was a renowned Confederate spy during the American Civil War. A socialite in Washington, D.C., during the period before the war, she moved in important political circles and cultivated friendships with presidents, generals, senators, and high-ranking military officers including John C. Calhoun and James Buchanan.[2] She used her connections to pass along key military information to the Confederacy at the start of the war. In early 1861, she was given control of a pro-Southern spy network in Washington, D.C., by her handler, Thomas Jordan, then a captain in the Confederate Army. She was credited by Jefferson Davis, the Confederate president, with ensuring the South's victory at the First Battle of Bull Run in late July 1861.

The government found that information was being leaked and the trail led to Rose Greenhow's residence. Greenhow was subject to house arrest; found to have continued her activities, in 1862 after an espionage hearing, she, with her daughter "Little Rose," was imprisoned for nearly five months in Washington, D.C. Deported to the Confederate States, she traveled to Richmond, Virginia and began new tasks. Running the blockade, she sailed to Europe to represent the Confederacy in a diplomatic mission to France and Britain from 1863 to 1864. In 1863, she also wrote and published her memoir in London, which was popular in Britain. After her returning ship ran aground in 1864 off the coast of Wilmington, North Carolina, she drowned when her rowboat overturned as she tried to escape a Union gunboat. She was honored with a Confederate military funeral.

During 1993, the women's auxiliary of the Sons of Confederate Veterans changed its name to the Order of the Confederate Rose in Greenhow's honor, following publicity about her exploits in a TV movie the previous year.

## Confederate spy

After losing her husband, Greenhow became more sympathetic to the Confederate cause. Greenhow was an advocate for secession and "preserving the Southern way of life," including slavery.[2] She was strongly influenced by her friendship with U.S. Senator John C. Calhoun from South Carolina. Greenhow's loyalty to the Confederacy was noted by those with similar sympathies in Washington, and she was recruited as a spy. Her recruiter was U.S. Army captain Thomas Jordan, who had set up a pro-Southern spy network in Washington.[11] He supplied her with a 26-symbol cipher for encoding messages.[4]

*Thomas Jordan*

After passing control of the espionage network to Greenhow, Jordan left the US Army, went South, and was commissioned as a captain in the Confederate Army.[11] He continued to receive and evaluate her reports. Jordan appeared to be Greenhow's handler for the Confederate Secret Service during its formative phase.[11]

On July 9 and July 16 of 1861, Greenhow passed secret messages to Confederate General P. G. T. Beauregard containing critical information regarding Union military movements for what would be the First Battle of Bull Run, including the plans of General Irvin McDowell.[12] Assisting in her conspiracy were pro-Confederate members of Congress, Union officers, courier Betty Duvall, and her dentist, Aaron Van Camp, as well as his son who was also a Confederate soldier, Eugene B. Van Camp.[13][2] Confederate President Jefferson Davis credited Greenhow's information with the Confederates securing victory at Manassas over the Union Army on July 21.[4]

After the battle she received the following telegram from Jordan: "Our President and our General direct me to thank you. We rely upon you for further information. The Confederacy owes you a debt." (Signed) JORDAN, Adjutant-General."[14] She became known as "Rebel Rose" for her work for the South.

## Capture and prison

*Rose O'Neal Greenhow with her youngest daughter and namesake, "Little" Rose, at the Old Capitol Prison, Washington, D.C., 1862*

Knowing she was suspected of spying for the Confederacy, Greenhow feared for her remaining daughters' safety. Leila was sent to Ohio to join her older sister Florence Greenhow Moore, whose husband Seymour Treadwell Moore had become a captain in the Union Army. (He was breveted a brigadier general in May 1865 for his services and achieved a rank of lieu-tenant colonel after the war in his army career.) Only Little Rose stayed with Greenhow in Washington.

Allan Pinkerton was made head of the recently formed Secret Service and one of his first orders was to watch Greenhow, because of her wide circle of con-tacts on both sides of the sectional split.[15] Due to the activities of visitors, he arrested Greenhow and placed her under house arrest at her 16th Street residence on August 23, 1861, along with one of her couriers, Lily

Mackall.[2] His agents traced other leaked information to Greenhow's home. While searching her house, Pinkerton and his men found extensive intelligence materials left from evidence she tried to burn, including scraps of coded messages, copies of what amounted to eight reports to Jordan over a month's time, and maps of Washington fortifications and notes on military movements.[4][16]

The materials included numerous love letters from the abolitionist Republican US Senator Henry Wilson from Massachusetts. She considered him her prize source, and said he gave her data on the "number of heavy guns and other artillery in the Washington defenses," but he likely knew far more from his work on the Military Affairs Committee. [17] The seized Greenhow papers are now held by the National Archives and Records Administration, with some available on line.[18]

Pinkerton supervised visitors to Greenhow's house and moved other suspected Southern sympathizers into it, giving rise to the nickname Fort Greenhow. He was pleased to oversee the visitors and messages, as it gave him more control of the Southern flow of information.[19] While messages continued to be sent to Jordan, he discounted them after Pinkerton mounted his control. When a letter from Greenhow to Seward complained of her treatment was publicized, there was Northern criticism for what was perceived as too lenient treatment of a spy. Pinkerton transferred Greenhow on January 18, 1862, to Old Capitol Prison, shutting down Fort Greenhow. So many political prisoners were detained that a two-man commission was set up to review their cases at what were called espionage hearings.[20] Greenhow was never subjected to trial.[4] Her youngest daughter, "Little Rose," then eight years old, was permitted to stay with her.

Greenhow continued to pass along messages while imprisoned.[4] Passers-by could see Rose's window from the street. Historians believe that the position of the blinds and number of candles burning in the window had special meaning to the "little birdies" passing by. Another account lists her prison room facing the prison yard "so that she could not see or be seen" and "every effort was made to keep Mrs. Greenhow away from the windows."[21] Greenhow also on one occasion flew the Confederate Flag from her prison window.[22]

## International acclaim

On May 31, 1862, Greenhow was released without trial (with her daughter), on condition she stay within Confederate boundaries. After they were escorted to Fortress Monroe at Hampton Roads, she and her daughter went on to Richmond, Virginia, where Greenhow was hailed by Southerners as a heroine. President Jefferson Davis welcomed her return and enlisted her as a courier to Europe. Greenhow ran the blockade and, from 1863 to 1864, traveled through France and Britain on a diplomatic mission building support for the Confederacy with the aristocrats.[4]

Many European aristocrats had sympathy for the South's elite; there were also strong commercial ties between Britain and the South. While in France, Greenhow was received in the court of Napoleon III at the Tuileries. In Britain, she had an audience with Queen

Victoria. Greenhow met, and in 1864 became engaged to, Granville Leveson-Gower, 2nd Earl Granville.[4] The details of her mission to Europe are recorded in her personal diaries, dated August 5, 1863, to August 10, 1864, when she wrote, "A sad sick feeling crept over me, of parting perhaps forever, from many dear to me . . . A few months before I had landed a stranger—I will not say in a foreign land—for it was the land of my ancestors—and many memories twined around my heart when my feet touched the shores of Merry England—but I was literally a stranger in the land of my fathers and a feeling of cold isolation was upon me."[1]

Two months after arriving in London, Greenhow wrote her memoir, titled *My Imprisonment and the First Year of Abolition Rule at Washington.* She published it that year in London and it sold well throughout Britain.[23]

## Death

On August 19, 1864,[24] Greenhow left Europe to return to the Confederacy, carrying dispatches. She traveled on the *Condor,* a British blockade runner. On October 1, 1864, the *Condor* ran aground at the mouth of the Cape Fear River near Wilmington, North Carolina, while being pursued by the Union gunboat USS *Niphon.* Fearing capture and reimprisonment, Greenhow fled the grounded ship by rowboat. A wave capsized the rowboat, and Greenhow drowned. She was weighed down by $2,000 worth of gold sewn into her underclothes and hung around her neck,[25] returns from her memoir royalties.

When Greenhow's body was recovered from the water near Wilmington, searchers found a small notebook[26] and a copy of her book *Imprisonment* hidden on her. Inside the book was a note meant for her daughter, Little Rose. She was honored with a military funeral at St. Thomas the Apostle Catholic Church in Wilmington, North Carolina,[4] and the Ladies Memorial Association, in 1888, marked her grave with a cross that read "Mrs. Rose O'Neal Greenhow. A Bearer of Dispatches to the Confederate Government."[1]

# Winfield Scott Hancock

**Winfield Scott Hancock** (February 14, 1824–February 9, 1886) was a United States Army officer and the Democratic nominee for President of the United States in 1880. He served with distinction in the Army for four decades, including service in the Mexican–American War and as a Union general in the American Civil War. Known to his Army colleagues as "Hancock the Superb," he was noted in particular for his personal leadership at the Battle of Gettysburg in 1863. His military service continued after the Civil War, as Hancock participated in the military Reconstruction of the South and the Army's presence at the Western frontier.

Hancock's reputation as a war hero at Gettysburg, combined with his status as a Unionist and supporter of states' rights, made him a potential presidential candidate. When the Democrats nominated him for President in 1880, he ran a strong campaign, but was narrowly defeated by Republican James A. Garfield.

## Civil War
*Joining the Army of the Potomac*

> Hancock stands the most conspicuous figure of all the general officers who did not exercise a separate command. He commanded a corps longer than any other one, and his name was never mentioned as having committed in battle a blunder for which he was responsible. He was a man of very conspicuous personal appearance . . . . His genial disposition made him friends, and his personal courage and his presence with his command in the thickest of the fight won for him the confidence of troops serving under him. No matter how hard the fight, the 2nd corps always felt that their commander was looking after them.
>
> —Ulysses S. Grant, Personal Memoirs[25]

Hancock returned east to assume quartermaster duties for the rapidly growing Union Army, but was quickly promoted to brigadier general on September 23, 1861, and given an infantry brigade to command in the division of Brig. Gen. William F. "Baldy" Smith, Army of the Potomac.[13] He earned his "Superb" nickname[13] in the Peninsula Campaign,

*General Winfield Scott Hancock*

in 1862, by leading a critical counterattack in the Battle of Williamsburg; army commander Maj. Gen. George B. McClellan telegraphed to Washington that "Hancock was superb today" and the appellation stuck.[26] McClellan did not follow through on Hancock's initiative, however, and Confederate forces were allowed to withdraw unmolested.[27]

In the Battle of Antietam, Hancock assumed command of the 1st Division, II Corps, following the mortal wounding of Maj. Gen. Israel B. Richardson in the horrific fighting at "Bloody Lane." Hancock and his staff made a dramatic entrance to the battlefield, galloping between his troops and the enemy, parallel to the Sunken Road. [28] His men assumed that Hancock would order counterattacks against the exhausted Confederates, but he carried orders from McClellan to hold his position.[29] He was promoted to major general of volunteers on November 29, 1862.[13] He led his division in the disastrous attack on Marye's Heights in the Battle of Fredericksburg the following month and was wounded in the abdomen. At the Battle of Chancellorsville, his division covered Maj. Gen. Joseph Hooker's withdrawal and Hancock was wounded again.[30] His corps commander, Maj. Gen. Darius N. Couch, transferred out of the Army of the Potomac in protest of actions Hooker took in the battle and Hancock assumed command of II Corps, which he would lead until shortly before the war's end.[26]

## Gettysburg

Hancock's most famous service was as a new corps commander at the Battle of Gettysburg, July 1 to 3, 1863.[26] After his friend, Maj. Gen. John F. Reynolds, was killed early on July 1, Maj. Gen. George G. Meade, the new commander of the Army of the Potomac, sent Hancock ahead to take command of the units on the field and assess the situation. Hancock thus was in temporary command of the "left wing" of the army, consisting of the I, II, III, and XI Corps. This demonstrated Meade's high confidence in him, because Hancock was not the most senior Union officer at Gettysburg at the time.[31] Hancock and the more senior XI Corps commander, Maj. Gen. Oliver O. Howard, argued briefly about this command arrangement, but Hancock prevailed and he organized the Union defenses on Cemetery Hill as more numerous Confederate forces drove the I and XI Corps back through the town. He had the authority from Meade to withdraw the forces, so he was responsible for the decision to stand and fight at Gettysburg.[32] At the conclusion of the day's action, Maj. Gen. Henry Warner Slocum arrived on the field and assumed command until Gen. Meade arrived after midnight.

On July 2, Hancock's II Corps was positioned on Cemetery Ridge, roughly in the center of the Union line, while Confederate General Robert E. Lee launched assaults on both ends of the line.[33] On the Union left, Lt. Gen. James Longstreet's assault smashed the III Corps and Hancock sent in his 1st Division, under Brig. Gen. John C. Caldwell, to reinforce the Union in the Wheatfield. As Lt. Gen. A.P. Hill's corps continued the attack toward the Union center, Hancock rallied the defenses and rushed units to the critical spots.[33] First, he issued the Third Brigade of his Third Division under Colonel George Willard into the fray to stop the advance of Confederate Brigadier General William Barksdale's Brigade.[34] In one famous incident, he sacrificed a regiment, the 1st Minnesota Volunteer Infantry Regiment, by ordering it to advance and charge a Confederate brigade four times its size, causing the Minnesotans to suffer 87 percent casualties.[35] While costly to the regiment, this heroic sacrifice bought time to organize the defensive line and saved the day for the Union army.[35] Following the action toward his right, he met the 13th Vermont Volunteer Infantry Regiment, a First Corps unit which had come from Cemetery Hill to help quell the crisis. Hancock sent them out to recover some artillery pieces Confederates had taken and were pulling away. The Vermonters were successful.[36] Having stabilized his line, he turned his attention to the sound of fighting on East Cemetery Hill. There, with darkness falling, Confederates from Major General Jubal Early's Division had gotten into Union batteries and were fighting the cannoneers hand-to-hand.[37] Hancock sent the First Brigade of his Third Division, under Colonel Samuel S. Carroll, to the fighting.[38] The brigade was crucial in flushing the enemy out of the batteries and dispatching them back down the face of East Cemetery Hill.

On July 3, Hancock continued in his position on Cemetery Ridge and thus bore the brunt of Pickett's Charge.[39] During the massive Confederate artillery bombardment that preceded the infantry assault, Hancock was prominent on horseback in reviewing and encouraging his troops. When one of his subordinates protested, "General, the corps commander ought not to risk his life that way," Hancock is said to have replied, "There are times when a corps commander's life does not count."[40] During the infantry assault, his old friend, Brig. Gen. Lewis A. Armistead, now leading a brigade in Maj. Gen. George Pickett's division, was wounded and died two days later. Hancock could not meet with his friend because he had just been wounded himself, a severe wound caused by a bullet striking the pommel of his saddle, entering his inner right thigh along with wood fragments and a large bent nail.[41] Helped from his horse by aides, and with a tourniquet applied to staunch the bleeding, he removed the saddle nail himself and, mistaking its source, remarked wryly, "They must be hard up for ammunition when they throw such shot as that."[42] News of Armistead's mortal wounding was brought to Hancock by a member of his staff, Captain Henry H. Bingham. Despite his pain, Hancock refused evacuation to the rear until the battle was resolved. He had been an inspiration for his troops throughout the three-day battle. Hancock later received the thanks of the U.S. Congress for " ... his gallant, meritorious and conspicuous share in that great and decisive victory."[13]

One military historian wrote, "No other Union general at Gettysburg dominated men by the sheer force of their presence more completely than Hancock."[26] As another wrote, "his tactical skill had won him the quick admiration of adversaries who had come to know him as the 'Thunderbolt of the Army of the Potomac'."[43]

## Virginia and the end of the war

Hancock suffered from the effects of his Gettysburg wound for the rest of the war. [26] After recuperating in Norristown, he performed recruiting services over the winter and returned in the spring to field command of the II Corps for Lt. Gen. Ulysses S. Grant's 1864 Overland Campaign, but he never regained full mobility and his former youthful energy.[44] Nevertheless, he performed well at the Battle of the Wilderness and commanded a critical breakthrough assault of the Mule Shoe at the "Bloody Angle" in the Battle of Spotsylvania Court House on May 12, shattering the Confederate defenders in his front, including the Stonewall Brigade.[45] His corps suffered enormous losses during a futile assault Grant ordered at Cold Harbor.[46]

After Grant's army slipped past Lee's army to cross the James River, Hancock found himself in a position from which he might have ended the war. His corps arrived to support William Farrar Smith's assaults on the lightly held Petersburg defensive lines, but he deferred to Smith's advice because Smith knew the ground and had been on the field all day, and no significant assaults were made before the Confederate lines were reinforced. One of the great opportunities of the war was lost.[2] After his corps participated in the assaults at Deep Bottom, Hancock was promoted to brigadier general in the regular army, effective August 12, 1864.[13]

Hancock's only significant military defeat occurred during the Siege of Petersburg. His II Corps moved south of the city, along the Wilmington and Weldon Railroad, tearing up track. On August 25, Confederate Maj. Gen. Henry Heth attacked and overran the faulty Union position at Reams's Station, shattering the II Corps, capturing many prisoners.[47] Despite a later victory at Hatcher's Run, the humiliation of Reams's Station contributed, along with the lingering effects of his Gettysburg wound, to his decision to give up field command in November.[48] He left the II Corps after a year in which it had suffered over 40,000 casualties, but had achieved significant military victories. His next assignment was to command the ceremonial First Veteran Corps.[48] He performed more recruiting, commanded the Middle Department, and relieved Maj. Gen. Philip Sheridan in command of forces in the now-quiet Shenandoah Valley.[2] He was promoted to brevet major general in the regular army for his service at Spotsylvania, effective March 13, 1865.[13]

## Post-war military service
### *Execution of Lincoln assassination conspirators*

At the close of the war, Hancock was assigned to supervise the execution of the Lincoln assassination conspirators.[49] Lincoln had been assassinated on April 14, 1865, and by May 9 of that year, a military commission had been convened to try the accused.[50] The actual assassin, John Wilkes Booth, was already dead, but the trial of his co-conspirators proceeded quickly, resulting in convictions. President Andrew Johnson ordered the executions

*The execution of the Lincoln assassination conspirators, July 7, 1865*

to be carried out on July 7. Although he was reluctant to execute some of the less-culpable conspirators, especially Mary Surratt, Hancock carried out his orders, later writing that "every soldier was bound to act as I did under similar circumstances."[51]

## Death

Hancock died in 1886 at Governors Island, still in command of the Military Division of the Atlantic, the victim of an infected carbuncle, complicated by diabetes.[26][2] He is buried in Montgomery Cemetery in West Norriton Township, Montgomery County, Pennsylvania, near Norristown, Pennsylvania.[13] Although he outlived both of his children, he was survived by the three grandchildren fathered by his son, Russell. Hancock's wife, Almira, published *Reminiscences of Winfield Scott Hancock* in 1887.

# David Herold

*Herold at the Washington Navy Yard after his arrest, 1865.*

**David Edgar Herold** (June 16, 1842–July 7, 1865) was an accomplice of John Wilkes Booth in the assassination of Abraham Lincoln on April 14, 1865. After the shooting, Herold accompanied Booth to the home of Dr. Samuel Mudd, who set Booth's injured leg. The two men then continued their escape through Maryland and into Virginia, and Herold remained with Booth until the authorities cornered them in a barn. Herold surrendered, but Booth was shot and died a few hours later. Herold was sentenced to death and hanged with three other conspirators at the Washington Arsenal, now known as Fort Lesley J. McNair.

## Biography

He became acquainted with John Surratt while attending classes at Charlotte Hall Military Academy in the late 1850s. A few years later, in December 1864, Surratt introduced him to John Wilkes Booth.

## Assassination plot

*Execution of Mary Surratt, Lewis Powell, David Herold, and George Atzerodt on July 7, 1865, at Fort McNair in Washington, D.C. Digitally restored.*

Herold and a group of co-conspirators had originally plotted to kidnap Lincoln, but later decided to kill him, the Vice President Andrew Johnson, and Secretary of State William H. Seward in a bid to help the Confederacy's cause.[5]

On the night of April 14, 1865, Herold guided Lewis Powell to Seward's house. Inside, Powell attempted to kill Seward, severely wounding him and other members of his household. The ensuing commotion frightened Herold and he rode off, leaving Powell to fend for himself. He then met with Booth outside of Washington, D.C., and they proceeded to Surrattsville, Maryland (now Clinton, Maryland) where they picked up weapons that Mary Surratt had left earlier for them at her property. Another conspirator, George Atzerodt, was supposed to kill Vice President Andrew Johnson, but never made the attempt.

It was at this point that John Wilkes Booth shot Lincoln at Ford's Theater. When Booth jumped onto the stage of Ford's theater, he broke his fibula. When Booth went across the bridge into Maryland, he met Herold there. They retrieved their weapons cache and proceeded to the home of Dr. Samuel Mudd, who set Booth's leg. Herold remained with Booth and continually aided him until Union cavalry caught up with them.

Herold and Booth were trapped by authorities on April 26, 1865, after taking refuge in a barn on the property of Richard Henry Garrett. Herold surrendered, but Booth refused to lay down his arms and was shot by Sergeant Boston Corbett through a crack in the barn wall. He died a few hours later. Herold was tried before a military tribunal. As he had already admitted his involvement in the assassination conspiracy, the only defense his lawyer Frederick Stone could offer was that David was feeble-minded[6] and under undue influence from Booth. His defense being unsuccessful, Herold was convicted and sentenced to death. He was hanged in Washington City on July 7, 1865. The fall from the gallows did not break his neck; he struggled for nearly five minutes, slowly strangling to death.

On February 15, 1869, David's mother and five of his sisters interred his remains in Congressional Cemetery (Washington, D.C.) in an unmarked grave, next to the grave of his father Adam.[7][8] The gravestone memorializing David now present in Congressional Cemetery was placed there in July 1917, at the time of the burial of his sister Mary Alice (Herold) Nelson (October 16, 1837–July 1, 1917) in the cemetery. Mary Alice was the wife of Frederick Massena Nelson (January 1827–May 11, 1909) of Pomonkey, Charles County, Maryland.

# A. P. Hill

**Ambrose Powell Hill Jr.** (November 9, 1825–April 2, 1865) was a Confederate general who was killed in the American Civil War. He is usually referred to as A. P. Hill to differentiate him from another, unrelated Confederate general, Daniel Harvey Hill.

A native Virginian, Hill was a career United States Army officer who had fought in the Mexican–American War and Seminole Wars prior to joining the Confederacy. After the start of the American Civil War, he gained early fame as the commander of the "Light Division" in the Seven Days Battles and became one of Stonewall Jackson's ablest subordinates, distinguishing himself in the 1862 battles of Cedar Mountain, Second Bull Run, Antietam, and Fredericksburg.

Following Jackson's death in May 1863 at the Battle of Chancellorsville, Hill was promoted to lieutenant general and commanded the Third Corps of Robert E. Lee's Army of Northern Virginia, which he led in the Gettysburg Campaign and the fall campaigns of 1863. His command of the corps in 1864–65 was interrupted on multiple occasions by illness, from which he did not return until just before the end of the war, when he was killed during the Union Army's offensive at the Third Battle of Petersburg.

## American Civil War

### Early months

On March 1, 1861, just before the outbreak of the Civil War, Hill resigned his U.S. Army commission. After Virginia seceded, he was appointed colonel of the 13th Virginia Infantry Regiment.[8] The 13th Virginia was one of the regiments in Brig. Gen. Joseph E. Johnston's army that were transported by railroad as reinforcements to the First Battle of Bull Run, but Hill and his men were sent to guard the Confederate right flank near Manassas and saw no action during the battle. Hill was promoted to brigadier general on February 26, 1862, and command of a brigade in the (Confederate) Army of the Potomac.[9]

## Light Division

In the Peninsula Campaign of 1862, Hill performed well as a brigade commander at the Battle of Williamsburg, where his brigade blunted a Union attack, and was promoted to major general and division command on May 26.[10] Hill's new division was composed mainly of brigades pulled from the Carolinas and Georgia.

His division did not participate in the Battle of Seven Pines (May 31–June 1), the battle in which Joseph E. Johnston was wounded and replaced in command of the Army of Northern Virginia by Robert E. Lee. June 1 was the first day that Hill began using a nickname for his division: the *Light Division*. This contradictory name for the largest division in

*General A.P. Hill*

all of the Confederate armies may have been selected because Hill wished his men to have a reputation for speed and agility. One of Hill's soldiers wrote after the war, "The name was applicable, for we often marched without coats, blankets, knapsacks, or any other burdens except our arms and haversacks, which were never heavy and sometimes empty."[11]

Hill's rookie division was in the thick of the fighting during the Seven Days Battles, being heavily engaged at Mechanicsville, Gaines Mill, and Glendale. Following the campaign, Hill became involved in a dispute with James Longstreet over a series of newspaper articles that appeared in the *Richmond Examiner*; relations between them deteriorated to the point that Hill was placed under arrest and Hill challenged Longstreet to a duel.[12] Following the Seven Days Battles, Lee reorganized the army into two corps and assigned Hill's division to Stonewall Jackson. Their relationship was less than amicable and the two quarreled many times. Hill frequently found himself under arrest by Jackson.[13]

At the Battle of Cedar Mountain on August 9, Hill launched a counterattack that stabilized the Confederate left flank, preventing it from being routed. Three weeks later at the Second Battle of Bull Run (Second Manassas), Hill was placed on the Confederate left along the unfinished railroad cut and held it against repeated Union attacks. During the campaign, Hill became involved in several minor disputes with Jackson concerning Jackson's marching orders to Hill.[14]

Hill's performance at The Battle of Antietam was particularly noteworthy. While Lee's army was enduring strong attacks by the Army of the Potomac outside Sharpsburg, Maryland, Hill's Light Division had been left behind to process Union prisoners at Harpers Ferry. Responding to an urgent call for assistance from Lee, Hill marched his men at a grueling pace and reached the battlefield just in time to counterattack a strong forward movement by the corps of Maj. Gen. Ambrose Burnside, which threatened to destroy Lee's right flank. Hill's arrival neutralized the threat, bringing an end to the battle with Lee's army battered but undefeated.[15] Hours after the battle, Hill told an inquisitive major that Burnside owed him $8,000.[16] During the retreat back to Virginia, he had his division push back a few regiments from the Union V Corps.[17]

At the Battle of Fredericksburg in December 1862, Hill was positioned near the Confederate right along a ridge; because of some swampy ground along his front, there was a 600-yard gap in Hill's front line, and the nearest brigade behind it was nearly a quarter mile away; the dense vegetation prevented the brigade commander from seeing any Union troops advancing on his position. During the battle, Maj. Gen. George Meade's division routed two of Hill's brigades and part of a third. Hill required the assistance from Maj. Gen. Jubal A. Early's division to repulse the Union attack. Hill's division suffered over 2,000 casualties during the battle, which was nearly two-thirds of the casualties in

Jackson's corps; two of his brigade commanders were wounded, one (Maxcy Gregg) mortally.[18] After the battle one of his brigade commanders, Brig. Gen. James J. Archer, criticized him about the gap left in the division's front line, saying that Hill had been warned about it before the battle but had done nothing to correct it. Hill was also absent from his division, and there is no record of where he was during the battle; this led to a rumor spread through the lines that he had been captured during the initial Union assault.[19]

Hill and Jackson argued several times during the Northern Virginia Campaign and the 1862 Maryland Campaign. During the invasion of Maryland, Jackson had Hill arrested and after the campaign charged him with eight counts of dereliction of duty.[20] During the lull in campaigning following the Battle of Fredericksburg, Hill repeatedly requested that Lee set up a court of inquiry, but the commanding general did not wish to lose the effective teamwork of his two experienced lieutenants and so refused to approve Hill's request.[21] Their feud was put aside whenever a battle was being fought and then resumed afterward, a practice that lasted until the Battle of Chancellorsville in May 1863.[22] There, Jackson was accidentally wounded by the 18th North Carolina Infantry of Hill's division. Hill briefly took command of the Second Corps and was wounded himself in the calves of his legs. While in the infirmary, he requested that the cavalry commander, J. E. B. Stuart, take his place in command.[23]

## Third Corps commander

After Jackson's death from pneumonia, Hill was promoted on May 24, 1863, to lieutenant general (becoming the Army of Northern Virginia's fourth highest-ranking general) and placed in command of the newly created Third Corps of Lee's army, which he led in the Gettysburg Campaign of 1863.[5] One of Hill's divisions, led by his West Point classmate Maj. Gen. Henry Heth, was the first to engage Union troops at the Battle of Gettysburg. Although the first day of the battle was a resounding Confederate success, Hill received much postbellum criticism from proponents of the Lost Cause movement, suggesting that he had unwisely brought on a general engagement against orders before Lee's army was fully concentrated.[24] His division under Maj. Gen. Richard H. Anderson fought in the unsuccessful second day assaults against Cemetery Ridge, while his favorite division commander, Maj. Gen. William Dorsey Pender, commanding the Light Division, was severely wounded, which prevented that division from cooperating with the assault. On the third day, two thirds of the men in Pickett's Charge were from Hill's corps, but Robert E. Lee chose James Longstreet to be overall commander of the assault.[25] Of all three infantry corps of the Army of Northern Virginia, Hill's suffered the most casualties at Gettysburg, which prompted Lee to order them to lead the retreat back into Virginia.[26]

During the autumn campaign of the same year, Hill launched his Corps "too hastily" in the Battle of Bristoe Station and was bloodily repulsed by Maj. Gen. Gouverneur K. Warren's II Corps. Lee did not criticize him for this afterward, but ordered him to detail himself to the dead and wounded after hearing his account. Hill's corps also took part in the Battle of Mine Run. Other than a brief visit to Richmond in January 1864, Hill remained with his corps in its winter encampments near Orange Court House.[27]

In the Overland Campaign of 1864, Hill's corps held back multiple Union attacks during the first day of the Battle of the Wilderness, but became severely disorganized as a result. Despite several requests from his division commanders, Hill refused to straighten and strengthen his line during the night, possibly due to Lee's plan to relieve them at daylight. At dawn on the second day of the battle, the Union army launched an attack that briefly drove Hill's corps back, with several units routed, but the First Corps under Longstreet arrived just in time to reinforce him.[28] Hill was medically incapacitated with an unspecified illness at Spotsylvania Court House, so Maj. Gen. Jubal Early temporarily took command of the Third Corps, but Hill was able to hear that his men were doing well and to observe the battle at Lee's side.[29] After recovering and regaining his corps, he was later rebuked by Lee for his piecemeal attacks at the Battle of North Anna. By then, Lee himself was too ill to coordinate his subordinates in springing a planned trap of the Union Army.[30] Hill held the Confederate left flank at Cold Harbor, but two divisions of his corps were used to defend against the main Union attack on the right flank on June 3; when part of the troops to his right gave way, Hill used one brigade to launch a successful counterattack.[31]

During the Siege of Petersburg of 1864–65, Hill and his men participated in several battles during the various Union offensives, particularly Jerusalem Plank Road, the Crater, Globe Tavern, Second Reams Station, and Peebles Farm. During the Battle of the Crater, he fought against his West Point classmate Ambrose Burnside, whom the former repulsed at Antietam and Fredericksburg. Hill was ill several times that winter; in March 1865, his health had deteriorated to the point where he had to recuperate in Richmond until April 1, 1865.[32]

## Death

Hill had said he had no desire to live to see the collapse of the Confederacy,[33] and on April 2, 1865, (during the Union breakthrough in the Third Battle of Petersburg, just seven days before Lee's surrender at Appomattox Court House), he was shot dead by a Union soldier, Corporal John W. Mauck of the 138th Pennsylvania, as he rode to the front of the Petersburg lines, accompanied by one staff officer. The Union soldiers called upon Hill to surrender. He refused their demands and was shot through the chest with a rifle. The bullet went through his heart, came out the other side of his chest, and sliced off his left thumb.[34] Hill fell to the ground and died within moments. His body was recovered by the Confederates shortly afterward. His family had hoped to take Hill to Richmond for burial, but the city's capture by Union forces caused him to be buried in Chesterfield County. In February 1867, his remains were re-interred in Hollywood Cemetery in Richmond. During the late 1880s, several former comrades raised funds for a monument to Hill in Richmond. Hill's remains were transferred to the base of the monument when it was dedicated on May 30, 1892.[35]

When Lee heard of Hill's death, he tearfully uttered, "He is now at rest, and we who are left are the ones to suffer."[36]

Per his last will and testament, he was interred standing up.[37]

# John Bell Hood

**John Bell Hood** (June 1[2] or June 29,[3] 1831– August 30, 1879) was a Confederate general during the American Civil War. Hood had a reputation for bravery and aggressiveness that sometimes bordered on recklessness. Arguably one of the best brigade and division commanders in the CSA, Hood gradually became increasingly ineffective as he was promoted to lead larger, independent commands late in the war; his career and reputation were marred by his decisive defeats leading an army in the Atlanta Campaign and the Franklin–Nashville Campaign.

Hood's education at the United States Military Academy led to a career as a junior officer in both the infantry and cavalry of the antebellum U.S. Army in California and Texas. At the start of the Civil War, he offered his services to his adopted state of Texas. He achieved his reputation for aggressive leadership as a brigade commander in the army of Robert E. Lee during the Seven Days Battles in 1862, after which he was promoted to division command. He led a division under James Longstreet in the campaigns of 1862–63. At the Battle of Gettysburg, he was severely wounded, rendering his left arm useless for the rest of his life. Transferred with many of Longstreet's troops to the Western Theater, Hood led a massive assault into a gap in the Union line at the Battle of Chickamauga, but was wounded again, requiring the amputation of his right leg.

Hood returned to field service during the Atlanta Campaign of 1864, and at the age of 33 was promoted to temporary full general and command of the Army of Tennessee at the outskirts of Atlanta, making him the youngest soldier on either side of the war to be given command of an army. There, he dissipated his army in a series of bold, calculated, but unfortunate assaults, and was forced to evacuate the besieged city. Leading his men through Alabama and into Tennessee, his army was severely damaged in a massive frontal assault at the Battle of Franklin and he was decisively defeated at the Battle of Nashville by his former West Point instructor, Maj. Gen. George H. Thomas, after which he was relieved of command.

After the war, Hood moved to Louisiana and worked as a cotton broker and in the insurance business. His business was ruined by a yellow fever epidemic in New Orleans during the winter of 1878–79 and he succumbed to the disease himself, dying just days after his wife and oldest child, leaving ten destitute orphans.

# Civil War

## Brigade and division command

Hood resigned from the United States Army immediately after the Battle of Fort Sumter and, dissatisfied with the neutrality of his native Kentucky, decided to serve his adopted state of Texas. He joined the Confederate army as a cavalry captain,[12] then was promoted to major and sent to command Brigadier General John B. Magruder's cavalry in the lower Virginia Peninsula. Hood and his horsemen took part in a "brilliant" July 12 skirmish at Newport News, capturing 12 men of the 7th New York Regiment of Volunteers as well as two deserters from Fort Monroe. They received high praise from Generals Lee and Magruder.[13][14] By September 30, the Texan was promoted to be colonel of the 4th Texas Infantry Regiment.[12]

On February 20, 1862, Hood was assigned to command a new brigade of mainly Texas regiments that would soon become known as the Texas Brigade. The brigade had been initially formed the previous fall and had initially been led by ex-US Senator Louis T. Wigfall, but he resigned his command to take a seat in the Confederate Congress. On March 26, Hood was promoted to brigadier general. Leading the Texas Brigade as part of the Army of Northern Virginia in the Peninsula Campaign, he established his reputation as an aggressive commander, eager to lead his troops personally into battle, and the Texans quickly gained a reputation as one of the army's elite combat units. At the Battle of Eltham's Landing, his men were instrumental in nullifying an amphibious landing by a Union division. When commanding general Joseph E. Johnston reflected upon the success Hood's men enjoyed in executing his order "to feel the enemy gently and fall back," he humorously asked, "What would your Texans have done, sir, if I had ordered them to charge and drive back the enemy?" Hood replied, "I suppose, General, they would have driven them into the river, and tried to swim out and capture the gunboats."[15] The Texas Brigade was held in reserve at Seven Pines.[16]

At the Battle of Gaines's Mill on June 27, Hood distinguished himself by leading his brigade in a charge that broke the Union line, which was the most successful Confederate performance in the Seven Days Battles. Hood himself survived unscathed, but over 400 men and most of the officers in the Texas Brigade were killed or wounded. He broke down and wept at the sight of the dead and dying men on the field. After inspecting the Union entrenchments, Maj. Gen Stonewall Jackson remarked "The men who carried this position were truly soldiers indeed."[17]

When Maj. Gen. William H.C. Whiting left the army on medical furlough July 26, Hood became permanent division commander, and his command was reassigned to Maj. Gen James Longstreet's corps. While the division had numbered five brigades at Seven Pines, a couple of army reorganizations since then reduced it to just two—the Texas Brigade and a brigade of Mississippians commanded by Col. Evander M. Law. Also accompanying them during the Northern Virginia Campaign was the independent South Carolina brigade of Brig. Gen Nathan G. Evans, who technically had authority over Hood, his junior in rank, for the campaign. At Second Bull Run, Hood spearheaded the assault on the Union left flank that forced them to retreat from the field. Hood's two brigades lost over 1000 men in the battle, and if Evans's brigade is also counted in, the total would be near 1500 casualties.[18]

In the pursuit of Union forces, Hood was involved in a dispute over captured ambulances with a superior officer, Brig. Gen. Nathan "Shanks" Evans. Evans arrested Hood, but Gen. Lee intervened and retained him in service. During the Maryland Campaign, just before the Battle of South Mountain, Hood was in the rear, still in virtual arrest. His Texas troops shouted to General Lee, "Give us Hood!" Lee restored Hood to command, despite Hood's refusal to apologize for his conduct.[19]

> It could scarcely be said that any [of the officers in Longstreet's corps] . . . save one had by this date displayed qualities that would dispose anyone to expect a career of eminence. The exception was Hood. . . . Anyone who had followed the operations of the Army after Gaines's Mill would have said that of all the officers under Longstreet, the most likely to be a great soldier was Hood.
> —Douglas Southall Freeman, *Lee's Lieutenants* [20]

During the Battle of Antietam, Hood's division came to the relief of Stonewall Jackson's corps on the Confederate left flank, fighting in the infamous cornfield, and turning back an assault by the Union I Corps in the West Woods. Afterward, they became engaged with the Union XII Corps. In the evening after the battle, Gen. Lee asked Hood where his division was. He responded, "They are lying on the field where you sent them. My division has been almost wiped out." Of his 2,000 men, almost 1,000 were casualties. Jackson was impressed with Hood's performance and recommended his promotion to major general, which occurred effective October 10, 1862.[21]

In the Battle of Fredericksburg in December, Hood's division saw little action, placed in the center, between Longstreet's lines on Marye's Heights, and Jackson's lines. And in the spring of 1863, he missed the great victory of the Battle of Chancellorsville because most of Longstreet's First Corps was on detached duty in Suffolk, Virginia, involving Longstreet himself and Hood's and George Pickett's divisions. When he heard news of Stonewall Jackson's death after Chancellorsville, he expressed grief for the man he most deeply admired, personally and militarily.[22]

## Gettysburg

It was to Hood that Lee wrote on May 21, 1863, prior to the Gettysburg Campaign on their growing confidence in the Army of Northern Virginia:

> I agree with you in believing that our army would be invincible if it could be properly organized and officered. There never were such men in an army before. They will go anywhere and do anything if properly led.[23]

At the Battle of Gettysburg, Longstreet's Corps arrived late on the first day, July 1, 1863. General Lee planned an assault for the second day that would feature Longstreet's Corps attacking northeast up the Emmitsburg Road into the Union left flank. Hood was dissatisfied with his assignment in the assault because it would face difficult terrain in the boulder-strewn area known as the Devil's Den. He requested permission from Longstreet to move around the left flank of the Union army, beyond the mountain known as [Big] Round Top, to strike the Union in their rear area. Longstreet refused permission, citing Lee's orders, despite repeated protests from Hood. Yielding to the inevitable, Hood finally gave in and his division stepped off around 4 p.m. on July 2, but a variety of factors caused it to veer to the east, away from its intended direction, where it would eventually meet with Union forces at Little Round Top. Just as the attack started, however, Hood was the victim of an artillery shell exploding overhead, severely damaging his left arm, which incapacitated him. (Although the arm was not amputated, he was unable to make use of it for the rest of his life.) His ranking brigade commander, Brig. Gen. Evander M. Law, assumed command of the division, but confusion as to orders and command status dissipated the direction and strength of the Confederate attack, significantly affecting the outcome of the battle.[24]

Hood recuperated in Richmond, Virginia, where he made a social impression on the ladies of the Confederacy. In August 1863, famous diarist Mary Boykin Chesnut wrote of Hood:

> When Hood came with his sad Quixote face, the face of an old Crusader, who believed in his cause, his cross, and his crown, we were not prepared for such a man as a beau-ideal of the wild Texans. He is tall, thin, and shy; has blue eyes and light hair; a tawny beard, and a vast amount of it, covering the lower part of his face, the whole appearance that of awkward strength. Some one said that his great reserve of manner he carried only into the society of ladies. Major [Charles S.] Venable added that he had often heard of the light of battle shining in a man's eyes. He had seen it once — when he carried to Hood orders from Lee, and found in the hottest of the fight that the man was transfigured. The fierce light of Hood's eyes I can never forget.[25]

As he recuperated, Hood began a campaign to win the heart of the young, prominent South Carolina socialite, Sally Buchanan Preston, known as "Buck" to her friends, whom he had first met while traveling through Richmond in March 1863. Hood later confessed that the flirtatious Southern belle had caused him to "surrender at first sight." As he prepared to return to duty in September, Hood proposed marriage to Buck, but received only a noncommittal response.[26]

## Chickamauga

Meanwhile, in the Western Theater, the Confederate army under General Braxton Bragg was faring poorly. Lee dispatched two divisions of Longstreet's Corps to Tennessee, and Hood was able to rejoin his men at Chickamauga Creek on September 18.[27] Bragg ordered him to form a "mini-corps," merging one of the brigades he had with him on the field with Brig. Gen. Bushrod Johnson's division. It was then that Hood participated in the Battle of Chickamauga, driving Col. Robert Minty's Union brigade from Reed's Bridge and stopping only at Alexander's Bridge, where John T. Wilder's men fired their Spencer repeating rifles on the Confederates.[28] As darkness set in, he chanced to have met Gen. John C. Breckinridge, former Vice-President of the United States, presidential candidate and Senator of Kentucky as well as a cousin of Buck Preston.[29] The remaining two units of Hood's division regrouped with their commander to prepare for the next day's battle.[30]

On the afternoon of the 19th, Hood repulsed an attack by Jefferson C. Davis's Union division.[31] He then advanced to assist Brig. Gen Henry D. Clayton's outnumbered men near the Lafayette Road.[32] Around this time, Longstreet had arrived; Hood was to be in temporary command of the I Corps, which would serve as part of the Confederate left wing under Longstreet.[33]

On the 20th, Hood led Longstreet's assault that exploited a gap in the Federal line, which led to the defeat of Maj. Gen. William Rosecrans's Union Army of the Cumberland. However, Hood was once again wounded severely; his right femur was fractured and his leg was amputated four inches (100 mm) below the hip. Hood's condition was so grave that the surgeon sent the severed leg along with him in the ambulance, assuming that they would be buried together. Because of Hood's bravery at Chickamauga, Longstreet recommended that he be promoted to lieutenant general as of that date, September 20, 1863; the confirmation by the Confederate Senate occurred on February 11, 1864, as Hood was preparing to return to duty.[34]

During Hood's second recuperation in Richmond that fall, he befriended Confederate President Jefferson Davis, who would subsequently promote him to a more important role. He also resumed his courtship of Buck Preston—a cousin of Breckinridge's—who, despite giving him some ambiguously positive signals, dashed his hopes on Christmas Eve. Hood confided to Mary Chesnut that the courtship "was the hardest battle he had ever fought in his life." In February, Hood proposed again to Buck and this time demanded a specific response, which was a reluctant, embarrassed agreement. However, the Preston family did not approve of Hood, who left for the field unmarried.[35]

## Atlanta Campaign and the Army of Tennessee

In the spring of 1864, the Confederate Army of Tennessee, under Gen. Joseph E. Johnston, was engaged in a campaign of maneuver against William T. Sherman, who was driving from Chattanooga toward Atlanta. Despite his two damaged limbs, Hood performed well in the field, riding as much as 20 miles a day without apparent difficulty, strapped to his horse with his artificial leg hanging stiffly, and an orderly following closely behind with crutches. The leg, made of cork, was donated (along with a couple of spares) by members of his Texas Brigade, who had collected $3,100 in a single day for that purpose; it had been

*Confederate General John Bell Hood*

imported from Europe through the Union blockade.[36] On May 12, Hood was baptized by Lieutenant General Leonidas Polk, the former Episcopal Bishop of Louisiana. Colonel Walter H. Rodgers, a witness to the baptism, stated that Hood "looked happy and as though a great burden had been lifted."[37]

During the Atlanta Campaign, Hood urged the normally cautious Johnston to act aggressively, but Johnston usually reacted to flanking maneuvers by Sherman with timely withdrawals, rather similar to his strategy in the Peninsula Campaign. One attempt by Johnston to act decisively in the offensive, during the Battle of Cassville, ironically was foiled by Hood, who had been ordered to attack the flank of one column of Sherman's army, but instead pulled back and entrenched when confronted by the unexpected arrival of a small detachment of that column.[38]

The Army of Tennessee continued withdrawing until it had crossed the last major water barrier before Atlanta, the Chattahoochee River. During this time, Hood had been sending the government in Richmond letters very critical of Johnston's conduct, bypassing official communication channels. The issue came to a head when Gen. Braxton Bragg was ordered by President Davis to travel to Atlanta to personally interview Johnston. After meeting with Johnston, he interviewed Hood and another subordinate, Joseph Wheeler, who told him that they had repeatedly urged Johnston to attack. Hood presented a letter that branded Johnston as being both ineffective and weak-willed. He told Bragg, "I have, General, so often urged that we should force the enemy to give us battle as to almost be regarded reckless by the officers high in rank in this army [meaning Johnston and senior corps commander William J. Hardee], since their views have been so directly opposite." Johnston's biographer, Craig L. Symonds, judges that Hood's letter "stepped over the line from unprofessional to outright subversive." Civil War historian Steven E. Woodworth wrote that Hood was "letting his ambition get the better of his honesty" because "the truth was that Hood, more often than Hardee, had counseled Johnston to retreat."[39] However, Hood was not alone in his criticism of Johnston's timidity. In William Hardee's June 22, 1864, letter to General Bragg, he stated, "If the present system continues we may find ourselves at Atlanta before a serious battle is fought." Other generals in the Army agreed with that assessment.[40]

On July 17, 1864, Jefferson Davis relieved Johnston. He considered replacing him with the more senior Hardee, but Bragg strongly recommended Hood. Bragg had not only been impressed by his interview with Hood, but he retained lingering resentments against Hardee from bitter disagreements in previous campaigns. Hood was promoted to the temporary rank of full general on July 18, and given command of the army just outside the gates of Atlanta. (Hood's temporary appointment as a full general was never confirmed by the Senate. His commission as a lieutenant general resumed on January 23, 1865.[12]) At 33, Hood was the youngest man on either side to be given command of an army. Robert E. Lee gave an ambiguous reply to Davis's request for his opinion about the promotion, calling Hood "a bold fighter, very industrious on the battlefield, careless off," but he could not say whether Hood possessed all of the qualities necessary to command an army in the field.[41] Lee also stated in the same letter to Jefferson Davis that he had a high opinion of Hood's gallantry, earnestness, and zeal.[42]

The change of command in the Army of Tennessee did not go unnoticed by Sherman. His subordinates, James B. McPherson and John M. Schofield, shared their knowledge of Hood from their time together at West Point. Upon learning of his new adversary's perceived reckless and gambling tendencies, Sherman planned to use that to his advantage.[43]

Hood conducted the remainder of the Atlanta Campaign with the strong aggressive actions for which he had become famous. He launched four major attacks that summer in an attempt to break Sherman's siege of Atlanta, starting almost immediately with an attack along Peachtree Creek. After hearing that McPherson was mortally wounded in the Battle of Atlanta, Hood deeply regretted his loss.[44] All of the offensives failed, particularly at the Battle of Ezra Church, with significant Confederate casualties. Finally, on September 2, 1864, Hood evacuated the city of Atlanta, burning as many military supplies and installations as possible.[45]

## Franklin–Nashville Campaign

As Sherman regrouped in Atlanta, preparing for his March to the Sea, Hood and Jefferson Davis met to devise a strategy to defeat him. Their plan was to attack Sherman's lines of communications between Chattanooga and Atlanta, and to move north through Alabama and into central Tennessee, assuming that Sherman would be threatened and follow. Hood's ambitious hope was that he could maneuver Sherman into a decisive battle, defeat him, recruit additional forces in Tennessee and Kentucky, and pass through the Cumberland Gap to come to the aid of Robert E. Lee, who was besieged at Petersburg. However, the plan proved a failure since Sherman felt this development furthered his current objective by removing opposing forces in his path, noting "If he [Hood] will go to the Ohio River, I'll give him rations. . . . my business is down south."[46] Instead of pursuing Hood with his army, he sent Maj. Gen. George H. Thomas to take control of the Union forces in Tennessee and coordinate the defense against Hood, while the bulk of Sherman's forces prepared to march toward Savannah.[47]

During their conference, Davis expressed his disappointment in Hood's performance in defending Atlanta, losing almost 20,000 men in ill-advised frontal assaults for no significant gains, and implied that he was considering replacing Hood in command of the army. After the president's departure for Montgomery, Alabama, he telegraphed Hood that he had decided to retain him in command and, acceding to Hood's request, transferred Hardee out of the Army of Tennessee. He also established a new theater commander to supervise Hood and the department of Lt. Gen. Richard Taylor, although the officer selected for the assignment, Gen. P.G.T. Beauregard, was not expected to exert any real operational control of the armies in the field.[48]

Hood's Tennessee Campaign lasted from September to December 1864, comprising seven battles and hundreds of miles of marching. He attempted to trap a large part of the Union Army of the Ohio under Maj. Gen. John M. Schofield at Spring Hill, Tennessee, before it could link up with Thomas in Nashville, but command failures and misunderstandings allowed Schofield's men to safely pass by Hood's army in the night. The next day at the Battle of Franklin, Hood sent his men across nearly two miles of open ground without the support of artillery in a last gasp effort to destroy Schofield's forces before they could withdraw across the Harpeth River and reach the safety of Nashville, which was only a night's march from Franklin. His troops were unsuccessful in their attempt to breach the Union breastworks, suffering severe casualties in an assault that is sometimes called the "Pickett's Charge of the West." Hood's exhausted army was unable to interfere as the Union force withdrew into Nashville. He later wrote that "Never did troops fight more gallantly" than at Franklin. Some popular histories assert that Hood acted rashly in a fit of rage, resentful that the Federal army had slipped past his troops the night before at Spring Hill and that he wanted to discipline his army by ordering his men to assault against strong odds. Recent scholarship by Eric Jacobson and Stephen M. Hood discounts this as unlikely, as it was not only militarily foolish, but Hood was observed to be determined, not angry, by the time he arrived in Franklin.[49]

> Never had there been such an overwhelming victory during the Civil War—indeed, never in American military history.
> —Wiley Sword, describing the Franklin–Nashville Campaign[50]

Unwilling to abandon his original plan, Hood stumbled toward the heavily fortified capital of Tennessee, and laid siege with inferior forces, which endured the beginning of a severe winter. Two weeks later, George Thomas attacked and completely routed Hood at the Battle of Nashville. During the battle and the subsequent relentless pursuit to the south, the Army of Tennessee ceased to be an effective fighting force, as the campaign cost the army about 23,500 of its initial strength of 38,000.[50] Hood and the remnants of the army retreated as far as Tupelo, Mississippi. Some of the survivors eventually joined Joseph E. Johnston for the Carolinas Campaign against Sherman. P.G.T. Beauregard sought permission to replace Hood with Lt. Gen. Richard Taylor, and the change of command occurred January 23, 1865. In a speech to his men, Hood expressed the hope that they would give their support to Taylor and avenge their comrades "whose bones lay bleaching upon the fields of Middle Tennessee." He returned to Richmond on February 8.[51]

## Final days of the war
In March 1865, Hood requested assignment to the Trans-Mississippi Theater to report on the situation there and to assess the possibility of moving troops across the Mississippi

River to reinforce the East. He met with Richard Taylor in Mississippi in late April and agreed with Taylor's proposal that his force should surrender. He departed to take this recommendation to the commanders remaining in the field, but before he arrived in Texas, General Edmund Kirby Smith surrendered his forces, and Hood surrendered himself in Natchez, Mississippi, where he was paroled on May 31, 1865.[52]

## Postbellum career

After the war, Hood moved to Louisiana and became a cotton broker and worked as president of the Life Association of America, an insurance business. In 1868, he married New Orleans native Anna Marie Hennen, with whom he had 11 children over 10 years, including three pairs of twins. He also served the community in numerous philanthropic endeavors, assisting in fund-raising for orphans, widows, and wounded soldiers.

During the postwar period, he began a memoir, *Advance and Retreat: Personal Experiences in the United States and Confederate States Armies*. Though rough, incomplete and not published until after his death, this work served to justify his actions, particularly in response to what he considered misleading or false accusations made by Joseph E. Johnston, and to unfavorable portrayals in William Tecumseh Sherman's memoirs.

His insurance business collapsed during a yellow fever epidemic in New Orleans during the winter of 1878–79. Soon after, in a single week, the epidemic killed Hood himself, Hood's wife, and his eldest daughter Lydia. His other ten children were left orphaned and penniless. The Texas Brigade Association provided support for the children for more than 20 years and all ten were eventually adopted by seven different families in Louisiana, Mississippi, Georgia, Kentucky, and New York.[53]

# Joseph Hooker

*Portrait by Mathew Brady or Levin C. Handy*

**Joseph Hooker** (November 13, 1814–October 31, 1879) was a career United States Army officer, achieving the rank of major general in the Union Army during the American Civil War. Although he served throughout the war, usually with distinction, Hooker is best remembered for his stunning defeat by Confederate General Robert E. Lee at the Battle of Chancellorsville in 1863.

After graduating from the United States Military Academy in 1837, Hooker served in the Seminole Wars and the Mexican–American War, receiving three brevet promotions. He resigned from the Army in 1853 and pursued farming, land development, and (unsuccessfully) politics in California. After the start of the Civil War he returned to the Army as a brigadier general. He distinguished himself as an aggressive combat commander leading a division in the Battle of Williamsburg, May 5, 1862, resulting in his promotion to major general. As a corps commander, he led the initial Union attacks at the Battle of Antietam, in which he was wounded. At the Battle of Fredericksburg, he commanded a "Grand Division" of two corps, and was ordered to conduct numerous futile frontal assaults that caused his men to suffer serious losses. Throughout this period, he conspired against and openly criticized his army commanders. Following the defeat at Fredericksburg, he was given command of the Army of the Potomac.

Hooker planned an audacious campaign against Robert E. Lee, but his Army was defeated by the Confederate Army at the Battle of Chancellorsville. Hooker's subordinate general's mistakes, and a loss of confidence on his part contributed to a failure to marshal the strength of his larger army against Lee, who boldly divided his army and routed a Union corps with a flank attack led by Stonewall Jackson. Casualties were heavy on both sides (approximately 17,000 of the Union's 117,000 troops, and 13,000 of the Confederate's 60,000 troops), and the defeat handed Lee the initiative, which allowed him to travel north to Gettysburg.[1]

Lincoln kept Hooker in command, but when General Halleck and Lincoln declined Hooker's request for troops from Harpers Ferry to reinforce his army while in pursuit of Lee's advance toward Pennsylvania, Hooker resigned his command. George G. Meade was appointed to the command of the Army of the Potomac on June 28, 1863, three days before Gettysburg, and was allowed to take the troops from Harpers Ferry.[1]

Hooker returned to combat in November, leading two corps from the Army of the Potomac to help relieve the besieged Union Army at Chattanooga, Tennessee, and achieving an important victory at the Battle of Lookout Mountain during the Chattanooga Campaign. He continued in the Western Theater under Maj. Gen. William T. Sherman, but departed in protest before the end of the Atlanta Campaign when he was passed over for promotion to command the Army of the Tennessee.

Hooker became known as "Fighting Joe" following a journalist's clerical error reporting from the Battle of Williamsburg; however, the nickname stuck. His personal reputation was as a hard-drinking ladies' man, and his headquarters were known for parties and gambling, although the historical evidence discounts any heavy drinking by the general himself.

## Civil War

At the start of the Civil War in 1861, Hooker requested a commission, but his first application was rejected, possibly because of the lingering resentment harbored by Winfield Scott, general-in-chief of the Army. He had to borrow money to make the trip east from California. After he witnessed the Union Army defeat at the First Battle of Bull Run, he wrote a letter to President Abraham Lincoln that complained of military mismanagement, promoted his own qualifications, and again requested a commission. He was appointed, in August 1861, as brigadier general of volunteers to rank from May 17. He commanded a brigade and then division around Washington, D.C., as part of the effort to organize and train the new Army of the Potomac, under Maj. Gen. George B. McClellan.[8]

## 1862

In the Peninsula Campaign of 1862, Hooker commanded the 2nd Division of the III Corps and made a good name for himself as a combat leader who handled himself well and aggressively sought out the key points on battlefields. He led his division with distinction at Williamsburg and at Seven Pines. Hooker's division did not play a major role in the Seven Days Battles, although he and fellow division commander Phil Kearny tried unsuccessfully to urge McClellan to counterattack the Confederates. He chafed at the cautious generalship of McClellan and openly criticized his failure to capture Richmond. Of his commander, Hooker said, "He is not only not a soldier, but he does not know what soldiership is." The Peninsula cemented two further reputations of Hooker's: his devotion to the welfare and morale of his men, and his hard drinking social life, even on the battlefield.

On July 26, Hooker was promoted to major general, to rank from May 5. During the Second Battle of Bull Run, the III Corps was sent to reinforce John Pope's Army of Virginia. Following Second Bull Run, Hooker replaced Irvin McDowell as commander of the Army of Virginia's III Corps, soon redesignated the I Corps of the Army of the Potomac. During the Maryland Campaign, Hooker led the I Corps at South Mountain and at Antietam, his corps launched the first assault of the bloodiest day in American history, driving south into the corps of Lt. Gen. Stonewall Jackson, where they fought each other to a standstill. Hooker, aggressive and inspiring to his men, left the battle early in the morning with a foot wound. He asserted that the battle would have been a decisive Union victory if he had managed to stay on the field, but General McClellan's caution once again failed the Northern troops and Lee's much smaller army eluded destruction. With his patience at an end, President Lincoln replaced McClellan with Maj. Gen. Ambrose Burnside. Although Hooker had criticized McClellan persistently, the latter was apparently unaware of it and in early October, shortly before his termination, had recommended that Hooker receive a promotion to brigadier general in the regular army. The War Department promptly acted on this recommendation, and Hooker received his brigadier's commission to rank from September 20. This promotion ensured that he would remain a general after the war was over and not revert to the rank of captain or lieutenant colonel.

The December 1862 Battle of Fredericksburg was another Union debacle. Upon recovering from his foot wound, Hooker was briefly made commander of V Corps, but was then promoted to "Grand Division" command, with a command that consisted of both III and V Corps. Hooker derided Burnside's plan to assault the fortified heights behind the city, deeming them "preposterous." His Grand Division (particularly V Corps) suffered serious losses in fourteen futile assaults ordered by Burnside over Hooker's protests. Burnside followed up this battle with the humiliating Mud March in January and Hooker's criticism of his commander bordered on formal insubordination. He described Burnside as a "wretch . . . of blundering sacrifice." Burnside planned a wholesale purge of his subordinates, including Hooker, and drafted an order for the president's approval. He stated that Hooker was "unfit to hold an important commission during a crisis like the present." But Lincoln's patience had again run out and he removed Burnside instead.

## Army of the Potomac

*Major General Joseph Hooker*

Lincoln appointed Hooker to command of the Army of the Potomac on January 26, 1863. Some members of the army saw this move as inevitable, given Hooker's reputation for aggressive fighting, something sorely lacking in his predecessors. During the "Mud March" Hooker was quoted by a *New York Times* army correspondent as saying that "Nothing would go right until we had a dictator, and the sooner the better."[9] Lincoln wrote a letter to the newly appointed general, part of which stated,

I have heard, in such way as to believe it, of your recently saying that both the Army and the Government needed a Dictator. Of course it was not for this, but in spite of it, that I have given you the command. Only those generals who gain success can set up dictators. What I now ask of you is military success, and I will risk the dictatorship.[10]

During the spring of 1863, Hooker established a reputation as an outstanding administrator and restored the morale of his soldiers, which had plummeted to a new low under Burnside. Among his changes were fixes to the daily diet of the troops, camp sanitary changes, improvements and accountability of the quartermaster system, addition of and monitoring of company cooks, several hospital reforms, and an improved furlough system (one man per company by turn, 10 days each). He also implemented corps badges as a means of identifying units during battle or when marching and to instill unit pride in the men. Other orders addressed the need to stem rising desertion (one from Lincoln combined with incoming mail review, the ability to shoot deserters, and better camp picket lines), more and better drills, stronger officer training, and for the first time, combining the federal cavalry into a single corps.[11] Hooker said of his revived army:

I have the finest army on the planet. I have the finest army the sun ever shone on. . . . If the enemy does not run, God help them. May God have mercy on General Lee, for I will have none.

Also during this winter Hooker made several high-level command changes, including with his corps commanders. Both "Left Grand Division" commander Maj. Gen. William B. Franklin, who vowed that he would not serve under Hooker, and II Corps commander Maj. Gen. Edwin Vose Sumner were relieved of command, on Burnside's recommendation, in the same order appointing Hooker to command. The IX Corps was a potential source of embarrassment or friction within the army because it was Burnside's old corps, so it was detached as a separate organization and sent to the Virginia Peninsula under the command of Brig. Gen. William F. "Baldy" Smith, former commander of VI Corps. (Both Franklin and Smith were considered suspect by Hooker because of their previous political maneuvering against Burnside and on behalf of McClellan.)[12]

For the important position of chief of staff, Hooker asked the War Department to send him Brig. Gen. Charles Stone, however this was denied. Stone had been relieved, arrested, and imprisoned for his role in the Battle of Ball's Bluff in the fall of 1861, despite the lack of any trial. Stone did not receive a command upon his release, mostly due to political pressures, which left him militarily exiled and disgraced. Army of the Potomac historian and author Bruce Catton termed this request by Hooker "a strange and seemingly uncharacteristic thing" and "one of the most interesting things he ever did."[13] Hooker never explained why he asked for Stone, but Catton believed:

[Hooker] laid schemes and calculations aside and for one brief moment stood up as a straightforward soldier who would defy politics and politicians. . . . It is a point to remember, because to speak up for General Stone took moral courage, a quality which Joe Hooker is rarely accused of possessing.[14]

Despite this, Fighting Joe would set a very bad example for the conduct of generals and their staffs and subordinates. His headquarters in Falmouth, Virginia, was described by cavalry officer Charles F. Adams, Jr., as being a combination of a "bar-room and a brothel."[15] He built a network of loyal political cronies that included Maj. Gen. Dan Butterfield for chief of staff, and the notorious political general, Maj. Gen. Daniel E. Sickles, for command of the III Corps.

## Chancellorsville

*General "Fightin' Joe" Hooker*

*Union General Joseph Hooker (seated 2nd to right) and his staff, 1863*

Hooker's plan for the spring and summer campaign was both elegant and promising. He first planned to send his cavalry corps deep into the enemy's rear, disrupting supply lines and distracting him from the main attack. He would pin down Robert E. Lee's much smaller army at Fredericksburg, while taking the large bulk of the Army of the Potomac on a flanking march to strike Lee in his rear. Defeating Lee, he could move on to seize Richmond. Unfortunately for Hooker and the Union, the execution of his plan did not match the elegance of the plan itself. The cavalry raid was conducted cautiously by its commander, Brig. Gen. George Stoneman, and met none of its objectives. The flanking march went well enough, achieving strategic surprise, but when he attempted to advance with three columns, Stonewall Jackson's surprise attack on May 1 pushed Hooker back and caused him to withdraw his troops. From there, Hooker pulled his army back to Chancellorsville and waited for Lee to attack. Lee audaciously split his smaller army in two to deal with both parts of Hooker's army. Then, he split again, sending Stonewall Jackson's corps on its own flanking march, striking Hooker's exposed right flank and routing the Union XI Corps. The Army of the Potomac dropped into a purely defensive mode and eventually was forced to retreat.

The Battle of Chancellorsville has been called "Lee's perfect battle" because of his ability to vanquish a much larger foe through audacious tactics. Part of Hooker's failure can be attributed to an encounter with a cannonball; while he was standing on the porch of his headquarters, the missile struck a wooden column against which he was leaning, initially knocking him senseless, and then putting him out of action for the rest of the day with a concussion. Despite his incapacitation, he refused entreaties to turn over temporary command of the army to his second-in-command, Maj. Gen. Darius N. Couch. Several of his subordinate generals, including Couch and Maj. Gen. Henry W. Slocum, openly questioned Hooker's command decisions. Couch was so disgusted that he refused to ever serve under Hooker again. Political winds blew strongly in the following weeks as generals maneuvered to overthrow Hooker or to position themselves if Lincoln decided on his own to do so.

Robert E. Lee once again began an invasion of the North, in June 1863, and Lincoln urged Hooker to pursue and defeat him. Hooker's initial plan was to seize Richmond instead, but Lincoln immediately vetoed that idea, so the Army of the Potomac began to march north, attempting to locate Lee's Army of Northern Virginia as it slipped down the Shenandoah Valley into Pennsylvania. Hooker's mission was first to protect Washington, D.C., and Baltimore and second to intercept and defeat Lee. Unfortunately, Lincoln was losing any remaining confidence he had in Hooker. Hooker's senior officers expressed to Lincoln their lack of confidence in Hooker, as did Henry Halleck, Lincoln's General-in-chief.[16] When Hooker got into a dispute with Army headquarters over the status of defensive forces in Harpers Ferry, he impulsively offered his resignation in protest, which was quickly accepted by Lincoln and General-in-chief Henry W. Halleck. On June 28, 1863, three days before the climactic Battle of Gettysburg, Hooker was replaced by Maj. Gen. George Meade. Hooker received the Thanks of Congress for his role at the start of the Gettysburg Campaign,[17] but the glory would go to Meade. Hooker's tenure as head of the Army of the Potomac had lasted 5 months.

## Western Theater

Hooker's military career was not ended by his poor performance in the summer of 1863. He went on to regain a reputation as a solid corps commander when he was transferred with the XI and XII Corps of the Army of the Potomac westward to reinforce the Army of the Cumberland around Chattanooga, Tennessee. Hooker was in command at the Battle of Lookout Mountain, playing an important role in Lt. Gen. Ulysses S. Grant's decisive victory at the Battle of Chattanooga. He was brevetted to major general in the regular army for his success at Chattanooga, but he was disappointed to find that Grant's official report of the battle credited his friend William Tecumseh Sherman's contribution over Hooker's.

Hooker led his corps (now designated the XX Corps) competently in the 1864 Atlanta Campaign under Sherman, but asked to be relieved before the capture of the city because of his dissatisfaction with the promotion of Maj. Gen. Oliver O. Howard to command of the Army of the Tennessee, upon the death of Maj. Gen. James B. McPherson. Not only did Hooker have seniority over Howard, but he also blamed Howard in large part for his defeat at Chancellorsville (Howard had commanded the XI Corps, which had borne the brunt of Jackson's flank attack). Hooker's biographer reports that there were numerous stories indicating that Abraham Lincoln attempted to intercede with Sherman, urging that Hooker be appointed to command the Army of the Tennessee, but Sherman threatened to resign if the president insisted. However, due to "obvious gaps" in the Official Records, the story cannot be verified.[18]

After leaving Georgia, Hooker commanded the Northern Department (comprising the states of Michigan, Ohio, Indiana, and Illinois), headquartered in Cincinnati, Ohio, from October 1, 1864, until the end of the war.[7] While in Cincinnati he married Olivia Groesbeck, sister of Congressman William S. Groesbeck.

## Final years

After the war, Hooker led Lincoln's funeral procession in Springfield on May 4, 1865. He served in command of the Department of the East and Department of the Lakes following the war. His postbellum life was marred by poor health and he was partially paralyzed by a stroke. He was mustered out of the volunteer service on September 1, 1866, and retired from the U.S. Army on October 15, 1868, with the regular army rank of major general. He died on October 31, 1879, while on a visit to Garden City, New York, and is buried in Spring Grove Cemetery, Cincinnati, Ohio,[7] his wife's home town.

# Stonewall Jackson

*General Jackson at Winchester, Virginia*
1862

**Thomas Jonathan "Stonewall" Jackson** (January 21, 1824–May 10, 1863) served as a Confederate general (1861–1863) during the American Civil War, and became one of the best-known Confederate commanders after General Robert E. Lee.[2] Jackson played a prominent role in nearly all military engagements in the Eastern Theater of the war until his death, and played a key role in winning many significant battles.

Born in what was then part of Virginia (in present-day West Virginia), Jackson received an appointment to the United States Military Academy at West Point, served in the U.S. Army during the Mexican–American War of 1846–1848 and distinguished himself at Chapultepec (1847). From 1851 to 1863 he taught at the Virginia Military Institute, where he was unpopular with his students. During this time, he married twice. His first wife died giving birth, but his second wife, Mary Anna Morrison, lived until 1915. When Virginia seceded from the Union in May 1861 after the attack on Fort Sumter (April 12, 1861), Jackson joined the Confederate Army. He distinguished himself commanding a brigade at the First Battle of Bull Run (July 21, 1861) the following month, providing crucial reinforcements and beating back a fierce Union assault. In this context Barnard Elliott Bee Jr. compared him to a "stone wall," hence his enduring nickname.

Jackson performed well in the campaigns in the Shenandoah Valley during 1862. Despite an initial defeat due largely to faulty intelligence, through swift and careful maneuvers Jackson was able to defeat three separate Union armies and prevent any of them from reinforcing General George B. McClellan's Army of the Potomac in its campaign against Richmond. Jackson then quickly moved his three divisions to reinforce General Lee's Army of Northern Virginia in defense of Richmond. His performance in the subsequent Seven Days Battles (June–July 1862) against George B. McClellan's Army of the Potomac was poor, but did not inhibit Confederate victory in the battles. During the Northern Virginia Campaign that summer, Jackson's troops captured and destroyed an important supply depot for General John Pope's Army of Virginia, and then withstood repeated assaults from Pope's troops at the Second Battle of Bull Run in August 1862. Jackson's troops played a prominent role in September's Maryland Campaign, capturing the town of Harpers Ferry, a strategic location, and providing a defense of the Confederate Army's left at Antietam on September 17, 1862. At Fredericksburg in December, Jackson's corps buckled but ultimately beat back an assault by the Union Army under Major General Ambrose Burnside.

In late April and early May 1863, faced with a larger Union army now commanded by Joseph Hooker at Chancellorsville, Lee divided his force three ways. On May 2, Jackson took his 30,000 troops and launched a surprise attack against the Union right flank, driving the opposing troops back about two miles. That evening he was accidentally shot by Confederate pickets. The general survived but lost his left arm to amputation; weakened by his wounds, he died of pneumonia eight days later.

Military historians regard Jackson as one of the most gifted tactical commanders in U.S. history.[3] His tactics are studied even today. His death proved a severe setback for the Confederacy, affecting not only its military prospects, but also the morale of its army and the general public. After Jackson's death, his military exploits developed a legendary quality, becoming an important element of the ideology of the "Lost Cause."[4]

## Slavery

*Stonewall Jackson in 1855*

Little as he was known to the white inhabitants of Lexington, Jackson was revered by many of the African Americans in town, both slaves and free blacks. In 1855, he was instrumental in the organization of Sunday School classes for blacks at the Presbyterian Church. His second wife, Mary Anna Jackson, taught with Jackson, as "he preferred that my labors should be given to the colored children, believing that it was more important and useful to put the strong hand of the Gospel under the ignorant African race, to lift them up."[27] The pastor, Dr. William Spottswood White, described the relationship between Jackson and his Sunday afternoon students: "In their religious instruction he succeeded wonderfully. His discipline was systematic and firm, but very kind. . . . His servants reverenced and loved him, as they would have done a brother or father. . . . He was emphatically the black man's friend." He addressed his students by name and they, in turn, referred to him affectionately as "Marse Major."[28]

Jackson's family owned six slaves in the late 1850s. Three (Hetty, Cyrus, and George, a mother and two teenage sons) were received as a wedding present. Another, Albert, requested that Jackson purchase him and allow him to work for his freedom; he was employed as a waiter in one of the Lexington hotels and Jackson rented him to VMI. Amy also requested that Jackson purchase her from a public slave auction and she served the family as a cook and housekeeper. The sixth, Emma, was a four-year-old orphan with a learning disability, accepted by Jackson from an aged widow and presented to his second wife, Mary Anna, as a welcome-home gift.[29] After the American Civil War began he appears to have hired out or sold his slaves, except, apparently at least, one slave: "A 'servant', Jim Lewis, had stayed with Jackson in the small house as he lay dying."[30] Mary Anna Jackson, in her 1895 memoir, said, "our servants . . . without the firm guidance and restraint of their master, the excitement of the times proved so demoralizing to them that he deemed it best for me to provide them with good homes among the permanent residents."[31] James Robertson wrote about Jackson's view on slavery:

> Jackson neither apologized for nor spoke in favor of the practice of slavery. He probably opposed the institution. Yet in his mind the Creator had sanctioned slavery, and man had no moral right to challenge its existence. The good Christian slaveholder was one who treated his servants fairly and humanely at all times.[32]

## John Brown raid aftermath

In November 1859, at the request of the governor of Virginia, Major William Gilham led a contingent of the VMI Cadet Corps to Charles Town to provide an additional military presence at the hanging of militant abolitionist John Brown on December 2, following his raid on the federal arsenal at Harpers Ferry on October 16. Major Jackson was placed in command of the artillery, consisting of two howitzers manned by twenty-one cadets.

## Civil War

In 1861, after Virginia seceded from the Union and as the American Civil War broke out, Jackson became a drill master for some of the many new recruits in the Confederate Army. On April 27, 1861, Virginia Governor John Letcher ordered Colonel Jackson to take command at Harpers Ferry, where he would assemble and command the unit which later gained fame as the "Stonewall Brigade," consisting of the 2nd, 4th, 5th, 27th, and 33rd Virginia Infantry regiments. All of these units were from the Shenandoah Valley region of Virginia, where Jackson located his headquarters throughout the first two years of the war. Jackson became known for his relentless drilling of his troops; he believed discipline was vital to success on the battlefield. Following raids on the B&O Railroad on May 24, he was promoted to brigadier general on June 17.[35]

## First Battle of Bull Run

Jackson rose to prominence and earned his most famous nickname at the First Battle of Bull Run (First Manassas) on July 21, 1861. As the Confederate lines began to crumble under heavy Union assault, Jackson's brigade provided crucial reinforcements on Henry House Hill, demonstrating the discipline he instilled in his men. Although under heavy fire for several continuous hours, Jackson received a wound, breaking the middle finger of his left hand; about midway between the hand and knuckle, the ball passing on the side next the index finger. The troops of South Carolina, commanded by Gen. Barnard Elliott Bee Jr. had been overwhelmed, and he rode up to Jackson in despair, exclaiming, "They are beating us back!" "Then," said Jackson, "we will give them the bayonet!" As he rode back to his command, Bee exhorted his own troops to re-form by shouting, "There is Jackson standing like a stone wall. Let us determine to die here, and we will conquer. Rally behind the Virginians!"[36] There is some controversy over Bee's statement and intent, which could not be clarified because he was killed almost immediately after speaking and none of his subordinate officers wrote reports of the battle. Major Burnett Rhett, chief of staff to General Joseph E. Johnston, claimed that Bee was angry at Jackson's failure to come immediately to the relief of Bee's and Francis S. Bartow's brigades while they were under heavy pressure. Those who subscribe to this opinion believe that Bee's statement was meant to be pejorative: "Look at Jackson standing there like a stone wall!"[37]

Regardless of the controversy and the delay in relieving Bee, Jackson's brigade, which would thenceforth be known as the Stonewall Brigade, stopped the Union assault and suffered more casualties than any other Southern brigade that day; Jackson has since then been generally known as Stonewall Jackson.[38] During the battle, Jackson displayed a gesture common to him and held his left arm skyward with the palm facing forward—interpreted by his soldiers variously as an eccentricity or an entreaty to God for success in combat. His hand was struck by a bullet or a piece of shrapnel and he suffered a small loss of bone in his middle finger. He refused medical advice to have the finger amputated.[39] After the battle, Jackson was promoted to major general (October 7, 1861)[35] and given command of the Valley District, with headquarters in Winchester.

## Valley Campaign

In the spring of 1862, Union Maj. Gen. George B. McClellan's Army of the Potomac approached Richmond from the southeast in the Peninsula Campaign. Maj. Gen. Irvin McDowell's large corps was poised to hit Richmond from the north, and Maj. Gen. Nathaniel P. Banks's army threatened the Shenandoah Valley. Jackson was ordered by Richmond to operate in the Valley to defeat Banks's threat and prevent McDowell's troops from reinforcing McClellan.

Jackson possessed the attributes to succeed against his poorly coordinated and sometimes timid opponents: a combination of great audacity, excellent knowledge and shrewd use of the terrain, and an uncommon ability to inspire his troops to great feats of marching and fighting.

The campaign started with a tactical defeat at Kernstown on March 23, 1862, when faulty intelligence led him to believe he was attacking a small detachment. But it became a strategic victory for the Confederacy, because his aggressiveness suggested that he possessed a much larger force, convincing President Abraham Lincoln to keep Banks' troops in the Valley and McDowell's 30,000-man corps near Fredericksburg, subtracting about 50,000 soldiers from McClellan's invasion force. As it transpired, it was Jackson's only defeat in the Valley.

By adding Maj. Gen. Richard S. Ewell's large division and Maj. Gen. Edward "Allegheny" Johnson's small division, Jackson increased his army to 17,000 men. He was still significantly outnumbered, but attacked portions of his divided enemy individually at McDowell, defeating both Brig. Gens. Robert H. Milroy and Robert C. Schenck. He defeated Banks at Front Royal and Winchester, ejecting him from the Valley. Lincoln decided that the defeat of Jackson was an immediate priority (though Jackson's orders were solely to keep Union forces occupied away from Richmond). He ordered Irvin McDowell to send 20,000 men to Front Royal and Maj. Gen. John C. Frémont to move to Harrisonburg. If both forces could converge at Strasburg, Jackson's only escape route up the Valley would be cut.

After a series of maneuvers, Jackson defeated Frémont's command at Cross Keys and Brig. Gen. James Shields at Port Republic on June 8–9. Union forces were withdrawn from the Valley.

It was a classic military campaign of surprise and maneuver. Jackson pressed his army to travel 646 miles (1,040 km) in 48 days of marching and won five significant victories with a force of about 17,000 against a combined force of 60,000. Stonewall Jackson's reputation for moving his troops so rapidly earned them the oxymoronic nickname "foot cavalry." He became the most celebrated soldier in the Confederacy (until he was eventually eclipsed by Lee) and lifted the morale of the Southern public.

## Peninsula

McClellan's Peninsula Campaign toward Richmond stalled at the Battle of Seven Pines on May 31 and June 1. After the Valley Campaign ended in mid-June, Jackson and his troops were called to join Robert E. Lee's Army of Northern Virginia in defense of the capital. By utilizing a railroad tunnel under the Blue Ridge Mountains and then transporting troops to Hanover County on the Virginia Central Railroad, Jackson and his forces made a surprise appearance in front of McClellan at Mechanicsville. Reports had last placed Jackson's forces in the Shenandoah Valley; their presence near Richmond added greatly to the Union commander's overestimation of the strength and numbers of the forces before him. This proved a crucial factor in McClellan's decision to re-establish his base at a point many miles downstream from Richmond on the James River at Harrison's Landing, essentially a retreat that ended the Peninsula Campaign and prolonged the war almost three more years.

Jackson's troops served well under Lee in the series of battles known as the Seven Days Battles, but Jackson's own performance in those battles is generally considered to be poor.[40] He arrived late at Mechanicsville and inexplicably ordered his men to bivouac for the night within clear earshot of the battle. He was late at Savage's Station. At White Oak Swamp he failed to employ fording places to cross White Oak Swamp Creek, attempting for hours to rebuild a bridge, which limited his involvement to an ineffectual artillery duel and a missed opportunity to intervene decisively at the Battle of Glendale, which was raging nearby. At Malvern Hill Jackson participated in the futile, piecemeal frontal assaults against entrenched Union infantry and massed artillery, and suffered heavy casualties (but this was a problem for all of Lee's army in that ill-considered battle). The reasons for Jackson's sluggish and poorly coordinated actions during the Seven Days are disputed, although a severe lack of sleep after the grueling march and railroad trip from the Shenandoah Valley was probably a significant factor. Both Jackson and his troops were completely exhausted. An explanation for this and other lapses by Jackson was tersely offered by his colleague and brother in-law General Daniel Harvey Hill: "Jackson's genius never shone when he was under the command of another."[41]

## Second Bull Run to Fredericksburg

*Montage of Thomas J. Jackson and staff.*

The military reputations of Lee's corps commanders are often characterized as Stonewall Jackson representing the audacious, offensive component of Lee's army, whereas his counterpart, James Longstreet, more typically advocated and executed defensive strategies and tactics. Jackson has been described as the army's hammer, Longstreet its anvil. [42] In the Northern Virginia Campaign of August 1862 this stereotype did not hold true. Longstreet commanded the Right Wing (later to become known as the First Corps) and Jackson commanded the Left Wing. Jackson started the campaign under Lee's orders with a sweeping flanking maneuver that placed his corps into the rear of Union Maj. Gen. John Pope's Army of Virginia. The Hotchkiss journal shows that Jackson, most likely, originally conceived the movement. In the journal entries for March 4 and 6, 1863, General Stuart tells Hotchkiss that "Jackson was entitled to all the credit" for the movement and that Lee thought the proposed movement "very hazardous" and "reluctantly consented" to the movement.[43] At Manassas Junction, Jackson was able to capture all of the supplies of the Union Army depot. Then he had his troops destroy all of it, for it was the main depot for the Union Army. Jackson then retreated and then took up a defensive position and effectively invited Pope to assault him. On August 28–29, the start of the Second Battle of Bull Run (Second Manassas), Pope launched repeated assaults against Jackson as Longstreet and the remainder of the army marched north to reach the battlefield.

On August 30, Pope came to believe that Jackson was starting to retreat, and Longstreet took advantage of this by launching a massive assault on the Union army's left with over 25,000 men. Although the Union troops put up a furious defense, Pope's army was forced to retreat in a manner similar to the embarrassing Union defeat at First Bull Run, fought on roughly the same battleground.

When Lee decided to invade the North in the Maryland Campaign, Jackson took Harpers Ferry, then hastened to join the rest of the army at Sharpsburg, Maryland, where they fought McClellan in the Battle of Antietam (Sharpsburg). Antietam was primarily a defensive battle against superior odds, although McClellan failed to exploit his advantage. Jackson's men bore the brunt of the initial attacks on the northern end of the battlefield and, at the end of the day, successfully resisted a breakthrough on the southern end when Jackson's subordinate, Maj. Gen. A. P. Hill, arrived at the last minute from Harpers Ferry.

The Confederate forces held their position, but the battle was extremely bloody for both sides, and Lee withdrew the Army of Northern Virginia back across the Potomac River, ending the invasion. On October 10, Jackson was promoted to lieutenant general, being ranked just behind Lee and Longstreet and his command was redesignated the Second Corps.

Before the armies camped for winter, Jackson's Second Corps held off a strong Union assault against the right flank of the Confederate line at the Battle of Fredericksburg, in what became a Confederate victory. Just before the battle, Jackson was delighted to receive a letter about the birth of his daughter, Julia Laura Jackson, on November 23.[44] Also before the battle, Maj. Gen. J. E. B. Stuart, Lee's dashing and well-dressed cavalry commander, presented to Jackson a fine general's frock coat that he had ordered from one of the best tailors in Richmond. Jackson's previous coat was threadbare and colorless from exposure to the elements, its buttons removed by admiring ladies. Jackson asked his staff to thank Stuart, saying that although the coat was too handsome for him, he would cherish it as a souvenir. His staff insisted that he wear it to dinner, which caused scores of soldiers to rush to see him in uncharacteristic garb. Jackson was so embarrassed with the attention that he did not wear the new uniform for months.[45]

## Chancellorsville

*General Jackson's "Chancellorsville" portrait, taken at a Spotsylvania County farm on April 26, 1863, seven days before he was wounded at the Battle of Chancellorsville*

At the Battle of Chancellorsville, the Army of Northern Virginia was faced with a serious threat by the Army of the Potomac and its new commanding general, Major General Joseph Hooker. General Lee decided to employ a risky tactic to take the initiative and offensive away from Hooker's new southern thrust—he decided to divide his forces. Jackson and his entire corps went on an aggressive flanking maneuver to the right of the Union lines: this flanking movement would be one of the most successful and dramatic of the war. While riding with his infantry in a wide berth well south and west of the Federal line of battle, Jackson employed Maj. Gen. Fitzhugh Lee's cavalry to provide for better reconnaissance regarding the exact location of the Union right and rear. The results were far better than even Jackson could have hoped. Fitzhugh Lee found the entire right side of the Federal lines in the middle of open field, guarded merely by two guns that faced westward, as well as the supplies and rear encampments. The men were eating and playing games in carefree fashion, completely unaware that an entire Confederate corps was less than a mile away. What happened next is given in Fitzhugh Lee's own words:

So impressed was I with my discovery, that I rode rapidly back to the point on the Plank road where I had left my cavalry, and back down the road Jackson was moving, until I met "Stonewall" himself. "General," said I, "if you will ride with me, halting your column here, out of sight, I will show you the enemy's right, and you will perceive the great advantage of attacking down the Old turnpike instead of the Plank road, the enemy's lines being taken in reverse. Bring only one courier, as you will be in view from the top of the hill." Jackson assented, and I rapidly conducted him to the point of observation. There had been no change in the picture. I only knew Jackson slightly. I watched him closely as he gazed upon Howard's troops. It was then about 2 pm. His eyes burned with a brilliant glow, lighting up a sad face. His expression was one of intense interest, his face was colored slightly with the paint of approaching battle, and radiant at the success of his flank movement. To the remarks made to him while the unconscious line of blue was pointed out, he did not reply once during the five minutes he was on the hill, and yet his lips were moving. From what I have read and heard of Jackson since that day, I know now what he was doing then. Oh! "beware of rashness," General Hooker. Stonewall Jackson is praying in full view and in rear of your right flank! While talking to the Great God of Battles, how could he hear what a poor cavalryman was saying. "Tell General Rodes," said he, suddenly whirling his horse towards the courier, "to move across the Old plank road; halt when he gets to the Old turnpike, and I will join him there." One more look upon the Federal lines, and then he rode rapidly down the hill, his arms flapping to the motion of his horse, over whose head it seemed, good rider as he was, he would certainly go. I expected to be told I had made a valuable personal reconnaissance – saving the lives of many soldiers, and that Jackson was indebted to me to that amount at least. Perhaps I might have been a little chagrined at Jackson's silence, and hence commented inwardly and adversely upon his horsemanship. Alas! I had looked upon him for the last time.

—Fitzhugh Lee, address to the Association of the Army of Northern Virginia, 1879

Jackson immediately returned to his corps and arranged his divisions into a line of battle to charge directly into the oblivious Federal right. The Confederates marched silently until they were merely several hundred feet from the Union position, then released a bloodthirsty cry and full charge. Many of the Federals were captured without a shot fired, the rest were driven into a full rout. Jackson pursued relentlessly back toward the center of the Federal line until dusk.

Darkness ended the assault. As Jackson and his staff were returning to camp on May 2, they were mistaken for a Union cavalry force by the 18th North Carolina Infantry regiment who shouted, "Halt, who goes there?," but fired before evaluating the reply. Frantic shouts by Jackson's staff identifying the party were replied to by Major John D. Barry with the retort, "It's a damned Yankee trick! Fire!"[46] A second volley was fired in response; in all, Jackson was hit by three bullets, two in the left arm and one in the right hand. Several other men in his staff were killed, in addition to many horses. Darkness and confusion prevented Jackson from getting immediate care. He was dropped from his stretcher while being evacuated because of incoming artillery rounds. Because of his injuries, Jackson's left arm had to be amputated by Dr. Hunter McGuire.[47] Jackson was moved to Thomas C. Chandler's 740 acres (3.0 km²) plantation named *Fairfield*. He was offered Chandler's home for recovery, but Jackson refused and suggested using Chandler's plantation office building instead. He was thought to be out of harm's way; but unknown to the doctors, he already had classic symptoms of pneumonia, complaining of a sore chest. This soreness was mistakenly thought to be the result of his rough handling in the battlefield evacuation.

## Death

Lee wrote to Jackson after learning of his injuries, stating: "Could I have directed events, I would have chosen for the good of the country to be disabled in your stead."[48] Jackson died of complications from pneumonia on May 10, 1863, eight days after he was shot. On his deathbed, though he became weaker, he remained spiritually strong, saying towards the end: "It is the Lord's Day; my wish is fulfilled. I have always desired to die on Sunday."

Dr. McGuire wrote an account of Jackson's final hours and last words:

A few moments before he died he cried out in his delirium, 'Order A.P. Hill to prepare for action! Pass the infantry to the front rapidly! Tell Major Hawks—' then stopped, leaving the sentence unfinished. Presently a smile of ineffable sweetness spread itself over his pale face, and he said quietly, and with an expression, as if of relief, 'Let us cross over the river, and rest under the shade of the trees.'[49]

His body was moved to the Governor's Mansion in Richmond for the public to mourn, and he was then moved to be buried in the Stonewall Jackson Memorial Cemetery, Lexington, Virginia. The arm that was amputated on May 2 was buried separately by Jackson's chaplain (Beverly Tucker Lacy), at the J. Horace Lacy house, "Ellwood," (now preserved at the Fredericksburg National Battlefield) in the Wilderness of Orange County, near the field hospital.[50]

Upon hearing of Jackson's death, Robert E. Lee mourned the loss of both a friend and a trusted commander. As Jackson lay dying, Lee sent a message through Chaplain Lacy, saying: "Give General Jackson my affectionate regards, and say to him: he has lost his left arm but I my right."[51] The night Lee learned of Jackson's death, he told his cook: "William, I have lost my right arm," and, "I'm bleeding at the heart."[52]

*Harper's Weekly* reported Jackson's death on May 23, 1863, as follows:

DEATH OF STONEWALL JACKSON.
General "Stonewall" Jackson was badly wounded in the arm at the battles of Chancellorsville, and had his arm amputated. The operation did not succeed, and pneumonia setting in, he died on the 10th inst., near Richmond, Virginia.[53]

## Command style

*A portrait of Stonewall Jackson (1864, J. W. King) in the National Portrait Gallery*

In command, Jackson was extremely secretive about his plans and extremely meticulous about military discipline. This secretive nature did not stand him in good stead with his subordinates, who were often not aware of his overall operational intentions until the last minute, and who complained of being left out of key decisions.[70]

Robert E. Lee could trust Jackson with deliberately undetailed orders that conveyed Lee's overall objectives, what modern doctrine calls the "end state." This was because Jackson had a talent for understanding Lee's sometimes unstated goals, and Lee trusted Jackson with the ability to take whatever actions were necessary to implement his end state requirements. Few of Lee's subsequent corps commanders had this ability. At Gettysburg, this resulted in lost opportunities. With a defeated and disorganized Union Army trying to regroup on high ground near town and vulnerable, Lee sent one of his new corps commanders, Richard S. Ewell, discretionary orders that the heights (Cemetery Hill and Culp's Hill) be taken "if practicable." Without Jackson's intuitive grasp of Lee's orders or the instinct to take advantage of sudden tactical opportunities, Ewell chose not to attempt the assault, and this failure is considered by historians to be the greatest missed opportunity of the battle.[71]

## Horsemanship

Jackson had a poor reputation as a horseman. One of his soldiers, Georgia volunteer William Andrews, wrote that Jackson was "a very ordinary looking man of medium size, his uniform badly soiled as though it had seen hard service. He wore a cap pulled down nearly to his nose and was riding a rawboned horse that did not look much like a charger, unless it would be on hay or clover. He certainly made a poor figure on a horseback, with his stirrup leather six inches too short, putting his knees nearly level with his horse's back, and his heels turned out with his toes sticking behind his horse's foreshoulder. A sorry description of our most famous general, but a correct one."[72] His horse was named "Little Sorrel" (also known as "Old Sorrel"), a small chestnut gelding which ironically was a captured Union horse from a Connecticut farm.[73][74] He rode Little Sorrel throughout the war, and was riding him when he was shot at Chancellorsville. Little Sorrel died at age 36 and is buried near a statue of Jackson on the parade grounds of VMI. (His mounted hide is on display in the VMI Museum.)[75]

# Harriet Ann Jacobs

**Harriet Ann Jacobs** (February 11, 1813–March 7, 1897) was an African-American writer who escaped from slavery and was later freed. She became an abolitionist speaker and reformer. Jacobs wrote an autobiography, *Incidents in the Life of a Slave Girl*, first serialized in a newspaper and published as a book in 1861 under the pseudonym Linda Brent. It was a reworking of the genres of slave narrative and sentimental novel, and was one of the first books to address the struggle for freedom by female slaves, explore their struggles with sexual harassment and abuse, and their effort to protect their roles as women and mothers.

After being overshadowed by the American Civil War, the book was rediscovered in the late 20th century, when there was new interest in minority and women writers. One scholar (Jean Fagan Yellin) researched the book, identifying Harriet Jacobs as the author and documenting many events and people in her life that corresponded to this autobiographical account.

## Biography

Harriet Ann Jacobs was born into slavery in Edenton, North Carolina, in 1813.[1] Her father was Elijah Knox, an enslaved biracial house carpenter owned by Andrew Knox. Elijah was said to be the son of Athena Knox, who was enslaved, and a white farmer, Henry Jacobs.[2] Harriet's mother was Delilah Horniblow, an enslaved black woman held by John Horniblow, a tavern owner. Under the principle of *partus sequitur ventrem*, both Harriet and her brother John were enslaved at birth, as their mother's status was passed to her children. Paternity from a free person—of any race—would not alter their status, according to law. Harriet lived with her mother until Delilah's death around 1819, when Harriet was six.[3] Then she lived with her mother's mistress, Margaret Horniblow, who taught Harriet to read, write and sew.

Three months before she died in 1825, Jacobs' mistress Margaret Horniblow had signed a will leaving her slaves to her mother. Dr. James Norcom and a man named Henry Flury witnessed a later codicil to the will directing that the girl Harriet be left to Norcom's daughter Mary Matilda, Horniblow's five-year-old niece. The codicil was not signed by Margaret Horniblow.[2] Norcom became Harriet's *de facto* master.

Norcom sexually harassed Harriet when she was still a child. He refused to allow her to marry, regardless of the man's status. Hoping to escape his attentions, Jacobs took Samuel Sawyer, a free white lawyer, as a consensual lover. Sawyer was later elected as a member of the US House of Representatives. With Sawyer, she had two children, Joseph and Louisa

Matilda Jacobs. Because she was enslaved, their biracial children were enslaved at birth by Norcom.[4] Harriet later wrote that Norcom threatened to sell her children if she refused his sexual advances, but she continued to evade him.

By 1835 her domestic situation had become unbearable, and Jacobs managed to escape. She hid in the home of a slaveowner in Edenton to keep an eye on her children. After a short stay, she took refuge in a swamp called Cabarrus Pocosin. She next hid in a crawl space above the ceiling of her grandmother Molly's shack.

Jacobs lived for seven years in her grandmother's attic before escaping in 1842 to the North by boat to Philadelphia, Pennsylvania. Sawyer had purchased their two children from Norcom. He let them live with Jacobs' grandmother but he did not free them.[4] The state had made manumission difficult following the Nat Turner slave rebellion of 1831. While in hiding, Jacobs had glimpses of her children from the attic and could hear their voices.

Jacobs escaped to the North in 1842, where she was taken in by anti-slavery friends from the Philadelphia Vigilant Committee. They helped her get to New York in September 1845.[5] There she found work as a nursemaid in the home of Nathaniel Parker Willis and made a new life. She was also able to reunite with her daughter, Louisa, who had been sent to New York at a young age to work as a "waiting-maid." By 1827, the last slaves had been freed in New York under its gradual abolition law.

In 1845, Jacobs' employer Mary Stace Willis died. Jacobs continued to care for Mary's daughter Imogen and to assist the widower Nathaniel Willis. In January she traveled to England with him and his daughter. In letters home, Jacobs claimed there was no prejudice against people of color in England. After returning from England, Jacobs left her employment with the Willises. She moved to Boston to visit with her daughter, son and brother for ten months. Her brother, John S. Jacobs, who had also escaped and was part of the anti-slavery movement, decided to open an anti-slavery reading room in Rochester, New York in 1849.[6] The black abolitionist, Frederick Douglass, was active in Rochester and it was a center of anti-slavery activities among whites as well.

John Jacobs found a school for Louisa and by November 1849, she was attending the Young Ladies Domestic Seminary School located in Clinton, New York. The school was founded in 1832 by abolitionist Hiram Huntington Kellogg. In 1849 Jacobs joined her brother in Rochester, where she met Quaker Amy Post. Amy and her husband Isaac Post were staunch abolitionists. As Jacobs became part of the American Anti-Slavery Society, she became very politicized. She helped support the Anti-Slavery Reading Room by speaking to audiences in Rochester to educate people and to raise money.

On October 1, 1850, John S. Jacobs' speech was quoted in *Meetings of Colored Citizens*. Following Congressional passage of the Fugitive Slave Act of 1850, both John and Harriet Jacobs feared for each other's safety, as legally they were still escaped slaves. The new law increased pressure to capture people who escaped slavery and required cooperation from officials and citizens of free states. The Jacobs' siblings left Rochester and returned to New York City. Furious about the act, John wanted to leave the country.

When he heard that the new state of California did not enforce the act, he decided to go there. He worked in the gold mines during the Gold Rush, where he was joined in 1852 by Joseph Jacobs, Harriet's son and his nephew.

On February 29, 1852, Harriet Jacobs was informed that Daniel Messmore, the husband of her young legal mistress Mary Matilda (Norcom) Messmore, had checked into a hotel in New York. To avert the risk of Jacobs being kidnapped, Cornelia Grinnell Willis (Willis' second wife) took Harriet and the Willis baby to a friend's house where they hid. Cornelia Willis encouraged Jacobs to take the baby and go to Willis relatives in Massachusetts. Without Jacobs' knowledge, Cornelia Willis paid $300 to Messmore for the rights to Harriet and gave Jacobs her freedom. Jacobs returned to New York with the Willis child.[7]

## Writing her memoir and other work

In late 1852 or early 1853, Amy Post suggested that Jacobs should write her life story. She also suggested that Jacobs contact the author Harriet Beecher Stowe, who was working on *A Key to Uncle Tom's Cabin*. When Stowe wanted to use Jacobs' history in her own book, Jacobs decided to write her own account.[8] She wrote secretly at night, in a nursery in the Willis' Idlewild estate.

Former First Lady Julia Tyler wrote a defense of slavery titled "The Women of England vs. the Women of America," in response to the "Stafford House Address" petition against slavery which the Duchess of Sutherland had helped to organize.[9][10] In response to "The Women of England vs. the Women of America," Jacobs wrote a letter to the *New York Tribune* which was her first published writing; it was published in 1853 and signed "Fugitive."[11][12]

Over the next several years, Jacobs continued to write her memoir, as well as letters to newspapers. In 1854, as Nathaniel Parker Willis was downstairs writing *Out-doors at Idlewild; Or, The Shaping of a Home on the Banks of the Hudson*, Jacobs was upstairs completing her own manuscript. Jacobs changed the names of all the people she depicted, including her own, to conceal their true identities and protect them from any adverse reaction. The slave owner "Dr. Flint" was based on Jacobs' former master, Dr. James Norcom.

In 1856, Jacobs' daughter Louisa became a governess in the home of James and Sara Payson Willis Parton, later known by the pen name Fanny Fern.[13]

## Publication of autobiography

Boston publishing house Phillips and Samson agreed to print Jacobs' autobiography, if she could convince Willis or Harriet Beecher Stowe to provide a preface, which they thought would help sales. She refused to ask Willis for help and Stowe turned her down. As it happened, the Phillips and Samson company soon closed shop.[14]

In 1860 Jacobs signed an agreement with the Thayer and Eldridge publishing house, which requested a preface by Lydia Maria Child.[14] Child also became involved in editing the manuscript, and the company introduced her to Jacobs. The two women remained in contact for much of their lives. Thayer and Eldridge went bankrupt before they could published the book. Jacobs herself ensured the publication of her book in both the United States and England in 1861.

Jacobs shaped her slave narrative to appeal to middle-class white Christian women in the North, focusing on the detrimental effect of slavery on women's chastity and sexual virtues. She insisted on showing that black slaves were women and mothers, too, challenging the white middle-class cult of womanhood as too narrowly construed.[8] Slave women had often been blamed when white men used them sexually, and Jacobs wanted to show how they were abused by the impossible power relationships. Christian women could perceive how slavery was a temptation to masculine lusts. The later part of *Incidents in the Life of a Slave Girl* was devoted to Jacobs' struggle to free her two children after she escaped.

## Life during the American Civil War

Starting in January, 1861, the United States suffered break-up; South Carolina, Mississippi, Florida, Alabama, Georgia, Louisiana, and Texas all seceded from the Union. The first six were the states that had the highest percentage of slaves to the total population among the 15 slave-holding states. In February, representatives from the southern states elected Jefferson Davis as President of the Confederacy. At this time, Harriet Jacobs and her editor, Lydia Maria Child, were trying to sell *Incidents in the Life of a Slave Girl*. They wrote to authors and editors of newspapers, to bookstore owners and to friends or frequent correspondents; they wanted anyone to advertise or sell Jacobs' narrative.

In May, 1861, John S. Jacobs, Harriet's younger brother, was in London to publish a much shorter narrative called *A True Tale of Slavery*. This book covered much of Harriet Jacobs' story, but it excluded the account of sexual harassment. John Jacobs' goal was to focus on slavery as an institution, trying to convince the people of England to support the Union. Not long after he published his narrative, the Civil War began in April, 1861, with the firing on Fort Sumter in South Carolina.

In the early years of the war, abolitionists were disturbed that Lincoln directed troops "to avoid any destruction of property," and they did not know what he was going to do about slavery. Unsure of what was to come, John S. Jacobs did not want to return to the United States until the government decided to abolish slavery. Many English had strong business ties to the South; southern cotton supplied British textile mills; and in addition to economic ties, aristocrats and others had some sympathies for the South. There was a threat that Great Britain might enter the war on the side of the Confederacy. John Jacobs stayed in London until the US government indicated it was serious about ending slavery. By January 14, 1862, John had already sold fifty copies of the narrative and stayed only two more weeks in England.

As the war continued, both *A True Tale of Slavery* and *Incidents in the Life of a Slave Girl* became more popular among abolitionists. Both books sold more copies in England than in the United States. The narratives encouraged the war as a fight against slavery.

In January 1862, Jacobs went with the Female Anti-Slavery Society to Philadelphia to lecture in support of her book. She also sent her book to a member of the Emancipation Committee in London. In England, the book was received as a major work of literature in addition to its anti-slavery position.

In August 1862, Jacobs worked in Alexandria, Virginia, and the Washington D.C. area to help organize, feed and shelter refugees from slavery and the poor free blacks of the region. She also tried to recruit more relief workers. During this period, she wrote to abolitionists Garrison and Charlotte Forten, both to share news and to ask for aid with work and supplies.

By March 1863, Jacobs noted the condition of poor refugees in Alexandria had improved, although there were 1,500 on a list for housing in the barracks, which could hold only 500. During this time, the marriage laws were changed to allow slaves and freedmen to marry, which she noted brought joy to many people.

In April, Julia A. Wilbur reported the needs of the black people in Alexandria to the Secretary of War, and he took immediate measures for their relief. Jacobs said she had the duty to go to Alexandria and act as a "visitor, advisor and instructor to the Contrabands of Alexandria." She ordered barracks to be built for the people of Alexandria, and the government honored her request. The additional barracks would house the old, disabled, women, children and orphans. Jacobs was sent to Alexandria to distribute donations among these people.

During this same period, Jacobs was working in Boston to help many poor blacks who had migrated there. An outbreak of smallpox caused many deaths. Other than the smallpox outbreak, the condition of the lives of these people had greatly improved. Jacobs noted that the people wanted to pay for their children to get schooling; they did not want to have a charity school. During this time, the newly freed people rejected being still referred to as "slaves," and hated being called "contrabands." Alexander Thomas Augusta, a free man of color from Virginia, had earned his medical degree in Canada and started practice there. After returning to the US after the outbreak of war, he appealed to President Lincoln to serve in the Army and received a commission. Jacobs reported that in 1863 he was appointed as a surgeon in the Union Army by the Secretary of War, the first African American to have such a position.

On June 5, 1863, Jacobs and two orphan children were featured at the New England Anti-Slavery Convention. She said she planned to bring many more orphaned black children from Virginia to Boston, and asked for help in placing them in new homes. People in the audience offered to take the two orphans home that day.[2]

From October 1863 to April 1865, Jacobs saw progress for the freedmen in Virginia. While living in Alexandria, again, she concentrated on setting up schools run by the community. Her daughter, Louisa Matilda Jacobs and a friend, Sarah Virginia Lawton of Cambridge, dedicated their lives to educating freedmen. "On January 11, 1864, the Jacobs Free School was named in her honor." She also contributed to organizing the communities of African Americans and to the building of hospitals, churches, schools and homes for newly freed people.[2]

Jacobs and her partner, Julia A. Wilbur, founded schools in Washington and Alexandria at the camps of black refugees from the South. But military officers took over houses they were using, as they needed quarters. In the camp areas, the loss of good housing was felt. Educating all people of color still was Jacobs' priority for improving their lives.[2]

According to records, Louisa Jacobs worked in a hospital throughout the Civil War.[2]

Jacobs mused about whether the lives of former slaves would be better because of their own efforts or those of "their white superiors." Jacobs' daughter taught in private homes until they could arrange a proper school. Soon after, a trustee meeting was called for her and other women who wished to teach. They gained a lease to have a building built for their use for five years.[2] Jacobs' students studied well and had steady progress. There was also a school at night for adults to learn. But the school lacked accommodations for the teachers, who had to board with families. Louisa needed more teachers to help her, and the school was $180.00 in debt with 275 children enrolled.

In May 1864, Jacobs wrote to the editors of *American Baptist* requesting help with the "Free Mission," an anti-slavery group. She wanted to collect clothing and basic necessities for the freedmen.[2]

On August 1, 1864, Jacobs returned to Arlington, Virginia. She set up an awareness day in Alexandria about the "struggle against chattel slavery," to celebrate the 30th anniversary of emancipation in the British West Indies and other colonies.[15] It was called the "First of August" celebration, and was Alexandria's first celebration of this kind. Festivals occurred throughout the North to raise awareness about slavery. This day gave a new meaning to the American flag because it now symbolized freedom for all.[2]

In October 1864, Jacobs wrote about the Small Pox Hospital in Claremont, which was used for both white soldiers and black people. All patients were properly cared for and treated alike. Other hospitals were struggling for lack of supplies. Jacobs worked to raise funds and acquire clothing and other supplies; she wanted to ensure quality treatment for black patients.[2]

By the end of October 1864, Jacobs updated her readers on the current conditions in Alexandria. She said that only a few of the freedmen relied on the government for food and shelter. Most were finding jobs and supporting themselves without additional assistance. Able to find housing in and around Washington, DC, they were living with improved conditions. In December, 1864, Alexandria School received donations to help provide for the children. Along with monetary donations they received books, slates and writing materials.

In 1865, Lydia Maria Child presented pages of Harriet Jacobs' narrative in *The Freedmen's Book*. She modified and republished certain passages from Jacobs' *Incidents in the Life of a Slave Girl*. Child emphasized the role of Jacobs' grandmother, focusing on her devotion and hard work. Such an account gave newly freed people an uplifting view to help them deal with their freedom.[2]

In April 1865, a New York committee reported on its visit to freedmen in Alexandria. It noted that African Americans were happy with the efforts of Harriet Jacobs. The school was under her management, and was successful.

On March 8, 1866, Jacobs wrote to Lydia Maria Child, noting that freedmen were being offered low wages in the Alexandria market. When they turned down job offers, whites complained they did not want to work. "Don't believe the stories so often repeated that the negroes are not willing to work. They are generally more than willing to work, if they can get anything for it," wrote Jacobs. Salaries were frequently offered to a group of laborers; for instance, Jacobs mentioned a group of former slaves who, for a salary, had to split a dollar and 50 cents.

Jacobs rejoiced when General Sherman gave freedmen 10–20 acres each of their rebel masters' land for three years. Even though it was late in the season to grow any crop, many freedmen were able to find success. "I visited some of the plantations, and I was rejoiced to see such a field of profitable labor opened for these poor people," says Jacobs. But President Andrew Johnson pardoned most rebels and restored their properties. The freedmen had to find new housing and work. When this happened, Jacobs told the freedmen to remain on the land until ordered to leave by the US government, hoping to stall until Congress stepped in. But the land was eventually returned. The freedmen suffered in winter weather, and the area had an outbreak of smallpox.[2]

In May 1866, Louisa Matilda Jacobs wrote a letter that was quoted in *The Fifth Report of New York Yearly Meeting of Friends on the Conditions and Wants of Freedmen*. She starts off saying how Harriet Jacobs was in Savannah with her daughter, where much help was needed with the expanding numbers of newly freed people. In the city, 3,933 slaves were freed by the 13th Amendment to the United States Constitution, but by 1866, more freedmen had left rural areas to settle there, reaching a total population of 10,500. She said starvation, sickness and disease were widespread. "Often in the cold weather were hundreds of them huddled together in misery and rags, over a few burning sticks, so desolate and filthy that they scarcely looked like human beings," wrote Louisa Jacobs. When spring came, some people were able to obtain some property to grow crops which were provided by the Committee that Harriet worked for. A school was also opened for freed children to go and get an education. The school acquired books and staff to teach the growing number of students.[2]

On May 26, 1866, a letter was written to Mr. and Mrs. Cheney from Louisa Jacobs. In the letter, she talks about the success of her school. She has been watching children who were at one time not able to read, begin to study arithmetic and geography with a full understanding of the English language. This, she says, is what brings her encouragement for all the work she has been doing. Jacobs then talks about how most freedmen now have their own land or are living on shares with other freedmen. Jacobs still knows that despite this glimpse of success, it will be hard for black people to really succeed in the south. She mentions that arrests are constant within the black community—even for the slightest offenses that a white man would get away with. A small charge could put a black person on the chain gang for six months or more. Jacobs stresses that, though things are going well, there are still obstacles ahead.

Around July 1866, there was a shooting that involved one African getting beaten severely and another being shot and killed. Two accounts circulated about the latter incident, one stating that the white man's life was in danger and he acted in self-defense, and the other stating that these incidents could have been avoided. Jacobs and her daughter decided to leave Savannah soon after the incident and head back North for the summer. On July 20, 1866, Harriet and Louisa boarded the steamship that took them to New York.

In November 1866, Harriet Jacobs received news that her son, Joseph, was sick in Australia and needed money for the trip home. Meanwhile, Louisa decided to join the American Equal Rights Association (AERA), which traveled from state to state advocating equal rights for all regardless of age, sex or color. She decided to leave the AERA, however, due to internal disagreements over the proposed 14th and 15th amendments to the Constitution, to provide citizenship and rights of suffrage to all African Americans. Jacobs and Louisa traveled to England to raise funds for the orphanage and home for the elderly they hoped to establish in Savannah. This refuge for destitute African Americans was never built.

In February 1867, Charles Lenox Remond, a prominent abolitionist, and Jacobs spoke to audiences in Johnstown, New York, thanks to arrangements made by Elizabeth Cady Stanton.

In 1868, Jacobs visited Britain to raise funds for orphans and freed, but poverty stricken, people in Savannah, Georgia. Jacobs published her appeal for funds in the Anti-Slavery Reporter and asked for them to be sent to Clementia Taylor, Robert Alsop or Stafford Allen. At least one hundred pounds was raised, but because of the prejudice in Georgia, Jacobs thought that the building would need to be delayed. This realization that the optimism of freedom would not be achieved as quickly as she hoped made this Jacobs' last visit to Britain.[16]

## Later years and death

Harriet Jacobs became less active in her later years, but supported her daughter and others in working for education of African Americans. Recently discovered letters written by her daughter, Louisa Matilda Jacobs, reveal aspects of her later life in 1880s and 1890s Washington, D.C.[17] She died in 1897 in Washington, DC. and was buried at Mount Auburn Cemetery in Cambridge, Massachusetts. Her headstone reads: "Patient in tribulation, fervent in spirit serving the Lord."[18]

# Andrew Johnson

**Andrew Johnson** (December 29, 1808–July 31, 1875) was the 17th president of the United States, serving from 1865 to 1869. Johnson assumed the presidency as he was vice president of the United States at the time of the assassination of Abraham Lincoln. A Democrat who ran with Lincoln on the National Union ticket, Johnson came to office as the Civil War concluded. He favored quick restoration of the seceded states to the Union. His plans did not give protection to the former slaves; he came into conflict with the Republican-dominated Congress, culminating in his impeachment by the House of Representatives. He was acquitted in the Senate by one vote. Johnson's main accomplishment as president is the Alaska purchase.

Johnson was born in poverty in Raleigh, North Carolina, and never attended school. Apprenticed as a tailor, he worked in several frontier towns before settling in Greeneville, Tennessee. He served as alderman and mayor there before being elected to the Tennessee House of Representatives in 1835. After brief service in the Tennessee Senate, Johnson was elected to the U.S. House of Representatives in 1843, where he served five two-year terms. He became Governor of Tennessee for four years, and was elected by the legislature to the U.S. Senate in 1857. In his congressional service, he sought passage of the Homestead Bill, which was enacted soon after he left his Senate seat in 1862. As Southern slave states, including Tennessee, seceded to form the Confederate States of America, Johnson remained firmly with the Union. He was the only sitting senator from a Confederate state who did not resign his seat upon learning of his state's secession. In 1862, Lincoln appointed him as military governor of Tennessee after most of it had been retaken. In 1864, Johnson, as a War Democrat and Southern Unionist, was a logical choice as running mate for Lincoln, who wished to send a message of national unity in his reelection campaign; their ticket easily won. When Johnson was sworn in as vice president in March 1865, he gave a rambling speech, after which he secluded himself to avoid public ridicule. Six weeks later, the assassination of Lincoln made him president.

Johnson implemented his own form of Presidential Reconstruction—a series of proclamations directing the seceded states to hold conventions and elections to reform their civil governments. When Southern states returned many of their old leaders, and passed Black Codes to deprive the freedmen of many civil liberties, Congressional Republicans refused to seat legislators from those states and advanced legislation to override the Southern actions. Johnson vetoed their bills, and Congressional Republicans overrode him, setting a pattern for the remainder of his presidency.[1] Johnson opposed the Fourteenth Amendment, which gave citizenship to former slaves. In 1866, Johnson went on an unprecedented national tour promoting his executive policies, seeking to destroy his Republican opponents.[2] As the conflict between the branches of government grew, Congress passed the Tenure of Office Act, restricting Johnson's ability to fire Cabinet officials. When he persisted in trying to dismiss Secretary of War Edwin Stanton, he was impeached by the House of Representatives, and narrowly avoided conviction in the Senate and removal from office. After failing to win the 1868 Democratic presidential nomination, Johnson left office in 1869.

Returning to Tennessee after his presidency, Johnson sought political vindication, and gained it in his eyes when he was elected to the Senate again in 1875, making Johnson the only former president to serve in the Senate. He died five months into his term. Johnson's strong opposition to federally guaranteed rights for African Americans is widely criticized. He is regarded by many historians as one of the worst presidents in American history.

## Secession crisis

*Johnson in 1860*

In October 1859, abolitionist John Brown and sympathizers raided the federal arsenal at Harpers Ferry, Virginia (today West Virginia). Tensions in Washington between pro- and anti-slavery forces increased greatly. Johnson gave a major speech in the Senate in December, decrying Northerners who would endanger the Union by seeking to outlaw slavery. The Tennessee senator stated that "all men are created equal" from the Declaration of Independence did not apply to African Americans, since the Constitution of Illinois contained that phrase—and that document barred voting by African Americans.[80][81] Johnson, by this time, was a wealthy man who owned a few household slaves,[82] 14 slaves, according to the 1860 Federal Census.[83]

Johnson hoped that he would be a compromise candidate for the presidential nomination as the Democratic Party tore itself apart over the slavery question. Busy with the Homestead Bill during the 1860 Democratic National Convention in Charleston, South Carolina, he sent two of his sons and his chief political adviser to represent his interests in the backroom deal-making. The convention deadlocked, with no candidate able to gain the required two-thirds vote, but the sides were too far apart to consider Johnson as a compromise. The party split, with Northerners backing Illinois Senator Stephen Douglas while Southerners, including Johnson, supported Vice President Breckinridge for president. With former Tennessee senator John Bell running a fourth-party candidacy and further dividing the vote, the Republican Party elected its first president, former Illinois representative Abraham Lincoln. The election of Lincoln, known to be against the spread of slavery, was unacceptable to many in the South. Although secession from the Union had not been an issue in the campaign, talk of it began in the Southern states.[84][85]

Johnson took to the Senate floor after the election, giving a speech well received in the

North, "I will not give up this government ... No; I intend to stand by it ... and I invite every man who is a patriot to ... rally around the altar of our common country ... and swear by our God, and all that is sacred and holy, that the Constitution shall be saved, and the Union preserved."[86][87] As Southern senators announced they would resign if their states seceded, he reminded Mississippi Senator Jefferson Davis that if Southerners would only hold to their seats, the Democrats would control the Senate, and could defend the South's interests against any infringement by Lincoln.[88] Gordon-Reed points out that while Johnson's belief in an indissoluble Union was sincere, he had alienated Southern leaders, including Davis, who would soon be the president of the Confederate States of America, formed by the seceding states. If the Tennessean had backed the Confederacy, he would have had small influence in its government.[89]

Johnson returned home when his state took up the issue of secession. His successor as governor, Isham G. Harris, and the legislature organized a referendum on whether to have a constitutional convention to authorize secession; when that failed, they put the question of leaving the Union to a popular vote. Despite threats on Johnson's life, and actual assaults, he campaigned against both questions, sometimes speaking with a gun on the lectern before him. Although Johnson's eastern region of Tennessee was largely against secession, the second referendum passed, and in June 1861, Tennessee joined the Confederacy. Believing he would be killed if he stayed, Johnson fled through the Cumberland Gap, where his party was in fact shot at. He left his wife and family in Greeneville.[90][91]

As the only member from a seceded state to remain in the Senate and the most prominent Southern Unionist, Johnson had Lincoln's ear in the early months of the war. [92] With most of Tennessee in Confederate hands, Johnson spent congressional recesses in Kentucky and Ohio, trying in vain to convince any Union commander who would listen to conduct an operation into East Tennessee.[93]

## Military Governor of Tennessee

Johnson's first tenure in the Senate came to a conclusion in March 1862 when Lincoln appointed him military governor of Tennessee. Much of the central and western portions of that seceded state had been recovered. Although some argued that civil government should simply resume once the Confederates were defeated in an area, Lincoln chose to use his power as commander in chief to appoint military governors over Union-controlled Southern regions.[94] The Senate quickly confirmed Johnson's nomination along with the rank of brigadier general.[95] In response, the Confederates confiscated his land and his slaves, and turned his home into a military hospital.[96] Later in 1862, after his departure from the Senate and in the absence of most Southern legislators, the Homestead Bill was finally enacted. Along with legislation for land-grant colleges and for the transcontinental railroad, the Homestead Bill has been credited with opening the American West to settlement.[97]

As military governor, Johnson sought to eliminate rebel influence in the state. He demanded loyalty oaths from public officials, and shut down all newspapers owned by

Confederate sympathizers. Much of eastern Tennessee remained in Confederate hands, and the ebb and flow of war during 1862 sometimes brought Confederate control again close to Nashville. However, the Confederates allowed his wife and family to pass through the lines to join him.[98][99] Johnson undertook the defense of Nashville as well as he could, though the city was continually harassed by cavalry raids led by General Nathan Bedford Forrest. Relief from Union regulars did not come until William S. Rosecrans defeated the Confederates at Murfreesboro in early 1863. Much of eastern Tennessee was captured later that year.[100]

When Lincoln issued the Emancipation Proclamation in January 1863, declaring freedom for all slaves in Confederate-held areas, he exempted Tennessee at Johnson's request. The proclamation increased the debate over what should become of the slaves after the war, as not all Unionists supported abolition. Johnson finally decided that slavery had to end. He wrote, "If the institution of slavery . . . seeks to overthrow it [the Government], then the Government has a clear right to destroy it."[101] He reluctantly supported efforts to enlist former slaves into the Union Army, feeling that African Americans should perform menial tasks to release white Americans to do the fighting.[102] Nevertheless, he succeeded in recruiting 20,000 black soldiers to serve the Union.[103]

## Vice President (1865)

In 1860, Lincoln's running mate had been Maine Senator Hannibal Hamlin. Vice President Hamlin had served competently, was in good health, and was willing to run again. Nevertheless, Johnson emerged as running mate for Lincoln's reelection bid in 1864.[104]

Lincoln considered several War Democrats for the ticket in 1864, and sent an agent to sound out General Benjamin Butler as a possible running mate. In May 1864, the President dispatched General Daniel Sickles to Nashville on a fact-finding mission. Although Sickles denied he was there either to investigate or interview the military governor, Johnson biographer Hans L. Trefousse believes Sickles's trip was connected to Johnson's subsequent nomination for vice president.[104] According to historian Albert Castel in his account of Johnson's presidency, Lincoln was impressed by Johnson's administration of Tennessee.[98] Gordon-Reed points out that while the Lincoln-Hamlin ticket might have been considered geographically balanced in 1860, "having Johnson, the *southern* War Democrat, on the ticket sent the right message about the folly of secession and the continuing capacity for union within the country."[105] Another factor was the desire of Secretary of State William Seward to frustrate the vice-presidential candidacy of his fellow New Yorker, former senator Daniel S. Dickinson, a War Democrat, as Seward would probably have had to yield his place if another New Yorker became vice president. Johnson, once he was told by reporters the likely purpose of Sickles' visit, was active on his own behalf, giving speeches and having his political friends work behind the scenes to boost his candidacy.[106]

To sound a theme of unity, Lincoln in 1864 ran under the banner of the National Union Party, rather than the Republicans.[105] At the party's convention in Baltimore in June, Lincoln was easily nominated, although there had been some talk of replacing him with a Cabinet officer or one of the more successful generals. After the convention backed Lincoln, former Secretary of War Simon Cameron offered a resolution to nominate Hamlin, but it was defeated. Johnson was nominated for vice president by C.M. Allen of Indiana with an Iowa delegate as seconder. On the first ballot, Johnson led with 200 votes to 150 for Hamlin and 108 for Dickinson. On the second ballot, Kentucky switched to vote for Johnson, beginning a stampede. Johnson was named on the second ballot with 491 votes to Hamlin's 17 and eight for Dickinson; the nomination was made unanimous. Lincoln expressed pleasure at the result, "Andy Johnson, I think, is a good man."[107] When word reached Nashville, a crowd assembled and the military governor obliged with a speech contending his selection as a Southerner meant that the rebel states had not actually left the Union.[107]

Although it was unusual at the time for a national candidate to actively campaign, Johnson gave a number of speeches in Tennessee, Kentucky, Ohio, and Indiana. He also sought to boost his chances in Tennessee while reestablishing civil government by making the loyalty oath even more restrictive, in that voters would now have to swear they opposed making a settlement with the Confederacy. The Democratic candidate for president, George McClellan, hoped to avoid additional bloodshed by negotiation, and so the stricter loyalty oath effectively disenfranchised his supporters. Lincoln declined to override Johnson, and their ticket took the state by 25,000 votes. Congress refused to count Tennessee's electoral votes, but Lincoln and Johnson did not need them, having won in most states that had voted, and easily secured the election.[108]

Now Vice President-elect, Johnson was anxious to complete the work of reestablishing civilian government in Tennessee, although the timetable for the election of a new governor did not allow it to take place until after Inauguration Day, March 4. He hoped to remain in Nashville to complete his task, but was told by Lincoln's advisers that he could not stay, but would be sworn in with Lincoln. In these months, Union troops finished the retaking of eastern Tennessee, including Greeneville. Just before his departure, the voters of Tennessee ratified a new constitution, abolishing slavery, on February 22, 1865. One of Johnson's final acts as military governor was to certify the results.[109]

Johnson traveled to Washington to be sworn in, although according to Gordon-Reed, "in light of what happened on March 4, 1865, it might have been better if Johnson had stayed in Nashville."[110] He may have been ill; Castel cited typhoid fever,[98] though Gordon-Reed notes that there is no independent evidence for that diagnosis.[110] On the evening of March 3, Johnson attended a party in his honor; he drank heavily. Hung over the following morning at the Capitol, he asked Vice President Hamlin for some whiskey. Hamlin produced a bottle, and Johnson took two stiff drinks, stating "I need all the strength for the occasion I can have." In the Senate Chamber, Johnson delivered a rambling address as Lincoln, the Congress, and dignitaries looked on. Almost incoherent at times, he finally meandered to a halt, whereupon Hamlin hastily swore him in as vice president.[111] Lincoln, who had watched sadly during the debacle, then went to his own swearing-in outside the Capitol, and delivered his acclaimed Second Inaugural Address.[112]

In the weeks after the inauguration, Johnson only presided over the Senate briefly, and hid from public ridicule at the Maryland home of a friend, Francis Preston Blair. When he did return to Washington, it was with the intent of leaving for Tennessee to reestablish his family in Greeneville. Instead, he remained after word came that General Ulysses S. Grant had captured the Confederate capital of Richmond, Virginia, presaging the end of the war.[113] Lincoln stated, in response to criticism of Johnson's behavior, that "I have known Andy Johnson for many years; he made a bad slip the other day, but you need not be scared; Andy ain't a drunkard."[114]

## Presidency (1865–1869)
*Accession*

On the afternoon of April 14, 1865, Lincoln and Johnson met for the first time since the inauguration. Trefousse states that Johnson wanted to "induce Lincoln not to be too lenient with traitors"; Gordon-Reed agrees.[115][116]

That night, President Lincoln was shot and mortally wounded by John Wilkes Booth, a Confederate sympathizer. The shooting of the President was part of a conspiracy to assassinate Lincoln, Johnson, and Seward the same night. Seward barely survived his wounds, while Johnson escaped attack as his would-be assassin, George Atzerodt, got drunk instead of killing the vice president. Leonard J. Farwell, a fellow boarder at the Kirkwood House, awoke Johnson with news of Lincoln's shooting at Ford's Theatre. Johnson rushed to the President's deathbed, where he remained a short time, on his return promising, "They shall suffer for this. They shall suffer for this."[117] Lincoln died at 7:22 a.m. the next morning; Johnson's swearing in occurred between 10 and 11 a.m. with Chief Justice Salmon P. Chase presiding in the presence of most of the Cabinet. Johnson's demeanor was described by the newspapers as "solemn and dignified."[118] Some Cabinet members had last seen Johnson, apparently drunk, at the inauguration.[119] At noon, Johnson conducted his first Cabinet meeting in the Treasury Secretary's office, and asked all members to remain in their positions.[120]

The events of the assassination resulted in speculation, then and subsequently, concerning Johnson and what the conspirators might have intended for him. In the vain hope of having his life spared after his capture, Atzerodt spoke much about the conspiracy, but did not say anything to indicate that the plotted assassination of Johnson was merely a ruse. Conspiracy theorists point to the fact that on the day of the assassination, Booth came to the Kirkwood House and left one of his cards. This object was received by Johnson's private secretary, William A. Browning, with an inscription, "Don't wish to disturb you. Are you at home? J. Wilkes Booth."[121]

Johnson presided with dignity over Lincoln's funeral ceremonies in Washington, before his predecessor's body was sent home to Springfield, Illinois, for interment.[122] Shortly after Lincoln's death, Union General William T. Sherman reported he had, without consulting Washington, reached an armistice agreement with Confederate General Joseph E. Johnston for the surrender of Confederate forces in North Carolina in exchange for the existing state government remaining in power, with private property rights to be respected. This did not even acknowledge the freedom of those in slavery. This was not acceptable to Johnson or the Cabinet who sent word for Sherman to secure the surrender without making political deals, which he did. Further, Johnson placed a $100,000 bounty (equivalent to $1.64 million in 2018) on Confederate President Davis, then a fugitive, which gave him the reputation of a man who would be tough on the South. More controversially, he permitted the execution of Mary Surratt for her part in Lincoln's assassination. Surratt was executed with three others, including Atzerodt, on July 7, 1865.[123]

# Joseph E. Johnston

*Johnston in uniform, ca. 1862*

**Joseph Eggleston Johnston** (February 3, 1807–March 21, 1891) was a career United States Army officer, serving with distinction in the Mexican–American War (1846–1848), and Seminole Wars. After Virginia seceded, he entered the Confederate States Army as one of its most senior general officers.

Johnston was trained as a civil engineer at the United States Military Academy at West Point, New York, graduating in the same class as Robert E. Lee. He served in Florida, Texas, and Kansas. By 1860 he achieved the rank of brigadier general as Quartermaster General of the U.S. Army.

Johnston's effectiveness in the American Civil War was undercut by tensions with Confederate president Jefferson Davis. Victory eluded him in most campaigns he personally commanded. He was the senior Confederate commander at the First Battle of Bull Run in July 1861, but the victory is usually credited to his subordinate, P.G.T. Beauregard. Johnston defended the Confederate capital of Richmond, Virginia, during the 1862 Peninsula Campaign, withdrawing under the pressure of Union Maj. Gen. George B. McClellan's superior force. He suffered a severe wound at the Battle of Seven Pines, and was replaced by Robert E. Lee.

In 1863, Johnston was placed in command of the Department of the West. In 1864, he commanded the Army of Tennessee against Union Maj. Gen. William Tecumseh Sherman in the Atlanta Campaign. In the final days of the war, Johnston was returned to command of the few remaining forces in the Carolinas Campaign. Union generals Ulysses S. Grant and Sherman both praised his actions in the war, and became friends with Johnston afterward.

After the war, Johnston served as an executive in the railroad and insurance businesses. He was elected as a Democrat in the United States House of Representatives, serving a single term. He was appointed as commissioner of railroads under Grover Cleveland. He died of pneumonia 10 days after attending Sherman's funeral in the pouring rain.

## Civil War

### Manassas and first friction with President Davis

When his native state, Virginia, seceded from the Union in 1861, Johnston resigned his commission as a brigadier general in the regular army, the highest-ranking U.S. Army officer to do so. He would go on to state, "I believed like most others, that the division of the country would be permanent; and that . . . the revolution begun was justified by the maxims so often repeated by Americans, that Free government is founded on the consent of the governed, and that every community strong enough to establish and maintain its independence, has a right to assert it. Having been educated in such opinions, I naturally determined to return to the State of which I was a native, join the people among whom I was born, and live with my kindred, and if necessary, fight in their defense."[11]

He was initially commissioned as a major general in the Virginia militia on May 4, but the Virginia Convention decided two weeks later that only one major general was required in the state army and Robert E. Lee was their choice. Johnston was then offered a state commission as a brigadier general, which he declined, accepting instead a commission as a brigadier general in the Confederate States Army on May 14. Johnston relieved Colonel Thomas J. "Stonewall" Jackson of command at Harpers Ferry in May and organized the Army of the Shenandoah in July.[12]

In the First Battle of Bull Run (First Manassas), July 21, 1861, Johnston rapidly moved his small army from the Shenandoah Valley to reinforce that of Brig. Gen. P. G. T. Beauregard, but he lacked familiarity with the terrain and ceded tactical planning of the battle to the more junior Beauregard as a professional courtesy. At midday, while Beauregard was still unclear about the direction his Union opponent was taking in the battle, Johnston decided that the critical point was to the north of his headquarters (the Lewis house, "Portici"), at Henry House Hill. He abruptly announced "The battle is there. I am going." Beauregard and the staffs of both generals followed his lead and rode off. Johnston encountered a scattered unit, the 4th Alabama, all of whose field grade officers had been killed, and personally rallied the men to reinforce the Confederate line. He consoled the despairing Brig. Gen. Barnard Bee and urged him to lead his men back into the fight. (General Bee's exhortation to his men was the inspiration for Stonewall Jackson's nickname.) Beauregard then convinced Johnston that he would be more valuable organizing the arrival of reinforcements for the remainder of the battle than providing at-the-front tactical leadership. Although Beauregard managed to claim the majority of public credit, Johnston's behind-the-scenes role was a critical factor in the Southern victory. After Bull Run, Johnston assisted Beauregard and William Porcher Miles in the design and production of the Confederate Battle Flag. It was Johnston's idea to make the flag square.[13]

It [the ranking of senior generals] seeks to tarnish my fair fame as a soldier and a man, earned by more than thirty years of laborious and perilous service. I had but this, the scars of many wounds, all honestly taken in my front and in the front of battle, and my father's Revolutionary sword. It was delivered to me from his venerated hand, without a stain of dishonor. Its blade is still unblemished as when it passed from his hand to mine. I drew it in the war, not for rank or fame, but to defend the sacred soil, the homes and hearths, the women and children; aye, and the men of my mother Virginia, my native South.

—Johnston's letter to Jefferson Davis, September 12, 1861 [14]

In August, Johnston was promoted to full general—what is called a four-star general in the modern U.S. Army—but was not pleased that three other men he had outranked in the "old Army" now outranked him, even though Davis backdated his promotion to July 4. Johnston felt that since he was the senior officer to leave the U.S. Army and join the Confederacy he should not be ranked behind Samuel Cooper, Albert Sidney Johnston, and Robert E. Lee. Only Beauregard was placed behind Johnston on the list of five new generals. This led to much bad blood between Johnston and Jefferson Davis, which would last throughout the war. The crux of Davis's counterargument was that Johnston's U.S. commission as a brigadier general was as a staff officer and that his highest line commission was as a lieutenant colonel; both Sidney Johnston and Lee had been full colonels. Johnston sent an intemperately worded letter to Davis, who was offended enough to discuss its tone with his cabinet.[15]

Johnston was placed in command of the Department of the Potomac and the Confederate Army of the Potomac on July 21, 1861, and the Department of Northern Virginia on October 22. From July to November 1861, he was headquartered at the Conner House in Manassas.[16] The winter of 1861–62 was relatively quiet for Johnston in his Centreville headquarters, concerned primarily with organization and equipment issues, as the principal Northern army, also named Army of the Potomac, was being organized by George B. McClellan. McClellan perceived Johnston's army as overwhelmingly strong in its fortifications, which prompted the Union general to plan an amphibious movement around Johnston's flank. In early March, learning of Union offensive preparations, Johnston withdrew his army to Culpeper Court House. This movement had repercussions on both sides. President Davis was surprised and disappointed by the unannounced move, which he considered a "precipitate retreat." At about this time, Davis moved to restrict Johnston's authority by bringing Robert E. Lee to Richmond as his military adviser and began issuing direct orders to some of the forces under Johnston's ostensible command. On the Northern side, McClellan was publicly embarrassed when it was revealed that the Confederate position had not been nearly as strong as he had portrayed. But more importantly, it required him to replan his spring offensive, and instead of an amphibious landing at his preferred target of Urbanna, he chose the Virginia Peninsula, between the James and York Rivers, as his avenue of approach toward Richmond.[17]

## Peninsula Campaign

In early April 1862, McClellan, having landed his troops at Fort Monroe at the tip of the Virginia Peninsula, began to move slowly toward Yorktown. Johnston's plan for the defense of the Confederate capital was controversial. Knowing that his army was half the size of McClellan's and that the Union Navy could provide direct support to McClellan from either river, Johnston attempted to convince Davis and Lee that the best course would be to concentrate in fortifications around Richmond. He was unsuccessful in persuading them and deployed most of his force on the Peninsula. Following lengthy siege preparations by McClellan at Yorktown, Johnston withdrew and fought a sharp defensive fight at Williamsburg (May 5) and turned back an attempt at an amphibious turning movement at Eltham's Landing (May 7). By late May the Union army was within six miles of Richmond.[18]

Realizing that he could not defend Richmond forever from the Union's overwhelming numbers and heavy siege artillery and that McClellan's army was divided by the rain-swollen Chickahominy River, Johnston attacked south of the river on May 31 in the Battle of Seven Pines or Fair Oaks. His plan was aggressive, but too complicated for his subordinates to execute correctly, and he failed to ensure they understood his orders in detail or to supervise them closely. The battle was tactically inconclusive, but it stopped McClellan's advance on the city and would turn out to be the high-water mark of his invasion. More significant, however, was that Johnston was wounded in his shoulder and chest by an artillery shell fragment near the end of the first day of the battle.[19] G.W. Smith commanded the army during the second day of the battle, before Davis quickly turned over command to the more aggressive Robert E. Lee, who would lead the Army of Northern Virginia for the rest of the war. Lee began by driving McClellan from the Peninsula during the Seven Days Battles of late June and beating a Union army a second time near Bull Run in August.[20]

## Appointment to the Western Theater and Vicksburg

Johnston was prematurely discharged from hospital on November 24, 1862, and appointed to command the Department of the West, the principal command of the Western Theater, which gave him titular control of Gen. Braxton Bragg's Army of Tennessee and Lt. Gen. John C. Pemberton's Department of Mississippi and East Louisiana. (The other major force in this area was the Trans-Mississippi Department, commanded by Lt. Gen. Theophilus H. Holmes, stationed principally in Arkansas. Johnston argued throughout his tenure that Holmes's command should be combined with Pemberton's under Johnston's control, or at least to reinforce Pemberton with troops from Holmes's command, but he was unable to convince the government to take either of these steps.)[21]

The first issue facing Johnston in the West was the fate of Braxton Bragg. The Confederate government was displeased with Bragg's performance at the Battle of Stones River, as were many of Bragg's senior subordinates. Jefferson Davis ordered Johnston to visit Bragg and determine whether he should be replaced. Johnston realized that if he recommended Bragg's replacement, he would be the logical choice to succeed him, and he considered that a field army command was more desirable than his current, mostly administrative post, but his sense of honor prevented him from achieving this personal gain at Bragg's expense. After interviewing Bragg and a number of his subordinates, he produced a generally positive report and refused to relieve the army commander. Davis ordered Bragg to a meeting in Richmond and designated Johnston to take command in the field, but Bragg's wife was ill and he was unable to travel. Furthermore, in early April Johnston was forced to bed with lingering problems from his Peninsula wound, and the attention of the Confederates shifted from Tennessee to Mississippi, leaving Bragg in place.[22]

The major crisis facing Johnston was defending Confederate control of Vicksburg, Mississippi, which was threatened by Union Maj. Gen. Ulysses S. Grant, first in a series of unsuccessful maneuvers during the winter of 1862–63 to the north of the fortress city, but followed in April 1863 with an ambitious campaign that began with Grant's Union army crossing the Mississippi River southwest of Vicksburg. Catching Lt. Gen. Pemberton by surprise, the Union army waged a series of successful battles as it moved northeast toward the state capital of Jackson. On May 9, the Confederate Secretary of War directed Johnston to "proceed at once to Mississippi and take chief command of the forces in the field." Johnston informed Richmond that he was still medically unfit, but would obey the order. When he arrived in Jackson on May 13 from Middle Tennessee, he learned that two Union army corps were advancing on the city and that there were only about 6,000 troops available to defend it. Johnston ordered a fighting evacuation (the Battle of Jackson, May 14) and retreated with his force to the north. Grant captured the city and then faced to the west to approach Vicksburg.[23]

Johnston began to move his force west to join Pemberton when he heard of that general's defeat at Champion Hill (May 16) and Big Black River Bridge (May 17). The survivors retreated to the fortifications of Vicksburg. Johnston urged Pemberton to avoid being surrounded by abandoning the city and to join forces with Johnston's troops, outnumbering Grant, but Davis had ordered Pemberton to defend the city as his highest priority. Grant launched two unsuccessful assaults against the fortifications and then settled in for a siege. The soldiers and civilians in the surrounded city waited in vain for Johnston's small force to come to their rescue. By late May Johnston had accumulated about 24,000 men but wanted additional reinforcements before moving forward. He considered ordering Bragg to send these reinforcements, but was concerned that this could result in the loss of Tennessee. He also bickered with President Davis about whether the order sending him to Mississippi could be construed as removing him from theater command; historian Steven E. Woodworth judges that Johnston "willfully misconstrued" his orders out of resentment of Davis's interference. Pemberton's army surrendered on July 4, 1863. Along with the capture of Port Hudson a week later, the loss of Vicksburg gave the Union complete control of the Mississippi River and cut the Confederacy in two. President Davis wryly ascribed the strategic defeat to a "want of provisions inside and a general outside [Johnston] who would not fight."[24]

The relationship between Johnston and Davis, difficult since the early days of the war, became bitter as recriminations were traded publicly about who was to blame for Vicksburg. That Johnston never wanted this theater command in the first place, difficulty in effectively moving troops due to lack of direct rail lines and the vast distances involved, lack of assistance from subordinate commanders, Pemberton's refusal to abandon Vicksburg as suggested, and President Davis' habit of communicating directly to Johnston's subordinates (which meant Johnston was often not aware of what was going on) all contributed to this defeat.[25] Davis considered firing Johnston, but he remained a popular officer and had many political allies in Richmond, most notably Sen. Louis

Wigfall. Instead, Bragg's army was removed from Johnston's command, leaving him in control of only Alabama and Mississippi.[26]

> The President detests Joe Johnston for all the trouble he has given him, and General Joe returns the compliment with compound interest. His hatred of Jeff Davis amounts to a religion. With him it colors all things.
>
> —Diarist Mary Chesnut[27]

While Vicksburg was falling, Union Maj. Gen. William S. Rosecrans was advancing against Bragg in Tennessee, forcing him to evacuate Chattanooga. Bragg achieved a significant victory against Rosecrans in the Battle of Chickamauga (September 19–20), but he was defeated by Ulysses S. Grant in the Battles for Chattanooga in November. Bragg resigned from his command of the Army of Tennessee and returned to Richmond in the role as military adviser to the president. Davis offered the position to William J. Hardee, the senior corps commander, who refused it. He considered P.G.T. Beauregard, another general with whom he had poor personal relations, and also Robert E. Lee. Lee, who was reluctant to leave Virginia, first recommended Beauregard, but sensing Davis's discomfort, changed his recommendation to Johnston. After much agonizing, Davis appointed Johnston to command the Army of Tennessee in Dalton, Georgia, on December 27, 1863.[28]

## Atlanta Campaign

Faced with Maj. Gen. William T. Sherman's advance from Chattanooga to Atlanta in the spring of 1864, Johnston conducted a series of withdrawals that appeared similar to his Peninsula Campaign strategy. He repeatedly prepared strong defensive positions, only to see Sherman maneuver around them in expert turning movements, causing him to fall back in the general direction of Atlanta. Johnston saw the preservation of his army as the most important consideration, and hence conducted a very cautious campaign. He handled his army well, slowing the Union advance and inflicting heavier losses than he sustained.

Sherman began his Atlanta Campaign on May 4. Johnston's Army of Tennessee fought defensive battles against the Federals at the approaches to Dalton, which was evacuated on May 13, then retreated 12 miles south to Resaca, and constructed defensive positions. However, after a brief battle, Johnston again yielded to Sherman, and retreated from Resaca on May 15. Johnston assembled the Confederate forces for an attack at Cassville.[29] As his troops advanced, an enemy force of unknown strength appeared unexpectedly on his right flank. A skirmish ensued, forcing the corps commander, Lt. Gen. John Bell Hood, to halt his advance and reposition his troops to face the threat. Faced with this unexpected threat, Johnston abandoned his attack and renewed his retreat. On May 20 they again retreated 8 miles further south to Cartersville. The month of May 1864 ended with Sherman's forces attempting to move away from their railroad supply line with another turning movement, but became bogged down by the Confederates' fierce defenses at the Battle of New Hope Church on May 25, the Battle of Pickett's Mill on May 27, and the Battle of Dallas on May 28.[30]

In June Sherman's forces continued maneuvers around the northern approaches to Atlanta, and a battle ensued at Kolb's Farm on June 22, followed by Sherman's first (and only) attempt at a massive frontal assault in the Battle of Kennesaw Mountain on June 27, which Johnston strongly repulsed. However, by this time Federal forces were within 17 miles of Atlanta, threatening the city from the west and north. Johnston had yielded over 110 miles of mountainous, and thus more easily defensible, territory in just two months, while the Confederate government became increasingly frustrated and alarmed. When Johnston retreated across the Chattahoochee River, the final major barrier before Atlanta, President Davis lost his patience.[31]

In early July, Davis sent Gen. Braxton Bragg to Atlanta to assess the situation. After several meetings with local civilian leaders and Johnston's subordinates, Bragg returned to Richmond and urged President Davis to replace Johnston. Davis removed Johnston from command on July 17, 1864, just outside Atlanta. "The fate of Atlanta, from the Confederate standpoint, was all but decided by Johnston."[32] (His replacement, Lt. Gen. Hood, was left with the "virtually impossible situation" of defending Atlanta [33] which he was forced to abandon in September.) Davis's decision to remove Johnston was one of the most controversial of the war.[34]

## North Carolina and surrender at Bennett Place

Johnston traveled to Columbia, South Carolina, to begin a virtual retirement. However, as the Confederacy became increasingly concerned about Sherman's March to the Sea across Georgia and then north through the Carolinas, the public clamored for Johnston's return. The general in charge of the Western Theater, P.G.T. Beauregard, was making little progress against the advancing Union force. Political opponents of Jefferson Davis, such as Sen. Louis Wigfall, added to the pressure in Congress. Diarist Mary Chesnut wrote, "We thought this was a struggle for independence. Now it seems it is only a fight between Joe Johnston and Jeff Davis." In January 1865, the Congress passed a law authorizing Robert E. Lee the powers of general in chief, and recommending that Johnston be reinstated as the commander of the Army of Tennessee. Davis immediately appointed Lee to the position, but refused to restore Johnston. In a lengthy unpublished memo, Davis wrote, "My opinion of General Johnston's unfitness for command has ripened slowly and against my inclinations into a conviction so settled that it would be impossible for me again to feel confidence in him as the commander of an army in the field."[35] Vice President Alexander H. Stephens and 17 senators petitioned Lee to use his new authority to appoint Johnston, bypassing Davis, but the general in chief declined. Instead, he recommended the appointment to Davis.[36]

Despite his serious misgivings, Davis restored Johnston to active duty on February 25, 1865. His new command comprised two military departments: the Department of South Carolina, Georgia, and Florida, and the Department of North Carolina and Southern

Virginia; he assumed command of the latter department on March 6. These commands included three Confederate field armies, including the remnants of the once formidable Army of Tennessee, but they were armies in name only. The Tennessee army had been severely depleted at Franklin and Nashville, lacked sufficient supplies and ammunition, and the men had not been paid for months; only about 6,600 traveled to South Carolina. Johnston also had available 12,000 men under William J. Hardee, who had been unsuccessfully attempting to resist Sherman's advance, Braxton Bragg's force in Wilmington, North Carolina, and 6,000 cavalrymen under Wade Hampton.[37]

Johnston, severely outnumbered, hoped to combine his force with a detachment of Robert E. Lee's army from Virginia, jointly defeat Sherman, and then return to Virginia for an attack on Ulysses S. Grant. Lee initially refused to cooperate with this plan. (Following the fall of Richmond in April, Lee attempted to escape to North Carolina to join Johnston, but it was too late.) Recognizing that Sherman was moving quickly, Johnston then planned to consolidate his own small armies so that he could land a blow against an isolated portion of Sherman's army, which was advancing in two separated columns. On March 19, 1865, Johnston was able to catch the left wing of Sherman's army by surprise at the Battle of Bentonville and briefly gained some tactical successes before superior numbers forced him to retreat to Raleigh, North Carolina. Unable to secure the capital, Johnston's army withdrew to Greensboro.[38]

After learning of Lee's surrender at Appomattox Court House on April 9, Johnston agreed to meet with General Sherman between the lines at a small farm known as Bennett Place near present-day Durham, North Carolina. After three separate days (April 17, 18, and 26, 1865) of negotiations, Johnston surrendered the Army of Tennessee and all remaining Confederate forces still active in North Carolina, South Carolina, Georgia, and Florida. It was the largest surrender of the war, totaling 89,270 soldiers. President Davis considered that Johnston, surrendering so many troops that had not been explicitly defeated in battle, had committed an act of treachery. Johnston was paroled on May 2 at Greensboro.[39]

After the surrender, Sherman issued ten days' rations to the hungry Confederate soldiers, as well as horses and mules for them to "insure a crop." He also ordered distribution of corn, meal, and flour to civilians throughout the South. This was an act of generosity that Johnston would never forget; he wrote to Sherman that his attitude "reconciles me to what I have previously regarded as the misfortune of my life, that of having you to encounter in the field."[40]

## Postwar years

Johnston struggled to make a living for himself and his wife, who was ailing. He became president of a small railroad, the Alabama and Tennessee River Rail Road Company, which during his tenure of May 1866 to November 1867, was renamed the Selma, Rome and Dalton Railroad. Johnston was bored with the position and the company failed for lack of capital. He established in 1868 an insurance company in Savannah, Georgia, acting as an agent for the Liverpool and London and Globe Insurance Company, and within four years had a network of more than 120 agents across the deep South.[41]

The income from this venture allowed him to devote time to his great postwar activity, writing his memoirs, as did several fellow officers. His *Narrative of Military Operations* (1874) was highly critical of Davis and many of his fellow generals. He repeated his grievance about his ranking as a general in the Confederate Army and attempted to justify his career as a cautious campaigner. The book sold poorly and its publisher failed to make a profit.[41]

Although many Confederate generals criticized Johnston, both Sherman and Grant portrayed him favorably in their memoirs. Sherman described him as a "dangerous and wily opponent" and criticized Johnston's nemeses, Hood and Davis. Grant supported his decisions in the Vicksburg Campaign: "Johnston evidently took in the situation, and wisely, I think, abstained from making an assault on us because it would simply have inflicted losses on both sides without accomplishing any result." Commenting on the Atlanta Campaign, Grant wrote,

> For my own part, I think that Johnston's tactics were right. Anything that could have prolonged the war a year beyond the time that it finally did close, would probably have exhausted the North to such an extent that they might then have abandoned the contest and agreed to a settlement.[42]

Johnston, like Lee, never forgot the magnanimity of the man to whom he surrendered. He would not allow criticism of Sherman in his presence. Sherman and Johnston corresponded frequently, and they met for friendly dinners in Washington whenever Johnston traveled there. When Sherman died, Johnston served as an honorary pallbearer at his funeral. During the procession in New York City on February 19, 1891, he kept his hat off as a sign of respect, although the weather was cold and rainy. Someone concerned for his health asked him to put on his hat, to which Johnston replied, "If I were in his place and he were standing here in mine, he would not put on his hat." He caught a cold that day, which developed into pneumonia. Johnston died several weeks later in Washington, D.C. He was buried next to his wife in Green Mount Cemetery, Baltimore, Maryland.[45]

# Robert E. Lee

*Lee in March* 1864

**Robert Edward Lee** (January 19, 1807–October 12, 1870) was an American and Confederate soldier, best known as a commander of the Confederate States Army. He commanded the Army of Northern Virginia in the American Civil War from 1862 until its surrender in 1865.

A son of Revolutionary War officer Henry "Light Horse Harry" Lee III, Lee was a top graduate of the United States Military Academy and an exceptional officer and military engineer in the United States Army for 32 years. During this time, he served throughout the United States, distinguished himself during the Mexican–American War, and served as Superintendent of the United States Military Academy. He was also the husband of Mary Anna Custis Lee, adopted great granddaughter of George Washington.

When Virginia's 1861 Richmond Convention declared secession from the Union, Lee chose to follow his home state, despite his desire for the country to remain intact and an offer of a senior Union command.[1] During the first year of the Civil War, he served as a senior military adviser to Confederate President Jefferson Davis. Once he took command of the Army of Northern Virginia in 1862, he soon emerged as an able tactician and battlefield commander, winning most of his battles, nearly all against far larger Union armies.[2][3]

Lee's two major strategic offensives into Union territory ended in defeat.[4][5][6] His aggressive tactics, especially at the Battle of Gettysburg, which resulted in high casualties at a time when the Confederacy had a shortage of manpower, have come under criticism in recent years.[7]

Lee surrendered the remnant of his army to Ulysses S. Grant at Appomattox Court House on April 9, 1865. Since Confederate Congress had appointed him supreme commander of Confederate armies, the remaining Confederate forces capitulated after his surrender. Lee rejected the proposal of a sustained insurgency against the Union and called for national reconciliation.

In 1865, Lee became president of Washington College (later Washington and Lee University) in Lexington, Virginia; in that position, he supported reconciliation between North and South.[8] He accepted "the extinction of slavery" provided for by the Thirteenth Amendment, but publicly opposed racial equality and granting African Americans the right to vote and other political rights.[9][10][11] Lee died in 1870. In 1975, the U.S. Congress posthumously restored Lee's citizenship effective June 13, 1865.[12]

## Lee's views on race and slavery

Several historians have noted the paradoxical nature of Lee's beliefs and actions concerning race and slavery. While Lee protested he had sympathetic feelings for blacks, they were subordinate to his own racial identity.[75] While Lee held slavery to be an evil institution, he also saw some benefit to blacks held in slavery.[76] While Lee helped assist individual slaves to freedom in Liberia, and provided for their emancipation in his own will,[77] he believed the enslaved should be eventually freed in a general way only at some unspecified future date as a part of God's purpose.[75][78] Slavery for Lee was a moral and religious issue, and not one that would yield to political solutions.[79] Emancipation would sooner come from Christian impulse among slave masters before "storms and tempests of fiery controversy" such as was occurring in "Bleeding Kansas."[75] Countering southerners who argued for slavery as a positive good, Lee in his well-known analysis of slavery from an 1856 letter called it a moral and political evil. While both Robert and his wife Mary Lee were disgusted with slavery, they also defended it against Abolitionist demands for immediate emancipation for all enslaved.[80]

Lee's father-in-law G. W. Parke Custis freed his slaves in his will.[81] In the same tradition, before leaving to serve in Mexico, Lee had written a will providing for the manumission of the only slaves he owned.[82] Parke Custis was a member of the American Colonization Society, which was formed to gradually end slavery by establishing a free republic in Liberia for African-Americans, and Lee assisted several ex-slaves to emigrate there. Also, according to historian Richard B. McCaslin, Lee was a gradual emancipationist, denouncing extremist proposals for immediate abolition of slavery. Lee rejected what he called evilly motivated political passion, fearing a civil and servile war from precipitous emancipation.[83]

Historian Elizabeth Brown Pryor offered an alternative interpretation of Lee's voluntary manumission of slaves in his will, and assisting slaves to a life of freedom in Liberia, seeing Lee as conforming to a "primacy of slave law." She wrote that Lee's private views on race and slavery,

"which today seem startling, were entirely unremarkable in Lee's world. No visionary, Lee nearly always tried to conform to accepted opinions. His assessment of black inferiority, of the necessity of racial stratification, the primacy of slave law, and even a divine sanction for it all, was in keeping with the prevailing views of other moderate slaveholders and a good many prominent Northerners."[84]

On taking on the role of administrator for the Parke Custis will, Lee used a provision to retain them in slavery to produce income for the estate to retire debt.[81] Lee did not welcome the role of planter while administering the Custis properties at Romancoke, another nearby the Pamunkey River and Arlington; he rented the estate's mill. While all the estates prospered under his administration, Lee was unhappy at direct participation in slavery as a hated institution.[82]

Even before what Michael Fellman called a "sorry involvement in actual slave management," Lee judged the experience of white mastery to be a greater moral evil to the white man than blacks suffering under the "painful discipline" of slavery which introduced Christianity, literacy and a work ethic to the "heathen African."[85] Columbia University historian Eric Foner notes that Lee:

> "was not a pro-slavery ideologue. But I think equally important is that, unlike some white southerners, he never spoke out against slavery"[86]

By the time of Lee's career in the U.S. Army, the officers of West Point stood aloof from political-party and sectional strife on such issues as slavery, as a matter of principle, and Lee adhered to the principle.[87][88] He considered it his patriotic duty to be apolitical while in active Army service,[89][90][91] and Lee did not speak out publicly on the subject of slavery prior to the Civil War.[92][93] Before the outbreak of the War, in 1860, Lee voted for John C. Breckinridge, who was the extreme pro-slavery candidate in the 1860 presidential election, not John Bell, the more moderate Southerner who won Virginia.[94]

Lee himself owned a small number of slaves in his lifetime and considered himself a paternalistic master.[94] There are various historical and newspaper hearsay accounts of Lee personally whipping a slave, but they are not direct eyewitness accounts. He was definitely involved in administering the day-to-day operations of a plantation and was involved in the recapture of runaway slaves.[95] One historian noted that Lee separated slave families, something that prominent slave-holding families in Virginia such as Washington and Custis did not do.[96] In 1862, Lee freed the slaves that his wife inherited, but that was in accordance with his father-in-law's will.[97]

Lee claimed that he found slavery bothersome and time-consuming as an everyday institution to run. In an 1856 letter to his wife, he maintained that slavery was a great evil, but primarily due to adverse impact that it had on white people:[98]

> In this enlightened age, there are few I believe, but what will acknowledge, that slavery as an institution, is a moral & political evil in any Country. It is useless to expatiate on its disadvantages. I think it however a greater evil to the white man than to the black race, & while my feelings are strongly enlisted in behalf of the latter, my sympathies are more strong for the former. The blacks are immeasurably better off here than in Africa, morally, socially & physically. The painful discipline they are undergoing, is necessary for their instruction as a race, & I hope will prepare & lead them to better things. How long their subjugation may be necessary is known & ordered by a wise Merciful Providence.[99]

Foner writes that "Lee's code of gentlemanly conduct did not seem to apply to blacks" during the War, as he did not stop his soldiers from kidnapping free black farmers and selling them into slavery.[86] Princeton University historian James M. McPherson noted that Lee initially rejected a prisoner exchange between the Confederacy and the Union when the Union demanded that black Union soldiers be included.[96] Lee did not accept the swap until a few months before the Confederacy's surrender.[96]

After the War, Lee told a congressional committee that blacks were "not disposed to work" and did not possess the intellectual capacity to vote and participate in politics.[97] Lee also said to the committee that he hoped that Virginia could "get rid of them," referring to blacks.[97] While not politically active, Lee defended Lincoln's successor, Andrew Johnson's approach to Reconstruction, which according to Foner, "abandoned the former slaves to the mercy of governments controlled by their former owners."[100] According to Foner, "A word from Lee might have encouraged white Southerners to accord blacks equal rights and inhibited the violence against the freed people that swept the region during Reconstruction, but he chose to remain silent."[97] Lee was also urged to condemn the white-supremacy [101] organization Ku Klux Klan, but opted to remain silent.[94]

In the generation following the war, Lee, though he died just a few years later, became a central figure in the Lost Cause interpretation of the war. The argument that Lee had always somehow opposed slavery, and freed his wife's slaves, helped maintain his stature as a symbol of Southern honor and national reconciliation.[94] Douglas Southall Freeman's Pulitzer prize-winning four-volume *R. E. Lee: A Biography* (1936), which was for a long period considered the definitive work on Lee, downplayed his involvement in slavery and emphasized Lee as a virtuous person. Eric Foner, who describes Freeman's volume as a "hagiography," notes that on the whole, Freeman "displayed little interest in Lee's relationship to slavery. The index to his four volumes contained 22 entries for 'devotion to duty', 19 for 'kindness', 53 for Lee's celebrated horse, Traveller. But 'slavery', 'slave emancipation' and 'slave insurrection' together received five. Freeman observed, without offering details, that slavery in Virginia represented the system 'at its best'. He ignored the postwar testimony of Lee's former slave Wesley Norris about the brutal treatment to which he had been subjected."[94]

## Harpers Ferry and Texas, 1859–1861

Both Harpers Ferry and the secession of Texas were monumental events leading up to the Civil War. Robert E. Lee was at both events. Lee initially remained loyal to the Union after Texas seceded.

## Harpers Ferry

John Brown led a band of 21 abolitionists who seized the federal arsenal at Harpers Ferry, Virginia, in October 1859, hoping to incite a slave rebellion. President James Buchanan gave Lee command of detachments of militia, soldiers, and United States Marines, to suppress the uprising and arrest its leaders.[102] By the time Lee arrived that night, the militia on the site had surrounded Brown and his hostages. At dawn, Brown refused the demand for surrender. Lee attacked, and Brown and his followers were captured after three minutes of fighting. Lee's summary report of the episode shows Lee believed it "was the attempt of a fanatic or madman." Lee said Brown achieved "temporary success" by creating panic and confusion and by "magnifying" the number of participants involved in the raid.[103]

## Texas

In 1860, Lt. Col. Robert E. Lee relieved Major Heintzelman at Fort Brown, and the Mexican authorities offered to restrain "their citizens from making predatory descents upon the territory and people of Texas . . . this was the last active operation of the Cortina War." Rip Ford, a Texas Ranger at the time, described Lee as "dignified without hauteur, grand without pride . . . he evinced an imperturbable self-possession, and a complete control of his passions . . . possessing the capacity to accomplish great ends and the gift of controlling and leading men."[104]

When Texas seceded from the Union in February 1861, General David E. Twiggs surrendered all the American forces (about 4,000 men, including Lee, and commander of the Department of Texas) to the Texans. Twiggs immediately resigned from the U.S. Army and was made a Confederate general. Lee went back to Washington and was appointed Colonel of the First Regiment of Cavalry in March 1861. Lee's colonelcy was signed by the new President, Abraham Lincoln. Three weeks after his promotion, Colonel Lee was offered a senior command (with the rank of Major General) in the expanding Army to fight the Southern States that had left the Union. Fort Mason, Texas was Lee's last command with the United States Army.[105]

## Civil War

### Resignation from United States Army

Unlike many Southerners who expected a glorious war, Lee correctly predicted it as protracted and devastating.[106] He privately opposed the new Confederate States of America in letters in early 1861, denouncing secession as "nothing but revolution" and an unconstitutional betrayal of the efforts of the Founding Fathers. Writing to George Washington Custis in January, Lee stated:

> The South, in my opinion, has been aggrieved by the acts of the North, as you say. I feel the aggression, and am willing to take every proper step for redress. It is the principle I contend for, not individual or private benefit. As an American citizen, I take great pride in my country, her prosperity and institutions, and would defend any State if her rights were invaded. But I can anticipate no greater calamity for the country than a dissolution of the Union. It would be an accumulation of all the evils we complain of, and I am willing to sacrifice everything but honor for its preservation. I hope, therefore, that all constitutional means will be exhausted before there is a resort to force. Secession is nothing but revolution. The framers

*Lee in uniform, 1863*

of our Constitution never exhausted so much labor, wisdom, and forbearance in its formation, and surrounded it with so many guards and securities, if it was intended to be broken by every member of the Confederacy at will. It was intended for "perpetual union," so expressed in the preamble, and for the establishment of a government, not a compact, which can only be dissolved by revolution, or the consent of all the people in convention assembled.[107]

Despite opposing secession, Lee said in January that "we can with a clear conscience separate" if all peaceful means failed. He agreed with secessionists in most areas, such as dislike of Northern anti-slavery criticisms and prevention of expanding slavery to new territories, and fear of its larger population. Lee supported the Crittenden Compromise, which would have constitutionally protected slavery.[1]

Lee's objection to secession was ultimately outweighed by a sense of personal honor, reservations about the legitimacy of a strife-ridden "Union that can only be maintained by swords and bayonets," and duty to defend his native Virginia if attacked.[107] He was asked while leaving Texas by a lieutenant if he intended to fight for the Confederacy or the Union, to which Lee replied, "I shall never bear arms against the Union, but it may be necessary for me to carry a musket in the defense of my native state, Virginia, in which case I shall not prove recreant to my duty."[108][1]

Although Virginia had the most slaves of any state, it was more similar to Maryland, which stayed in the Union, than the Deep South; a convention voted against secession in early 1861. Scott, commanding general of the Union Army and Lee's mentor, told Lincoln he wanted him for a top command, telling Secretary of War Simon Cameron that he had "entire confidence" in Lee. He accepted a promotion to colonel of the 1st Cavalry Regiment on March 28, again swearing an oath to the United States.[109][1] Meanwhile, Lee ignored an offer of command from the Confederacy. After Lincoln's call for troops to put down the rebellion, a second Virginia convention in Richmond voted to secede[110] on April 17, and a May 23 referendum would likely ratify the decision. That night Lee dined with brother Smith and cousin Phillips, naval officers. Because of Lee's indecision, Phillips went to the War Department the next morning to warn that the Union might lose his cousin if the government did not act quickly.[1]

In Washington that day,[106] Lee was offered by presidential advisor Francis P. Blair a role as major general to command the defense of the national capital. He replied:

Mr. Blair, I look upon secession as anarchy. If I owned the four millions of slaves in the South I would sacrifice them all to the Union; but how can I draw my sword upon Virginia, my native state?[110]

Lee immediately went to Scott, who tried to persuade him that Union forces would be large enough to prevent the South from fighting, so he would not have to oppose his state; Lee disagreed. When Lee asked if he could go home and not fight, the fellow Virginian said that the army did not need equivocal soldiers and that if he wanted to resign, he should do so before receiving official orders. Scott told him that he had made "the greatest mistake of your life."[1]

Lee agreed that to avoid dishonor he had to resign before receiving unwanted orders. While historians have usually called his decision inevitable ("the answer he was born to make," wrote Douglas Southall Freeman; another called it a "no-brainer") given the ties to family and state, an 1871 letter from his eldest daughter, Mary Custis Lee, to a biographer described Lee as "worn and harassed" yet calm as he deliberated alone in his office. People on the street noticed Lee's grim face as he tried to decide over the next two days, and he later said that he kept the resignation letter for a day before sending it on April 20. Two days later the Richmond convention invited Lee to the city. It elected him as commander of Virginia state forces before his arrival on April 23, and almost immediately gave him George Washington's sword as symbol of his appointment; whether he was told of a decision he did not want without time to decide, or did want the excitement and opportunity of command, is unclear.[27][1][106]

A cousin on Scott's staff told the family that Lee's decision so upset Scott that he collapsed on a sofa and mourned as if he had lost a son, and asked to not hear Lee's name. When Lee told family his decision he said "I suppose you will all think I have done very wrong," as the others were mostly pro-Union; only Mary Custis was a secessionist, and her mother especially wanted to choose the Union but told her husband that she would support whatever he decided. Many younger men like nephew Fitzhugh wanted to support the Confederacy, but Lee's three sons joined the Confederate military only after their father's decision.[1][106]

Most family members like brother Smith reluctantly also chose the South, but Smith's wife and Anne, Lee's sister, still supported the Union; Anne's son joined the Union Army, and no one in his family ever spoke to Lee again. Many cousins fought for the Confederacy, but Phillips and John Fitzgerald told Lee in person that they would uphold their oaths; John H. Upshur stayed with the Union military despite much family pressure; Roger Jones stayed in the Union army after Lee refused to advise him on what to do; and two of Philip Fendall's sons fought for the Union. Forty percent of Virginian officers stayed with the North.[1][106]

## Early role

At the outbreak of war, Lee was appointed to command all of Virginia's forces, but upon the formation of the Confederate States Army, he was named one of its first five full generals. Lee did not wear the insignia of a Confederate general, but only the three stars of a Confederate colonel, equivalent to his last U.S. Army rank.[111] He did not intend to wear a general's insignia until the Civil War had been won and he could be promoted, in peacetime, to general in the Confederate Army.

Lee's first field assignment was commanding Confederate forces in western Virginia, where he was defeated at the Battle of Cheat Mountain and was widely blamed for Confederate setbacks.[112] He was then sent to organize the coastal defenses along the Carolina and Georgia seaboard, appointed commander, "Department of South Carolina, Georgia and Florida" on November 5, 1861. Between then and the fall of Fort Pulaski, April 11, 1862, he put in place a defense of Savannah that proved successful in blocking Federal advance on Savannah. Confederate fort and naval gunnery dictated night time movement and construction by the besiegers. Federal preparations required four months. In those four months, Lee developed a defense in depth. Behind Fort Pulaski on the Savannah River, Fort Jackson was improved, and two additional batteries covered river approaches.[113] In the face of the Union superiority in naval, artillery and infantry deployment, Lee was able to block any Federal advance on Savannah, and at the same time, well-trained Georgia troops were released in time to meet McClellan's Peninsula Campaign. The city of Savannah would not fall until Sherman's approach from the interior at the end of 1864.

At first, the press spoke to the disappointment of losing Fort Pulaski. Surprised by the effectiveness of large caliber Parrott Rifles in their first deployment, it was widely speculated that only betrayal could have brought overnight surrender to a Third System Fort. Lee was said to have failed to get effective support in the Savannah River from the three sidewheeler gunboats of the Georgia Navy. Although again blamed by the press for Confederate reverses, he was appointed military adviser to Confederate President Jefferson Davis, the former U.S. Secretary of War. While in Richmond, Lee was ridiculed as the 'King of Spades' for his excessive digging of trenches around the capitol. These trenches would later play a pivotal role in battles near the end of the war.[114]

## Commander, Army of Northern Virginia (June 1862–June 1863)

In the spring of 1862, in the Peninsula Campaign, the Union Army of the Potomac under General George B. McClellan advanced on Richmond from Fort Monroe to the east. McClellan forced Gen. Joseph E. Johnston and the Army of Virginia to retreat to just north and east of the Confederate capital.

Then Johnston was wounded at the Battle of Seven Pines, on June 1, 1862. Lee now got his first opportunity to lead an army in the field—the force he renamed the Army of *Northern* Virginia, signalling his confidence that the Union army would be driven away from Richmond. Early in the war, Lee had been called "Granny Lee" for his allegedly timid style of command.[115] Confederate newspaper editorials objected to him replacing Johnston, opining that Lee would be passive, waiting for Union attack. And for the first three weeks of June, he did not attack, instead strengthening Richmond's defenses.

*Lee mounted on Traveller (September 1866)*

But then he launched a series of bold attacks against McClellan's forces, the Seven Days Battles. Despite superior Union numbers, and some clumsy tactical performances by his subordinates, Lee's attacks derailed McClellan's plans and drove back part of his forces. Confederate casualties were heavy, but McClellan was unnerved, retreated 25 miles (40 km) to the lower James River, and abandoned the Peninsula Campaign. This success completely changed Confederate morale, and the public's regard for Lee. After the Seven Days Battles, and until the end of the war, his men called him simply "Marse Robert," a term of respect and affection.

The setback, and the resulting drop in Union morale, impelled Lincoln to adopt a new policy of relentless, committed warfare.[116][117] After the Seven Days, Lincoln decided he would move to emancipate most Confederate slaves by executive order, as a military act, using his authority as commander-in-chief.[118] But he needed a Union victory first.

Meanwhile, Lee defeated another Union army under Gen. John Pope at the Second Battle of Bull Run. In less than 90 days after taking command, Lee had run McClellan off the Peninsula, defeated Pope, and moved the battle lines from 6 miles (9.7 km) outside Richmond, to 20 miles (32 km) outside Washington.

Lee now invaded Maryland and Pennsylvania, hoping to collect supplies in Union territory, and possibly win a victory that would sway the upcoming Union elections in favor of ending the war. But McClellan's men found a lost Confederate dispatch, Special Order 191, that revealed Lee's plans and movements. McClellan always exaggerated Lee's numerical strength, but now he knew the Confederate army was divided and could be destroyed in detail. However, McClellan moved slowly, not realizing a spy had informed Lee that McClellan had the plans. Lee quickly concentrated his forces west of Antietam Creek, near Sharpsburg, Maryland, where McClellan attacked on September 17. The Battle of Antietam was the single bloodiest day of the war, with both sides suffering enormous losses. Lee's army barely withstood the Union assaults, then retreated to Virginia the next day. This narrow Confederate defeat gave President Abraham Lincoln the opportunity to issue his Emancipation Proclamation,[119] which put the Confederacy on the diplomatic and moral defensive.[120]

Disappointed by McClellan's failure to destroy Lee's army, Lincoln named Ambrose Burnside as commander of the Army of the Potomac. Burnside ordered an attack across the Rappahannock River at Fredericksburg, Virginia. Delays in bridging the river allowed Lee's army ample time to organize strong defenses, and the Union frontal assault on December 13, 1862, was a disaster. There were 12,600 Union casualties to 5,000

Confederate; one of the most one-sided battles in the Civil War.[121] After this victory, Lee reportedly said "It is well that war is so terrible, else we should grow too fond of it."[121] At Fredericksburg, according to historian Michael Fellman, Lee had completely entered into the "spirit of war, where destructiveness took on its own beauty."[121]

After the bitter Union defeat at Fredericksburg, President Lincoln named Joseph Hooker commander of the Army of the Potomac. In May 1863, Hooker maneuvered to attack Lee's army via Chancellorsville, Virginia. But Hooker was defeated by Lee's daring maneuver: dividing his army and sending Stonewall Jackson's corps to attack Hooker's flank. Lee won a decisive victory over a larger force, but with heavy casualties, including Jackson, his finest corps commander, who was accidentally killed by his own troops.[122]

## Battle of Gettysburg

The critical decisions came in May–June 1863, after Lee's smashing victory at the Battle of Chancellorsville. The western front was crumbling, as multiple uncoordinated Confederate armies were unable to handle General Ulysses S. Grant's campaign against Vicksburg. The top military advisers wanted to save Vicksburg, but Lee persuaded Davis to overrule them and authorize yet another invasion of the North. The immediate goal was to acquire urgently needed supplies from the rich farming districts of Pennsylvania; a long-term goal was to stimulate peace activity in the North by demonstrating the power of the South to invade. Lee's decision proved a significant strategic blunder and cost the Confederacy control of its western regions, and nearly cost Lee his own army as Union forces cut him off from the South.[123]

In the summer of 1863, Lee invaded the North again, marching through western Maryland and into south central Pennsylvania. He encountered Union forces under George G. Meade at the three-day Battle of Gettysburg in Pennsylvania in July; the battle would produce the largest number of casualties in the American Civil War. With some of his subordinates being new and inexperienced in their commands, J .E. B. Stuart's cavalry being out of the area, and Lee being slightly ill, he was less than comfortable with how events were unfolding. While the first day of battle was controlled by the Confederates, key terrain that should have been taken by General Ewell was not. The second day ended with the Confederates unable to break the Union position, and the Union being more solidified. Lee's decision on the third day, against the judgment of his best corps commander General Longstreet, to launch a massive frontal assault on the center of the Union line turned out to be disastrous. The assault known as Pickett's Charge was repulsed and resulted in heavy Confederate losses. The general rode out to meet his retreating army and proclaimed, "All this has been my fault."[124] Lee was compelled to retreat. Despite flooded rivers that blocked his retreat, he escaped Meade's ineffective pursuit. Following his defeat at Gettysburg, Lee sent a letter of resignation to President Davis on August 8, 1863, but Davis refused Lee's request. That fall, Lee and Meade met again in two minor campaigns that did little to change the strategic standoff. The Confederate Army never fully recovered from the substantial losses incurred during the three-day battle in southern

Pennsylvania. The historian Shelby Foote stated, "Gettysburg was the price the South paid for having Robert E. Lee as commander."

## Ulysses S. Grant and the Union offensive

In 1864 the new Union general-in-chief, Lt. Gen. Ulysses S. Grant, sought to use his large advantages in manpower and material resources to destroy Lee's army by attrition, pinning Lee against his capital of Richmond. Lee successfully stopped each attack, but Grant with his superior numbers kept pushing each time a bit farther to the southeast. These battles in the Overland Campaign included the Wilderness, Spotsylvania Court House and Cold Harbor.

Grant eventually was able to stealthily move his army across the James River. After stopping a Union attempt to capture Petersburg, Virginia, a vital railroad link supplying Richmond, Lee's men built elaborate trenches and were besieged in Petersburg, a development which presaged the trench warfare of World War I. Lee attempted to break the stalemate by sending Jubal A. Early on a raid through the Shenandoah Valley to Washington, D.C., but Early was defeated early on by the superior forces of Philip Sheridan. The Siege of Petersburg lasted from June 1864 until March 1865, with Lee's outnumbered and poorly supplied army shrinking daily because of desertions by disheartened Confederates.

## General in Chief

*Lee with son Custis (left) and aide Walter H. Taylor (right) by Brady, April 16, 1865*

On February 6, 1865, Lee was appointed General in Chief of the Armies of the Confederate States.

As the South ran out of manpower the issue of arming the slaves became paramount. Lee explained, "We should employ them without delay . . . [along with] gradual and general emancipation." The first units were in training as the war ended.[125][126] As the Confederate army was devastated by casualties, disease and desertion, the Union attack on Petersburg succeeded on April 2, 1865. Lee abandoned Richmond and retreated west. Lee then made an attempt to escape to the southwest and join up with Joseph E. Johnston's Army of Tennessee in North Carolina. However, his forces were soon surrounded and he surrendered them to Grant on April 9, 1865, at the Battle of Appomattox Court House.[127] Other Confederate armies followed suit and the war ended. The day after his surrender, Lee issued his Farewell Address to his army.

Lee resisted calls by some officers to reject surrender and allow small units to melt away into the mountains, setting up a lengthy guerrilla war. He insisted the war was over and energetically campaigned for inter-sectional reconciliation. "So far from engaging in a war to perpetuate slavery, I am rejoiced that slavery is abolished. I believe it will be greatly for the interests of the South."[128]

## Postbellum life

*Lee in 1869 (photo by Levin C. Handy)*

After the war, Lee was not arrested or punished (although he was indicted[134]), but he did lose the right to vote as well as some property. Lee's prewar family home, the Custis-Lee Mansion, was seized by Union forces during the war and turned into Arlington National Cemetery, and his family was not compensated until more than a decade after his death.[135]

Lee somewhat supported President Johnson's plan of Reconstruction. In 1866 Lee counseled southerners not to resume fighting, of which Grant said Lee was "setting an example of forced acquiescence so grudging and pernicious in its effects as to be hardly realized."[136] Lee joined with Democrats in opposing the Radical Republicans who demanded punitive measures against the South, distrusted its commitment to the abolition of slavery and, indeed, distrusted the region's loyalty to the United States.[137][138] Lee supported a system of free public schools for blacks, but forthrightly opposed allowing blacks to vote. "My own opinion is that, at this time, they [black Southerners] cannot vote intelligently, and that giving them the [vote] would lead to a great deal of demagogism, and lead to embarrassments in various ways," Lee stated.[139] Emory Thomas says Lee had become a suffering Christ-like icon for ex-Confederates. President Grant invited him to the White House in 1869, and he went. Nationally he became an icon of reconciliation between the North and South, and the reintegration of former Confederates into the national fabric.[140]

*General Lee and his Confederate officers in their first meeting since Appomattox, August 1869.*

Lee hoped to retire to a farm of his own, but he was too much a regional symbol to live in obscurity. From April to June 1865, he and his family resided in Richmond at the Stewart-Lee House.[141] He accepted an offer to serve as the president of Washington College (now

Washington and Lee University) in Lexington, Virginia, and served from October 1865 until his death. The Trustees used his famous name in large-scale fund-raising appeals and Lee transformed Washington College into a leading Southern college, expanding its offerings significantly, adding programs in commerce and journalism, and incorporating the Lexington Law School. Lee was well liked by the students, which enabled him to announce an "honor system" like that of West Point, explaining that "we have but one rule here, and it is that every student be a gentleman." To speed up national reconciliation Lee recruited students from the North and made certain they were well treated on campus and in town.[142]

Several glowing appraisals of Lee's tenure as college president have survived, depicting the dignity and respect he commanded among all. Previously, most students had been obliged to occupy the campus dormitories, while only the most mature were allowed to live off-campus. Lee quickly reversed this rule, requiring most students to board off-campus, and allowing only the most mature to live in the dorms as a mark of privilege; the results of this policy were considered a success. A typical account by a professor there states that "the students fairly worshipped him, and deeply dreaded his displeasure; yet so kind, affable, and gentle was he toward them that all loved to approach him. . . . No student would have dared to violate General Lee's expressed wish or appeal; if he had done so, the students themselves would have driven him from the college."[143]

While at Washington College, Lee told a colleague that the greatest mistake of his life was taking a military education.[144]

## President Johnson's amnesty pardons

On May 29, 1865, President Andrew Johnson issued a Proclamation of Amnesty and Pardon to persons who had participated in the rebellion against the United States. There were fourteen excepted classes, though, and members of those classes had to make special application to the President. Lee sent an application to Grant and wrote to President Johnson on June 13, 1865:

> Being excluded from the provisions of amnesty & pardon contained in the proclamation of the 29th Ulto; I hereby apply for the benefits, & full restoration of all rights & privileges extended to those included in its terms. I graduated at the Mil. Academy at West Point in June 1829. Resigned from the U.S. Army April '61. Was a General in the Confederate Army, & included in the surrender of the Army of N. Virginia 9 April '65.[145]

On October 2, 1865, the same day that Lee was inaugurated as president of Washington College in Lexington, Virginia, he signed his Amnesty Oath, thereby complying fully with the provision of Johnson's proclamation. Lee was not pardoned, nor was his citizenship restored.[145]

Three years later, on December 25, 1868, Johnson proclaimed a second amnesty which removed previous exceptions, such as the one that affected Lee.[146]

## Illness and death

On September 28, 1870, Lee suffered a stroke. He died two weeks later, shortly after 9 a.m. on October 12, 1870, in Lexington, Virginia, from the effects of pneumonia. According to one account, his last words on the day of his death, were "Tell Hill he *must* come up! Strike the tent,"[156] but this is debatable because of conflicting accounts and because Lee's stroke had resulted in aphasia, possibly rendering him unable to speak.[157]

At first no suitable coffin for the body could be located. The muddy roads were too flooded for anyone to get in or out of the town of Lexington. An undertaker had ordered three from Richmond that had reached Lexington, but due to unprecedented flooding from long-continued heavy rains, the caskets were washed down the Maury River. Two neighborhood boys, C.G. Chittum and Robert E. Hillis, found one of the coffins that had been swept ashore. Undamaged, it was used for the General's body, though it was a bit short for him. As a result, Lee was buried without shoes.[158] He was buried underneath Lee Chapel at Washington and Lee University, where his body remains.

# James Lewis

*Lewis in* 1908

**James Lewis** (1832–July 11, 1914) was notable as a soldier and Republican Party politician in Louisiana. Born into slavery and of mixed race, during the American Civil War he left a position as steward on a Confederate steamboat to move to New Orleans, which had been taken over by Union troops. There he helped organize the First Louisiana Volunteer Native Guards, becoming captain of Company K and serving until 1864. After the war he became politically active in the Republican Party during the Reconstruction era, where he was an ally of several other leading men of color in the city and state. This was an especially violent time in Louisiana and New Orleans politics, but Lewis survived for decades as a political leader. He initially worked for the Freedmen's Bureau, where he was an agent to raise money and establish schools for freed slaves. He was appointed as a federal custom's inspector for a short period, the first man of African descent to gain a federal civil position in the state. He was recalled for political reasons.

Lewis entered the New Orleans Metropolitan Police force, but left in 1872 after more political machinations. He emerged from the immediate postwar period as a leader in the New Orleans Republican Party . For much of the 1870s, 1880s, 1890s, and 1900s, he held state and federal-level Republican-appointee government positions, usually in the United States Treasury Department. He also served for years under Republican administrations as the surveyor-general of Louisiana and Mississippi. He was a Freemason and a leader in the Grand Army of the Republic, a civil war veterans organization.

## Early life

James Lewis was born into slavery in Wilkinson County, Mississippi in 1832.[1] His father was a white planter, his master, and his mother was an enslaved woman of mixed race (mulatto).[2] He was raised in Bayou Sara, Louisiana.[3] Before the American Civil War (1861–1865), Lewis worked on steamboats on the Mississippi River, including the steamboat *Ingomar*, where he served and formed a friendship with Robert Reed Church; he also befriended Norris Wright Cuney by steamboat work. All three became political leaders after the Civil War.[4][5][6]

## Civil War

At the beginning of the Civil War, Lewis served as a steward on the CSS *De Soto* and was present at the fighting at the Battle of Belmont in November 1861 and the Battle of Island

Number Ten and New Madrid in February, March, and April 1862. Lewis believed the war was a chance to fight for the freedom of all blacks. He fled through danger to New Orleans shortly after its capture by Union Forces under David Farragut and Benjamin Butler in late April and early May 1862, in order to join Union forces.

In New Orleans, Lewis resolved to become a soldier. Together with other blacks, he asked for permission to raise a regiment of colored troops. Lewis raised two companies of colored infantry and was mustered into the First Louisiana Volunteer Native Guards as captain of one of these, Company K.[1] While a minority of the members had been free men of color before the war, the majority of troops were slaves newly freed by their escape from plantations and joining Union lines.

Lewis resigned his commission after the Red River Campaign led by Nathaniel Banks in 1864.[1] Lewis later wrote that he resigned because he was ordered to appear before a Board of Examiners that would rule on his ability to continue as captain, and a member of the board told him that no black officers would be passed. In November 1864, Lewis was authorized to recruit another company of infantry to join the 1st United States Colored Infantry. He offered to do so if allowed to appear before a Board of Examiners and be commissioned as an officer.[7]

In 1864 Lewis married Josephine Joubert of New Orleans, a free woman of color whose family had been slaveholders. For many years the couple lived in a fine house on Canal Street across from Straight University.[2]

## Reconstruction era

After the war, Lewis returned to New Orleans, where he worked as a permit and custom-house broker until the opening of ocean trade and the start of the Reconstruction Era. He was appointed as traveling agent for the educational department of the Freedmen's Bureau and worked to establish schools for freed slaves throughout Louisiana. He was frequently threatened during his work by ex-Confederates who opposed his efforts. At one point he was captured in North Louisiana and risked death but was rescued by the intervention of a group of fellow Freemasons.[1] He may have been one of the injured in the 1866 New Orleans riot at the Mechanics Institute, when whites rioted against a parade of blacks celebrating suffrage.[8]

When the Freedmen's Bureau closed, Lewis was appointed by Republican Governor William P. Kellogg as the United States inspector of customs for Louisiana, making him the first black man to have a civil position in the Federal service in Louisiana. In 1869, Lewis refused to support Seymour and Blair's presidential ticket, and as a result, Perry Fuller removed him from the position. Lewis became sergeant of the Metropolitan Police in New Orleans. He was successful in this position and was promoted to captain of the police. In 1870, Governor Henry Clay Warmouth appointed Lewis as colonel of the Second Regiment of the State Militia. That year Lewis was also elected to a two-year term as administer of police.[1]

## Personal life and death

Lewis was described as having "the massive build and pleasing features of that one of Napoleon's marshals who enjoyed the most human and tender sentiments of the master," and that his "lordly manners" gave him "the peculiar charm of the gentleman of the old school" although more "French than Southern Gentleman."[20]

Lewis' son, James Lewis Jr., was an active member of the New Orleans black elite. [21] His daughter, Julia (Lewis) Nickerson (c. 1878–December 7, 1908), was a violinist and cellist in her husband William J. Nickerson's orchestra.[22]

Lewis died in New Orleans on July 11, 1914.[13]

# Maria Lewis

**Maria Lewis alias George Harris** was a Union Civil War soldier, and former slave, who gained distinction in the Eighth New York Cavalry.[1]

## Biography

Lewis was born around 1846, in Albemarle County, Virginia, where she and her family were kept as slaves.[2] At the age of seventeen, she emancipated herself from slavery by disguising herself as a "darkly tanned" white man, and joining company C of the 8th New York Cavalry. [3]She adopted the name George Harris, after the character from *Uncle Tom's Cabin*, who similarly escaped by passing himself for a Spanish man.[4] She originally planned to use the identity to travel North; she decided to stay with the army after finding she enjoyed the freedom life as a white man brought her. Lewis remained with General Philip Sheridan's cavalry unit in the Shenandoah Valley for an additional eighteen months. [4] While serving, she fought at the Battle of Waynesboro on the second of March.[2] Lewis distinguished herself amongst her fellow soldiers, and became a member of the honor guard assigned to present seventeen captured rebel flags to the Secretary of War, Edwin Stanton.[4] She became friends with an abolitionist family from New York, the Wilburs, and after her service, she came to them and confessed to being a woman. The family gave her skirts, and found her a place to work. Lewis later received "lessons" from Julia's sister, Frances, presumably learning to read and write, which was barred to enslaved people prior to the civil war.[5] Little is known about her life after the war.

# Abraham Lincoln

*Lincoln in November 1863*

**Abraham Lincoln** (February 12, 1809–April 15, 1865) was an American statesman and lawyer who served as the 16th president of the United States from March 1861 until his assassination in April 1865. Lincoln led the nation through the American Civil War, its bloodiest war and its greatest moral, constitutional, and political crisis.[2][3] He preserved the Union, abolished slavery, strengthened the federal government, and modernized the U.S. economy.

Born in Kentucky, Lincoln grew up on the frontier in a poor family. Self-educated, he became a lawyer, Whig Party leader, Illinois state legislator, and Congressman. In 1849, he left government to resume his law practice, but angered by the Kansas–Nebraska Act's opening of the prairie lands to slavery, reentered politics in 1854. He became a leader in the new Republican Party and gained national attention in the 1858 debates against national Democratic leader Stephen Douglas in the U.S. Senate campaign in Illinois. He then ran for President in 1860, sweeping the North and winning. Southern pro-slavery elements took his win as proof that the North was rejecting the constitutional rights of Southern states to practice slavery. They began the process of seceding from the union. To secure its independence, the new Confederate States of America fired on Fort Sumter, one of the few U.S. forts in the South. Lincoln called up volunteers and militia to suppress the rebellion and restore the Union.

As the leader of the moderate faction of the Republican Party, Lincoln confronted Radical Republicans, who demanded harsher treatment of the South; War Democrats, who rallied a large faction of former opponents into his camp; anti-war Democrats (called Copperheads), who despised him; and irreconcilable secessionists, who plotted his assassination. Lincoln fought the factions by pitting them against each other, by carefully distributing political patronage, and by appealing to the American people. [4]:65–87 His Gettysburg Address became an iconic call for nationalism, republicanism, equal rights, liberty, and democracy. He suspended *habeas corpus*, and he averted British intervention by defusing the *Trent* Affair. Lincoln closely supervised the war effort, including the selection of generals and the naval blockade that shut down the South's trade. As the war progressed, he maneuvered to end slavery, issuing the Emancipation Proclamation of 1863; ordering the Army to protect escaped slaves, encouraging border states to outlaw slavery, and pushing through Congress the Thirteenth Amendment to the United States Constitution, which outlawed slavery across the country.

Lincoln managed his own re-election campaign. He sought to reconcile his damaged nation by avoiding retribution against the secessionists. A few days after the Battle of Appomattox Court House, he was shot by John Wilkes Booth, an actor and Confederate sympathizer, on April 14, 1865, and died the following day. Abraham Lincoln is remembered as the United States' martyr hero. He is consistently ranked both by scholars[5] and the public[6] as among the greatest U.S. presidents.

## Emergence as Republican leader

*Lincoln in 1858, the year of his debates with Stephen Douglas over slavery.*

The debate over the status of slavery in the territories exacerbated sectional tensions between the slave-holding South and the free North. The Compromise of 1850 failed to defuse the issue.[12]:175–176 In the early 1850s, Lincoln supported sectional mediation, and his 1852 eulogy for Clay focused on the latter's support for gradual emancipation and opposition to "both extremes" on the slavery issue.[12]:182–185 As the 1850s progressed, the debate over slavery in the Nebraska Territory and Kansas Territory became particularly acrimonious, and Senator Douglas proposed popular sovereignty as a compromise measure; the proposal would allow the electorate of each territory to decide the status of slavery. The proposal alarmed many Northerners, who hoped to prevent the spread of slavery into the territories. Despite this Northern opposition, Douglas's Kansas–Nebraska Act narrowly passed Congress in May 1854.[12]:188–190

For months after its passage, Lincoln did not publicly comment, but he came to strongly oppose it.[12]:196–197 On October 16, 1854, in his "Peoria Speech," Lincoln declared his opposition to slavery, which he repeated en route to the presidency.[18]:148–152 Speaking in his Kentucky accent, with a powerful voice,[12]:199 he said the Kansas Act had a "*declared* indifference, but as I must think, a covert *real* zeal for the spread of slavery. I cannot but hate it. I hate it because of the monstrous injustice of slavery itself. I hate it because it deprives our republican example of its just influence in the world . . . "[41]:255 Lincoln's attacks on the Kansas–Nebraska Act marked his return to political life.[12]:203–205

Nationally, the Whigs were irreparably split by the Kansas–Nebraska Act and other efforts to compromise on the slavery issue. Reflecting the demise of his party, Lincoln wrote in 1855, "I think I am a Whig, but others say there are no Whigs, and that I am an abolitionist [ . . . ] I do no more than oppose the *extension* of slavery."[12]:215–216 Drawing on the antislavery portion of the Whig Party, and combining Free Soil, Liberty, and antislavery Democratic Party members, the new Republican Party formed as a northern party dedicated to antislavery.[43]:38–39 Lincoln resisted early recruiting attempts, fearing that it would serve as a platform for extreme abolitionists.[12]:203–204 Lincoln hoped to rejuvenate the Whigs, though he lamented his party's growing closeness with the nativist Know Nothing movement.[12]:191–194

In the 1854 elections, Lincoln was elected to the Illinois legislature but declined to take his seat.[12]:203–205 In the elections' aftermath, which showed the power and popularity of the movement opposed to the Kansas–Nebraska Act, Lincoln instead sought election to the United States Senate.[12]:204–205 At that time, senators were elected by the state legislature. [35]:119 After leading in the first six rounds of voting, he was unable to obtain a majority. Lincoln instructed his backers to vote for Lyman Trumbull. Trumbull was an antislavery Democrat, and had received few votes in the earlier ballots; his supporters, also antislavery Democrats, had vowed not to support any Whig. Lincoln's decision to withdraw enabled his Whig supporters and Trumbull's antislavery Democrats to combine and defeat the mainstream Democratic candidate, Joel Aldrich Matteson.[12]:205–208

## 1856 campaign

In part due to the ongoing violent political confrontations in Kansas, opposition to the Kansas–Nebraska Act remained strong throughout the North. As the 1856 elections approached, Lincoln joined the Republicans. He attended the May 1856 Bloomington Convention, which formally established the Illinois Republican Party. The convention platform asserted that Congress had the right to regulate slavery in the territories and called for the immediate admission of Kansas as a free state. Lincoln gave the final speech of the convention, in which he endorsed the party platform and called for the preservation of the Union.[12]:216–221 At the June 1856 Republican National Convention, Lincoln received significant support to run for vice president, though the party nominated William Dayton to run with John C. Frémont. Lincoln supported the Republican ticket, campaigning throughout Illinois. The Democrats nominated former Ambassador James Buchanan, who had been out of the country since 1853 and thus had avoided the slavery debate, while the Know Nothings nominated former Whig President Millard Fillmore. [12]:224–228 Buchanan defeated both his challengers. Republican William Henry Bissell won election as Governor of Illinois. Lincoln's vigorous campaigning had made him the leading Republican in Illinois.[12]:229–230

## Principles

Eric Foner (2010) contrasts the abolitionists and anti-slavery Radical Republicans of the Northeast, who saw slavery as a sin, with the conservative Republicans, who thought it was bad because it hurt white people and blocked progress. Foner argues that Lincoln was a moderate in the middle, opposing slavery primarily because it violated the republicanism principles of the Founding Fathers, especially the equality of all men and democratic self-government as expressed in the Declaration of Independence.[33]:84–88

## *Dred Scott*

In March 1857, in *Dred Scott v. Sandford,* Supreme Court Chief Justice Roger B. Taney wrote that blacks were not citizens and derived no rights from the Constitution. While many Democrats hoped that *Dred Scott* would end the dispute over slavery in the territories, the decision sparked further outrage in the North.[12]:236–238 Lincoln denounced it, alleging it was the product of a conspiracy of Democrats to support the Slave Power.[53]:69–110 Lincoln argued, "The authors of the Declaration of Independence never intended 'to say all were equal in color, size, intellect, moral developments, or social capacity,' but they 'did consider all men created equal—equal in certain inalienable rights, among which are life, liberty, and the pursuit of happiness.'"[54]:299–300

## Lincoln–Douglas debates and Cooper Union speech

Douglas was up for re-election in 1858, and Lincoln hoped to defeat him. With the former Democrat Trumbull now serving as a Republican senator, many in the party felt that a former Whig should be nominated in 1858, and Lincoln's 1856 campaigning and willingness to support Trumbull in 1854 had earned him favor.[12]:247–248 Some eastern Republicans favored Douglas's re-election in 1858, since he had led the opposition to the Lecompton Constitution, which would have admitted Kansas as a slave state.[35]:138–139 Many Illinois Republicans resented this eastern interference. For the first time, Illinois Republicans held a convention to agree upon a Senate candidate, and Lincoln won the nomination with little opposition.[12]:247–250

Accepting the nomination, Lincoln delivered his House Divided Speech, drawing on Mark 3:25, "A house divided against itself cannot stand. I believe this government

cannot endure permanently half slave and half free. I do not expect the Union to be dissolved—I do not expect the house to fall—but I do expect it will cease to be divided. It will become all one thing, or all the other."[12]:251 The speech created an evocative image of the danger of disunion.[36]:98 The stage was then set for the campaign for statewide election of the Illinois legislature which would, in turn, select Lincoln or Douglas.[7]:209 When informed of Lincoln's nomination, Douglas stated, "[Lincoln] is the strong man of the party . . . and if I beat him, my victory will be hardly won."[12]:257–258

The Senate campaign featured seven debates, the most famous political debates in American history.[55]:182 The principals stood in stark contrast both physically and politically.

*Abraham Lincoln (1860) by Mathew Brady, taken the day of the Cooper Union speech.*

Lincoln warned that "The Slave Power" was threatening the values of republicanism, and accused Douglas of distorting the values of the Founding Fathers that all men are created equal, while Douglas emphasized his Freeport Doctrine, that local settlers were free to choose whether to allow slavery, and accused Lincoln of having joined the abolitionists.[7]:214–224 The debates had an atmosphere of a prize fight and drew crowds in the thousands. Lincoln's argument was rooted in morality. He claimed that Douglas represented a conspiracy to extend slavery to free states. Douglas's argument was legal, claiming that Lincoln was defying the authority of the U.S. Supreme Court and the *Dred Scott* decision.[7]:223

Though the Republican legislative candidates won more popular votes, the Democrats won more seats, and the legislature re-elected Douglas. Lincoln's articulation of the issues gave him a national political presence.[56]:89–90 In May 1859, Lincoln purchased the *Illinois Staats-Anzeiger*, a German-language newspaper that was consistently supportive; most of the state's 130,000 German Americans voted Democratic but the German-language paper mobilized Republican support.[7]:242, 412 In the aftermath of the 1858 election, newspapers frequently mentioned Lincoln as a potential Republican presidential candidate, rivaled by William H. Seward, Salmon P. Chase, Edward Bates, and Simon Cameron. While Lincoln was popular in the Midwest, he lacked support in the Northeast, and was unsure whether to seek the office.[12]:291–293 In January 1860, Lincoln told a group of political allies that he would accept the nomination if offered, and in the following months several local papers endorsed his candidacy.[12]:307–308

On February 27, 1860, New York party leaders invited Lincoln to give a speech at Cooper Union to a group of powerful Republicans. Lincoln argued that the Founding Fathers had little use for popular sovereignty and had repeatedly sought to restrict slavery. Lincoln insisted that morality required opposition to slavery, and rejected any "groping for some middle ground between the right and the wrong."[54]:473 Despite his inelegant appearance—many in the audience thought him awkward and even ugly[40]:108–111—Lincoln demonstrated intellectual leadership that brought him into contention. Journalist Noah Brooks reported, "No man ever before made such an impression on his first appeal to a New York audience."[56]:97[40]:157

Historian David Herbert Donald described the speech as a "superb political move for an unannounced candidate, to appear in one rival's (Seward) own state at an event sponsored by the second rival's (Chase) loyalists, while not mentioning either by name during its delivery."[7]:240 In response to an inquiry about his ambitions, Lincoln said, "The taste *is* in my mouth a little."[7]:241

## 1860 presidential election

*A Timothy Cole wood engraving taken from a May 20, 1860, ambrotype of Lincoln, two days following his nomination for president*

On May 9–10, 1860, the Illinois Republican State Convention was held in Decatur.[7]:244 Lincoln's followers organized a campaign team led by David Davis, Norman Judd, Leonard Swett, and Jesse DuBois, and Lincoln received his first endorsement.[35]:175–176 Exploiting his embellished frontier legend (clearing land and splitting fence rails), Lincoln's supporters adopted the label of "The Rail Candidate."[7]:245 In 1860, Lincoln described himself: "I am in height, six feet, four inches, nearly; lean in flesh, weighing, on an average, one hundred and eighty pounds; dark complexion, with coarse black hair, and gray eyes."[57]

On May 18, at the Republican National Convention in Chicago, Lincoln won the nomination on the third ballot, beating candidates such as Seward and Chase. A former Democrat, Hannibal Hamlin of Maine, was nominated for

Vice President to balance the ticket. Lincoln's success depended on his campaign team, his reputation as a moderate on the slavery issue, and his strong support for Whiggish programs of internal improvements and the tariff.[58]:609–629

Pennsylvania put him over the top, led by Pennsylvania iron interests who were reassured by his tariff support.[59]:50–55 Lincoln's managers had focused on this delegation, while following Lincoln's dictate to "Make no contracts that bind me."[7]:247–250

Most Republicans agreed with Lincoln that the North was the aggrieved party, as the Slave Power tightened its grasp on the national government. Throughout the 1850s, Lincoln doubted the prospects of civil war, and his supporters rejected claims that his election would incite secession.[34]:10, 13, 18 Douglas was selected as the candidate of the Northern Democrats. Delegates from eleven slave states walked out of the Democratic convention, disagreeing with Douglas's position on popular sovereignty, and ultimately selected incumbent Vice President John C. Breckinridge as their candidate.[7]:253 A group of former Whigs and Know Nothings formed the Constitutional Union Party and nominated John Bell of Tennessee. Lincoln and Douglas competed for votes in the North, while Bell and Breckinridge primarily found support in the South.[12]:247–248

Lincoln's campaign team carefully projected his image as an ideal candidate. Michael Martinez wrote:

> Lincoln and his political advisers manipulated his image and background . . . . Sometimes he appeared as a straight-shooting, plain-talking, common-sense-wielding man of the people. His image as the "Rail Splitter" dates from this era. His supporters also portrayed him as "Honest Abe," the country fellow who was simply dressed and not especially polished or formal in his manner but who was as honest and trustworthy as his legs were long. Even Lincoln's tall, gangly frame was used to good advantage during the campaign as many drawings and posters show the candidate sprinting past his vertically challenged rivals. At other times, Lincoln appeared as a sophisticated, thoughtful, articulate, "presidential" candidate.[60]

Prior to the Republican convention, the Lincoln campaign began cultivating a nationwide youth organization, the Wide Awakes, which it used to generate popular support throughout the country to spearhead voter registration drives, thinking that new voters and young voters tended to embrace new parties.[61] Lincoln's ideas of abolishing slavery grew, drawing more supporters. People of the Northern states knew the Southern states would vote against Lincoln and rallied supporters for Lincoln.[62]

As Douglas and the other candidates campaigned, Lincoln was the only one to give no speeches. Instead, he relied on the enthusiasm of the Republican Party. The party did the leg work that produced majorities across the North, and produced an abundance of campaign posters, leaflets, and newspaper editorials. Thousands of Republican speakers focused first on the party platform, and second on Lincoln's life story, emphasizing his childhood poverty. The goal was to demonstrate the superior power of "free labor," whereby a common farm boy could work his way to the top by his own efforts.[7]:254–256 The Republican Party's production of campaign literature dwarfed the combined opposition; a *Chicago Tribune* writer produced a pamphlet that detailed Lincoln's life, and sold 100,000–200,000 copies.[7]:254

On November 6, Lincoln was elected the 16th president of the United States. He was the first Republican president and his victory was entirely due to his support in the North and West; no ballots were cast for him in 10 of the 15 Southern slave states, and he won only two of 996 counties in all the Southern states.[63]:61 Lincoln received 1,866,452 votes, or 39.8 percent of the total in a four-way race. He won the free Northern states, as well as California and Oregon.[12]:350

Lincoln's victory in the electoral college was decisive: Lincoln had 180 and his opponents added together had only 123.[64]:4:312

## Presidency

### Secession and inauguration

After the November election, secessionists planned to leave the Union before he took office in March.[65]:350 On December 20, 1860, South Carolina took the lead by adopting an ordinance of secession; by February 1, 1861, Florida, Mississippi, Alabama, Georgia, Louisiana, and Texas had followed.[7]:267[66]:498 Six of these states declared themselves to be a sovereign nation, the Confederate States of America, and adopted a constitution. [7]:267 The upper South and border states (Delaware, Maryland, Virginia, North Carolina, Tennessee, Kentucky, Missouri, and Arkansas) listened to, but initially rejected, the secessionist appeal.[12]:362 President Buchanan and President-elect Lincoln refused to recognize the Confederacy, declaring secession illegal.[66]:520, 569–570 The Confederacy selected Jefferson Davis as its provisional President on February 9, 1861.[12]:369

Attempts at compromise followed. Lincoln and the Republicans rejected the proposed Crittenden Compromise as contrary to the Party's free-soil in the territories platform.[12]:360–361 Lincoln rejected the idea, saying, "I will suffer death before I consent . . . to any concession or compromise which looks like buying the privilege to take possession of this government to which we have a constitutional right."[7]:268

Lincoln did tacitly support the proposed Corwin Amendment to the Constitution, which passed Congress before Lincoln came into office and was then awaiting ratification by the states. That proposed amendment would have protected slavery in states where it already existed.[67]:22[68]:280–281 A few weeks before the war, Lincoln sent a letter to every governor informing them Congress had passed a joint resolution to amend the Constitution. [69] Lincoln was open to the possibility of a constitutional convention to make further amendments to the Constitution.[68]:281

En route to his inauguration, Lincoln addressed crowds and legislatures across the North.[7]:273–277 The president-elect evaded possible assassins in Baltimore. On February 23, 1861, he arrived in disguise in Washington, D.C., which was placed under substantial military guard.[7]:277–279 Lincoln directed his inaugural address to the South, proclaiming once again that he had no intention, or inclination, to abolish slavery in the Southern states:

Apprehension seems to exist among the people of the Southern States that by the accession of a Republican Administration their property and their peace and personal security are to be endangered. There has never been any reasonable cause for such apprehension. Indeed, the most ample evidence to the contrary has all the while existed and been open to their inspection. It is found in nearly all the published speeches of him who now addresses you. I do but quote from one of those speeches when I declare that "I have no purpose, directly or indirectly, to interfere with the institution of slavery in the States where it exists. I believe I have no lawful right to do so, and I have no inclination to do so."

*— First inaugural address, 4 March 1861*[70]:212

Lincoln cited his plans for banning the expansion of slavery as the key source of conflict between North and South, stating "One section of our country believes slavery is right and ought to be extended, while the other believes it is wrong and ought not to be extended. This is the only substantial dispute." The President ended his address with an appeal to the people of the South: "We are not enemies, but friends. We must not be enemies . . . The mystic chords of memory, stretching from every battlefield, and patriot grave, to every living heart and hearthstone, all over this broad land, will yet swell the chorus of the Union, when again touched, as surely they will be, by the better angels of our nature."[7]:283–284 The failure of the Peace Conference of 1861 signaled that legislative compromise was impossible. By March 1861, no leaders of the insurrection had proposed rejoining the Union on any terms. Meanwhile, Lincoln and the Republican leadership agreed that the dismantling of the Union could not be tolerated.[7]:268, 279 Lincoln said in his second inaugural address:

Both parties deprecated war, but one of them would make war rather than let the Nation survive, and the other would accept war rather than let it perish, and the war came.

## The Civil War

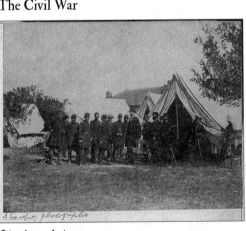

*A Gardner, photographer*

*Lincoln at Antietam*

Fort Sumter's commander, Major Robert Anderson, sent a request for provisions to Washington, and the execution of Lincoln's order to meet that request was seen by the secessionists as an act of war. On April 12, 1861, Confederate forces fired on Union troops at Fort Sumter and began the fight. Historian Allan Nevins argued that the newly inaugurated Lincoln made three miscalculations: underestimating the gravity of the crisis, exaggerating the strength of Unionist sentiment in the South, and not realizing the Southern Unionists were insisting there be no invasion.[71]:5:29

William Tecumseh Sherman talked to Lincoln during inauguration week and was "sadly disappointed" at his failure to realize that "the country was sleeping on a volcano" and that the South was preparing for war.[72]:185–186 Donald concludes that, "His repeated efforts to avoid collision in the months between inauguration and the firing on Ft. Sumter showed he adhered to his vow not to be the first to shed fraternal blood. But he also vowed not to surrender the forts. The only resolution of these contradictory positions was for the confederates to fire the first shot; they did just that."[7]:293

On April 15, Lincoln called on the states to send detachments totaling 75,000 troops to recapture forts, protect Washington, and "preserve the Union," which, in his view, remained intact despite the seceding states. This call forced states to choose sides. Virginia seceded and was rewarded with the Confederate capital, despite the exposed position of Richmond close to Union lines. North Carolina, Tennessee, and Arkansas followed over the following two months. Secession sentiment was strong in Missouri and Maryland, but did not prevail; Kentucky remained neutral.[17]:226 The Fort Sumter attack rallied Americans north of the Mason-Dixon line to defend the nation.

States sent Union regiments south. On April 19, mobs in Baltimore, which controlled rail links, attacked Union troops who were changing trains. Local leaders' groups later burned critical rail bridges to the capital. The Army responded by arresting local Maryland officials. Lincoln suspended the writ of *habeas corpus* in areas the army felt it needed to secure for troops to reach Washington.[73]:174 John Merryman, a Maryland official involved in hindering the U.S. troop movements, petitioned Supreme Court Chief Justice and Marylander, Roger B. Taney, author of the *Dred Scott* opinion, to issue a writ of *habeas corpus*. In June Taney, acting as a circuit judge and not speaking for the Supreme Court, issued the writ, because in his opinion only Congress could suspend the writ. Lincoln continued the army policy that the writ was suspended in limited areas despite the ex parte Merryman ruling.[74][75]:3–31

## Union military strategy

After the Battle of Fort Sumter, Lincoln took executive control of the war and formed an overall Union military strategy. Lincoln responded to this unprecedented political and military crisis as commander-in-chief, using unprecedented powers. He expanded his war powers, imposed a blockade on Confederate ports, disbursed funds before appropriation by Congress, suspended *habeas corpus*, and arrested and imprisoned thousands of suspected Confederate sympathizers. Lincoln was supported by Congress and the northern public for these actions. In addition, Lincoln had to reinforce Union sympathies in the border slave states and keep the war from becoming an international conflict.[7]:303–304[56]:163–164

The war dominated Lincoln's time and attention. From the start, it was clear that bipartisan support would be essential to success, and that any compromise would alienate factions on both sides of the aisle, such as the appointment of Republicans and Democrats to command positions. Copperheads criticized Lincoln for refusing to compromise on slavery. The Radical Republicans criticized him for moving too slowly in abolishing slavery.[7]:315, 331–333, 338–339, 417 On August 6, 1861, Lincoln signed the Confiscation Act that authorized judicial proceedings to confiscate and free slaves who were used to support the Confederates. In practice, the law had little effect, but it did signal political support for abolishing slavery.[7]:314[56]:178

In late August 1861, General John C. Frémont, the 1856 Republican presidential nominee, without consulting his superiors in Washington, proclaimed a very harsh martial law in Missouri. Lincoln cancelled the proclamation, saying its emancipation plan was political, lacking military necessity and a legal basis.[7]:314–317 After Lincoln acted, Union enlistments from Maryland, Kentucky, and Missouri increased by over 40,000.[56]:181

In foreign policy, Lincoln's main goal was to stop military aid to the Confederacy. [34]:213–214 Lincoln left most diplomatic matters to his Secretary of State, William Seward. [34]:213–214 At times Seward was too bellicose, so for balance Lincoln maintained a close working relationship with Senate Foreign Relations Committee chairman Charles Sumner. [7]:322 The *Trent* Affair of late 1861 threatened war with Great Britain. The U.S. Navy had illegally intercepted a British mail ship, the *Trent*, on the high seas and seized two Confederate envoys; Britain protested vehemently while the U.S. cheered. Lincoln ended the crisis by releasing the two diplomats. Biographer James G. Randall dissected Lincoln's successful techniques:[76] his restraint, his avoidance of any outward expression of truculence, his early softening of State Department's attitude toward Britain, his deference toward Seward and Sumner, his withholding of his own paper prepared for the occasion, his readiness to arbitrate, his golden silence in addressing Congress, his shrewdness in recognizing that war must be averted, and his clear perception that a point could be clinched for America's true position at the same time that full satisfaction was given to a friendly country.

Lincoln painstakingly monitored the telegraph reports coming into the War Department. He tracked all phases of the effort, consulted with governors, and selected generals based on their success (as well as their state and party). In January 1862, after many complaints of inefficiency and profiteering in the War Department, Lincoln replaced Simon Cameron with Edwin Stanton as War Secretary. Stanton centralized the War Department's activities, auditing and cancelling contracts, saving the federal government $17,000,000. [35]:115 Stanton was a staunchly Unionist, pro-business, conservative Democrat who moved toward the Radical Republican faction. He worked more often and more closely with Lincoln than any other senior official. "Stanton and Lincoln virtually conducted the war together," say Thomas and Hyman.[77]

In terms of war strategy, Lincoln articulated two priorities: to ensure that Washington was well-defended, and to conduct an aggressive war effort leading to prompt, decisive victory. However major Northern newspapers demanded more—they expected victory within 90 days.[7]:295–296 Twice a week, Lincoln met with his cabinet in the afternoon. Occasionally Mary would force him to take a carriage ride, concerned that he was working too hard.[7]:391–392 Lincoln learned from reading his chief of staff General Henry Halleck's book, a disciple of the European strategist Jomini; he began to appreciate the critical need to control strategic points, such as the Mississippi River.[78]:7, 66, 159 Lincoln saw the importance of Vicksburg and understood the necessity of defeating the enemy's army, rather than simply capturing territory.[7]:432–436

## General McClellan

After the Union rout at Bull Run and Winfield Scott's retirement, Lincoln appointed Major General George B. McClellan general-in-chief.[7]:318–319 McClellan then took months to plan his Peninsula Campaign. McClellan's slow progress frustrated Lincoln, as did his position that no troops were needed to defend Washington. McClellan blamed Lincoln's holding troops back for his campaign's subsequent failure.[7]:349–352 Lincoln went as far as meeting with General McClellan in his home to discuss matters privately. Once McClellan heard Lincoln was in his home, McClellan stayed hidden away until Lincoln left.

Lincoln removed McClellan in March 1862, after McClellan offered unsolicited political advice.[7]:360–361 In July Lincoln elevated Henry Halleck.[79] Lincoln appointed John Pope as head of the new Army of Virginia. Pope complied with Lincoln's desire to advance on

*Lincoln and McClellan*

Richmond from the north, thus protecting Washington from counterattack.[64]:2:159–162

Pope was then soundly defeated at the Second Battle of Bull Run in the summer of 1862, forcing the Army of the Potomac back to defend Washington.[80]:2:159–162

Despite his dissatisfaction with McClellan's failure to reinforce Pope, Lincoln restored him to command of all forces around Washington.[81]:478–479 Two days after McClellan's return to command, General Robert E. Lee's forces crossed the Potomac River into Maryland, leading to the Battle of Antietam in September.[81]:478–480 The ensuing Union victory was among the bloodiest in American history, but it enabled Lincoln to announce that he would issue an Emancipation Proclamation in January. Lincoln had waited for a military victory so that the Proclamation would not be perceived as the product of desperation.[81]:481

McClellan then resisted the president's demand that he pursue Lee's army, while General Don Carlos Buell likewise refused orders to move the Army of the Ohio against rebel forces in eastern Tennessee. Lincoln replaced Buell with William Rosecrans; and, after the 1862 midterm elections, replaced McClellan with Ambrose Burnside. Both were presumably more supportive of the commander-in-chief.[7]:389–390

Burnside, against presidential advice, launched an offensive across the Rappahannock River and was defeated by Lee at Fredericksburg in December. Desertions during 1863 came in the thousands and increased after Fredericksburg.[7]:429–431 Lincoln promoted Joseph Hooker.[64]:6:433–44

The midterm elections in 1862 cost the Republicans severe losses due to rising inflation, high taxes, rumors of corruption, suspension of *habeas corpus*, military draft law, and fears that freed slaves would come North and undermine the labor market. The Emancipation Proclamation gained votes for Republicans in rural New England and the upper Midwest, but cost votes in the Irish and German strongholds and in the lower Midwest, where many Southerners had lived for generations.[64]:6:322

In the spring of 1863, Lincoln became optimistic about upcoming military campaigns to the point of thinking the end of the war could be near if a string of victories could be put together; these plans included attacks by Hooker on Lee north of Richmond, Rosecrans on Chattanooga, Grant on Vicksburg, and a naval assault on Charleston.[7]:422–423

Hooker was routed by Lee at the Battle of Chancellorsville in May.[64]:6:432–450 He then resigned and was replaced by George Meade as Lee moved north. Meade followed Lee into Pennsylvania and beat him in the Gettysburg Campaign, but then failed to follow up despite Lincoln's demands. At the same time, Grant captured Vicksburg and gained control of the Mississippi River, splitting off the far western rebel states.[7]:444–447

## Emancipation Proclamation

The Federal government's power to end slavery was limited by the Constitution, which before 1865, committed the issue to individual states. Lincoln argued that slavery would end by preventing its expansion into new territories. He sought to persuade the states to accept compensated emancipation in return for their prohibition of slavery. Lincoln believed that curtailing slavery would make it obsolete.[82] Lincoln rejected Frémont's two emancipation attempts in August 1861 and one by Major General David Hunter in May 1862, on the grounds that it was not within their power, and would upset loyal border states.[83]:290–291

On June 19, 1862, endorsed by Lincoln, Congress passed an act banning slavery on all federal territory. In July, the Confiscation Act of 1862 was enacted, which set up court procedures to free the slaves of those convicted of aiding the rebellion. Although Lincoln believed this was not within Congress's power, he approved the bill in deference to the legislature. He felt such action could be taken only by the Commander-in-Chief, using Constitutional war powers, which he planned to do. Lincoln discussed a draft of the Emancipation Proclamation with his cabinet.[7]:364–365

Privately, Lincoln concluded that the Confederacy's slave base had to be eliminated. However, Copperheads argued that emancipation was a stumbling block to peace and reunification. Republican editor Horace Greeley of the *New York Tribune* agreed. [84]:124 Lincoln rejected this argument directly in his letter of August 22, 1862. Although he said he personally wished all men could be free, Lincoln stated that the primary goal of his actions as president (he used the first person pronoun and explicitly refers to his "official duty") was that of preserving the Union:[85]:147–153

> My paramount object in this struggle is to save the Union, and is not either to save or to destroy slavery. If I could save the Union without freeing any slave I would do it, and if I could save it by freeing all the slaves I would do it; and if I could save it by freeing some and leaving others alone I would also do that. What I do about slavery, and the colored race, I do because I believe it helps to save the Union; and what I forbear, I forbear because I do not believe it would help to save the Union ... I have here stated my purpose according to my view of official duty; and I intend no modification of my oft-expressed personal wish that all men everywhere could be free.[41]:388

The Emancipation Proclamation, issued on September 22, 1862, with effect on January 1, 1863, declared free the slaves in 10 states not then under Union control, with exemptions specified for areas under Union control in two states.[7]:364, 379 Lincoln spent the next 100 days preparing the army and the nation for emancipation, while Democrats rallied their voters by warning of the threat that freed slaves posed to northern whites.[86]

Once the abolition of slavery in the rebel states became a military objective, Union armies advancing south liberated three million slaves. Lincoln's comment on the signing of the Proclamation was: "I never, in my life, felt more certain that I was doing right, than I do in signing this paper."[7]:407 Lincoln continued earlier plans to set up colonies for the newly freed slaves. He supported this in the Proclamation, but the undertaking failed.[7]:408

Enlisting former slaves became official policy. By the spring of 1863, Lincoln was ready to recruit black troops in more than token numbers. In a letter to Tennessee military governor Andrew Johnson encouraging him to lead the way in raising black troops, Lincoln wrote, "The bare sight of 50,000 armed and drilled black soldiers on the banks of the Mississippi would end the rebellion at once."[7]:430–431 By the end of 1863, at Lincoln's direction, General Lorenzo Thomas had recruited 20 regiments of blacks from the Mississippi Valley.[7]:431

## Gettysburg Address (1863)

Lincoln spoke at the Gettysburg battlefield cemetery on November 19, 1863.[7]:453–460 Defying his prediction that "the world will little note, nor long remember what we say here," the Address became the most quoted speech in American history.[11]:222

In 272 words, and three minutes, Lincoln asserted that the nation was born not in 1789, but in 1776, "conceived in Liberty, and dedicated to the proposition that all men are created equal." He defined the war as dedicated to the principles of liberty and equality for all. He declared that the deaths of so many brave soldiers would not be in vain, that slavery would end, and the future of democracy would be assured, that "government of the people, by the people, for the people, shall not perish from the earth."[7]:460–466[87]:20, 27, 105, 146

## General Grant

Grant's victories at the Battle of Shiloh and in the Vicksburg campaign impressed Lincoln. Responding to criticism of Grant after Shiloh, Lincoln had said, "I can't spare this man. He fights."[18]:315 With Grant in command, Lincoln felt the Union Army could advance in multiple theaters, and incorporate black troops. Meade's failure to capture Lee's army after Gettysburg and the continued passivity of the Army of the Potomac persuaded Lincoln to promote Grant to supreme commander. Grant stayed with Meade's army and told Meade what to do.[64]:4:6–17

Lincoln was concerned that Grant might be considering a presidential candidacy in 1864, as was McClellan. Lincoln arranged for an intermediary to inquire into Grant's political intentions. Assured that he had none, Lincoln submitted Grant's appointment to the Senate. He obtained Congress's consent to make him Lieutenant General, a rank that had remained unoccupied since George Washington.[7]:490–492

Grant waged his bloody Overland Campaign in 1864, with heavy losses on both sides. [88]:113 Despite this, when Lincoln asked what Grant's plans were, the general replied, "I propose to fight it out on this line if it takes all summer."[7]:501

Grant's army moved steadily south. Lincoln traveled to Grant's headquarters at City Point, Virginia, to confer with Grant and William Tecumseh Sherman.[89] Lincoln replaced the Union losses by mobilizing support throughout the North.[18]:422–424

Lincoln authorized Grant to target infrastructure—plantations, railroads, and bridges—hoping to destroy the South's morale and weaken its fighting ability. Lincoln emphasized defeat of the Confederate armies rather than destruction (which was considerable) for its own sake.[90]:434–458

In 1864 Confederate general Jubal Early raided Washington, D.C., while Lincoln watched from an exposed position; Captain Oliver Wendell Holmes shouted at him, "Get down, you damn fool, before you get shot!"[18]:434

As Grant continued to attrit Lee's forces, efforts to discuss peace began. Confederate Vice President Stephens led a group to meet with Lincoln, Seward, and others at Hampton Roads. Lincoln refused to allow any negotiation with the Confederacy as a coequal; his sole objective was an agreement to end the fighting and the meetings produced no results. [7]:565 On April 1, 1865, Grant nearly encircled Petersburg. The Confederate government evacuated and the city fell. Lincoln visited the conquered capital. On April 9, Lee surrendered to Grant at Appomattox officially ending the war.[7]:589

## Re-election

Lincoln ran again in 1864. He united the main Republican factions, along with War Democrats such as Edwin M. Stanton and Andrew Johnson. Lincoln used conversation and his patronage powers—greatly expanded from peacetime—to build support and fend off the Radicals' efforts to replace him.[91]:53–69[92]:77–90 At its convention, the Republicans selected Johnson as his running mate. To broaden his coalition to include War Democrats as well as Republicans, Lincoln ran under the label of the new Union Party.[7]:494–507

Grant's bloody stalemates damaged Lincoln's re-election prospects, and many Republicans feared defeat. Lincoln confidentially pledged in writing that if he should lose the election, he would still defeat the Confederacy before turning over the White House.[93]:80 Lincoln did not show the pledge to his cabinet, but asked them to sign the sealed envelope.

While the Democratic platform followed the "Peace wing" of the party and called the war a "failure," their candidate, McClellan, supported the war and repudiated the platform. Lincoln provided Grant with more troops and led his party to renew its support for Grant. Sherman's capture of Atlanta in September and David Farragut's capture of Mobile ended defeatism.[7]:531 The Democratic Party was deeply split, with some leaders and most soldiers openly for Lincoln. The National Union Party was united by Lincoln's support for emancipation. State Republican parties stressed the perfidy of the Copperheads.[94]:307 On November 8, Lincoln carried all but three states, including 78 percent of Union soldiers.[93]:80[95]:274–293

On March 4, 1865, Lincoln delivered his second inaugural address. In it, he deemed the endless casualties to be God's will. Historian Mark Noll claims this speech to rank "among the small handful of semi-sacred texts by which Americans conceive their place in the world."[96]:426 Lincoln said:

> Fondly do we hope—fervently do we pray—that this mighty scourge of war may speedily pass away. Yet, if God wills that it continue, until all the wealth piled by the bond-man's 250 years of unrequited toil shall be sunk, and until every drop of blood drawn with the lash, shall be paid by another drawn with the sword, as was said 3,000 years ago, so still it must be said, "the judgments of the Lord, are true and righteous altogether." With malice toward none; with charity for all; with firmness in the right, as God gives us to see the right, let us strive on to finish the work we are in; to bind up the nation's wounds; to care for him who shall have borne the battle, and for his widow, and his orphan—to do all which may achieve and cherish a just and lasting peace, among ourselves, and with all nations.[97]

## Reconstruction

Reconstruction began during the war, as Lincoln and his associates considered how to reintegrate the nation, and the fates of Confederate leaders and freed slaves. Shortly after Lee's surrender, a general asked Lincoln how to treat defeated Confederates. Lincoln replied, "Let 'em up easy."[18]:509–512 Lincoln was determined to find meaning in the war even when it had passed, and did not want to continue to outcast the southern states. His main goal was to keep the union together. He planned to go forward not by focusing on who to blame, but on how to rebuild the nation as one.[98] Lincoln led the moderates regarding Reconstruction policy, and was opposed by the Radicals, under Rep. Thaddeus Stevens, Sen. Charles Sumner and Sen. Benjamin Wade, who otherwise remained Lincoln's allies. Determined to reunite the nation and not alienate the South, Lincoln urged that

THE 'RAIL SPLITTER' AT WORK REPAIRING THE UNION.

*A political cartoon of Vice President Andrew Johnson (a former tailor) and Lincoln, 1865, entitled The 'Rail Splitter' At Work Repairing the Union. The caption reads (Johnson): "Take it quietly Uncle Abe and I will draw it closer than ever." (Lincoln): "A few more stitches Andy and the good old Union will be mended."*

speedy elections under generous terms be held. His Amnesty Proclamation of December 8, 1863, offered pardons to those who had not held a Confederate civil office, had not mistreated Union prisoners, and would sign an oath of allegiance.[7]:471–472

As Southern states fell, they needed leaders while their administrations re-formed. In Tennessee and Arkansas, Lincoln appointed Johnson and Frederick Steele as military governors, respectively. In Louisiana, Lincoln ordered General Nathaniel P. Banks to promote a plan that would restore statehood when 10 percent of the voters agreed. Democratic opponents accused Lincoln of using the military to ensure his and the Republicans' political aspirations. The Radicals denounced his policy as too lenient, and passed their own plan, the Wade–Davis Bill, in 1864, which Lincoln vetoed. The Radicals retaliated by refusing to seat elected representatives from Louisiana, Arkansas, and Tennessee.[7]:485–486

Lincoln's appointments were designed to harness both moderates and Radicals. To fill Chief Justice Taney's seat on the Supreme Court, he named the Radicals' choice, Salmon P. Chase, who Lincoln believed would uphold his emancipation and paper money policies. [64],4:206

After implementing the Emancipation Proclamation, Lincoln increased pressure on Congress to outlaw slavery throughout the nation with a constitutional amendment. He declared that such an amendment would "clinch the whole matter."[7]:561 By December 1863, an amendment was brought to Congress. This first attempt failed, falling short of the required two-thirds majority on June 15, 1864, in the House of Representatives. Passage became part of the Republican/Unionist platform. After a House debate, the second attempt passed on January 31, 1865.[7]:562–563[99] With ratification, it became the Thirteenth Amendment to the United States Constitution on December 6, 1865.[100]

Lincoln believed the federal government had limited responsibility to the millions of freedmen. He signed Senator Charles Sumner's Freedmen's Bureau bill that set up a temporary federal agency designed to meet the immediate needs of former slaves. The law opened land for a lease of three years with the ability to purchase title for the freedmen. Lincoln announced a Reconstruction plan that involved short-term military control, pending readmission under the control of southern Unionists.[56]:242–243

## Assassination

Abraham Lincoln was assassinated by John Wilkes Booth on Good Friday, April 14, 1865, while attending a play at Ford's Theatre, five days after Lee's surrender. Booth was a well-known actor and a Confederate spy from Maryland; though he never joined the Confederate army, he had contacts with the Confederate secret service.[7]:586–587 After attending an April 11, 1865, speech in which Lincoln promoted voting rights for blacks, Booth decided to assassinate the President.[111]:3–4 Learning of Lincoln's intent to attend the play with Grant, Booth and his co-conspirators planned to assassinate Lincoln and Grant at the theater and to kill Vice President Johnson and Secretary of State Seward at their respective homes. Lincoln left to attend the play *Our American Cousin* on April 14. At the last minute, Grant decided to go to New Jersey to visit his children instead of attending the play.[7]:594–597

Booth crept up from behind and at about 10:13 pm, fired at the back of Lincoln's head, mortally wounding him. Lincoln's guest Major Henry Rathbone momentarily grappled with Booth, but Booth stabbed him and escaped.[7]:597[112]

Lincoln was taken across the street to Petersen House. After remaining in a coma for nine hours, Lincoln died at 7:22 am on April 15. After death his face relaxed into a smile. [113][114][115][116] Stanton saluted and said, "Now he belongs to the ages."[117]

Lincoln's flag-enfolded body was then escorted in the rain to the White House by bare-headed Union officers, while the city's church bells rang. President Johnson was sworn in at 10:00 am, less than 3 hours after Lincoln's death.

Booth was tracked to a farm in Virginia. Refusing to surrender, he was shot on April 26.[25]:153[7]:599

## Funeral and burial

The late President lay in state, first in the East Room, and then in the Capitol Rotunda from April 19 through April 21. The caskets containing Lincoln's body and the body of his son Willie traveled for three weeks on the *Lincoln Special* funeral train.[118] The train followed a circuitous route from Washington, D.C., to Springfield, Illinois, stopping at many cities for memorials attended by hundreds of thousands. Many others gathered along the tracks as the train passed with bands, bonfires, and hymn singing[118]:31–58[119]:231–238 or in silent grief. Poet Walt Whitman composed *When Lilacs Last in the Dooryard Bloom'd* to eulogize him, one of four poems he wrote about Lincoln.[120] African-Americans were especially moved; they had lost "their Moses."[121]:164 In a larger sense, the reaction was in response to the deaths of so many men in the war.[121]:197–199 Historians emphasized the widespread shock and sorrow, but noted that some Lincoln haters celebrated his death. [121](pp84, 86, 96–97)

## Legacy

The successful reunification of the states had consequences for the name of the country. The term "the United States" has historically been used, sometimes in the plural ("these

United States"), and other times in the singular, without any particular grammatical consistency. The Civil War was a significant force in the eventual dominance of the singular usage by the end of the 19th century.[129]

*Lincoln in February 1865, two months before his death*

Historians such as Harry Jaffa, Herman Belz, John Diggins, Vernon Burton, and Eric Foner stress Lincoln's redefinition of *republican values*. As early as the 1850s, a time when most political rhetoric focused on the Constitution, Lincoln redirected emphasis to the Declaration of Independence as the foundation of American political values—what he called the "sheet anchor" of republicanism.[54]:399 The Declaration's emphasis on equality and freedom for all, in contrast to the Constitution's tolerance of slavery, shifted the debate. Regarding the 1860 Cooper Union speech, Diggins notes, "Lincoln presented Americans a theory of history that offers a profound contribution to the theory and destiny of republicanism itself."[130]:307 He highlights the moral basis of republicanism, rather than its legalisms.[33]:215 Nevertheless, Lincoln justified the war via legalisms (the Constitution was a contract, and for one party to get out of a contract all the other parties had to agree), and then in terms of the national duty to guarantee a republican form of government in every state.[54]:263 Burton argues that Lincoln's republicanism was taken up by the emancipated Freedmen.[131]

In Lincoln's first inaugural address, he explored the nature of democracy. He denounced secession as anarchy, and explained that majority rule had to be balanced by constitutional restraints. He said "A majority held in restraint by constitutional checks and limitations, and always changing easily with deliberate changes of popular opinions and sentiments, is the only true sovereign of a free people."[132]:86

## Historical reputation

> In his company, I was never reminded of my humble origin, or of my unpopular color.
>
> — *Frederick Douglass* [133]:259–260

In surveys of U.S. scholars ranking presidents conducted since the 1940s, Lincoln is consistently ranked in the top three, often as number one.[5][6] A 2004 study found that scholars in the fields of history and politics ranked Lincoln number one, while legal scholars placed him second after George Washington.[134]:264 In presidential ranking polls conducted in the United States since 1948, Lincoln has been rated at the top in the majority of polls. Generally, the top three presidents are rated as 1. Lincoln; 2. Washington; and 3. Franklin Delano Roosevelt, although the order varies.[135][136]

# James Longstreet

**James Longstreet** (January 8, 1821–January 2, 1904) was one of the foremost Confederate generals of the American Civil War and the principal subordinate to General Robert E. Lee, who called him his "Old War Horse." He served under Lee as a corps commander for most of the famous battles fought by the Army of Northern Virginia in the Eastern Theater, and briefly with Braxton Bragg in the Army of Tennessee in the Western Theater.

After graduating from the United States Military Academy at West Point, Longstreet served in the Mexican–American War. He was wounded in the thigh at the Battle of Chapultepec, and afterward married his first wife, Louise Garland. Throughout the 1850s, he served on frontier duty in the American Southwest. In June 1861, Longstreet resigned his U.S. Army commission and joined the Confederate Army. He commanded Confederate troops during an early victory at Blackburn's Ford in July and played a minor role at the First Battle of Bull Run.

Longstreet made significant contributions to several important Confederate victories, mostly in the Eastern Theater as one of Robert E. Lee's chief subordinates in the Army of Northern Virginia. He performed poorly at Seven Pines by accidentally marching his men down the wrong road, causing them to be late in arrival, but played an important role in the success of the Seven Days Battles in the summer of 1862. Longstreet led a devastating counterattack that routed the Union army at Second Bull Run in August. His men held their ground in defensive roles at Antietam and Fredericksburg. Longstreet's most controversial service was at the Battle of Gettysburg in July 1863, where he openly disagreed with General Lee on the tactics to be employed and reluctantly supervised several unsuccessful attacks on Union forces, including the disastrous Pickett's Charge. Afterwards, Longstreet was, at his own request, sent to the Western Theater to fight under Braxton Bragg, where his troops launched a ferocious assault on the Union lines at Chickamauga, which carried the day. Afterwards, his performance in semiautonomous command during the Knoxville Campaign resulted in a Confederate defeat. Longstreet's tenure in the Western Theater was marred by his central role in numerous conflicts amongst Confederate generals. Unhappy serving under Bragg, Longstreet and his men were sent back to Lee. He ably commanded troops during the Battle of the Wilderness in 1864, where he was seriously wounded by friendly fire. He later returned to the field, serving under Lee in the Siege of Petersburg and the Appomattox Campaign.

He enjoyed a successful post-war career working for the U.S. government as a diplomat, civil servant, and administrator. His conversion to the Republican Party and his cooperation with his old friend, President Ulysses S. Grant, as well as critical comments he wrote about Lee's wartime performance, made him anathema to many of his former Confederate colleagues. His reputation in the South further suffered when he led African-American militia against the anti-Reconstruction White League at the Battle of Liberty Place in 1874. Authors of the Lost Cause movement focused on Longstreet's actions at Gettysburg as a primary reason for the Confederacy's loss of the war. Since the late 20th century, his reputation has undergone a slow reassessment. Many Civil War historians now consider him among the war's most gifted tactical commanders.

## American Civil War

*Joining the Confederacy and initial hostilities*

At the time of the Battle of Fort Sumter at the beginning of the American Civil War, Longstreet was paymaster for the United States Army and stationed in Albuquerque, having not yet resigned his commission. After news of the engagement, he joined his fellow Southerners in leaving the post. In his memoirs, Longstreet calls it a "sad day," and records that a number of Northern officers attempted to persuade him not to go. He states that he asked one of them "what course he would pursue if his State should pass ordinances of secession and call him to its defence. He confessed that he would obey the call."[42]

Longstreet was not enthusiastic about secession from the Union, but he had long been infused with the concept of states' rights, and felt he could not go against his homeland. [43] Although he was born in South Carolina and reared in Georgia, he offered his services to the state of Alabama, which had appointed him to West Point and where his mother still lived. Furthermore, he was the senior West Point graduate from that state, which implied a commensurate rank in the state's forces would be available.[44] After settling his accounts, he resigned from the U.S. Army on May 8, 1861, to cast his lot with the Confederacy in the Civil War.[45]

Longstreet arrived in Richmond, Virginia with a commission as a lieutenant colonel in the Confederate States Army. He met with Confederate President Jefferson Davis at the executive mansion on June 22, 1861, where he was informed that he had been appointed a brigadier general with date of rank on June 17, a commission he accepted on June 25. He was ordered to report to Brig. Gen. P. G. T. Beauregard at Manassas, where he was given command of a brigade of three Virginia regiments—the 1st, 11th, and 17th Virginia Infantry regiments in the Confederate Army of the Potomac.[46][47]

GEN. LONGSTREET, C. S. A.

*Sketch of Longstreet, 1861*

Longstreet assembled his staff and trained his brigade incessantly. On July 16, Union General Irvin McDowell began marching his army toward Manassas Junction. Longstreet's brigade first saw action at Blackburn's Ford on July 18, when it collided with McDowell's advance division under Brigadier

General Daniel Tyler. An infantry charge pushed Longstreet's men back, and in his own words Longstreet "rode with sabre in hand for the leading files, determined to give them all that was in the sword and my horse's heels, or stop the break." A second attack soon began, but Confederate successes were hampered when inexperienced soldiers from Colonel Jubal Early's brigade sent to reinforce Longstreet began firing on their own men. Tyler eventually withdrew, as he had orders not to bring on a general engagement.[48] The battle preceded the First Battle of Bull Run (First Manassas). When the main attack came at the opposite end of the line on July 21, the brigade played a relatively minor role, although it endured artillery fire for nine hours.[49][50] Between 5 and 6 in the evening, Longstreet received an order from General Joseph E. Johnston instructing him to take part in pursuit of the Federal troops, who had been defeated and were fleeing the battlefield. He obeyed, but when he met the brigade of Brigadier General Milledge Bonham, Bonham, who outranked Longstreet, ordered him to retreat. An order soon arrived from Johnston ordering the same. Longstreet was infuriated that his commanders would not allow a vigorous pursuit of the defeated Union Army.[51] His trusted Chief of Staff, Moxley Sorrel, recorded that he was "in a fine rage. He dashed his hat furiously to the ground, stamped, and bitter words escaped him." He quoted Longstreet as saying afterwards, "Retreat! Hell, the Federal army has broken to pieces."[52]

On October 7, Longstreet was promoted to major general and assumed command of a division in the newly reorganized and renamed Confederate Army of Northern Virginia under Johnston (formed from the previous Army of the Potomac and the Army of the Shenandoah)—with four infantry brigades commanded by Generals Daniel Harvey Hill, David R. Jones, Bonham, and Louis Wigfall, as well as Hampton's Legion commanded by Wade Hampton III.[53]

## Family tragedy

On January 10, 1862, Longstreet traveled under orders from Johnston to Richmond, where he discussed with Davis the creation of a draft or conscription program. He spent much of the intervening time with Louise and their children, and was back at army headquarters in Centreville by the 20th. After only a day or two, he received a telegram informing him that all four of his children were extremely sick in an outbreak of scarlet fever. Longstreet immediately returned to Richmond.[54]

Longstreet arrived in Richmond before the death of his one-year old daughter Mary Anne on January 25. Four-year old James died the following day. Eleven-year-old Augustus Baldwin ("Gus") died on February 1. His 13-year-old son Garland remained ill but appeared to be out of mortal danger. George Pickett and his future wife LaSalle Corbell were in the Longstreet's company throughout the affair. They arranged the funeral and burial, which for unknown reasons neither Longstreet nor his wife attended. Longstreet waited a very short time to return to the army, doing so on February 5. He rushed back to Richmond later in the month when Garland took a turn for the worse, but came back after he recovered. The losses were devastating for Longstreet and he became withdrawn, both personally and socially. In 1861 his headquarters were noted for parties, drinking, and poker games. After he returned from the funeral the headquarters social life became for a time more somber. He rarely drank, and his religious devotion increased.[55][56]

## Peninsula

That spring, Union Maj. Gen. George B. McClellan, commander of the Army of the Potomac, launched the Peninsula Campaign intending to capture the Confederate capital of Richmond.[57] In his memoirs, Longstreet would write that while in temporary command of the Confederate army he wrote to Thomas J. "Stonewall" Jackson proposing that he march to Jackson in the Shenandoah Valley and combine forces. No evidence has emerged for this claim.[58][59]

Following the delay of the Union offensive against Richmond at the Siege of Yorktown, Johnston oversaw a tactical withdrawal to the outskirts of Richmond, where defenses had already been prepared. Longstreet's division formed the rearguard, which was heavily engaged at the Battle of Williamsburg on May 5. There, Union troops beginning with Joseph Hooker's division of the Union III Corps, which was commanded by Samuel P. Heintzelman, came out of a forest into open ground to attack Longstreet's men.[60] To protect the army's supply wagons, Longstreet launched a strong counterattack with the brigades of Cadmus M. Wilcox, A. P. Hill, Pickett and two other regiments. The assault drove the Union soldiers back.[61] Finding the ground he occupied untenable, Longstreet requested reinforcements from D. H. Hill's division a little further up the road and received among others Early's brigade.[62] Early then launched a fruitless and bloody attack well after the wagons had already been safely evacuated. Overall, the battle was a success, protecting the passage of Confederate supply wagons and delaying the advance of McClellan's army toward Richmond.[63] The affair resulted in the capture of nine Union artillery pieces.[60] Longstreet reported 9,000 Confederate troops engaged compared to 12,000 Union troops, and the Confederates suffered fewer casualties.[64] McClellan inaccurately characterized the battle as a Union victory in a dispatch to Washington.[60]

On May 31, during the Battle of Seven Pines, Longstreet received his orders verbally from Johnston, but ended up apparently misremembering them. He marched his men in the wrong direction down the wrong road, causing congestion and confusion with other Confederate units, diluting the effect of the massive Confederate counterattack against McClellan. He then got into an argument with Maj. Gen. Benjamin Huger over who had seniority, causing significant delay.[65] When D. H. Hill subsequently asked Longstreet for reinforcements, he complied, but failed to properly coordinate his brigades.[66] Late in the day, General Edwin Vose Sumner crossed the rain-swollen Chickahominy River with two divisions.[67] General Johnston was wounded during the battle. Although Johnston preferred Longstreet as his replacement, command of the Army of Northern Virginia shifted to G. W. Smith, the senior major general, for a single day.[68] On June 1, Richardson's division of Sumner's corps engaged Longstreet's men, routing Lewis Armistead's brigade, but the brigades of Pickett, William Mahone, and Roger Atkinson Pryor positioned in the woods managed to hold it back. After six hours of fighting, the battle ended in a draw.[69] Johnston praised Longstreet's performance in the battle. Biographer William Garrett Piston marks it as "the lowest point in Longstreet's military career."[65] Longstreet's report unfairly blamed Huger for the mishaps.[70] On June 1, the President's military advisor Robert E. Lee assumed command of the Army of Northern Virginia. In his memoirs, Longstreet suggested that he initially doubted Lee's capacity for command.[71] He wrote that his arrival "was far from reconciling the troops to the loss of our beloved chief, Joseph E. Johnston." He wrote that Lee did not have much of a reputation at the time that he took command and that there were therefore "misgivings" about Lee's "power and skill for field service."[72]

In late June, Lee organized a plan to drive McClellan's army away from the capital, which culminated in what became known as the Seven Days Battles. At daybreak on June 27 at Gaines's Mill, the Confederate Army attacked the V Corps of the Union Army under Brigadier General Fitz John Porter, which was positioned south of the Chickahominy River. Federal troops held their lines for most of the day against attacks from the divisions of A.P. Hill and D.H. Hill, and Jackson did not arrive until afternoon. At about 5 p.m., Longstreet received orders from Lee to join the battle. Longstreet's fresh troops, accompanied by the brigades of Brigadier General John Bell Hood and Colonel Evander M. Law from William H.C. Whiting's division, charged the Union lines, forcing them to retreat across the Chickahominy.[73][74][75] Longstreet was engaged again on June 30 with about 20,000 men at Glendale.[76] He departed from his usual strategy of placing troops several lines deep and instead spread them out, which in the opinion of some military historians cost him the battle. His efforts were further damaged by the slowness of other Confederate commanders, and McClellan was able to withdraw his army to the high plateau of Malvern Hill.[77] Jackson, engaged at White Oak Swamp, ignored reports of ways in which to cross the swamp, and refused to answer an inquiry from Longstreet's staff officer John Fairfax. Huger's advance was slow enough to allow Federal troops to be transported away from guarding him and towards Longstreet, and Theophilus Holmes also performed poorly. Nearly 50,000 Confederate troops stood within a few miles of the field at Glendale and rendered little to no assistance.[78] In a reconnaissance on the evening of June 30, Longstreet reported to Lee that conditions were favorable enough to justify assault. In the fighting the next day, Longstreet surrendered A.P. Hill's entire division to Magruder, and marched his remaining troops toward the Union positions on the Confederate extreme right. His men were exposed to fire on their flanks from McClellan's troops and were forced to withdraw without success.[79]

Throughout the Seven Days Battles, Longstreet had operational command of nearly half of Lee's army—15 brigades—as it drove McClellan back down the Peninsula. Longstreet performed aggressively and quite well in his new, larger command, particularly at Gaines's Mill and Glendale. Lee's army in general suffered from poor maps, organizational flaws, and weak performances by Longstreet's peers, including, uncharacteristically, Stonewall Jackson, and was unable to destroy the Union Army.[50][70][80] Moxley Sorrel wrote of Longstreet's confidence and calmness in battle: "He was like a rock in steadiness when sometimes in battle the world seemed flying to pieces." General Lee said shortly after Seven Days, "Longstreet was the staff in my right hand." He had been established as Lee's principal lieutenant.[81] Lee reorganized the Army of Northern Virginia after Seven Days, increasing Longstreet's command from six brigades to 28.[82] Over time, Lee and Longstreet became good friends, and set up headquarters very near each other. Despite sharing with Jackson a belief in temperance as well as a deep religious conviction, Lee never developed as strong a friendship with him. Piston speculates that the more relaxed atmosphere of Longstreet's headquarters, which included gambling and drinking, allowed Lee to relax and take his mind off the war, and reminded him of his more happy younger days.[83]

After the campaign, an editorial appeared in the *Richmond Examiner* inaccurately claiming that that the Battle of Glendale "was fought exclusively by General A.P. Hill and the forces under his command." Longstreet then drafted a letter refuting the article, which was published in the *Richmond Whig*. Hill took offense and requested that his division be transferred out of Longstreet's command. Longstreet agreed, but Lee took no action. Then, Hill refused to accede to Longstreet's repeated requests for information, and was eventually arrested on Longstreet's orders. He challenged Longstreet to a duel, who accepted, but Lee intervened and transferred Hill's division out of Longstreet's command and into Jackson's.[84]

## Second Bull Run

The military reputations of Lee's corps commanders are often characterized as Stonewall Jackson representing the audacious, offensive component of Lee's army, with Longstreet more typically advocating and executing strong defensive strategies and tactics. Jackson has been described as the army's hammer, Longstreet its anvil. [85] In the first part of the Northern Virginia Campaign of August 1862, this stereotype held true, but in the climactic battle, it did not. In June, the Federal Government created the 50,000-strong Army of Virginia, and put Major Gen. John Pope in command.[86] For the Confederate Army, Longstreet commanded the Right Wing (later to become known as the First Corps) and Jackson commanded the Left Wing.[87] Pope moved south in an attempt to attack Lee and threaten Richmond through an overland march. Lee left Longstreet near Richmond to guard the city and dispatched Jackson to hinder Pope's advance. Jackson won a major victory at the Battle of Cedar Mountain. [88] After learning that McClellan, as ordered, had dispatched troops north to assist Pope, Lee ordered Longstreet north as well, leaving only three divisions under G.W. Smith to protect Richmond against McClellan's reduced force. Longstreet's men began their march on August 17, aided by Stuart's cavalry.[89] On August 23, Longstreet engaged Pope's position in a minor artillery duel at the First Battle of Rappahannock Station. The Confederate Washington Artillery was heavily damaged and a Union shell landed feet away from Longstreet and Wilcox but failed to explode. Meanwhile, Stuart's cavalry rode around the Army of Virginia and captured hundreds of soldiers and horses as well as some of Pope's personal belongings.[90]

Jackson executed a sweeping flanking maneuver that captured Pope's main supply depot. He placed his corps in the rear of Pope's army, but he then took up a defensive position and effectively invited Pope to assault him. On August 28 and August 29, the start of the Second Battle of Bull Run (Second Manassas), Pope pounded Jackson as Longstreet and the remainder of the army marched from the west, through Thoroughfare Gap, to reach the battlefield. On the afternoon of the 28th, Longstreet engaged a 5,000-man federal division under James B. Ricketts at the Battle of Thoroughfare Gap. Ricketts had been ordered to delay Longstreet's march towards the main Confederate army, but he took up his position too late, allowing George T. Anderson's brigade to occupy the high ground. Lee and Longstreet watched the battle together and decided to flank the Union position. Hood's division and a brigade under Henry L. Benning advanced towards the gap from the north and the south, respectively, while Wilcox's division followed in a six mile march northward. Ricketts realized his position was untenable and withdrew that evening, allowing Longstreet to join up with the rest of Lee's army. Postwar criticism of Longstreet claimed that he marched his men too slowly, leaving Jackson to bear the brunt of the fighting for two days, but they covered roughly 30 miles (50 km) in a little over 24 hours and Lee did not attempt to get his army concentrated any faster.[91]

When Longstreet's men arrived at Second Manassas, around midday on August 29, Lee planned a flanking attack on the Union Army, which was concentrating its attention on

*Longstreet circa 1862*

Jackson. Longstreet demurred against three suggestions from Lee, urging him to attack, recommending instead that a reconnaissance in force be conducted to survey the ground in front of him. By 6:30 p.m., Hood's division moved forward against Porter's corps, and Longstreet withdrew it at 8:30 p.m., having a better idea of the terrain and enemy soldiers in the area. Despite the smashing victory that followed, Longstreet's performance at the battle was criticized by postbellum advocates of the Lost Cause, claiming that his slowness, reluctance to attack, and disobedience to General Lee were a harbinger of his controversial performance to come on July 2, 1863, at the Battle of Gettysburg.[55][92][93] Lee's biographer, Douglas Southall Freeman, wrote: "The seeds of much of the disaster at Gettysburg were sown in that instant—when Lee yielded to Longstreet and Longstreet discovered that he would."[94] Longstreet biographer Jeffry D. Wert disputes this conclusion, pointing out that in a post-war letter to Longstreet, Porter told him that had he attacked him that day, his "loss would have been enormous."[95]

Despite this criticism, the following day, August 30, was one of Longstreet's finest performances of the war. After his attacks on the 29th, Pope came to believe with little evidence that Jackson was in retreat.[96] He ordered a reluctant Porter to move his corps forward in pursuit, and they collided with Jackson's men and suffered heavy casualties. The attack exposed the Union left flank, and Longstreet took advantage of this by launching a massive assault on the Union flank with over 25,000 men. For over four hours they "pounded like a giant hammer"[97] with Longstreet actively directing artillery fire and sending brigades into the fray. Longstreet and Lee were together during the assault and both of them came under Union artillery fire. Although the Union troops put up a furious defense, Pope's army was forced to retreat in a manner similar to the embarrassing Union defeat at First Bull Run, fought on roughly the same battleground.[70][98] Longstreet gave all of the credit for the victory to Lee, describing the campaign as "clever and brilliant." It established a strategic model he believed to be ideal—the use of defensive tactics within a strategic offensive.[99] On September 1, Jackson's corps moved to cut off the Union retreat at the Battle of Chantilly. Longstreet's men remained on the field in order to fool Pope into thinking that Lee's entire army was still on his front.[100]

## Antietam and Fredericksburg

Longstreet's actions in the final two major Confederate defensive battles of 1862 would be the proving grounds for his development of dominant defensive tactics.[101] After the Confederate success at Second Manassas, Lee, holding the strategic initiative, decided to take the war to Maryland to relieve Virginia and hopefully induce foreign nations to come to the Confederates' aid. Longstreet supported the plan. "The situation called for action," he later said, "and there was but one opening—across the Potomac." His men crossed into Maryland on September 6 and arrived in Frederick the following day.[102] In the Maryland Campaign of September, at the Battle of Antietam, Longstreet held his part of the Confederate defensive line against Union forces twice as numerous. After the delaying action Longstreet's corps fought at South Mountain, he retired to Sharpsburg to join Stonewall Jackson, and prepared to fight a defensive battle. Using terrain to his advantage, Longstreet validated his idea that the tactical defense was now vastly superior to the exposed offense. While the offense dominated in the time of Napoleon, the technological advancements had overturned this. Lt. Col. Harold M. Knudsen claims that Longstreet was one of the few Civil War officers sensible of this development.[103] At the end of that bloodiest day of the Civil War, Lee greeted his subordinate by saying, "Ah! Here is Longstreet; here's my old *war-horse!*"[104] On October 9, a few weeks after Antietam, Longstreet was promoted to lieutenant general. Lee arranged for Longstreet's promotion to be dated one day earlier than Jackson's, making the Old War-Horse the senior lieutenant general in the entire Confederate Army. In an army reorganization in November, Longstreet's command, now designated the First Corps, consisted of five divisions, approximately 41,000 men.[105][106][107]

In December, Longstreet's First Corps played the decisive role in the Battle of Fredericksburg, midway between the two opposing capitals, where the Confederate army made its stand to protect Richmond from the Army of the Potomac, now commanded by Ambrose Burnside. Since Lee moved Longstreet to Fredericksburg early, it allowed Longstreet to take the time to dig in portions of his line, methodically site artillery, and set up a kill zone over the axis of advance he thought the Union attack would follow. Remembering the slaughter at Antietam, in which the Confederates did not build defensive works, Longstreet ordered trenches, abatis, and fieldworks to be constructed south of the town along a stonewall at the foot of Marye's Heights, which would set a precedent for future defensive battles by the Army of Northern Virginia. This was completed in the days before the battle. After failing to cross the Rappahannock on December 11, Burnside ordered an artillery bombardment of the town, and forced his way across the following day.[108]

Longstreet had his men firmly entrenched along Marye's Heights. On December 13, under Burnside's orders, troops from the Union Right Grand Division under Sumner launched fourteen frontal assaults against Longstreet's troops on Marye's Heights, which unexpectedly became the center of the battle.[109] When Lee expressed apprehension that the Federal troops might overrun Longstreet's men on Marye's Heights, Longstreet replied that as long as he had sufficient ammunition he would "kill them all" before any of them reached his line. He advised him to look towards Jackson's more tenuous position to the right. Longstreet was proven correct, for from their strong position, Longstreet's men easily held off all of the Union assaults, while Jackson managed to repel a much stronger Union attack by the division of George Meade. One Union general compared the scene before Marye's Heights to "a great slaughter pen" and said that his men "might as well have tried to take Hell."[110]

Burnside intended to attack again the next day, but several of his officers, particularly Sumner, advised him against it. He entrenched his men instead and withdrew on December 15.[111] The Union army suffered almost 8,000 casualties at Marye's Heights; Longstreet lost only 1,900. His great defensive success was not based entirely on the advantage of terrain; this time it was the combination of terrain, defensive works, and a centralized coordination of artillery.[112][113]

## Suffolk

Shortly after Fredericksburg, Longstreet vaguely suggested to Lee that "one corps could hold the Rappahannock while the other was operating elsewhere." In February of 1863, he made a more specific request, suggesting to Wigfall that his corps be detached from the Army of Northern Virginia and sent to reinforce the Army of Tennessee, where Gen. Braxton Bragg was being challenged in Middle Tennessee by the Army of the Cumberland under Union Maj. Gen. William S. Rosecrans, Longstreet's roommate at West Point.[114] By this time, Longstreet could be identified as part of a "western concentration bloc" which believed that reinforcing Confederate armies operating in the Western Theater of the war to protect the states in that part of the Confederacy from invasion was more important than offensive campaigns in the East. This group also included Joe Johnston and Louis Wigfall, now a Confederate senator, both of whom Longstreet was very close with. These people were generally cautious and believed that the Confederacy, with its limited resources, should engage in a defensive rather than an offensive war. [115] Lee did detach two divisions from the First Corps, but ordered them to Richmond, not Tennessee. Seaborne movements of the Union IX Corps potentially threatened vital ports on the mid-Atlantic coast. The division of George Pickett started for the capital in mid-February, was followed by John Hood's, and then Longstreet himself was told to take command of the detached divisions and the Departments of North Carolina and Southern Virginia.[116][18] The divisions of McLaws and Anderson remained with Lee.[117]

In April, Longstreet besieged Union forces in the city of Suffolk, Virginia, a minor operation, but one that was very important to Lee's army, still stationed in war-devastated central Virginia. It enabled Confederate authorities to collect huge amounts of provisions that had been under Union control. However, this operation caused Longstreet and 15,000 men of the First Corps to be absent from the Battle of Chancellorsville in May. Despite Lee's brilliant victory at Chancellorsville, Longstreet once again came under criticism, claiming that he could have marched his men back from Suffolk in time to join Lee. [55][118][119][120] However, from the Chancellorsville and Suffolk scenario, Longstreet brought forward the beginnings of a new Confederate strategy. These events proved that the Army of Northern Virginia could manage with fewer troops for periods of time, and units could be shifted to create windows of opportunity in other theaters. Longstreet advocated the first strategic movements to utilize rail, interior lines, and create temporary numerical advantages in Mississippi or Tennessee prior to Gettysburg.[121]

## Gettysburg

### Campaign plans

Following Chancellorsville and the death of Stonewall Jackson, Longstreet and Lee met in mid-May to discuss options for the army's summer campaign. Longstreet once more pushed for the detachment of all or part of his corps to be sent to Tennessee. The justification for this course of action was becoming more urgent as Union Maj. Gen. Ulysses S. Grant was advancing on the critical Confederate stronghold on the Mississippi River, Vicksburg. Longstreet argued that a reinforced army under Bragg could defeat Rosecrans and drive toward the Ohio River, which would compel Grant to break his hold on Vicksburg.[122] He advanced these views during a meeting with Confederate Secretary of War James Seddon, who approved of the idea but doubted that Lee would do so, and opined that Davis was unlikely to go against Lee's wishes. Longstreet had criticized Bragg's generalship and may have been hoping to replace him, although he also might have wished to see Joseph Johnston take command, and indicated that he would be content to serve under him as a corps commander. Lee prevented this plan from taking place by telling Davis that parting with large numbers of troops would force him to move his army closer to Richmond, and instead advancing a plan to invade Pennsylvania. A campaign in the North would relieve agricultural and military pressure that the war was placing on Virginia and North Carolina, and, by threatening a federal city, disrupt Union offensives elsewhere and erode support for the war among Northern civilians.[123] In his memoirs, Longstreet described his reaction to Lee's proposal:

> His plan or wishes announced, it became useless and improper to offer suggestions leading to a different course. All that I could ask was that the policy of the campaign should be one of defensive tactics; that we should work so as to force the enemy to attack us, in such good position as we might find in our own country, so well adapted to that purpose—which might assure us of a grand triumph. To this he readily assented as an important and material adjunct to his general plan.[124]

There is conflicting evidence for the veracity of Longstreet's account. It was written years after the campaign and is affected by hindsight, both of the results of the battle and of the postbellum criticism of the Lost Cause authors. In letters of the time Longstreet made no reference to such a bargain with Lee. In April 1868, Lee said that he "had never made any such promise, and had never thought of doing any such thing."[125][126] Yet in his post-battle report, Lee wrote, "It had not been intended to fight a general battle at such a distance from our base, unless attacked by the enemy."[127]

The Army of Northern Virginia was reorganized after Jackson's death. Two division commanders, Richard S. Ewell and A. P. Hill, were promoted to lieutenant general and assumed command of the Second and the newly created Third Corps respectively. Longstreet's First Corps gave up the division of Maj. Gen. Richard H. Anderson during the reorganization, leaving him with the divisions of Hood, McLaws, and Pickett.[128][129]

After it was determined that an advance north was inevitable, Longstreet dispatched the scout Henry Thomas Harrison, whom he had met during the Suffolk Campaign, to gather information. He paid Harrison in gold and told him that he "did not care to see him till he could bring information of importance."[130] In the initial movements of the campaign, Longstreet's corps followed Ewell's through the Shenandoah Valley. Harrison reported to Longstreet on the evening of June 28, and was instrumental in warning the Confederates that the Army of the Potomac was advancing north to meet them more quickly than they had anticipated, and were already massing around Frederick, Maryland. Lee was initially skeptical, but the report prompted him to order the immediate concentration of his army north of Frederick near Gettysburg, Pennsylvania. Harrison also brought news that Joseph Hooker had been replaced as commander of the Army of the Potomac by George Meade.[131]

## July 1–2

Longstreet's actions at the Battle of Gettysburg would become the centerpiece of the controversy that surrounded him for over a century.[132] Longstreet arrived on the battlefield late in the afternoon of the first day, July 1, 1863, hours ahead of his troops. By then, two Union corps had been driven by Ewell and Hill back through the town into defensive positions on Cemetery Hill. Lee had not intended to fight before his army was fully concentrated, but chance and questionable decisions by A. P. Hill brought on the battle, which—on the first day—was an impressive Confederate victory. Meeting with Lee, Longstreet was concerned about the strength of the Union defensive position on elevated ground and advocated a strategic movement around the left flank of the enemy, to "secure good ground between him and his capital," which would presumably compel Meade to attack defensive positions erected by the Confederates.[133][134][135] Instead, Lee exclaimed, "If the enemy is there tomorrow, I will attack him." Longstreet replied, "If he is there tomorrow it is because he wants you to attack."[136]

Lee's plan for July 2 called for Longstreet to attack the Union's left flank, which would be followed up by Hill's attack on Cemetery Ridge near the center, while Ewell demonstrated on the Union right. Longstreet was not ready to attack as early as Lee envisioned. He received permission from Lee to wait for Brig. Gen. Evander M. Law's brigade (Hood's division) to reach the field before he advanced any of his other brigades; Law marched his men quickly, covering 28 miles in eleven hours, but did not arrive until noon. Three of Longstreet's brigades were still in march column, and some distance from the attack positions they would need to reach.[137] All of Longstreet's divisions were forced to take a long detour while approaching the enemy position, misled by inadequate reconnaissance that failed to identify a completely concealed route.[138]

Postbellum criticism of Longstreet claims that he was ordered by Lee to attack in the early morning and that his delays were a significant contributor to the loss of the battle.[106] However, Lee agreed to the delays for arriving troops and did not issue his formal order for the attack until 11 a.m. Although Longstreet's motivations have long been clouded by the vitriol of the Lost Cause partisans, many historians agree that Longstreet did not aggressively pursue Lee's orders to launch an attack as early as possible. Biographer Jeffry D. Wert wrote, "Longstreet deserves censure for his performance on the morning of July 2. He allowed his disagreement with Lee's decision to affect his conduct. Once the commanding general determined to assail the enemy, duty required Longstreet to comply with the vigor and thoroughness that had previously characterized his generalship. The concern for detail, the regard for timely information, and the need for preparation were absent."[139] Military historians Herman Hattaway and Archer Jones wrote, "Unenthusiastic about the attack, Longstreet consumed so much time in properly assembling and aligning the corps that the assault did not commence until 4 p.m. During all the time that passed, Meade continued to move in troops to bring about a more and more complete concentration; by 6 p.m. he had achieved numerical superiority and had his left well covered."[140] Campaign historian Edwin Coddington presents a lengthy description of the approach march, which he described as "a comedy of errors such as one might expect of inexperienced commanders and raw militia, but not of Lee's "War Horse" and his veteran troops." He called the episode "a dark moment in Longstreet's career as a general."[141] Gettysburg historian Harry Pfanz concluded that "Longstreet's angry dissidence had resulted in further wasted time and delay."[142] David L. Callihan, in a 2002 reassessment of Longstreet's legacy, wrote, "It is appalling that a field commander of Longstreet's experience and caliber would so cavalierly and ineptly march and prepare his men for battle."[143] An alternative view has been expressed by John Lott, "General Longstreet did all that could be expected on the 2nd day and any allegations of failing to exercise his duty by ordering a morning assault can be repudiated. It would have been impossible to have commenced an attack much earlier than it occurred, and it is doubtful that the Confederacy could have placed the attack in any more secure hands than General Longstreet."[144]

Regardless of the controversy regarding the preparations, however, once the assault began around 4 p.m., Longstreet pressed the assault by McLaws and Hood (Pickett's division had not yet arrived) competently against fierce Union resistance, but it was largely unsuccessful, with significant casualties.[145]

## July 3

On the night of July 2, Longstreet did not follow his usual custom of meeting Gen. Lee at his headquarters to discuss the day's battle, claiming that he was too fatigued to make the ride. Instead, he spent part of the night planning for a movement around Big Round Top that would allow him to attack the enemy's flank and rear. (Longstreet, despite his use of scouting parties, was apparently unaware that a considerable body of troops from the Union VI Corps was in position to block this move.) Shortly after issuing orders for the attack, around sunrise, Longstreet was joined at his headquarters by Lee, who was dismayed at this turn of events. The commanding general had intended for Longstreet to attack the Union left early in the morning in a manner similar to the attack of July 2, using Pickett's newly arrived division, in concert with a resumed attack by Ewell on Culp's Hill. What Lee found was that no one had ordered Pickett's division forward from its bivouac in the rear and that Longstreet had been planning an independent operation without consulting with him.[146] Lee wrote with some restraint in his after-battle report that Longstreet's "dispositions were not completed as early as was expected."[127]

Since his plans for an early-morning coordinated attack were now infeasible, Lee instead ordered Longstreet to coordinate a massive assault on the center of the Union line, employing the division of George Pickett and brigades from A. P. Hill's corps. Longstreet knew this assault had little chance of success. The Union Army was in a position reminiscent of the one Longstreet had taken at Fredericksburg to defeat Burnside's assault. The Confederates would have to cover almost a mile of open ground and spend time negotiating sturdy fences under fire. The lessons of Fredericksburg and Malvern Hill were lost to Lee on this day. In his memoirs, Longstreet claims to have told Lee that he believed the attack on the Union center would fail:

General, I have been a soldier all my life. I have been with soldiers engaged in fights by couples, by squads, companies, regiments, divisions, and armies, and should know, as well as any one, what soldiers can do. It is my opinion that no fifteen thousand men ever arranged for battle can take that position.[147]

During the artillery barrage that preceded the infantry assault, Longstreet began to agonize over an assault that was going to cost dearly. He attempted to pass the responsibility for launching Pickett's division to his artillery chief, Col. Edward Porter Alexander. When the time came to actually order Pickett forward, Longstreet could only nod in assent, unable to verbalize the order. The assault, known as Pickett's Charge, suffered the heavy casualties that Longstreet anticipated. It was the decisive point in the Confederate loss at Gettysburg and Lee ordered a retreat back to Virginia the following day.[148][149][150][151]

Criticism of Longstreet after the war was based not only on his reputed conduct at the Battle of Gettysburg and support for Reconstruction, but also intemperate remarks he made about Robert E. Lee. For example, in his memoirs, he commented:

> That he [Lee] was excited and off his balance was evident on the afternoon of the 1st, and he labored under that oppression until enough blood was shed to appease him.[152]

For years after the war Longstreet's reputation suffered and was blamed for the failed attack even though Lee ordered the advance after Longstreet's repeated advice to cancel the attack.[153]

## Chickamauga

In mid-August 1863, Longstreet once again resumed his attempts to be transferred to the Western Theater. He wrote a private letter to Seddon, requesting that he be transferred to serve under his old friend Gen. Joseph Johnston. He followed this up in conversations with his congressional ally Wigfall, who had long considered Longstreet a suitable replacement for Braxton Bragg. Bragg had a poor combat record and was very unpopular with his men and officers. Since Bragg's army was under increasing pressure from Rosecrans outside of Chattanooga, Lee and President Davis agreed to the request on September 5. In one of the most daunting logistical efforts of the Confederacy, Longstreet, with the divisions of Lafayette McLaws and John Hood, a brigade from George Pickett's division, and Porter Alexander's 26-gun artillery battalion, traveled over 16 railroads on a 775-mile (1,247 km) route through the Carolinas to reach Bragg in northern Georgia.[154] Although the entire operation would take over three weeks, lead elements of the corps arrived on September 17.[155]

On September 19 at the Battle of Chickamauga, Bragg began an unsuccessful attempt to interpose his army between Rosecrans and Chattanooga before the arrival of most of Longstreet's corps.[156] Throughout the day, Confederate troops launched largely unsuccessful assaults on Union positions that were highly costly for both sides. One of Longstreet's own divisions under Hood successfully resisted a strong Union counterattack from Jefferson C. Davis's division of the XX Corps that afternoon.[157] When Longstreet himself arrived on the field in the late evening, he failed to find Bragg's headquarters. He and his staff spent considerable time riding looking for them. They accidentally came across a federal picket line and were nearly captured.[158] When the two finally met at Bragg's headquarters late at night, Bragg placed Longstreet in command of the left wing of his army; Lt. Gen. Leonidas Polk commanded the right. On September 20, Longstreet lined up eight brigades in a deep column against a narrow front, an attack very similar to future German tank tactics in World War II.[159] The attack was supposed to begin early in the morning shortly after an assault by Polk's wing. However, confusion and mishandled orders caused Polk's attack to be delayed, and Longstreet's advance did not begin until just after 11 after hearing gunfire from his left.[160] By chance, a mistaken order from General Rosecrans caused a gap to appear in the Union line by transferring Thomas J. Wood's division from the right to reinforce the XIV Corps under George Henry Thomas in the center.[161]

Longstreet took additional advantage of the confusion to increase his chances of success. The organization of the attack was well suited to the terrain and would have penetrated the Union line regardless. Bushrod Johnson's division poured through the gap, driving the Union forces back.[162] After Longstreet ordered Thomas C. Hindman's division forward, the Union right collapsed entirely.[163] Rosecrans fled the field as units began to retreat in panic. Thomas managed to rally the retreating units and solidify a defensive position on Snodgrass Hill. He held that position against repeated afternoon attacks by Longstreet, who was not adequately supported by the Confederate right wing. Once night fell, the battle was over, and Thomas was able to extricate the units under his control to Chattanooga. Bragg's failure to coordinate the right wing and cavalry to further envelop Thomas prevented a total rout of the Union Army.[164][165] Bragg also neglected to pursue the retreating Federals aggressively, resulting in the futile Siege of Chattanooga. He had dismissed a proposal from Longstreet that he do so, citing a lack of transportation and calling the plan a "visionary scheme."[166] Nevertheless, Chickamauga was the greatest Confederate victory in the Western Theater and Longstreet deserved and received a good portion of the credit.[167]

## Tennessee

Not long after the Confederates entered Tennessee following their victory at Chickamauga, Longstreet clashed with Bragg and became leader of the group of senior commanders of the army who conspired to have him removed. Bragg's subordinates had long been dissatisfied with his abrasive personality and poor battlefield record; the arrival of Longstreet (the senior lieutenant general in the Army) and his officers, and the fact that they quickly took their side, added credibility to the earlier claims, and was a catalyst toward action. Longstreet wrote to Seddon, "I am convinced that nothing but the hand of God can save us or help us as long as we have our present commander." The situation became so grave that President Davis was forced to intercede in person. What followed was one of the most bizarre scenes of the war, with Bragg sitting red faced as a procession of his commanders condemned him. Longstreet stated that Bragg "was incompetent to manage an army or put men into a fight" and that he "knew nothing of the business." On October

*Carte de Visite portrait of*
*Longstreet*

12, Davis declared his support for Bragg. He left him and his dissatisfied subordinates in their positions, doing nothing to resolve the conflict.[168]

Bragg relieved or reassigned the generals who had testified against him, and retaliated against Longstreet by reducing his command to only those units that he brought with him from Virginia. Despite the dysfunctional command climate under Bragg, and the lack of support from the War Department and President Davis concerning Bragg's removal, Longstreet did the best he could to continue to seek options in the Chattanooga Campaign. [169] Bragg resigned himself and his army to the siege of the Union Army of the Cumberland in Chattanooga. At about this time, Longstreet learned of the birth of a son, who was named Robert Lee.[170] Grant arrived in Chattanooga on October 23 and took overall command of the new Union Military Division of the Mississippi. He replaced Rosecrans with Thomas.[171]

While Longstreet's relations with Bragg were extremely poor, his connection with his subordinates also soured. He had a strong prewar friendship with McLaws, but it began to show signs of souring after McLaws blamed Longstreet for the defeat at Gettysburg and was accused by Longstreet of displaying lethargy after Chickamauga.[172] Hood's old division was under the temporary command of Brigadier General Micah Jenkins. The brigadier general who had been in the division the longest was Evander M. Law. Both men disliked each other and desired permanent command of the division. Longstreet favored Jenkins, while most of the men favored Law. Longstreet had asked Davis to name a permanent commander, but he refused.[173]

On October 27, Union troops managed to open up a "cracker line" to bring food to their troops by defeating Law's brigade of Hood's division, temporarily commanded by Jenkins, at the Battle of Brown's Ferry. In the nighttime Battle of Wauhatchie from October 28–29, Jenkins failed to regain the lost position. He blamed Law and Brigadier General Jerome B. Robertson for the lack of success. Longstreet sided with Jenkins in the dispute. Longstreet took no immediate action against Law but complained about Robertson. A court of inquiry was set up, but its proceedings were suspended and Robertson returned to command.[174] After the Confederate failures, Longstreet devised a strategy to prevent reinforcement and a lifting of the siege by Grant. He knew this Union reaction was underway, and that the nearest railhead was Bridgeport, Alabama, where portions of two Union corps would soon arrive. After sending his artillery commander, Porter Alexander, to reconnoiter the Union-occupied town, he devised a plan to shift most of the Army of Tennessee away from the siege, setting up logistical support in Rome, Georgia, to go after Bridgeport to take the railhead, possibly catching Maj. Gen. Joseph Hooker and arriving Union troops from the Eastern Theater in a disadvantageous position. The plan was well received and approved by President Davis,[175] but it was disapproved by Bragg, who objected to the significant logistical challenges it posed. Longstreet accepted Bragg's arguments[176] and agreed to a plan in which he and his men were dispatched to East Tennessee to deal with an advance by the Union Army of the Ohio, commanded by Maj. Gen. Ambrose Burnside. Longstreet was selected for this assignment partially due to enmity on Bragg's part, but also because the War Department intended for Longstreet's men to return to Lee's army and this movement was in that direction.[177][178]

Longstreet was criticized for the slow pace of his advance toward Knoxville in November and some of his troops began using the nickname "Peter the Slow" to describe him.[179] At the Battle of Campbell's Station on November 16, the Federals evaded Longstreet's troops. This was due both to the poor performance of Law, who exposed his brigade to the enemy and thus ruined what was supposed to be a surprise attack, and Burnside's skillful retreat. The Confederates also dealt with muddy roads and a shortage of good supplies.[180]

Burnside settled into entrenchments around the city, which Longstreet besieged. Longstreet soon learned that Bragg had been defeated at Chattanooga on November 25, and that William Tecumseh Sherman's men were marching to relieve Burnside. He decided to risk a frontal attack on Union entrenchments before they arrived. On November 29, he sent his troops forward at the Battle of Fort Sanders. The attack was repulsed, and Longstreet was forced to retreat.[181] When Bragg was defeated by Grant, Longstreet was ordered to join forces with the Army of Tennessee in northern Georgia. He demurred and began to move back to Virginia, soon pursued by Sherman. Longstreet defeated federal troops in an engagement at Bean's Station on December 14 before the armies went into winter quarters. The greatest effect of the campaign was to deprive Bragg of troops he sorely needed in Chattanooga. Longstreet's second independent command (after Suffolk) was a failure and his self-confidence was damaged. He reacted to the failure of the campaign by blaming others. He relieved Lafayette McLaws from command and requested the court martial of Robertson and Law. He also submitted a letter of resignation to Adjutant General Samuel Cooper on December 30, 1863, but his request to be relieved was denied.[182][183]

The sufferings of the Confederate troops were to continue into the winter. Longstreet set up his headquarters in Rogersville. He attempted to keep communications open with Lee's army in Virginia, but Federal cavalry general William W. Averell's raids destroyed the railroads, isolating him and forcing him to rely only on Eastern Tennessee for supplies. Longstreet's corps suffered through a severe winter in Eastern Tennessee with inadequate shelter and provisions. More than half of the men were without shoes.[184] Writing to Georgia's Quartermaster General, Ira Roe Foster on January 24, 1864, Longstreet noted: "There are five Georgia Brigades in this Army – Wofford's, G.T. Anderson's, Bryan's, Benning's, and Crews' cavalry brigade. They are all alike in excessive need of shoes, clothing of all kinds, and blankets. All that you can send will be thankfully received."[185] Meanwhile,

Longstreet again developed strategic plans. He called for an offensive through Tennessee into Kentucky in which his command would be bolstered by P. G. T. Beauregard and 20,000 men. Although he had the concurrence of General Lee, Longstreet was unable to convince President Davis or his newly appointed military advisor, Braxton Bragg, who had finally been relieved and replaced by Joe Johnston as commander of the Army of Tennessee following the defeat at Chattanooga.[186][187]

In February 1864, the lines of communication were repaired. Once the weather warmed, Longstreet's men marched north and returned to the Army of Northern Virginia at Gordonsville.[184]

## Wilderness to Appomattox

Longstreet found out that his old friend Ulysses S. Grant had been appointed General-in-Chief of the Union Army, with headquarters in the field alongside the Army of the Potomac. Longstreet told his fellow officers that "he will fight us every day and every hour until the end of the war."[188] Longstreet helped save the Confederate Army from defeat in his first battle back with Lee's army, the Battle of the Wilderness in May 1864. [189] After Grant moved south of the Rapidan River in an attempt to take Richmond, Lee intended to delay battle in order to give Longstreet's 14,000 men time to arrive on the field. Grant disrupted these plans by attacking him on May 5, and the fighting was inconclusive. The following morning at 5 a.m., Hancock led two divisions in a ferocious attack on A. P. Hill's corps, driving the men back two miles. Just as this was happening, Longstreet's men arrived on the field. They took advantage of an old roadbed built for an out-of-use railroad to creep through a densely wooded area unnoticed before launching a powerful flanking attack.[190] Longstreet's men moved forward along the Orange Plank Road against the II Corps and in two hours nearly drove it from the field. Once again he developed

innovative tactics to deal with difficult terrain, ordering the advance of six brigades by heavy skirmish lines, which allowed his men to deliver a continuous fire into the enemy, while proving to be elusive targets themselves. Historian Edward Steere attributed much of the success of the Army to "the display of tactical genius by Longstreet which more than redressed his disparity in numerical strength."[191] After the war, Hancock said to Longstreet of this flanking maneuver: "You rolled me up like a wet blanket."[192]

Longstreet was wounded during the assault— accidentally shot by his own men only about 4 miles (6.4 km) away from the place where Jackson suffered

*James Longstreet in 1865*

the same fate a year earlier. A bullet passed through his shoulder, severing nerves, and tearing a gash in his throat. Jenkins, who was riding with Longstreet, was also shot and died from his wounds. The momentum of the attack subsided. As he was taken from the field, Longstreet urged Lee to press the attack. Instead, Lee delayed further movement until units could be realigned, giving the Union defenders adequate time to reorganize. The subsequent attack was a failure.[193] Alexander called the removal of Longstreet the critical juncture of the battle: "I have always believed that, but for Longstreet's fall, the panic which was fairly underway in Hancock's [II] Corps would have been extended & have resulted in Grant's being forced to retreat back across the Rapidan."[194]

Longstreet missed the rest of the 1864 spring and summer campaign, where Lee sorely missed his skill in handling the army.[195] On May 1, he was confirmed as an Episcopalian. [196] He was treated in Lynchburg, Virginia, and recuperated in Augusta, Georgia, with his cousin, Emma Eve Longstreet Sibley, the daughter of his father's brother, Gilbert. [195] While in Augusta, he participated in the funeral service for Lt. Gen. Leonidas Polk at Saint Paul's Church, joining the Bishops of Mississippi and Arkansas in casting earth onto the coffin.[197] He rejoined Lee in October 1864, with his right arm paralyzed and in a sling, initially unable to ride a horse. He had taught himself to write with his left hand; by periodically pulling on his arm, as advised by doctors, he was able to regain use of his right hand in later years.[198] At this time, Longstreet's staff underwent major changes. The most significant was the transfer of Sorrel, Longstreet's Chief of Staff, to brigade command. He was replaced by Major Osmun Latrobe.[199] For the remainder of the Siege of Petersburg, Longstreet commanded the defenses in front of the capital of Richmond, including all forces north of the James River and Pickett's Division at Bermuda Hundred. He retreated with Lee in the Appomattox Campaign, commanding both the First and Third Corps, following the death of A. P. Hill on April 2.[200][201][202]

As Lee's army attempted to escape to Farmville, Longstreet was engaged at Sailor's Creek on April 6.[203] The Confederates were unable to reach the town, but with the assistance of troops under Anderson and Ewell, managed to prevent federal troops from blocking the army's last path of escape. The overall battle ended in disaster, with nearly 7,000 of the 10,000 Confederate troops engaged killed, wounded, or captured.[204] By April 7, Lee's army had been reduced from nearly 40,000 men on March 31 to 25,000. A group of Confederate officers including William N. Pendleton concluded that the time had come to ask Lee to open negotiations for the army's surrender. Pendleton approached Longstreet and asked him to intercede with Lee, but he refused, saying, "If General Lee doesn't know when to surrender until I tel him, he will never know." Nevertheless, Pendleton approached Lee, who was in communication with Grant on the subject of Confederate surrender, but refused to surrender the army.[205] Lee held his last conference of war on the night of April 8. It was decided that at daybreak, Longstreet would hold the Union troops back while John B. Gordon would lead an escape towards Lynchburg, and then cover his retreat.[206] At the Battle of Appomattox Court House that morning, Longstreet was heavily engaged with the Union II Corps under Andrew A. Humphreys. Gordon's troops were surrounded, and he requested reinforcements which Longstreet could not furnish. Lee was left with no alternative but to meet General Grant to discuss surrender.[207]

Lee worried that his refusal to meet with Grant to discuss surrender terms at the latter's first request would cause him to demand harsher terms this time. Longstreet advised him of his belief that Grant would treat them fairly. As Lee rode toward Appomattox Court House on April 9, Longstreet said that if Grant gave too strong demands, he ought to "break off the interview and tell General Grant to do his worst."[208] After Lee's surrender,

*James Longstreet after the War*

Longstreet arrived in the McLean House, where Grant happily greeted him. He offered Longstreet a cigar and invited him to play a card game. "Why do men fight who were born to be brothers? . . . His whole greeting and conduct towards us was as though nothing had ever happened to mar our pleasant relations," Longstreet told a reporter.[209]

## Postbellum life

After the war, Longstreet and his family settled in New Orleans, a location popular with a number of former Confederate generals. He entered into a cotton brokerage partnership there and also became the president of the newly created and prominent insurance company. He actively sought the presidency of the Mobile and Ohio Railroad but was unsuccessful, and also failed in an attempt to get investors for a proposed railroad from New Orleans around the northwestern coast of the Gulf of Mexico south across the Rio Grande river and American-Mexican border to Monterrey, Mexico. In 1870, he was named president of the newly organized New Orleans and Northeastern Railroad. With Grant's support, he applied for a pardon from President Andrew Johnson. Johnson refused, however, telling Longstreet in a meeting: "There are three persons of the South who can never receive amnesty: Mr. Davis, General Lee, and yourself. You have given the Union cause too much trouble." Regardless of such opposition the Radical Republican-controlled United States Congress restored his citizenship rights in June 1868.[210][211]

Longstreet was one of a small group of former Confederate generals, including James L. Alcorn and William Mahone, to join or ally with the nationally dominant Republican Party during the Reconstruction era. He endorsed Grant for president in the election of 1868, attended his inauguration ceremonies in Washington, D.C., and six days later was appointed by Grant as surveyor of customs in New Orleans. For these acts he lost favor with many white Southerners. His old friend Harvey Hill wrote to a newspaper: "Our scalawag is the local leper of the community." Unlike Northerners who moved South and were sometimes referred to as "Carpetbaggers," Hill wrote, Longstreet "is a native, which is so much the worse."

A major element of the Lost Cause movement, aside from attacking Longstreet's war record, was the idea that the central cause of the Civil War was the protection of states' rights, not slavery. Responding to such arguments, Longstreet once remarked, "I never heard of any other cause of the quarrel than slavery."[212]

In April 1873, Longstreet dispatched a police force under Colonel Theodore W. DeKlyne to the Louisiana town of Colfax to help the local government and its majority-black supporters defend themselves against an insurrection by white supremacists. DeKlyne did not arrive until April 14, one day after the Colfax massacre. By then, his men's task consisted mainly of burying the bodies of blacks who had been killed and attempting to arrest the culprits.[213] During protests of election irregularities in 1874, referred to as the Battle of Liberty Place, an armed force of 8,400 members of the anti-Reconstructionist White League advanced on the State House in New Orleans, which was the capitol of Louisiana at the time, after Republican William Pitt Kellogg was declared the winner of a close and heavily-disputed gubernatorial election. Longstreet commanded a force of 3,600 Metropolitan Police, city policemen, and African-American militia troops, armed with two Gatling guns and a battery of artillery. He rode to meet the protesters but was pulled from his horse, shot by a spent bullet, and taken prisoner. The White League charged, causing many of Longstreet's men to flee or surrender. There were total casualties of 38 killed and 79 wounded. Federal troops sent by President Grant were required to restore order. Longstreet's use of armed black troops during the disturbances increased the denunciations by anti-Reconstructionist and former Southern Confederates.[214]

After bearing criticism of his war record from other Confederates for decades, Longstreet refuted most of their arguments in his memoirs entitled *From Manassas to Appomattox*, a labor of five years that was published in 1896.[198] Piston describes the prose as "entertaining, if occasionally labored." In the book, Longstreet praises several Civil War officers but frequently disparages others, most heavily his postwar detractors Jubal Early and Fitzhugh Lee. Although Longstreet expressed personal affection for Robert E. Lee, he was at times sharply critical of his strategy. The quality of the book was said to have been diminished by bitterness and a lack of objectivity, and it did little if anything to alter the views of Longstreet's opponents.[222]

His final years were marked by poor health and partial deafness. In 1902 he suffered from severe rheumatism and was unable to stand for more than a few minutes at a time. His weight diminished from 200 to 135 pounds by January 1903. Cancer developed in his right eye, and in December he had X-ray therapy in Chicago to treat it.[198] He contracted pneumonia and died in Gainesville on January 2, 1904, six days before his 83rd birthday. At his funeral, Mass was said by Bishop Benjamin Joseph Keiley of Savannah, Georgia, a veteran of the Army of Northern Virginia.[217] Longstreet's remains are buried in Alta Vista Cemetery, in Gainesville. He outlived most of his detractors, and was one of only a few general officers from the Civil War to live into the 20th century.[223]

# George B. McClellan

**George Brinton McClellan** (December 3, 1826–October 29, 1885) was an American soldier, civil engineer, railroad executive, and politician. A graduate of West Point, McClellan served with distinction during the Mexican–American War (1846–1848), and later left the Army to work in railroads until the outbreak of the American Civil War (1861–1865). Early in the conflict, McClellan was appointed to the rank of major general and played an important role in raising a well-trained and organized army, which would become the Army of the Potomac in the Eastern Theater; he served a brief period (November 1861 to March 1862) as general-in-chief of the Union Army.

McClellan organized and led the Union army in the Peninsula Campaign in southeastern Virginia from March through July 1862. It was the first large-scale offensive in the Eastern Theater. Making an amphibious clockwise turning movement around the Confederate Army in northern Virginia, McClellan's forces turned west to move up the Virginia Peninsula, between the James and York Rivers, landing from the Chesapeake Bay, with the Confederate capital, Richmond, as their objective. Initially, McClellan was somewhat successful against General Joseph E. Johnston, but the emergence of General Robert E. Lee to command the Army of Northern Virginia turned the subsequent Seven Days Battles into a partial Union defeat. However, historians note that Lee's victory was in many ways pyrrhic as he failed to destroy the Army of the Potomac and suffered a bloody repulse at Malvern Hill. Historian Stephan Sears in *To the Gates of Richmond* notes McClellan's Army of the Potomac inflicted 20,204 losses while only sustaining 15,855 themselves. McClellan's army would be withdrawn from the Peninsula in August 1862. Military theorist Emory Upton noted at the time that "The worst that could be said of the Peninsula campaign was that thus far it had not been successful. To make it a failure was reserved for the agency of General Halleck."

General McClellan failed to maintain the trust of President Abraham Lincoln, who did not trust his commander-in-chief and was privately derisive of him. McClellan was removed from command in November in the aftermath of the 1862 midterm elections. This decision contributed to McClellan's supposed failure to decisively pursue Lee's Army following the tactically inconclusive but strategic Union victory at the Battle of Antietam outside Sharpsburg, Maryland. Future commander of the Army of the Potomac George Gordon Meade noted in his letters that the decision was for political rather than military reasons. Even critics such as William Swinton lamented the timing of McClellan's removal: "The moment chosen was an inopportune and an ungracious one; for never had McClellan acted with such vigor and rapidity - never had he shown so much confidence in himself or the army in him." McClellan would never receive another field command and went on to become the unsuccessful Democratic Party nominee in the 1864 presidential election against the Republican Lincoln's reelection. The effectiveness of his campaign was damaged when he repudiated his party's platform, which promised an end to the war and negotiations with the southern Confederacy. He served as the 24th Governor of New Jersey from 1878 to 1881; eventually became a writer, and vigorously defended his Civil War conduct.

Most classic histories have presented McClellan as a poor battlefield general. In recent decades, however, this view has been challenged. Some historians view him as a highly capable commander whose reputation suffered unfairly at the hands of pro-Lincoln partisans who made him a scapegoat for the Union's military setbacks. In particular, McClellan's role in the Maryland Campaign has undergone a positive reassessment. Notably, after the war, subsequent commanding general and 18th President Ulysses S. Grant was asked for his opinion of McClellan as a general; he replied, "McClellan is to me one of the mysteries of the war."[2]

## Civil War

### Ohio and strategy

At the start of the Civil War, McClellan's knowledge of what was called "big war science" and his railroad experience suggested he might excel at military logistics. This placed him in great demand as the Union mobilized. The governors of Ohio, Pennsylvania, and New York, the three largest states of the Union, actively pursued him to command their states' militia. Ohio Governor William Dennison was the most persistent, so McClellan was commissioned a major general of volunteers and took command of the Ohio militia on April 23, 1861. Unlike some of his fellow Union officers who came from abolitionist families, he was opposed to federal interference with slavery. For this reason, some of his Southern colleagues approached him informally about siding with the Confederacy, but he could not accept the concept of secession.[22]

On May 3 McClellan re-entered federal service as commander of the Department of the Ohio, responsible for the defense of the states of Ohio, Indiana, Illinois, and, later, western Pennsylvania, western Virginia, and Missouri. On May 14, he was commissioned a major general in the regular army. At age 34, he outranked everyone in the Army except Lt. Gen. Winfield Scott, the general-in-chief. McClellan's rapid promotion was partly due to his acquaintance with Salmon P. Chase, Treasury Secretary and former Ohio governor and senator.[23]

As McClellan scrambled to process the thousands of men who were volunteering for service and to set up training camps, he also applied his mind to grand strategy. He wrote a letter to Gen. Scott on April 27, four days after assuming command in Ohio, that presented the first proposal for a strategy for the war. It contained two alternatives, each envisioning a prominent role for himself as commander. The first would use 80,000 men to invade Virginia through the Kanawha Valley toward Richmond. The second would use the same force to drive south instead, crossing the Ohio River into Kentucky and Tennessee. Scott rejected both plans as logistically unfeasible. Although he complimented McClellan and expressed his "great confidence in your intelligence, zeal, science, and energy," he replied by letter that the 80,000 men would be better used on a river-based expedition to control the Mississippi River and split the Confederacy, accompanied by a strong Union blockade of Southern ports. This plan, which would require considerable patience of the Northern public, was derided in newspapers as the Anaconda Plan, but eventually proved to be the outline of the successful prosecution of the war. Relations between the two generals became increasingly strained over the summer and fall.[24]

## Western Virginia

McClellan's first military operations were to occupy the area of western Virginia that wanted to remain in the Union and subsequently became the state of West Virginia. He had received intelligence reports on May 26 that the critical Baltimore and Ohio Railroad bridges in that portion of the state were being burned. As he quickly implemented plans to invade the region, he triggered his first serious political controversy by proclaiming to the citizens there that his forces had no intentions of interfering with personal property—including slaves. "Notwithstanding all that has been said by the traitors to induce you to believe that our advent among you will be signalized by interference with your slaves, understand one thing clearly—not only will we abstain from all such interference but we will on the contrary with an iron hand, crush any attempted insurrection on their part." He quickly realized that he had overstepped his bounds and apologized by letter to President Lincoln. The controversy was not that his proclamation was diametrically opposed to the administration's policy at the time, but that he was so bold in stepping beyond his strictly military role.[25]

His forces moved rapidly into the area through Grafton and were victorious at the tiny skirmish called the Battle of Philippi, arguably the first land conflict of the war. His first personal command in battle was at Rich Mountain, which he also won. His subordinate commander, William S. Rosecrans, bitterly complained that his attack was not reinforced as McClellan had agreed.[26] Nevertheless, these two minor victories propelled McClellan to the status of national hero.[27] The *New York Herald* entitled an article about him "Gen. McClellan, the Napoleon of the Present War."[28]

## Building an army

After the defeat of the Union forces at Bull Run on July 21, 1861, Lincoln summoned McClellan from western Virginia, where McClellan had given the North the only engagements bearing a semblance of victory. He traveled by special train on the main Pennsylvania line from Wheeling through Pittsburgh, Philadelphia, and Baltimore, and on to Washington City, and was greeted by enthusiastic crowds that met his train along the way.[29]

Carl Sandburg wrote, "McClellan was the man of the hour, pointed to by events, and chosen by an overwhelming weight of public and private opinion."[30] On July 26, the day he reached the capital, McClellan was appointed commander of the Military Division of the Potomac, the main Union force responsible for the defense of Washington. On August 20, several military units in Virginia were consolidated into his department and he immediately formed the Army of the Potomac, with himself as its first commander.[31] He reveled in his newly acquired power and influence:[29]

> I find myself in a new and strange position here—Presdt, Cabinet, Genl Scott & all deferring to me—by some strange operation of magic I seem to have become *the* power of the land. . . . I almost think that were I to win some small success now I could become Dictator or anything else that might please me—but nothing of that kind would please me—*therefore* I *won't* be Dictator. Admirable self-denial!
>
> —George B. McClellan, letter to Ellen, July 26, 1861

*General George B. McClellan with staff & dignitaries (from left to right): Gen. George W. Morell, Lt. Col. A.V. Colburn, Gen. McClellan, Lt. Col. N.B. Sweitzer, Prince de Joinville (son of King Louis Phillippe of France), and on the very right – the prince's nephew, Count de Paris*

During the summer and fall, McClellan brought a high degree of organization to his new army, and greatly improved its morale with frequent trips to review and encourage his units. It was a remarkable achievement, in which he came to personify the Army of the Potomac and reaped the adulation of his men.[32] He created defenses for Washington that were almost impregnable, consisting of 48 forts and strong points, with 480 guns manned by 7,200 artillerists.[33] The Army of the Potomac grew in number from 50,000 in July to 168,000 in November, becoming the largest military force the United States had raised until that time.[30] But this was also a time of tension in the high command, as he continued to quarrel frequently with the government and the general-in-chief, Lt. Gen. Scott, on matters of strategy. McClellan rejected the tenets of Scott's Anaconda Plan, favoring instead an overwhelming grand battle, in the Napoleonic style. He proposed that his army should be expanded to 273,000 men and 600 guns and "crush the rebels in one campaign." He favored a war that would impose little impact on civilian populations and require no emancipation of slaves.

McClellan's antipathy to emancipation added to the pressure on him, as he received bitter criticism from Radical Republicans in the government.[34] He viewed slavery as an institution recognized in the Constitution, and entitled to federal protection wherever it existed (Lincoln held the same public position until August 1862).[35] McClellan's writings after the war were typical of many Northerners: "I confess to a prejudice in favor of my own race, & can't learn to like the odor of either Billy goats or niggers."[33] But in November 1861, he wrote to his wife, "I will, if successful, throw my sword onto the scale to force an improvement in the condition of those poor blacks." He later wrote that had it been his place to arrange the terms of peace, he would have insisted on gradual emancipation, guarding the rights of both slaves and masters, as part of any settlement. But he made no secret of his opposition to the radical Republicans. He told Ellen, "I will not fight for the abolitionists." This put him in opposition with officials of the administration who believed he was attempting to implement the policies of the opposition party.[36]

The immediate problem with McClellan's war strategy was that he was convinced the Confederates were ready to attack him with overwhelming numbers. On August 8, believing that the Confederacy had over 100,000 troops facing him (in contrast to the 35,000 they had actually deployed at Bull Run a few weeks earlier), he declared a state of emergency in the capital. By August 19, he estimated 150,000 rebel soldiers on his front. McClellan's subsequent campaigns were strongly influenced by the overblown enemy strength estimates of his secret service chief, detective Allan Pinkerton, but in August 1861, these estimates were entirely McClellan's own. The result was a level of extreme caution that sapped the initiative of McClellan's army and dismayed the government. Historian and biographer Stephen W. Sears observed that McClellan's actions would have been "essentially sound" for a commander who was as outnumbered as McClellan thought he was, but McClellan in fact rarely had less than a two-to-one advantage over the armies that opposed him in 1861 and 1862. That fall, for example, Confederate forces ranged from 35,000 to 60,000, whereas the Army of the Potomac in September numbered 122,000 men; in early December 170,000; by year end, 192,000.[37] Confederate returns for December 1861, found in the *Official Record*, Ser 4: Vol 1, place Confederate aggregate present and absent in Virginia at 133,876 men. This places McClellan's estimates as significantly closer than previously thought.

The dispute with Scott became increasingly personal. Scott (as well as many in the War Department) was outraged that McClellan refused to divulge any details about his strategic planning, or even such basic information as the strengths and dispositions of his units. McClellan claimed he could not trust anyone in the administration to keep his plans secret from the press, and thus the enemy. In the course of a disagreement about defensive forces on the Potomac River, McClellan wrote to his wife on August 10: "Genl Scott is the great obstacle—he will not comprehend the danger & is either a traitor, or an incompetent. I have to fight my way against him."[38] Scott became so disillusioned with the young general that he offered his resignation to President Lincoln, who initially refused to accept it. Rumors traveled through the capital that McClellan might resign, or instigate a military coup, if Scott were not removed. Lincoln's Cabinet met on October 18 and agreed to accept Scott's resignation for "reasons of health."[39]

However, the subsequently formed Army of the Potomac had high morale and was extremely proud of their general, some even referring to McClellan as the saviour of Washington. He prevented the army's morale from collapsing at least twice, in the aftermath of the First and Second Battles of Bull Run. Many historians argue that he was talented in this aspect.

## General-in-chief

*"Quaker guns" (logs used as ruses to imitate cannons) in former Confederate fortifications at Manassas Junction*

On November 1, 1861, Winfield Scott retired and McClellan became general-in-chief of all the Union armies. The president expressed his concern about the "vast labor" involved in the dual role of army commander and general-in-chief, but McClellan responded, "I can do it all."[39]

Lincoln, as well as many other leaders and citizens of the northern states, became increasingly impatient with McClellan's slowness to attack the Confederate forces still massed near Washington. The Union defeat at the minor Battle of Ball's Bluff near Leesburg in October added to the frustration and indirectly damaged McClellan. In December, the Congress formed a Joint Committee on the Conduct of the War, which became a thorn in the side of many generals throughout the war, accusing them of incompetence and, in some cases, treason. McClellan was called as the first witness on December 23, but he contracted typhoid fever and could not attend. Instead, his subordinate officers testified, and their candid admissions that they had no knowledge of specific strategies for advancing against the Confederates raised many calls for McClellan's dismissal.[40]

McClellan further damaged his reputation by his insulting insubordination to his commander-in-chief. He privately referred to Lincoln, whom he had known before the war as a lawyer for the Illinois Central, as "nothing more than a well-meaning baboon," a "gorilla," and "ever unworthy of . . . his high position."[41] On November 13, he snubbed the president, who had come to visit McClellan's house, by making him wait for 30 minutes, only to be told that the general had gone to bed and could not receive him.[42]

On January 10, Lincoln met with top generals (McClellan did not attend) and directed them to formulate a plan of attack, expressing his exasperation with General McClellan with the following remark: "If General McClellan does not want to use the army, I would like to borrow it for a time."[43] On January 12, 1862, McClellan was summoned to the White House, where the Cabinet demanded to hear his war plans. For the first time, he revealed his intentions to transport the Army of the Potomac by ship to Urbanna, Virginia, on the Rappahannock River, outflanking the Confederate forces near Washington, and proceeding 50 miles (80 km) overland to capture Richmond. He refused to give any specific details of the proposed campaign, even to his friend, newly appointed War Secretary Edwin M. Stanton. On January 27, Lincoln issued an order that required all of his armies to begin offensive operations by February 22, Washington's birthday. On January 31, he issued a supplementary order for the Army of the Potomac to move overland to attack the Confederates at Manassas Junction and Centreville. McClellan immediately replied with a 22-page letter objecting in detail to the president's plan and advocating instead his Urbanna plan, which was the first written instance of the plan's details being presented to the president. Although Lincoln believed his plan was superior, he was relieved that McClellan finally agreed to begin moving, and reluctantly approved. On March 8, doubting McClellan's resolve, Lincoln again interfered with the army commander's prerogatives. He called a council of war at the White House in which McClellan's subordinates were asked about their confidence in the Urbanna plan. They expressed their confidence to varying degrees. After the meeting, Lincoln issued another order, naming specific officers as corps commanders to report to McClellan (who had been reluctant to do so prior to assessing his division commanders' effectiveness in combat, even though this would have meant his direct supervision of twelve divisions in the field).[44]

Two more crises would confront McClellan before he could implement his plans. The Confederate forces under General Joseph E. Johnston withdrew from their positions before Washington, assuming new positions south of the Rappahannock, which completely nullified the Urbanna strategy. McClellan revised his plans to have his troops disembark at Fort Monroe, Virginia, and advance up the Virginia Peninsula to Richmond, an operation that would be known as the Peninsula Campaign. Then, however, McClellan came under extreme criticism in the press and Congress when it was learned that Johnston's forces had not only slipped away unnoticed, but had for months fooled the Union Army with logs painted black to appear as cannons, nicknamed Quaker Guns. Congress's joint committee visited the abandoned Confederate lines and radical Republicans introduced a resolution demanding the dismissal of McClellan, but it was narrowly defeated by a parliamentary maneuver.[45] The second crisis was the emergence of the Confederate ironclad CSS *Virginia*, which threw Washington into a panic and made naval support operations on the James River seem problematic.

On March 11, 1862, Lincoln removed McClellan as general-in-chief, leaving him in command of only the Army of the Potomac, ostensibly so that McClellan would be free to devote all his attention to the move on Richmond. Lincoln's order was ambiguous as to whether McClellan might be restored following a successful campaign. In fact, the general-in-chief position was left unfilled. Lincoln, Stanton, and a group of officers who formed the "War Board" directed the strategic actions of the Union armies that spring. Although

McClellan was assuaged by supportive comments Lincoln made to him, in time he saw the change of command very differently, describing it as a part of an intrigue "to secure the failure of the approaching campaign."[46]

## Peninsula Campaign

McClellan's army began to sail from Alexandria on March 17. It was an armada that dwarfed all previous American expeditions, transporting 121,500 men, 44 artillery batteries, 1,150 wagons, over 15,000 horses, and tons of equipment and supplies. An English observer remarked that it was the "stride of a giant."[47] The army's advance from Fort Monroe up the Virginia Peninsula proved to be slow. McClellan's plan for a rapid seizure of Yorktown was foiled by the removal of 1st Corps from the Army of the Potomac for the defense of Washington. McClellan had hoped to use the 1st Corps to capture Glouchester Point and thus outflank the Confederate position. When he discovered that the Confederates had fortified a line across the Peninsula he hesitated to attack. As Swinton notes "It is possible, however — and there is a considerable volume of evidence bearing upon this point — that General McClellan, during all the earlier portion of the month before Yorktown, had it in his mind, even without McDowell's corps, to undertake the decisive turning movement by the north side of the York. In this event, it would not only be in the direction of his plan to make no attack, but it would play into his hands that his opponent should accumulate his forces on the Peninsula. Yet this halting between two opinions had the result that, when he had abandoned the purpose of making the turning movement, it had become too late for him to make a direct attack." McClellan asked for the opinion of his chief engineer John G. Barnard, who recommended against an assault. This caused him to decide on a siege of the city, which required considerable preparation.

McClellan continued to believe intelligence reports that credited the Confederates with two or three times the men they actually had. Early in the campaign, Confederate General John B. "Prince John" Magruder defended the Peninsula against McClellan's advance with a vastly smaller force. He created a false impression of many troops behind the lines and of even more troops arriving. He accomplished this by marching small groups of men repeatedly past places where they could be observed at a distance or were just out of sight, accompanied by great noise and fanfare.[48] During this time, General Johnston was able to provide Magruder with reinforcements, but even then there were far fewer troops than McClellan believed were opposite him.

After a month of preparation, just before he was to assault the Confederate works at Yorktown, McClellan learned that Johnston had withdrawn up the Peninsula towards Williamsburg. McClellan was thus required to give chase without any benefit of the heavy artillery so carefully amassed in front of Yorktown. The Battle of Williamsburg on May 5 is considered a Union victory—McClellan's first—but the Confederate army was not destroyed and a bulk of their troops were successfully moved past Williamsburg to Richmond's outer defenses while the battle was waged and for several days thereafter.[49]

McClellan had also placed hopes on a simultaneous naval approach to Richmond via the James River. That approach failed following the Union Navy's defeat at the Battle of Drewry's Bluff, about 7 miles (11 km) downstream from the Confederate capital, on May 15. Basing artillery on a strategic bluff high above a bend in the river, and sinking boats to create an impassable series of obstacles in the river itself, the Confederates effectively blocked this potential approach to Richmond.[50]

McClellan's army moved towards Richmond over the next three weeks, coming to within four miles (6 km) of it. He established a supply base on the Pamunkey River (a navigable tributary of the York River) at White House Landing where the Richmond and York River Railroad extending to Richmond crossed, and commandeered the railroad, transporting steam locomotives and rolling stock to the site by barge.[51]

On May 31, as McClellan planned an assault, his army was surprised by a Confederate attack. Johnston saw that the Union army was split in half by the rain-swollen Chickahominy River and hoped to defeat it in detail at Seven Pines and Fair Oaks. McClellan was unable to command the army personally because of a recurrence of malarial fever, but his subordinates were able to repel the attacks. Nevertheless, McClellan received criticism from Washington for not counterattacking, which some believed could have opened the city of Richmond to capture. Johnston was wounded in the battle, and General Robert E. Lee assumed command of the Army of Northern Virginia. McClellan spent the next three weeks repositioning his troops and waiting for promised reinforcements. As Lee recounted McClellan was attempted to make "this a battle of posts" which would lock the Confederate army in an atrittional battle with superior Union firepower.

At the end of June, Lee began a series of attacks that became known as the Seven Days Battles. The first major battle, at Mechanicsville, was poorly coordinated by Lee and his subordinates and resulted in heavy casualties for little tactical gain. However the battle had a significant impact on McClellan's nerve. The surprise appearance of Maj. Gen. Stonewall Jackson's troops in the battle (when they had last been reported to be many miles away in the Shenandoah Valley) convinced McClellan that he was even more outnumbered than he had thought. He reported to Washington that he faced 200,000 Confederates, perhaps due to a false report on the arrival of another Confederate army P.G.T. Beauregard. The number of men McClellan actually faced varies with Joseph Harsh in *Confederate Tide Rising* placing Lee's army at 112,220 men compared with the 105,857 under McClellan.

Lee continued his offensive at Gaines's Mill to the east. That night, McClellan decided to withdraw his army to a safer base, well below Richmond, on a portion of the James River that was under control of the Union Navy. In doing so, Lee had assumed that the Union army would withdraw to the east toward its existing supply base and McClellan's move to the south delayed Lee's response for at least 24 hours.[52] Ethan Rafuse notes"McClellan's change of base to the James, however, thwarted Lee's attempt to do this. Not only did McClellan's decision allow the Federals to gain control of the time and place for the battles that took place in late June and early July, it enabled them to fight in a way that inflicted terrible beating on the Confederate army . . . . More importantly, by the end of the Seven Days Battles, McClellan had dramatically improved his operational situation."

But McClellan was also tacitly acknowledging that he would no longer be able to invest Richmond, the object of his campaign; the heavy siege artillery required would be almost impossible to transport without the railroad connections available from his original supply base on the York River. In a telegram to Secretary of War Edwin Stanton, reporting on these events, McClellan blamed the Lincoln administration for his reversals. "If I save this army now, I tell you plainly I owe no thanks to you or to any other persons in Washington. You have done your best to sacrifice this army."[53] Fortunately for McClellan, Lincoln never saw that inflammatory statement (at least at that time) because it was censored by the War Department telegrapher.

McClellan was also fortunate that the failure of the campaign left his army mostly intact, because he was generally absent from the fighting and neglected to name any second-in-command who might direct his retreat.[54] Military historian Stephen W. Sears wrote, "When he deserted his army on the Glendale and Malvern Hill battlefields during the Seven Days, he was guilty of dereliction of duty. Had the Army of the Potomac been wrecked on either of these fields (at Glendale the possibility had been real), that charge under the Articles of War would likely have been brought against him."[55] In the battle of Glendale, McClellan was five miles (8 km) away behind Malvern Hill, without telegraph communications and too distant to command his army. In the battle of Malvern Hill, he was on a gunboat, the USS *Galena*, which at one point was ten miles (16 km) away, down the James River.[56] In both battles, effective command of the army fell to his friend and V Corps commander Brigadier General Fitz John Porter. When the public heard about the *Galena*, it was yet another great embarrassment, comparable to the Quaker Guns at Manassas. Editorial cartoons published in the course of the 1864 presidential campaign lampooned McClellan for having preferred the safety of a ship while a battle was fought in the distance.[57]

McClellan was reunited with his army at Harrison's Landing on the James. Debates were held as to whether the army should be evacuated or attempt to resume an offensive toward Richmond. McClellan maintained his estrangement from Abraham Lincoln with his repeated call for reinforcements and by writing a lengthy letter in which he proposed strategic and political guidance for the war, continuing his opposition to abolition or seizure of slaves as a tactic. He concluded by implying he should be restored as general-in-chief, but Lincoln responded by naming Maj. Gen. Henry W. Halleck to the post without consulting, or even informing, McClellan.[58] Lincoln and Stanton also offered command of the Army of the Potomac to Maj. Gen. Ambrose Burnside, who refused the appointment.[59]

Back in Washington, a reorganization of units created the Army of Virginia under Maj. Gen. John Pope, who was directed to advance toward Richmond from the northeast. McClellan, not wishing to abandon his campaign, delayed the return of the Army of the Potomac from the Peninsula enough so that the reinforcements arrived while the northern

Virginia campaign was already underway. The Sixth Corps under Porter from the Army of the Potomac would serve with Pope during the campaign. A frustrated McClellan wrote to his wife before the battle, "Pope will be thrashed . . . & be disposed of [by Lee]. . . . Such a villain as he is ought to bring defeat upon any cause that employs him."[60] Lee had gambled on removing significant units from the Peninsula to attack Pope, who was beaten decisively at Second Bull Run in August.

## Maryland campaign

After the defeat of Pope at Second Bull Run, President Lincoln reluctantly returned to the man who had mended a broken army before. He realized that McClellan was a strong organizer and a skilled trainer of troops, able to recombine the units of Pope's army with the Army of the Potomac faster than anyone. On September 2, 1862, Lincoln named McClellan to command "the fortifications of Washington, and all the troops for the defense of the capital." The appointment was controversial in the Cabinet, a majority of whom signed a petition declaring to the president "our deliberate opinion that, at this time, it is not safe to entrust to Major General McClellan the command of any Army of the United States."[61] The president admitted that it was like "curing the bite with the hair of the dog." But Lincoln told his secretary, John Hay, "We must use what tools we have. There is no man in the Army who can man these fortifications and lick these troops of ours into shape half as well as he. If he can't fight himself, he excels in making others ready to fight."[62]

Northern fears of a continued offensive by Robert E. Lee were realized when he launched his Maryland campaign on September 4, hoping to arouse pro-Southern sympathy in the slave state of Maryland. McClellan's pursuit began on September 5. He marched toward Maryland with six of his reorganized corps. Numbers vary as to the size of McClellan's forc with its paper strength at 87,164, Steven R. Stotelmyer in *Too Useful to Sacrifice* places it about 60,000 men noting that the 87,000 number includes non-combat soldiers and units not immediately available. McClellan would leave two corps behind to defend Washington.[62] McClellan's reception in Frederick, Maryland, as he marched towards Lee's army, was described by the correspondent for Harper's Magazine:

> The General rode through the town on a trot, and the street was filled six or eight deep with his staff and guard riding on behind him. The General had his head uncovered, and received gracefully the salutations of the people. Old ladies and men wept for joy, and scores of beautiful ladies waved flags from the balconies of houses upon the street, and their joyousness seemed to overcome every other emotion. When the General came to the corner of the principal street the ladies thronged around him. Bouquets, beautiful and fragrant, in great numbers were thrown at him, and the ladies crowded around him with the warmest good wishes, and many of them were entirely overcome with emotion. I have never witnessed such a scene. The General took the gentle hands which were offered to him with many a kind

and pleasing remark, and heard and answered the many remarks and compliments with which the people accosted him. It was a scene which no one could forget—an event of a lifetime.[63]

Lee divided his forces into multiple columns, spread apart widely as he moved into Maryland and also maneuvered to capture the federal arsenal at Harpers Ferry. This was a risky move for a smaller army, but Lee was counting on his knowledge of McClellan's temperament. He told one of his generals, "He is an able general but a very cautious one. His army is in a very demoralized and chaotic condition, and will not be prepared for offensive operations—or he will not think it so—for three or four weeks. Before that time I hope to be on the Susquehanna."[64] Lee's assessment proved to be inaccurate as McClellan reacted quickly, with the Confederate leader remarking that McClellan was "advancing more rapidly than was convenient." Many classic histories have portrayed McClellan's army was moving lethargically, averaging only 6 miles (9.7 km) a day.[65] However, as noted by Stotelmyer this number comes from Halleck and does not match the primary source data. Numerous regimental histories from the period recall movements more than double the reported six miles.

Meanwhile, Union soldiers accidentally found a copy of Lee's orders dividing his army, wrapped around a package of cigars in an abandoned camp. They delivered the order to McClellan's headquarters in Frederick on September 13. Upon realizing the intelligence value of this discovery, McClellan threw up his arms and exclaimed, "Now I know what to do!" He waved the order at his old Army friend, Brig. Gen. John Gibbon, and said, "Here is a paper with which if I cannot whip Bobbie Lee, I will be willing to go home." He telegraphed President Lincoln: "I have the whole rebel force in front of me, but I am confident, and no time shall be lost. I think Lee has made a gross mistake, and that he will be severely punished for it. I have all the plans of the rebels, and will catch them in their own trap if my men are equal to the emergency. . . . Will send you trophies."[66]

## Battle of South Mountain

Despite this initial show of bravado, McClellan soon became faced with the fact that the Lee's order was now obsolete, incomplete missing the first two sections and was not clear as to troop numbers. Despite its acclaim by many historians, the order gave McClellan little he did not already know. McClellan within hours of receiving the order dispatched his cavalry to assess its accuracy. By 6:20 he was issuing his orders for the following day. Some have inaccurately claimed McClellan delayed some 18 hours before reacting. This, however, is easily disproven by the fact that his army was in motion all day on the 13th due to orders from McClellan for the following day. It was McClellan's practice to write his orders the night before for the following day.

McClellan ordered his units to set out for the South Mountain passes and was able to punch through the defended passes that separated them from Lee. The stubborn Confederate defenses gave Lee enough time to concentrate many of his men at Sharpsburg, Maryland. As noted by historians such as Stotelmyer the significance of the Union victory at South Mountain should not be underestimated. It ruined Lee's plans to invade Pennsylvania and took the initiative away from the Confederate commander. The Battle of South Mountain also presented McClellan with an opportunity for one of the great theatrical moments of his career, as historian Sears describes:

> The mountain ahead was wreathed in smoke eddies of battle smoke in which the gun flashes shone like brief hot sparks. The opposing battle lines on the heights were marked by heavier layers of smoke, and columns of Federal troops were visible winding their way up the mountainside, each column . . . looking like a 'monstrous, crawling, blue-black snake' . . . McClellan posed against this spectacular backdrop, sitting motionless astride his warhorse Dan Webster with his arm extended, point-ing Hooker's passing troops toward the battle. The men cheered him until they were hoarse . . . and some broke ranks to swarm around the martial figure and indulge in the 'most extravagant demonstrations'.[67]

The Union army reached Antietam Creek, to the east of Sharpsburg, on the evening of September 15. A planned attack on September 16 was put off because of early morn-ing fog, allowing Lee to prepare his defenses with an army less than half the size of McClellan's.[68]

## Battle of Antietam

*Lincoln with McClellan and staff after the Battle of Antietam. Notable figures (from left) are 5. Alexander S. Webb, Chief of Staff, V Corps; 6. McClellan;. 8. Dr. Jonathan Letterman; 10. Lincoln; 11. Henry J. Hunt; 12. Fitz John Porter; 15. Andrew A. Humphreys; 16. Capt. George Armstrong Custer*

The Battle of Antietam on September 17, 1862, was the single bloodiest day in American military history. McClellan devel-oped a complex battle plan to defeat Lee's army, as Ethan Rafuse in *McClellan's War* out-lines: "It was an excellent tactical plan that took advantage of the merits of attacks on both the left and the right, ensured that McClellan had the ability to control his army and the flexibility to respond to events and conver all contingencies." The outnum-bered Confederate forces, however, fought desperately and well. Lee was able to shift his defenders to parry each of three Union thrusts, launched separately and sequen-tially against the Confederate left, center, and finally the right. Union efforts were also frustrated by the wounding of two corps commanders and difficult terrain. Some classic Histories and James M. McPherson have criticized McClellan from keeping two corps

*Lincoln in McClellan's tent after the Battle of Antietam*

reserve during the battle.[69] Stotelmyer, however, believes that McClellan's reserve poll was far smaller than previously thought. Further, he states that the two corps in question were not in reserve per existing doctrine as they were manning portions of the line. He additionally notes that McClellan did not display his famed caution at the battle as he attacked an enemy he believed outnumbered him on high ground.

The battle was tactically inconclusive, with the Union suffering a higher overall number of casualties, although Lee technically was defeated because he withdrew first from the battlefield and retreated back to Virginia, and lost a larger percentage of his army than McClellen did. McClellan wired to Washington, "Our victory was complete. The enemy is driven back into Virginia." Yet there was obvious disappointment that McClellan had not crushed Lee, who was fighting with a smaller army with its back to the Potomac River. Although McClellan's subordinates can claim their share of responsibility for delays (such as Ambrose Burnside's misadventures at Burnside Bridge) and blunders (Edwin V. Sumner's attack without reconnaissance), these were localized problems from which the full army could have recovered. Historians have faulted McClellan for accepting the cautious advice about saving his reserves, such as when a significant breakthrough in the center of the Confederate line could have been exploited, but Fitz John Porter is said to have told McClellan, "Remember, General, I command the last reserve of the last Army of the Republic."[70] However, the veracity of this supposed statement is in doubt. Porter in the post-war period never claimed to have made the statement and it also fails to note the several Union corps at that time defending Washington.

Despite being a tactical draw, Antietam is considered a turning point of the war and a victory for the Union because it ended Lee's strategic campaign (his first invasion of the North) and it allowed President Lincoln to issue the Emancipation Proclamation on September 22, taking effect on January 1, 1863. Although Lincoln had intended to issue the proclamation earlier, he was advised by his Cabinet to wait until a Union victory to avoid the perception that it was issued out of desperation. The Union victory and Lincoln's proclamation played a considerable role in dissuading the governments of France and Britain from recognizing the Confederacy; some suspected they were planning to do so in the aftermath of another Union defeat.[71] McClellan had no prior knowledge that the plans for emancipation rested on his battle performance.

Lincoln ordered McClellan's removal from command on November 5, 1862. Maj. Gen. Ambrose Burnside assumed command of the Army of the Potomac on November 9, 1862.[72] McClellan wrote to his wife, "Those in whose judgment I rely tell me that I fought the battle splendidly and that it was a masterpiece of art. . . . I feel I have done all that can be asked in twice saving the country. . . . I feel some little pride in having, with a beaten & demoralized army, defeated Lee so utterly. . . . Well, one of these days history will I trust do me justice."[73]

## 1864 Presidential election

Secretary Stanton ordered McClellan to report to Trenton, New Jersey, for further orders, although none were issued. As the war progressed, there were various calls to return McClellan to an important command, following the Union defeats at Fredericksburg and Chancellorsville, as Robert E. Lee moved north at the start of the Gettysburg campaign, and as Jubal Early threatened Washington in 1864. When Ulysses S. Grant became general-in-chief, he discussed returning McClellan to an unspecified position. But all of these opportunities were impossible, given the opposition within the administration and the knowledge that McClellan posed a potential political threat. McClellan worked for months on a lengthy report describing his two major campaigns and his successes in organizing the Army, replying to his critics and justifying his actions by accusing the administration of undercutting him and denying him necessary reinforcements. The War Department was reluctant to publish his report because, just after completing it in October 1863, McClellan openly declared his entrance to the political stage as a Democrat.[74]

McClellan was nominated by the Democrats to run against Abraham Lincoln in the 1864 U.S. presidential election. Following the example of Winfield Scott, he ran as a U.S. Army general still on active duty; he did not resign his commission until election day, November 8, 1864. McClellan supported continuation of the war and restoration of the Union (but not the abolition of slavery), but the party platform, written by Copperhead leader Clement Vallandigham of Ohio, was opposed to this position. The platform called for an immediate cessation of hostilities and a negotiated settlement with the Confederacy. McClellan was forced to repudiate the platform, which made his campaign inconsistent and difficult. He also was not helped by the party's choice for vice president, George H. Pendleton, a peace candidate from Ohio.[75]

The deep division in the party, the unity of the Republicans (running under the label "National Union Party"), the absence of a large portion of the Democrats' base (the South) from the voter pool, and the military successes by Union forces in the fall of 1864 doomed McClellan's candidacy. Lincoln won the election handily, with 212 Electoral College votes to 21 and a popular vote of 2,218,388 to 1,812,807 or 55 percent to 45 percent.[76] For all his popularity with the troops, McClellan failed to secure their support and the military vote went to Lincoln nearly 3–1. Lincoln's share of the vote in the Army of the Potomac was 70 percent.[77]

## Postbellum years

In 1877 the Democrats nominated McClellan for Governor of New Jersey, an action that took him by surprise because he had not expressed an interest in the position. He accepted the nomination, won election, and served a single term from 1878 to 1881, a tenure marked by careful, conservative executive management and by minimal political rancor. The concluding chapter of his political career was his strong support in 1884 for the election of Grover Cleveland. He sought the position of Secretary of War in Cleveland's cabinet, for which he was well qualified, but political rivals from New Jersey succeeded in blocking his nomination.[84]

McClellan devoted his final years to traveling and writing; he produced his memoirs, *McClellan's Own Story* (published posthumously in 1887), in which he stridently defended his conduct during the war. He died unexpectedly of a heart attack at age 58 at Orange, New Jersey, after suffering from chest pains for a few weeks. His final words, at 3 a.m., October 29, 1885, were, "I feel easy now. Thank you." He was buried at Riverview Cemetery in Trenton.[85]

# Benjamin McCulloch

**Benjamin McCulloch** (November 11, 1811–March 7, 1862) was a soldier in the Texas Revolution, a Texas Ranger, a major general in the Texas militia and thereafter a major in the United States Army (United States Volunteers) during the Mexican–American War, a U.S. marshal, and a brigadier general in the army of the Confederate States during the American Civil War.

## Civil War service

Texas seceded from the union on February 1, 1861, and on February 14, McCulloch received a colonel's commission from Confederate President Jefferson Davis, with the comment that "to Texans, a moment's notice is sufficient when their State demands their service." He was authorized to demand the surrender of all federal military posts in the state. Subsequently, on the morning of February 16, U.S. Army General Twiggs, finding that more than 1,000 Texas troops had surrounded his installations in an orderly manner during the night, turned over to McCulloch all federal property in San Antonio. In return Twigg's troops were to be allowed to leave the state unharmed. On May 11, President Davis appointed McCulloch a brigadier general.

McCulloch was placed in command of the Indian Territory. He set up his headquarters at Little Rock, and began piecing together an Army of the West, with regiments

*Benjamin McCulloch*

from Texas, Arkansas, and Louisiana. He disagreed strongly with General Sterling Price of Missouri, but with the assistance of Brigadier General Albert Pike, he was able to build alliances for the Confederacy with the Cherokee, Choctaw, and Creek nations.

On August 10, 1861, McCulloch's troops, though relatively poorly armed, handily defeated the army of General Nathaniel Lyon at the Battle of Wilson's Creek, Missouri. "We have an average of only twenty-five rounds of ammunition to the man," McCulloch reported, "and no more to be had short of Fort Smith and Baton Rouge." He did not have a high opinion of Price's Missourians, noting that they were undisciplined, commanded mostly by incompetent and inexperienced politicians, and possessed only a poor mix of weapons and equipment. For some 5,000 of them, their enlistment time was up and they were anxious to go home. Cooperation between the Arkansas and Missouri contingents was feeble, with "little cordiality of feeling between the two armies." His lack of confidence in the Missourians led McCulloch to hesitate when a bold attack might well have destroyed Lyon's smaller force and given Missouri to the Confederacy.

The continuing feud between McCulloch and Price led to the appointment of Major General Earl Van Dorn to overall command, Henry Heth and Braxton Bragg having declined the appointment. When Van Dorn launched an expedition against St. Louis, a strategy McCulloch strongly opposed, it was again McCulloch's reconnaissance that contributed most to what little success Van Dorn's plan was able to achieve.

McCulloch commanded the Confederate right wing at the Battle of Pea Ridge (or Elkhorn Tavern), Arkansas, and on March 7, 1862, after much maneuvering his troops overran a key Union artillery battery. Union resistance stiffened late in the morning, however, and as McCulloch rode forward to scout out enemy positions, he was shot out of the saddle and died instantly. McCulloch always disliked army uniforms and was wearing a black velvet civilian suit and Wellington boots at the time of his death. Credit for the fatal shot was claimed by sharpshooter Peter Pelican of the 36th Illinois Infantry.

McCulloch's next in command, Brig. Gen. James M. McIntosh, head of the cavalry, was killed a few minutes later in a charge to recover McCulloch's body. Confederate Col. Louis Hébert was captured in the same charge, and the Confederate forces, with no remaining leadership, slowly fell apart and withdrew. Historians generally blame the Confederate disaster at Pea Ridge and the subsequent loss of undefended Arkansas on the death of General Ben McCulloch.

McCulloch's body was buried on the field at Pea Ridge, but was subsequently removed with other victims of the battle to a cemetery in Little Rock. He was later reinterred in the Texas State Cemetery in Austin; the gravesite is in the cemetery's Republic Hill section, Row N, No. 4. His papers are housed at the Dolph Briscoe Center for American History (previously the Barker Texas History Center) at the University of Texas at Austin. McCulloch County, Texas, formed in 1856 and located in the present geographical center of the state, was named for him.[2] He is also one of thirty men inducted into the Texas Ranger Hall of Fame at Fort Fisher, Waco.

Shortly after Pea Ridge, Albert Pike, now a brigadier general, constructed Fort McCulloch as the principal Confederate fortification in the southern section of the Indian Territory, naming it after his late commander. It was built on a bluff on the south bank of the Blue River and is now located in Bryan County, Oklahoma. It was placed on the U.S. National Register of Historic Places in 1971.

Camp Ben McCulloch (*see* External Links below) was established near Austin in 1896 as a reunion site for the United Confederate Veterans and is the last such site still owned by the UCV's descendant group, the Sons and Daughters of the Confederacy. It is now a public recreation facility of some 200 acres (0.8 km²), operated by the County of Hays, and is a popular location for Central Texas family reunions, picnics, and musical festivals.

Several other members of McCulloch's family followed him to Texas, including his mother. She died in Ellis County in 1866 at the home of another of her sons, John C. McCulloch, who had been a captain in the Confederate army. Her remains were exhumed in 1938 by the State of Texas and reinterred beside those of Gen. Ben McCulloch, and a joint monument was erected. Other siblings lived in Gonzales and in Walker County.

# Wilmer McLean

**Wilmer McLean** (May 3, 1814–June 5, 1882) was an American wholesale grocer from Virginia. His house near Manassas, Virginia, was involved in the First Battle of Bull Run in 1861. After the battle he moved to Appomattox, Virginia to escape the war, thinking that it would be safe. Instead, in 1865, General Robert E. Lee surrendered to Ulysses S. Grant in McLean's house in Appomattox. His houses were, therefore, involved in one of the first and one of the last encounters of the American Civil War. He lived in his house with his wife, Virginia.

## American Civil War
### *First Battle of Bull Run*

*Wilmer McLean, c.1860*

The initial engagement on July 21, 1861, of what would become the First Battle of Bull Run (First Manassas) took place on McLean's farm, the Yorkshire Plantation, in Manassas, Prince William County, Virginia. Union Army artillery fired at McLean's house, which was being used as a headquarters for Confederate Brigadier General P. G. T. Beauregard, and a cannonball dropped through the kitchen fireplace. Beauregard wrote after the battle, "A comical effect of this artillery fight was the destruction of the dinner of myself and staff by a Federal shell that fell into the fire-place of my headquarters at the McLean House."[1]

McLean was a retired major in the Virginia militia but, at age 47, he was too old to return to active duty at the outbreak of the Civil War. He made his living during the war as a sugar broker supplying the Confederate States Army. He decided to move because his commercial activities were centered mostly in southern Virginia and the Union army presence in his area of northern Virginia made his work difficult. He undoubtedly was also motivated by a desire to protect his family from a repetition of their combat experience. In the spring of 1863, he and his family moved about 120 miles (190 km) south to Appomattox County, Virginia, near a dusty, crossroads community called Appomattox Court House.[2]

## Appomattox Court House

On April 9, 1865, the war revisited McLean. Confederate General Robert E. Lee was about to surrender to Lieutenant General Ulysses S. Grant. He sent a messenger to Appomattox Court House to find a place to meet. On April 8, 1865, the messenger knocked on

McLean's door and requested the use of his home, to which McLean reluctantly agreed. Lee surrendered to Grant in the parlor of McLean's house, effectively ending the Civil War.[2] Later, McLean is supposed to have said "The war began in my front yard and ended in my front parlor."[3]

Once the ceremony was over, members of the Army of the Potomac began taking the tables, chairs, and various other furnishings in the house—essentially, anything that was not tied down—as souvenirs. They simply handed money to the protesting McLean as they made off with his property.[4] Major General Edward Ord paid $40 (equivalent to $655 in today's dollars)[5] for the table Lee had used to sign the surrender document, while Major General Philip Sheridan took the table on which Grant had drafted the document for $20 (equivalent to $327 in today's dollars) in gold.[6][7] Sheridan then asked George Armstrong Custer to carry it away on his horse.[7] The table was presented to Custer's wife and is now on exhibit at the American History Museum at the Smithsonian.[8] An authentic recreation of McLean's second home is now part of the Appomattox Court House National Historical Park operated by the National Park Service of the United States Department of the Interior.

## After the war

After the war, McLean and his family sold their house in 1867, unable to keep up the mortgage payments, and returned to their home in Manassas.[9] They later moved to Alexandria, Virginia. He worked for the Internal Revenue Service from 1873 to 1876.

Wilmer McLean died in Alexandria and is buried there at St. Paul's Episcopal Cemetery.

# George Meade

**George Gordon Meade** (December 31, 1815–November 6, 1872) was a career United States Army officer and civil engineer best known for defeating Confederate General Robert E. Lee at the Battle of Gettysburg in the American Civil War. He previously fought with distinction in the Second Seminole War and the Mexican–American War. During the Civil War, he served as a Union general, rising from command of a brigade to that of the Army of the Potomac. Earlier in his career, he was an engineer and was involved in the coastal construction of several lighthouses.

Meade's Civil War combat experience started as a brigade commander in the Peninsula Campaign and the Seven Days Battles. He was severely wounded while leading his brigade at the Battle of Glendale.

*Meade, portrait by Mathew Brady*

As a division commander, he had notable success at the Battle of South Mountain and assumed temporary corps command at the Battle of Antietam. Meade's division was arguably the most successful of any at the Battle of Fredericksburg in December. It was part of a force charged with driving the Confederate troops under Stonewall Jackson back from their position on Prospect Hill. The division made it further than any other, but was forced to turn back due to a lack of reinforcements. Meade was promoted to commander of the V Corps, which he led during the Battle of Chancellorsville.

During the Gettysburg Campaign, he was appointed to command the Army of the Potomac just three days before the Battle of Gettysburg. Arriving on the field after the first day's action on July 1, Meade organized his army on favorable ground to fight an effective defensive battle against Robert E. Lee's Army of Northern Virginia, repelling a series of massive assaults throughout the next two days. Lee was forced to retreat to Virginia, ending his hope of winning the war through a successful invasion of the North. This victory was marred by Meade's ineffective pursuit during the retreat, allowing Lee and his army to escape instead of completely destroying them. The Union Army also failed to follow up on its success during the Bristoe Campaign and Battle of Mine Run that fall, which ended inconclusively. Meade suffered from intense political rivalries within the Army, notably with Daniel Sickles, who tried to discredit his role in the victory at Gettysburg.

In 1864–65, Meade continued to command the Army of the Potomac through the Overland Campaign, the Richmond-Petersburg Campaign, and the Appomattox Campaign, but he was overshadowed by the direct supervision of the general-in-chief, Lt. Gen. Ulysses S. Grant, who accompanied him throughout these campaigns. Grant conducted most of the strategy during these campaigns, leaving Meade with significantly less influence than before. His image was harmed by his notoriously short temper and disdain for the press. After the war, he commanded several important departments during Reconstruction.

## American Civil War
*Early commands*

*General Meade's horse, Old Baldy*

Meade was appointed brigadier general of volunteers on August 31, 1861, a few months after the start of the American Civil War, based on the strong recommendation of Pennsylvania Governor Andrew Curtin. He was assigned command of the 2nd Brigade of the Pennsylvania Reserves, recruited early in the war, which he led competently, initially in the construction of defenses around Washington, D.C. He eventually came to command a brigade in the Pennsylvania Reserves Division of the Army of the Potomac. In early 1862, with the army being reorganized into corps, Meade served as part of the I Corps under Maj. Gen Irvin McDowell. The I Corps was stationed in the Rappahannock area, but in June, the Pennsylvania Reserves were detached and sent to the Peninsula to reinforce the main army. With the onset of the Seven Days Battles on June 25, the Reserves were in the thick of the fighting. At Mechanicsville and Gaines Mill, Meade's brigade was mostly held in reserve, but at Glendale on June 30, it was heavily engaged and Meade was shot three times, in the arm, leg, and back. He partially recovered his strength in time for the Northern Virginia Campaign and the Second Battle of Bull Run, in which he led his brigade, then assigned to Maj. Gen. Irvin McDowell's corps of the Army of Virginia. His brigade made a heroic stand on Henry House Hill to protect the rear of the retreating Union Army. At the start of the Maryland Campaign a few days later, he received command of the 3rd Division, I Corps, Army of the Potomac, and distinguished himself during the Battle of South Mountain. When Meade's brigade stormed the heights at South Mountain, Maj. Gen. Joseph Hooker, his corps commander, was heard to exclaim, "Look at Meade! Why, with troops like those, led in that way, I can win anything!" In the Battle of Antietam, Meade replaced the wounded Hooker in command of I Corps, selected personally by McClellan over other generals his superior in rank. He performed well at Antietam, but was wounded in the thigh.[7]

During the Battle of Fredericksburg, Meade's division made the only breakthrough of the Confederate lines, spearheading through a gap in Lt. Gen. Thomas J. "Stonewall" Jackson's corps at the southern end of the battlefield. For this action, Meade was promoted to major general of volunteers, to rank from November 29, 1862, and major in the regular army, to rank from June 18. However, his attack was not reinforced, resulting in the loss of much of his division. After the battle, he received command of V Corps, which he led in the Battle of Chancellorsville the following spring. General Hooker, then commanding the Army of the Potomac, had grand, aggressive plans for the campaign, but was too timid in execution, allowing the Confederates to seize the initiative. Meade's corps was left in reserve for most of the battle, contributing to the Union defeat. Afterward, Meade argued strongly with Hooker for resuming the attack against Lee, but to no avail.[8]

## Army of the Potomac and Gettysburg

*Commanders of the Army of the Potomac, Gouverneur K. Warren, William H. French, George G. Meade, Henry J. Hunt, Andrew A. Humphreys, and George Sykes in September 1863*

*General Meade's headquarters, Gettysburg, Pennsylvania*

Hooker resigned from command of the Army of the Potomac while pursuing Lee in the Gettysburg Campaign.[9] In the early morning hours of June 28, 1863, a messenger from President Abraham Lincoln arrived to inform Meade of his appointment as Hooker's replacement. Meade was taken by surprise and later wrote to his wife that when the officer entered his tent to wake him, he assumed that Army politics had caught up with him and he was being arrested. He had not actively sought command and was not the president's first choice. John F. Reynolds, one of four major generals who outranked Meade in the Army of the Potomac, had earlier turned down the president's suggestion that he take over.[10]

Meade assumed command at Prospect Hall in Frederick, Maryland.[11] Lee's Army of Northern Virginia was invading Pennsylvania and, as a former corps commander, Meade had little knowledge of the disposition of the rest of his new army. Lee was aware of Meade's inexperience and wanted to exploit it. Only three days later he confronted Lee in the Battle of Gettysburg, July 1–3, 1863, when he won the battle that is considered a turning point of the war. The battle began almost by accident, as the result of a chance meeting engagement between Confederate infantry and Union cavalry in Gettysburg on July 1. By the end of the first day, two Union infantry corps had been almost destroyed, but had taken up positions on favorable ground. Meade rushed the remainder of his army to Gettysburg and skillfully deployed his forces for a defensive battle, reacting swiftly to fierce assaults on his line's left, right, and center, culminating in Lee's disastrous assault on the center, known as Pickett's Charge.[12]

During the three days, Meade made excellent use of capable subordinates, such as Maj. Gens. John F. Reynolds and Winfield S. Hancock, to whom he delegated great responsibilities. Unfortunately for Meade's reputation, he did not skillfully manage the political manipulators he inherited from Hooker. Maj. Gens. Daniel Sickles, III Corps commander, and Daniel Butterfield, Meade's chief of staff, caused him difficulty later in the war, questioning his command decisions and courage. Sickles had developed a personal vendetta against Meade because of Sickles's allegiance to Joseph Hooker, whom Meade had replaced, and because of controversial disagreements at Gettysburg. Sickles had either mistakenly or deliberately disregarded Meade's orders about placing his corps in the defensive line, which led to that corps' destruction and placed the entire army at risk on the second day of battle. Radical Republicans, some of whom like Thaddeus Stevens were former Know Nothings and hostile to Irish Catholics like Meade's family, in the Joint Committee on the Conduct of the War suspected that Meade was a Copperhead and tried in vain to relieve him from command.[13]

Following their severe losses at Gettysburg, General Lee's army retreated to Virginia. Meade was criticized by President Lincoln and others for not aggressively pursuing the Confederates during their retreat. At one point, the Army of Northern Virginia was extremely vulnerable with its back to the rain-swollen, almost impassable Potomac River, but was able to erect strong defensive positions before Meade could organize an effective attack. Lincoln believed that this wasted an opportunity to end the war. Nonetheless, Meade was rewarded for his actions at Gettysburg by a promotion to brigadier general in the regular army and the Thanks of Congress, which commended Meade " . . . and the officers and soldiers of [the Army of the Potomac], for the skill and heroic valor which at Gettysburg repulsed, defeated, and drove back, broken and dispirited, beyond the Rappahannock, the veteran army of the rebellion."[14] Meade wrote the following to his wife after meeting President Lincoln:

> Yesterday I received an order to repair to Washington, to see the President. . . . The President was, as he always is, very considerate and kind. He found no fault with my operations, although it was very evident he was disappointed that I had not got a battle out of Lee. He coincided with me that there was not much to be gained by any farther advance; but General Halleck was very urgent that something should be done, but what that something was he did not define. As the Secretary of War was absent in Tennessee, final action was postponed till his return.[15]
>
> — *General Meade*

For the remainder of the fall campaigning season in 1863, hobbled by the transfer of his XI and XII Corps to the Western Theater, during both the Bristoe Campaign and the Mine Run Campaign, Meade outmaneuvered Lee in the Bristoe Campaign but failed to win a decisive victory against Lee during the Mine Run Campaign because of General French and the Third Corps.[16]

Meade was a competent and outwardly modest man, although correspondence with his wife throughout the war suggests he was disguising his ego and ambition. A London newspaperman described Meade: "He is a very remarkable looking man—tall, spare, of a commanding figure in presence, his manner pleasant and easy but having much dignity. His head is partially bald and is small and compact, but the forehead is high. He has the late Duke of Wellington class of nose, and his eyes, which have a serious and almost sad expression, are rather sunken, or appear so from the prominence of the curve nasal appearance. He has a decidedly patrician and distinguished appearance." Meade's short temper earned him notoriety, and while he was respected by most of his peers, he was not well loved by his army. Some referred to him as "a damned old goggle-eyed snapping turtle."[17]

## Meade and Grant

*Horse artillery headquarters in Brandy Station, Virginia, February 1864. Meade stands at the far right with Generals John Sedgwick and Alfred Torbert, along with staff officers.*

When Lt. Gen. Ulysses S. Grant was appointed commander of all Union armies in March 1864, Meade offered to resign. He stated the task at hand was of such importance that he would not stand in the way of Grant choosing the right man for the job and offered to serve wherever placed. Grant assured Meade he had no intentions of replacing him. Grant later wrote that this incident gave him a more favorable opinion of Meade than the great victory at Gettysburg.[18]

Grant made his headquarters with Meade for the remainder of the war, which caused Meade to chafe at the close supervision he received. Following an incident in June 1864, in which Meade disciplined reporter Edward Cropsey from *The Philadelphia Inquirer* newspaper for an unfavorable article, all of the press assigned to his army agreed to mention Meade only in conjunction with setbacks. Meade apparently knew nothing of this arrangement, and the reporters giving all of the credit to Grant angered Meade.[19]

Additional differences caused further friction between Grant and Meade. Waging a war of attrition in his Overland Campaign against Robert E. Lee, Grant was willing to suffer previously unacceptable losses with the knowledge that the Union Army had replacement soldiers available, whereas the Confederates did not. Meade, despite his aggressive performance in lesser commands in 1862, had become a more cautious general and more concerned about the futility of attacking entrenched positions. Most of the bloody repulses his army suffered in the Overland Campaign were ordered by Grant, although the aggressive maneuvering that eventually cornered Lee in the trenches around Petersburg were Grant's initiative as well.

Meade was additionally frustrated by the manner in which Grant sometimes gave preferable treatment to subordinates that he had brought with him from the Western Theater. A primary example of this was Grant's interference with Meade's direction of Maj. Gen. Philip Sheridan's Cavalry Corps. The Army of the Potomac had used cavalry for couriers, scouting, and headquarters guards for most of its existence. Only Joe Hooker had contemplated using them in an aggressive fashion, and Meade had largely continued established practice. Sheridan objected and told Meade that he could "whip Stuart" if Meade let him. Meade reported the conversation to Grant, who replied, "Well, he generally knows what he is talking about. Let him start right out and do it." Meade deferred to Grant's judgment and issued orders to Sheridan to "proceed against the enemy's cavalry" and from May 9 through May 24, sent him on a raid toward Richmond, directly challenging the Confederate cavalry.[20]

*Generals George G. Meade, Andrew A. Humphreys and staff in Culpeper, Virginia outside Meade's headquarters, 1863*

*General Meade and other generals of Army of the Potomac in Washington, D.C., June 1865*

Although Meade generally performed effectively under Grant's supervision in the Overland Campaign and the Richmond-Petersburg Campaign, a few instances of bad judgment marred his legacy. During the Battle of Cold Harbor, Meade inadequately supervised his corps commanders and did not insist they perform reconnaissance before their disastrous frontal assault. Inexplicably, Meade wrote to his wife immediately after the attack and expressed pride that it was he who had ordered the attack. During the initial assaults on Petersburg, Meade again failed to coordinate the attacks of his corps before General Lee could reinforce the line, resulting in the ten-month stalemate, the Siege of Petersburg. He approved the plan of Maj. Gen. Ambrose Burnside to plant explosives in a mine shaft dug underneath the Confederate line east of Petersburg, but at the last minute he changed Burnside's plan to lead the attack with a well-trained African-American division that was highly drilled just for this action, instructing him to take a politically less risky course and substitute an untrained and poorly led white division. The resulting Battle of the Crater was one of the great fiascoes of the war. In all of these cases, Grant bears some of

*General George G. Meade and staff in Washington, D.C., in June 1865*

the responsibility for approving Meade's plans, but Meade's performance was not at the same level of competence he displayed on other occasions.[21]

After Spotsylvania, Grant requested that Meade be promoted to major general of the regular army. In a telegram to Secretary of War Edwin Stanton on May 13, 1864, Grant stated that "Meade has more than met my most sanguine expectations. He and [William T.] Sherman are the fittest officers for large commands I have come in contact with."[22] Meade felt slighted that his promotion was processed after that of Sherman and Philip Sheridan, the latter his subordinate.[23] However, his date of rank meant that he was outranked at the end of the war only by Grant, Halleck, and Sherman.[24] Although he fought during the Appomattox Campaign, Grant and Sheridan received most of the credit. He was not present when Robert E. Lee surrendered at Appomattox Court House.[19]

## Command decisions

Meade's decisions in command of the Army of the Potomac have been the focus of controversy. He has been accused of not being aggressive enough in pursuit of Confederate forces, and being reluctant to attack on occasion. His reputation among the public and 19th century historians suffered as a result of his short temper, his bad relationship with the press, his place in the shadow of the victorious Grant, and particularly the damaging fallout from the controversies with Dan Sickles. Recent historical works have portrayed him in a more positive light. They have acknowledged that Meade displayed and acted upon an understanding of the necessary changes in tactics brought about by improvements in weapons technology, such as his decisions to entrench when practicable and not to launch frontal assaults on fortified positions. In addition, the Army of the Potomac had suffered very heavily at Gettysburg, with over 20,000 casualties and the loss of many of its best officers and enlisted men, including three corps commanders, and Meade may have been fully justified in not attempting a rapid pursuit with his army in such a battered condition.[25]

## Later life and death

In 1865, Meade was admitted as an honorary member of the Pennsylvania Society of the Cincinnati.[26]

Meade was a commissioner of Fairmount Park in Philadelphia from 1866 until his death. The people of Philadelphia gave his widow a house at 1836 Delancey Place (Philadelphia), where he lived. The house still has the word "Meade" over the door, but it is now used as apartments. He also held various military commands, including the Military Division of the Atlantic, the Department of the East, and the Department of the South.

He replaced Major General John Pope as governor of the Reconstruction Third Military District in Atlanta on January 10, 1868.

Meade received an honorary doctorate in law (LL.D.) from Harvard University, and his scientific achievements were recognized by various institutions, including the American Philosophical Society and the Philadelphia Academy of Natural Sciences.[27]

Having long suffered from complications caused by his war wounds, Meade died on November 6, 1872, at the age of 56, still on active duty, following a battle with pneumonia. [26] He was buried at Laurel Hill Cemetery.[28][29]

# John S. Mosby

**John Singleton Mosby** (December 6, 1833– May 30, 1916), also known by his nickname, the "Gray Ghost," was a Confederate army cavalry battalion commander in the American Civil War. His command, the 43rd Battalion, Virginia Cavalry, known as *Mosby's Rangers* or *Mosby's Raiders*, was a partisan ranger unit noted for its lightning-quick raids and its ability to elude Union Army pursuers and disappear, blending in with local farmers and townsmen. The area of northern central Virginia in which Mosby operated with impunity was known during the war and ever since as *Mosby's Confederacy*. After the war, Mosby became a Republican and worked as an attorney, supporting his former enemy's commander, U.S. President Ulysses S. Grant. He also served as the American consul to Hong Kong and in the U.S. Department of Justice.

## Military career in the American Civil War

### 1861

Mosby spoke out against secession, but joined the Confederate army as a private at the outbreak of the war. He first served in William "Grumble" Jones's Washington Mounted Rifles. Jones became a Major and was instructed to form a more collective "Virginia Volunteers," which he created with two mounted companies and eight companies of infantry and riflemen, including the Washington Mounted Rifles. Mosby thought the Virginia Volunteers lacked congeniality, and he wrote to the governor requesting to be transferred. However, his request was not granted. The Virginia Volunteers participated in the First Battle of Bull Run (First Manassas) in July 1861.

### 1862

In April 1862, the Confederate Congress passed the Partisan Ranger Act which "provides that such partisan rangers, after being regularly received into service, shall be entitled to the same pay, rations, and quarters, during their term of service, and be subject to the same regulations, as other soldiers."

*John Singleton Mosby*

By June 1862, Mosby was scouting for J .E. B. Stuart during the Peninsular Campaign, including supporting Stuart's "Ride around McClellan."[17] He was captured on July 20 by Union cavalry while waiting for a train at the Beaverdam Depot in Hanover County, Virginia. Mosby was imprisoned in the Old Capitol Prison in Washington, D.C. for ten days before being exchanged as part of the war's first prisoner exchange. Even as a prisoner Mosby spied on his enemy. During a brief stopover at Fort Monroe he detected an unusual buildup of shipping in Hampton Roads and learned they were carrying thousands of troops under Ambrose Burnside from North Carolina on their way to reinforce John Pope in the Northern Virginia Campaign. When he was released, Mosby walked to the army headquarters outside Richmond and personally related his findings to Robert E. Lee.[18]

After the Battle of Fredericksburg, in December 1862, Mosby and his senior officer J .E. B. Stuart led raids behind Union lines in Prince William, Fairfax and Loudoun counties, seeking to disrupt federal communications and supplies between Washington D.C., and Fredericksburg, as well as provision their own forces. As the year ended, at Oakham Farm in Loudoun County, Virginia Mosby gathered with various horsemen from Middleburg, Virginia who decided to form what became known as Mosby's Rangers.[19]

## 1863

In January 1863, Stuart, with Lee's concurrence, authorized Mosby to form and take command of the 43rd Battalion Virginia Cavalry. This was later expanded into Mosby's Command, a regimental-sized unit of partisan rangers operating in Northern Virginia. The 43rd Battalion operated officially as a unit of the Army of Northern Virginia, subject to the commands of Lee and Stuart, but its men (1,900 of whom served from January 1863 through April 1865) lived outside of the norms of regular army cavalrymen. The Confederate government certified special rules to govern the conduct of partisan rangers. These included sharing in the disposition of spoils of war. They had no camp duties and lived scattered among the civilian population. Mosby required proof from any volunteer that he had not deserted from the regular service, and only about 10 percent of his men had served previously in the Confederate Army.[20]

In March 1863, Mosby conducted a daring raid far inside Union lines near the Fairfax County courthouse—helped according to his own account by a deserter from the 5th New York Cavalry regiment named James Ames—who served under Mosby until he

*Mosby's Rangers - Top row (left to right): Lee Herverson, Ben Palmer, John Puryear, Tom Booker, Norman Randolph, Frank Raham. # Second row: Robert Blanks Parrott, John Troop, John W. Munson, John S. Mosby, Newell, Neely, Quarles. # Third row: Walter Gosden, Harry T. Sinnott, Butler, Gentry.*

*Edwin H. Stoughton.*

was killed in 1864.[21][22] He and his men captured three Union officers, including Brig. Gen. Edwin H. Stoughton. Mosby wrote in his memoirs that he found Stoughton in bed and roused him with a "spank on his bare back." [23][24] Upon being so rudely awakened the general indignantly asked what this meant. Mosby quickly asked if he had ever heard of "Mosby." The general replied, "Yes, have you caught him?" "I *am* Mosby," the Confederate ranger said. "Stuart's cavalry has possession of the Court House; be quick and dress." Mosby and his 29 men had captured a Union general, two captains, 30 enlisted men, and 58 horses without firing a shot.[25][26] Mosby was formally promoted to the rank of captain two days later, on March 15, 1863, and major on March 26, 1863.[27] On May 3, 1863, Mosby attacked and captured supply depot Warrenton Junction, Virginia guarded by about 80 men of the 1st West Virginia Volunteer Cavalry Regiment; Mosby losses were 1 killed and 20 wounded/and or captured; Union losses were 6 officers and 14 privates killed and wounded.[28] On May 29, 1863, Mosby with 40 men [29] led a raid in Greenwich, Virginia derailing a supply train; a battle occurred between Mosby forces and the Union Cavalry under Colonel Mann who commanded the 1st Vermont Cavalry; 5th New York Cavalry; 7th Michigan Cavalry. Mosby forces were obliged to retreat losing 6 killed; 20 wounded and 10 men and 1 howitzer captured; Union losses were 4 killed and 15 wounded.[30] On June 10, 1863, Mosby led 100 men on a raid across the Potomac River to attack the Union camp at Seneca, Maryland. After routing a company of the Sixth Michigan Cavalry and burning their camp, Mosby reported the success to J .E. B. Stuart. This drew Stuart's attention to Rowser's Ford. Mosby had crossed the Potomac there, and during the night of June 27 Stuart's forces would use the same crossing while separated from Lee's army, and thus didn't arrive at Gettysburg until the afternoon of the second day of the battle. Thus, some analysts claim Lee stumbled into the battle without his cavalry, partly because of Mosby's successful skirmish at Seneca three weeks earlier.[31]

Mosby endured his first serious wound of the war on August 24, 1863, during a skirmish near Annandale, Virginia, when a bullet hit him through his thigh and side. He retired from the field with his troops and returned to action a month later.[32]

## 1864

The partisan rangers proved controversial among Confederate army regulars, who thought they encouraged desertion as well as morale problems in the countryside as potential soldiers would favor sleeping in their own (or friendly) beds and capturing booty to the hardships and privations of traditional military campaigns. Mosby was thus enrolled in the Provisional Army of the Confederate States and soon promoted to lieutenant colonel on January 21, 1864, and to colonel, December 7, 1864.[27] Mosby carefully screened potential recruits, and required each to bring his own horse.

The *Personal Memoirs of Ulysses S. Grant* tell of an incident near Warrenton, Virginia on about May 1, 1864, when Mosby unknowingly missed by only a few minutes a chance to kill or capture Grant, who was traveling unguarded on a special train from Washington back to his headquarters to launch the Overland Campaign.

Mosby endured a second serious wound on September 14, 1864, while taunting a Union regiment by riding back and forth in front of it. A Union bullet shattered the handle of his revolver before entering his groin. Barely staying on his horse to make his escape, he resorted to crutches during a quick recovery and returned to command three weeks later.[33]

Mosby's successful disruption of supply lines, attrition of Union couriers, and disappearance in the disguise of civilians caused Lt. Gen. Ulysses S. Grant to tell Maj. Gen. Philip Sheridan:

> The families of most of Mosby's men are know[n] and can be collected. I think they should be taken and kept at Fort McHenry or some secure place as hostages for good conduct of Mosby and his men. When any of them are caught with nothing to designate what they are hang them without trial.[34]

On September 22, 1864, Union forces executed six of Mosby's men who had been captured out of uniform (i.e. as spies) in Front Royal, Virginia; a seventh (captured, according to Mosby's subsequent letter to Sheridan, "by a Colonel Powell on a plundering expedition into Rappahannock") was reported by Mosby to have suffered a similar fate.[35] William Thomas Overby was one of the men selected for execution on the hill in Front Royal. His captors offered to spare him if he would reveal Mosby's location, but he refused. According to reports at the time, his last words were, "My last moments are sweetened by the reflection that for every man you murder this day Mosby will take a tenfold vengeance."[36] After the executions a Union soldier pinned a piece of paper to one of the bodies that read: "This shall be the fate of all Mosby's men."[37]

After informing General Robert E. Lee and Confederate Secretary of War James A.

*Captain Montjoy, wood engraving 1867*[38]

Seddon of his intention to respond in kind, Mosby ordered seven Union prisoners, chosen by lot, to be executed in retaliation on November 6, 1864, at Rectortown, Virginia. Although seven men were duly chosen in the original "death lottery," in the end just three men were actually executed. One numbered lot fell to a drummer boy who was excused because of his age, and Mosby's men held a second drawing for a man to take his place. Then, on the way to the place of execution a prisoner recognized Masonic regalia on the uniform of Confederate Captain Montjoy, a recently inducted Freemason then returning from a raid. The condemned captive gave him a secret Masonic distress signal. Captain Montjoy substituted one of his own prisoners for his fellow Mason[39] (though one source speaks of *two* Masons being substituted).[40] Mosby upbraided Montjoy, stating that his command was "not a Masonic lodge." The soldiers charged with carrying out the executions of the revised group of seven successfully hanged three men. They shot two more in the head and left them for dead (remarkably, both survived). The other two condemned men managed to escape separately.[41]

On November 11, 1864, Mosby wrote to Philip Sheridan, the commander of Union forces in the Shenandoah Valley, requesting that both sides resume treating prisoners with humanity. He pointed out that he and his men had captured and returned far more of Sheridan's men than they had lost.[42] The Union side complied. With both camps treating prisoners as "prisoners of war" for the duration, there were no more executions.

On November 18, 1864, Mosby's command defeated Blazer's Scouts at the Battle of Kabletown.[43]

Mosby had his closest brush with death on December 21, 1864, near Rector's Crossroads in Virginia. While dining with a local family, Mosby was fired on through a window, and the ball entered his abdomen two inches below the navel.[32] He managed to stagger into the bedroom and hide his coat, which had his only insignia of rank. The commander of the Union detachment, Maj. Douglas Frazar of the 13th New York Cavalry, entered the house and—not knowing Mosby's identity—inspected the wound and pronounced it mortal. Although left for dead, Mosby recovered and returned to the war effort once again two months later.[44]

## 1865

Several weeks after General Robert E. Lee's surrender, Mosby's status was uncertain, as some posters above the signature of Gen. Winfield S. Hancock stated that marauding bands would be destroyed and specifically named Mosby as a guerrilla chief and not included in the parole, although Mosby received a copy on April 12 at a letter drop in the Valley along with a letter from Hancock's chief of staff, Gen. C.H. Morgan, calling on Mosby to surrender and promising the same terms as extended to Gen. Lee. Further negotiations followed, at Winchester and Millwood. Finally, on April 21, 1865, in Salem, Virginia, Mosby disbanded the rangers, and on the following day many former rangers rode their worst horses to Winchester to surrender, receive paroles and return to their homes.[45]

Mosby instead rode south with several officers, planning to fight with General Joseph E. Johnston's army in North Carolina. However, before he reached his fellow Confederates, he read a newspaper article about Johnston's surrender. Some proposed that they return to Richmond and capture the Union officers who were occupying the White House of the Confederacy, but Mosby rejected the plan, telling them, "Too late! It would be murder and highway robbery now. We are soldiers, not highwaymen."[46] By early May, Mosby confirmed the $5,000 bounty on his head, but still managed to evade capture, including at a raid near Lynchburg, Virginia which terrified his mother. When Mosby finally confirmed the arrest order had been rescinded, he surrendered on June 17, one of the last Confederate officers to do so.[47][48]

## Later life

Blind in one eye and cantankerous, he spent his final years in Washington, D.C., living in a boardinghouse and watched over by his remaining daughters to the extent he would let them or others.

Mosby also continued writing about his wartime exploits, as he had been in 1887 *Mosby's War Reminiscences and Stuart's Cavalry Campaigns*, which had defended the reputation of J .E. B. Stuart, who some partisans of the "Lost Cause" blamed for the Confederacy's defeat at the Battle of Gettysburg. Mosby had served under Stuart and was fiercely loyal to the late general, writing, "He made me all that I was in the war. . . . But for his friendship I would never have been heard of." He lectured in New England in connection with that first book and wrote numerous articles for popular publications. He published a book length treatise in 1908, a work that relied on his skills as a lawyer to refute categorically all of the claims laid against Stuart. A recent comprehensive study of the Stuart controversy, written by Eric J. Wittenberg and J. David Petruzzi, called Mosby's work a *"tour de force."*[71]

He attended only one reunion of his Rangers, in Alexandria, Virginia, in January 1895, noticing with bemusement how many had become clergymen but preferring to look forward not back.[72] During the war, he had kept a slave, Aaron Burton, to whom he occasionally sent money in Brooklyn, New York after the war and with whom he kept in contact into the 1890s.[73] In 1894, Mosby wrote to a former comrade regarding the cause of the war, stating: "I've always understood that we went to war on account of the thing we quarreled with the North about. I've never heard of any other cause than slavery."[74][75][76]

In June 1907, Mosby wrote a letter to Samuel "Sam" Chapman, in which he expressed his displeasure over people, namely George Christian, downplaying and denying the importance of slavery in its causing the American Civil War. In the letter, Mosby explained his reasons as to why he fought for the Confederacy, despite personally disapproving of slavery. While he admitted that the Confederate states had seceded to protect and defend their institution of slavery, he had felt it was his patriotic duty as a Virginian to fight on behalf of the Confederacy, stating that "I am not ashamed of having fought on the side of slavery—a soldier fights for his country—right or wrong—he is not responsible for the political merits of the course he fights in" and that "The South was my country."[77][78]

## Death and legacy

In January 1915 the University of Virginia awarded Mosby a medal and written tribute, which touched him deeply. Throughout his life, Mosby remained loyal to those he believed fair-minded, such as Stuart and Grant, but refused to cater to Southern sympathies. He proclaimed that there was "no man in the Confederate Army who had less of the spirit of knight-errantry in him, or took a more practical view of war than I did."[76] He died of complications after throat surgery in a Washington, D.C. hospital on May 30, 1916, noting at the end that it was Memorial Day. He is buried at the Warrenton Cemetery in Warrenton, Virginia.[27]

# Samuel Mudd

**Samuel Alexander Mudd** (December 20, 1833–January 10, 1883) was an American physician who was imprisoned for conspiring with John Wilkes Booth in the assassination of President Abraham Lincoln.

Working as a doctor and tobacco farmer in Southern Maryland, Mudd was a Democrat and declared his belief in slavery as a God-given institution. The Civil War seriously damaged his business, especially when Maryland abolished slavery in 1864. That year, he first met Booth, who was planning to kidnap Lincoln, and Mudd was seen in company with three of the conspirators. However, his part in the plot, if any, remains unclear.

After mortally wounding Lincoln on April 14, 1865, Booth rode with conspirator David Herold to Mudd's home in the early hours of April 15 for surgery on his fractured leg before he crossed into Virginia. Sometime that day, Mudd must have learned of the assassination but did not report Booth's visit to the authorities for another 24 hours. That appeared to link him to the crime, as did his various changes of story under interrogation. A military commission found him guilty of aiding and conspiring in a murder, and he was sentenced to life imprisonment, escaping the death penalty by a single vote.

Mudd was pardoned by President Andrew Johnson and released from prison in 1869. Despite repeated attempts by family members and others to have it expunged, his conviction has not been overturned.

## Early years

Born in Charles County, Maryland, Mudd was the fourth of 10 children of Henry Lowe and Sarah Ann Reeves Mudd. He grew up on Oak Hill, his father's tobacco plantation of several hundred acres, 30 miles (48 km) southeast of Washington, DC, and worked by 89 slaves.[1][2]

At 15, after several years of home tutoring, Mudd went off to boarding school at St. John's Literary Institute, now known as Saint John's Catholic Prep School in Frederick, Maryland. Two years later, he enrolled at Georgetown College in Washington, DC. He then studied medicine at the University of Maryland, Baltimore, writing his thesis on dysentery.

Upon graduation in 1856, Mudd returned to Charles County to practice medicine, marrying his childhood sweetheart, Sarah Frances (Frankie) Dyer Mudd one year later.[3]

As a wedding present, Mudd's father gave the couple 218 acres (0.88 km²) of his best farmland and a new house named St. Catherine. While the house was under construction,

the young Mudds lived with Frankie's bachelor brother, Jeremiah Dyer, finally moving into their new home in 1859. They had nine children in all: four before Mudd's arrest and five after his release from prison.[4] To supplement his income from his medical practice, Mudd became a small scale tobacco grower, using five slaves according to the 1860 census.
[5] Mudd believed that slavery was divinely ordained and wrote a letter to the theologian Orestes Brownson to that effect.[6]

With the advent of the American Civil War in 1861, the Southern Maryland slave system and the economy that it supported rapidly began to collapse. In 1863, the Union Army established Camp Stanton, just 10 miles (16 km) from the Mudd farm to enlist black freedmen and runaway slaves. Six regiments totaling over 8,700 black soldiers, many from Southern Maryland, were trained there. In 1864, Maryland, which was exempt from Lincoln's 1863 Emancipation Proclamation, abolished slavery, making it difficult for growers like Mudd to operate their plantations. As a result, Mudd considered selling his farm and depending on his medical practice. As Mudd pondered his alternatives, he was introduced to someone who said he might be interested in buying his property, a 26-year-old actor, John Wilkes Booth.

## Booth connection

*Lincoln's assassin, John Wilkes Booth*

Many historians agree that President Abraham Lincoln's future assassin, John Wilkes Booth, visited Bryantown, Maryland, in November and December 1864, claiming to look for real estate investments. Bryantown is about 25 miles (40 km) from Washington, DC, and about 5 miles (8.0 km) from Mudd's farm. The real estate story was merely a cover; Booth's true purpose was to plan an escape route as part of a plan to kidnap Lincoln. Booth believed the federal government would ransom Lincoln by releasing a large number of Confederate prisoners of war.

Historians agree that Booth met Mudd at St. Mary's Catholic Church in Bryantown during one of those visits, probably in November. Booth visited Mudd at his farm the next day, and stayed there overnight. The following day, Booth purchased a horse from Mudd's neighbor and returned to Washington. Some historians[7] believe that Booth used his visit to Bryantown to recruit Mudd to his kidnapping plot, but others believe that Mudd would have had no interest in such a scheme.

A short time later, on December 23, 1864, Mudd went to Washington where he met Booth again. Some historians believe the meeting had been arranged, but others disagree. The two men, as well as John Surratt, Jr., and Louis J. Weichmann, had a conversation and drinks together, first at Booth's hotel and later at Mudd's.

According to a statement made by associated conspirator George Atzerodt, found long after his death and taken down while he was in federal custody on May 1, 1865, Mudd knew in advance about Booth's plans; Atzerodt was sure the doctor knew, he said, because Booth had "sent (as he told me) liquors & provisions . . . about two weeks before the murder to Dr. Mudd's."[8]

Although that is true, some historians believe that there may be other reasons behind Mudd's relationship to Booth. The trial brought forth many theories of Mudd's involvement in the assassination of Lincoln. One theory posits that Mudd was involved in a completely different conspiracy to gain an upper hand for the southern states. Prior to the assassination of Lincoln, Booth originally intended to kidnap the president and hold him and other political affiliates of the Union for a large sum of money.[9] The plan was in effect until the night of the assassination, when Booth met up with Atzerodt, David Herold and Lewis Powell (who gave his name as Lewis Payne when he was arrested at Mary Surratt's house days after the murder)[10] and disclosed the plot to assassinate the president.[9] Following the assassination, Powell came forth by stating that Booth had not told him until the meeting and that the other men did not know about the plot until the night of the assassination.[9] That supports the theory that Mudd may have been an accomplice to the plot to kidnap the president but not a conspirator to the assassination.

After Booth shot Lincoln on April 14, 1865, he broke his left fibula while fleeing Ford's Theater. Booth met up with Herold and both made for Virginia, via southern Maryland. They stopped at Mudd's house around 4 a.m. on April 15. Mudd splinted Booth's leg. He also arranged for a carpenter, John Best, to make a pair of crutches for Booth, and gave him a shoe to wear.[8] Booth paid Mudd $25 in greenbacks for his services. He and Herold spent between twelve and fifteen hours at Mudd's house. They slept in the front bedroom on the second floor. It is unclear whether Mudd had yet been informed that Booth had killed Lincoln.

Mudd went to Bryantown during the day on April 15 to run errands; if he did not already know the news of the assassination from Booth, he certainly learned of it on the trip. He returned home that evening, and accounts differ as to whether Booth and Herold had already left, whether Mudd met them as they were leaving, and whether they left at Mudd's urging and with his assistance.

It is certain that Mudd did not immediately contact the authorities. When questioned, he stated that he had not wanted to leave his family alone in the house in case the assassins returned and found him absent and his family unprotected. He waited until Mass the following day, Easter Sunday, when he asked his second cousin, Dr. George Mudd, a resident of Bryantown, to notify the 13th New York Cavalry in Bryantown, under the command of Lieutenant David Dana. The delay in contacting the authorities drew suspicion and was a significant factor in tying Mudd to the conspiracy.

During his initial investigative interview on April 18, Mudd stated that he had never seen either of the parties before.[11][12] In his sworn statement of April 22, he told about Booth's visit to Bryantown in November 1864 but then said, "I have never seen Booth since that time to my knowledge until last Saturday morning."[13] He hid his meeting with Booth in Washington in December 1864. In prison, Mudd admitted the Washington meeting and said he ran into Booth by chance during a Christmas shopping trip. Mudd's failure to mention the meeting in his interview with detectives was a big mistake. When Weichmann later told the authorities of the meeting, they realized that Mudd had misled them and immediately began to treat him as a suspect, rather than a witness.

During the conspiracy trial, Lieutenant Alexander Lovett testified, "On Friday, the 21st of April, I went to Mudd's again, for the purpose of arresting him. When he found we were going to search the house, he said something to his wife, and she went upstairs and brought down a boot. Mudd said he had cut it off the man's leg. I turned down the top of the boot, and saw the name 'J. Wilkes' written in it."[14]

## Trial

After Booth's death on April 26, 1865, Mudd was arrested and charged with conspiracy to murder Lincoln. Representative Frederick Stone was the senior defense counsel for Mudd.[15]

On May 1, 1865, President Johnson ordered the formation of a nine-man military commission to try the conspirators. Mudd was represented by General Thomas Ewing, Jr.. The trial began on May 10, 1865. Mary Surratt, Lewis Powell, George Atzerodt, David Herold, Samuel Mudd, Michael O'Laughlen, Edmund Spangler and Samuel Arnold were all charged with conspiring to murder Lincoln.[16] The prosecution called 366 witnesses.[17]

The defense sought to prove that Mudd was a loyal citizen, citing his self-description as a "Union man" and asserting that he was "a deeply religious man, devoted to family, and a kind master to his slaves."[17] The prosecution presented witnesses who testified that he had shot one of his slaves in the leg and threatened to send others to Richmond, Virginia, to assist in the construction of Confederate defenses. The prosecution also contended that he had been a member of a Confederate communications distribution agency and had sheltered Confederate soldiers on his plantation.[17]

On June 29, 1865, Mudd was found guilty with the others. The testimony of Louis J. Weichmann was crucial in obtaining the convictions. According to historian Edward Steers, the testimony presented by former slaves was also crucial, but it faded from public memory.[17] Mudd escaped the death penalty by one vote and was sentenced to life imprisonment. Four of the defendants (Surratt, Powell, Atzerodt and Herold) were hanged at the Old Penitentiary at the Washington Arsenal on July 7, 1865.

## Imprisonment

Mudd, O'Laughlen, Arnold, and Spangler were imprisoned at Fort Jefferson, in the Dry Tortugas, about 70 miles (110 km) west of Key West, Florida. The fort housed Union Army deserters and held about 600 prisoners when Mudd and the others arrived. Prisoners lived on the second tier of the fort, in unfinished, open-air gun rooms called casemates. Mudd

*Dr. Mudd as he appeared while working in the carpenter's shop in the prison at Fort Jefferson, circa 1866–1867.*

and his three companions lived in the casemate directly above the fort's main entrance, called the sally port.

In September 1865, two months after Mudd arrived, the control of Fort Jefferson was transferred from the 161st New York Volunteer Infantry Regiment to the 82nd US Colored Troops. On September 25, 1865, he attempted to escape from Fort Jefferson by stowing away on the transport *Thomas A. Scott*.[18]

He was quickly discovered and placed, along with Arnold, O'Laughlen, Spangler, and George St. Leger Grenfell, in a large empty ground-level gunroom that soldiers referred to as "the dungeon." The men were let out of the dungeon every working day for 12 hours and were required to wear leg irons. However, following a December 22 letter from his wife to President Johnson, the War Department ordered the discontinuance of the shackles and the move to better quarters, which was accomplished by January.[18]:88–89,95–99,101,103

After three months in the dungeon, Mudd and the others were returned to the general prison population. However, because of his attempted escape, Mudd lost his privilege of working in the prison hospital and was assigned to work in the prison carpentry shop with Spangler.

There was an outbreak of yellow fever in the fall of 1867 at the fort. O'Laughlen eventually died of it on September 23. The prison doctor died, and Mudd agreed to take over the position. He was able to help stem the spread of the disease. The soldiers in the fort wrote a petition to Johnson in October 1867 stating the degree of Mudd's assistance: "He inspired the hopeless with courage and by his constant presence in the midst of danger and infection . . . . [Many] doubtless owe their lives to the care and treatment they received at his hands."[19] Probably as a reward for his work in the yellow fever epidemic, Mudd was reassigned from the carpentry shop to a clerical job in the Provost Marshal's office, where he remained until his pardon.

## Later life

The influence of his defense attorney, Thomas Ewing Jr., who was also influential in the President's administration, was one reason why Mudd was pardoned by Johnson on February 8, 1869. He was released from prison on March 8, 1869, and returned to his home in Maryland on March 20, 1869.[20] On March 2, 1869, three weeks after he pardoned Mudd, Johnson also pardoned Spangler and Arnold.[21]

When Mudd returned home, well-wishing friends and strangers, as well as inquiring newspaper reporters, besieged him. Mudd was very reluctant to talk to the press because he felt it had misquoted him in the past. He gave one interview to the *New York Herald* after his release but immediately regretted it and complained that the article had several factual errors and misrepresented his work during the yellow fever epidemic. On the whole, though, Mudd continued to enjoy the support of his friends and neighbors. He resumed his medical practice and slowly brought the family farm back to productivity.

## Death

Mudd was just 49 years old when he died of pneumonia, on January 10, 1883, and was buried in the cemetery at St. Mary's Catholic Church in Bryantown, the same church in which he once met Booth.[20]:326

# John Frederick Parker

**John Frederick Parker** (May 19, 1830–June 28, 1890) was an American police officer for the Metropolitan Police Department of the District of Columbia. Parker was one of four men detailed to act as United States President Abraham Lincoln's bodyguard on April 14, 1865, the night Lincoln was assassinated at Ford's Theatre.

## Biographic Information

Parker was born in 1830, in Virginia.[1][2] No government or bible record regarding Parker's specific birth date or more specific birth location other than Virginia has been published in government records. By 1855, Parker had moved to Washington, District of Columbia, where he married Mary L.C. Maus on July 16, 1855.[3] U.S. Census population schedules reflect that he lived in the District of Columbia in 1860, 1870, and 1880.[4][5][6] U.S. Census Records for 1890, which began shortly before Parker's death are incomplete, as a result of a fire, and he does not appear in remaining incomplete records.

## Career

He moved to Washington, D.C., where he worked as a carpenter. He became one of Washington's original police officers when the Metropolitan Police Department of the District of Columbia was created in 1861.[7]

During his time as an officer, he was charged with dereliction of duty and conduct unbecoming an officer several times for being drunk on duty, sleeping on streetcars while at work, and visiting a brothel (Parker claimed the madam had sent for him). Parker was typically reprimanded for these acts but never fired.[7]

## Lincoln's assassination

On April 14, 1865, President Lincoln, his wife Mary Todd Lincoln, Major Henry Rathbone and his fiancée Clara Harris were attending the play *Our American Cousin* at Ford's Theatre. Parker was assigned to guard the entrance to the President's box where the four were seated. He is known to have, at first, stayed at his assigned post, but he later told family members that he was then released by Lincoln until the end of the play. During the intermission, Parker went to a nearby tavern with Lincoln's valet and coachman.[7]

It is unclear whether Parker ever returned to the theater, but he was not at his post when John Wilkes Booth shot the President. Parker was charged with neglect of duty and tried on May 3, 1865, but no transcripts of the case were kept. The complaint was dismissed on June 2, 1865. Despite leaving his post the night Lincoln was shot, Parker was still assigned to work security at the White House. Before Mary Todd Lincoln moved out of the White House following her husband's death, Parker was assigned as her bodyguard. Mrs. Lincoln's dressmaker Elizabeth Keckley overheard Mrs. Lincoln yell to Parker, "So you are on guard tonight, on guard in the White House after helping to murder the

President."[8] Parker attempted to defend himself stating that he "could never stoop to murder much less to the murder of so good and great a man as the President. I did wrong, I admit, and have bitterly repented." Mrs. Lincoln told Parker that she would always think he was responsible for the President's death and angrily dismissed him from the room.[8]

## Later years and death

Parker remained on the police force until 1868 when he was fired for sleeping on duty. He later went back to work as a carpenter.[8]

He died of pneumonia complicated by asthma and exhaustion in Washington, D.C., on June 28, 1890. He was buried in an unmarked grave at Glenwood Cemetery.[9] His widow, Mary America Maus, was buried next to him upon her death in 1904 as were their three children. There are no known images of him and his grave is unmarked to signify his contribution to the president's death.[8]

# J. Johnston Pettigrew

**James Johnston Pettigrew** (July 4, 1828–July 17, 1863) was an author, lawyer, linguist, diplomat, and soldier. As a Confederate general in the American Civil War, he was one of three division commanders in the disastrous assault known as Pickett's Charge on the final day of the Battle of Gettysburg. He was badly wounded during the assault and killed by a Union attack during the Confederate retreat to Virginia.

## Civil War

When war began, Pettigrew joined the Hampton Legion, a force raised in South Carolina by Wade Hampton, as a private, although he quickly accepted a commission as colonel of the 1st South Carolina Rifle Militia Regiment. He returned to North Carolina to command the 12th (later renamed the 22nd) North Carolina Infantry. Both Jefferson Davis and Gen. Joseph E. Johnston urged him to accept higher command, but he declined because of his lack of military experience. However, as the need for qualified officers in the Confederate States Army became acute, the new colonel was soon ordered to Virginia to accept a promotion to brigadier general on February 26, 1862.

When a young relative requested a "safe place" on Pettigrew's staff, he replied: "I assure you that the most unsafe place in the Brigade is about me. By all means let him get rid of this idea of a safe place, which he will regret after time. The post of danger is certainly the post of honor." He was true to his word.

## Peninsula Campaign

During the Peninsula Campaign in the summer of 1862, Pettigrew was severely wounded at the Battle of Seven Pines. He was hit by a Minié ball that damaged his throat, windpipe, and shoulder. Pettigrew nearly bled to death, and while lying wounded, he received another bullet wound in the arm and was bayoneted in the right leg. Believing his wounds mortal, Pettigrew did not permit any of his men to leave the ranks to carry him to the rear. Left for dead on the field, he recovered consciousness as a Union prisoner of war. [2] Exchanged two months later, the general recovered from his wounds, spent the fall commanding a brigade in Maj. Gen. Daniel Harvey Hill's division around Richmond, and in the winter commanded a brigade in North Carolina and southern Virginia. He returned to his North Carolina brigade just in time to begin the Gettysburg Campaign in June 1863.

## Gettysburg Campaign

The Confederate War Department had assigned Pettigrew's Brigade to Gen. Robert E. Lee's Army of Northern Virginia, and Pettigrew traveled to Fredericksburg, Virginia, to rejoin that army in late May. Pettigrew's Brigade was the strongest in Maj. Gen. Henry Heth's Division of Lt. Gen. A.P. Hill's Third Corps. Freshly uniformed and armed with rifles from state military depots, his regiments presented a fine military appearance during the march through Maryland and Pennsylvania. Some of his regimental officers were also members of the North Carolina planter "aristocracy," including Colonel Collett Leventhorpe leading the 11th North Carolina Infantry and twenty-one-year-old Harry Burgwyn at the head of the 26th North Carolina Regiment, the largest Confederate regiment at Gettysburg. Not having been in serious combat for nearly a year, his brigade mustered a strength over 2,500 officers and men.[3]

Pettigrew's Brigade tangled with the Iron Brigade on July 1, 1863, at the McPherson and Herbst farms to the west of Gettysburg, where all four of his regiments suffered devastating losses—over 40 percent—but were successful in driving the Union forces off of McPherson's Ridge.[3] General Pettigrew assumed command of the division after the wounding of Gen. Heth that afternoon, and attempted to reorganize the battered division during the next day's battle as they lay behind Seminary Ridge.

On July 3, 1863, Gen. Lee selected Pettigrew's division to march at the left of Maj. Gen. George Pickett's in the famous infantry assault popularly known as Pickett's Charge (sometimes called "Longstreet's Assault" or the "Pickett-Pettigrew-Trimble Assault," since Pickett led only one third of the men engaged in the attack). Lee had not consulted with Pettigrew beforehand and was unaware of the terrible condition of Pettigrew's division.

As the division advanced, it received murderous fire. After Pettigrew's horse was shot out from under him, he continued on foot. As he approached within 100 yards (90 meters) of the stone wall on Cemetery Ridge (which was partially held by his cousin John Gibbon, leading Second Division of the Union II Corps), he was severely wounded in the left hand by canister fire. Despite being in great pain, Pettigrew remained with his soldiers until it was obvious that the attack had failed. Holding his bloody hand, as Pettigrew was retreating towards Seminary Ridge, he encountered General Lee. Pettigrew attempted to speak, but Lee, seeing the wound, spoke first: "General, I am sorry to see you are wounded; go to the rear." With a painful salute, Pettigrew continued to the rear.

During the Confederate retreat from Gettysburg, Pettigrew remained in command until Heth recovered. Stopped by the flooded Potomac River at Falling Waters, West Virginia, Pettigrew's brigade was deployed in a dense skirmish line on the Maryland side, in order to protect the road to the river crossing. Union cavalry probed the southern defenses throughout the night as Lee's army crossed the pontoon bridges into West Virginia. On the morning of July 14, 1863, Pettigrew's brigade was one of the last Confederate units still north of the Potomac River when the Union attacked his position. On foot and in the front line, Pettigrew was directing his soldiers when he was shot by a Union cavalryman from the Michigan Brigade at close range, the bullet striking him in the abdomen. He was immediately carried to the rear and across the Potomac, having refused to be left in federal hands. He died three days later at Edgewood Manor plantation near Bunker Hill, West Virginia.[4] His brigade, which lost an estimated 56 percent casualties, had been ruined as an effective combat organization.[5]

# George Pickett

**George Edward Pickett** (January 16,[1] 1825–July 30, 1875) was a career United States Army officer who became a major general in the Confederate States Army during the American Civil War. He is best remembered for leading Pickett's Charge, the futile and bloody Confederate offensive on the third day of the Battle of Gettysburg that bears his name.

Pickett graduated last out of 59 cadets in the United States Military Academy class of 1846. He served as a second lieutenant in the United States Army during the Mexican–American War and is noted for his service in the Battle of Chapultepec in September 1847. After this, he served in the Washington Territory and eventually reached the rank of captain. Pickett participated in the Pig War of 1859. Near the beginning of the American Civil War, he commissioned in the Confederate States Army, and he attained the rank of brigadier general in January 1862. He commanded a brigade that saw heavy action during the Peninsula Campaign of 1862. Pickett was wounded at the Battle of Gaines's Mill on June 27.

He did not return to command until September, following the Battle of Antietam, when he was given command of a division in the Right Wing of the Army of Northern Virginia, in the command of Major General James Longstreet, which became the I Corps that December. His division was lightly engaged at the Battle of Fredericksburg and, along with most of Longstreet's Corps, missed the Battle of Chancellorsville while participating in the Suffolk Campaign in 1863. During the Gettysburg Campaign, his division was, much to Pickett's frustration, the last to arrive on the field. However, it was one of three divisions under the command of General Longstreet to participate in a disastrous assault on Union positions on July 3, the final day of the battle. The attack has been given the name "Pickett's Charge." In February 1864, Pickett ordered 22 North Carolinians in Union uniform hanged as deserters, after a failed assault on New Berne. Brigadier General John Peck sent Pickett a note telling him the men were US soldiers and should be treated as prisoners of war. Pickett thanked him for giving him the names, as he now knew who he was hanging. His military career came to an inglorious end when his division was overwhelmed and defeated at the Battle of Five Forks.

Following the war, Pickett feared prosecution for his execution of deserters and temporarily fled to Canada. An old Army friend, Ulysses S. Grant, interceded on his behalf, and he returned to Virginia in 1866. He could not rejoin the Army, so he tried his hand at farming, then selling insurance. He died at age 50 in July 1875 from an "abscess of the liver."[2]

# Civil War

## *Early assignments*

On April 19, after the firing on Battle of Fort Sumter and in response to President Lincoln's call for 75,000 volunteers to suppress the rebellion, Virginia joined three more Southern states in seceding from the Union.[24] Native son Pickett sailed from San Juan Island to Bellingham, Washington to resign his commission and was told by his commander that he had to resign it in Washington, D.C. To accomplish this he sailed to Fort Steilacoom, south of Tacoma, Washington and caught transport aboard a mail steamer to the Isthmus of Panama, trekked 40 miles overland to Colon, caught another ship to Richmond, Virginia to obtain a commission in the Army of Northern Virginia, and then to Washington, D.C. to turn in his resignation. Arriving after the First Battle of Bull Run, he resigned his commission in the U.S. Army on June 25, 1861; he had been holding a commission as a major in the Confederate States Army Artillery since March 16.[4] Within a month he was appointed colonel in command of the Rappahannock Line of the Department of Fredericksburg, Virginia, under the command of Major General Theophilus H. Holmes. Holmes's influence obtained a commission for Pickett as a brigadier general, dated January 14, 1862.[4][25]

*Confederate Major General George E. Pickett*

Pickett made a colorful general. He rode a sleek black charger named "Old Black," and wore a small blue kepi-style cap, with buffed gloves over the sleeves of an immaculately tailored uniform that had a double row of gold buttons on the coat, and shiny gold spurs on his highly polished boots. He held an elegant riding crop whether mounted or walking. His moustache drooped gracefully beyond the corners of his mouth and then turned upward at the ends. His hair was the talk of the Army: "long ringlets flowed loosely over his shoulders, trimmed and highly perfumed, his beard likewise was curling and giving up the scent of Araby."[26]

Pickett's first combat command was during the Peninsula Campaign, leading a brigade that was nicknamed the Gamecocks (the brigade would eventually be led by Richard B. Garnett in Pickett's Charge). Pickett led his brigade ably in the battles of Williamsburg and Seven Pines, earning commendations from his superiors. At Gaines's Mill on June 27 he was shot off his horse while leading his brigade in its first assault.[27] Pickett continued to move forward with his men for a while, leading his horse on foot. A second assault by Pickett's brigade, led by Colonel Eppa Hunton, along with the brigade led by Cadmus M. Wilcox, broke the Union line. Pickett feared that he had taken a mortal blow to his shoulder, but the wound was initially assessed by others as minor.[28] The shoulder wound turned out to be severe enough that, while not fatal, Pickett was out of action for the next three months, and his arm would remain stiff for at least a year.[29]

When Pickett returned to the Army in September 1862, following the Battle of Antietam, he was given command of a two-brigade division in the corps commanded by his old colleague from Mexico, Major General Longstreet. Pickett was promoted to major general on October 10. Shortly afterwards his division was upgraded to five brigades, commanded by Generals Garnett, James L. Kemper, Lewis Armistead, Montgomery Dent Corse and Micah Jenkins. The division was only lightly engaged at the Battle of Fredericksburg in December.[30] His division would not see serious combat until the Gettysburg Campaign the following summer.

## Suffolk and courtship

Longstreet and two of his divisions—those commanded by Pickett and John Bell Hood—were detached from Lee's main army in April while participating in the Suffolk Campaign. They thus missed the Battle of Chancellorsville. The Suffolk Campaign was minor and inconclusive, while the Battle of Chancellorsville was an enormous Confederate victory.[31]

Before the Gettysburg Campaign, Pickett fell in love with a Virginia teenager, LaSalle "Sallie" Corbell (1843–1931), commuting back and forth from his duties in Suffolk to be with her. Although Sallie would later insist that she met him in 1852 (at age 9), she did not marry the 38-year-old widower until November 13, 1863. The couple had two children, George Edward Pickett, Jr. (born July 17, 1864)[32] and David Corbell Pickett (born 1865 or 1866).[33] David died in late 1873 or January 1874[34] of measles.[35]

At Suffolk, Longstreet grew impatient with Pickett's frequent trips away from his division to see Sallie at her home in nearby Chuckatuck. Pickett then decided to ask for permission for the visits from Longstreet's chief of staff, Moxley Sorrel, who referred him to Longstreet. Instead of asking Longstreet, Pickett went without permission.[36] After the war, Sorrel commented, "I don't think his division benefitted by such carpet-knight doings in the field."[37]

## Gettysburg and Pickett's Charge

Pickett's division arrived at the Battle of Gettysburg on the evening of the second day, July 2, 1863. It was reduced to three brigades present, Corse's still being detached in Virginia and Jenkins' transferred. It had been delayed by the assignment of guarding the Confederate lines of communication through Chambersburg, Pennsylvania. After two days of heavy fighting, General Robert E. Lee's Army of Northern Virginia, which had initially driven the Union Army of the Potomac to the high ground south of Gettysburg, had been unable to dislodge the Union soldiers from their position.[38] Lee's plan for July 3 called for a massive assault on the center of the Union lines on Cemetery Ridge, calculating that Meade had concentrated his forces to protect his flanks while leaving his center weak. Lee directed General Longstreet to assemble a force of three divisions for the attack—two divisions from the corps of Lieutenant General A. P. Hill, under the temporary command of J. Johnston Pettigrew and Major General Isaac R. Trimble, which had both seen action on July 1, and Pickett's fresh division from Longstreet's own corps.[39] The center was occupied by the Union II Corps, commanded by Major General Winfield Scott Hancock. [40] Longstreet was technically in command, not Pickett. Nevertheless, the attack became known as "Pickett's Charge." In addition, much of the mythology of the Charge arose from newspaper reports. As Pickett was the only major general from Virginia to partici- pate in the charge, the Virginia newspapers both played up their native son's role and made the assault a more "glamorous" event.[41]

Following a two-hour artillery barrage meant to soften up the Union defenses, the three divisions stepped off across open fields almost a mile from Cemetery Ridge. Pickett inspired his men by shouting, "Up, Men, and to your posts! Let no man forget today that you are from Old Virginia."[42] Pickett's division, with the brigades of Brigadier Generals Armistead, Garnett, and Kemper, was on the right flank of the assault. It received pun- ishing artillery fire, and then volleys of massed musket fire as it approached its objective. Armistead's brigade made the farthest progress through the Union lines. Armistead was mortally wounded, falling near "The Angle," at what is now termed the "High Water Mark of the Confederacy." Neither of the other two divisions made comparable progress across the fields; Armistead's success was not reinforced, and his men were quickly killed or captured.[40]

Pickett's Charge was a bloodbath. While the Union suffered 1,500 casualties, the Confederates had over 6,000. Over 50 percent of the men sent across the fields were killed or wounded.[43] Pickett's division alone, out of about 5,500 men, lost 224 killed, 1,140 wounded, and 1,499 missing/captured.[44] Pickett's three brigade commanders and all thir- teen of his regimental commanders were casualties. Kemper was wounded, Garnett killed, and Armistead mortally wounded. Trimble and Pettigrew were the most senior casualties of the entire Confederate assault, the former losing a leg and the latter wounded in the hand and later mortally wounded during the retreat to Virginia. Pickett has received some historical criticism for establishing his final position well to the rear of his troops. Thomas R. Friend, who served Pickett as a courier, defended Pickett by writing that he "went as far as any Major General, Commanding a division, ought to have gone, and farther."[45]

As soldiers straggled back to the Confederate lines along Seminary Ridge, Lee feared a Union counteroffensive and tried to rally his center, telling returning soldiers that the fail- ure was "all my fault." Pickett was inconsolable. When Lee told Pickett to rally his division for the defense, Pickett allegedly replied, "General Lee, I have no division."[46] Pickett's official report for the battle has never been found. While it is rumored that Lee rejected it for its bitter negativity and demanded that it be rewritten, an updated version was never filed.[47]

## North Carolina

After the Battle of Gettysburg, Pickett commanded the Department of Southern Virginia and North Carolina. In February, Pickett was ordered to capture New Bern,

North Carolina from Federal forces. The subsequent Battle of New Bern resulted in a Confederate defeat. Following the battle, Pickett ordered the execution of 22 United States Army soldiers from North Carolina who were captured during the failed raid.[48] Confederates claimed they were merely executing deserters.[49] In fact many of the US soldiers put to death offered good evidence that they refused service in the Confederate States Army, serving only in the North Carolina home guard on the basis of refusing to take up arms against the United States.[50]

(After the war Pickett fled to Canada to escape an investigation into the executions, but he returned to the United States after being promised by General Grant, to public controversy, that he would not face prosecution.[50])

## Overland Campaign and Siege of Petersburg

Following the New Bern battle, Pickett served as a division commander in the Defenses of Richmond. After P. G. T. Beauregard bottled up Benjamin Butler in the Bermuda Hundred Campaign, Pickett's division was detached in support of Robert E. Lee's operation in the Overland Campaign, just before the Battle of Cold Harbor, in which Pickett's division occupied the center of the defensive line, a place in which the main Union attack did not occur.[51] His division participated in the Siege of Petersburg.[30]

## Battle of Five Forks

General Pickett had received orders from Robert E. Lee to, with the Cavalry divisions of Major Generals William Henry Fitzhugh Lee and Thomas L. Rosser, hold the vital railroad crossing at Five Forks at all costs. On April 1, at the Battle of Five Forks, their troops were attacked by a combined force under Major General Philip Henry Sheridan, which consisted of the V Corps of the Army of the Potomac, commanded by Major General Gouverneur K. Warren, and the Cavalry Corps of the Army, commanded by Brigadier General Wesley Merritt. Pickett, W.H.L. Lee, and Rosser were located behind the lines of their troops at the time of the attack, enjoying a shad bake while failing to inform their subordinate officers of their location. Meanwhile, Warren's troops overwhelmed Pickett's left flank, and the Cavalry troops pinned the Confederates down elsewhere. By the time the Confederate commanders realized the catastrophe, it was too late to prevent the defeat. The result of the battle, as well as that of the Third Battle of Petersburg the following day, forced Lee to abandon his entrenchments at Petersburg, leading to the capture of Richmond and surrender of his army on April 9.[52]

## Relief controversy

A controversy existed over whether or not Pickett was relieved of his command in the final days of the war. After the war, Lee's Chief of Staff, Lieutenant Colonel Walter H. Taylor, wrote that following the Battle of Sayler's Creek on April 6, 1865, he had issued orders for Lee relieving Major Generals Richard H. Anderson and Bushrod Johnson, whose forces had been lost in the battle and who thereby no longer had troops under their command. In fact, Anderson had returned to his home in South Carolina following the battle. In addition, Taylor recollected that he had issued an order relieving Pickett as well. Pickett's division was still intact, though reduced in number to about the size of a brigade.[53] No copies of these orders exist. Douglas Southall Freeman, a biographer of Lee, supported this assertion, writing in 1935 that at the same time Lee relieved Anderson of command, he took the same action regarding Pickett and Bushrod Johnson, but the order regarding Pickett apparently never reached him. As late as April 11, he signed himself, "Maj. Genl. Commdg."[54]

In contradiction to this assertion, in his 1870 book *Pickett's Men* Walter Harrison reprinted an order from Lieutenant Colonel Taylor to Pickett dated April 10, 1865, in which Taylor addressed Pickett as "Maj Gen G E Picket [*sic*], General Commanding" The order was a request for an account of the movements and actions of Pickett's Division from the time of the Battle of Five Forks on April 1 to the surrender at Appomattox on April 9. In the report Pickett submitted, he said:

> The second day after the battle referred to (Five Forks) not being able to find General Anderson's headquarters, I reported to Lieut. Gen. Longstreet, and continued to receive orders from him until the army was paroled and disbursed."[55]

Pickett's official report to Taylor was signed "G.E. Pickett, Major-Gen., Commd'g."[56] This is the April 11 report mentioned by Freeman above. Thus in Pickett's official report to Taylor he speaks of commanding his men and interacting with his superior officer right up until the surrender at Appomattox. Taylor attempted to explain the apparent contradiction by telling Fitzhugh Lee that he addressed his request in the manner he did because Pickett was not dismissed from the Army, and for the period in question, Pickett was initially in command.[57] This explanation, however, leaves unanswered the question of how Taylor expected Pickett to answer for the period of time Pickett purportedly was not in command. The explanation does not explain Pickett's report which covered the entire period, nor the fact that Pickett signed the report as the acting commander, nor did it explain Longstreet's interactions with Pickett over this period of time. Furthermore, there is no record of Taylor requesting reports from any other officers dismissed from the service on the movements of their former troops, nor of his referring to such officers in a manner which would connote active command.

The medical officer of Pickett's division, Dr. M. G. Elzey, was with Pickett at the time of these events. When an elderly Colonel John S. Mosby raised this issue in 1911, Elzey wrote a letter to the *Richmond Times-Dispatch* in answer to Mosby:

> I was General Pickett's personal medical advisor, and continued to be such until the time of his death. We rode together a greater part of the way during the retreat of our army from Petersburg to Appomattox. We escaped together from the battlefield at Sailor's Creek and were constantly together until we reached Appomattox.

I repeat it, therefore, with all confidence, that I am a competent witness to the fact that he was never under arrest, but remained in command of his Division until the last scene at Appomattox.

—M. G. Elzey[58]

In Longstreet's final report, he makes no mention of Pickett or his division. Nor does Longstreet mention any other officer being in charge of the unit, nor Pickett commanded the men remaining in his division and reported to Longstreet.[59] These men surrendered with Pickett at Appomattox. Regarding Pickett and his division, no source can be produced which asserts anything otherwise.

## Appomattox

On April 9, Pickett commanded his remaining troops in the Battle of Appomattox Courthouse, forming up in the final battle line of the Army of Northern Virginia. He surrendered with Lee's army and was paroled at Appomattox Court House on April 12, 1865.[60]

A legend told by Pickett's widow stated that when the Union Army marched into Richmond, she received a surprise visitor. He acted graciously and inquired whether he had found the Pickett house. Abraham Lincoln himself, the story goes, had come to determine the fate of an old acquaintance before the wars, and Sallie, astonished, admitted she was his wife and held out her infant for the president to cradle.[61] Lincoln historian Gerald J. Prokopowicz has called this story a "fantasy."[62]

## Postbellum life

Pickett's execution of 22 captured Union Army soldiers, from North Carolina at New Bern, was then under investigation. Pickett, fearing prosecution, fled with his wife and son to Canada. Testimony at the hearings, including that of wartime North Carolina Governor Zebulon Vance, alleged that at least some of the executed men had belonged to local militias and been unwillingly transferred to the regular Confederate army in "violation of their enlistment agreement," and thus should not have been treated as deserters and shot.[63] Pickett remained out of the country for a year until hearing that, at the recommendation of Ulysses S. Grant, the investigation had ended. Pickett returned to the United States with his family in 1866 to work as an insurance agent and farmer in Norfolk, Virginia.[9]

On June 23, 1874, House Resolution 3086, an "act to remove the political disabilities of George E. Pickett of Virginia," was passed by the U.S. Congress. Pickett was granted a full pardon, about a year before his death.[64]

Pickett lamented his men, lost in great number at Gettysburg. Late in his life, Colonel John S. Mosby, who had served under General J. E. B. Stuart, was present when Lee and Pickett met briefly after the war. He claimed their interaction was cold and reserved. Others present at the meeting disputed this, stating Lee only acted in his usual reserved and gentlemanly fashion.[65] Pickett, Mosby said, complained bitterly to him after this meeting that "That man destroyed my division."[46] Mosby allegedly replied, "Yes, but he made you immortal." Most historians find the encounter as Mosby interpreted it unlikely. Asked by reporters why Pickett's Charge failed, Pickett frequently replied, "I've always thought the Yankees had something to do with it."[66]

George E. Pickett died in Norfolk, Virginia, on July 30, 1875.[67] The cause of death was a liver abscess, although whether it was alcohol-related, amoebic or bacterial is not clear. [68] He was initially interred in Cedar Grove Cemetery in Norfolk.[69] His remains were disinterred on October 23 and he was buried in Hollywood Cemetery in Richmond, Virginia on October 24, 1875. More than 40,000 people lined the funeral route, while another 5,000 marched in the funeral procession.[70] A memorial to Pickett was erected over his grave site and dedicated on October 5, 1888.[71] The memorial was not, however, placed directly above Pickett's burial site, and the exact location of his remains is not clear.[72]

# Leonidas Polk

*Lt. Gen. Leonidas Polk c.1863–1864 as commander of the First Corps, Army of Tennessee.*

**Leonidas Polk** (April 10, 1806–June 14, 1864) was a planter in Maury County, Tennessee, USA, and a second cousin of President James K. Polk. He was bishop of the Episcopal Diocese of Louisiana. He resigned his ecclesiastical position to become a major general in the Confederate army (called "Sewanee's Fighting Bishop"). His official portrait at the University of the South depicts him dressed as a bishop with his army uniform hanging nearby.

He is often erroneously named "Leonidas K. Polk." He had no middle name and never signed any documents as such. The errant "K" was derived from his listing in the *post-bellum* New Orleans press as "Polk, Leon. (k)," signifying "killed in action."

Polk was one of the more notable, yet controversial, political generals of the war. Recognizing his indispensable familiarity with the Mississippi Valley, Confederate President Jefferson Davis commissioned his elevation to a high military position regardless of his lack of prior combat experience. He commanded troops in the Battle of Shiloh, the Battle of Perryville, the Battle of Stones River, the Tullahoma Campaign, the Battle of Chickamauga, the Chattanooga Campaign, and the Atlanta Campaign. He is remembered for his bitter disagreements with his immediate superior, the likewise-controversial General Braxton Bragg of the Army of Tennessee, and for his general lack of success in combat. While serving under the command of General Joseph E. Johnston, he was killed in action in 1864 during the Atlanta Campaign.

## Civil War
### Kentucky

At the outbreak of the Civil War, Polk pulled the Louisiana Convention out of the Episcopal Church of the United States to form the Protestant Episcopal Church in the Confederate States of America. Although he hoped that secession would result in a peaceful separation of the North and South, and suggested that he was reluctant to take up arms personally, he did not hesitate to write to his friend and former classmate at West Point, Jefferson Davis,[9] offering his services in the Confederate States Army. Polk was commissioned a major general on June 25, 1861, and ordered to command Department No. 2 (roughly, the area between the Mississippi River and the Tennessee River).[10] He committed one of the great blunders of the Civil War by dispatching troops to occupy Columbus, Kentucky, in September 1861; the critical border state of Kentucky had declared its neutrality between the Union and the Confederacy, but Polk's action was instrumental in prompting the Kentucky legislature to request Federal aid to resist his advance, ending the state's brief attempt at neutrality and effectively ceding it to Union control for the remainder of the war.[11]

During this period Polk argued about strategy with his subordinate, Pillow, and his superior, Gen. Albert Sidney Johnston, commander of Confederate forces in the Western Theater. Resentful that his former West Point roommate was giving him orders, he submitted a letter of resignation to President Davis on November 6, but Davis rejected the request.[12] Polk's command saw its first combat on November 7, 1861, in the minor, inconclusive Battle of Belmont between Polk's subordinate, Brig. Gen. Gideon Johnson Pillow and Union Brig. Gen. Ulysses S. Grant. Although not present on the battlefield himself, Polk was wounded nearby on November 11 when the largest cannon in his army, nicknamed "Lady Polk" in honor of his wife, exploded during demonstration firing. The explosion stunned Polk and blew his clothes off, requiring a convalescence of several weeks.

## Army of Mississippi

> Besides being a basically incompetent general, Polk had the added fault of hating to take orders.
>
> —Steven E. Woodworth, *Jefferson Davis and His Generals*[13]

In April 1862, Polk commanded the First Corps of Albert Sidney Johnston's Army of Mississippi at the Battle of Shiloh and continued in that role for much of the rest of the year under Beauregard, who had assumed command following the death of A. S. Johnston on the first day at Shiloh, and then under Gen. Braxton Bragg. At various times his command was considered a corps and at other times the "Right Wing" of the army. In the fall, during the invasion of Kentucky by Bragg and Maj. Gen. Edmund Kirby Smith, Polk was in temporary command of the Army of Mississippi while Bragg visited Frankfort to preside over the inauguration of a Confederate governor for the state. Polk disregarded an order from Bragg to attack the flank of the pursuing Union Army near Frankfort.[14]

> Bragg thoroughly despised . . . the genial but pompous and often incompetent Bishop Polk. Bragg considered Polk "an old woman, utterly worthless," especially at disciplining men. Unfortunately for Bragg and for the Confederacy as a whole, Polk remained a great favorite of Jefferson Davis despite carefully couched hints from Bragg, which protected the irritatingly self-righteous Polk from the increasingly sycophantic Bragg and made his appointment to wing command a political necessity.
>
> —Kenneth W. Noe, *Perryville*[15]

At the Battle of Perryville, Polk's right wing constituted the main attacking force against Maj. Gen. Don Carlos Buell's Army of the Ohio, but Polk was reluctant to attack the small portion of Buell's army that faced him until Bragg arrived at the battlefield. One of the enduring legends of the Civil War is that Polk witnessed his subordinate, Maj. Gen. Benjamin F. Cheatham, advancing his division. Cheatham allegedly shouted, "Give 'em hell, boys!" and Polk, retaining the sensibility of his role as an Episcopal bishop, seconded the cheer: "Give it to 'em boys; give 'em what General Cheatham says!"[16]

## Army of Tennessee

After Perryville, Polk began a year-long campaign to get Bragg relieved of command, hoping to use his close relationship with President Davis to accomplish his goal.[17] Despite the failure of his Kentucky campaign, Bragg was retained in command, but this did nothing to reduce the enmity between Polk and Bragg. Polk was promoted to lieutenant general on October 11, 1862, with date of rank of October 10. He became the second most senior Confederate of that rank during the war, behind James Longstreet.[18] In November, the Army of Mississippi was renamed the Army of Tennessee and Polk commanded its First Corps until September 1863.[19]

Polk fought under Bragg at the Battle of Stones River in late 1862 and once again Bragg's subordinates politicked to remove their army commander after an unsuccessful battle (the battle was tactically inconclusive, but Bragg was unable to stop the advance of the Union Army of the Cumberland under Maj. Gen. William S. Rosecrans and Bragg withdrew his army to Tullahoma, Tennessee). Bragg was also unsuccessful in resisting Rosecrans's advance in the Tullahoma Campaign, which began to threaten the important city of Chattanooga. In the face of Rosecrans's expert maneuvering of his army, Polk counseled Bragg to retreat rather than stand and fight in their Tullahoma fortifications.[20]

Rosecrans eventually maneuvered Bragg out of Chattanooga and the Army of Tennessee withdrew into the mountains of northwestern Georgia with the Army of the Cumberland in hot pursuit. Bragg planned to attack and destroy at least one of Rosecrans's corps, advancing separately over mountainous roads. He was infuriated when Polk's division under Maj. Gen. Thomas C. Hindman failed to attack an isolated Union corps at Davis's Cross Roads as ordered on September 11. Two days later, Polk disregarded orders from Bragg to attack another isolated corps, the second failed opportunity. At the Battle of Chickamauga, Polk was given command of the Right Wing and the responsibility for initiating the attack on the second day of battle (September 19). He failed to inform his subordinates of the plan and his wing was late in attacking, allowing the Union defenders time to complete their field fortifications. Bragg wrote after the war that if it were not for the loss of these hours, "our independence might have been won."[21]

Chickamauga was a great tactical victory for Bragg, but instead of pursuing and destroying the Union Army as it retreated, he laid siege to it in Chattanooga, concentrating his effort against the enemies inside his army instead of his enemies from the North. He demanded an explanation from Polk on the bishop's failure to attack in time on September

20 and Polk placed the blame entirely on one of his subordinates, Maj. Gen. D. H. Hill. Bragg wrote to President Davis, "Gen'l Polk by education and habit is unfit for executing the plans of others. He will convince himself his own are better and follow them without reflecting on the consequences." Bragg relieved Polk of his command and ordered him to Atlanta to await further orders. Although Polk protested the "arbitrary and unlawful order" to the Secretary of War and demanded a court of inquiry, he was not restored to his position and Davis once again retained Bragg in army command, despite the protestations of a number of his subordinate generals.[22]

## Mississippi

President Davis transferred his friend Polk to command the Department of Mississippi and East Louisiana (December 23, 1863–January 28, 1864) and then the Department of Alabama and East Mississippi (January 28–May 4, 1864), giving him effective command of the state of Mississippi following the departure of Gen. Joseph E. Johnston to replace Bragg in command of the Army of Tennessee. Polk unsuccessfully attempted to oppose Maj. Gen. William Tecumseh Sherman's raid against Meridian, Mississippi, in February 1864. In May, he was ordered to take his forces and join with Johnston in resisting Sherman's advance in the Atlanta Campaign. He assumed command of the Third Corps of the Army of Tennessee on May 4.[23] His command remained commonly known as the "Army of Mississippi."

## Atlanta Campaign and death

Polk brought more than 20,000 men with him to Georgia. Because of his elevated rank, he became the army's second in command under Johnston. By using successive flanking maneuvers, Sherman forced Johnston to withdraw his army from strong defensive positions to protect the Confederate line of communication. This forced Johnston ever closer to the critically important city of Atlanta.[24]

> The army had suffered a severe loss. It was not that Polk had been a spectacular corps officer. His deficiencies as a commander and his personal traits of stubbornness and childishness had played no small role in several of the army's disasters in earlier times. The loss was one of morale and experience. Polk was the army's most beloved general, a representative of that intangible identification of the army with Tennessee.
>
> —*Thomas L. Connelly, Autumn of Glory*[25]

On June 14, 1864, Polk was scouting enemy positions near Marietta, Georgia, with his staff when he was killed in action by a Federal 3-inch (76 mm) shell at Pine Mountain.[26] The artillery fire was initiated when Sherman spotted a cluster of Confederate generals—Polk, William J. Hardee, and Johnston, with their staffs—in an exposed area. He pointed them out to Maj. Gen. Oliver Otis Howard, commander of the IV Corps, and ordered him to fire upon them. Battery I of the 1st Ohio Light Artillery, commanded by Capt. Hubert Dilger, obeyed the order within minutes. The first round from the battery came close and a second came even closer, causing the men to disperse. The third shell struck Polk's left arm, went through his chest, and exited hitting his right arm, then exploded against a tree; it nearly cut Polk in two.[27]

# David Dixon Porter

*Porter in the 1860s, during the American Civil War. Photo taken by Mathew Brady; restoration copyright © Adam Cuerden; used with permission.*

**David Dixon Porter** (June 8, 1813–February 13, 1891) was a United States Navy admiral and a member of one of the most distinguished families in the history of the U.S. Navy. Promoted as the second U.S. Navy officer ever to attain the rank of admiral, after his adoptive brother David G. Farragut, Porter helped improve the Navy as the Superintendent of the U.S. Naval Academy after significant service in the American Civil War.

Porter began naval service as a midshipman at the age of 10 years under his father, Commodore David Porter, on the frigate USS *John Adams*. For the remainder of his life, he was associated with the sea. Porter served in the Mexican War in the attack on the fort at the City of Vera Cruz. At the outbreak of the Civil War, he was part of a plan to hold Fort Pickens, near Pensacola, Florida, for the Union; its execution disrupted the effort to relieve the garrison at Fort Sumter, leading to its fall. Porter commanded an independent flotilla of mortar boats at the capture of New Orleans. Later, he was advanced to the rank of (acting) rear admiral in command of the Mississippi River Squadron, which cooperated with the army under Major General Ulysses S. Grant in the Vicksburg Campaign. After the fall of Vicksburg, he led the naval forces in the difficult Red River Campaign in Louisiana. Late in 1864, Porter was transferred from the interior to the Atlantic coast, where he led the U.S. Navy in the joint assaults on Fort Fisher, the final significant naval action of the war.

Porter worked to raise the standards of the U.S. Navy in the position of Superintendent of the Naval Academy when it was restored to Annapolis. He initiated reforms in the curriculum to increase professionalism. In the early days of President Grant's administration, Porter was *de facto* Secretary of the Navy. When his adoptive brother David G. Farragut was advanced from rank of vice-admiral to admiral, Porter took his previous position; likewise, when Farragut died, Porter became the second man to hold the newly created rank of admiral. He gathered a corps of like-minded officers devoted to naval reform.

Porter's administration of the Navy Department aroused powerful opposition by some in Congress, who forced the Secretary of the Navy Adolph E. Borie to resign. His replacement, George Robeson, curtailed Porter's power and eased him into semi-retirement.

# Civil War

## Powhatan *and the relief of Fort Pickens*

*Porter*

The seceded states[24] laid claim to the national forts within their boundaries, but they did not make good their claim to Fort Sumter in South Carolina and Forts Pickens, Zachary Taylor, and Jefferson in Florida. [25] They soon made it clear that they would use force if necessary to gain possession of Fort Sumter and Fort Pickens. President Abraham Lincoln resolved not to cede them without a fight. Secretary of State William H. Seward, Captain Montgomery C. Meigs of the U.S. Army, and Porter devised a plan for the relief of Fort Pickens. The principal element of their plan required use of the steam frigate USS *Powhatan*, which would be commanded by Porter and would carry reinforce-

ments to the fort from New York. Because no one was above suspicion in those days, the plan had to be implemented in complete secrecy; not even Secretary of the Navy Gideon Welles was to be advised.[26]

Welles was in the meantime preparing an expedition for the relief of the garrison at Fort Sumter. As he was unaware that *Powhatan* would not be available, he included it in his plans. When the other vessels assigned to the effort showed up, the South Carolina troops at Charleston began to bombard Fort Sumter, and the Civil War was on. The relief expedition could only wait outside the harbor. The expedition had little chance to be successful in any case; without the support of the guns on *Powhatan*, it was completely impotent. The only contribution made by the expedition was to carry the soldiers who had defended Fort Sumter back to the North following their surrender and parole.[27]

Lincoln did not punish Seward for his part in the incident, so Welles felt that he had no choice but to forgive Porter, whose culpability was less. Later, he reasoned that it had at least a redeeming feature in that Porter, whose loyalty had been suspect, was henceforth firmly attached to the Union. As he wrote,[28]

> In detaching the Powhatan from the Sumter expedition and giving the command to Porter, Mr. Seward extricated that officer from Secession influences, and committed him at once, and decisively, to the Union cause."

## Mortar fleet at New Orleans and Vicksburg

In late 1861, the Navy Department began to develop plans to open the Mississippi River.[29] The first move would be to capture New Orleans. For this Porter, by this time advanced to rank of commander, was given the responsibility of organizing a flotilla of some twenty mortar boats that would participate in the reduction of the forts defending the city from the south. The flotilla was a semi-autonomous part of the West

Gulf Blockading Squadron, which was to be commanded by Porter's adoptive brother Captain David G. Farragut.[30]

The bombardment of Fort Jackson and Fort St. Philip began on April 18, 1862. Porter had opined that two days of concentrated fire would be enough to reduce the forts, but after five days they seemed as strong as ever. The mortars were beginning to run low on ammunition. Farragut, who put little reliance on the mortars anyway, made the decision to bypass the forts on the night of April 24. The fleet successfully ran past the forts; the mortars were left behind, but they bombarded the forts during the passage in order to distract the enemy gunners. Once the fleet was above the forts, nothing significant stood between them and New Orleans; Farragut demanded the surrender of the city, and it fell to his fleet on April 29. The forts were still between him and Porter's mortar fleet, but when the latter again began to pummel Fort Jackson, its garrison mutinied and forced its surrender. Fort St. Philip had to follow suit. Surrender of the two forts was accepted by Commander Porter on April 28.[31]

Following orders from the Navy Department, Farragut took his fleet upstream to capture other strongpoints on the river, with the aim of complete possession of the Mississippi. At Vicksburg, Mississippi he found that the bluffs were too high to be reached by the guns of his fleet, so he ordered Porter to bring his mortar flotilla up. The mortars suppressed the Rebel artillery well enough that Farragut's ships could pass the batteries at Vicksburg and link up with a Union flotilla coming down from the north. The city could not be taken, however, without active participation by the army, which did not happen. On July 8, the bombardment ceased when Porter was ordered to Hampton Roads to assist in Major General George B. McClellan's Peninsula Campaign. A few days later, Farragut followed, and the first attempt to take Vicksburg was over.[32]

## Acting rear admiral: the Vicksburg Campaign

*Porter and George Gordon Meade*

In the summer of 1862, shortly after Porter left Vicksburg, the U.S. Navy was extensively modified; among the features of the revised organization were a set of officer ranks from ensign to rear admiral that paralleled the ranks in the Army. Among the new ranks created were those of commodore and rear admiral.[33] According to the organization charts, the persons in command of the blockading squadrons were to be rear admirals. Another part of the reorganization transferred the Western gunboat flotilla from the army to the navy, and retitled it the Mississippi River Squadron. The change of title implied that it was formally equivalent to the other squadrons, so its commanding officer would likewise be a rear admiral. The problem was that the commandant of the gunboat flotilla, Flag Officer Charles H. Davis, had not shown the initiative that the Navy Department wanted, so he had to be removed. He was made rear admiral, but he was recalled to Washington to serve as chief of the Bureau of Navigation.[34]

Most of the men who could have replaced Davis were either less suitable or were unavailable because of other assignments, so finally Secretary Welles decided to appoint Porter to the position. He did this despite some doubt. As he wrote in his *Diary*,[35]

> Relieved Davis and appointed D. D. Porter to the Western Flotilla, which is hereafter to be recognized as a squadron. Porter is but a Commander. He has, however, stirring and positive qualities, is fertile in resources, has great energy, excessive and sometimes not over-scrupulous ambition, is impressed with and boastful of his own powers, given to exaggeration in relation to himself, —a Porter infirmity, —is not generous to older and superior living officers, whom he is too ready to traduce, but is kind and patronizing to favorites who are juniors, and generally to official inferiors. Is given to cliquism but is brave and daring like all his family . . . It is a question, with his mixture of good and bad traits, how he will succeed.

Thus Commander Porter became Acting Rear Admiral Porter without going through the intermediate ranks of captain and commodore. He was assigned to command the Mississippi Squadron and left Washington for his new command on October 9, 1862, and arrived in Cairo, Illinois on October 15.[36]

Secretary of War Edwin Stanton considered Porter "a gas bag . . . blowing his own trumpet and stealing credit which belongs to others."[37] Historian John D. Winters, in his *The Civil War in Louisiana*, describes Porter as having "possessed the qualities of abundant energy, recklessness, resourcefulness, and fighting spirit needed for the trying role ahead. Porter was assigned the task of aiding General John A. McClernand in opening the upper Mississippi. The choice of McClernand, a volunteer political general, pleased Porter because he felt that all West Point men were 'too self-sufficient, pedantic, and unpractical.'"[38]

Winters also writes that Porter "revealed a weakness he was to display many times: he belittled a superior officer [Charles H. Poor]. He often heaped undue praise upon a subordinate, but rarely could find much to admire in a superior."[39]

The Army was showing renewed interest in opening the Mississippi River at just this time, and Porter met two men who would have great influence on the campaign. First was Major General William T. Sherman, a man of similar temperament to his own, with whom he immediately formed a particularly strong friendship.[40] The other was Major General McClernand, whom he just as quickly came to dislike.[41] Later they would be joined by Major General Ulysses S. Grant; Grant and Porter became friends and worked together quite well, but it was on a more strictly professional level than his relation with Sherman. [42][43]

Close cooperation between the Army and Navy was vital to the success of the siege of Vicksburg. The most prominent contribution to the campaign was the passage of the batteries at Vicksburg and Grand Gulf by a major part of the Mississippi River Squadron. Grant had asked merely for a few gunboats to shield his troops, but Porter persuaded him to use more than half of his fleet. After nightfall on April 16, 1863, the fleet moved downstream past the batteries. Only one vessel was lost in the ensuing firefight. Six nights later, a similar run past the batteries gave Grant the transports he needed for crossing the river.[44] Now south of Vicksburg, Grant at first tried to attack the Rebels through Grand Gulf, and requested Porter to eliminate the batteries there before his troops would be sent across. On April 29, the gunboats spent most of the day bombarding two Confederate forts. They succeeded in silencing the lower of the two, but the upper fort remained. Grant called off the assault and moved downstream to Bruinsburg, where he was able to cross the river unopposed.[45]

Although the fleet made no major offensive contributions to the campaign after Grand Gulf, it remained important in its secondary role of keeping the blockade against the city. When Vicksburg was besieged, the encirclement was made complete by the Navy's control of the Mississippi and Yazoo Rivers. When it finally fell on July 4, 1863, Grant was unstinting in his praise of the assistance he had received from Porter and his men.[46]

For his contribution to the victory, Porter's appointment as "acting" rear admiral was made permanent, dated from July 4.[47]

## Red River Expedition

After the opening of the Mississippi, the political general Nathaniel P. Banks, who was in charge of army forces in Louisiana, brought pressure on the Lincoln administration to mount a campaign across Louisiana and into Texas along the line of the Red River. The ostensible purpose was to extend Union control into Texas,[48] but Banks was influenced by numerous speculators to convert the campaign into little more than a raid to seize cotton. Admiral Porter was not in favor; he thought that the next objective of his fleet should be to capture Mobile, but he received direct orders from Washington to cooperate with Banks.[49]

After considerable delays caused by Banks's attention to political rather than military matters, the Red River expedition got under way in early March 1864. From the start, navigation of the river presented as great a problem for Porter and his fleet as did the Confederate army that opposed them. The army under Banks and the navy under Porter did little to cooperate, and instead often became rivals in a race to seize cotton. Confederate opposition under Major General Richard Taylor[a] succeeded in keeping them apart by defeating Banks at the Battle of Mansfield, following which Banks gave up the expedition. From that time on, Porter's primary task was to extricate his fleet. The task was made difficult by falling water levels in the river, but he ultimately got most out, with the help of heroic efforts by some of the soldiers who stayed to protect the fleet.[50]

## Capture of Fort Fisher

*Porter and staff, December 1864.*

By late summer 1864, Wilmington, North Carolina, was the only port open for running the blockade, and the Navy Department began to plan to close it. Its major defense was Fort Fisher, a massive structure at the New Inlet to the Cape Fear River.[51] Secretary Welles believed that the head of the North Atlantic Blockading Squadron, Rear Admiral Samuel Phillips Lee, was inadequate for the task, so he at first assigned Rear Admiral Farragut to be Lee's replacement. Farragut was too ill to serve, however, so Welles then decided to switch Lee with Porter: Lee would command the Mississippi River Squadron, and Porter would come east and prepare for the attack on Fort Fisher.[52]

The planned attack on Fort Fisher required the cooperation of the army, and the troops were taken from the Army of the James. It was expected that Brigadier General Godfrey Weitzel would command, but Major General Benjamin F. Butler, the commander of the Army of the James, exercised one of the prerogatives of his position to install himself as leader of the expedition. Butler proposed that the fort could be flattened by exploding a ship filled with gunpowder near it, and Porter accepted the idea; if successful, the scheme would avoid a protracted siege or its alternative, a frontal assault. Accordingly, the old steamer USS *Louisiana* was packed with powder and blown up in the early morning of December 24, 1864. It had, however, no discernible effect on the fort. Butler brought part of his troops ashore, but he was already convinced that the effort was hopeless, so he removed his force before making an all-out assault.[53]

Porter, enraged by Butler's timorousness, went to U. S. Grant and demanded that Butler be removed. Grant agreed, and placed Major General Alfred H. Terry in charge of a second assault on the fort. The second assault began on January 13, 1865, with unopposed landings and bombardment of the fort by the fleet. Porter imposed new methods of bombardment this time: each ship was assigned a specific target, with intent to destroy the enemy's guns rather than to knock down the walls. They were also to continue firing after the men ashore started their assault; the ships would shift their aim to points ahead of the advancing troops. The bombardment continued for two more days, while Terry got his men into position. On the 15th, frontal assaults on opposite faces by Terry's soldiers on the land side and 2000 sailors and marines on the beach vanquished the fort. This was the last significant naval operation of the war.[54]

## Tour of Richmond

By April 1865, the Civil War drawing to a close, U.S. victory in the war was all but guaranteed.

After the Confederate capital of Richmond was captured by U.S. forces, Porter toured the city on foot, accompanying U.S. President Abraham Lincoln with several armed body-guards. He fondly recalled the events in his 1885 book, *Incidents and Anecdotes of the Civil War*, where he described witnessing scores of many freed slaves rushing to get a glimpse of Lincoln, whom they admired as a hero and credited for their emancipation, kissing his clothing and singing odes to him:

> Twenty years have passed since that event; it is almost too new in history to make a great impression, but the time will come when it will loom up as one of the greatest of man's achievements, and the name of Abraham Lincoln — who of his own will struck the shackles from the limbs of four millions of people — will be honored thousands of years from now as man's name was never honored before. [ . . . ] The scene was so touching I hated to disturb it, yet we could not stay there all day; we had to move on; so I requested the patriarch to withdraw from about the President with his companions and let us pass on.
>
> —David Dixon Porter, *Incidents and Anecdotes of the Civil War, (1885), pp. 295–296.*[55]

## Assassination of Abraham Lincoln

A few weeks after his visit to Virginia, Lincoln was assassinated. Porter, upon learning of Lincoln's assassination, was greatly upset by the news, as he admired Lincoln greatly. Porter called Lincoln the best man he ever knew and ever will know. He stated that he felt some responsibility for Lincoln's death, feeling that had he been with him on the night of his death, he might have prevented his murder.[56]

## Final years

In 1866, the rank of admiral was created in the U.S. Navy. Naval hero David G. Farragut, his adoptive brother, was named as the nation's first admiral, and Porter became vice admiral at the same time. In 1870, Farragut died, and it was expected that Porter would be promoted to fill the vacancy.

Eventually, he did become the second admiral, but it was after much controversy that was provoked by his many enemies. Among them were several very powerful politicians, including some of the political generals he had contended with in the war.[60] Porter reached the mandatory retirement age of 62 in June 1875 but was allowed to remain on active duty.

Despite the prestige of the high rank, Porter's eclipse in influence continued. For the last twenty years of his life, he had little to do with the operations of the Navy. Porter turned to writing, producing some histories that are of doubtful reliability but provide insights into his own beliefs and character. He also wrote some fiction that has not with-stood the test of time.

In 1890 he became the founding president of the District of Columbia Society of the Sons of the American Revolution. He was assigned national membership number 1801 and District of Columbia Society membership number 1. He served as president of the society until his death the next year. He was also an honorary member of the Society of the Cincinnati.

After twenty years of semi-retirement, his health began to give way. In the summer of 1890, he suffered a heart attack; he survived but his health was clearly in decline. He died at the age of 77 on the morning of February 13, 1891.[61]

Porter is interred at Arlington National Cemetery.[62]

# Lewis Powell

*Powell in wrist irons aboard the USS Saugus, photograph by Alexander Gardner, 1865*

**Lewis Thornton Powell** (April 22, 1844–July 7, 1865), also known as Lewis Payne and Lewis Paine, was an American who attempted to assassinate United States Secretary of State William H. Seward on April 14, 1865. He was a conspirator with John Wilkes Booth, who assassinated President Abraham Lincoln that same night.

Powell was a Confederate soldier wounded at Gettysburg. He later served in Mosby's Rangers before working with the Confederate Secret Service in Maryland. He met Booth and was recruited into an unsuccessful plot to kidnap Lincoln. On April 14, 1865, Booth resolved to have Lincoln, Seward, and Vice President Andrew Johnson all assassinated.

Powell was given the task to kill Seward. He was assisted by David Herold, who guided Powell to Seward's home and kept horses ready for the escape. Powell severely injured Seward, and Herold fled before Powell could exit the Seward home. Powell lost his way in the city, and three days later arrived at a boarding house run by Mary Surratt, mother of co-conspirator John Surratt. By chance, the police were searching the house at that moment, and arrested Powell. Powell and three others, including Mary Surratt, were sentenced to death by a military tribunal and were executed at the Washington Arsenal.

## Civil War service

### 2nd Florida Infantry and capture

On May 30, 1861, Lewis Powell left home and traveled to Jasper, Florida, where he enlisted in Company I of the 2nd Florida Infantry. He was accepted because he lied about his age (he claimed to be 19).[10] Powell's unit fought in March and April 1862 in the Peninsula Campaign. Powell became a battle-hardened and effective soldier. He won praise from his commanding officers, and claimed that when he shot his rifle he did so to kill (never to wound). He was alleged to have carried the skull of a Union soldier with him, which he used as an ashtray.[11] His one-year enlistment having expired, Powell received a two-month furlough, during which time he returned home to visit his family. He re-enlisted at Jasper on May 8, 1862.[12] In November 1862, Powell fell ill and was hospitalized at General Hospital No. 11 in Richmond, Virginia.[12] He returned to active duty within a few weeks, and fought in the Battle of Fredericksburg (December 11–15, 1862) near Fredericksburg, Virginia.[13] His unit was then assigned to Third Corps, Army of Northern Virginia, which was organized at the beginning of 1863. Third Corps finally went into combat at the Battle of Gettysburg, July 1–3, 1863.

Powell was shot in the right wrist on July 2[11] (preventing him from participating in Pickett's Charge on July 3), captured, and sent to a POW hospital at Pennsylvania College.[14] Transferred to Camp Letterman, the vast medical field hospital northeast of Gettysburg, on July 6,[15] Powell worked as a nurse in the camp and at Pennsylvania College[16] until September 1, when he was turned over to the Provost Marshal. He was taken by train to Baltimore, Maryland, and (still a POW) began working on September 2 at West Buildings Hospital.[17] In Baltimore, Powell met and developed a relationship with a woman named Margaret "Maggie" Branson, who was volunteering as a nurse. It is believed that Branson assisted Lewis in escaping from the hospital on September 7.[17] Some historians contend that she actually provided him with a Union Army uniform.[18][19]

## Escape and Mosby's Rangers

*Colonel John S. Mosby, who permitted Powell to join "Mosby's Rangers" as a partisan.*

Margaret Branson took Powell to her mother's boarding house at 16 North Eutaw Street in Baltimore. Many, perhaps most, Marylanders were Confederate sympathizers, and the Bransons were fervent believers in the Southern cause. The Branson boarding house was a well-known Confederate safe house and frequent rendezvous point for members of the Confederate Secret Service (the Confederacy's spy agency). [20] Powell may have spent up to two weeks at the Branson house[18] before heading south. While still in Maryland, he learned the location of Harry Gilmor and his "Gilmor's Raiders" (a unit of Confederate cavalry detached from Second Corps) and spent a few days with them.[21] He crossed into Virginia and on September 30 he ended up at the home of John Scott Payne, a prominent doctor and Confederate sympathizer who lived at Granville Tract, a plantation about 4 miles (6.4 km) from Warrenton. By now, Powell was wearing a ragged Confederate uniform, and Payne welcomed him into the home for a meal and a night's stay. They discussed the exploits of Colonel John S. Mosby's 43rd Battalion Virginia Cavalry (or "Mosby's Rangers"), a very large detached unit of partisans based in Warrenton. Powell joined Mosby the following day (October 1, 1863).[22]

For more than a year, Powell served under Mosby. Mosby considered Powell to be one of his most effective soldiers, and Powell earned the nickname "Lewis the Terrible" for his ferocity and murderousness in combat.[23] He lived as a civilian with the Paynes, putting on his uniform and participating in military activities only when conducting a partisan raid.[21] Powell participated in a number of actions, including the Wagon Raids of October and November 1863; the Battle of Loudoun Heights on January 10, 1864; the battle of Second Dranesville on February 20–21, 1864; the Action at Mount Zion Church on July 3 and 6, 1864; the Berryville Wagon Raid on August 13, 1864; the Raid on Merritt's Cavalry Division in September 1864; the Mansassas Gap Railroad Raid on October 3–7, 1864; the Greenback Raid on October 14, 1864;[24] the Valley Pike Raid on October 25, 1864; and the Rout of Blazer's Command on November 17, 1864. This last raid proved to be a turning point for Powell. Union Army Lieutenant Richard R. "Dick" Blazer was a noted Indian fighter who'd been sent to destroy Mosby's Rangers. Instead, Blazer's unit was routed and Blazer captured. Powell and three others were given the privilege of taking Blazer to prison in Richmond, Virginia, in late November.[21]

Powell's visit to Richmond changed him. He returned to Warrenton morose and intro-spective. Historian Michael W. Kauffman argues that Powell saw a Baltimore acquaintance in Richmond, and that turned his thoughts back to the time he'd spent in September 1863 romancing Margaret Branson and her sister, Mary, at the Branson boarding house. [21] Powell biographer Betty Ownsbey, however, argues that his Richmond trip made him aware that the Confederate cause was lost, and his depression was caused by his desire to get out of the fighting.[25] Several other historians claim that the Confederate Secret Service had already recruited him into its ranks during the previous year (with Mosby's consent), and that Powell's moodiness came from moral misgivings he had as he contemplated being sent north to assist with various kidnap plots against Abraham Lincoln.[26][27][28][a][29][30]

## Involvement in conspiracy
### Recruitment

*John Surratt in* 1868.

For whatever reason, Powell deserted on January 1, 1865.[31] He made his way to Richmond, where he sold his horse and purchased a ticket on a train headed for Alexandria, Virginia.[32] On January 13, he entered the Union Army's lines at Alexandria, claimed to be a civilian refugee,[32] and—under the name "Lewis Payne" (or "Paine," sources vary)—took an oath of allegiance to the United States.[33][34][21][b][31] On January 14, Powell arrived in Baltimore and checked into Miller's Hotel.[24][35] He made contact with the Bransons, and soon took up residence in their boarding house again.[36][37] He used the name "Lewis Payne," and the Bransons introduced him to David Preston Parr, a merchant whose china shop was used for meetings, as a mail drop, and as a safe house for Confederate agents and spies. Over the next few weeks, Powell met frequently with Parr,[38] a Confederate Secret Service agent.[39][32]

The same day that Powell arrived in Baltimore, John Surratt and Louis J. Weichmann purchased a boat at Port Tobacco in Charles County, Maryland. Surratt, and to a much lesser degree Weichmann, were members of a group led by John Wilkes Booth which planned to kidnap President Abraham Lincoln and spirit him into Virginia, where he could be turned over to Confederate military authorities. The boat was needed to ferry Lincoln across the Potomac River. The two men then traveled to Baltimore on January 21.[38] In testimony for the prosecution in June 1865, Weichmann said that Surratt had $300 which he needed to give to a man in Baltimore. Although Surratt never revealed the man's name, the prosecution at Powell's 1865 trial attempted to show that this man was Lewis Powell.[36] Historian Edward Steers Jr. agrees that it is likely that Surratt met Powell at this time,[36] while historians David Griffin Chandler and Elizabeth Trindal present their meeting at Parr's China Hall store as fact.[40][41]

In either late January[40] or early February 1865,[35] Powell encountered John Wilkes Booth outside Barnum's Hotel in Baltimore.[35][42] Booth treated Powell to lunch at the hotel, and recruited him into the plot to kidnap Lincoln.[40] Powell became a fervent believer in Booth, and Booth came to trust Powell implicitly. Although several others had been part of the conspiracy for some time, Powell swiftly became the second most important person in the plot (next to John Surratt).[40] Booth made arrangements for Powell to stay at Herndon House boarding house under the name "Reverend Lewis Payne" whenever he traveled to Washington, D.C.[40] During this time, Powell used a variety of aliases in addition to "Lewis Payne," including use of the last names Hall, Kensler, Mosby, Paine, and Wood.[43]

## Kidnap conspiracy at Surratt's boarding house

One evening in early February, Powell (using the alias "Mr. Wood") appeared at Mary Surratt's boarding house 604 H Street NW in Washington, D.C., Mary was John's mother, and she had taken up residence in the boarding house in the fall of 1864 after renting out her tavern in Surrattsville (now Clinton), Maryland, to former D.C., police officer John M. Lloyd. Powell asked for John Surratt, who was not at home. He then requested something to eat and a place to stay, and Mrs. Surratt granted both requests after her son returned home and vouched for "Mr. Wood." Powell told Louis Weichmann, who was a boarder in the house, that "Wood" was a clerk in Parr's china shop in Baltimore. Powell left the next day.[44][45][46]

Powell's role in the plot almost came to an end when, on March 12, 1865, he beat a black maid at the Branson boarding house. She had him arrested and accused him of being a Confederate spy. It was a serious charge: Maryland was under martial law, and the Union Army's Provost Marshal had supervision over such cases. Using the name "Lewis Paine," Powell swore he was from Fauquier County, Virginia, and knew nothing about the war. Declaring he was only 18 years old, he pretended to be stupid and not understand the English language too well. Lacking evidence that he was a spy, the Provost Marshal released Powell on March 14. Powell took an oath of allegiance to the United States, and the Provost Marshal wrote on his allegiance form that "Lewis Paine" was to live north of Philadelphia, Pennsylvania, for the duration of the war.[33][47][43][48] (The Provost Marshal had foolishly written the "stay north" order in pencil. Powell later erased it from his oath of allegiance.)[47]

*John Wilkes Booth in 1865.*

The day before Powell was released, John Surratt sent a telegram to Parr in Baltimore, telling him to send Powell immediately to Washington. Powell was freed just in time to take the 6:00 p.m. train to the capital.[49][50][c][43][47][36] Powell arrived at the Surratt boarding house and identified himself as "Reverend Lewis Payne," a Baptist preacher. When members of the boarding house recognized him as "Mr. Wood" from several weeks earlier, Powell explained that he knew a "Mr. Wood" and that they had been confused. In a new suit, his demeanor suave and cultured (quite unlike his previous surly attitude), the members of the household accepted his explanation. But when "Reverend Payne" met with John Surratt, he claimed not to know him—even though on his previous visit he claimed to be a friend of John's. To Louis Weichmann, this was highly suspicious behavior, but Mrs. Surratt said she was happy with "Reverend Payne's" explanations. Powell stayed for three days, then left.[51][52][53]

Powell was not the only conspirator to have arrived in the city. Booth had assembled his entire team—which consisted of John Surratt, Lewis Powell, Samuel Arnold, George Atzerodt, David Herold, and Michael O'Laughlen—because he wanted the men to plan to kidnap Lincoln the next time he attended a play at Ford's Theatre. Booth rented the President's Box at the theater on March 15, and he provided tickets to Powell and Surratt so that they could familiarize themselves with the layout of the theater and how to access the box. The two attended the theater as planned (in the company of two of Mrs. Surratt's female boarders). The group then had a late-night planning meeting at Gautier's Restaurant at 252 Pennsylvania Avenue. It was the first time that Arnold and O'Laughlen were meeting the others, and it was the first time Booth revealed his plan to kidnap Lincoln from Ford's Theatre. Booth assigned Powell (whom he called "Mosby") the job of catching a handcuffed Lincoln as he was lowered from the President's Box onto the stage. Arnold said that Powell, the strongest of the men, should be the one to subdue and handcuff Lincoln, not catch him from below. As the men argued, Booth kept altering his plan and Powell's role in it.[54] Throughout the meeting, Arnold and O'Laughlen expressed their anger at Booth. They said they had joined a plot to kidnap Lincoln in the country, where the president would be unguarded and there was little chance of encountering a military patrol. Now Booth was changing that plan significantly, and they didn't like it. The meeting broke up at 5:00 a.m. after Arnold said trying to kidnap Lincoln from a theater full of people in the middle of the city was suicidal.[55][56]

On the morning of March 17, Booth learned that President Lincoln had been invited to attend a matinee theatrical performance at the Soldiers' Home. The Soldiers' Home was in a rural part of the District of Columbia about 1 mile (1.6 km) from the city limits (at that time Florida Avenue), and Lincoln usually visited the facility without an escort. The group met in front of the Surratt boarding house at 2:00 p.m. to receive instructions from Booth. Booth sent Herold out to the Surratt tavern with equipment, and informed the others that they should wait at a local saloon while he rode out to the Soldier's Home to scout the area. When Booth arrived at the Soldier's Home, he learned that Lincoln had decided to address a group of Indiana soldiers at a downtown hotel instead.[55] Powell and the other conspirators never left the tavern.[57]

Powell returned to the Branson boarding house that evening, then traveled to New York City with Booth on March 21.[58] Powell stayed at the Revere House, a fashionable hotel, and later moved to a boarding house.[59][d][60] There is evidence that Booth and Powell then traveled to Toronto, Upper Canada, a major center of Confederate activity. Richard Montgomery, a Confederate spy, said that he saw Powell meet with Jacob Thompson and Clement Claiborne Clay, the two heads of the Confederate Secret Service, in Toronto.[61] On March 23, Booth sent a coded telegram to Louis Weichmann, which John Surratt understood to mean that Powell should stay at the Herndon House after he returned to Washington.[62][63][60] Powell returned to the capital on the night of March 27 and checked into the Herndon House using the alias "Kensler."[64] Powell joined Booth that night to watch a performance of the opera *La Forza del Destino* at Ford's Theatre.[65]

On April 11, President Lincoln addressed a crowd from the balcony on the north side of the White House. In this speech, Lincoln discussed his plans for accepting the rebellious states back into the Union, and singled out Louisiana as the first he'd like to see do so. Lincoln announced that he also wanted to see African Americans given the right to vote. Booth and Powell stood on the White House lawn listening to the speech. Booth seethed at the idea of giving blacks political power, and told Powell, "That means nigger citizenship. Now, by God, I will put him through. That will be the last speech he will ever make."[66]

## Lincoln assassination plot

It is unclear just when Powell learned that the kidnap plot had turned to an assassination. There is testimony from the nurse attending the Secretary of State indicating that Powell may have learned of his role to assassinate Seward on Thursday, April 13. A man fitting Powell's description appeared at the Seward home that day to inquire about the Secretary's health. Powell himself was inconsistent. He once said he learned he was to kill Seward on the morning of Friday, April 14, but later claimed he did not know until the evening of April 14.[67]

*William H. Seward, the object of Powell's murder attempt.*

On the afternoon of April 14, Booth learned that Abraham Lincoln would be attending a play at Ford's Theatre that night. Booth decided that the time had come to kill Lincoln.[68][69] Booth sent David Herold to tell Powell the news. The two men probably spent the afternoon and early evening at the Canterbury Music Hall on Pennsylvania Avenue, where Powell met and possibly had a tryst with Mary Gardner, a performer there.[70]

At 8:00 p.m. that night, Booth, Atzerodt, Herold, and Powell met in Powell's room at the Herndon House in Washington, D.C., where Booth assigned roles.[68][69] They would strike that very night, Booth said. Powell (accompanied by Herold) was to go to the home of Secretary of State William H. Seward and kill him. Atzerodt was to assassinate Vice President Andrew Johnson.[e][71] Booth was to murder Lincoln at Ford's Theatre.

## The attack on Seward

*Lithograph of Powell attacking Frederick Seward.*

At about 10:13 p.m., Powell was escorted to the Seward residence on Lafayette Square near the White House by David Herold. Seward had been injured in a carriage accident on April 5, and suffered a concussion, broken jaw, broken right arm, and many serious bruises. Local newspapers reported that Seward was at home convalescing, so Powell and Herold knew where to find him. Powell was armed with a Whitney revolver and large knife, and wore black pants, a long overcoat, a grey vest, a grey dress coat, and a hat with a wide brim.[72][73] Herold waited outside, holding Powell's horse. Powell knocked and rang the bell, and the door was answered by William Bell, Seward's African American maitre d'. Holding up a small bottle, Powell claimed that Seward's physician, Dr. T.S. Verdi, had sent some medicine to the house. Bell was suspicious, as Dr. Verdi had departed the home only an hour earlier and left instructions for Seward not to be disturbed. Bell asked Powell to wait, but Powell pushed past him and began mounting the stairs to the second-floor bedrooms.[73]

Seward's son, Frederick, appeared at the top of the steps in his nightclothes. As Powell reached the second floor, Frederick ordered Powell to stop.[73] Seward's daughter, Fanny, stuck her head out of her father's bedroom door and warned the men that Seward was sleeping. She then returned to the bedroom.[74] Powell said he was delivering medicine, and Frederick asked for the bottle. Powell gave it to him, then pulled out his revolver and pulled the trigger with the barrel of the gun against Frederick's chest.[73] The revolver misfired, and Powell pistol-whipped Frederick over and over. Bell fled the house screaming "Murder! Murder!" and raced to the office of General Christopher C. Augur next door for help. Terrified, Herold tied Powell's horse to a tree and fled on his own steed.[73]

Powell now drew out his knife and burst through Seward's bedroom door. Inside were Seward's Army nurse, Sergeant George F. Robinson, and Fanny Seward. Powell slashed Robinson on the forearm, and the soldier fell. Powell punched Fanny in the face, and leapt onto the bed. He savagely began knifing Seward in the head and throat. Seward, however, was wearing a metal and canvas splint on his jaw, which deflected most of Powell's blows. However, Powell managed to cut through Seward's right cheek and along his right throat, causing a large amount of blood flow. Believing Seward to be dead, Powell hesitated. Just then, Seward's other son, Augustus, burst into the room. Powell stabbed him several times. Augustus dragged Powell onto the floor. Robinson and Augustus Seward wrestled with the strong, uninjured Powell. Powell stabbed Robinson in the chest and shoulder, and slashed a portion of Augustus' scalp from his head.[75]

Powell shouted, "I'm mad! I'm mad!" and fled the room. Powell was confronted by State Department messenger Emerick "Bud" Hansell in the hallway. Hansell had just arrived at the house moments earlier and found the front door ajar. As Hansell turned to flee, Powell stabbed him in the back. Powell ran out of the house, and threw his knife in the gutter of the street.[76]

## Flight and capture

Powell now realized that Herold had abandoned him. Powell had almost no knowledge of the streets of Washington, D.C., and without Herold he had no way of locating the streets he was to use for his escape route.[76][g][77] He mounted his horse, and began riding at a relatively slow pace north on 15th Street.[76]

Powell's exact movements from the time he was seen cantering up 15th Street until the time he appeared at the Surratt boarding house three days later are not clear. It is well-established that he ended up (by riding or walking) in the far northeast part of the District of Columbia near Fort Bunker Hill, where he discarded his overcoat.[h][77] In the overcoat pockets were Powell's riding gloves, a false mustache, and a piece of paper with Mary Gardner's name and hotel room number on it.[78] Sources differ widely on what happened. Historian Ernest B. Furguson says Powell's horse gave out near Lincoln Hospital (now Lincoln Park), a mile east of the United States Capitol on East Capitol Street. He then hid in "a cemetery" (without specifying which).[79] Ownsbey says Powell hid in a tree for three days.[77] Historians William C. Edwards and Edward Steers Jr. claim Powell made it to both Fort Bunker Hill and Congressional Cemetery (at 18th and E Streets SE),[80] while Ralph Gary claims that Powell hid out in a marble burial vault at Congressional Cemetery.[81] Andrew Jampoler, however, says Powell just wandered the streets of the city.[82] Whether Powell abandoned his horse,[83][84][85][86] was thrown by it,[85] or both[77] is unclear, and Powell never gave a public or formal statement about what happened.[i][87][j][88]

Powell decided to return to Surratt's boarding house to seek help. His clothes were somewhat bloody from the attack at Seward's home, and he'd dropped his hat at the Seward home.[89] During much of the Victorian era, it was considered unseemly for any man (even a menial laborer) to be seen in public without a hat, and Powell would have been viewed with suspicion had he tried to enter the city without one.[90] Ripping the sleeve from his undershirt, Powell placed the sleeve on his head in the hope that people would think it was a stocking cap.[91][92] To complete his disguise as a common laborer, he then stole a pickaxe from a farmyard.[90] Powell then headed for Surratt's.

Members of the D.C., Metropolitan Police Department already suspected John Surratt of complicity in Lincoln's murder, and had visited the Surratt boarding house for the first time as early as 2:00 a.m. on April 15, less than four hours after the attacks. [93][94][95] Nothing incriminating was found. Federal authorities decided to make a second visit. Military investigators arrived at about 11:00 p.m. on Monday, April 17, to bring Mrs. Surratt and others in for questioning. As they were about to depart at 11:45 p.m., Powell showed up on the doorstep.[96] Powell claimed to be a menial laborer who'd been hired that morning by Mrs. Surratt to dig a gutter in the street. He explained his arrival at the house by saying that he wanted to know what time he should begin work in the morning. His clothes aroused intense suspicion, as he wore rather good quality boots, pants, dress shirt, vest, and coat. [97] His pickaxe seemed unused,[98] and his hands were uncalloused and well manicured (unlike those of a common laborer).[99] Mrs. Surratt denied knowing him. (She would later claim that her extremely poor eyesight and the darkness of the room prevented her from recognizing Powell. Powell stood under a bright lamp just five feet from her when she made her denial.)[100]

Taken into custody, Powell was discovered to have a box of pistol cartridges, a compass, hair pomade, a brush and comb, two fine handkerchiefs, and a copy of his oath of allegiance (signed "L. Paine") in his pockets. These were not the possessions of a menial laborer. Although he claimed he was a poor man who barely earned a dollar a day for ditch-digging, Powell's wallet contained $25.[101] About 3:00 a.m. on April 18, William Bell identified Powell as the man who assaulted Seward. Powell was formally arrested, and imprisoned aboard the monitor USS *Saugus*, then at anchor in the Anacostia River at the Washington Navy Yard.[102] A second identification was made around mid-morning on April 18 when Augustus Seward visited the *Saugus* and positively identified Powell as the man who attacked him and his father.[103]

## Trial and execution

The federal government arrested a great many people for their role in the Lincoln assassination. Arrests included John T. Ford, owner of Ford's Theatre; Ford's brothers, James and Harry Clay Ford; John "Peanuts" Burroughs, the African American boy who unwittingly held Booth's horse in the alley behind Ford's Theatre; Mary Surratt's brother, John

Zadoc "Zad" Jenkins; Surratt's boarder, 15-year-old Honora Fitzpatrick; and many others. Some, like Judson Jarboe, had merely seen one of the key conspirators walk by. All were released, although many were incarcerated for up to 40 days or more.[104]

The most important prisoners were kept aboard monitors, to prevent escape as well as any effort to free them. Along with Powell on the *Saugus* were Michael O'Laughlen, Samuel Arnold, Edmund Spangler (scene shifter at Ford's Theatre), and George Atzerodt's cousin, Hartmann Richter (who had harbored Atzerodt for four days). Aboard the USS *Montauk* were David Herold, George Atzerodt (he was later moved to the *Saugus*), and the body of John Wilkes Booth. Dr. Samuel Mudd and Mary Surratt were held at the Old Capitol Prison (now the site of the United States Supreme Court Building).[105][k][106]

## Confinement

*Powell in the hat and overcoat he wore the night he attacked Seward.*

*Powell aboard the USS Saugus by Alexander Gardner.*

Reporters were denied access to the prisoners, but photographer Alexander Gardner received clearance. On April 27, Gardner began taking photographs of those who were caught up in the government's dragnet.[l] One by one, each prisoner was brought on deck and photographed in a few positions. Gardner took far more photographs of Powell than anyone else. Powell obliged Gardner by posing seated, standing (with and without restraints), and modeling the overcoat and hat that he had worn the night of the Seward attacks. Among the most famous of the photographs is one in which Powell sits against the gun turret of the *Saugus*, staring into the camera in a modern fashion, relaxed and direct.[107]

Powell's confinement was not easy. He was constantly shackled with a form of manacles known as "lily irons," a riveted handcuff that had two separate iron bands on each wrist that prevented bending of the wrist or use of the hands independently.[108] Like all the male prisoners, a heavy iron ball at the end of a 6-foot (1.8 m) long chain was manacled to one of his legs.[109] Shackles were riveted closed about the ankles, which caused Powell's feet to swell considerably.[110][m][111] Like all the prisoners, he had only a straw pallet on which to sit or lie and a single blanket for warmth.[112][113] The same meal was served four times a day: coffee or water, bread, salted pork, and beef or beef soup.[109] On April 29, all the prisoners aboard the monitors and at the Old Capitol Prison were moved to newly constructed cells at the Washington Arsenal (now Fort Lesley J. McNair).[114]

The prisoners were not permitted to bathe or wash until May 4, when all bindings and clothes were removed and they were permitted to bathe in cold water in the presence of a soldier.[115] In early May, General John F. Hartranft, special provost marshal overseeing the prisoners, began improving the living conditions. Powell and the other prisoners began to receive fresh clothing (including undergarments) more frequently, more food, and writing instruments (paper, pen, ink).[116] When Powell was observed raising the iron ball to his head, Hartranft feared Powell might be contemplating suicide, and had the ball removed on June 2.[116] Living conditions improved again on June 18, when the prisoners were given a box to sit on, outdoor exercise time each day, and reading material and chewing tobacco after each meal.[112]

On April 22, Powell repeatedly banged his head into the iron walls of his cell aboard the *Saugus*.[117] Whether it was a suicide attempt, as his jailers believed, or not, it deeply alarmed military officials. A canvas padded hood, with only a slit for the mouth and nostrils, was fashioned. Powell and all the other prisoners aboard the monitors were forced to wear them 24 hours a day, seven days a week, to prevent any further suicide attempts. [108] Only Mary Surratt and Dr. Mudd were not required to wear the hoods.[118][119] Powell cried when the hood was placed on him.[109] The hoods were hot, claustrophobic, and uncomfortable, and in the humid confines of the monitors in the steaming Washington summer, the prisoners suffered immensely. On June 6, Hartranft ordered them removed except for Powell's.[120][121]

The apparent suicide attempt worried prison officials for another reason. Powell allegedly could not remember what state or country he had been born in or his age. Military personnel became concerned that he was insane or was being driven mad by his confinement. Three physicians were called in to determine his sanity, and on June 17, he was interviewed for three hours and 40 minutes by Major Thomas Akaryote and Dr. John T. Gray. (The military tribunal later ruled him sane.)[122]

With Booth dead and John Surratt still at large, Powell was the individual who knew most about the conspiracy, and government officials pressed him for information. Major Thomas T. Eckert spent hours with Powell over the weeks until his execution, trying to get him to talk. During this time, Powell told many stories, some true and some obviously not) about his war experiences and various plots to kill Lincoln or commit other crimes (such as burn New York City).[123]

## Trial

The trial of the alleged conspirators began on May 9.[124] A military tribunal, rather than a civilian court, was chosen as the prosecutorial venue because government officials thought that its more lenient rules of evidence would enable the court to get to the bottom of what was then perceived by the public as a vast conspiracy.[125] A military tribunal also avoided the possibility of jury nullification since federal officials worried that a jury drawn from the pro-Southern populace of the District of Columbia might free the prisoners. [126] All eight alleged conspirators were tried simultaneously.[127]

*The leaders of the prosecution: John A. Bingham, Joseph Holt, Henry Lawrence Burnett.*

The prosecution was led by Judge Advocate General Brigadier General Joseph Holt, assisted by Assistant Judge Advocate General Colonel Henry Lawrence Burnett, and Judge Advocate Major John Bingham. [128] A panel of nine judges, all military officers, sat in judgment over the accused. Conviction required a simple majority of judges, while imposition of the death sentence required a two-thirds majority. The only appeal was directly to the President of the United States.[129][130][131][n][132]

A room on the northeast corner of the third floor of the Arsenal was used as a courtroom.[133][134][135] The prisoners sat together on long benches[133][136] wearing wrist and ankle manacles[137] and an armed guard on either side of each of them.[136][138] The exception was Surratt, who sat in a chair unmanacled.[133][136][139][140] Surratt and Powell received the most press attention during the trial.[141]

Powell did not have legal representation until the third day of the trial. James Mason Campbell, son-in-law of late Supreme Court Chief Justice Roger B. Taney,[142][143] declined to represent him. On the second day, Burnett asked Colonel William E. Doster to assume Powell's defense.[144] John Atzerodt had hired Doster to represent his brother, George Atzerodt, during the trial. Although reluctant since he had his hands full with one client, Doster agreed,[145] but for weeks, Powell refused to speak to Doster.[112]

The prosecution opened its case against Powell on May 13. Weichmann tied Powell strongly to the Booth-led conspiracies against Lincoln.[146] Slowly, the public realized that "Lewis Payne," the name used to formally charge the individual with conspiracy, attempted murder, and murder, was really someone named Lewis Powell.[146] Court testimony turned to other issues for a week before the prosecution's case against Powell resumed. Seward butler William Bell, Augustus Seward, and Sergeant George F. Robinson testified about the attack on the Secretary of State and identified Powell as the assailant. The Herndon House landlady testified that Powell rented a room from her, while two police officers discussed Powell's arrest.[147] A long list of other witnesses testified about minor pieces of evidence (such as the discovery of Powell's knife in the gutter and the recovery of his abandoned horse).[148]

Bell's testimony proved to be a turning point. Powell was freed from his restraints and was obliged to put on his hat and overcoat. He placed his hands on Bell as if to shove him aside. Bell's reaction provoked much laughter in the courtroom, even from Powell. [149] However, Powell was rattled by the testimony and finally agreed to speak with Doster about himself and his case. Powell expressed remorse for hurting Frederick Seward, but most of his discussion was disjointed and rambling, and he still could not remember his age or place of birth. Doster became convinced that Powell was half-witted. Although

Powell revealed his real name, the name of his father, and where his parents lived, Powell's many fabrications left Doster too distrustful of those facts to act on them. (Doster did not write to George Powell in Florida until nearly a month had passed.)[150]

The defense opened its case on June 21.[151] Doster's defense of Powell was essentially a plea for his life. The weight of evidence against Powell was so overwhelming that Doster never attempted to disprove his guilt. Rather, Doster characterized Powell's actions as those of a soldier who "aimed at the head of a department instead of a corps."[152] On June 2, Doster suggested to the court that Powell was insane. Dr. Charles Nichols, superintendent of the Government Hospital for the Insane, testified as to his belief that Powell was insane, as did the two guards who watched over Powell. However, despite additional examinations by a number of physicians, none of them found Powell insane. Many claimed he was stupid or slow-witted, but none found him insane.[153]

Doster made one last bid to save Powell's life by arguing that Powell had not killed Lincoln or Seward and so his life should be spared.[154] Doster ignored the conspiracy laws of the day, which incorporated the concept of vicarious liability, which meant that Powell was responsible for Lincoln's murder even if the original conspiracy were to kidnap, rather than kill, and even if Booth had acted to kill without Powell's knowledge or consent.[155]

# Execution

## *Execution eve*

The nine judges of the military tribunal began considering the guilt and sentencing of the co-conspirators on June 29. About an hour was spent considering each defendant's guilt. On June 30, the tribunal began voting on the charges facing each individual. They disposed of the Herold and Atzerodt cases before considering Powell's guilt. He was found guilty of all charges, except the two counts of conspiracy with Edmund Spangler. The tribunal sentenced Powell to death.[156][157] President Johnson affirmed the verdicts and sentences on July 5 following an inevitable appeal.[158][159]

On July 6, the verdicts were made public.[160] General Winfield Scott Hancock and General Hartranft began informing the prisoners of their sentences at noon the same day.[161] Powell was the first to be told that he was found guilty and sentenced to die, and he accepted his fate stoically. Powell asked to see two ministers: Reverend Augustus P. Stryker, an Episcopalian minister at St. Barnabas Church in Baltimore and a Confederate sympathizer, and the Reverend Doctor Abram Dunn Gillette, a loyal Unionist and pastor at the First Baptist Church in Washington, D.C., Gillette arrived shortly after Powell made his request. Powell spent several hours with Gillette, whom he had seen preach in Baltimore in February 1865. Powell told Gillette about his background, how he came to be involved in the conspiracy, and how much he regretted his actions (which he still justified as those of a soldier). Powell wept profusely during portions of their interview, and blamed Confederate leaders for his predicament.[162]

Powell strenuously attempted to exonerate Mary Surratt. According to one source, Powell asked Gillette to bring Captain Christian Rath to him. Rath came, and Powell declared that Surratt knew nothing of the conspiracy and was innocent. Rath conferred with Eckert, and within an hour had taken down Powell's statement for consideration by President Johnson.[163] Another source, however, says that it was the two Roman Catholic priests who were consoling Mary Surratt, Father Jacob Walter and Father B.F. Wiget, and Surratt's daughter, Anna, who visited Powell that evening and elicited the statement declaring Mrs. Surratt innocent.[164] Whichever version is true (perhaps both), Powell's statement had no effect on anyone with authority to prevent Surratt's execution.[164] Powell was the only one of the conspirators to make a statement exonerating Surratt.[164]

Gillette spent the night with Powell. The condemned man alternately wept and prayed, and fell asleep for three hours near dawn.[163] Reverend Stryker was on his way to Washington, but would not receive permission to see Powell until noon the following day.[165]

## Execution

*Execution of (left to right) Mary Surratt, Lewis Powell, David Herold, and George Atzerodt on July 7, 1865, at the Washington Arsenal in Washington, D.C.*

A gallows was constructed in the Arsenal courtyard[166] 12 feet (3.7 m) high and large enough for all four condemned to be hanged at once.[167]

Powell asked to see General Hartranft and impressed upon him once more Mary Surratt's innocence. Hartranft wrote a memorandum to President Johnson outlining Powell's statement, adding that he believed Powell to be telling the truth. Powell then made a statement exonerating Atzerodt and declared that Atzerodt refused to kill Vice President Johnson even though Booth had ordered him to do so.[168]

At 1:15 p.m., July 7, 1865,[169][170] the prisoners were taken through the courtyard and up the steps of the gallows.[169][171] Each prisoner's ankles and wrists were manacled. [172] More than 1,000 people, including government officials, members of the US armed forces, friends and family of the condemned, official witnesses, and reporters, watched from the Arsenal courtyard and the tops of its walls.[173] Alexander Gardner, who had photographed Powell and the others two months before, photographed the execution for the government.[174]

Hartranft read the execution order[169] as the condemned sat in chairs.[175] White cloth was used to bind their arms to their sides, and to tie their ankles and thighs together.[170] [172] On Powell's behalf Gillette thanked the prison officials for their kindness, and said a prayer for Powell's soul; Powell's eyes filled with tears.[176] Powell said, "Mrs. Surratt is innocent. She doesn't deserve to die with the rest of us."[177]

The prisoners were asked to stand and move forward a few feet to the nooses.[175][178] A white bag was placed over the head of each prisoner after the noose was put in place. [172] Powell said to Rath through his hood, "I thank you, goodbye."[176] Rath clapped his hands,[179][170][178] and soldiers knocked the supports from under the drops.[172][180] Surratt and Atzerodt[179] seemed to die quickly.[181][182] Herold and Powell struggled for nearly five minutes.[179][181][182] Powell's body swung about wildly, and once or twice his legs came up so that he was almost in a sitting position.[183][184]

## Burial

The bodies were allowed to hang for about 30 minutes before being cut down[173][178] [185] and placed in wooden gun boxes.[186][172][173] The name of each deceased was written on a piece of paper and placed in the box in a glass vial.[173] They were buried, along with Booth, against the east wall of the prison yard.[187]

In 1867, the coffins were reburied elsewhere within the Arsenal.[187][188] In February 1869, after much pleading from the Booths and Surratts, President Johnson agreed to turn the bodies over to their families.[187]

There is some dispute about what happened next. Historian Betty Ownsbey says that Powell's family expressed a wish to reclaim the remains, but did not do so.[189] Historian Richard Bak believes Powell's remains were interred at Graceland Cemetery in Washington, D.C. Powell's remains were disinterred and reburied at Holmead's Burying Ground. According to Powell family legend, Bak says, the family went to Washington in 1871 to retrieve Lewis' remains; the skull was missing. On the return trip to Florida, George Powell fell ill, and Lewis Powell's remains were temporarily interred on a nearby farm. In 1879, the remains were retrieved and the headless corpse was buried in Geneva, Florida.[190] Betty Ownsbey says this is nothing more than a fanciful story.[187] She argues that the events could not have occurred as related by family members, for the city of Washington, D.C., would have issued a disinterment order as well as issued a receipt for the body—neither of which occurred.[191] There are also other reasons to believe the family legend is inaccurate. Graceland Cemetery (a burial ground primarily for African Americans) did not open until 1872, but Powell was reburied before that. Graceland closed in 1894,[192] a date which does not fit with the date of the Holmead's burial as related by Bak or Ownsbey.[p][193]

Other documents describe an alternative series of events. According to this version, Powell's family declined to retrieve the body, at which point Powell was buried at Holmead's Burying Ground[194] in either June 1869[195] or February 1870.[196] A.H. Gawler of Gawler's Funeral Home handled the reburial. The burial site was unmarked, and only Gawler and a few Army personnel knew where Powell was interred at Holmead's.[196] Holmead's closed in 1874, and for the next decade bodies were disinterred and reburied elsewhere. Family members and friends reclaimed about 1,000 bodies. The remains of 4,200 Caucasians were removed to Rock Creek Cemetery, while several hundred African American remains were reinterred at Graceland Cemetery.[197] According to the *Washington Evening Star* newspaper, Powell's body was exhumed by Gawler's on December 16, 1884. The identifying glass vial was recovered, but the paper it was supposed to contain was missing.[198] Wesley Pippenger, a historian who has studied Holmead's Burying Ground, asserts that Powell's remains were buried at Graceland Cemetery.[199][q] With unclaimed white remains at Graceland moved to mass graves at Rock Creek Cemetery,[197] Powell's remains may lie there.

Powell biographer Betty Ownsbey suggests a third sequence of events. She argues Powell was interred at Graceland Cemetery, but that his remains were disinterred some time between 1870 and 1884 and moved to Holmead's Burying Ground. Powell's remains were disinterred in 1884, and buried in a mass grave in Section K, Lot 23, at Rock Creek Cemetery.[200]

# William Quantrill

**William Clarke Quantrill** (July 31, 1837–June 6, 1865) was a Confederate guerrilla leader during the American Civil War.

Having endured a tempestuous childhood before later becoming a schoolteacher, Quantrill joined a group of bandits who roamed the Missouri and Kansas countryside apprehending escaped slaves. Later on this group became Confederate soldiers, who were referred to as "Quantrill's Raiders." This group was a pro-Confederate partisan ranger outfit best known for their often brutal guerrilla tactics, which made use of effective Native American field skills. Also notable, William's group included the infamous young Jesse James and his older brother Frank James. Quantrill is often noted as influential in the minds of many bandits, outlaws and hired guns of the Old West as it was being settled. In May 1865, Quantrill was mortally wounded by Union troops in Central Kentucky, in one of the last engagements of the Civil War.

## Guerrilla leader

In 1861, Quantrill went to Texas with a slaveholder named Marcus Gill. There they met Joel B. Mayes and joined the Cherokee Nations. Mayes was a half Scots-Irish, half Cherokee Indian Confederate sympathizer and a war chief of the Cherokee Nations in Texas. He had moved from Georgia to the old Indian Territory in 1838. Mayes enlisted and served as a private in Company A of the 1st Cherokee Regiment in the Confederate army. It was Mayes who taught Quantrill guerrilla warfare tactics. He would learn the ambush fighting tactics used by the Native Americans as well as sneak attacks and camouflage. Quantrill, in the company of Mayes and the Cherokee Nations, joined with General Sterling Price and fought at the Battle of Wilson's Creek and Lexington in August and September 1861.[8]

Quantrill deserted General Price's army and went to Blue Springs, Missouri, to form his own "Army" of loyal men who had great belief in him and the Confederate cause; they came to be known as "Quantrill's Raiders." By Christmas of 1861, he had ten men who would follow him full-time into his pro-Confederate guerrilla organization.[9] These men were: William Haller, George Todd, Joseph Gilcrist, Perry Hoy, John Little, James Little, Joseph Baughan, William H. Gregg, James A. Hendricks, and John W. Koger. Later in 1862, John Jarrett, John Brown, Cole Younger, as well as William T. "Bloody Bill" Anderson and the James brothers would join Quantrill's army.[10]

## Lawrence Massacre

The most significant event in Quantrill's guerrilla career took place on August 21, 1863. Lawrence had been seen for years as the stronghold of the anti-slavery forces in Kansas and as a base of operation for incursions into Missouri by Jayhawkers and pro-Union forces. It was also the home of James H. Lane, a senator known in Missouri for his staunch anti-slavery views and also a leader of the Jayhawkers.

During the weeks immediately preceding the raid, Union General Thomas Ewing, Jr., had ordered the detention of any civilians giving aid to Quantrill's Raiders. Several female relatives of the guerrillas had been imprisoned in a makeshift jail in Kansas City, Missouri. On August 14, the building collapsed, killing four young women and seriously injuring others. Among the dead was Josephine Anderson, sister of one of Quantrill's key guerrilla allies, "Bloody Bill" Anderson. Another of Anderson's sisters, Mary, was permanently crippled in the collapse. Quantrill's men believed the collapse was deliberate, and the event fanned them into a fury.

Some historians have suggested that Quantrill had actually planned to raid Lawrence in advance of the building's collapse, in retaliation for earlier Jayhawker attacks[11] as well as the burning of Osceola, Missouri.

Early on the morning of August 21, Quantrill descended from Mount Oread and attacked Lawrence at the head of a combined force of as many as 450 guerrilla fighters. Senator Lane, a prime target of the raid, managed to escape through a cornfield in his nightshirt, but the guerrillas, on Quantrill's orders, killed around 150 men and boys who were able to carry a rifle.[12] When Quantrill's men rode out at 9 a.m., most of Lawrence's buildings were burning, including all but two businesses.

On August 25, in retaliation for the raid, General Ewing authorized General Order No. 11 (not to be confused with General Ulysses S. Grant's order of the same name). The edict ordered the depopulation of three and a half Missouri counties along the Kansas border (with the exception of a few designated towns), forcing tens of thousands of civilians to abandon their homes. Union troops marched through behind them, burning buildings, torching planted fields and shooting down livestock to deprive the guerrillas of food, fodder and support. The area was so thoroughly devastated that it became known thereafter as the "Burnt District." Quantrill and his men rode south to Texas, where they passed the winter with the Confederate forces. On May 18, 1864, Quantrill's forces lynched Texas Sheriff James L. Read in Collin County, Texas.

## Last years

While in Texas, Quantrill and his 400 men quarreled. His once-large band broke up into several smaller guerrilla companies. One was led by his lieutenant, "Bloody Bill" Anderson, Quantrill joined them briefly in the fall of 1864 during fighting north of the Missouri River.

In the spring of 1865, now leading only a few dozen pro-confederates, Quantrill staged a series of raids in western Kentucky. Confederate General Robert E. Lee surrendered to Ulysses Grant on April 9, and General Johnston surrendered most of the rest of the Confederate Army to General Sherman on April 26. On May 10, Quantrill and his band were caught in a Union ambush at Wakefield Farm. Unable to escape on account of a skittish horse, he was shot in the back and paralyzed from the chest down. The unit that successfully ambushed Quantrill and his followers was led by Edwin W. Terrell, a guerrilla hunter charged with finding and eliminating high profile targets by General John M. Palmer, commander of the District of Kentucky. Union officials, namely Palmer and Governor Thomas E. Bramlette had no interest in Quantrill staging a repeat of his performance in Missouri circa 1862–1863 [13] He was brought by wagon to Louisville, Kentucky, and taken to the military prison hospital, located on the north side of Broadway at 10th Street. He died from his wounds on June 6, 1865, at the age of 27.[14]

## Burial

Quantrill was buried in an unmarked grave (which is now marked) in what later became known as St. John's Cemetery in Louisville. A boyhood friend of Quantrill's, newspaper reporter William W. Scott, claimed to have dug up the Louisville grave in 1887 and brought Quantrill's remains back to Dover at the request of Quantrill's mother. These remains were supposedly buried in Dover in 1889. However, Scott attempted unsuccessfully to sell what he said were Quantrill's bones, so it is not known whether the remains he returned to Dover or buried in Dover were genuine. In the early 1990s the Missouri division of the Sons of Confederate Veterans convinced the Kansas State Historical Society to negotiate with authorities in Dover, which led to three arm bones, two leg bones, and some hair, all allegedly Quantrill's, being buried in 1992 at the Old Confederate Veteran's Home Cemetery in Higginsville, Missouri. As a result of these events, there are grave markers for Quantrill in Louisville, Dover, and Higginsville.[15]

## Claim of post-1865 survival

In August 1907, news articles appeared in Canada and the U.S. claiming that J.E. Duffy, a member of a Michigan cavalry troop that dealt with Quantrill's raiders during the Civil War, had met Quantrill at Quatsino Sound, on northern Vancouver Island while investigating timber rights in the area. Duffy claimed to recognize the man, living under the name of John Sharp, as Quantrill. Duffy said that Sharp admitted he was Quantrill and discussed in detail raids in Kansas and elsewhere. Sharp claimed that he had survived the ambush in Kentucky, though receiving a bayonet and bullet wound, making his way to South America where he lived some years in Chile. He returned to the U.S., working as a cattleman in Fort Worth, Texas. He then moved to Oregon, acting as a cowpuncher and drover, before reaching British Columbia in the 1890s, where he worked in logging, trapping and finally as a mine caretaker at Coal Harbour at Quatsino.

Within some weeks after the news stories were published, two men came to British Columbia, travelling to Quatsino from Victoria, leaving Quatsino on a return voyage of a coastal steamer the next day. On that day, Sharp was found severely beaten, dying several hours later without giving information about his attackers. The police were unable to solve the murder.[16]

## Reputation and legacy

Quantrill's actions remain controversial to this day. Some historians view him as an opportunistic, bloodthirsty outlaw; James M. McPherson, one of America's most prominent experts on the Civil War today, calls him and Anderson "pathological killers" who "murdered and burned out Missouri Unionists." [17] Historian Matthew Christopher Hulbert argues that Quantrill "ruled the bushwhacker pantheon" established by ex-Confederate officer and propagandist John Newman Edwards in the 1870s to provide the state of Missouri with its own "irregular Lost Cause."[18] Some of Quantrill's celebrity later rubbed off on other ex-Raiders, like John Jarrett, George and Oliver Shepard, Jesse and Frank James, and Cole Younger, who went on after the war to apply Quantrill's hit-and-run tactics to bank and train robbery.[19] The William Clarke Quantrill Society continues to celebrate Quantrill's life and deeds.[20]

# Henry Rathbone

**Henry Reed Rathbone** (July 1, 1837–August 14, 1911) was a United States military officer and diplomat who was present at the assassination of President Abraham Lincoln. Rathbone was sitting with his fiancée, Clara Harris, next to the President and his wife, Mary Todd Lincoln, when John Wilkes Booth entered the president's box at Ford's Theatre and fatally shot Lincoln in the head. When Rathbone attempted to prevent Booth from fleeing the scene, Booth stabbed and seriously wounded him.

## Lincoln assassination

On April 14, 1865, Major Rathbone and his fiancee Clara Harris accepted an invitation to see a play at Ford's Theatre from President Abraham Lincoln and his wife, First Lady Mary Todd Lincoln. The couple, who had been friends with the President and his wife for some time, were invited after Ulysses S. Grant and his wife Julia, Thomas Eckert, and several others had declined Mrs. Lincoln's invitation.[8]

During the play, noted stage actor John Wilkes Booth stealthily entered the Presidential box and fatally shot Lincoln in the head with a pistol. As Rathbone attempted to apprehend Booth, Booth slashed Rathbone's left arm with a dagger from the elbow to his shoulder. Rathbone later recalled that he was horrified at the anger on Booth's face.[9][10] [11] Rathbone again grabbed at Booth as Booth prepared to jump from the sill of the box. He grabbed onto Booth's coat, causing Booth to fall awkwardly to the stage, perhaps breaking his leg. Booth nonetheless escaped, and remained at large for twelve days.[12][13]

Despite his serious wound, Rathbone escorted Mary Lincoln to the Petersen House across the street, where the president had been taken.[14] Shortly thereafter he passed out due to blood loss.[15] Harris arrived soon after and held his head in her lap while he lay semiconscious. When a surgeon who had been attending Lincoln finally examined him, it was realized that his wound was more serious than initially thought. Booth had cut him nearly to the bone and severed an artery. Rathbone was taken home while Harris remained with Mary Todd Lincoln as the President lay dying over the next nine hours. [16] This death vigil lasted through the night, until morning, when Lincoln died at 7:22 a.m. on April 15, 1865.[17]

## Diplomatic career and mental decline

Although Rathbone's physical wounds healed, his mental state deteriorated in the years following Lincoln's death as he anguished over his perceived inability to thwart the assassination attempt.[18] He married Harris on July 11, 1867, and the couple had three children: Henry Riggs (born February 12, 1870, who later became a U.S. Congressman), Gerald Lawrence (born August 26, 1871), and Clara Pauline (born September 15, 1872).[19]

Rathbone resigned from the Army in 1870, having risen to the rank of brevet colonel. [20] After his resignation, he struggled to find and keep a job due to his mental instability. He became convinced that Harris was unfaithful. He also resented the attention Harris paid their children and reportedly threatened his wife on several occasions after suspecting that she was going to divorce him and take the children.[11] Nonetheless, President Chester A. Arthur appointed Rathbone as the U.S. Consul to the Province of Hanover in 1882. The family relocated to Germany, where Rathbone's mental health continued to decline.[21]

On December 23, 1883, Rathbone attacked his children in a fit of madness. Rathbone fatally shot and stabbed his wife, who was attempting to protect the children. Rathbone then stabbed himself five times in the chest in an attempted suicide.[22] He was charged with murder but was declared insane by doctors after blaming the murder on an intruder. He was convicted and committed to an asylum for the criminally insane in Hildesheim, Germany. The couple's children were sent to live with their uncle, William Harris, in the United States.[11]

## Final years and death

Rathbone spent the rest of his life in the asylum. He died on August 14, 1911, and was buried next to his wife in the city cemetery at Hanover/Engesohde.[11] As time passed, the cemetery management, looking over records concerning plots without recent activity or family interest, decided in 1952 that both sets of remains could be exhumed and disposed of.[23]

# William H. Seward

**William Henry Seward** (May 16, 1801–October 10, 1872) was United States Secretary of State from 1861 to 1869, and earlier served as governor of New York and United States Senator. A determined opponent of the spread of slavery in the years leading up to the American Civil War, he was a prominent figure in the Republican Party in its formative years, and was praised for his work on behalf of the Union as Secretary of State during the Civil War.

Seward was born in 1801 in the village of Florida, in Orange County, New York State, where his father was a farmer and owned slaves. He was educated as a lawyer and moved to the Central New York town of Auburn. Seward was elected to the New York State Senate in 1830 as an Anti-Mason. Four years later, he became the gubernatorial nominee of the Whig Party. Though he was not successful in that race, Seward was elected governor in 1838 and won a second two-year term in 1840. During this period, he signed several laws that advanced the rights of and opportunities for black residents, as well as guaranteeing fugitive slaves jury trials in the state. The legislation protected abolitionists, and he used his position to intervene in cases of freed black people who were enslaved in the South.

After many years of practicing law in Auburn, he was elected by the state legislature to the U.S. Senate in 1849. Seward's strong stances and provocative words against slavery brought him hatred in the South. He was re-elected to the Senate in 1855, and soon joined the nascent Republican Party, becoming one of its leading figures. As the 1860 presidential election approached, he was regarded as the leading candidate for the Republican nomination. Several factors, including attitudes to his vocal opposition to slavery, his support for immigrants and Catholics, and his association with editor and political boss Thurlow Weed, worked against him, and Abraham Lincoln secured the presidential nomination. Although devastated by his loss, he campaigned for Lincoln, who appointed him Secretary of State after winning the election.

Seward did his best to stop the southern states from seceding; once that failed, he devoted himself wholeheartedly to the Union cause. His firm stance against foreign intervention in the Civil War helped deter the United Kingdom and France from possibly gaining the independence of the Confederate States. He was one of the targets of the 1865 assassination plot that killed Lincoln, and was seriously wounded by conspirator Lewis Powell. Seward remained in his post through the presidency of Andrew Johnson, during which he negotiated the Alaska Purchase in 1867 and supported Johnson during his impeachment. His contemporary Carl Schurz described Seward as "one of those spirits who sometimes will go ahead of public opinion instead of tamely following its footprints."[1]

## Secession crisis

*Seward photographed by the studio of Mathew Brady*

Lincoln's election had been anticipated in Southern states, and South Carolina and other Deep South states began to call conventions for the purpose of secession. In the North, there was dissent over whether to offer concessions to the South to preserve the Union, and if conciliation failed, whether to allow the South to depart in peace. Seward favored compromise. He had hoped to remain at home until the New Year, but with the deepening crisis left for Washington in time for the new session of Congress in early December.[105]

The usual tradition was for the leading figure of the winning party to be offered the position of Secretary of State, the most senior Cabinet post. Seward was that person, and around December 12, the vice president-elect, Maine Senator Hannibal Hamlin, offered Seward the position on Lincoln's behalf. At Weed's advice, Seward was slow to formally accept, doing so on December 28, 1860, though well before Inauguration Day, March 4, 1861.[106] Lincoln remained in Illinois until mid-February, and he and Seward communicated by letter.[107][108]

As states in the Deep South prepared to secede in late 1860, Seward met with important figures from both sides of the sectional divide.[109] Seward introduced a proposed constitutional amendment preventing federal interference with slavery. This was done at Lincoln's private request; the president-elect hoped that the amendment, and a change to the Fugitive Slave Act to allow those captured a jury trial, would satisfy both sides. Congressmen introduced many such proposals, and Seward was appointed to a committee of 13 senators to consider them. Lincoln was willing to guarantee the security of slavery in the states that currently had it, but he rejected any proposal that would allow slavery to expand. It was increasingly clear that the deep South was committed to secession; the Republican hope was to provide compromises to keep the border slave states in the Union. Seward voted against the Crittenden Compromise on December 28, but quietly continued to seek a compromise that would keep the border states in the Union.[110]

Seward gave a major speech on January 12, 1861. By then, he was known to be Lincoln's choice as Secretary of State, and with Lincoln staying silent, it was widely expected that he would propound the new administration's plan to save the Union. Accordingly, he spoke to a crowded Senate, where even Jefferson Davis attended despite Mississippi's secession, and to packed galleries.[111] He urged the preservation of the Union, and supported an amendment such as the one he had introduced, or a constitutional convention, once passions had cooled. He hinted that New Mexico Territory might be a slave state, and urged the construction of two transcontinental railroads, one northern, one southern. He suggested the passage of legislation to bar interstate invasions such as that by John Brown. Although Seward's speech was widely applauded, it gained a mixed reaction in the border states to which he had tried to appeal. Radical Republicans were not willing to make concessions to the South, and were angered by the speech.[112] Pennsylvania Congressman Thaddeus Stevens, a radical, warned that if Lincoln, like Seward, ignored the Republican platform and tried to purchase peace through concessions, he would retire, as too old[a] to bear the years of warfare in the Republican Party that would result.[113]

Lincoln applauded Seward's speech, which he read in Springfield, but refused to approve any compromise that could lead to a further expansion of slavery. Once Lincoln left Springfield on February 11, he gave speeches, stating in Indianapolis that it would not be coercing a state if the federal government insisted on retaining or retaking property that belonged to it.[114] This came as the United States Army still held Fort Sumter; the president-elect's words upset moderate southerners. Virginia Congressman Sherrard Clemens wrote,

Mr. Lincoln, by his speech in the North, has done vast harm. If he will not be guided by Mr. Seward but puts himself in the hands of Mr. Chase and the ultra [that is, Radical] Republicans, nothing can save the cause of the Union in the South."[115]

Lincoln arrived in Washington, unannounced and incognito, early on the morning of February 23, 1861. Seward had been advised by General Winfield Scott that there was a plot to assassinate Lincoln in Baltimore when he passed through the city. Senator Seward sent his son Frederick to warn Lincoln in Philadelphia, and the president-elect decided to travel alone but for well-armed bodyguards. Lincoln travelled without incident, and came to regret his decision as he was widely mocked for it. Later that morning, Seward accompanied Lincoln to the White House, where he introduced the Illinoisan to President Buchanan.[116]

Seward and Lincoln differed over two issues in the days before the inauguration: the composition of Lincoln's cabinet, and his inaugural address. Given a draft of the address, Seward softened it to make it less confrontational toward the South; Lincoln accepted many of the changes, though he gave it, according to Seward biographer Glyndon G. Van Deusen, "a simplicity and a poetic quality lacking in Seward's draft."[117] The differences regarding the Cabinet revolved around the inclusion of Salmon Chase, a radical. Lincoln wanted all elements of the party, as well as representation from outside it; Seward opposed Chase, as well as former Democrats such as Gideon Welles and Montgomery Blair. Seward did not get his way, and gave Lincoln a letter declining the post of Secretary of State.[118] Lincoln felt, as he told his private secretary, John Nicolay, that he could not "afford to let Seward take the first trick."[119] No reply or acknowledgement was made by Lincoln until after the inaugural ceremonies were over on March 4, when he asked Seward to remain. Seward did[120] and was both nominated and confirmed by the Senate, with minimal debate, on March 5, 1861.[121]

## Secretary of State
## War breaks out

Lincoln faced the question of what to do about Fort Sumter in Charleston harbor, held by the Army against the will of South Carolinians, who had blockaded it. The fort's commander, Major Robert Anderson, had sent word that he would run out of supplies. Seward, backed by most of the Cabinet, recommended to Lincoln that an attempt to resupply Sumter would be provocative to the border states, that Lincoln hoped to keep from seceding. Seward hinted to the commissioners who had come to Washington on behalf of the Confederacy that Sumter would be surrendered. Lincoln was loath to give up Sumter, feeling it would only encourage the South in its insurgency.[122]

With the Sumter issue unresolved, Seward sent Lincoln a memorandum on April 1, proposing various courses of action, including possibly declaring war on France and Spain if certain conditions were not met, and reinforcing the forts along the Gulf of Mexico. In any event, vigorous policies were needed and the president must either establish them himself or allow a Cabinet member to do so, with Seward making it clear he was willing to do it.[123] Lincoln drafted a reply indicating that whatever policy was adopted, "I must do it," though he never sent it, but met with Seward instead, and what passed between them is not known.[124] Seward's biographers make the point that the note was sent to a Lincoln who had not yet proved himself in office.[125][126]

Lincoln decided on expeditions to try to relieve Sumter and Florida's Fort Pickens. Meanwhile, Seward was assuring Justice John Archibald Campbell, the intermediary with the Confederate commissioners who had come to Washington in an attempt to secure recognition, that no hostile action would be taken. Lincoln sent a notification to South Carolina's governor of the expedition, and on April 12, Charleston's batteries began firing on Sumter, beginning the Civil War.[127]

## Diplomacy

When the war started, Seward turned his attention to making sure that foreign powers did not interfere in the conflict.[128] When, in April 1861, the Confederacy announced that it would authorize privateers, Seward sent word to the American representatives abroad that the U.S. would become party to the Paris Declaration Respecting Maritime Law of 1856. This would outlaw such vessels, but Britain required that, if the U.S. were to become a party, the ratification would not require action to be taken against Confederate vessels.[129]

The Palmerston government considered recognizing the Confederacy as an independent nation. Seward was willing to wage war against Britain if it did, and drafted a strong letter for the American Minister in London, Charles Francis Adams, to read to the Foreign Secretary, Lord Russell. Seward submitted it to Lincoln, who, realizing that the Union was in no position to battle both the South and Britain, toned it down considerably, and made it merely a memorandum for Adams's guidance.[130]

In May 1861, Britain and France declared the South to be belligerents by international law, and their ships were entitled to the same rights as U.S.-flagged vessels, including the right to remain 24 hours in neutral ports.[131] Nevertheless, Seward was pleased that both nations would not meet with Confederate commissioners or recognize the South as a nation. Britain did not challenge the Union blockade of Confederate ports, and Seward wrote that if Britain continued to avoid interfering in the war, he would not be overly sensitive to what wording they used to describe their policies.[132]

In November 1861, the USS *San Jacinto*, commanded by Captain Charles Wilkes, intercepted the British mail ship RMS *Trent* and removed two Confederate diplomats, James Mason and John Slidell. They were held in Boston amid jubilation in the North and outrage in Britain. The British minister in Washington, Lord Lyons, demanded their release, as the U.S. had no right to stop a British-flagged ship traveling between neutral ports. The British drew up war plans to attack New York and sent reinforcements to Canada. Seward worked to defuse the situation. He persuaded Lyons to postpone delivering an ultimatum, and told Lincoln that the prisoners would have to be released. Lincoln did let them go, reluctantly, on technical grounds.[133] Relations between the U.S. and Britain soon improved; in April 1862, Seward and Lyons signed a treaty they had negotiated allowing each nation to inspect the other's ships for contraband slaves.[134] In November 1862, with America's image in Britain improved by the issuance of the preliminary Emancipation Proclamation, the British cabinet decided against recognition of the Confederacy as a nation.[135]

Confederate agents in Britain had arranged for the construction of Confederate ships; most notably the CSS *Alabama*, which ravaged Union shipping after her construction in 1862. With two more such vessels under construction the following year, supposedly for French interests, Seward pressed Palmerston not to allow them to leave port, and, nearly complete, they were seized by British officials in October 1863.[136]

## Involvement in wartime detentions

From the start of the war until early 1862, when responsibility was passed to the War Department, Seward was in charge of determining who should be detained without charges or trial. Approximately 800 men and a few women, believed to be Southern sympathizers or spies, were detained, usually at the initiation of local officials. Once Seward was informed, he would often order that the prisoner be transferred to federal authorities. Seward was reported to have boasted to Lord Lyons that "I can touch a bell on my right hand, and order the arrest of a citizen . . . and no power on earth, except that of the President, can release them. Can the Queen of England do so much?"[b][137]

In September 1861, Maryland legislators planned to vote to leave the Union. Seward took action against them: his son Frederick, the United States Assistant Secretary of State, reported to his father that the disloyal legislators were in prison.[138] On evidence provided by detective Allen Pinkerton, Seward in 1862 ordered the arrest of Rose Greenhow, a Washington socialite with Confederate sympathies. Greenhow had sent a stream of reports south, which continued even after she was placed under house arrest. From

Washington's Old Capitol Prison, the "Rebel Rose" provided newspaper interviews until she was allowed to cross into Confederate territory.[139]

When Seward received allegations that former president Pierce was involved in a plot against the Union, he asked Pierce for an explanation. Pierce indignantly denied it. The matter proved to be a hoax, and the administration was embarrassed. On February 14, 1862, Lincoln ordered that responsibility for detentions be transferred to the War Department, ending Seward's part in them.[140]

## Relationship with Lincoln

Seward had mixed feelings about the man who had blocked him from the presidency. One story is that when Seward was told that to deny Carl Schurz an office would disappoint him, Seward angrily stated, "Disappointment! You speak of me of disappointment! To me, who was justly entitled to the Republican nomination for the presidency, and who had to stand aside and see it given to a little Illinois lawyer!"[141] Despite his initial reservations about Lincoln's abilities, he came to admire Lincoln as the president grew more confident in his job. Seward wrote to his wife in June 1861, "Executive skill and vigor are rare qualities. The President is the best of us, but he needs constant and assiduous cooperation."[142] According to Goodwin, "Seward would become his most faithful ally in the cabinet . . . Seward's mortification at not having received his party's nomination never fully abated, but he no longer felt compelled to belittle Lincoln to ease his pain."[143] Lincoln, a one-term congressman, was inexperienced in Washington ways, and relied on Seward's advice on protocol and social etiquette.[144]

The two men built a close personal and professional relationship. Lincoln fell into the habit of entrusting Seward with tasks not within the remit of the State Department, for example asking him to examine a treaty with the Delaware Indians. Lincoln would come to Seward's house and the two lawyers would relax before the fire, chatting. Seward began to feature in the president's humorous stories. For example, Lincoln would tell of Seward remonstrating with the president, whom he found polishing his boots, "In Washington, we do not blacken our own boots," with Lincoln's response, "Indeed, then whose boots *do* you blacken, Mr. Secretary?"[145]

Other cabinet members became resentful of Seward, who seemed to be always present when they discussed their departments' concerns with Lincoln, yet they were never allowed to be there when the two men discussed foreign affairs. Seward announced when cabinet meetings would be; his colleagues eventually persuaded Lincoln to set a regular date and time for those sessions.[146] Seward's position on the Emancipation Proclamation when Lincoln read it to his cabinet in July 1862 is uncertain; Secretary of War Edwin Stanton wrote at the time that Seward opposed it in principle, feeling the slaves should simply be freed as Union armies advanced. Two later accounts indicate that Seward felt that it was not yet time to issue it, and Lincoln did wait until after the bloody stalemate at Antietam that ended Confederate General Robert E. Lee's incursion into the North to issue it. In the interim, Seward cautiously investigated how foreign powers might react to such a proclamation, and learned it would make them less likely to interfere in the conflict. [147]

Seward was not close to Lincoln's wife Mary, who by some accounts had opposed his appointment as Secretary of State. Mary Lincoln developed such a dislike for Seward that she instructed her coachman to avoid passing by the Seward residence. The Secretary of State enjoyed the company of the younger Lincoln boys, Willie and Tad, presenting them with two cats from his assortment of pets.[148]

Seward accompanied Lincoln to Gettysburg, Pennsylvania, in November 1863, where Lincoln was to deliver a short speech, that would become famous as the Gettysburg Address. The night before the speech, Lincoln met with Seward. There is no surviving evidence that Seward authored any changes: he stated after the address, when asked if had had any hand in it, that only Lincoln could have made that speech. Seward also proposed to Lincoln that he proclaim a day of national thanksgiving, and drafted a proclamation to that effect. Although post-harvest thanksgiving celebrations had long been held, this first formalized Thanksgiving Day as a national observance.[149]

## 1864 election; Hampton Roads Conference

It was far from certain that Lincoln would even be nominated in 1864, let alone re-elected, as the tide of war, though generally favoring the North, washed back and forth. Lincoln sought nomination by the National Union Party, composed of Republicans and War Democrats. No one proved willing to oppose Lincoln, who was nominated. Seward was by then unpopular among many Republicans and opponents sought to prompt his replacement by making Lincoln's running mate former New York Democratic senator Daniel S. Dickinson; under the political customs of the time, one state could not hold two positions as prestigious as vice president and Secretary of State. Administration forces turned back Dickinson's bid, nominating instead Military Governor of Tennessee Andrew Johnson, with whom Seward had served in the Senate. Lincoln was re-elected in November; Seward sat with Lincoln and the assistant presidential secretary, John Hay, as the returns came in.[150]

In January 1865, Francis Preston Blair, father of former Lincoln Postmaster General Montgomery Blair, went, with Lincoln's knowledge, to the Confederate capital of Richmond to propose to Davis that North and South unite to expel the French from their domination of Mexico. Davis appointed commissioners (Vice President Alexander Stephens, former U.S. Supreme Court justice Campbell, and former Confederate Secretary of State Robert M. T. Hunter) to negotiate. They met with Lincoln and Seward at the Hampton Roads Conference the following month. Lincoln would settle for nothing short of a cession of resistance to the federal government and an end to slavery; the Confederates would not even concede that they and the Union were one nation. There was much friendly talk, as most of them had served together in Washington, but no agreement.[151] After the conference broke up, Seward sent a bucket of champagne to the Confederates, conveyed by a black oarsman in a rowboat, and called to the southerners, "keep the champagne, but return the Negro."[152]

## Assassination attempt

John Wilkes Booth had originally planned to kidnap Lincoln, and recruited conspirators, including Lewis Powell. Having found no opportunity to abduct the president, on April 14, 1865, Booth assigned Powell to assassinate Seward, with George Atzerodt to kill Vice President Johnson and himself to kill Lincoln, which would slay the three senior members of the Executive Branch. Accordingly, another member of the conspiracy, David Herold, led Powell to the Seward home on horseback and was responsible for holding Powell's horse while he committed the attack. Seward had been hurt in an accident some days before, and Powell gained entry to the home on the excuse he was delivering medicine to the injured man, but was stopped at the top of the stairs by Seward's son Frederick, who insisted Powell give him the medicine. Powell instead attempted to fire on Frederick, and beat him over the head with the barrel of his gun when it misfired. Powell burst through the door, threw Fanny Seward (Seward's daughter) to one side, jumped on the bed, and stabbed William Seward in the face and neck five times. A soldier assigned to guard and nurse the secretary, Private George F. Robinson, jumped on Powell, forcing him from the bed. Private Robinson and Augustus Henry Seward, another of Seward's sons, were also injured in their struggle with the would-be assassin. Ultimately, Powell fled, stabbing a messenger, Emerick Hansell, as he went, only to find that Herold, panicked by the screams from the house, had left with both horses. Seward was at first thought dead, but revived enough to instruct Robinson to send for the police and lock the house until they arrived.[153]

Almost simultaneously with the attack on Seward, Booth had mortally wounded Lincoln at Ford's Theatre. Atzerodt, however, decided not to go through with the attack on Johnson. When Secretary of War Edwin Stanton and Navy Secretary Gideon Welles hurried to Seward's home to find out what had happened, they found blood everywhere.[154]

All five men injured that night at the Seward home survived. Powell was captured the next day at the boarding house of Mary Surratt, and was executed on July 7, 1865, along with Herold, Atzerodt, and Surratt, convicted as conspirators in the Lincoln assassination. Their deaths occurred only weeks after that of Seward's wife Frances, who never recovered from the shock of the assassination attempt.[155]

## Death and family matters

Back in Auburn, Seward began his memoirs, but only reached his thirties before putting it aside to write of his travels. In these months he was steadily growing weaker. On October 10, 1872, he worked at his desk in the morning as usual, then complained of trouble breathing. Seward grew worse during the day, as his family gathered around him. Asked if he had any final words, he said, "Love one another."[183] Seward died that afternoon. His funeral a few days later was preceded by the people of Auburn and nearby filing past his open casket for four hours. Thurlow Weed was there for the burial of his friend, and Harriet Tubman, a former slave whom the Sewards had aided, sent flowers. President Grant sent his regrets he could not be there.[184][185]

William Seward rests with his wife Frances and daughter Fanny (1844–1866), in Fort Hill Cemetery in Auburn.[184][185] They had three surviving sons: Augustus Henry Seward (1826–1876), William H. Seward Jr. (1839–1920) (both of whom had served as Union officers before successful business careers) and Frederick W. Seward (1830–1915) (who served under his father in the State Department), and one daughter.

# Robert Gould Shaw

*May 1863*

**Robert Gould Shaw** (October 10, 1837–July 18, 1863) was an American officer in the Union Army during the American Civil War. Born into a prominent Boston abolitionist family, he accepted command of the first all-black regiment (54th Massachusetts) in the Northeast. Supporting the promised equal treatment for his troops, he encouraged the men to refuse their pay until it was equal to that of white troops' wage.

He led his regiment at the Second Battle of Fort Wagner in July 1863. They attacked a beachhead near Charleston, South Carolina, and Shaw was killed while leading his men to the parapet of the Confederate-held fort. Although the regiment was overwhelmed by firing from the defenses and driven back, suffering many casualties, Shaw's leadership and the regiment became legendary. They inspired tens of thousands more African Americans to enlist for the Union and contribute to its ultimate victory.

## American Civil War

With the outbreak of the American Civil War, Shaw volunteered to serve with the 7th New York Militia. On 19 April 1861 Private Shaw marched down Broadway in lower Manhattan as his unit traveled south to man the defense of Washington, D.C.[5] Lincoln's initial call up asked volunteers to make a 90-day commitment, and after three months Shaw's new regiment was dissolved.[6] Following this Shaw joined a newly forming regiment from his home state, the 2nd Massachusetts Infantry.[7]

On 28 May 1861 Shaw was commissioned as a second lieutenant in the regiment's Company H. Over the next year and a half, he fought with his fellow Massachusetts soldiers in the first Battle of Winchester, the Battle of Cedar Mountain and at the bloody battle of Antietam.[8] Shaw served both as a line officer in the field and as a staff officer for General George H Gordon.[9] Twice wounded, by the fall of 1862 he was promoted to the rank of captain.[7][10]

Since the start of the war, abolitionists such as Massachusetts governor John A. Andrew urged enlistment of African Americans as soldiers to fight the Confederacy. This proposal was broadly opposed. Many men believed that colored troops would lack discipline, be difficult to train, and would break and run in battle. The general attitude in the North was that colored troops would prove to be an embarrassment and hindrance to regular army units.[11]

Andrew traveled to Washington, DC in early January 1863 to meet with Secretary of War Edwin Stanton and repeat his argument for the use of colored troops in the Union army. Stanton was won to his side; on January 26, 1863, Stanton issued an order to Andrew to raise further volunteer regiments to fight for the Union, adding the new recruits "may include persons of African descent, organized into special corps."[12] Andrew immediately set about doing so, and the 54th Massachusetts Volunteer Infantry began to be formed.

For the unit's officers, Andrew sought a certain type of white gentleman, " . . . young men of military experience, of firm antislavery principles, ambitious, superior to a vulgar contempt for color, and having faith in the capacity of colored men for military service." Most importantly, he wanted men who understood the stakes, that the success or failure of the endeavor would elevate or depress the manner in which the character of colored persons were viewed throughout the world for many years to come.[13] Andrew wrote to many individuals prominent in the abolitionist movement, including Morris Hallowell of Philadelphia and Francis Shaw of Boston.

To command the unit, Andrew already had Shaw's son in mind. Andrew wrote to Francis Shaw about the need to find a leader who would accept the responsibility of the command " . . . with a full sense of its importance, with an earnest determination for its success."[14] Included in Andrew's letter was a commission for Robert Shaw to take command of the new regiment.[15]

Carrying the commission, Francis Shaw traveled to Virginia to speak with his son.[16] Robert Shaw was hesitant to take the post,[10] as he did not believe that authorities would send the unit to the front lines, and he did not want to leave his fellow soldiers. Finally he agreed to take the command.[17] On February 6 he telegraphed his father with his decision. [18] He was 24 years old. The command came with a colonelcy, the rank commensurate with the position of regimental commander.

Andrew had some difficulty finding enough colored volunteers in Massachusetts to form the regiment. Andrew assured recruits that they would receive the standard pay of 13 dollars a month, and that if they were captured, the government of the United States would insist they be treated as any other soldier.[19] The Boston area provided enough recruits to form the regiment's "C" Company.[20] The remainder of the regiment was formed with black recruits from all across the North. Few were former slaves from the South.[21] Two sons of the prominent African-American abolitionist leader Frederick Douglass volunteered to serve with the 54th.[22]

Captain Shaw arrived in Boston on 15 February 1863 and immediately assumed his position.[23] He was a strict disciplinarian, determined to train the men to high standards.[10] On 25 March 1863 Shaw wrote to his father of his fledgling regiment:

> Everything goes on prosperously. The intelligence of the men is a great surprise to me. They learn all the details of guard duty and camp service infinitely more readily than most of the Irish that I have had under my command. There is not the least doubt that we will leave the State with as good a regiment as any that has marched.[24]

Shaw was promoted to major on March 31, 1863, and two weeks later on April 17 was made full colonel. On April 30 the regiment drew 950 Enfield rifled muskets and swords for non-commissioned officers (NCOs)[25] By May 11, more troops had arrived in Boston than were required to man the regiment. The 55th Massachusetts was begun with the next round of new recruits.[26]

On May 28 Shaw led the men of the 54th through the streets of Boston to the docks, where the regiment boarded a transport steamer and sailed south. The regiment was to be used in a Union campaign against Charleston, South Carolina, a major port.[7] The 54th arrived at Port Royal Island on June 4, and was placed under the overall command of Major General David Hunter.[27] Initially the regiment was used to provide manual labor at the loading docks, but Colonel Shaw applied for action. Four days later his regiment boarded onto transport and was sent to Hilton Head, South Carolina.[28] From there they moved further south to St. Simons Island, Georgia, which served as their base of operations.

On June 11, 1863, the 54th was sent with the 2nd South Carolina Volunteers (who were also of African-American descent) for a raid against the town of Darien, Georgia. Overall command of the force was with the senior officer, colonel James Montgomery of the 2nd South Carolina. Upon reaching the town, Montgomery set his troops to looting it. Shaw was outraged by this behavior by Union troops.

He ordered his troops to limit their seizures to those items that would be useful for the camp, and committed only one company to the task. After the town had been emptied of all valuables and livestock, Montgomery told Shaw, "I shall burn this town." To Shaw the burning of the town appeared to serve no military purpose, and he knew it would create a great hardship to its residents. In a letter to his family he recalled, "I told him I did not want to take the responsibility of it, and he was only too happy to take all of it on his own shoulders."[29] Montgomery had the town burned to the ground.[30]

After the regiment's return to camp Shaw wrote to X Corps Assistant Adjutant General Lieutenant-Colonel Charles G. Halpine, seeking clarification of what was required of him. He asked if Montgomery was acting under orders from General Hunter, stating in part "I am perfectly willing to burn any place which resists, or gives some reason for such a proceeding; but it seems to me barbarous to turn women and children adrift in that way; and if I am only assisting Colonel Montgomery in a private enterprise of his own, it is very distasteful to me." It is not clear if Shaw ever received an answer from Halpine, but Montgomery was in fact carrying out a policy supported by Hunter.[31]

## Second Battle of Fort Wagner

Colonel Shaw and the 54th Regiment were placed under the command of General Quincy Gilmore and sent to Charleston, South Carolina to take part in the second attempt to defeat the Confederate garrison stationed there. The fort was well armed with an assortment of heavy guns and whose overall strength was underestimated by Union command. [32] At the battle, July 18, 1863, along with two brigades of white troops, the 54th assaulted Confederate batteries at Fort Wagner. As the unit hesitated in the face of overwhelming

Confederate fire, Shaw led his men into battle by shouting, "Forward, Fifty-Fourth, forward!" He mounted a parapet and urged his men forward, but was shot through the chest three times and died almost instantly. According to the Color Sergeant of the 54th, he was shot and killed early in the battle while trying to lead the unit forward and fell on the outside of the fort.[33][34] Some Confederate reports claim his body was hit a total of seven times. The battle had continued to 10 p.m. which ended with heavy Union losses. Among the other fatalities was Gen. George Crockett Strong, mortally wounded; Col. Haldimand S. Putnam shot and killed instantly; Col. John Lyman Chatfield, mortally wounded.[35] Shaw's 54th Regiment suffered the heaviest losses.[36] The Confederates buried Shaw in a mass grave with many of his men, an act they intended as an insult.[37]

Two sons of Fredrick Douglass, Charles Douglass and his eldest son, Lewis Douglass, belonged to the 54th regiment. Lewis was wounded at the Battle of Fort Wagner shortly after Shaw fell, and barely managed to retreat to safety.[38]

Following the battle, commanding Confederate General Johnson Hagood returned the bodies of the other Union officers who had died, but left Shaw's where it was, for burial in a mass grave with the black soldiers. Hagood told a captured Union surgeon that "Had he [Shaw] been in command of white troops . . . " he would have returned Shaw's body, as was customary for officers, instead of burying it with the fallen black soldiers.[39]

Although the gesture was intended as an insult by Hagood, Shaw's friends and family believed it was an honor for him to be buried with his soldiers. Efforts had been made to recover Shaw's body (which had been stripped and robbed prior to burial). His father publicly proclaimed that he was proud to know that his son was buried with his troops, befitting his role as a soldier and a crusader for emancipation.[40]

In a letter to the regimental surgeon, Lincoln Stone, Frank Shaw wrote:

We would not have his body removed from where it lies surrounded by his brave and devoted soldiers. . . . We can imagine no holier place than that in which he lies, among his brave and devoted followers, nor wish for him better company. – what a body-guard he has![41]

After the war, the Union Army disinterred and reburied all the remains—including, presumably, those of Col. Shaw—at the Beaufort National Cemetery in Beaufort, South Carolina. Their gravestones were marked as "unknown."[42]

Shaw's sword had been stolen from the first gravesite but was recovered in 1865 and returned to his parents. It disappeared after being passed down within the family. In June 2017 it was discovered in a family attic of Mary Minturn Wood and brother Robert Shaw Wood, descendants of Shaw's sister Susanna. They donated it to the Massachusetts Historical Society.[43]

# Philip Sheridan

**Philip Henry Sheridan** (March 6, 1831[1]–August 5, 1888) was a career United States Army officer and a Union general in the American Civil War. His career was noted for his rapid rise to major general and his close association with General-in-chief Ulysses S. Grant, who transferred Sheridan from command of an infantry division in the Western Theater to lead the Cavalry Corps of the Army of the Potomac in the East. In 1864, he defeated Confederate forces under General Jubal Early in the Shenandoah Valley and his destruction of the economic infrastructure of the Valley, called "The Burning" by residents, was one of the first uses of scorched-earth tactics in the war. In 1865, his cavalry pursued Gen. Robert E. Lee

*Sheridan during the 1860s*

and was instrumental in forcing his surrender at Appomattox.

Sheridan fought in later years in the Indian Wars of the Great Plains. Both as a soldier and private citizen, he was instrumental in the development and protection of Yellowstone National Park. In 1883, Sheridan was appointed general-in-chief of the U.S. Army, and in 1888 he was promoted to the rank of General of the Army during the term of President Grover Cleveland.

## Civil War

### Western Theater

In the fall of 1861, Sheridan was ordered to travel to Jefferson Barracks, near St. Louis, Missouri, for assignment to the 13th U.S. Infantry. He departed from his command of Fort Yamhill, Oregon, by way of San Francisco, across the Isthmus of Panama, and through New York City to home in Somerset for a brief leave. On the way to his new post, he made a courtesy call to Maj. Gen. Henry W. Halleck in St. Louis, who commandeered his services to audit the financial records of his immediate predecessor, Maj. Gen. John C. Frémont, whose administration of the Department of the Missouri was tainted by charges of wasteful expenditures and fraud that left the status of $12 million in debt. Sheridan sorted out the mess, impressing Halleck in the process. Much to Sheridan's dismay, Halleck's vision for Sheridan consisted of a continuing role as a staff officer. Nevertheless, Sheridan performed the task assigned to him and entrenched himself as an excellent staff officer in Halleck's view.[8] According to biographer Brenda Wineapple, he was sometimes called "Little Phil" because he stood 5'6." In December, Sheridan was appointed chief commissary officer of the Army of Southwest Missouri, but convinced the department commander, Halleck, to give him the position of quartermaster general as well. In January 1862, he reported for duty to Maj. Gen. Samuel Curtis and served under him at the Battle of Pea Ridge. Sheridan soon discovered that officers were engaged in profiteering. They stole horses from civilians and demanded payment from Sheridan. He refused to pay for the stolen property and confiscated the horses for the use of Curtis's army. When Curtis ordered him to pay the officers, Sheridan brusquely retorted, "No authority can compel me to jayhawk or steal." Curtis had Sheridan arrested for insubordination but Halleck's influence appears to have ended any formal proceedings. Sheridan performed aptly in his role under Curtis and, now returned to Halleck's headquarters, he accompanied the army on the Siege of Corinth[9] and served as an assistant to the department's topographical engineer, but also made the acquaintance of Brig. Gen. William T. Sherman, who offered him the colonelcy of an Ohio infantry regiment. This appointment fell through, but Sheridan was subsequently aided by friends (including future Secretary of War Russell A. Alger), who petitioned Michigan Governor Austin Blair on his behalf. Sheridan was appointed colonel of the 2nd Michigan Cavalry on May 27, 1862, despite having no experience in the mounted arm.[10][11]

A month later, Sheridan commanded his first forces in combat, leading a small brigade that included his regiment. At the Battle of Booneville, Mississippi, July 1, 1862, he held back several regiments of Brig. Gen. James R. Chalmers's Confederate cavalry, deflected a large flanking attack with a noisy diversion, and reported critical intelligence about enemy dispositions.[12] His actions so impressed the division commanders, including Brig. Gen. William S. Rosecrans, that they recommended Sheridan's promotion to brigadier general. They wrote to Halleck, "Brigadiers scarce; good ones scarce. . . . The undersigned respectfully beg that you will obtain the promotion of Sheridan. He is worth his weight in gold." The promotion was approved in September, but dated effective July 1 as a reward for his actions at Booneville.[13] It was just after Booneville that one of his fellow officers gave him the horse that he named Rienzi (after the skirmish of Rienzi, Mississippi), which he would ride throughout the war.[14]

Sheridan was assigned to command the 11th Division, III Corps, in Maj. Gen. Don Carlos Buell's Army of the Ohio. On October 8, 1862, Sheridan led his division in the Battle of Perryville. Under orders from Buell and his corps commander, Maj. Gen. Charles Gilbert, Sheridan sent Col. Daniel McCook's brigade to secure a water supply for the army. McCook drove off the Confederates and secured water for the parched Union troops at Doctor's Creek. Gilbert ordered McCook not to advance any further and then rode to consult with Buell. Along the way, Gilbert ordered his cavalry to attack the Confederates in Dan McCook's front. Sheridan heard the gunfire and came to the front with another brigade. Although the cavalry failed to secure the heights in front of McCook, Sheridan's reinforcements drove off the Southerners. Gilbert returned and ordered Sheridan to return to McCook's original position. Sheridan's aggressiveness convinced the opposing Confederates under Maj. Gen. Leonidas Polk, that they should remain on the defensive. His troops repulsed Confederate attacks later that day, but did not participate in the heaviest fighting of the day, which occurred on the Union left.[15]

*Union Cavalry General Philip Sheridan*

On December 31, 1862, the first day of the Battle of Stones River, Sheridan anticipated a Confederate assault and positioned his division in preparation for it. His division held back the Confederate onslaught on his front until their ammunition ran out and they were forced to withdraw. This action was instrumental in giving the Union army time to rally at a strong defensive position. For his actions, he was promoted to major general on April 10, 1863, (with date of rank December 31, 1862). In six months, he had risen from captain to major general.[16]

The Army of the Cumberland recovered from the shock of Stones River and prepared for its summer offensive against Confederate General Braxton Bragg. Sheridan's division participated in the advance against Bragg in Rosecrans's brilliant Tullahoma Campaign, and was the lead division to enter the town of Tullahoma.[17] On the second day of the Battle of Chickamauga, September 20, 1863, Rosecrans was shifting Sheridan's division behind the Union battle line when Bragg launched an attack into a gap in the Union line. Sheridan's division made a gallant stand on Lytle Hill against an attack by the Confederate corps of Lt. Gen. James Longstreet, but was swamped by retreating Union soldiers. The Confederates drove Sheridan's division from the field in confusion. He gathered as many men as he could and withdrew toward Chattanooga, rallying troops along the way. Learning of Maj. Gen. George H. Thomas's XIV Corps stand on Snodgrass Hill, Sheridan ordered his division back to the fighting, but they took a circuitous route and did not participate in the fighting as some histories claim. His return to the battlefield ensured that he did not suffer the fate of Rosecrans who rode off to Chattanooga leaving the army to its fate, and was soon relieved of command.[18]

During the Battle of Chattanooga, at Missionary Ridge on November 25, 1863, Sheridan's division and others in George Thomas's army broke through the Confederate lines in a wild charge that exceeded the orders and expectations of Thomas and Ulysses S. Grant. Just before his men stepped off, Sheridan told them, "Remember Chickamauga," and many shouted its name as they advanced as ordered to a line of rifle pits in their front. Faced with enemy fire from above, however, they continued up the ridge. Sheridan spotted a group of Confederate officers outlined against the crest of the ridge and shouted, "Here's at you!" An exploding shell sprayed him with dirt and he responded, "That's damn ungenerous! I shall take those guns for that!" The Union charge broke through the Confederate lines on the ridge and Bragg's army fell into retreat. Sheridan impulsively ordered his men to pursue Bragg to the Confederate supply depot at Chickamauga Station, but called them back when he realized that his was the only command so far forward. General Grant reported after the battle, "To Sheridan's prompt movement, the

Army of the Cumberland and the nation are indebted for the bulk of the capture of prisoners, artillery, and small arms that day. Except for his prompt pursuit, so much in this way would not have been accomplished."[19]

## Overland Campaign

Gen. Ulysses S. Grant, newly promoted to be general-in-chief of all the Union armies, summoned Sheridan to the Eastern Theater to command the Cavalry Corps of the Army of the Potomac. Unbeknownst to Sheridan, he was actually Grant's second choice, after Maj. Gen. William B. Franklin, but Grant agreed to a suggestion about Sheridan from Chief of Staff Henry W. Halleck. After the war, and in his memoirs, Grant claimed that Sheridan was the very man he wanted for the job. Sheridan arrived at the headquarters of the Army of the Potomac on April 5, 1864, less than a month before the start of Grant's massive Overland Campaign against Robert E. Lee.[20]

In the early battles of the campaign, Sheridan's cavalry was relegated by army commander Maj. Gen. George Meade to its traditional role—screening, reconnaissance, and guarding trains and rear areas—much to Sheridan's frustration. In the Battle of the Wilderness (May 5–6, 1864), the dense forested terrain prevented any significant cavalry role. As the army swung around the Confederate right flank in the direction of Spotsylvania Court House, Sheridan's troopers failed to clear the road from the Wilderness, losing engagements along the Plank Road on May 5 and Todd's Tavern on May 6 through May 8, allowing the Confederates to seize the critical crossroads before the Union infantry could arrive.[21]

When Meade quarreled with Sheridan for not performing his duties of screening and reconnaissance as ordered, Sheridan told Meade that he could "whip Stuart" if Meade let him. Meade reported the conversation to Grant, who replied, "Well, he generally knows what he is talking about. Let him start right out and do it." Meade deferred to Grant's judgment and issued orders to Sheridan to "proceed against the enemy's cavalry" and from

*Maj. Gen. Philip Sheridan and his generals in front of Sheridan's tent, 1864. Left to right: Henry E. Davies, David McM. Gregg, Sheridan, Wesley Merritt, Alfred Torbert, and James H. Wilson.*

May 9 through May 24, sent him on a raid toward Richmond, directly challenging the Confederate cavalry. The raid was less successful than hoped; although his raid managed to mortally wound Confederate cavalry commander Maj. Gen. J .E. B. Stuart at Yellow Tavern on May 11 and beat Maj. Gen. Fitzhugh Lee at Meadow Bridge on May 12, the raid never seriously threatened Richmond and it left Grant without cavalry intelligence for Spotsylvania and North Anna. Historian Gordon C. Rhea wrote, "By taking his cavalry from Spotsylvania Court House, Sheridan severely handicapped Grant in his battles against Lee.

The Union Army was deprived of his eyes and ears during a critical juncture in the campaign. And Sheridan's decision to advance boldly to the Richmond defenses smacked of unnecessary showboating that jeopardized his command."[22]

Rejoining the Army of the Potomac, Sheridan's cavalry fought inconclusively at Haw's Shop (May 28), a battle with heavy casualties that allowed the Confederate cavalry to obtain valuable intelligence about Union dispositions. They seized the critical crossroads that triggered the Battle of Cold Harbor (June 1 to June 12) and withstood a number of assaults until reinforced. Grant then ordered Sheridan on a raid to the northwest to break the Virginia Central Railroad and to link up with the Shenandoah Valley army of Maj. Gen. David Hunter. He was intercepted by the Confederate cavalry under Maj. Gen. Wade Hampton at the Battle of Trevilian Station (June 11–12), where in the largest all-cavalry battle of the war, he achieved tactical success on the first day, but suffered heavy casualties during multiple assaults on the second. He withdrew without achieving his assigned objectives. On his return march, he once again encountered the Confederate cavalry at Samaria (St. Mary's) Church on June 24, where his men suffered significant casualties, but successfully protected the Union supply wagons they were escorting.[23]

History draws decidedly mixed opinions on the success of Sheridan in the Overland Campaign, in no small part because the very clear Union victory at Yellow Tavern, highlighted by the death of Jeb Stuart, tends to overshadow other actions and battles. In Sheridan's report of the Cavalry Corps' actions in the campaign, discussing the strategy of cavalry fighting cavalry, he wrote, "The result was constant success and the almost total annihilation of the rebel cavalry. We marched when and where we pleased; we were always the attacking party, and always successful." A contrary view has been published by historian Eric J. Wittenberg, who notes that of four major strategic raids (Richmond, Trevilian, Wilson-Kautz, and First Deep Bottom) and thirteen major cavalry engagements of the Overland and Richmond–Petersburg campaigns, only Yellow Tavern can be considered a Union victory, with Haw's Shop, Trevilian Station, Meadow Bridge, Samaria Church, and Wilson-Kautz defeats in which some of Sheridan's forces barely avoided destruction.[24]

## Army of the Shenandoah

Throughout the war, the Confederacy sent armies out of Virginia through the Shenandoah Valley to invade Maryland and Pennsylvania and threaten Washington, D.C., Lt. Gen. Jubal Early, following the same pattern in the Valley Campaigns of 1864, and hoping to distract Grant from the Siege of Petersburg, attacked Union forces near Washington and raided several towns in Pennsylvania. Grant, reacting to the political commotion caused by the invasion, organized the Middle Military Division, whose field troops were known as the Army of the Shenandoah. He considered various candidates for command, including George Meade, William B. Franklin, and David Hunter, with the latter two intended for the military division while Sheridan would command the army. All of these choices were rejected by either Grant or the War Department and, over the objection of Secretary of War Edwin Stanton, who believed him to be too young for such a high

*Union Cavalry General Philip Sheridan*

post, Sheridan took command in both roles at Harpers Ferry on August 7, 1864. His mission was not only to defeat Early's army and to close off the Northern invasion route, but to deny the Shenandoah Valley as a productive agricultural region to the Confederacy. Grant told Sheridan, "The people should be informed that so long as an army can subsist among them recurrences of these raids must be expected, and we are determined to stop them at all hazards. . . . Give the enemy no rest . . . Do all the damage to railroads and crops you can. Carry off stock of all descriptions, and negroes, so as to prevent further planting. If the war is to last another year, we want the Shenandoah Valley to remain a barren waste."[25]

Sheridan got off to a slow start, needing time to organize and to react to reinforcements reaching Early; Grant ordered him not to launch an offensive "with the advantage against you." And yet Grant expressed frustration with Sheridan's lack of progress. The armies remained unengaged for over a month, causing political consternation in the North as the 1864 election drew near. The two generals conferred on September 16 at Charles Town and agreed that Sheridan would begin his attacks within four days.[26]

On September 19, Sheridan beat Early's much smaller army at Third Winchester and followed up on September 22 with a victory at Fisher's Hill. As Early attempted to regroup, Sheridan began the punitive operations of his mission, sending his cavalry as far south as Waynesboro to seize or destroy livestock and provisions, and to burn barns, mills, factories, and railroads. Sheridan's men did their work relentlessly and thoroughly, rendering over 400 square miles uninhabitable. The destruction presaged the scorched-earth tactics of Sherman's March to the Sea through Georgia—deny an army a base from which to operate and bring the effects of war home to the population supporting it. The residents referred to this widespread destruction as "The Burning." There has been much controversy over the scorched-earth tactics. Sheridan's troops told of the wanton attack in their letters home, calling themselves "barn burners" and "destroyers of homes." One soldier wrote to his family that he had personally set 60 private homes on fire and opined that "it was a hard looking sight to see the women and children turned out of doors at this season of the year" (winter). A Sergeant William T. Patterson wrote that "the whole country around is wrapped in flames, the heavens are aglow with the light thereof . . . such mourning, such lamentations, such crying and pleading for mercy [by defenseless women] . . . I never saw or want to see again."[27] For this reason, many still consider Sheridan and Sherman to be war criminals, protected by the loopholes of the Lieber Code. The Confederates were not idle during this period and Sheridan's men were plagued by guerrilla raids by partisan ranger Col. John S. Mosby.[28]

Although Sheridan assumed that Jubal Early was effectively out of action and he considered withdrawing his army to rejoin Grant at Petersburg, Early received reinforcements and, on October 19 at Cedar Creek, launched a well-executed surprise attack while Sheridan was absent from his army, ten miles away at Winchester.[29] Hearing the distant sounds of artillery, he rode aggressively to his command. He reached the battlefield about 10:30 a.m. and began to rally his men. Fortunately for Sheridan, Early's men were too occupied to take notice; they were hungry and exhausted and fell out to pillage the Union camps. Sheridan's actions are generally credited with saving the day (although Maj. Gen. Horatio G. Wright, commanding Sheridan's VI Corps, had already rallied his men and stopped their retreat). Early had been dealt his most significant defeat, rendering his army almost incapable of future offensive action. Sheridan received a personal letter of thanks from Abraham Lincoln and a promotion to major general in the regular army as of November 8, 1864, making him the fourth ranking general in the Army, after Grant, Sherman, and Meade. Grant wrote to Secretary of War Edwin M. Stanton after he ordered a 100-gun salute to celebrate Sheridan's victory at Cedar Creek, "Turning what bid fair to be a disaster into glorious victory stamps Sheridan, what I have always thought him, one of the ablest of generals." A famous poem, *Sheridan's Ride*, was written by Thomas Buchanan Read to commemorate the general's return to the battle. Sheridan reveled in the fame that Read's poem brought him, renaming his horse Rienzi to "Winchester," based on the poem's refrain, "Winchester, twenty miles away." The poem was widely used in Republican campaign efforts and some have credited Abraham Lincoln's margin of victory to it.[30] As for Lincoln himself, the President, pleased at Sheridan's performance as a commander, wrote to Sheridan and playfully confessed his reassessment of the relatively short officer, "When this peculiar war began, I thought a cavalryman should be six feet four inches, but I have changed my mind. Five foot four will do in a pinch."[31]

Sheridan spent the next several months occupied with light skirmishing and fighting guerrillas. Although Grant continued his exhortations for Sheridan to move south and break the Virginia Central Railroad supplying Petersburg, Sheridan resisted. Wright's VI Corps returned to join Grant in November. Sheridan's remaining men, primarily cavalry and artillery, finally moved out of their winter quarters on February 27, 1865, and headed east. The orders from Gen. Grant were largely discretionary: they were to destroy the Virginia Central Railroad and the James River Canal, capture Lynchburg if practicable, then either join William T. Sherman in North Carolina or return to Winchester.[32]

## Appomattox Campaign

Sheridan interpreted Grant's orders liberally and instead of heading to North Carolina in March 1865, he moved to rejoin the Army of the Potomac at Petersburg. He wrote in his memoirs, "Feeling that the war was nearing its end, I desired my cavalry to be in at the death."[33] His finest service of the Civil War was demonstrated during his relentless pursuit of Robert E. Lee's Army, effectively managing the most crucial aspects of the Appomattox Campaign for Grant.[34]

On the way to Petersburg, at the Battle of Waynesboro, March 2, he trapped the remainder of Early's army and 1,500 soldiers surrendered. On April 1, he cut off Gen.

Lee's lines of support at Five Forks, forcing Lee to evacuate Petersburg. During this battle he ruined the military career of Maj. Gen. Gouverneur K. Warren by removing him from command of the V Corps under circumstances that a court of inquiry later determined were unjustified. President Rutherford B. Hayes ordered a court of inquiry that convened in 1879 and, after hearing testimony from dozens of witnesses over 100 days, found that Sheridan's relief of Warren had been unjustified. Unfortunately for Warren, these results were not published until after his death.[35]

*Sheridan portrait by Mathew Brady or Levin C. Handy*

Sheridan's aggressive and well-executed performance at the Battle of Sayler's Creek on April 6 effectively sealed the fate of Lee's army, capturing over 20 percent of his remaining men.[36] President Lincoln sent Grant a telegram on April 7: "Gen. Sheridan says 'If the thing is pressed I think that Lee will surrender.' Let the thing be pressed." At Appomattox Court House, April 9, 1865, Sheridan blocked Lee's escape, forcing the surrender of the Army of Northern Virginia later that day. Grant summed up Little Phil's performance in these final days: "I believe General Sheridan has no superior as a general, either living or dead, and perhaps not an equal."[37]

## Reconstruction

After Gen. Lee's surrender, and that of Gen. Joseph E. Johnston in North Carolina, the only significant Confederate field force remaining was in Texas under Gen. Edmund Kirby Smith. Sheridan was supposed to lead troops in the Grand Review of the Armies in Washington, D.C., but Grant appointed him commander of the Military District of the Southwest on May 17, 1865,[6] six days before the parade, with orders to defeat Smith without delay and restore Texas and Louisiana to Union control. However, Smith surrendered before Sheridan reached New Orleans.

## Death and burial

In 1888 Sheridan suffered a series of massive heart attacks two months after sending his memoirs to the publisher. Although thin in his youth, by 57 years of age he had reached a weight of over 200 pounds. After his first heart attack, the U.S. Congress quickly passed legislation to promote him to general on June 1, 1888, and he received the news from a congressional delegation with joy, despite his pain.

His family moved him from the heat of Washington to his summer cottage in the Nonquitt section of Dartmouth, Massachusetts, where he died of heart failure on August 5, 1888.[60]

His body was returned to Washington and he was buried on a hillside facing the capital city near Arlington House in Arlington National Cemetery.[61][62] The sculpture on the marker was executed by English sculptor Samuel James Kitson. The burial helped elevate Arlington to national prominence.[63] His wife Irene never remarried, saying, "I would rather be the widow of Phil Sheridan than the wife of any man living."[64]

# William Tecumseh Sherman

**William Tecumseh Sherman** (February 8, 1820–February 14, 1891) was an American soldier, businessman, educator, and author. He served as a general in the Union Army during the American Civil War (1861–65), for which he received recognition for his outstanding command of military strategy as well as criticism for the harshness of the scorched earth policies he implemented in conducting total war against the Confederate States.[2]

Sherman was born into a prominent political family. He graduated from the United States Military Academy in 1840 and was stationed in California. He married Ellen Ewing Sherman and together they raised eight children. Sherman's wife and children were all devout Catholics, while Sherman was originally a member of the faith but later left it. In 1859, he gained a position as superintendent of the Louisiana State Seminary of Learning & Military Academy. Living in the South, Sherman grew to respect Southern culture and sympathize with the practice of Southern slavery, although he opposed secession.

Sherman began his Civil War career serving with distinction in the First Battle of Bull Run before being transferred to the Western Theater. He served in Kentucky in 1861, where he acted overly paranoid, exaggerating the presence of spies in the region and providing what seemed to be alarmingly high estimates of the number of troops needed to pacify Kentucky. He was granted leave, and fell into depression. Sherman returned to serve under General Ulysses S. Grant in the winter of 1862 during the battles of forts Henry and Donelson. Before the Battle of Shiloh, Sherman commanded a division. Failing to make proper preparations for a Confederate offensive, his men were surprised and overrun. He later rallied his division and helped drive the Confederates back. Sherman later served in the Siege of Corinth and commanded the XV Corps during the Vicksburg Campaign, which led to the fall of the critical Confederate stronghold of Vicksburg on the Mississippi River. After Grant was promoted to command of all Western armies, Sherman took over the Army of the Tennessee and led it during the Chattanooga Campaign, which culminated with the routing of the Confederate armies in the state of Tennessee.

In 1864, Sherman succeeded Grant as the Union commander in the western theater of the war. He proceeded to lead his troops to the capture of the city of Atlanta, a military success that contributed to the re-election of Abraham Lincoln. Sherman's subsequent march through Georgia and the Carolinas further undermined the Confederacy's ability to continue fighting by destroying large amounts of supplies and demoralizing the Southern people. The tactics that he used during this march, though effective, remain a subject of controversy. He accepted the surrender of all the Confederate armies in the Carolinas,

Georgia, and Florida in April 1865, after having been present at most major military engagements in the West. When Grant assumed the U.S. presidency in 1869, Sherman succeeded him as Commanding General of the Army, in which capacity he served from 1869 until 1883. As such, he was responsible for the U.S. Army's engagement in the Indian Wars over the next 15 years. Sherman advocated total war against hostile Indians to force them back onto their reservations. He was skeptical of the Reconstruction era policies of the federal government in the South. Sherman steadfastly refused to be drawn into politics and in 1875 published his *Memoirs*, one of the best-known first-hand accounts of the Civil War. British military historian B. H. Liddell Hart declared that Sherman was "the first modern general."[3]

## Civil War service
### *First commissions and Bull Run*

*Portrait by Mathew Brady, c. 1864*

Sherman was first commissioned as colonel of the 13th U.S. Infantry Regiment, effective May 14, 1861. This was a new regiment yet to be raised, and Sherman's first command was actually of a brigade of three-month volunteers,[41] at the head of which he became one of the few Union officers to distinguish himself at the First Battle of Bull Run on July 21, 1861, where he was grazed by bullets in the knee and shoulder. The disastrous Union defeat at Bull Run led Sherman to question his own judgment as an officer and the capacities of his volunteer troops. President Lincoln, however, was impressed by Sherman while visiting the troops on July 23 and promoted him to brigadier general of volunteers (effective May 17, 1861, with seniority in rank to Ulysses S. Grant, his future commander).[42] He was assigned to serve under Robert Anderson in the Department of the Cumberland in Louisville, Kentucky, and in October Sherman succeeded Anderson in command of the department. Sherman considered that his new assignment broke a promise from Lincoln that he would not be given such a prominent position.[43]

## Breakdown

Having succeeded Anderson at Louisville, Sherman now had principal military responsibility for Kentucky, a border state in which Confederate troops held Columbus and Bowling Green and were present near the Cumberland Gap.[44] He became exceedingly pessimistic about the outlook for his command and he complained frequently to Washington, D.C., about shortages while providing exaggerated estimates of the strength of the rebel forces. Critical press reports appeared about him after an October visit to Louisville by the secretary of war, Simon Cameron, and in early November 1861 Sherman insisted that he be relieved.[45] He was promptly replaced by Brigadier General Don Carlos Buell and transferred to St. Louis, Missouri. In December, he was put on leave by Maj. Gen. Henry W. Halleck, commander of the Department of the Missouri, who considered him unfit for duty. Sherman went to Lancaster, Ohio, to recuperate. While he was at home, his wife Ellen wrote to his brother, Senator John Sherman, seeking advice. She complained of "that melancholy insanity to which your family is subject."[46] Sherman later wrote that the concerns of command "broke me down," and he admitted contemplating suicide.[47] His problems were compounded when the *Cincinnati Commercial* described him as "insane."[48]

By mid-December 1861 Sherman had recovered sufficiently to return to service under Halleck in the Department of the Missouri. (In March, Halleck's command was redesignated the Department of the Mississippi and enlarged to unify command in the West). Sherman's initial assignments were rear-echelon commands, first of an instructional barracks near St. Louis and then in command of the District of Cairo.[49] Operating from Paducah, Kentucky, he provided logistical support for the operations of Brig. Gen. Ulysses S. Grant to capture Fort Donelson (February 1862). Grant, the previous commander of the District of Cairo, had recently won a major victory at Fort Henry (February 6, 1862) and been given command of the ill-defined District of West Tennessee. Although Sherman was technically the senior officer at this time, he wrote to Grant, "I feel anxious about you as I know the great facilities [the Confederates] have of concentration by means of the River and R Road, but [I] have faith in you—Command me in any way."[50]

## Shiloh

After Grant captured Fort Donelson, Sherman got his wish to serve under Grant when he was assigned on March 1, 1862, to the Army of West Tennessee as commander of the 5th Division.[51] His first major test under Grant was at the Battle of Shiloh. The massive Confederate attack on the morning of April 6, 1862, took most of the senior Union commanders by surprise. Sherman had dismissed the intelligence reports received from militia officers, refusing to believe that Confederate General Albert Sidney Johnston would leave his base at Corinth. He took no precautions beyond strengthening his picket lines, and refused to entrench, build abatis, or push out reconnaissance patrols. At Shiloh, he may have wished to avoid appearing overly alarmed in order to escape the kind of criticism he had received in Kentucky. He had written to his wife that, if he took more precautions, "they'd call me crazy again."[52]

Despite being caught unprepared by the attack, Sherman rallied his division and conducted an orderly, fighting retreat that helped avert a disastrous Union rout. Finding Grant at the end of the day sitting under an oak tree in the darkness and smoking a cigar, Sherman felt, in his words, "some wise and sudden instinct not to mention retreat." In what would become one of the most notable conversations of the war, Sherman said simply: "Well, Grant, we've had the devil's own day, haven't we?" After a puff of his cigar, Grant replied calmly: "Yes. Lick 'em tomorrow, though."[53] Sherman proved instrumental to the successful Union counterattack of April 7, 1862. At Shiloh, Sherman was wounded twice—in the hand and shoulder—and had three horses shot out from under him. His performance was praised by Grant and Halleck and after the battle, and he was promoted to major general of volunteers, effective May 1, 1862.[51]

Beginning in late April, a Union force of 100,000 moved slowly against Corinth, under Halleck's command with Grant relegated to second-in-command; Sherman commanded the division on the extreme right of the Union's right wing (under George H. Thomas). Shortly after the Union forces occupied Corinth on May 30, Sherman persuaded Grant not to leave his command, despite the serious difficulties he was having with Halleck. Sherman offered Grant an example from his own life, "Before the battle of Shiloh, I was cast down by a mere newspaper assertion of 'crazy', but that single battle gave me new life, and I'm now in high feather." He told Grant that, if he remained in the army, "some happy accident might restore you to favor and your true place."[54] In July, Grant's situation improved when Halleck left for the East to become general-in-chief, and Sherman became the military governor of occupied Memphis.[55]

## Vicksburg

The careers of both officers ascended considerably after that time. In Sherman's case, this was in part because he developed close personal ties to Grant during the two years they served together in the West.[56] During the long and complicated campaign against Vicksburg, one newspaper complained that the "army was being ruined in mud-turtle expeditions, under the leadership of a drunkard [Grant], whose confidential adviser [Sherman] was a lunatic."[57]

Sherman's military record in 1862–63 was mixed. In December 1862, forces under his command suffered a severe repulse at the Battle of Chickasaw Bayou, just north of Vicksburg, Mississippi.[58] Soon after, his XV Corps was ordered to join Maj. Gen. John A. McClernand in his successful assault on Arkansas Post, generally regarded as a politically motivated distraction from the effort to capture Vicksburg.[59] Before the Vicksburg Campaign in the spring of 1863, Sherman expressed serious reservations about the wisdom of Grant's unorthodox strategy,[60] but he went on to perform well in that campaign under Grant's supervision.

The historian John D. Winters in *The Civil War in Louisiana* (1963) describes Sherman:

> . . . He had yet [before Vicksburg] to display any marked talents for leadership. Sherman, beset by hallucinations and unreasonable fears and finally contemplating suicide, had been relieved from command in Kentucky. He later began a new climb to success at Shiloh and Corinth under Grant. Still, if he muffed his Vicksburg assignment, which had begun unfavorably, he would rise no higher. As a man, Sherman was an eccentric mixture of strength and weakness. Although he was impatient, often irritable and depressed, petulant, headstrong, and unreasonably gruff, he had solid soldierly qualities. His men swore by him, and most of his fellow officers admired him.[61]

## Chattanooga

After the surrender of Vicksburg to the Union forces under Grant on July 4, 1863, Sherman was given the rank of brigadier general in the regular army, in addition to his rank as a major general of volunteers. Sherman's family came from Ohio to visit his camp near Vicksburg; his nine-year-old son, Willie, the Little Sergeant, died from typhoid fever contracted during the trip.[62]

Command in the West was unified under Grant (Military Division of the Mississippi), and Sherman succeeded Grant in command of the Army of the Tennessee. Following the defeat of the Army of the Cumberland at the Battle of Chickamauga by Confederate General Braxton Bragg's Army of Tennessee, the army was besieged in Chattanooga, Tennessee. Sherman's troops were sent to relieve them. While traveling to Chattanooga, Sherman departed Memphis on a train that arrived at the Battle of Collierville, Tennessee, while the Union garrison there was under attack on October 11, 1863. General Sherman took command of the 550 men and successfully defended against an attack of 3,500 Confederate cavalry.

During the Chattanooga Campaign in November, under Grant's overall command, Sherman quickly took his assigned target of Billy Goat Hill at the north end of Missionary Ridge, only to discover that it was not part of the ridge at all, but rather a detached spur separated from the main spine by a rock-strewn ravine. When he attempted to attack the main spine at Tunnel Hill, his troops were repeatedly repelled by Patrick Cleburne's heavy division, the best unit in Bragg's army. Sherman's efforts were assisted by George Henry Thomas's army's successful assault on the center of the Confederate line, a movement originally intended as a diversion.[63] Subsequently, Sherman led a column to relieve Union forces under Ambrose Burnside thought to be in peril at Knoxville. In February 1864, he led an expedition to Meridian, Mississippi, to disrupt Confederate infrastructure.[64]

## Atlanta

Despite this mixed record, Sherman enjoyed Grant's confidence and friendship. When Lincoln called Grant east in the spring of 1864 to take command of all the Union armies, Grant appointed Sherman (by then known to his soldiers as "Uncle Billy") to succeed him as head of the Military Division of the Mississippi, which entailed command of Union troops in the Western Theater of the war. As Grant took overall command of the armies of the United States, Sherman wrote to him outlining his strategy to bring the war to an end concluding that "if you can whip Lee and I can march to the Atlantic I think ol' Uncle Abe will give us twenty days leave to see the young folks."[65]

Sherman proceeded to invade the state of Georgia with three armies: the 60,000-strong Army of the Cumberland under George Henry Thomas, the 25,000-strong Army of the Tennessee under James B. McPherson, and the 13,000-strong Army of the Ohio under John M. Schofield.[66] He fought a lengthy campaign of maneuver through mountainous terrain against Confederate General Joseph E. Johnston's Army of Tennessee, attempting a direct assault only at the disastrous Battle of Kennesaw Mountain. In July, the cautious Johnston was replaced by the more aggressive John Bell Hood, who played to Sherman's strength by challenging him to direct battles on open ground. Meanwhile, in August, Sherman "learned that I had been commissioned a major-general in the regular army, which was unexpected, and not desired until successful in the capture of Atlanta."[67]

Sherman's Atlanta Campaign concluded successfully on September 2, 1864, with the capture of the city, which Hood had been forced to abandon. This success made Sherman a household name and helped ensure Lincoln's presidential re-election in November. In August, the Democratic Party had nominated as its candidate George B. McClellan, the popular former Union army commander, and it had seemed likely that Lincoln would lose to McClellan. Lincoln's defeat could well have meant the victory of the Confederacy, as the Democratic Party platform called for peace negotiations based on the acknowledgment of the Confederacy's independence. Thus the capture of Atlanta, coming when it did, may have been Sherman's greatest contribution to the Union cause.[68]

After ordering almost all civilians to leave the city in September, Sherman gave instructions that all military and government buildings in Atlanta be burned, although many private homes and shops were burned as well.[69] This was to set a precedent for future behavior by his armies.

## March to the Sea

During September and October, Sherman and Hood played cat-and-mouse in north Georgia (and Alabama) as Hood threatened Sherman's communications to the north. Eventually, Sherman won approval from his superiors for a plan to cut loose from his communications and march south, having advised Grant that he could "make Georgia howl."[70] This created the threat that Hood would move north into Tennessee. Trivializing that threat, Sherman reportedly said that he would "give [Hood] his rations" to go in that direction as "my business is down south."[71] However, Sherman left forces under Maj. Gens. George H. Thomas and John M. Schofield to deal with Hood; their forces eventually smashed Hood's army in the battles of Franklin (November 30) and Nashville (December 15–16).[72] Meanwhile, after the November elections, Sherman began a march with 62,000 men to the port of Savannah, Georgia, living off the land and causing, by his own estimate, more than $100 million in property damage.[73] Sherman called this harsh tactic of material war "hard war," often seen as a species of total war.[74] At the end of this campaign, known as Sherman's March to the Sea, his troops captured Savannah on December 21, 1864.[75] Sherman then dispatched a famous message to Lincoln, offering him the city as a Christmas present.[76]

Sherman's success in Georgia received ample coverage in the Northern press at a time when Grant seemed to be making little progress in his fight against Confederate General Robert E. Lee's Army of Northern Virginia. A bill was introduced in Congress to promote Sherman to Grant's rank of lieutenant general, probably with a view towards having him replace Grant as commander of the Union Army. Sherman wrote both to his brother, Senator John Sherman, and to General Grant vehemently repudiating any such promotion.[77] According to a war-time account,[78] it was around this time that Sherman made his memorable declaration of loyalty to Grant:

*General Sherman with Generals Howard, Logan, Hazen, Davis, Slocum, and Mower, photographed by Mathew Brady, May 1865*

General Grant *is a great general.* I know him well. He stood by me when I was crazy, and I stood by him when he was drunk; and now, sir, we stand by each other always.

While in Savannah, Sherman learned from a newspaper that his infant son Charles Celestine had died during the Savannah Campaign; the general had never seen the child.[79]

## Final campaigns in the Carolinas

Grant then ordered Sherman to embark his army on steamers and join the Union forces confronting Lee in Virginia, but Sherman instead persuaded Grant to allow him to march north through the Carolinas, destroying everything of military value along the way, as he had done in Georgia. He was particularly interested in targeting South Carolina, the first state to secede from the Union, because of the effect that it would have on Southern morale.[80] His army proceeded north through South Carolina against light resistance from the troops of Confederate General Joseph E. Johnston. Upon hearing that Sherman's men were advancing on corduroy roads through the Salkehatchie swamps at a rate of a dozen miles per day, Johnston "made up his mind that there had been no such army in existence since the days of Julius Caesar."[81]

Sherman captured the state capital of Columbia, South Carolina, on February 17, 1865. Fires began that night and by next morning most of the central city was destroyed. The burning of Columbia has engendered controversy ever since, with some claiming the fires were accidental, others a deliberate act of vengeance, and still others that the retreating Confederates burned bales of cotton on their way out of town.[82]

Local Native American Lumbee guides helped Sherman's army cross the Lumber River, which was flooded by torrential rains, into North Carolina. According to Sherman, the trek across the Lumber River, and through the swamps, pocosins, and creeks of Robeson County was "the damnedest marching I ever saw."[83] Thereafter, his troops did little damage to the civilian infrastructure, as North Carolina, unlike its southern neighbor, was regarded by his men as a reluctant Confederate state, having been the second from last state to secede from the Union, before Tennessee. Sherman's final significant military engagement was a victory over Johnston's troops at the Battle of Bentonville, March 19–21. He soon rendezvoused at Goldsborough, North Carolina, with Union troops awaiting him there after the capture of Fort Fisher and Wilmington.

In late March, Sherman briefly left his forces and traveled to City Point, Virginia, to consult with Grant. Lincoln happened to be at City Point at the same time, allowing the only three-way meetings of Lincoln, Grant, and Sherman during the war.[84]

## Confederate surrender

Following Lee's surrender to Grant at Appomattox Court House and the assassination of President Lincoln, Sherman met with Johnston in mid-April at Bennett Place in Durham, North Carolina, to negotiate a Confederate surrender. At the insistence of Johnston and of Confederate President Jefferson Davis, Sherman conditionally agreed to generous terms that dealt with both political and military issues. Sherman thought that those terms were consistent with the views Lincoln had expressed at City Point, but the general had not been given the authority, by General Grant, the newly installed President Andrew Johnson, or the Cabinet, to offer those terms.

The government in Washington, D.C., refused to approve Sherman's terms and the Secretary of War, Edwin M. Stanton, denounced Sherman publicly, precipitating a long-lasting feud between the two men. Confusion over this issue lasted until April 26, 1865, when Johnston, ignoring instructions from President Davis, agreed to purely military terms and formally surrendered his army and all the Confederate forces in the Carolinas, Georgia, and Florida, in what was the largest single capitulation of the war.[85] Sherman proceeded with 60,000 of his troops to Washington, D.C., where they marched in the Grand Review of the Armies, on May 24, 1865, and were then disbanded. Having become the second most important general in the Union army, he thus had come full circle to the city where he started his war-time service as colonel of a non-existent infantry regiment.

## Slavery and emancipation

*Portrait by Mathew Brady or Levin C. Handy, between 1865 and 1880*

Sherman was not an abolitionist before the war and, like others of his time and background, he did not believe in "Negro equality."[86][87] Before the war, Sherman at times even expressed some sympathy with the view of Southern whites that the black race was benefiting from slavery, although he opposed breaking up slave families and advocated teaching slaves to read and write.[30] During the Civil War, Sherman declined to employ black troops in his armies.[88]

Sherman's military campaigns of 1864 and 1865 freed many slaves, who greeted him "as a second Moses or Aaron"[86] and joined his marches through Georgia and the Carolinas by the tens of thousands. The fate of these refugees became a pressing military and political issue. Some abolitionists accused Sherman of doing little to alleviate the precarious living conditions of the freed slaves.[89] To address this issue, on January 12, 1865, Sherman met in Savannah with Secretary of War Stanton and with twenty local black leaders. After Sherman's departure, Garrison Frazier, a Baptist minister, declared in response to an inquiry about the feelings of the black community:

We looked upon General Sherman, prior to his arrival, as a man, in the providence of

God, specially set apart to accomplish this work, and we unanimously felt inexpressible gratitude to him, looking upon him as a man that should be honored for the faithful performance of his duty. Some of us called upon him immediately upon his arrival, and it is probable he did not meet [Secretary Stanton] with more courtesy than he met us. His conduct and deportment toward us characterized him as a friend and a gentleman.[90]

Four days later, Sherman issued his Special Field Orders, No. 15. The orders provided for the settlement of 40,000 freed slaves and black refugees on land expropriated from white landowners in South Carolina, Georgia, and Florida. Sherman appointed Brig. Gen. Rufus Saxton, an abolitionist from Massachusetts who had previously directed the recruitment of black soldiers, to implement that plan.[91] Those orders, which became the basis of the claim that the Union government had promised freed slaves "40 acres and a mule," were revoked later that year by President Andrew Johnson.

Although the context is often overlooked, and the quotation usually chopped off, one of Sherman's most famous statements about his hard-war views arose in part from the racial attitudes summarized above. In his *Memoirs*, Sherman noted political pressures in 1864–1865 to encourage the escape of slaves, in part to avoid the possibility that "'able-bodied slaves will be called into the military service of the rebels.'"[92] Sherman thought concentration on such policies would have delayed the "successful end" of the war and the "liberat[ion of] *all* slaves."[93] He went on to summarize vividly his hard-war philosophy and to add, in effect, that he really did not want the help of liberated slaves in subduing the South:

My aim then was to whip the rebels, to humble their pride, to follow them to their inmost recesses, and make them fear and dread us. "Fear of the Lord is the beginning of wisdom." I did not want them to cast in our teeth what General Hood had once done at Atlanta, that we had to call on their slaves to help us to subdue them. But, as regards kindness to the race . . . , I assert that no army ever did more for that race than the one I commanded at Savannah.[94]

## Strategies

Sherman's record as a tactician was mixed, and his military legacy rests primarily on his command of logistics and on his brilliance as a strategist. The influential 20th-century British military historian and theorist B. H. Liddell Hart ranked Sherman as one of the most important strategists in the annals of war, along with Scipio Africanus, Belisarius, Napoleon Bonaparte, T. E. Lawrence, and Erwin Rommel. Liddell Hart credited Sherman with mastery of maneuver warfare (also known as the "indirect approach"), as demonstrated by his series of turning movements against Johnston during the Atlanta Campaign. Liddell Hart also stated that study of Sherman's campaigns had contributed significantly to his own "theory of strategy and tactics in mechanized warfare," which had in turn influenced Heinz Guderian's doctrine of *Blitzkrieg* and Rommel's use of tanks during the Second World War.[95] Another World War II-era student of Liddell Hart's writings about

Sherman was George S. Patton, who "'spent a long vacation studying Sherman's campaigns on the ground in Georgia and the Carolinas, with the aid of [Liddell Hart's] book'" and later "'carried out his [bold] plans, in super-Sherman style'."[96]

Sherman's greatest contribution to the war, the strategy of total warfare—endorsed by General Grant and President Lincoln—has been the subject of controversy. Sherman himself downplayed his role in conducting total war, often saying that he was simply carrying out orders as best he could in order to fulfill his part of Grant's master plan for ending the war.

## Total warfare

Like Grant, Sherman was convinced that the Confederacy's strategic, economic, and psychological ability to wage further war needed to be definitively crushed if the fighting were to end. Therefore, he believed that the North had to conduct its campaign as a war of conquest and employ scorched earth tactics to break the backbone of the rebellion. He called this strategy "hard war."

Sherman's advance through Georgia and South Carolina was characterized by widespread destruction of civilian supplies and infrastructure. Although looting was officially forbidden, historians disagree on how well this regulation was enforced.[97] Union soldiers who foraged from Southern homes became known as bummers. The speed and efficiency of the destruction by Sherman's army was remarkable. The practice of heating rails and bending them around trees, leaving behind what came to be known as "Sherman's neckties," made repairs difficult. Accusations that civilians were targeted and war crimes were committed on the march have made Sherman a controversial figure to this day, particularly in the American South.

The damage done by Sherman was almost entirely limited to the destruction of property. Though exact figures are not available, the loss of civilian life appears to have been very small.[98] Consuming supplies, wrecking infrastructure, and undermining morale were Sherman's stated goals, and several of his Southern contemporaries noted this and commented on it. For instance, Alabama-born Major Henry Hitchcock, who served in Sherman's staff, declared that "it is a terrible thing to consume and destroy the sustenance of thousands of people," but if the scorched earth strategy served "to paralyze their husbands and fathers who are fighting . . . it is mercy in the end."[99]

The severity of the destructive acts by Union troops was significantly greater in South Carolina than in Georgia or North Carolina. This appears to have been a consequence of the animosity among both Union soldiers and officers to the state that they regarded as the "cockpit of secession."[100] One of the most serious accusations against Sherman was that he allowed his troops to burn the city of Columbia. In 1867, Gen. O. O. Howard, commander of Sherman's 15th Corps, reportedly said, "It is useless to deny that our troops burnt Columbia, for I saw them in the act."[101] However, Sherman himself stated that "[i]f I had made up my mind to burn Columbia I would have burnt it with no more feeling than I would a common prairie dog village; but I did not do it . . . "[102] Sherman's official report on the burning placed the blame on Confederate Lt. Gen. Wade Hampton III, who Sherman said had ordered the burning of cotton in the streets. In his memoirs,

Sherman said, "In my official report of this conflagration I distinctly charged it to General Wade Hampton, and confess I did so pointedly to shake the faith of his people in him, for he was in my opinion a braggart and professed to be the special champion of South Carolina."[103] Historian James M. McPherson has concluded that:

> The fullest and most dispassionate study of this controversy blames all parties in varying proportions—including the Confederate authorities for the disorder that characterized the evacuation of Columbia, leaving thousands of cotton bales on the streets (some of them burning) and huge quantities of liquor undestroyed . . . Sherman did not deliberately burn Columbia; a majority of Union soldiers, including the general himself, worked through the night to put out the fires.[104]

In this general connection, it is also noteworthy that Sherman and his subordinates (particularly John A. Logan) took steps to protect Raleigh, North Carolina, from acts of revenge after the assassination of President Lincoln.[105]

## Modern assessment

After the fall of Atlanta in 1864, Sherman ordered the city's evacuation. When the city council appealed to him to rescind that order, on the grounds that it would cause great hardship to women, children, the elderly, and others who bore no responsibility for the conduct of the war, Sherman sent a written response in which he sought to articulate his conviction that a lasting peace would be possible only if the Union were restored, and that he was therefore prepared to do all he could do to quash the rebellion:

> You cannot qualify war in harsher terms than I will. War is cruelty, and you cannot refine it; and those who brought war into our country deserve all the curses and maledictions a people can pour out. I know I had no hand in making this war, and I know I will make more sacrifices to-day than any of you to secure peace. But you cannot have peace and a division of our country. If the United States submits to a division now, it will not stop, but will go on until we reap the fate of Mexico, which is eternal war . . . I want peace, and believe it can only be reached through union and war, and I will ever conduct war with a view to perfect and early success. But, my dear sirs, when peace does come, you may call on me for anything. Then will I share with you the last cracker, and watch with you to shield your homes and families against danger from every quarter.[106]

Literary critic Edmund Wilson found in Sherman's *Memoirs* a fascinating and disturbing account of an "appetite for warfare" that "grows as it feeds on the South."[107] Former U.S. Defense Secretary Robert McNamara refers equivocally to the statement that "war is cruelty and you cannot refine it" in both the book *Wilson's Ghost*[108] and in his interview for the film *The Fog of War*.

But when comparing Sherman's scorched-earth campaigns to the actions of the British

Army during the Second Boer War (1899–1902)—another war in which civilians were targeted because of their central role in sustaining an armed resistance—South African historian Hermann Giliomee declares that it "looks as if Sherman struck a better balance than the British commanders between severity and restraint in taking actions proportional to legitimate needs."[109] The admiration of scholars such as Victor Davis Hanson, B. H. Liddell Hart, Lloyd Lewis, and John F. Marszalek for General Sherman owes much to what they see as an approach to the exigencies of modern armed conflict that was both effective and principled.

In May 1865, after the major Confederate armies had surrendered, Sherman wrote in a personal letter:

> I confess, without shame, I am sick and tired of fighting—its glory is all moonshine; even success the most brilliant is over dead and mangled bodies, with the anguish and lamentations of distant families, appealing to me for sons, husbands and fathers . . . tis only those who have never heard a shot, never heard the shriek and groans of the wounded and lacerated . . . that cry aloud for more blood, more vengeance, more desolation.[110]

## Later years

He lived most of the rest of his life in New York City. He was devoted to the theater and to amateur painting and was much in demand as a colorful speaker at dinners and banquets, in which he indulged a fondness for quoting Shakespeare.[129] During this period, he stayed in contact with war veterans, and through them accepted honorary membership into the Phi Kappa Psi Fraternity and the Irving Literary Society. Sherman was proposed as a Republican candidate for the presidential election of 1884, but declined as emphatically as possible, saying, "I will not accept if nominated and will not serve if elected."[130] Such a categorical rejection of a candidacy is now referred to as a "Shermanesque statement."

In 1888 he joined the newly formed Boone and Crockett Club, a wildlife conservation organization founded by Theodore Roosevelt and George Bird Grinnell.[131]

## Death

Sherman died of pneumonia in New York City at 1:50 p.m. on February 14, 1891, six days after his 71st birthday. President Benjamin Harrison sent a telegram to General Sherman's family and ordered all national flags to be flown at half mast. Harrison, in a message to the Senate and the House of Representatives, wrote that:

> He was an ideal soldier, and shared to the fullest the esprit du corps of the army, but he cherished the civil institutions organized under the Constitution, and was only a soldier that these might be perpetuated in undiminished usefulness and honor.[132]

*Sherman's death mask*

# Robert Smalls

**Robert Smalls** (April 5, 1839– February 23, 1915) was an American businessman, publisher, and politician. Born into slavery in Beaufort, South Carolina, he freed himself, his crew, and their families during the American Civil War by commandeering a Confederate transport ship, CSS *Planter*, in Charleston harbor, on May 13, 1862, and sailing it from Confederate-controlled waters of the harbor to the U.S. blockade that surrounded it. He then piloted the ship to the Union-controlled enclave in Beaufort-Port Royal-Hilton Head area, where she became a Union warship. His example and persuasion helped convince President Abraham Lincoln to accept African-American soldiers into the Union Army.

After the American Civil War he returned to Beaufort and became a politician, winning election as a Republican to the South Carolina State legislature and the United States House of Representatives during the Reconstruction era. Smalls authored state legislation providing for South Carolina to have the first free and compulsory public school system in the United States. He founded the Republican Party of South Carolina. Smalls was the last Republican to represent South Carolina's 5th congressional district until 2010.

## Early life

Robert Smalls was born in 1839 to Lydia Polite, a woman enslaved by Henry McKee, who was most likely Smalls's father.[1] She gave birth to him in a cabin behind McKee's house, at 511 Prince Street in Beaufort, South Carolina.[2] He grew up in the city under the influence of the Lowcountry Gullah culture of his mother. His mother lived as a servant in the house but grew up in the fields. Robert was favored over other slaves, so his mother worried that he might grow up not understanding the plight of field slaves, and asked for him to be made to work in the fields and to witness whipping.[3]

When he was 12, at the request of his mother, Smalls's master sent him to Charleston to hire out as a laborer for one dollar a week, with the rest of the wage being paid to his master. The youth first worked in a hotel, then became a lamplighter on Charleston's streets. In his teen years, his love of the sea led him to find work on Charleston's docks and wharves. Smalls worked as a longshoreman, a rigger, a sail maker, and eventually worked his way up to become a wheelman, more or less a pilot, though slaves were not honored by that title. As a result, he was very knowledgeable about Charleston harbor.[4]

At age 17, Smalls married Hannah Jones, an enslaved hotel maid, in Charleston on

December 24, 1856. She was five years his senior and already had two daughters. Their own first child, Elizabeth Lydia Smalls, was born in February 1858. Three years later they had a son, Robert Jr., who later died at age two.[5] Robert aimed to pay for their freedom by purchasing them outright, but the price was steep, $800 (equivalent to $22,308 in 2018). He had managed to save up only $100. It could take decades for him to reach $800.[3]

## Civil war

### *Escape from slavery*

In April 1861, the American Civil War began with the Battle of Fort Sumter in nearby Charleston Harbor. In the fall of 1861, Smalls was assigned to steer the CSS *Planter*, a lightly armed Confederate military transport under the command of Charleston's District Commander Brigadier General Roswell S. Ripley.[6] *Planter*'s duties were to deliver dispatches, troops and supplies, to survey waterways, and to lay mines. Smalls piloted the *Planter* throughout Charleston harbor and beyond, on area rivers and along the South Carolina, Georgia and Florida coasts.[7][8] From Charleston harbor, Smalls and the *Planter*'s crew could see the line of Federal blockade ships in the outer harbor, seven miles away.[9] Smalls appeared content and had the confidence of the *Planter*'s crew and owners, and at some time in April 1862, Smalls began to plan an escape. He discussed the matter with the other slaves in the crew except one, whom he did not trust.[2]

On May 12, 1862, the *Planter* traveled ten miles southwest of Charleston to stop at Coles Island, a Confederate post on the Stono River that was being dismantled.[10] There the ship picked up four large guns to transport to a fort in Charleston harbor. Back in Charleston, the crew loaded 200 pounds of ammunition and 20 cords of firewood onto the *Planter*.[7] At some point family members hid aboard another steamer docked at the North Atlantic wharf.[11][12]

On the evening of May 12, the *Planter* was docked as usual at the wharf below General Ripley's headquarters.[2] Her three white officers disembarked to spend the night ashore, leaving Smalls and the crew on board, "as was their custom."[13] (Afterward, the three Confederate officers were court-martialed and two convicted, but the verdicts were later overturned.[2]) About 3 a.m. May 13, Smalls and seven of the eight slave crewmen made their previously planned escape to the Union blockade ships. Smalls put on the captain's uniform and wore a straw hat similar to the captain's. He sailed the *Planter* past what was then called Southern Wharf, and stopped at another wharf to pick up his wife and children and the families of other crewmen.

Smalls guided the ship past the five Confederate harbor forts without incident, as he gave the correct signals at checkpoints. The *Planter* had been commanded by a Captain Charles C.J. Relyea and Smalls copied Relyea's manners and straw hat on deck to fool Confederate onlookers from shore and the forts.[14] The *Planter* sailed past Fort Sumter at about 4:30 a.m. The alarm was only raised by the time they were out of gun range. Smalls headed straight for the Union Navy fleet, replacing the rebel flags with a white bed sheet his wife had brought aboard. The *Planter* had been seen by the USS *Onward*, which was about to fire until a crewman spotted the white flag.[4] In the dark, the sheet was hard to see, but the sunrise came just in time.[3]

Witness account:

"Just as No. 3 port gun was being elevated, someone cried out, 'I see something that looks like a white flag'; and true enough there was something flying on the steamer that would have been white by application of soap and water. As she neared us, we looked in vain for the face of a white man. When they discovered that we would not fire on them, there was a rush of contrabands out on her deck, some dancing, some singing, whistling, jumping; and others stood looking towards Fort Sumter, and muttering all sorts of maledictions against it, and 'de heart of de Souf,' generally. As the steamer came near, and under the stern of the Onward, one of the Colored men stepped forward, and taking off his hat, shouted, 'Good morning, sir! I've brought you some of the old United States guns, sir!'" That man was Robert Smalls.[3]

The *Onward*'s captain, John Frederick Nickels,[14] boarded the *Planter*, and Smalls asked for a United States flag to display. He surrendered the *Planter* and her cargo to the United States Navy.[4] Smalls's escape plan had succeeded.

The *Planter* and description of Smalls's actions were forwarded by Lt. Nickels to his commander, Capt. E.G. Parrott. In addition to her own light guns, *Planter* carried the four loose artillery pieces from Coles Island and the 200 pounds of ammunition. Most valuable, however, were the captain's code book containing the Confederate signals and a map of the mines and torpedoes that had been laid in Charleston's harbor. Smalls's own extensive knowledge of the Charleston region's waterways and military configurations proved highly valuable. Parrott again forwarded the *Planter* to flag officer Du Pont at Port Royal, describing Smalls as very intelligent. Smalls gave detailed information about Charleston's defenses to Du Pont, commander of the blockading fleet. Federal officers were surprised to learn from Smalls that contrary to their calculations, only a few thousand troops remained to protect the area, the rest having been sent to Tennessee and Virginia. They also learned that the Coles Island fortifications on Charleston's southern flank were being abandoned and were without protection.[7] This intelligence allowed Union forces to capture Coles Island and its string of batteries without a fight on May 20, a week after Smalls's escape. The Union would hold the Stono inlet as a base for the remaining three years of the war.[2] Du Pont was impressed, and wrote the following to the Navy secretary in Washington: "Robert, the intelligent slave and pilot of the boat, who performed this bold feat so skillfully, informed me of [the capture of the Sumter gun], presuming it would be a matter of interest." He "is superior to any who have come into our lines—intelligent as many of them have been."[3]

## Service to the Union

Smalls, having just turned 23, quickly became known in the North as a hero for his daring exploit. Newspapers and magazines reported his actions. The U.S. Congress passed a bill awarding Smalls and his crewmen the prize money for the *Planter* (valuable not only for its guns but low draft in Charleston bay); Southern newspapers demanded harsh discipline for the Confederate officers whose joint shore leave had allowed the slaves to steal the boat.[15] Smalls's share of the prize money came to US$1,500 (equivalent to $37,645 in 2018). Immediately after the capture, Smalls was invited to travel to New York to help raise money for ex-slaves, but Admiral DuPont vetoed the proposal and Smalls began to serve the Union Navy, especially with his detailed knowledge of mines laid near Charleston. However, with the encouragement of Major General David Hunter, the Union commander at Port Royal, Smalls went to Washington, D.C., in August 1862 with Rev. Mansfield French, a Methodist minister who had helped found Wilberforce University in Ohio and had been sent by the American Missionary Association to help former slaves at Port Royal.[16] They wanted to persuade Lincoln and Secretary of War Edwin Stanton to permit black men to fight for the Union. Although Lincoln had previously rescinded orders by Hunter and Generals Fremont and Sherman to mobilize black troops,[16] Stanton soon signed an order permitting up to 5,000 African Americans to enlist in the Union forces at Port Royal. Those who did were organized as the 1st and 2nd South Carolina Regiments (Colored). Smalls worked as a civilian with the Navy until March 1863, when he was transferred to the Army. By his own account, Smalls was present at 17 major battles and engagements in the Civil War.[2]

After capture, the *Planter* required some repairs, which were performed locally, and went into Union service near Fort Pulaski. The boat was valued for its shallow draft, compared to other boats in the fleet.[17] Smalls was made pilot of the *Crusader* under Captain Alexander Rhind. In June of that year, Smalls was piloting the *Crusader* on Edisto in Wadmalaw Sound when the *Planter* returned to service, and an infantry regiment engaged in the Battle of Simmon's Bluff at the head of the Edisto River. He continued to pilot the *Crusader* and the *Planter*. As a slave, he had assisted in laying mines (then called "torpedoes") along the coast and river. Now, as a pilot, he helped find and remove them and serviced the blockade between Charleston and Beaufort. He was also present when the *Planter* was fired upon at several fights at Adam's Run on the Dawho River and at battles at Rockville, at John's Island, and at the Second Battle of Pocotaligo.[14]

He was made pilot of the ironclad USS *Keokuk*, again under captain Rhind, and took part in the attack on Fort Sumter on April 7, 1863, which was a preamble to the Second Battle of Fort Sumter later that fall. The *Keokuk* took 96 hits and retired for the night, sinking the next morning. Smalls and much of the crew moved to the *Ironside* and the fleet returned to Hilton Head.[14]

In June 1863, David Hunter was replaced as commander of the Department of the South by Quincy Adams Gillmore. With Gillmore's arrival, Smalls was transferred to the quartermaster's department. Smalls was pilot of the USS *Isaac Smith*, later recommissioned in the Confederate Navy the *Stono* in the expedition on Morris Island. When Union troops took the south end of the Island, Smalls was put in charge of the Light House Inlet as pilot.[14]

On December 1, 1863, Smalls was piloting the *Planter* under Captain James Nickerson on Folly Island Creek when Confederate batteries at Secessionville opened. Nickerson fled the pilot house for the coal-bunker. Smalls refused to surrender, fearing that the black crewmen would not be treated as prisoners of war and might be summarily killed. Smalls entered the pilothouse and took command of the boat and piloted her to safety. For this, he was reportedly promoted by Gillmore to the rank of captain and made acting captain of the *Planter*.[14][4]

In May 1864, he was voted an unofficial delegate to the Republican National Convention in Baltimore. Later that spring, Smalls piloted the *Planter* to Philadelphia for an overhaul. In Philadelphia, he supported what was known as the Port Royal Experiment, an effort to raise money to support the education and development of ex-slaves. At the outset of the Civil War, Smalls could not read or write, but he achieved literacy in Philadelphia. In 1864, Smalls was in a streetcar in Philadelphia and was ordered to give his seat to a white passenger. Rather than ride on the open overflow platform, Smalls left the car. This incident of humiliating a heroic veteran was cited in the debate that resulted in the legislature's passing a bill to integrate public transportation in Pennsylvania in 1867.[2]

In December 1864, Smalls and the *Planter* moved to support William T. Sherman's army in Savannah, Georgia, at the destination point of his March to the Sea. Smalls returned with the *Planter* to Charleston harbor in April 1865 for the ceremonial raising of the American flag again at Fort Sumter.[2] Smalls was discharged on June 11, 1865. Other vessels Smalls piloted during the war include the *Huron* and the *Paul Jones*.[18] He continued to pilot the *Planter,* serving a humanitarian mission of taking food and supplies to freedmen who lost their homes and livelihoods during the war. On September 30, the *Planter* entered the service of the Freedmen's Bureau.[19]

## Commission and prize money

Smalls's position in the Union Army and Navy has been disputed and Smalls's reward for the capture of the *Planter* has been criticized. During Smalls's life, articles about Smalls state that when he was assigned to pilot the *Planter*, the Navy did not allow him to hold the rank of pilot because he was not a graduate of a naval academy, a requirement at that time. To assure he received proper pay for a captain, he was commissioned second lieutenant of the 1st South Carolina Volunteers (later re-designated as the 33rd US Colored Infantry) and detailed to act as pilot. Many sources also state that General Gillmore promoted Smalls to captain in December 1863 when he saved the *Planter* when it was under attack near Secessionville.[20] Later sources state that Smalls did receive a commission either in the Army or the Navy, but he was likely officially a civilian throughout the war.[2]

Later in his life, when Smalls sought a Navy pension, he learned that he had not been officially commissioned. He claimed he had received an official commission from Gillmore but had lost it. In 1883, a bill passed committee to put him on the Navy retired list, but in the end was halted, allegedly due to Smalls's being black.[21] In 1897, a special act of congress granted Smalls a pension of $30 per month, equal to the pension for a Navy captain.[2]

In 1883, during discussion of the bill to put Smalls on the Navy retired list, a report stated that the 1862 appraisal of the *Planter* was "absurdly low" and that a fair valuation would have been over $60,000. However, Smalls received no further payment until 1900. That year, Congress passed a statute paying Smalls $5,000 less the amount paid to him in 1862 ($1,500) for his capture of the steamship. Many still felt that this was less than his due.[2]

## After the Civil War

Immediately following the war, Smalls returned to his native Beaufort, where he purchased his former master's house at 511 Prince St, which Union tax authorities had seized in 1863 for refusal to pay taxes. Later, the former owner sued to regain the property, but Smalls retained ownership in the court case. The case became an important precedent in other, similar cases.[2] His mother, Lydia, lived with him for the remainder of her life. He allowed his former master's wife, the elderly Jane Bond McKee, to move into her former home prior to her death. Smalls spent nine months learning to read and write. He purchased a two-story Beaumont building to use as a school for African-American children.[19]

## Business ventures

*Richard Gleaves, Smalls's business partner after the war*

In 1866 Smalls went into business in Beaufort with Richard Howell Gleaves, a businessman from Philadelphia. They opened a store to serve the needs of freedmen. Smalls also hired a teacher to help him study.[18] That April, the Radical Republicans who controlled Congress overrode President Andrew Johnson's vetoes and passed a Civil Rights Act. In 1868, they passed the 14th Amendment, which was ratified by the states to extend full citizenship to all Americans regardless of race.

Smalls invested significantly in the economic development of the Charleston-Beaufort region. In 1870, in anticipation of a Reconstruction-based prosperity, Smalls, with fellow representatives Joseph Rainey, Alonzo Ransier and others, formed the Enterprise Railroad, an 18-mile horse-drawn railway line that carried cargo and passengers between the Charleston wharves and inland depots.[22] Except for one white director,[23] the railroad's board of directors was entirely African American. Richard H. Cain was its first president. Author Bernard E. Powers describes it as "the most impressive commercial venture by members of Charleston's black elite."[24][25] He owned and helped publish a black-owned newspaper, the *Beaufort Southern Standard* starting in 1872.[19]

## Political career

Small's wartime fame and his fluency with the Gullah dialect gave him an avenue for political advancement.[18]

## State politics

Smalls was a delegate at the 1868 South Carolina Constitutional Convention where he was a part of the effort to make free, compulsory schooling available to all South Carolina children.[19] He also served as a delegate at several Republican National Conventions; he also participated in the South Carolina Republican State conventions.

In 1868, Smalls was elected to the South Carolina House of Representatives. He was very effective, and introduced the Homestead Act and introduced and worked to pass the Civil Rights bill. In 1870, Jonathan Jasper Wright was elected judge of the South Carolina Supreme Court and Smalls was elected to fill his unexpired time in the Senate. He continued in the Senate, winning the 1872 election against W. J. Whipper. In the senate he was considered a very good speaker and debater. He was on the Finance Committee and chairman of the Public Printing Committee.[26][19]

He was a delegate to the National Republican Conventions in 1872 in Philadelphia, which nominated Grant for president; in 1876 in Cincinnati, which nominated Hayes; and in 1884 in Chicago, which nominated Blaine[26]—and then continuously to all conventions until 1896.[27] He was also elected vice-president of the South Carolina Republican Party at their 1872 state convention.

In 1873, he was appointed lieutenant-colonel of the Third Regiment, South Carolina State Militia. He was later promoted to brigadier-general of the Second Brigade, South Carolina Militia, and the major-general of the Second Division, South Carolina State Militia. He held this position until 1877, when Democrats took control of the state government.[26][19]

## National politics

In 1874, Smalls was elected to the United States House of Representatives, where he served two terms from 1875 to 1879. From 1882 to 1883, he represented South Carolina's 5th congressional district in the House. The state legislature gerrymandered to change the district boundaries, including Beaufort and other heavily black, coastal areas in South Carolina's 7th congressional district, giving the others substantial white majorities. Smalls was elected from the 7th district and served from 1884 to 1887. He was a member of the 44th, 45th, 47th, 48th, 49th U.S. Congresses.[2]

In 1875, he opposed the transfer of troops out of the South, fearing the effect of such a move on the safety of blacks in the South.[18] During consideration of a bill to reduce and restructure the United States Army, Smalls introduced an amendment that "Hereafter in

*George D. Tillman, one of Smalls's chief rivals in Congressional races*

the enlistment of men in the Army . . . no distinction whatsoever shall be made on account of race or color." However, the amendment was not considered by Congress. He was the last Republican elected from the 5th district until 2010 when Mick Mulvaney took office. He was the second-longest serving African-American member of Congress (behind his contemporary Joseph Rainey) until the mid-20th century.[2]

After the Compromise of 1877, the U.S. government withdrew its remaining forces from South Carolina and other Southern states. Conservative Southern Bourbon Democrats, who called themselves the Redeemers, had resorted to violence and election fraud to regain control of the state legislature. As part of wide-ranging white efforts to reduce African-American political power, Smalls was charged and convicted of taking a bribe five years earlier in connection with the awarding of a printing contract. He was pardoned as part of an agreement by which charges were also dropped against Democrats accused of election fraud.[27]

The scandal took a political toll, and he was defeated by Democrat George D. Tillman in 1878, and again, narrowly, in 1880. He successfully contested the 1880 result and regained the seat in 1882. In 1884, he was elected to fill a seat in a different district. He was nominated for Senate but defeated by Wade Hampton in 1886. During this period in Congress he supported racial integration legislation, supported a pension for the widow of his former Major General, David Hunter, and advised South Carolina blacks to refrain from emigrating to the North and Midwest or to Liberia.[18]

In 1890, he was appointed by President Benjamin Harrison as collector of the Port of Beaufort, which he held until 1913 except during Democrat Grover Cleveland's second term.[2] Smalls was active into the twentieth century. He was a delegate to the 1895 South Carolina constitutional convention. Together with five other black politicians, he strongly opposed white Democratic efforts that year to disfranchise black citizens. They wrote an article for the *New York World* to publicize the issues, but the state constitution was ratified. It and similar constitutions across the South for some time passed challenges that reached the US Supreme Court, resulting in the exclusion of African Americans from politics across the South and crippling of the Republican Party in the region.

In the late 1890s, he began to suffer from diabetes. He turned down an offer of a colonelcy of a black regiment in the Spanish-American War and to the post of minister to Liberia.

## Local politics

Though Smalls was not officially involved with politics on the local level, he had some influence. In 1913, in one of his final actions as community leader, he played an important role in stopping a lynch mob from killing two black suspects in the murder of a white man. He pressured the mayor, saying that blacks he had sent throughout the city would burn the town down if the mob was not stopped. The mayor and sheriff stopped the mob.[18]

## Death

Smalls died of malaria and diabetes in 1915 at the age of 75.[19] He was buried in his family's plot in the churchyard of the Tabernacle Baptist Church in downtown Beaufort. The monument to Smalls in this churchyard is inscribed with a statement he made to the South Carolina legislature in 1895: "My race needs no special defense, for the past history of them in this country proves them to be the equal of any people anywhere. All they need is an equal chance in the battle of life."[29][30]

# Edwin Stanton

**Edwin McMasters Stanton** (December 19, 1814–December 24, 1869) was an American lawyer and politician who served as Secretary of War under the Lincoln Administration during most of the American Civil War. Stanton's management helped organize the massive military resources of the North and guide the Union to victory. However, he was criticized by many Union generals for perceived over-cautiousness and micromanagement.[1] He also organized the manhunt for Abraham Lincoln's assassin, John Wilkes Booth.

After Lincoln's assassination, Stanton remained as the Secretary of War under the new U.S. President Andrew Johnson during the first years of Reconstruction. He opposed the lenient policies of Johnson towards the former Confederate States. Johnson's attempt to dismiss Stanton ultimately led to Johnson being impeached by the Radical Republicans in the House of Representatives. Stanton returned to law after retiring as Secretary of War, and in 1869 was nominated as an Associate Justice of the Supreme Court by Johnson's successor, Ulysses S. Grant; however, he died four days after his nomination was confirmed by the Senate.

## Early work in politics (1860–1862)
### In Buchanan's cabinet
In late 1860 President Buchanan was formulating his yearly State of the Union address to Congress, and asked Attorney General Black to offer insight into the legality and constitutionality of secession. Black then asked Stanton for advice.[58] Stanton approved a strongly worded draft of Black's response to Buchanan, which denounced secession from the Union as illegal. Buchanan gave his address to Congress on December 3.[59] Meanwhile, Buchanan's cabinet were growing more discontent with his handling of secession, and several members deemed him too weak on the issue. On December 5 his Secretary of the Treasury, Howell Cobb resigned. On December 9 Secretary of State Lewis Cass, disgruntled over Buchanan's failure to defend the government's interests in the South, tendered his resignation. Black was nominated to replace Cass on December 12.[60] About a week later, Stanton, at the time in Cincinnati, was told to come to Washington at once, for he had been confirmed by the Senate as Buchanan's new Attorney General. He was sworn in on December 20.[60][61]

Stanton met a cabinet in disarray over the issue of secession. Buchanan did not want to agitate the South any further, and sympathized with the South's cause.[62] On December 9 Buchanan had agreed with South Carolinian congressmen that the military installations in the state would not be reinforced unless force against them was perpetrated. However, on the day that Stanton assumed his position, Maj. Robert Anderson moved his unit to Fort Sumter, South Carolina, which the Southerners viewed as Buchanan reneging on his promise. South Carolina issued an ordinance of secession soon after, declaring itself independent of the United States.[63] The South Carolinians demanded that federal forces leave Charleston Harbor altogether; they threatened carnage if they did not get compliance.[64] The following day, Buchanan gave his cabinet a draft of his response to the South Carolinians. Secretaries Thompson and Philip Francis Thomas, of the Treasury Department, thought the President's response too pugnacious; Stanton, Black and Postmaster General Joseph Holt thought it too placatory. Isaac Toucey, Secretary of the Navy, was alone in his support of the response.[65]

Stanton was unnerved by Buchanan's ambivalence towards the South Carolina secession crisis, and wanted to stiffen him against complying to the South's demands.[66] On December 30 Black came to Stanton's home, and the two agreed to pen their objections to Buchanan ordering a withdrawal from Fort Sumter. If he did such a thing, the two men, along with Postmaster General Holt, agreed that they would resign, delivering a crippling blow to the administration. Buchanan obliged them.[67][Note 2] The South Carolinian delegates got their response from President Buchanan on New Year's Eve 1860; the President would not withdraw forces from Charleston Harbor.[69]

By February 1, six Southern states had followed South Carolina's lead and passed ordinances of secession, declaring themselves to no longer be a part of the United States. [70] On February 18 Jefferson Davis was sworn in as the President of the Confederate States.[71] Meanwhile, Washington was astir with talk of coups and conspiracies. Stanton thought that discord would ravage the capital on February 13, when electoral votes were being counted; nothing happened. Again, Stanton thought, when Lincoln was sworn in on March 4 there would be violence; this did not come to pass. Lincoln's inauguration did give Stanton a flickering of hope that his efforts to keep Fort Sumter defended would not be in vain, and that Southern aggression would be met with force in the North. In his inauguration speech, Lincoln did not say he would outlaw slavery throughout the nation, but he did say that he would not support secession in any form, and that any attempt to leave the Union was not lawful. In Stanton, Lincoln's words were met with cautious optimism. [72] The new President submitted his choices for his cabinet on March 5,[73] and by that day's end, Stanton was no longer the attorney general.[74] He lingered in his office for a while to help settle in and guide his replacement, Edward Bates.[73]

## Cameron's advisor

On July 21, the North and the South experienced their first major clash at Manassas Junction in Virginia, the First Battle of Bull Run. Northerners thought the battle would end the war, and defeat the Confederacy decisively; however, the bloody encounter ended with the Union Army retreating to Washington. Lincoln wanted to bolster Northern numbers afterwards, with many in the North believing the war would be more arduous than

*Simon Cameron, Lincoln's Secretary of War before Stanton*

they initially expected, but when more than 250,000 men signed up, the federal government did not have enough supplies for them. The War Department had states buy the supplies, assuring them that they would be reimbursed. This led to states selling the federal government items that were usually damaged or worthless at very high prices. Nonetheless, the government bought them.[75]

Soon, Simon Cameron, Lincoln's Secretary of War, was being accused of incompetently handling his department, and some wanted him to resign. Cameron sought out Stanton to advise him on legal matters concerning the War Department's acquisitions, among other things. [76] Calls for Cameron to resign grew louder when he endorsed a bombastic November 1861 speech given by Col. John Cochrane to his unit. "[W]e should take the slave by the hand, placing a musket in it, and bid him in God's name strike for the liberty of the human race," Cochrane said.[77] Cameron embraced Cochrane's sentiment that slaves should be armed, but it was met with repudiation in Lincoln's cabinet. Caleb B. Smith, the Secretary in the Department of the Interior, scolded Cameron for his support of Cochrane.[78]

Cameron inserted a call to arm the slaves in his report to Congress, which would be sent along with Lincoln's address to the legislature.[78] Cameron gave the report to Stanton, who amended it with a passage that went even further in demanding that slaves be armed,[79] stating that those who rebel against the government lose their claims to any type of property, including slaves, and that it was "clearly the right of the Government to arm slaves when it may become necessary as it is to use gunpowder or guns taken from the enemy."[80] Cameron gave the report to Lincoln, and sent several copies to Congress and the press. Lincoln wanted the portions containing calls to arm the slaves removed, and ordered the transmission of Cameron's report be stopped and replaced with an altered version. Congress received the version without the call to arm slaves, while the press received a version with it. When newspapers published the document in its entirety, Lincoln was excoriated by Republicans, who thought him weak on the issue of slavery, and disliked that he wanted the plea to arm slaves removed.[79]

The President resolved to dismiss Cameron when abolitionists in the North settled over the controversy. Cameron would not resign until he was sure of his successor, and that he could leave the cabinet without damaging his reputation. When a vacancy in the post of Minister to Russia presented itself, Cameron and Lincoln agreed that he would fill the post when he resigned. As for a successor, Lincoln thought Joseph Holt best for the job, but his Secretary of State, William H. Seward, wanted Stanton to succeed Cameron. Salmon Chase, Stanton's friend and Lincoln's Treasury Secretary, agreed.[81] Stanton had been preparing for a partnership with Samuel L. M. Barlow in New York, but abandoned these plans when he heard of his possible nomination.[82] Lincoln nominated Stanton to the post of Secretary of War on January 13. He was confirmed two days following.[83]

## Lincoln's Secretary of War (1862–1865)

### Early days in office

Under Cameron, the War Department had earned the moniker "the lunatic asylum."[84] The department was barely respected among soldiers or government officials, and its authority was routinely disregarded. The army's generals held the brunt of the operating authority in the military, while the President and the War Department interceded only in exceptional circumstances.[85] The department also had strained relations with Congress, especially Representative John Fox Potter, head of the House's "Committee on Loyalty of Federal employees," which sought to root out Confederate sympathizers in the government. Potter had prodded Cameron to remove about fifty individuals he suspected of Confederate sympathies; Cameron had paid him no mind.[86]

Stanton was sworn in on January 20.[87] Immediately, he set about repairing the fractious relationship between Congress and the War Department. Stanton met with Potter on his first day as secretary, and on the same day, dismissed four persons whom Potter deemed unsavory. This was well short of the fifty people Potter wanted gone from the department, but he was nonetheless pleased. Stanton also met with Senator Benjamin Wade and his Joint Committee on the Conduct of the War. The committee was a necessary and fruitful ally; it had subpoena power, thus allowing it to acquire information Stanton could not, and could help Stanton remove War Department staffers. Wade and his committee were happy to find an ally in the executive branch, and met with Stanton often thereafter. [88] Stanton made a number of organizational changes within the department as well. He appointed John Tucker, an executive at the Philadelphia and Reading Railroad, and Peter H. Watson, his partner in the reaper case, to be his assistant secretaries,[89] and had the staff at the department expanded by over sixty employees.[84] Further, Stanton appealed to the Senate to cease appointments of military officials until he could review the more than 1,400 individuals up for promotion. Hitherto, military promotions were a spoils system, where individuals favorable to the administration were given promotions, regardless of merit. This ceased under Stanton.[90][Note 3]

On January 29 Stanton ordered that all contracts to manufacturers of military materials and supplies outside the United States be voided and replaced with contracts within the country, and that no such further contracts be made with foreign companies. The order provoked apprehension in Lincoln's cabinet.[93] The United Kingdom and France were searching for cause to recognize and support the Confederates, and Stanton's order may have given it to them.[94] Secretary of State Seward thought the order would "complicate the foreign situation." Stanton persisted, and his January 29 order stood.[95]

Meanwhile, Stanton worked to create an effective transportation and communication network across the North. His efforts focused on the railroad system and the telegraph lines. Stanton worked with Senator Wade to push through Congress a bill that would codify the ability of the President and his administration to forcibly seize railroad and telegraph lines for their purposes. Railroad companies in the North were accommodating to the needs and desires of the federal government for the most part, and the law was rarely used.[96] Stanton also secured the government's use of telegraph. He relocated the military's telegraphing operations from McClellan's army headquarters to his department, a decision the general was none too pleased with. The relocation gave Stanton closer control over the military's communications operations, and he exploited this. Stanton forced all members of the press to work through Assistant Secretary Watson, where unwanted journalists would be disallowed access to official government correspondence. If a member of the press went elsewhere in the department, they would be charged with espionage.[97]

Prior to Stanton's incumbency as War Secretary, President Lincoln apportioned responsibility for the security of government against treachery and other unsavory activities to several members of his cabinet, mostly Secretary Seward, as he did not trust Attorney General Bates or Secretary Cameron. Under Secretary Stanton, the War Department would have consolidated responsibility for internal security. A lynch-pin of Seward's strategy to maintain internal security was the use of arbitrary arrests and detentions, and Stanton continued this practice. Democrats harshly criticized the use of arbitrary arrests, but Lincoln contented that it was his primary responsibility to maintain the integrity and security of the government, and that waiting until possible betrayers committed guilty acts would hurt the government.[98] At Stanton's behest Seward continued the detention of only the most risky inmates, and released all others.[99]

## General-in-Chief

Lincoln eventually grew tired of McClellan's inaction, especially after his January 27, 1862, order of advance against the Confederates in the Eastern Theatre had provoked little military response from McClellan. On March 11 Lincoln relieved McClellan of his post as general-in-chief of U.S. forces—leaving him in charge of only the Army of the Potomac—and replaced him with Stanton. This created a bitter chasm in the relationship between Stanton and McClellan, and implored McClellan's supporters to claim that Stanton "usurped" the role of general-in-chief, and that a Secretary of War should be subordinate to military commanders.[100][101] Lincoln ignored such calls, leaving military power consolidated within himself and Stanton.[102]

*Photograph of Edwin Stanton*

Meanwhile, McClellan was preparing for the first major military operation in the Eastern Theatre, the Peninsula Campaign. The Army of the Potomac began their movement to the Virginia Peninsula on March 17.[103] The first action of the campaign was at Yorktown. Lincoln wanted McClellan to attack the town outright, but McClellan's inspection of the Confederate defensive works there compelled him to lay siege to the town instead.[104] Washington politicians were angered at McClellan's choice to delay an attack. McClellan, however, requested reinforcements for his siege—the 11,000 men in Maj. Gen. William B. Franklin's division, of Maj. Gen. Irvin McDowell's corps. Stanton wanted Maj. Gen. McDowell's corps to stay together and march on to Richmond, but McClellan persisted, and Stanton eventually capitulated.[105]

McClellan's campaign lasted several months. However, after Gen. Robert E. Lee became the commander of local Confederate forces on June 1, he launched a series of offensives against the Army of the Potomac, which, by late June 1862, was just a few miles from the Confederate capital, Richmond.[106] In addition, Stanton ordered McClellan to transfer one of his corps east to defend Washington.[107] McClellan and the Army of the Potomac were pushed back to Harrison's Landing in Virginia, where they were protected by Union gunboats.[108] In Washington, Stanton was blamed for McClellan's defeat by the press and the public. On April 3 Stanton had suspended military recruiting efforts under the mistaken impression that McClellan's Peninsula Campaign would end the war. With McClellan retreating and the casualties from the campaign piling up, the need for more men rose significantly. Stanton restored recruiting operations on July 6, when McClellan's defeat on the Peninsula was firmly established, but the damage was done. The press, angered by Stanton's strict measures regarding journalistic correspondence, unleashed torrents of scorn on Stanton, furthering the narrative that he was the only encumbrance to McClellan's victory.[109]

The attacks hurt Stanton, and he considered resigning, but he remained in his position, at Lincoln's request.[110] As defeats piled up, Lincoln sought to give some order to the disparate divisions of Union forces in Virginia. He decided to consolidate the commands of Maj. Gens. McDowell, John C. Frémont, and Nathaniel P. Banks into the Army of Virginia, which was to be commanded by Maj. Gen. John Pope.[111] Lincoln was also convinced that the North's army needed reform at the highest ranks; he and Stanton being the *de facto* commanders of Union forces had proved too much to bear, so Lincoln would need a skilled commander. He chose Gen. Henry W. Halleck. Halleck arrived in Washington on July 22, and was confirmed as the general-in-chief of Union forces the following day.[112]

## War rages on

In the final days of August 1862, Gen. Lee had delivered the Union a second rout at Manassas Junction in the Second Battle of Bull Run; this time, against Maj. Gen. Pope and his Army of Virginia. A number of people, including Maj. Gen. Halleck and Secretary Stanton, thought Lee would turn his attention to Washington. Instead, Lee began the Maryland Campaign. The campaign started with a skirmish at Mile Hill on September 4, followed by a major confrontation at Harpers Ferry. Lincoln, without consulting Stanton, perhaps knowing Stanton would object, merged Pope's Army of Virginia into

McClellan's Army of the Potomac. With 90,000 men, McClellan launched his army into the bloody Battle of Antietam, and emerged victorious, pushing the Army of Northern Virginia back into Virginia, and effectively ending Lee's Maryland offensive.[113] McClellan's success at Antietam Creek emboldened him to demand that Lincoln and his government cease obstructing his plans, Halleck and Stanton be removed, and he be made general-in-chief of the Union Army. Meanwhile, he refused to move aggressively against Lee and the Army of Northern Virginia, which was withdrawing towards Richmond. McClellan's unreasonable requests continued, as did his indolence, and Lincoln's patience with him soon grew thin.[114] He dismissed him from leadership of the Army of the Potomac on November 5. Maj. Gen. Ambrose Burnside replaced McClellan days later.[115]

Burnside, at Halleck's request, submitted a plan to create a ruse at Culpeper and Gordonsville, while the brunt of his force took Fredericksburg, then moved on to Richmond. Halleck's response was sent on November 14: "The President has just assented to your plan. He thinks that it will succeed, if you move rapidly; otherwise not."[116] The following Battle of Fredericksburg was a disaster, and the Army of the Potomac was handily defeated.[117]

Maj. Gen. Joseph Hooker replaced Burnside on January 26, 1863. Stanton did not much care for Hooker, who had loudly denounced Lincoln's administration, and had been insubordinate while serving under Burnside. He would have preferred for Maj. Gen. William Rosecrans to head the army; Lincoln disregarded Stanton's opinion. As Thomas and Hyman tell it, Lincoln "chose Hooker because that general had a reputation as a fighter and stood higher in popular esteem at that moment than any other eastern general."[118] Hooker spent considerable time strengthening the Army of the Potomac, especially regarding morale. Hooker's first major engagement with Lee's Army of Northern Virginia was the Battle of Chancellorsville in early May 1863. Lee had Thomas "Stonewall" Jackson engage Hooker's rearguard in a precipitous flanking maneuver. Stonewall Jackson's maneuver was skilfully employed, resulting a Confederate victory when the fighting ended on May 6, leaving 17,000 casualties.[119]

Stanton's attempts to raise Northern spirits after the defeat were hampered by news that, under Hooker, the Army of the Potomac had become grossly undisciplined. Indeed, Hooker's camps were described as "combination of barroom and brothel." Stanton petitioned for liquor and women to be forbidden in Hooker's ranks.[120] Meanwhile, Lee was again pushing into the North. Lee's movements were racking nerves in Washington by mid-June, more so when disturbing reports came from Hooker's subordinates, such as that of Brig. Gen. Marsena Patrick: "[Hooker] acts like a man without a plan, & is entirely at a loss what to do, or how to match the enemy, or counteract his movements."[121] Further, like McClellan, Hooker kept overestimating Lee's numbers, and said Lincoln's administration did not have full confidence in him. Hooker resigned on June 27; Stanton and Lincoln decided that his replacement would be Maj. Gen. George Meade, who was appointed the following day.[122]

Lee and Meade first clashed in the Battle of Gettysburg on July 1. News of a victory at Gettysburg, and a great Confederate retreat, came on July 4. Soon after, word came of Maj. Gen. Grant's victory at Vicksburg. Northerners were exultant. Stanton even gave a rare speech to a huge crowd outside of the War Department's headquarters.[123] The administration's celebrations soon ended, however, when Maj. Gen. Meade refused to launch an attack against Lee while the Army of Northern Virginia was stuck on the banks of the Potomac river. When Lee crossed the river untouched on July 14, Lincoln and Stanton were upset.[124] Stanton affirmed in a letter to a friend that Meade would have his support unreservedly, but that "since the world began no man ever missed so great an opportunity of serving his country as was lost by his neglecting to strike his adversary." Stanton knew, though, that Meade's reluctance came at the advice of his division commanders, who outranked him.[125]

While action in the Eastern Theater winded down, action in the west heated up. After the two-day Battle of Chickamauga in late September, Maj. Gen. Rosecrans, the commander of the Army of the Cumberland, was left trapped in Chattanooga, Tennessee and beset on all sides by Gen. Braxton Bragg's forces. Rosecrans telegraphed Washington: "We have met a serious disaster, extent not yet ascertained." The situation in Chattanooga was desperate. The North needed the town in its hands. According to journalist Charles Anderson Dana, who had been Stanton's assistant secretary since March 1863,[126] Rosecrans might only be able to fight for another 15–20 more days and that without at least 20,000 to 25,000 men, Chattanooga would be lost.[127] Stanton organized the secret transportation of thousands of Union troops by rail.[107] Lincoln and Stanton agreed to make Maj. Gen. Grant the commander of almost all forces in the west, while dismissing Rosecrans from command of the Army of the Cumberland, and replacing him with Maj. Gen. George Henry Thomas.[128] Grant and Maj. Gen. William Tecumseh Sherman broke the Gen. Bragg's siege at Chattanooga in late November. Confederate Lt. Gen. James Longstreet attempted to besiege Maj. Gen. Burnside's army at Knoxville, but Sherman attacked the Confederates, sending them retreating.[129]

## End of the war

Grant, having been promoted to the rank of lieutenant general and made the commanding general of the Union Army, crossed the Rapidan River on May 4, 1864. The following day, he and Lee's armies clashed in the Battle of the Wilderness. The result was inconclusive, but Grant, unlike previous commanders, was loath to stop his onward push; "there would be no turning back," he told Lincoln.[130] Grant again engaged Lee at Spotsylvania Court House, emerging victorious.[131] Several days later, Grant and Lee battled at Cold Harbor, where Grant launched numerous assaults in an open field, incurring heavy losses. Grant pushed on, moving his army to a position just south of Richmond, near Petersburg; so began the Siege of Petersburg.[132] "Long lines of parallel entrenchments curled south and east of Richmond as both armies dug in," say Thomas and Hyman. "Grant stabbed at Lee's fortifications, always keeping the pressure on, and at the same time probed westward, feeling for the railroads that brought Lee's supplies."[133]

In the 1864 presidential election, Lincoln and his new Vice President, Andrew Johnson, emerged victorious against their Democratic opponents, George B. McClellan and George H. Pendleton. Republicans also won major congressional and gubernatorial victories in Ohio, Indiana, Kentucky and New York.[134] Stanton played no small part in securing the victory. Several days prior to the election, he ordered soldiers from key states such as Illinois, Lincoln's home state, to be returned home to vote. "The men who were doing the fighting had voted for more of it in order to make their efforts worth while," Thomas and Hyman state. Stanton also used his powers at the War Department to ensure that Republican voters were not harassed or threatened at the polls. Thomas and Hyman credit Stanton's troop furlough and other moves with much of the Republican success in the 1864 elections.[135]

On March 3, 1865, the day before Lincoln's second inauguration, Grant wired to Washington that Lee had sent representatives to him to sue for peace. Lincoln initially told Grant that he should get peace with the South by any means necessary. Stanton declared, however, that it is the president's duty to sue for peace; otherwise, the president is useless and little more than a figure-head. This engendered an immediate change of tone from the president. Stanton, at Lincoln's urging, told Grant that he was to "have no conference with General Lee unless it be for the capitulation of Gen. Lee's army, or on some minor, and purely, military matter." Further, Grant was not to "decide, discuss, or confer upon any political questions. Such matters the President holds in his own hands; and will submit them to no military conferences or conventions." Grant agreed.[136] Days later, Lincoln visited Grant at his siege headquarters (the Siege of Petersburg was still ongoing). Once Maj. Gen. Philip Sheridan had rejoined his army from the Shenandoah Valley, Grant was prepared to make his final push into Richmond.[137] On April 1, 1865, Sheridan defeated Lee's army in the Battle of Five Forks, forcing a retreat from Petersburg. Stanton, who had stayed close to his telegraph for days, told his wife the following evening: "Petersburg is evacuated and probably Richmond. Put out your flags."[138] Stanton was worried that President Lincoln, who had stayed around to watch Grant's push into Richmond, was in danger of being captured, and warned him. Lincoln disagreed, but was happy for Stanton's concern. The President wrote Stanton: "It is certain now that Richmond is in our hands, and I think I will go there to-morrow."[138]

News of Richmond's fall, which came on April 3,[139] touched off a furious excitement throughout the North. "The news spread fast, and people streaming from stores and offices speedily filled the thoroughfares. Cannons began firing, whistles tooted, horns blew, horsecars were forced to a standstill, the crowd yelled and cheered," say Thomas and Hyman.[140] Stanton was overjoyed. At his bidding, candles were put in the windows of each of the Department's properties, while bands played "The Star-Spangled Banner." Further, the department's headquarters was adorned with American flags, along with an image of a bald eagle holding in its talons a scroll with "Richmond" written on it.[140] The night Richmond fell, Stanton tearily gave an impromptu speech to the crowd outside the War Department.[139]

Lee and his army had slipped out of Richmond before its fall, though.[140] Grant marched west to stymie Lee's retreat, while Lincoln remained in Richmond. News of Grant's victories over the withdrawing Confederates lit up Washington's telegraphs. The Union Army was pressing on Lee's tail, and capturing thousands of Confederate prisoners of war. On April 9 Lee finally surrendered, ending the war.[141] On April 13, Stanton suspended conscription and recruiting, as well as the army's acquisition efforts.[142]

## Lincoln assassinated

On April 13, Lincoln invited Stanton, Grant and their wives to join him at Ford's Theatre the next evening. Lincoln had invited Stanton to go with him to the theatre several times, invitations Stanton routinely rejected. Further, neither Stanton's nor Grant's wives would go unless the other went. The Grants used a visit to their children in New Jersey as their excuse. Finally, Lincoln decided to go to the theatre with Major Henry Rathbone and his betrothed. Stanton retired home that night after visiting a bedridden Secretary Seward. He went to bed at about 10 p.m. Soon after, he heard Ellen yell from downstairs: "Mr. Seward is murdered!"[143] Stanton rushed downstairs. Upon hearing that Lincoln, too, might be dead, Stanton grew intensely animated. He wanted to leave immediately. He was cautioned: "You mustn't go out . . . As I came up to the house I saw a man behind the tree-box, but he ran away, and I did not follow him."[143] Stanton paid little mind to the man; he found a taxi and went to Seward's home.[143]

At his arrival, Stanton was told that Lincoln had in fact been attacked. Stanton ordered that the homes of all members of the cabinet and the Vice President be put under guard. [144] Stanton pushed through a crowd at the Secretary's home to find an unconscious Seward being attended to by a doctor in a bloody third-floor room. Seward's son, Frederick, was

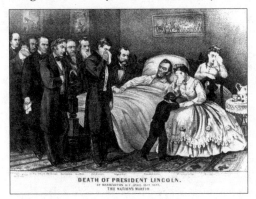

DEATH OF PRESIDENT LINCOLN.

*Abraham Lincoln lay on his deathbed at the Petersen House in Washington, surrounded by family, friends and government officials.*

left paralyzed by the attack. Stanton and Secretary of the Navy Gideon Welles, who had come to Seward's home moments before, decided to go to Ford's Theatre to see the President. The two secretaries went by carriage, accompanied by Quartermaster General Meigs and David K. Cartter, a justice of the District Court for the District of Columbia.[145]

Stanton found Lincoln at the Petersen House across from the theatre. Lincoln lay on a bed diagonally, because of his height.[145] When he saw the dying President, several accounts say Stanton began to weep. However, William Marvel states in his book, *Lincoln's Autocrat: The Life of Edwin Stanton* that "Stanton's emotional detachment and his domineering persona made him valuable that night, as others wallowed in anguish."[146] Thomas and Hyman also state: "Always before, death close at hand had unsettled him close to the point of imbalance. Now he seemed calm, grim, decisive, in complete outward control of himself."[147] Andrew Johnson, about whom Stanton, and the country, knew little, was sworn in as President at 11 a.m. on April 15, in the Kirkwood Hotel.[148] However, Stanton, who had planned to retire at the end of the war, "was indeed in virtual control of the government," say Thomas and Hyman. "He had charge of the Army, Johnson was barely sworn in and vastly unsure of himself, and Congress was not in session."[149]

Stanton ordered testimony taken from those who saw the attack. Witnesses blamed actor John Wilkes Booth for the assassination.[150] Stanton put all soldiers in Washington on guard,[151] and ordered a lockdown of the city.[152] Rail traffic to the south was to be halted, and fishing boats on the Potomac were not to come ashore.[151] Stanton also called Grant back to the capital from New Jersey.[146]

On April 15, Washington was, as journalist George A. Townsend said, "full of Detective Police." At Stanton's request, the United States Secret Service and the New York Police Department joined the War Department's detectives' tireless search for Booth and any accomplices.[153] Stanton had the lower deck of the monitor USS *Montauk*, which was placed near the Washington Navy Yard,[154] host several of the conspirators, Lewis Powell, Michael O'Laughlen, Edmund Spangler, and George Atzerodt. The other plotters, except Booth and Mary Surratt, were confined aboard the USS *Saugus*. The prisoners on both boats were bound by ball and chain, with handcuffs attached to an iron rod. Stanton also ordered a bag placed over the captives' heads, with a hole in it to allow for eating and breathing.[155] Surratt was kept at Old Capitol Prison, where she had been since her arrest. [156] Booth, the remaining culprit, had been shot at a barn in Virginia, and died soon after. Booth's body was put aboard the *Montauk*. After an autopsy was performed, and Booth's identity confirmed beyond any doubt, he was buried in a "secret, unmarked, and unhallowed grave," on Stanton's orders. Stanton knew Booth would be lionized in the South, and thought he would not give anyone the opportunity.[157] The conspirators went on to be tried and convicted. All but three were hanged.[158]

## Johnson administration (1865–1868)
### Sherman's truce

Lt. Gen. Grant, failing to find Stanton at the War Department, sent a note to his home by courier on the evening of April 21. The matter was urgent.[159] Maj. Gen. Sherman, who had established his army headquarters in Raleigh, North Carolina, had negotiated a peace deal with Confederate commander Gen. Joseph E. Johnston, with the grace of Confederate States Secretary of War John C. Breckinridge. Sherman had been authorized to negotiate with the Southerners only in matters regarding the military, as Grant had been with Lee. Sherman explicitly acknowledged that his negotiations with Confederate leaders were to stay firmly in the realm of military policy, but flouted the limitations anyway. Sherman's deal contained, as expected, a termination of hostilities with the South, but also specified

*Maj. Gen. William Tecumseh Sherman*

that Southern governments who had rebelled against the United States were to be recognized by the federal government once they swore allegiance to the United States. Further, the deal's terms provided for federal courts to be reinstated in rebellious states, as well as the restoration of property and voting rights to Southerners, and a blanket pardon for Southerners who had rebelled. The deal went even further, allowing Southern troops to place their weapons in the hands of their states' governments, which would effectively rearm the Southern states. Sherman's truce also allotted power to the Supreme Court to resolve jurisdictional disputes between state and local governments in the South, which was a political issue, and not a legal issue, making that a power the court did not constitutionally have.[160]

The courier arrived at Stanton's residence breathless, interrupting his dinner. When he heard the news, Stanton, "in a state of high excitement," rushed to the War Department. He sent for all members of the cabinet in the name of the President. Johnson's cabinet, along with Grant and Preston King, Johnson's advisor, convened at 8 p.m. that night. Word of Sherman's actions was met with unanimous condemnation by those present. President Johnson instructed Stanton to tell Sherman his deal had been rejected, and that "hostilities should be immediately resumed after giving the Confederates the forty-eight hours' notice required to terminate the truce." Grant would go to Raleigh at once to inform Sherman of Stanton's edict, as well as to assume command of troops in the South.[161]

Stanton took the matter to the press. In addition to publicizing the details of Sherman's deal, Stanton said Sherman intentionally flouted direct orders from both Lincoln and Johnson, listed nine reasons Sherman's deal had been categorically rejected. Further, Stanton accused Sherman of recklessly opening a path by which Jefferson Davis might flee the country with specie Davis purportedly took with him after abandoning Richmond. [162] The latter claim was based in Sherman's removal of Maj. Gen. George Stoneman's forces from the Greensboro railway—Greensboro was the place to which Davis and other Confederate officials fled.[161] Stanton's words were damning. "It amounted to a castigation of Sherman and virtually accused him of disloyalty," say Thomas and Hyman. Moreover, Sherman being among the most respected generals in the country, Stanton's publication endangered his place in the administration.[162]

Having not seen Stanton's dispatch to the press, Sherman wrote Stanton a conciliatory letter, calling his agreement "folly" and saying that, though he still felt his deal with Johnston and Breckinridge was solid, it was not his place to contest his superior's decision and that he would follow orders.[163] Meantime, Maj. Gen. Halleck, at Grant's request, communicated to several of Sherman's subordinates that they were to move their forces to North Carolina, regardless of what Sherman said. Halleck sent another dispatch to Sherman's generals telling them not to listen to Sherman's edicts at all. After Halleck's order, and reading Stanton's message to the press in a newspaper, Sherman's fury reached a dizzying, explosive tenor. Sherman thought Stanton had unjustifiably characterized him as a disloyal pariah. "I respect [Stanton's] office but I cannot him personally, till he undoes the injustice of the past," Sherman said to Grant.[164] Sherman's brother, Senator John Sherman, wanted the general censured for his actions, but still treated fairly. Sherman himself, and his wife's powerful family, the Ewings, wanted Stanton to publicly take back his statements. Stanton characteristically refused.[165]

In late May, there would be a Grand Review of the Armies, where the Union Army would parade through the streets of Washington. Halleck offered the hospitality of his home to Sherman; the general bluntly refused. He informed Grant of his rejection, stating as well that he would only listen to orders from Stanton if they were explicitly sanctioned by the President as well. Sherman further stated that "retraction or pusillanimous excusing" would no longer cut it. The only thing acceptable to Sherman would be for Stanton to declare himself a "common libeller." "I will treat Mr. Stanton with like scorn & contempt, unless you have reasons otherwise, for I regard my military career as ended, save and except so far as necessary to put my army into your hands."[166]

Sherman made well on his promise. At the Grand Review, Sherman saluted the President and Grant, but slighted the secretary of war by walking past him without a handshake, in full view of the public. Stanton gave no immediate response. Journalist Noah Brooks wrote "Stanton's face, never very expressive, remained immobile."[167] The affront touched off speculation that Stanton was about to resign. Stanton, too, considered leaving his post, but at the request of the President and numerous others, including people in the military, he kept on. In reparative efforts, Sherman's wife brought the Stantons flowers, and spent time at their home, but Sherman continued to harbor resentment toward Stanton.[168]

## Death and funeral

On the night of December 23 Stanton complained of pains in his head, neck and spine. His doctor, Surgeon General Joseph Barnes, was called. As had happened on many nights before, Stanton's asthma had made breaths come with some difficulty. Stanton's lungs and heart felt constricted, which kept Stanton's wife and children, as well as Barnes, by his bedside.[206] Stanton's condition began to improve at midnight, until he began, as Marvin states, "[gasping] so strenuously for air that someone ran for the pastor of the Church of the Epiphany, and soon after he arrived Stanton lost consciousness."[205] At about 3 a.m., Barnes checked Stanton's pulse and breathing but felt nothing. Stanton died on December 24, 1869, at the age of 55.[205]

Stanton's body was placed in a black, linen-inlaid coffin in his second-story bedroom.[207] President Grant had wanted a state funeral, but Ellen Stanton wanted as simple an affair as could be had. Nonetheless, Grant ordered all public offices closed, and federal buildings draped in "raiments of sorrow." Flags in several major cities were lowered to half-staff, and gun salutes sounded at army installations around the country.[208] On December 27, his body was carried by artillerymen to his home's parlor. President Grant, Vice President Schuyler Colfax, the Cabinet, the entire Supreme Court, senators, representatives, army officers and other important officials all attended Stanton's funeral. After the eulogy, Stanton's casket was placed atop a caisson, and drawn by four horses to Washington D.C.'s Oak Hill Cemetery at the head of a mile-long cavalcade.[209]

Stanton was interred beside the grave of his son James Hutchinson Stanton, who had died in infancy several years earlier. An assortment of Cabinet officials, generals, justices and senators carried Stanton's coffin to its final resting place. One of Stanton's professors from Kenyon College performed a service at the graveyard, and a three-volley salute was issued, ending the ceremony.[210]

# Harriet Beecher Stowe

**Harriet Elisabeth Beecher Stowe** (/stoʊ/; June 14, 1811–July 1, 1896) was an American abolitionist and author. She came from the Beecher family, a famous religious family, and is best known for her novel *Uncle Tom's Cabin* (1852), which depicts the harsh conditions for enslaved African Americans. The book reached millions as a novel and play, and became influential in the United States and Great Britain, energizing anti-slavery forces in the American North, while provoking widespread anger in the South. Stowe wrote 30 books, including novels, three travel memoirs, and collections of articles and letters. She was influential for both her writings and her public stances and debates on social issues of the day.

## Life and work

Harriet Elisabeth Beecher was born in Litchfield, Connecticut, on June 14, 1811.[1] She was the sixth of 11 children [2] born to outspoken Calvinist preacher Lyman Beecher. Her mother was his first wife, Roxana (Foote), a deeply religious woman who died when Stowe was only five years old. Roxana's maternal grandfather was General Andrew Ward of the Revolutionary War. Her notable siblings included a sister, Catharine Beecher, who became an educator and author, as well as brothers who became ministers: including Henry Ward Beecher, who became a famous preacher and abolitionist, Charles Beecher, and Edward Beecher.[3]

Harriet enrolled in the Hartford Female Seminary run by her older sister Catharine. There she received a traditional academic education, usually only reserved for males at the time, with a focus in the classics, including studies of languages and mathematics. Among her classmates was Sarah P. Willis, who later wrote under the pseudonym Fanny Fern.[4]

In 1832, at the age of 21, Harriet Beecher moved to Cincinnati, Ohio, to join her father, who had become the president of Lane Theological Seminary. There, she also joined the Semi-Colon Club, a literary salon and social club whose members included the Beecher sisters, Caroline Lee Hentz, Salmon P. Chase (future governor of the state and Secretary of Treasury under President Lincoln), Emily Blackwell and others.[5] Cincinnati's trade and shipping business on the Ohio River was booming, drawing numerous migrants from different parts of the country, including many escaped slaves, as well as Irish immigrants who worked on the state's canals and railroads. Areas of the city had been wrecked in the Cincinnati riots of 1829, when ethnic Irish attacked blacks, trying to push competitors for jobs out of the city. Beecher met a number of African Americans who had suffered in those attacks, and their experience contributed to her later writing about slavery. Riots took place again in 1836 and 1841, driven also by native-born anti-abolitionists.

The most famous event to ever take place at Lane was the series of debates held on 18 days in February 1834, between colonization and abolition defenders, decisively won by Theodore Weld and other abolitionists. Elizabeth attended most of the debates. [6]:171 Her father and the trustees, afraid of more violence from anti-abolitionist whites, prohibited any further discussions of the topic. The result was a mass exodus of the Lane students, together with a supportive trustee and a professor, who moved as a group to the new Oberlin Collegiate Institute after its trustees agreed, by a close and acrimonious vote, to accept students regardless of "race" and to allow discussions of any topic.

It was in the literary club at Lane that she met Rev. Calvin Ellis Stowe, a widower who was a professor of Biblical Literature at the seminary.[7] The two married at the Seminary on January 6, 1836.[8] He was an ardent critic of slavery, and the Stowes supported the Underground Railroad, temporarily housing several fugitive slaves in their home. Most slaves continued north to secure freedom in Canada. The Stowes had seven children together, including twin daughters.

## *Uncle Tom's Cabin* and Civil War

In 1850, Congress passed the Fugitive Slave Law, prohibiting assistance to fugitives and strengthening sanctions even in free states. At the time, Stowe had moved with her family to Brunswick, Maine, where her husband was now teaching at Bowdoin College. Their home near the campus is protected as a National Historic Landmark.[9]

Stowe claimed to have a vision of a dying slave during a communion service at Brunswick's First Parish Church, which inspired her to write his story.[10] However, what more likely allowed her to empathize with slaves was the loss of her eighteen-month-old son, Samuel Charles Stowe. She even stated the following, "Having experienced losing someone so close to me, I can sympathize with all the poor, powerless slaves at the unjust auctions. You will always be in my heart Samuel Charles Stowe."[11] On March 9, 1850, Stowe wrote to Gamaliel Bailey, editor of the weekly anti-slavery journal *The National Era*, that she planned to write a story about the problem of slavery: "I feel now that the time is come when even a woman or a child who can speak a word for freedom and humanity is bound to speak . . . I hope every woman who can write will not be silent."[12]

Shortly after in June 1851, when she was 40, the first installment of her *Uncle Tom's Cabin* was published in serial form in the newspaper *The National Era*. She originally used the subtitle "The Man That Was A Thing," but it was soon changed to "Life Among the Lowly."[1] Installments were published weekly from June 5, 1851, to April 1, 1852.[12] For the newspaper serialization of her novel, Stowe was paid $400.[13] *Uncle Tom's Cabin* was published in book form on March 20, 1852, by John P. Jewett with an initial print run of 5,000 copies.[14] Each of its two volumes included three illustrations and a title-page designed by Hammatt Billings.[15] In less than a year, the book sold an unprecedented

300,000 copies.[16] By December, as sales began to wane, Jewett issued an inexpensive edition at 37½ cents each to stimulate sales.[17]

According to Daniel R. Lincoln, the goal of the book was to educate Northerners on the realistic horrors of the things that were happening in the South. The other purpose was to try to make people in the South feel more empathetic towards the people they were forcing into slavery.[18]

*Portrait of Harriet Beecher Stowe by Francis Holl, 1853*

The book's emotional portrayal of the effects of slavery on individuals captured the nation's attention. Stowe showed that slavery touched all of society, beyond the people directly involved as masters, traders and slaves. Her novel added to the debate about abolition and slavery, and aroused opposition in the South. In the South, Stowe was depicted as out of touch, arrogant, and guilty of slander. Within a year, 300 babies in Boston alone were named Eva (one of the book's characters), and a play based on the book opened in New York in November.[19] Southerners quickly responded with numerous works of what are now called anti-Tom novels, seeking to portray Southern society and slavery in more positive terms. Many of these were bestsellers, although none matched the popularity of Stowe's work, which set publishing records.

After the start of the Civil War, Stowe traveled to the capital, Washington, D.C., where she met President Abraham Lincoln on November 25, 1862.[20] Stowe's daughter, Hattie, reported, "It was a very droll time that we had at the White house I assure you . . . I will only say now that it was all very funny—and we were ready to explode with laughter all the while."[21] What Lincoln said is a minor mystery. Her son later reported that Lincoln greeted her by saying, "so you are the little woman who wrote the book that started this great war."[22] Her own accounts are vague, including the letter reporting the meeting to her husband: "I had a real funny interview with the President."[21]

## Later years

A year after the war, Stowe purchased property near Jacksonville, Florida. In response to a newspaper article in 1873 she wrote, "I came to Florida the year after the war and held property in Duval County ever since. In all this time I have not received even an incivility from any native Floridian."[23]

Following the death of her husband, Calvin Stowe, in 1886, Harriet started rapidly to decline in health. By 1888, the *Washington Post* reported that as a result of dementia the 77-year-old Stowe started writing *Uncle Tom's Cabin* over again. She imagined that she was engaged in the original composition, and for several hours every day she industriously used pen and paper, inscribing passages of the book almost exactly word for word. This was done unconsciously from memory, the authoress imagining that she composed the matter as she went along. To her diseased mind the story was brand new, and she frequently exhausted herself with labor which she regarded as freshly created.[30]

Mark Twain, a neighbor of Stowe's in Hartford, recalled her last years in the following passage of his autobiography:

> Her mind had decayed, and she was a pathetic figure. She wandered about all the day long in the care of a muscular Irish woman. Among the colonists of our neighborhood the doors always stood open in pleasant weather. Mrs. Stowe entered them at her own free will, and as she was always softly slippered and generally full of animal spirits, she was able to deal in surprises, and she liked to do it. She would slip up behind a person who was deep in dreams and musings and fetch a war whoop that would jump that person out of his clothes. And she had other moods. Sometimes we would hear gentle music in the drawing-room and would find her there at the piano singing ancient and melancholy songs with infinitely touching effect.[31]

Modern researchers now speculate that at the end of her life Harriet was suffering from Alzheimer's disease.[32]

Harriet Beecher Stowe died on July 1, 1896, at age eighty-five in Hartford, Connecticut. She is buried in the historic cemetery at Phillips Academy in Andover, Massachusetts,[33] along with her husband and their son Henry Ellis.

# J. E. B. Stuart

**James Ewell Brown "Jeb" Stuart** (February 6, 1833–May 12, 1864) was a United States Army officer from Virginia who became a Confederate States Army general during the American Civil War. He was known to his friends as "Jeb," from the initials of his given names. Stuart was a cavalry commander known for his mastery of reconnaissance and the use of cavalry in support of offensive operations. While he cultivated a cavalier image (red-lined gray cape, yellow sash, hat cocked to the side with an ostrich plume, red flower in his lapel, often sporting cologne), his serious work made him the trusted eyes and ears of Robert E. Lee's army and inspired Southern morale.[3]

Stuart graduated from West Point in 1854, and served in Texas and Kansas with the U.S. Army. In 1855, he married Flora Cooke. His father-in-law was the "Father of the US Cavalry," Philip St. George Cooke. Stuart was a veteran of the frontier conflicts with American Indians and the violence of Bleeding Kansas, and he participated in the capture of John Brown at Harpers Ferry. He resigned, when his home state of Virginia seceded, to serve in the Confederate Army, first under Stonewall Jackson in the Shenandoah Valley, but then in increasingly important cavalry commands of the Army of Northern Virginia, playing a role in all of that army's campaigns until his death.

He established a reputation as an audacious cavalry commander and on two occasions (during the Peninsula Campaign and the Maryland Campaign) circumnavigated the Union Army of the Potomac, bringing fame to himself and embarrassment to the North. At the Battle of Chancellorsville, he distinguished himself as a temporary commander of the wounded Stonewall Jackson's infantry corps.

Stuart's most famous campaign, the Gettysburg Campaign, was flawed when his long separation from Lee's army left Lee unaware of Union troop movements so that Lee was surprised and almost trapped at the Battle of Gettysburg. Stuart received significant criticism from the Southern press as well as the proponents of the Lost Cause movement after the war. During the 1864 Overland Campaign, Union Maj. Gen. Philip Sheridan's cavalry launched an offensive to defeat Stuart, who was mortally wounded at the Battle of Yellow Tavern. Stuart's widow wore black for the rest of her life in remembrance of her deceased husband.

## Confederate Army
*Early service*

[Stuart] is a rare man, wonderfully endowed by nature with the qualities necessary for an officer of light cavalry. . . . Calm, firm, acute, active, and enterprising, I know no one more competent than he to estimate the occurrences before him at their true value. If you add to this army a real brigade of cavalry, you can find no better brigadier-general to command it.

—General Joseph E. Johnston, letter to Confederate President Jefferson Davis, August 1861[28]

Stuart was commissioned as a lieutenant colonel of Virginia Infantry in the Confederate Army on May 10, 1861.[1] Maj. Gen. Robert E. Lee, now commanding the armed forces of Virginia, ordered him to report to Colonel Thomas J. Jackson at Harper's Ferry. Jackson chose to ignore Stuart's infantry designation and assigned him on July 4 to command all the cavalry companies of the Army of the Shenandoah, organized as the 1st Virginia Cavalry Regiment.[29] He was promoted to colonel on July 16.[1]

After early service in the Shenandoah Valley, Stuart led his regiment in the First

Battle of Bull Run (where Jackson got his nickname, "Stonewall"), and participated in the pursuit of the retreating Federals. He then commanded the Army's outposts along the upper Potomac River until given command of the cavalry brigade for the army then known as the Army of the Potomac (later named the Army of Northern Virginia). He was promoted to brigadier general on September 24, 1861.[1]

## Peninsula

In 1862, the Union Army of the Potomac began its Peninsula Campaign against Richmond, Virginia, and Stuart's cavalry brigade assisted Gen. Joseph E. Johnston's army as it withdrew up the Virginia Peninsula in the face of superior numbers. Stuart

*Stonewall Jackson assigned Stuart to cavalry.*

fought at the Battle of Williamsburg, but in general the terrain and weather on the Peninsula did not lend themselves to cavalry operations.

Stuart and Jackson were an unlikely pair: one outgoing, the other introverted; one flashily uniformed, the other plainly dressed; one Prince Rupert and the other Cromwell. Yet Stuart's self-confidence, penchant for action, deep love of Virginia, and total abstinence from such vices as alcohol, tobacco, and pessimism endeared him to Jackson. . . . Stuart was the only man in the Confederacy [who] could make Jackson laugh—and who dared to do so.

—James I. Robertson, Jr., *Stonewall Jackson*[30]

However, when Gen. Robert E. Lee became commander of the Army of Northern Virginia, he requested that Stuart perform reconnaissance to determine whether the right flank of the Union army was vulnerable. Stuart set out with 1,200 troopers on the morning of June 12 and, having determined that the flank was indeed vulnerable, took his men on a complete circumnavigation of the Union army, returning after 150 miles on July 15 with 165 captured Union soldiers, 260 horses and mules, and various quartermaster and ordnance supplies. His men met no serious opposition from the more decentralized Union cavalry, coincidentally commanded by his father-in-law, Col. Cooke, and their total casualties amounted to one man killed. The maneuver was a public relations sensation and Stuart was greeted with flower petals thrown in his path at Richmond. He had become as famous as Stonewall Jackson in the eyes of the Confederacy.[31]

## Northern Virginia

*CSA Cavalry General J.E. B. Stuart*

Early in the Northern Virginia Campaign, Stuart was promoted to major general on July 25, 1862, and his command was upgraded to the Cavalry Division. [32] He was nearly captured and lost his signature plumed hat and cloak to pursuing Federals during a raid in August, but in a retaliatory raid at Catlett's Station the following day, managed to overrun Union army commander Maj. Gen. John Pope's headquarters, and not only captured Pope's full uniform, but also intercepted orders that provided Lee with valuable intelligence concerning reinforcements for Pope's army.[32]

At the Second Battle of Bull Run (Second Manassas), Stuart's cavalry followed the massive assault by Longstreet's infantry against Pope's army, protecting its flank with artillery batteries. Stuart ordered Brig. Gen. Beverly Robertson's brigade to pursue the Federals and in a sharp fight against Brig. Gen. John Buford's brigade, Col. Thomas T. Munford's 2nd Virginia Cavalry was overwhelmed until Stuart sent in two more regiments as reinforcements. Buford's men, many of whom were new to combat, retreated across Lewis's Ford and Stuart's troopers captured over 300 of them. Stuart's men harassed the retreating Union columns until the campaign ended at the Battle of Chantilly.[33]

## Maryland

During the Maryland Campaign of September 1862, Stuart's cavalry screened the army's movement north. He bears some responsibility for Robert E. Lee's lack of knowledge of the position and celerity of the pursuing Army of the Potomac under George B. McClellan. For a five-day period, Stuart rested his men and entertained local civilians at a gala ball at Urbana, Maryland. His reports make no reference to intelligence gathering by his scouts or patrols.[34] As the Union Army drew near to Lee's divided army, Stuart's men skirmished at various points on the approach to Frederick and Stuart was not able to keep his brigades concentrated enough to resist the oncoming tide. He misjudged the Union routes of advance, ignorant of the Union force threatening Turner's Gap, and required assistance from the infantry of Maj. Gen. D.H. Hill to defend the South Mountain passes in the Battle of South Mountain.[35] His horse artillery bombarded the flank of the Union army as it opened its attack in the Battle of Antietam. By mid-afternoon, Stonewall Jackson ordered Stuart to command a turning movement with his cavalry against the Union right flank and rear, which if successful would be followed up by an infantry attack from the West Woods. Stuart began probing the Union lines with more artillery barrages, which were answered with "murderous" counterbattery fire and the cavalry movement intended by Jackson was never launched.[36]

Three weeks after Lee's army had withdrawn back to Virginia, on October 10–12, 1862, Stuart performed another of his audacious circumnavigations of the Army of the Potomac, his Chambersburg Raid—126 miles in under 60 hours, from Darkesville, West Virginia to as far north as Mercersburg, Pennsylvania and Chambersburg and around to the east through Emmitsburg, Maryland and south through Hyattstown, Maryland and White's Ford to Leesburg, Virginia—once again embarrassing his Union opponents and seizing horses and supplies, but at the expense of exhausted men and animals, without gaining much military advantage. Jubal Early referred to it as "the greatest horse stealing expedition" that only "annoyed" the enemy.[37] Stuart gave his friend Jackson a fine, new officer's tunic, trimmed with gold lace, commissioned from a Richmond tailor, which he thought would give Jackson more of the appearance of a proper general (something to which Jackson was notoriously indifferent).[38]

McClellan pushed his army slowly south, urged by President Lincoln to pursue Lee, crossing the Potomac starting on October 26. As Lee began moving to counter this, Stuart screened Longstreet's Corps and skirmished numerous times in early November against Union cavalry and infantry around Mountville, Aldie, and Upperville. On November 6, Stuart received sad news by telegram that his daughter Flora had died just before her fifth birthday of typhoid fever on November 3.[39]

## Fredericksburg and Chancellorsville

In the December 1862 Battle of Fredericksburg, Stuart and his cavalry—most notably his horse artillery under Major John Pelham—protected Stonewall Jackson's flank at Hamilton's Crossing. General Lee commended his cavalry, which "effectually guarded our right, annoying the enemy and embarrassing his movements by hanging on his flank, and attacking when the opportunity occurred." Stuart reported to Flora the next day that he had been shot through his fur collar but was unhurt.[40]

After Christmas, Lee ordered Stuart to conduct a raid north of the Rappahannock River to "penetrate the enemy's rear, ascertain if possible his position & movements, & inflict upon him such damage as circumstances will permit." With 1,800 troopers and a horse artillery battery assigned to the operation, Stuart's raid reached as far north as four miles south of Fairfax Court House, seizing 250 prisoners, horses, mules, and supplies. Tapping telegraph lines, his signalmen intercepted messages between Union commanders and Stuart sent a personal telegram to Union Quartermaster General Montgomery C. Meigs, "General Meigs will in the future please furnish better mules; those you have furnished recently are very inferior."[41]

On March 17, 1863, Stuart's cavalry clashed with a Union raiding party at Kelly's Ford. The minor victory was marred by the death of Major Pelham, which caused Stuart profound grief, as he thought of him as close as a younger brother. He wrote to a Confederate Congressman, "The noble, the chivalric, the gallant Pelham is no more. . . . Let the tears of agony we have shed, and the gloom of mourning throughout my command bear witness." Flora was pregnant at the time and Stuart told her that if it were a boy, he wanted him to be named John Pelham Stuart. (Virginia Pelham Stuart was born October 9.)[42]

At the Battle of Chancellorsville, Stuart accompanied Stonewall Jackson on his famous flanking march of May 2, 1863, and started to pursue the retreating soldiers of the Union XI Corps when he received word that both Jackson and his senior division commander, Maj. Gen. A.P. Hill, had been wounded. Hill, bypassing the next most senior infantry general in the corps, Brig. Gen. Robert E. Rodes, sent a message ordering Stuart to take command of the Second Corps. Although the delays associated with this change of command effectively ended the flanking attack the night of May 2, Stuart performed credibly as an infantry corps commander the following day, launching a strong and well-coordinated attack against the Union right flank at Chancellorsville. When Union troops abandoned Hazel Grove, Stuart had the presence of mind to quickly occupy it and bombard the Union positions with artillery. Stuart relinquished his infantry command on May 6 when Hill returned to duty.[43] Stephen W. Sears wrote:

> . . . It is hard to see how Jeb Stuart, in a new command, a cavalryman commanding infantry and artillery for the first time, could have done a better job. The astute Porter Alexander believed all credit was due: "Altogether, I do not think there was a more brilliant thing done in the war than Stuart's extricating that command from the extremely critical position in which he found it."[44]

Stonewall Jackson died on May 10 and Stuart was once again devastated by the loss of a close friend, telling his staff that the death was a "national calamity." Jackson's wife, Mary Anna, wrote to Stuart on August 1, thanking him for a note of sympathy: "I need not assure you of which you already know, that your friendship & admiration were cordially reciprocated by him. I have frequently heard him speak of Gen'l Stuart as one of his warm personal friends, & also express admiration for your Soldierly qualities."[45]

## Brandy Station

The grand review of June 5 was surely the proudest day of Jeb Stuart's thirty years. As he led a cavalcade of resplendent staff officers to the reviewing stand, trumpeters heralded his coming and women and girls strewed his path with flowers. Before all of the spectators the assembled cavalry brigade stretched a mile and a half. After Stuart and his entourage galloped past the line in review, the troopers in their turn saluted the reviewing stand in columns of squadrons. In performing a second "march past," the squadrons started off at a trot, then spurred to a gallop. Drawing sabers and breaking into the Rebel yell, the troopers rush toward the horse artillery drawn up in battery. The gunners responded defiantly, firing blank charges. Amidst this tumult of cannon fire and thundering hooves, a number of ladies swooned in their escorts' arms.

—Stephen W. Sears, *Gettysburg*[46]

Returning to the cavalry for the Gettysburg Campaign, Stuart endured the two low points in his career, starting with the Battle of Brandy Station, the largest predominantly cavalry engagement of the war. By June 5, two of Lee's infantry corps were camped in and around Culpeper. Six miles northeast, holding the line of the Rappahannock River, Stuart bivouacked his cavalry troopers, mostly near Brandy Station, screening the Confederate Army against surprise by the enemy. Stuart requested a full field review of his troops by Gen. Lee. This grand review on June 5 included nearly 9,000 mounted troopers and four batteries of horse artillery, charging in simulated battle at Inlet Station, about two miles (three km) southwest of Brandy Station.[47]

Lee was not able to attend the review, however, so it was repeated in his presence on June 8, although the repeated performance was limited to a simple parade without battle simulations.[48] Despite the lower level of activity, some of the cavalrymen and the newspaper reporters at the scene complained that all Stuart was doing was feeding his ego and exhausting the horses. Lee ordered Stuart to cross the Rappahannock the next day and raid Union forward positions, screening the Confederate Army from observation or interference as it moved north. Anticipating this imminent offensive action, Stuart ordered his tired troopers back into bivouac around Brandy Station.[49]

Army of the Potomac commander Maj. Gen. Joseph Hooker interpreted Stuart's presence around Culpeper to be indicative of preparations for a raid on his army's supply lines. In reaction, he ordered his cavalry commander, Maj. Gen. Alfred Pleasonton, to take a combined arms force of 8,000 cavalrymen and 3,000 infantry on a "spoiling raid" to "disperse and destroy" the 9,500 Confederates.[50] Pleasonton's force crossed the Rappahannock in two columns on June 9, 1863, the first crossing at Beverly's Ford (Brig. Gen. John Buford's division) catching Stuart by surprise, waking him and his staff to the sound of gunfire. The second crossing, at Kelly's Ford, surprised Stuart again, and the Confederates found themselves assaulted from front and rear in a spirited melee of mounted combat. A series of confusing charges and countercharges swept back and forth across Fleetwood Hill, which had been Stuart's headquarters the previous night. After ten hours of fighting, Pleasonton ordered his men to withdraw across the Rappahannock.[51]

> If Gen. Stuart is to be the eyes and ears of the army we advise him to see more, and be seen less. . . . Gen. Stuart has suffered no little in public estimation by the late enterprises of the enemy.
>
> —*Richmond Enquirer,* June 12, 1863[52]

Although Stuart claimed a victory because the Confederates held the field, Brandy Station is considered a tactical draw, and both sides came up short. Pleasonton was not able to disable Stuart's force at the start of an important campaign and he withdrew before finding the location of Lee's infantry nearby. However, the fact that the Southern cavalry had not detected the movement of two large columns of Union cavalry, and that they fell victim to a surprise attack, was an embarrassment that prompted serious criticism from fellow generals and the Southern press. The fight also revealed the increased competency of the Union cavalry, and foreshadowed the decline of the formerly invincible Southern mounted arm.[53]

## Stuart's ride in the Gettysburg Campaign

Following a series of small cavalry battles in June as Lee's army began marching north through the Shenandoah Valley, Stuart may have had in mind the glory of circumnavigating the enemy army once again, desiring to erase the stain on his reputation of the surprise at Brandy Station. General Lee gave orders to Stuart on June 22 on how he was to participate in the march north. The exact nature of those orders has been argued by the participants and historians ever since, but the essence was that Stuart was instructed to guard the mountain passes with part of his force while the Army of Northern Virginia was still south of the Potomac, and that he was to cross the river with the remainder of the army and screen the right flank of Ewell's Second Corps. Instead of taking a direct route north near the Blue Ridge Mountains, however, Stuart chose to reach Ewell's flank by taking his three best brigades (those of Brig. Gen. Wade Hampton, Brig. Gen. Fitzhugh Lee, and Col. John R. Chambliss, the latter replacing the wounded Brig. Gen. W. H. F. "Rooney" Lee) between the Union army and Washington, moving north through Rockville to Westminster and on into Pennsylvania, hoping to capture supplies along the way and cause havoc near the enemy capital. Stuart and his three brigades departed Salem Depot at 1 a.m. on June 25.[54]

Unfortunately for Stuart's plan, the Union army's movement was underway and his proposed route was blocked by columns of Federal infantry, forcing him to veer farther to the east than either he or General Lee had anticipated. This prevented Stuart from linking up with Ewell as ordered and deprived Lee of the use of his prime cavalry force, the "eyes and ears" of the army, while advancing into unfamiliar enemy territory.[55]

Stuart's command crossed the Potomac River at 3 a.m. on June 28. At Rockville they captured a wagon train of 140 brand-new, fully loaded wagons and mule teams. This wagon train would prove to be a logistical hindrance to Stuart's advance, but he interpreted Lee's orders as placing importance on gathering supplies. The proximity of the Confederate raiders provoked some consternation in the national capital and two Union cavalry brigades and an artillery battery were sent to pursue the Confederates. Stuart supposedly said that were it not for his fatigued horses "he would have marched down the 7th Street Road [and] took Abe & Cabinet prisoners."[56]

In Westminster on June 29, his men clashed briefly with and overwhelmed two companies of Union cavalry, chasing them a long distance on the Baltimore road, which Stuart claimed caused a "great panic" in the city of Baltimore.[57] The head of Stuart's column encountered Brig. Gen. Judson Kilpatrick's cavalry as it passed through Hanover and scattered it on June 30; the Battle of Hanover ended after Kilpatrick's men regrouped and drove the Confederates out of town. Stuart's brigades had been better positioned to guard their captured wagon train than to take advantage of the encounter with Kilpatrick. After a 20-mile trek in the dark, his exhausted men reached Dover on the morning of July 1, as the Battle of Gettysburg was commencing without them.[58]

Stuart headed next for Carlisle, hoping to find Ewell. He lobbed a few shells into town during the early evening of July 1 and burned the Carlisle Barracks before withdrawing to the south towards Gettysburg. He and the bulk of his command reached Lee at Gettysburg the afternoon of July 2. He ordered Wade Hampton to cover the left rear of the Confederate battle lines, and Hampton fought with Brig. Gen. George Armstrong Custer at the Battle of Hunterstown before joining Stuart at Gettysburg.[59]

## Gettysburg and its aftermath

When Stuart arrived at Gettysburg on the afternoon of July 2—bringing with him the caravan of captured Union supply wagons—he received a rare rebuke from Lee. No one witnessed the private meeting between Lee and Stuart, but reports circulated at headquarters that Lee's greeting was "abrupt and frosty." Colonel Edward Porter Alexander wrote, "Although Lee said only, 'Well, General, you are here at last,' his manner implied rebuke, and it was so understood by Stuart."[60] On the final day of the battle, Stuart was ordered to move into the enemy's rear and disrupt its line of communications at the same time Pickett's Charge was sent against the Union positions on Cemetery Ridge, but his attack on East Cavalry Field was repulsed by Union cavalry under Brig. Gens. David Gregg and George Custer.[61]

During the retreat from Gettysburg, Stuart devoted his full attention to supporting the army's movement, successfully screening against aggressive Union cavalry pursuit and escorting thousands of wagons with wounded men and captured supplies over difficult roads and through inclement weather. Numerous skirmishes and minor battles occurred during the screening and delaying actions of the retreat. Stuart's men were the final units to cross the Potomac River, returning to Virginia in "wretched condition—completely worn out and broken down."[62]

The failure to crush the Federal army in Pennsylvania in 1863, in the opinion of almost all of the officers of the Army of Northern Virginia, can be expressed in five words—*the absence of the cavalry.*

—Confederate Maj. Gen. Henry Heth[63]

The Gettysburg Campaign was the most controversial of Stuart's career. He became one of the scapegoats (along with James Longstreet) blamed for Lee's loss at Gettysburg by proponents of the postbellum Lost Cause movement, such as Jubal Early.[64] This was fueled in part by opinions of less partisan writers, such as Stuart's subordinate, Thomas L. Rosser, who stated after the war that Stuart did, "on this campaign, *undoubtedly*, make the fatal blunder which lost us the battle of Gettysburg." In General Lee's report on the campaign, he wrote:

> . . . the absence of the cavalry rendered it impossible to obtain accurate information. . . . By the route [Stuart] pursued, the Federal Army was interposed between his command and our main body, preventing any communication with him until his arrival at Carlisle. The march toward Gettysburg was conducted more slowly than it would have been had the movements of the Federal Army been known.[63]

One of the most forceful postbellum defenses of Stuart was by Col. John S. Mosby, who had served under him during the campaign and was fiercely loyal to the late general, writing, "He made me all that I was in the war. . . . But for his friendship I would never have been heard of." He wrote numerous articles for popular publications and published a book length treatise in 1908, a work that relied on his skills as a lawyer to refute categorically all of the claims laid against Stuart.[65]

Historians remain divided on how much the defeat at Gettysburg was due to Stuart's failure to keep Lee informed. Edward G. Longacre argues that Lee deliberately gave Stuart wide discretion in his orders. Edwin B. Coddington refers to the "tragedy" of Stuart in the Gettysburg Campaign and judges that when Fitzhugh Lee raised the question of "whether Stuart exercised the discretion *undoubtedly given to him, judiciously,*" the answer is no. Agreeing that Stuart's absence permitted Lee to be surprised at Gettysburg, Coddington points out that the Union commander was just as surprised. Eric J. Wittenberg and J. David Petruzzi have concluded that there was "plenty of blame to go around" and the fault should be divided between Stuart, the lack of specificity in Lee's orders, and Richard S. Ewell, who might have tried harder to link up with Stuart northeast of Gettysburg. Jeffry D. Wert acknowledges that Lee, his officers, and fighting by the Army of the Potomac bear the responsibility for the Confederate loss at Gettysburg, but states that "Stuart failed Lee and the army in the reckoning at Gettysburg. . . . Lee trusted him and gave him discretion, but Stuart acted injudiciously."[66]

Although Stuart was not reprimanded or disciplined in any official way for his role in the Gettysburg campaign, it is noteworthy that his appointment to corps command on September 9, 1863, did not carry with it a promotion to lieutenant general. Edward

Bonekemper wrote that since all other corps commanders in the Army of Northern Virginia carried this rank, Lee's decision to keep Stuart at major general rank, while at the same time promoting Stuart's subordinates Wade Hampton and Fitzhugh Lee to major generals, could be considered an implied rebuke.[67] Jeffry D. Wert wrote that there is no evidence Lee considered Stuart's performance during the Gettysburg Campaign and that it is "more likely that Lee thought the responsibilities in command of a cavalry corps did not equal those of an infantry corps."[68]

## Fall 1863 and the 1864 Overland Campaign

Lee reorganized his cavalry on September 9, creating a Cavalry Corps for Stuart with two divisions of three brigades each. In the Bristoe Campaign, Stuart was assigned to lead a broad turning movement in an attempt to get into the enemy's rear, but General Meade skillfully withdrew his army without leaving Stuart any opportunities to take advantage of. On October 13, Stuart blundered into the rear guard of the Union III Corps near Warrenton, resulting in the First Battle of Auburn.

> [The cavalry's success in the Bristoe Campaign can be attributed] to the generalship, boldness, and untiring energy of Major-General Stuart, for it was he who directed every movement of importance, and his generalship, boldness, and energy won the unbounded confidence of officers and men, and gave the prestige of success.
> —Confederate Colonel Oliver Funsten[69]

Ewell's corps was sent to rescue him, but Stuart hid his troopers in a wooded ravine until the unsuspecting III Corps moved on, and the assistance was not necessary. As Meade withdrew towards Manassas Junction, brigades from the Union II Corps fought a rearguard action against Stuart's cavalry and the infantry of Brig. Gen. Harry Hays's division near Auburn on October 14. Stuart's cavalry boldly bluffed Warren's infantry and escaped disaster. After the Confederate repulse at Bristoe Station and an aborted advance on Centreville, Stuart's cavalry shielded the withdrawal of Lee's army from the vicinity of Manassas Junction. Judson Kilpatrick's Union cavalry pursued Stuart's cavalry along the Warrenton Turnpike, but were lured into an ambush near Chestnut Hill and routed. The Federal troopers were scattered and chased five miles (eight km) in an affair that came to be known as the "Buckland Races." The Southern press began to mute its criticism of Stuart following his successful performance during the fall campaign.[70]

The Overland Campaign, Lt. Gen. Ulysses S. Grant's offensive against Lee in the spring of 1864, began at the Battle of the Wilderness, where Stuart aggressively pushed Thomas L. Rosser's Laurel Brigade into a fight against George Custer's better-armed Michigan Brigade, resulting in significant losses. General Lee sent a message to Stuart: "It is very important to save your Cavalry & not wear it out. . . . You must use your good judgment to make any attack which may offer advantages." As the armies maneuvered toward their next confrontation at Spotsylvania Court House, Stuart's cavalry fought delaying actions against the Union cavalry. His defense at Laurel Hill, also directing the infantry of Brig. Gen. Joseph B. Kershaw, skillfully delayed the advance of the Federal army for nearly 5 critical hours.[71]

## Yellow Tavern and death

The commander of the Army of the Potomac, Maj. Gen. George Meade, and his cavalry commander, Maj. Gen. Philip Sheridan, quarreled about the Union cavalry's performance in the first two engagements of the Overland Campaign. Sheridan heatedly asserted that he wanted to "concentrate all of cavalry, move out in force against Stuart's command, and whip it." Meade reported the comments to Grant, who replied "Did Sheridan say that? Well, he generally knows what he is talking about. Let him start right out and do it." Sheridan immediately organized a raid against Confederate supply and railroad lines close to Richmond, which he knew would bring Stuart to battle.[72]

Sheridan moved aggressively to the southeast, crossing the North Anna River and seizing Beaver Dam Station on the Virginia Central Railroad, where his men captured a train, liberating 3,000 Union prisoners and destroying more than one million rations and medical supplies destined for Lee's army. Stuart dispatched a force of about 3,000 cavalrymen to intercept Sheridan's cavalry, which was more than three times their numbers. As he

rode in pursuit, accompanied by his aide, Maj. Andrew R. Venable, they were able to stop briefly along the way to be greeted by Stuart's wife, Flora, and his children, Jimmie and Virginia. Venable wrote of Stuart, "He told me he never expected to live through the war, and that if we were conquered, that he did not want to live."[73]

The Battle of Yellow Tavern occurred May 11, at an abandoned inn located six miles (9.7 km) north of Richmond. The Confederate troops resisted from the low ridgeline bordering the road to Richmond, fighting for over three hours. After receiving a scouting report from Texas Jack Omohundro, Stuart led a countercharge and pushed the advancing Union troopers back from

*"Dorsey . . . save your men."*  the hilltop. Stuart, on horseback, shouted encouragement from in front of Company K of the 1st Virginia Cavalry while firing his revolver at the Union troopers.

As the 5th Michigan Cavalry streamed in retreat past Stuart, a dismounted Union private, 44-year-old John A. Huff, turned and shot Stuart with his .44-caliber revolver from a distance of 10–30 yards.[74] Huff's bullet struck Stuart in the left side. It then sliced through his stomach and exited his back, one inch to the right of his spine.[75] Stuart fell into the arms of Company K's commander Gus W. Dorsey. Dorsey caught him and took him from his horse. Stuart told him: "Dorsey . . . save your men." Dorsey refused to leave him and brought Stuart to the rear.[76][77][78]

He suffered great pain as an ambulance took him to Richmond to await his wife's arrival at the home of Dr. Charles Brewer, his brother-in-law. As he was being driven from the field in an ambulance wagon, Stuart noticed disorganized ranks of retreating men and called out to them his last words on the battlefield: "Go back, go back, and do your duty, as I have done mine, and our country will be safe. Go back, go back! I had rather die than be whipped."[79]

Stuart ordered his sword and spurs be given to his son. As his aide Major McClellan left his side, Confederate President Jefferson Davis came in, took General Stuart's hand, and asked, "General, how do you feel?" Stuart answered "Easy, but willing to die, if God and my country think I have fulfilled my destiny and done my duty."[79] His last whispered words were: "I am resigned; God's will be done." He died at 7:38 p.m. on May 12, the following day, before Flora Stuart reached his side. He was 31 years old. Stuart was buried in Richmond's Hollywood Cemetery. Upon learning of Stuart's death, General Lee is reported to have said that he could hardly keep from weeping at the mere mention of Stuart's name and that Stuart had never given him a bad piece of information.[80] John Huff, the private who had fatally wounded Stuart, was killed in action just a few weeks later at the Battle of Haw's Shop.

Flora wore the black of mourning for the remainder of her life, and never remarried. She lived in Saltville, Virginia, for 15 years after the war, where she opened and taught at a school in a log cabin. She worked from 1880 to 1898 as principal of the Virginia Female Institute in Staunton, Virginia, a position for which Robert E. Lee had recommended her before his death ten years earlier.[81] In 1907, the Institute was renamed Stuart Hall School in her honor. Upon the death of her daughter Virginia, from complications in childbirth in 1898, Flora resigned from the Institute and moved to Norfolk, Virginia, where she helped Virginia's widower, Robert Page Waller, in raising her grandchildren. She died in Norfolk on May 10, 1923, after striking her head in a fall on a city sidewalk. She is buried alongside her husband and their daughter, Little Flora, in Hollywood Cemetery in Richmond.[82]

# John Surratt

*John H. Surratt Jr. in 1868*

**John Harrison Surrat Jr.** (April 13, 1844–April 21, 1916) was accused of plotting with John Wilkes Booth to kidnap U.S. President Abraham Lincoln; he was also suspected of involvement in the Abraham Lincoln assassination. His mother, Mary Surratt, was convicted of conspiracy and hanged by the U.S. government; she owned the boarding house that the conspirators used as a safe house and to plot the scheme.

He avoided arrest immediately after the assassination by fleeing to Canada and then to Europe. He thus avoided the fate of the other conspirators, who were hanged. He served briefly as a Pontifical Zouave but was recognized and arrested. He escaped to Egypt but was eventually arrested and extradited. By the time of his trial, the statute of limitations had expired on most of the potential charges which meant that he was never convicted of anything.

## Plot to kidnap Lincoln

Surratt served as a Confederate Secret Service courier and spy. After he had been carrying dispatches about Union troop movements across the Potomac River. Dr. Samuel Mudd introduced Surratt to Booth on December 23, 1864, and Surratt agreed to help Booth kidnap Lincoln. The meeting took place at the National Hotel, in Washington, D.C., where Booth lived.

Booth's plan was to seize Lincoln and take him to Richmond, Virginia, to exchange him for thousands of Confederate prisoners of war. On March 17, 1865, Surratt and Booth, along with their comrades, waited in ambush for Lincoln's carriage to leave the Campbell General Hospital to return to Washington. However, Lincoln had changed his mind and remained in Washington.

## Assassination of Lincoln

After the assassination of Lincoln, on April 14, 1865, Surratt denied any involvement and said that he was then in Elmira, New York. He was one of the first people suspected of the attempt to assassinate Secretary of State William H. Seward, but the culprit was soon discovered to be Lewis Powell.

## In hiding

When he learned of the assassination, Surratt fled to Montreal, Lower Canada, arriving on April 17, 1865. He then went to St. Liboire, where a Catholic priest, Father Charles Boucher, gave him sanctuary. Surratt remained there while his mother was arrested, tried, and hanged in the US for conspiracy.

Aided by ex-Confederate agents Beverly Tucker and Edwin Lee, Surratt, disguised, booked passage under a false name. He landed at Liverpool, United Kingdom, in September, where he lodged in the oratory at the Church of the Holy Cross.[3]

Surratt would later serve for a time in the Ninth Company of the Pontifical Zouaves, in the Papal States, under the name John Watson.[4][5]

An old friend, Henri Beaumont de Sainte-Marie, recognized Surratt and notified papal officials and the US minister in Rome, Rufus King.[6]

On November 7, 1866, Surratt was arrested and sent to the Velletri prison. He escaped and lived with the supporters of Garibaldi, who gave him safe passage. Surratt traveled to the Kingdom of Italy and posed as a Canadian citizen named Walters. He booked passage to Alexandria, Egypt, but was arrested there by US officials on November 23, 1866, still in his Pontifical Zouaves uniform.[7] He returned to the US on the USS *Swatara* to the Washington Navy Yard in early 1867.[8]

## Trial

Eighteen months after his mother was hanged, Surratt was tried in a Maryland civilian court. It was not before a military commission, unlike the trials of his mother and the others, as a US Supreme Court decision, *Ex parte Milligan*, had declared the trial of civilians before military tribunals to be unconstitutional if civilian courts were still open.

*John Harrison Surratt Jr. in Papal Zouave uniform, c. 1867*

Judge David Carter presided over Surratt's trial, and Edwards Pierrepont conducted the federal government's case against him. Surratt's lead attorney, Joseph Habersham Bradley, admitted Surratt's part in plotting to kidnap Lincoln but denied any involvement in the murder plot. After two months of testimony, Surratt was released after a mistrial; eight jurors had voted not guilty, four voted guilty.

The statute of limitations on charges other than murder had run out, and Surratt was released on bail.[9]

## Later life

Surratt tried to farm tobacco and then taught at the Rockville Female Academy. In 1870, as one of the last surviving members of the conspiracy, Surratt began a much-heralded public lecture tour. On December 6, at a small courthouse in Rockville, Maryland, in a 75-minute speech, Surratt admitted his involvement in the scheme to kidnap Lincoln. However, he maintained that he knew nothing of the assassination plot and reiterated that he was then in Elmira. He disavowed any participation by the Confederate government, reviled Weichmann as a "perjurer" who was responsible for his mother's death and said his friends had kept from him the seriousness of her plight in Washington. After that revelation, it was reported in Washington's *Evening Star* that the band played "Dixie" and a small concert was improvised, with Surratt the center of female attention.

Three weeks later, Surratt was to give a second lecture in Washington, but it was canceled because of public outrage.[10]

Surratt later took a job as a teacher in St. Joseph Catholic School in Emmitsburg, Maryland. In 1872, Surratt married Mary Victorine Hunter, a second cousin of Francis Scott Key. The couple lived in Baltimore and had seven children.[11]

Some time after 1872, he was hired by the Baltimore Steam Packet Company. He rose to freight auditor and, ultimately, treasurer of the company. Surratt retired from the steamship line in 1914 and died of pneumonia in 1916, at the age of 72.

He was buried in the New Cathedral Cemetery, in Baltimore.[12]

# Mary Surratt

*Surratt in 1850*

**Mary Elizabeth Jenkins Surratt**[1][2][3] (1820 or May 1823–July 7, 1865) was an American boarding house owner who was convicted of taking part in the conspiracy to assassinate U.S. President Abraham Lincoln. Sentenced to death, she was hanged and became the first woman executed by the US federal government. She maintained her innocence until her death, and the case against her was and is controversial. Surratt was the mother of John H. Surratt, Jr., who was later tried but was not convicted of involvement in the assassination.

Born in Maryland in the 1820s, Surratt converted to Catholicism at a young age and remained a practicing Catholic for the rest of her life. She wed John Harrison Surratt in 1840 and had three children by him. An entrepreneur, John became the owner of a tavern, an inn, and a hotel. The Surratts were sympathetic to the Confederate States of America and often hosted fellow Confederate sympathizers at their tavern.

Upon her husband's death in 1862, Surratt had to manage his estate. Tired of doing so without help, Surratt moved to her townhouse in Washington, D.C., which she then ran as a boardinghouse. There, she was introduced to John Wilkes Booth. Booth visited the boardinghouse numerous times, as did George Atzerodt and Lewis Powell, Booth's co-conspirators in the Lincoln assassination. Shortly before leaving Washington to kill Lincoln, Booth spoke with Surratt and handed her a package containing binoculars for one of her tenants, John M. Lloyd.

After Lincoln was assassinated, Surratt was arrested and put on military tribunal trial the following month, along with the other conspirators. She was convicted primarily due to the testimonies of Lloyd, who said that she told him to have the "shooting irons" ready, and Louis J. Weichmann, who testified about Surratt's relationships with Confederate groups and sympathizers. Five of the nine judges at her trial asked that Surratt be granted clemency by President Andrew Johnson because of her age and sex. Johnson did not grant her clemency, though accounts differ as to whether or not he received the clemency request. Surratt was hanged on July 7, 1865, and later buried in Mount Olivet Cemetery. She has since been portrayed in film, theater and television.

## Civil War and widowhood

The American Civil War began on April 12, 1861. The border state of Maryland remained part of the United States ("the Union"), but the Surratts were Confederate sympathizers,[32]

[43][55][56] and their tavern regularly hosted fellow sympathizers.[43][55][57] The Surratt tavern was being used as a safe house for Confederate spies,[43][58] and at least one author concludes that Mary had "de facto" knowledge of this.[43] Confederate scout and spy Thomas Nelson Conrad visited Surratt's boarding house before and during the Civil War.[59]

On March 7, 1861, three days after Abraham Lincoln's inauguration as President of the United States, Isaac left Maryland and traveled to Texas, where he enlisted in the Confederate States Army (serving in the 33rd Cavalry, or Duff's Partisan Rangers, 14th Cavalry Battalion).[46][48][60] John Jr. quit his studies at St. Charles College in July 1861 and became a courier for the Confederate Secret Service, moving messages, cash, and contraband back and forth across enemy lines.[61] The Confederate activities in and around Surrattsville drew the attention of the Union government. In late 1861, Lafayette C. Baker, a detective with the Union Intelligence Service, and 300 Union soldiers camped in Surrattsville and investigated the Surratts and others for Confederate activities.[62] He quickly uncovered evidence of a large Confederate courier network operating in the area, but despite some arrests and warnings, the courier network remained intact.[62]

*John H. Surratt, Jr. in 1868. Mary Surratt's son was a Confederate courier.*

John Surratt collapsed suddenly and died on either August 25[10][63] or August 26[64][65] in 1862 (sources differ as to the date). The cause of death was a stroke.[46] [63][66] The Surratt family affairs were in serious financial difficulties.[64] John Jr. and Anna both left school to help their mother run the family's remaining farmland and businesses.[43] On September 10, 1862, John Jr. was appointed postmaster of the Surrattsville post office.[67] [68][69] Lafayette Baker swept through Surrattsville again in 1862, and several postmasters were dismissed for disloyalty,[62] but John Jr. was not one of them. In August 1863, he sought a job in the paymaster's department in the United States Department of War, but his application caused federal agents to be suspicious about his family's loyalties to the Union.[69] On November 17, 1863, he was dismissed as postmaster for disloyalty.[70][68][71]

The loss of John Jr.'s job as postmaster caused a financial crisis for the Surratt family. [54] When John Sr.'s estate was probated in late November 1862, the family owned only two middle-age male slaves.[67] However, by 1863, Louis J. Weichmann, a friend of John Jr. from St. Charles College, observed that the family had six or more slaves working on the property.[72] By 1864, Mary Surratt found that her husband's unpaid debts and bad business deals had left her with many creditors.[55] Several of her slaves ran away.[54][65][73][74] When he was not meeting with Confederate sympathizers in the city, her son was selling vegetables to raise cash for the family.[75] Mary was tired of running the farm, tavern, and other businesses without her son's help.[76] In the fall of 1864, she began considering moving to her townhouse in the city.[36]

On October 1, 1864, she took possession of the townhouse at 604 H Street NW in Washington, D.C.[54] The house was made of gray brick, 29 feet (8.8 m) wide, 100 feet (30 m) deep, and had four stories.[6][36][77] The first floor, which was level with the street, had two large rooms, used as the kitchen and dining room.[6][77] The second floor had a front and back parlor, with the room in the rear used as Mary Surratt's bedroom.[6][78] The third floor had three rooms: two in the front and a larger one at the back.[6][79] The fourth floor, which was considered an attic, had two large and one small room, occupied by a servant.[6][79] Surratt began moving her belongings into the townhouse that month,[80] and on November 1, 1864, Anna and John Jr. took up residence there.[81] Mary Surratt herself moved into the home on December 1.[81] That same day, she leased the tavern in Surrattsville to a former Washington, D.C., policeman and Confederate sympathizer John M. Lloyd for $500 a year.[29][81][82] On November 30, December 8, and December 27, Mary Surratt advertised for lodgers in the *Daily Evening Star* newspaper.[29][54][83][84] She had initially said that she wanted only lodgers who were known to her personally or were recommended by friends, but in her advertisements, she said rooms were "available for 4 gentlemen."[84][85]

Some scholars have raised questions about Surratt's move into the city. Historians Kate Larson and Roy Chamlee have noted that although there is no definite proof, a case can be made that Surratt made the move into the city in furtherance of her and her son's espionage activities.[36][77] For example, Larson and Chamlee say that on September 21, 1864, John Surratt wrote to Louis J. Weichmann, observing that the family's plans to move into the city were advancing rapidly "on account of certain events having turned up,"[36][77] perhaps a cryptic reference to either his Confederate activities in general or the conspiracy to kidnap or kill Lincoln.[36] Larson has observed that although the move made long-term economic sense for Surratt, it also, in the short term, would have meant moving expenses and furnishing up to 10 rooms in the townhouse, money that she did not have.[77]

Chamlee, too, found little economic reason to move into the city and concluded that it would have been more profitable to rent the H Street boarding house entirely to lodgers. [36] During her time in the city, Surratt tried to keep her daughter away from what she felt were negative influences.[36] Moreover, Surratt still owed money on both the tavern and the townhouse and would take out yet another mortgage against the townhouse in January 1865.[36]

John Jr. transferred all his title to the family property to his mother in January 1865. That act may have additional implications. A traitor's property could be seized, and John's spy knowledge was certainly his motivation for relinquishing his title to the houses and land. Mary may have known of his motivation as well or at least suspected. If she did, she would have possessed at least *de facto* knowledge of the conspiracy.[86]

## Conspiracy

Louis J. Weichmann moved into Surratt's boarding house on November 1, 1864.[87] On December 23, 1864, Dr. Samuel Mudd introduced John Surratt, Jr. to John Wilkes Booth.

*Surratt's boarding house, c. 1890, little changed from how it looked during her occupancy.*

[88][89] Booth recruited John Jr. into his conspiracy to kidnap Lincoln.[88][90] Confederate agents began frequenting the boarding house.[88][91] Booth visited the boarding house many times over the next few months,[88][92][93] sometimes at Mary's request.[88]

George Atzerodt and Lewis Powell boarded at the townhouse for short periods.[88] Atzerodt, a friend of both John Jr. and Booth and a co-conspirator in the plot [94] to kidnap Lincoln, visited the boarding house several times in the first two months of 1865.[95] He stayed at the Surratt boarding house in February 1865 (for one night or several, sources differ), but he proved to be a heavy drinker, and Surratt evicted him after just a few days.[93][96]

He continued to visit the townhouse frequently afterward, however.[97] Powell posed as a Baptist preacher and stayed at the boarding house for three days in March 1865.[93][98] David Herold also called at the home several times.[91][97]

As part of the plot to kidnap Lincoln in March 1865, John, Atzerodt, and Herold hid two Spencer carbines, ammunition, and some other supplies at the Surratt tavern in Surrattsville.[88][99][100] On April 11, Mary Surratt rented a carriage and drove to the Surratt tavern.[101] She said that she made the trip to collect a debt owed her by a former neighbor. [101] However, according to her tenant, John Lloyd, Surratt told him to get the "shooting irons" ready to be picked up.[88][102] On April 14, Surratt said that she would once again visit the family tavern in Surrattsville to collect a debt.[88][103] Shortly before she left the city, Booth visited the boarding house and spoke privately with her.[88][104][105] He gave her a package, later found to contain binoculars, for Lloyd to pick up later that evening.[88][104][105] Surratt did so and, according to Lloyd, again told Lloyd to have the "shooting irons" ready for pickup and handed him a wrapped package from Booth.[88][99][106][107]

Booth's plan was to assassinate Lincoln and have Atzerodt kill Vice President Andrew Johnson and Powell kill Secretary of State William H. Seward. Booth killed Lincoln, Atzerodt never attempted to kill Johnson, and Powell stabbed Seward repeatedly but failed to murder him.[108] As they fled the city after Lincoln's assassination, Booth and Herold picked up the rifles and binoculars from Surratt's tavern.[88] Lloyd repaired a broken spring on Surratt's wagon before she left.[106][109][110]

## Arrest and incarceration

Around 2 a.m. on April 15, 1865, members of the District of Columbia police visited the Surratt boarding house, seeking John Wilkes Booth and John Surratt.[88][111][112] Why the police came to the house is not entirely clear. Most historians conclude that Weichmann's friend, Department of War employee Daniel Gleason, had alerted federal authorities to Confederate activity centered on the Surratt house, but that does not explain why police rather than federal agents appeared there.[111] (Historian Roy Chamlee, however, says that there is evidence that Gleason did not tell police about his suspicions of Weichmann for several days.)[113] Within 45 minutes of the attack on Lincoln, John Surratt's name had become associated with the attack on Secretary of State William H. Seward.[114] The police as well as the Provost Marshal's office both had files on John Surratt, Jr., and knew he was a close friend of Booth.[114] (It is possible that either James L. Maddox, property supervisor at Ford's Theatre and a friend of Booth's, or actor John Matthews, both of whom may have known about the plot to attack government officials, mentioned Surratt's name.) [114] Historian Otto Eisenschiml has argued that David Herold's attempt to steal a horse from John Fletcher may have led them to the Surratt boarding house,[115] but at least one other scholar has called the link uncertain.[111] Other sources claim that eyewitnesses had identified Booth as Lincoln's attacker, and the detectives had information (a tip from an unnamed actor and a bartender) linking John Jr. to Booth.[88][116] Mary lied to the detectives that her son had been in Canada for two weeks.[88][117] She also did not reveal that she had delivered a package to the tavern on Booth's behalf, only hours earlier.[118]

*Lewis Powell was the co-conspirator whose untimely arrival at the Surratt boarding house on April 17 convinced many of Mary Surratt's guilt.*

On April 17, a Surratt neighbor told US military authorities that he overheard one of the Surratt's servants saying that three men had come to the house on the night of Lincoln's assassination and that one of the men had mentioned Booth in a theater.[119][120] [121] (The servant was mistaken about the date, as John Surratt Jr. had indeed been in Elmira, New York, on a mission for a Confederate general).[122] Other pieces of information also mentioned the boarding house as a key meeting place of the possible conspirators.[118] Either Colonel Henry H. Wells, Provost Marshal (head of the military police) of the District of Columbia, or General Christopher C. Augur told Colonel Henry Steel Olcott to arrest everyone in the house.[118][119] Federal soldiers visited the Surratt boarding house again late on the evening of April 17.[118][123][124] John Jr. could not be found, but after a search of the house, the agents found in Mary's room a picture of Booth, hidden behind another photograph, pictures of Confederate leaders including Jefferson Davis, a pistol, a mold for making bullets, and percussion caps.[120][123][125] As Mary was being arrested for conspiracy to assassinate Lincoln, Powell appeared at her door in disguise.[126][127][128] Although Surratt denied knowing him,[92][127][129] Powell claimed that he was a laborer hired by Surratt to dig a ditch the next morning. The discrepancy and Powell's unusually well-groomed appearance, quite unlike a ditch-digger, prompted his arrest.[92][127][129] He was later identified as the man who had attempted to assassinate Secretary of State William Seward.[126]

After her arrest, she was held at an annex to the Old Capitol Prison before being transferred to the Washington Arsenal on April 30.[126][130] Two armed guards stood before the door to her cell from the beginning of her imprisonment until her death.[131] Her cell, while airy and larger than the others,[132] was sparsely furnished, with a straw mattress, table, wash basin, chair, and a bucket.[133][134][135] Food was served four times a day, always of bread; salt pork, beef, or beef soup; and coffee or water.[136] The other arrested conspirators had their heads enclosed in a padded canvas bag to prevent a suicide attempt.[137] Sources disagree as to whether Surratt was forced to wear it as well.[132][137] Although the others wore iron manacles on their feet and ankles, she was not manacled.[132] (Rumors to the contrary were raised by reporters at the trial who could not see her or "heard" the clank of chains about her feet. The rumors were repeatedly investigated and denied.)[138] She began to suffer menstrual bleeding and became weak during her detention.[133][134][139] She was given a rocking chair and allowed visits from her daughter, Anna.[140][141] She and Powell received the most attention from the press.[142] The Northern press was also highly critical of her, claiming that she had a "criminal face" due to her small mouth and dark eyes.[143]

John Surratt, Jr., was in Elmira at the time of the assassination, delivering messages on behalf of a Confederate general.[122] After learning of Lincoln's death, he fled to Montreal, Quebec, Canada.[144]

## Trial

The trial for the alleged conspirators began on May 9.[64] A military tribunal, rather than a civilian court, was chosen as the venue because government officials thought that its more lenient rules of evidence would enable the court to get to the bottom of what was then perceived by the public as a vast conspiracy.[145] All eight alleged conspirators were tried simultaneously.[127] Historians have conflicting views regarding Surratt's innocence. Historian Laurie Verge commented, "Only in the case of Dr. Samuel Alexander Mudd is there as much controversy as to the guilt or innocence of one of the defendants."[146] Lincoln assassination scholar Thomas Reed Turner says that of the eight people accused of plotting to kill Lincoln, the case against Surratt remains "the most controversial . . . at that time and since."[99]

A room on the northeast corner of the third floor of the Arsenal was made into a courtroom, and the prisoners were brought into the room through a side door, which prevented them from passing by or being harassed by spectators.[133][147] Surratt was given special considerations during the trial because of her illness and sex. In the courtroom, she sat apart from the other prisoners.[133][148] Sources differ as to whether an armed guard sat on either side of her, as was done for other prisoners during the trial.[148][149] While the others wore wrist and ankle manacles in the courtroom, she did not.[132][138][150] She was also permitted a bonnet, fan, and veil to hide her face from spectators.[150] As her illness worsened during the trial, she was moved to a larger and more comfortable prison cell.[150]

Surratt was charged with abetting, aiding, concealing, counseling, and harboring her co-defendants.[151] The federal government initially attempted to find legal counsel for her and the others, but almost no attorneys were willing to take the job for fear they would be accused of disloyalty to the Union.[152] Surratt retained Reverdy Johnson as her legal counsel.[126][153] A member of the military commission trying the conspirators challenged Johnson's right to defend Surratt, as he had objected to requiring loyalty oaths from voters in the 1864 presidential election.[126][154] After much discussion, this objection was withdrawn, but damage had been done to his influence, and he did not attend most of the court sessions.[126][155] Most of Surratt's legal defense was presented by two other lawyers: Frederick Aiken and John Wesley Clampitt.[126][152]

The prosecution's strategy was to tie Surratt to the conspiracy. Powell's arrival at her boarding house, three days after the president's murder, was critical evidence against her,

*Louis J. Weichmann, whose testimony proved critical in convicting Mary Surratt.*

the government argued.[126] The prosecution presented nine witnesses, but most of their case rested on the testimony of just two men: John M. Lloyd and Louis J. Weichmann.[126][127] Lloyd testified on May 13 and 15, 1865[156] on the hiding of the carbines and other supplies at the tavern in March and the two conversations he had with her in which she told him to get the "shooting irons" ready.[99][126][157] Weichmann's testimony was important, as it established an intimate relationship between her and the other conspirators.[99][127] Weichmann testified May 16 to 19[156] and said that he had resided at the boarding house since November 1864. He had seen or overheard John Jr. meeting and talking with Atzerodt, Booth, and Powell many times over the past four and a half months.[129] Weichmann had driven Surratt to the tavern on April 11 and 14, confirmed that she and Lloyd had spent much time in private conversation, testified that he saw Booth give her the package of binoculars, and attested that she

had turned the package over to Lloyd.[129][158] Weichmann also testified at length about the Surratt family's ties to the Confederate spy and courier rings operating in the area and their relationships with Atzerodt and Powell.[129] He also testified about the December 23 meeting with Booth and John (which he also attended) and their subsequent meeting with Booth at Booth's room at the National Hotel.[129] Finally, he told the military tribunal about the general excitement in the boarding house in March 1865 after the failed attempt to kidnap Lincoln.[129]

Other prosecution witnesses reinforced Weichmann's testimony. Lodger Honora

Fitzpatrick confirmed visits by Atzerodt, Booth, and Powell to the boarding house.[129] Emma Offut, Lloyd's sister-in-law, testified that she saw (but did not hear) Surratt speaking for long periods of time with Lloyd on April 11 and 14.[129] Government agents testified about their arrest of Surratt, Powell's arrival, and her denial that she knew Powell. [129] The fact that Powell sought refuge in the boarding house after Lincoln's murder left a bad impression on her.[99] Surratt's refusal (or failure) to recognize him also weighed against her.[127] The agents also testified about their search of the house, and the evidence (the photographs, the weapons, etc.) discovered there.[129] Lloyd's testimony was the most important for the prosecution's case,[92][158][159] for it indicated that she had played an active role in the conspiracy in the days before Lincoln's death.[109] The prosecution rested its case on May 22.[129]

The defense strategy was to impeach the testimony of the key prosecution witnesses: Lloyd and Weichmann. It also wished to show that she was loyal to the Union, her trips to Surrattsville were of an innocent nature, and she had not been aware of Booth's plans. [109] There were 31 witnesses who testified for the defense.[109] George H. Calvert testified that he had pressed Surratt to pay a debt, Bennett Gwynn said Surratt had sought payment from John Nothey to satisfy the Calvert debt, and Nothey agreed that he had received a letter from Surratt for him to appear at the tavern on April 11 to pay what was owed.[109] Several witnesses impugned Lloyd's character by testifying about his alcoholism,[109] while others said he was too intoxicated on the day of Lincoln's assassination to remember that day clearly.[109][160] Augustus Howell, a Confederate agent, testified Weichmann was an untrustworthy witness, as he had sought to become a Confederate spy himself.[160][161] (The prosecution had attempted to show that Howell was a Confederate spy and should not be trusted.)[162] Anna Surratt testified that it was Weichmann who had brought Atzerodt into the boarding house, that the photograph of Booth was hers, and that she owned photographs of Union political and military leaders.[162][163] Anna denied ever overhearing any discussions of disloyal activities or ideas in the boarding house, and that Booth's visits to the house were always short.[162] Anna explained her mother's failure to recognize Powell by asserting she could not see well.[162][164] Augusta Howell, Honora Fitzpatrick, a former servant and a former slave testified to Mary's poor eyesight as well.[160][161][162][164][163] The former servant and the former slave both said Surratt had given Union soldiers food. [162][163] Numerous witnesses were called at the end of the defense's case to testify to her loyalty to the Union, her deep Christian faith, and her kindness.[162][164] During the prosecution's rebuttal, government lawyers called four witnesses to the stand, who testified as to Weichmann's unimpeachable character.[162]

Johnson and Aiken presented the closing arguments for the defense. Johnson attacked the jurisdiction of a military tribunal over civilians, as had Mudd's attorney.[162] Aiken challenged the court's jurisdiction as well.[165] He also reiterated that Lloyd and Weichmann were unreliable witnesses and that the evidence against her was all circumstantial.[166] The only evidence linking Surratt to the conspiracy to kill Lincoln, he said, came from Lloyd and Weichmann, and neither man was telling the truth.[166] (Dorothy Kunhardt has written that there is evidence the latter's perjured testimony was suborned by Secretary of War Edwin M. Stanton.)[167]

Judge Advocate John Bingham presented the closing argument for the prosecution.[166] The military tribunal had jurisdiction, he said, not only because the court itself had ruled at the beginning of the trials that it did but because they were crimes committed in a military zone, during a time of war, and against high government officials in carrying out treasonous activities.[166] Bingham pointed out that the Surratt boarding house was where the conspiracy was planned, and Atzerodt, Booth, and Powell had all met with Surratt.[166] Booth had paid for the rental of the carriage that took Surratt to Surrattsville each time, and Bingham said that was evidence that Surratt's trips were critical to the conspiracy.[166] Bingham also said that Lloyd's testimony had been corroborated by others and that his unwillingness to reveal the cache of weapons in the tavern was prompted by his subservient tenant relationship to Surratt.[166] Bingham concluded by reiterating the government's key point: Powell had returned to the Surratt house seeking Surratt, and that alone was proof of her guilt.[166] Bingham also pointed out for the tribunal that the charge a person was indicted for was irrelevant. Under the law of conspiracy, if one person carries out a crime, all conspirators are guilty of the same crime.[166][168]

The trial ended on June 28, 1865.[64][169] Surratt was so ill the last four days of the trial that she was permitted to stay in her cell.[169] In the opinion of historian Roy Z. Chamlee, both legal teams appeared to have flaws in their cases, and except for Reverdy Johnson, neither team employed highly-skilled attorneys.[169] The government's case was hindered by its failure to call as a witness the man who shared Lloyd's carriage when he talked with Surratt and could have verified Lloyd's version of the "shooting irons" story or Metropolitan Police Chief A.C. Richards whose investigation had had the most success in the early days of the investigation.[169] The government did not fully investigate Booth's meetings with Surratt at noon or the evening of the murder, and its questioning and cross-examination of witnesses was poorly prepared and weak.[169] What is most important, according to historian Roy Z. Chamber Jr., is that the government had botched the attempt to apprehend John Jr.[169] The defense's case, too, had a problem. The defense never followed up on inconsistencies in Weichmann's chronology of Mary's last visit to the tavern, which could have undermined Weichmann's entire credibility.[169]

The military tribunal considered guilt and sentencing on June 29 and 30.[169] Surratt's guilt was the second-last to be considered, as her case had problems of evidence and witness reliability.[169] The sentence was handed down on June 30.[170] The military tribunal found her guilty on all charges but two.[171] A death sentence required six of the nine votes of the judges.[170][172] Surratt was sentenced to death, the first woman executed by the federal government.[6][24] The sentence was announced publicly on July 5.[173][174][175] When Powell learned of his sentence, he declared that she was completely innocent of all charges.[176] The night before the execution, Surratt's priests and Anna Surratt both visited Powell and elicited from him a strong statement declaring Mary innocent. Although it was delivered to Captain Christian Rath, who was overseeing the execution, Powell's statement had no effect on anyone with authority to prevent Surratt's death.[177] George Atzerodt bitterly condemned her, implicating her even further in the conspiracy.[176] Powell's was the only statement by any conspirator exonerating Surratt.[177]

Anna Surratt pleaded repeatedly for her mother's life with Judge Advocate General Joseph Holt, but he refused to consider clemency.[64] She also attempted to see President Andrew Johnson several times to beg for mercy but was not granted permission to see him.[64]

Five of the nine judges signed a letter asking President Johnson to give Surratt clemency and commute her sentence to life in prison because of her age and sex.[170][178] Holt did not deliver the recommendation to Johnson until July 5, two days before Surratt and the others were to hang.[170] Johnson signed the order for execution but did not sign the order for clemency.[170][178] Johnson later said he never saw the clemency request; Holt said he showed it to Johnson, who refused to sign it.[64][170] Johnson, according to Holt, said in signing the death warrant that she had "kept the nest that hatched the egg."[178]

## Execution

Construction of the gallows for the hanging of the conspirators condemned to death began immediately on July 5, after the execution order was signed.[173] It was constructed in the south part of the Arsenal courtyard, was 12 feet (3.7 m) high and about 20 square feet (1.9 m$^2$) in size.[179] Rath, who oversaw the preparations for the executions, made the nooses.[180] Tired of making nooses and thinking that the government would never hang a woman, he made Surratt's noose the night before the execution with five loops rather than the regulation seven.[177][180] He tested the nooses that night by tying them to a tree limb and a bag of buckshot and then tossing the bag to the ground (the ropes held).[180] Civilian workers did not want to dig the graves out of superstitious fear, so Rath asked for volunteers among the soldiers at the Arsenal and received more help than he needed.[180]

At noon on July 6, Surratt was informed she would be hanged the next day. She wept profusely.[181] She was joined by two Catholic priests (Jacob Walter and B.F. Wiget)[140][182] and her daughter Anna.[179] Father Jacob remained with her almost until her death.[183] Her menstrual problems had worsened, and she was in such pain and suffered from such severe cramps that the prison doctor gave her wine and medication.[140][184] She repeatedly asserted her innocence.[140] She spent the night on her mattress, weeping and moaning in pain and grief, ministered to by the priests.[177][185] Anna left her mother's side at 8 a.m. on July 7 and went to the White House to beg for her mother's life one last time.[185] Her entreaty rejected, she returned to the prison and her mother's cell at about 11 a.m.[186] The soldiers began testing the gallows about 11:25 a.m.; the sound of the tests unnerved all the prisoners.[187] Shortly before noon, Mary Surratt was taken from her cell and then allowed to sit in a chair near the entrance to the courtyard.[187] The heat in the city that day was oppressive. By noon, it had already reached 92.3°F (33.5°C).[188] The guards ordered all visitors to leave at 12:30 p.m.[186] When she was forced to part from her mother, Anna's hysterical screams of grief could be heard throughout the prison.[189][190]

Clampitt and Aiken had not finished trying to save their client, however. On the morning of July 7, they asked a District of Columbia court for a writ of *habeas corpus*, arguing that the military tribunal had no jurisdiction over their client.[191][192][193] The court issued the writ at 3 a.m., and it was served on General Winfield Scott Hancock.[191][192][194] Hancock was ordered to produce Surratt by 10 a.m.[194] General Hancock sent an aide to General John F. Hartranft, who commanded the Old Capitol Prison, ordering him not to admit any US marshal, as that would prevent the marshal from serving a similar writ on Hartranft.[191] Johnson was informed that the court had issued the writ and promptly cancelled it at 11:30 a.m. under the authority granted to him by the Habeas Corpus Suspension Act of 1863. [191][193][195] General Hancock and United States Attorney General James Speed personally appeared in court and informed the judge of the cancellation of the writ.[194]

*Aftermath of the execution of Mary Surratt, Lewis Powell, David Herold, and George Atzerodt on July 7, 1865.*

On July 7, 1865, at 1:15 p.m.,[196][197] a procession led by General Hartranft escorted the four condemned prisoners through the courtyard and up the steps to the gallows. [190][196] Each prisoner's ankles and wrists were bound by manacles.[198] Surratt led the way,[190][199] wearing a black bombazine dress, black bonnet, and black veil.[200][201] More than 1,000 people, including government officials, members of the US armed forces, friends and family of the accused, official witnesses, and reporters, watched. [202] General Hancock limited attendance to those who had a ticket, and only those who had a good reason to be present were given a ticket.[203] (Most of those present were military officers and soldiers, as fewer than 200 tickets had been printed.)[199] Alexander Gardner, who had photographed the body of Booth and taken portraits of several of the male conspirators while they were imprisoned aboard naval ships, photographed the execution for the government.[203] Hartranft read the order for their execution.[196] Surratt, either weak from her illness or swooning in fear (perhaps both), had to be supported by two soldiers and her priests.[190][199] The condemned were seated in chairs, Surratt almost collapsing into hers.[201] She was seated to the right of the others, the traditional "seat of honor" in an execution.[180] White cloth was used to bind their arms to their sides and their ankles and thighs together.[197][198] The cloths around Surratt's legs were tied around her dress below the knees.[197] Each person was ministered to by a member of the clergy. From the scaffold, Powell said, "Mrs. Surratt is innocent. She doesn't deserve to die with the rest of us."[204] Fathers Jacob and Wiget prayed over her and held a crucifix to her lips. [201][205] About 16 minutes elapsed from the time the prisoners entered the courtyard until they were ready for execution.[201]

A white bag was placed over the head of each prisoner after the noose was put in place.

[198] Surratt's bonnet was removed, and the noose put around her neck by a US Secret Service officer.[197][201][206] She complained that the bindings about her arms hurt, and the officer preparing said, "Well, it won't hurt long."[207] Finally, the prisoners were asked to stand and move forward a few feet to the nooses.[201][206] The chairs were removed.[206] Her last words, spoken to a guard as he moved her forward to the drop, were "Please don't let me fall."[204][207]

Surratt and the others stood on the drop for about 10 seconds,[200] and then Captain Rath clapped his hands.[180][197][206] Four soldiers of Company F of the 14th Veteran Reserves knocked out the supports holding the drops in place, and the condemned fell.[198] [208] Surratt, who had moved forward enough to barely step onto the drop, lurched forward and slid partway down the drop, her body snapping tight at the end of the rope, swinging back and forth.[180] Surratt's death appeared to be the roughest. "Unlike the others', her neck does not break, and she does not die right away. [Instead, she] swings for five long minutes before her larynx is crushed and her body stops fighting for air." [209] Atzerodt's stomach heaved once and his legs quivered; then, he was still.[210][211] Herold and Powell struggled for nearly five minutes, strangling to death.[180][210][211]

## Burial

Each body was inspected by a physician to ensure that death had occurred.[198][202][210] The bodies of the executed were allowed to hang for about 30 minutes[202][206][212] and soldiers began to cut them down at 1:53 p.m.[198] A corporal raced to the top of the gallows and cut down Atzerodt's body, which fell to the ground with a thud.[198] He was reprimanded, and the other bodies were cut down more gently.[198] Herold's body was next, followed by Powell's.[198] Surratt's body was cut down at 1:58 p.m.[198] As Surratt's body was cut loose, her head fell forward. A soldier joked, "She makes a good bow" and was rebuked by an officer for his poor use of humor.[24][198]

Upon examination, the military surgeons determined that no one's neck had been broken by the fall.[24][198] The manacles and cloth bindings were removed but not the white execution masks, and the bodies were placed into the pine coffins.[198][202] The name of each person was written on a piece of paper by acting Assistant Adjutant R. A. Watts,[206] and inserted in a glass vial, which was placed into the coffin.[202] The coffins were buried against the prison wall in shallow graves, just a few feet from the gallows.[202] A white picket fence marked the burial site.[213] The night that she died, a mob attacked the Surratt boarding house and began stripping it of souvenirs until the police stopped them.[207]

Anna Surratt unsuccessfully asked for her mother's body for four years.[214] In 1867, the War Department decided to tear down the portion of the Washington Arsenal where the bodies of Surratt and the other executed conspirators lay.[215] On October 1, 1867, the coffins were disinterred and reburied in Warehouse No. 1 at the Arsenal, with a wooden marker placed at the head of each burial vault.[213][215] Booth's body lay alongside them.[213] In February 1869, Edwin Booth asked Johnson for the body of his brother.[215] Johnson agreed to turn the body over to the Booth family, and on February 8 Surratt's body was turned over to the Surratt family.[213][214][216][217] She was buried in Mount Olivet Cemetery in Washington, D.C., on February 9, 1869.[216][217] Lloyd is buried 100 yards (91 m) from her grave in the same cemetery.[218]

# George Henry Thomas

**George Henry Thomas** (July 31, 1816–March 28, 1870) was a United States Army officer and a Union general during the American Civil War, one of the principal commanders in the Western Theater.

Thomas served in the Mexican–American War and later chose to remain with the U.S. Army for the Civil War as a Southern Unionist, despite his heritage as a Virginian (whose home state would join the Confederate States of America). He won one of the first Union victories in the war, at Mill Springs in Kentucky, and served in important subordinate commands at Perryville and Stones River. His stout defense at the Battle of Chickamauga in 1863 saved the Union Army from being completely routed, earning him his most famous nickname, "the Rock of Chickamauga." He followed soon after with a dramatic breakthrough on Missionary Ridge in the Battle of Chattanooga. In the Franklin–Nashville Campaign of 1864, he achieved one of the most decisive victories of the war, destroying the army of Confederate General John Bell Hood, his former student at West Point, at the Battle of Nashville.

Thomas had a successful record in the Civil War, but he failed to achieve the historical acclaim of some of his contemporaries, such as Ulysses S. Grant and William T. Sherman. He developed a reputation as a slow, deliberate general who shunned self-promotion and who turned down advancements in position when he did not think they were justified. After the war, he did not write memoirs to advance his legacy. He also had an uncomfortable personal relationship with Grant, which served him poorly as Grant advanced in rank and eventually to the Presidency.

## American Civil War
### Remaining with the Union
At the outbreak of the Civil War, 19 of the 36 officers in the 2nd U.S. Cavalry resigned, including three of Thomas's superiors—Albert Sidney Johnston, Robert E. Lee, and William J. Hardee.[21] Many Southern-born officers were torn between loyalty to their states and loyalty to their country. Thomas struggled with the decision but opted to remain with the United States. His Northern-born wife probably helped influence his decision. In response, his family turned his picture against the wall, destroyed his letters, and never spoke to him again. (During the economic hard times in the South after the war, Thomas sent some money to his sisters, who angrily refused to accept it, declaring they had no brother.)[22]

Nevertheless, Thomas stayed in the Union Army with some degree of suspicion surrounding him. On January 18, 1861, a few months before Fort Sumter, he had applied for a job as the commandant of cadets at the Virginia Military Institute.[23] Any real tendency to the secessionist cause, however, could be refuted when he turned down Virginia Governor John Letcher's offer to become chief of ordnance for the Virginia Provisional Army.[24] On June 18, his former student and fellow Virginian, Confederate Col. J .E. B. Stuart, wrote to his wife, "Old George H. Thomas is in command of the cavalry of the enemy. I would like to hang, *hang* him as a traitor to his native state."[25] Nevertheless, as the Civil War carried on, he won the affection of Union soldiers serving under him as a "soldier's soldier," who took to affectionately referring to Thomas as "Pap Thomas."[26]

## Kentucky

Thomas was promoted in rapid succession to be lieutenant colonel (on April 25, 1861, replacing Robert E. Lee) and colonel (May 3, replacing Albert Sidney Johnston) in the regular army, and brigadier general of volunteers (August 17).[27] In the First Bull Run Campaign, he commanded a brigade under Maj. Gen. Robert Patterson in the Shenandoah Valley,[28] but all of his subsequent assignments were in the Western Theater. Reporting to Maj. Gen. Robert Anderson in Kentucky, Thomas was assigned to training recruits and to command an independent force in the eastern half of the state. On January 18, 1862, he defeated Confederate Brig. Gens. George B. Crittenden and Felix Zollicoffer at Mill Springs, gaining the first important Union victory in the war, breaking Confederate strength in eastern Kentucky, and lifting Union morale.[29]

## Shiloh and Corinth

On December 2, 1861, Brig. Gen. Thomas was assigned to command the 1st Division of Maj. Gen. Don Carlos Buell's Army of the Ohio. He was present at the second day of the Battle of Shiloh (April 7, 1862), but arrived after the fighting had ceased. The victor at Shiloh, Maj. Gen. Ulysses S. Grant, came under severe criticism for the bloody battle and his superior, Maj. Gen. Henry W. Halleck, reorganized his Department of the Mississippi to ease Grant out of direct field command. The three armies in the department were divided and recombined into three "wings." Thomas, promoted to major general effective April 25, 1862, was given command of the Right Wing, consisting of four divisions from Grant's former Army of the Tennessee and one from the Army of the Ohio. Thomas successfully led this putative army in the siege of Corinth. On June 10, Grant returned to command of the original Army of the Tennessee.

## Perryville, Stones River, Chickamauga, and Chattanooga

Thomas resumed service under Don Carlos Buell. During Confederate General Braxton Bragg's invasion of Kentucky in the fall of 1862, the Union high command became nervous about Buell's cautious tendencies and offered command of the Army of the Ohio to Thomas, who refused. Thomas served as Buell's second-in-command at the Battle of

Perryville; although tactically inconclusive, the battle halted Bragg's invasion of Kentucky as he voluntarily withdrew to Tennessee. Again frustrated with Buell's ineffective pursuit of Bragg, the Union replaced him with Maj. Gen. William Rosecrans. Thomas wrote on October 30, 1862, a letter of protest to Secretary Stanton, feeling that Rosecrans was junior to him, but Stanton wrote back on November 15, telling him that that was not the case (Rosecrans had in fact been his junior, but his commission as major general had been backdated to make him senior to Thomas) and reminding him of his earlier refusal to accept command; Thomas demurred and withdrew his protest.[30]

Fighting under Rosecrans, commanding the "Center" wing of the newly renamed Army of the Cumberland, Thomas gave an impressive performance at the Battle of Stones River, holding the center of the retreating Union line and once again preventing a victory by Bragg. He was in charge of the most important part of the maneuvering from Decherd to Chattanooga during the Tullahoma Campaign (June 22–July 3, 1863) and the crossing of the Tennessee River. At the Battle of Chickamauga on September 19, 1863, now commanding the XIV Corps, he once again held a desperate position against Bragg's onslaught while the Union line on his right collapsed. Thomas rallied broken and scattered units together on Horseshoe Ridge to prevent a significant Union defeat from becoming a hopeless rout. Future president James Garfield, a field officer for the Army of the Cumberland, visited Thomas during the battle, carrying orders from Rosecrans to retreat; when Thomas said he would have to stay behind to ensure the Army's safety, Garfield told Rosecrans that Thomas was "standing like a rock."[31] After the battle he became widely known by the nickname "The Rock of Chickamauga," representing his determination to hold a vital position against strong odds.

Thomas succeeded Rosecrans in command of the Army of the Cumberland shortly before the Battles for Chattanooga (November 23–25, 1863), a stunning Union victory that was highlighted by Thomas's troops storming the Confederate line on Missionary Ridge. As the Army of the Cumberland advanced further than ordered, General Grant, on Orchard Knob asked Thomas, "Who ordered the advance?" Thomas replied, "I don't know. I did not."

## Atlanta and Franklin/Nashville

During Maj. Gen. William Tecumseh Sherman's advance through Georgia in the spring of 1864, the Army of the Cumberland numbered over 60,000 men, and Thomas's staff did the logistics and engineering for Sherman's entire army group, including developing a novel series of Cumberland pontoons. At the Battle of Peachtree Creek (July 20, 1864), Thomas's defense severely damaged Lt. Gen. John B. Hood's army in its first attempt to break the siege of Atlanta.

When Hood broke away from Atlanta in the autumn of 1864, menaced Sherman's long line of communications, and endeavored to force Sherman to follow him, Sherman abandoned his communications and embarked on the March to the Sea. Thomas stayed behind to fight Hood in the Franklin-Nashville Campaign. Thomas, with a smaller force, raced with Hood to reach Nashville, where he was to receive reinforcements.

At the Battle of Franklin on November 30, 1864, a large part of Thomas's force, under command of Maj. Gen. John M. Schofield, dealt Hood a strong defeat and held him in check long enough to cover the concentration of Union forces in Nashville. At Nashville, Thomas had to organize his forces, which had been drawn from all parts of the West and which included many young troops and even quartermaster employees. He declined to attack until his army was ready and the ice covering the ground had melted enough for his men to move. The North, including General Grant himself (now general-in-chief of all Union armies), grew impatient at the delay. Maj. Gen. John A. Logan was sent with an order to replace Thomas, and soon afterwards Grant started a journey west from City Point, Virginia to take command in person.

Thomas attacked on December 15, 1864, in the Battle of Nashville and effectively destroyed Hood's command in two days of fighting. Thomas sent his wife, Frances Lucretia Kellogg Thomas, the following telegram, the only communication surviving of the Thomases' correspondence: "We have whipped the enemy, taken many prisoners and considerable artillery."

Thomas was appointed a major general in the regular army, with date of rank of his Nashville victory, and received the Thanks of Congress:

> . . . to Major-General George H. Thomas and the officers and soldiers under his command for their skill and dauntless courage, by which the rebel army under General Hood was signally defeated and driven from the state of Tennessee.

Thomas may have resented his late promotion to major general (which made him junior by date of rank to Sheridan); upon receiving the telegram announcing it, he remarked to Surgeon George Cooper: "I suppose it is better late than never, but it is too late to be appreciated. I earned this at Chickamauga."[32]

Thomas also received another nickname from his victory: "The Sledge of Nashville."

## Later life and death

After the end of the Civil War, Thomas commanded the Department of the Cumberland in Kentucky and Tennessee, and at times also West Virginia and parts of Georgia, Mississippi and Alabama, through 1869. During the Reconstruction period, Thomas acted to protect freedmen from white abuses. He set up military commissions to enforce labor contracts since the local courts had either ceased to operate or were biased against blacks. Thomas also used troops to protect places threatened by violence from the Ku Klux Klan. [33] In a November 1868 report, Thomas noted efforts made by former Confederates to paint the Confederacy in a positive light, stating:

> [T]he greatest efforts made by the defeated insurgents since the close of the war

have been to promulgate the idea that the cause of liberty, justice, humanity, equality, and all the calendar of the virtues of freedom, suffered violence and wrong when the effort for southern independence failed. This is, of course, intended as a species of political cant, whereby the crime of treason might be covered with a counterfeit varnish of patriotism, so that the precipitators of the rebellion might go down in history hand in hand with the defenders of the government, thus wiping out with their own hands their own stains; a species of self-forgiveness amazing in its effrontery, when it is considered that life and property—justly forfeited by the laws of the country, of war, and of nations, through the magnanimity of the government and people—was not exacted from them.

*— George Henry Thomas, November 1868.*[34]

President Andrew Johnson offered Thomas the rank of lieutenant general—with the intent to eventually replace Grant, a Republican and future president, with Thomas as general in chief—but the ever-loyal Thomas asked the Senate to withdraw his name for that nomination because he did not want to be party to politics. In 1869 he requested assignment to command the Military Division of the Pacific with headquarters at the Presidio of San Francisco. He died there of a stroke on March 28, 1870, while writing an answer to an article criticizing his military career by his wartime rival John Schofield. Sherman, by then general-in-chief, personally conveyed the news to President Grant at the White House. None of Thomas's blood relatives attended his funeral as they had never forgiven him for his loyalty to the Union. He was buried in Oakwood Cemetery, in Troy, New York. His gravestone was sculpted by Robert E. Launitz and comprises a white marble sarcophagus topped by a bald eagle.[35]

# Harriet Tubman

*Tubman c. 1885*

**Harriet Tubman** (born Araminta Ross, c. March 1822[1] – March 10, 1913) was an American abolitionist and political activist. Born into slavery, Tubman escaped and subsequently made some 13 missions to rescue approximately 70 enslaved people, including family and friends,[2] using the network of antislavery activists and safe houses known as the Underground Railroad. She later helped abolitionist John Brown recruit men for his raid on Harpers Ferry. During the American Civil War, she served as an armed scout and spy for the Union Army. In her later years, Tubman was an activist in the struggle for women's suffrage.

Born a slave in Dorchester County, Maryland, Tubman was beaten and whipped by her various masters as a child. Early in life, she suffered a traumatic head wound when an irate slave owner threw a heavy metal weight intending to hit another slave, but hitting her instead. The injury caused dizziness, pain, and spells of hypersomnia, which occurred throughout her life. After her injury, Tubman began experiencing strange visions and vivid dreams, which she ascribed to premonitions from God. These experiences, combined with her Methodist upbringing, led her to become devoutly religious.

In 1849, Tubman escaped to Philadelphia, then immediately returned to Maryland to rescue her family. Slowly, one group at a time, she brought relatives with her out of the state, and eventually guided dozens of other slaves to freedom. Traveling by night and in extreme secrecy, Tubman (or "Moses," as she was called) "never lost a passenger."[3] After the Fugitive Slave Act of 1850 was passed, she helped guide fugitives farther north into British North America, and helped newly freed slaves find work. Tubman met John Brown in 1858, and helped him plan and recruit supporters for his 1859 raid on Harpers Ferry.

When the Civil War began, Tubman worked for the Union Army, first as a cook and nurse, and then as an armed scout and spy. The first woman to lead an armed expedition in the war, she guided the raid at Combahee Ferry, which liberated more than 700 slaves. After the war, she retired to the family home on property she had purchased in 1859 in Auburn, New York, where she cared for her aging parents. She was active in the women's suffrage movement until illness overtook her, and she had to be admitted to a home for elderly African Americans that she had helped to establish years earlier. After her death in 1913, she became an icon of courage and freedom.

## Birth and family

Tubman was born Araminta "Minty" Ross to enslaved parents, Harriet ("Rit") Green and Ben Ross. Rit was owned by Mary Pattison Brodess (and later her son Edward). Ben was held by Anthony Thompson, who became Mary Brodess's second husband, and who ran a large plantation near the Blackwater River in the Madison area of Dorchester County, Maryland. As with many slaves in the United States, neither the exact year nor place of Tubman's birth is known, and historians differ as to the best estimate. Kate Larson records the year as 1822, based on a midwife payment and several other historical documents, including her runaway advertisement,[1] while Jean Humez says "the best current evidence suggests that Tubman was born in 1820, but it might have been a year or two later."[4] Catherine Clinton notes that Tubman reported the year of her birth as 1825, while her death certificate lists 1815 and her gravestone lists 1820.[5]

Modesty, Tubman's maternal grandmother, arrived in the United States on a slave ship from Africa; no information is available about her other ancestors.[6] As a child, Tubman was told that she seemed like an Ashanti person because of her character traits, though no evidence exists to confirm this lineage.[7] Her mother Rit (who may have had a white father)[7][8] was a cook for the Brodess family.[4] Her father Ben was a skilled woodsman who managed the timber work on Thompson's plantation.[7] They married around 1808 and, according to court records, had nine children together: Linah, Mariah Ritty, Soph, Robert, Minty (Harriet), Ben, Rachel, Henry, and Moses.[9]

Rit struggled to keep her family together as slavery threatened to tear it apart. Edward Brodess sold three of her daughters (Linah, Mariah Ritty, and Soph), separating them from the family forever.[10] When a trader from Georgia approached Brodess about buying Rit's youngest son, Moses, she hid him for a month, aided by other slaves and free blacks in the community.[11] At one point she confronted her owner about the sale.[12] Finally, Brodess and "the Georgia man" came toward the slave quarters to seize the child, where Rit told them, "You are after my son; but the first man that comes into my house, I will split his head open."[12] Brodess backed away and abandoned the sale.[13] Tubman's biographers agree that stories told about this event within the family influenced her belief in the possibilities of resistance.[13][14]

## Childhood

Tubman's mother was assigned to "the big house"[15][16] and had scarce time for her family; consequently, as a child Tubman took care of a younger brother and baby, as was typical in large families.[17] When she was five or six years old, Brodess hired her out as a nursemaid to a woman named "Miss Susan." Tubman was ordered to care for the baby and rock its cradle as it slept; when it woke up and cried, she was whipped. She later recounted a particular day when she was lashed five times before breakfast. She carried the scars for the rest of her life.[18] She found ways to resist, such as running away for five days,[19] wearing layers of clothing as protection against beatings, and fighting back.[20]

As a child, Tubman also worked at the home of a planter named James Cook. She had to check the muskrat traps in nearby marshes, even after contracting measles. She became so ill that Cook sent her back to Brodess, where her mother nursed her back to health.

Brodess then hired her out again. She spoke later of her acute childhood homesickness, comparing herself to "the boy on the Swanee River," an allusion to Stephen Foster's song "Old Folks at Home."[21] As she grew older and stronger, she was assigned to field and forest work, driving oxen, plowing, and hauling logs.[22]

As an adolescent, Tubman suffered a severe head injury when an overseer threw a two-pound metal weight at another slave who was attempting to flee. The weight struck Tubman instead, which she said "broke my skull." Bleeding and unconscious, she was returned to her owner's house and laid on the seat of a loom, where she remained without medical care for two days.[23] After this incident, Tubman frequently experienced extremely painful headaches.[24] She also began having seizures and would seemingly fall unconscious, although she claimed to be aware of her surroundings while appearing to be asleep. This condition remained with her for the rest of her life; Larson suggests she may have suffered from temporal lobe epilepsy as a result of the injury.[25][26]

After her injury, Tubman began experiencing visions and vivid dreams, which she interpreted as revelations from God. These spiritual experiences had a profound effect on Tubman's personality and she acquired a passionate faith in God.[27] Although Tubman was illiterate, she was told Bible stories by her mother and likely attended a Methodist church with her family.[28][29] She rejected the teachings of the New Testament that urged slaves to be obedient, and found guidance in the Old Testament tales of deliverance. This religious perspective informed her actions throughout her life.[30]

## Family and marriage

Anthony Thompson promised to manumit Tubman's father at the age of 45. After Thompson died, his son followed through with that promise in 1840. Tubman's father continued working as a timber estimator and foreman for the Thompson family.[31] Several years later, Tubman contacted a white attorney and paid him five dollars to investigate her mother's legal status. The lawyer discovered that a former owner had issued instructions that Tubman's mother, Rit, like her husband, would be manumitted at the age of 45. The record showed that a similar provision would apply to Rit's children, and that any children born after she reached 45 years of age were legally free, but the Pattison and Brodess families ignored this stipulation when they inherited the slaves. Challenging it legally was an impossible task for Tubman.[32]

Around 1844, she married a free black man named John Tubman.[33] Although little is known about him or their time together, the union was complicated because of her slave status. The mother's status dictated that of children, and any children born to Harriet and John would be enslaved. Such blended marriages—free people of color marrying enslaved people—were not uncommon on the Eastern Shore of Maryland, where by this time, half the black population was free. Most African-American families had both free and enslaved members. Larson suggests that they might have planned to buy Tubman's freedom.[34]

Tubman changed her name from Araminta to Harriet soon after her marriage, though the exact timing is unclear. Larson suggests this happened right after the wedding,[33] and

Clinton suggests that it coincided with Tubman's plans to escape from slavery.[35] She adopted her mother's name, possibly as part of a religious conversion, or to honor another relative.[33][35]

## Escape from slavery

In 1849, Tubman became ill again, which diminished her value as a slave. Edward Brodess tried to sell her, but could not find a buyer.[36] Angry at him for trying to sell her and for continuing to enslave her relatives, Tubman began to pray for her owner, asking God to make him change his ways.[37] She said later: "I prayed all night long for my master till the first of March; and all the time he was bringing people to look at me, and trying to sell me." When it appeared as though a sale was being concluded, "I changed my prayer," she said. "First of March I began to pray, 'Oh Lord, if you ain't never going to change that man's heart, kill him, Lord, and take him out of the way.'"[38] A week later, Brodess died, and Tubman expressed regret for her earlier sentiments.[39]

As in many estate settlements, Brodess's death increased the likelihood that Tubman would be sold and her family broken apart.[40] His widow, Eliza, began working to sell the family's slaves.[41] Tubman refused to wait for the Brodess family to decide her fate, despite her husband's efforts to dissuade her.[42] "[T]here was one of two things I had a right to," she explained later, "liberty or death; if I could not have one, I would have the other."[43]

Tubman and her brothers, Ben and Henry, escaped from slavery on September 17, 1849. Tubman had been hired out to Dr. Anthony Thompson (the son of her father's former owner), who owned a large plantation in an area called Poplar Neck in neighboring Caroline County; it is likely her brothers labored for Thompson as well. Because the slaves were hired out to another household, Eliza Brodess probably did not recognize their absence as an escape attempt for some time. Two weeks later, she posted a runaway notice in the Cambridge *Democrat*, offering a reward of up to $100 for each slave returned. [44] Once they had left, Tubman's brothers had second thoughts. Ben may have just become a father. The two men went back, forcing Tubman to return with them.[45]

Soon afterward, Tubman escaped again, this time without her brothers.[46] She tried to send word of her plans beforehand to her mother. She sang a coded song to Mary, a trusted fellow slave, that was a farewell. "I'll meet you in the morning," she intoned, "I'm bound for the promised land."[47] While her exact route is unknown, Tubman made use of the network known as the Underground Railroad. This informal but well-organized system was composed of free and enslaved blacks, white abolitionists, and other activists. Most prominent among the latter in Maryland at the time were members of the Religious Society of Friends, often called Quakers.[46] The Preston area near Poplar Neck contained a substantial Quaker community and was probably an important first stop during Tubman's escape.[48] From there, she probably took a common route for fleeing slaves—northeast along the Choptank River, through Delaware and then north into Pennsylvania.[49] A journey of nearly 90 miles (145 kilometers) by foot would have taken between five days and three weeks.[50]

Tubman had to travel by night, guided by the North Star and trying to avoid slave catchers eager to collect rewards for fugitive slaves.[51] The "conductors" in the Underground Railroad used deceptions for protection. At an early stop, the lady of the house instructed Tubman to sweep the yard so as to seem to be working for the family. When night fell, the family hid her in a cart and took her to the next friendly house.[52] Given her familiarity with the woods and marshes of the region, Tubman likely hid in these locales during the day.[49] Particulars of her first journey remain shrouded in secrecy; because other fugitive slaves used the routes, Tubman did not discuss them until later in life.[53] She crossed into Pennsylvania with a feeling of relief and awe, and recalled the experience years later:

> When I found I had crossed that line, I looked at my hands to see if I was the same person. There was such a glory over everything; the sun came like gold through the trees, and over the fields, and I felt like I was in Heaven.[47]

## Nicknamed "Moses"

*Harriet Ross Tubman*

After reaching Philadelphia, Tubman thought of her family. "I was a stranger in a strange land," she said later. "[M]y father, my mother, my brothers, and sisters, and friends were [in Maryland]. But I was free, and *they* should be free."[54] She worked odd jobs and saved money.[55] The U.S. Congress meanwhile passed the Fugitive Slave Law of 1850, which heavily punished abetting escape and forced law enforcement officials—even in states that had outlawed slavery—to assist in their capture. The law increased risks for escaped slaves, more of whom therefore sought refuge in Southern Ontario (then part of the United Province of Canada) which, as part of the British Empire, had abolished slavery.[56] Racial tensions were also increasing in Philadelphia as waves of poor Irish immigrants competed with free blacks for work.[57]

In December 1850, Tubman was warned that her niece Kessiah and her two children, six-year-old James Alfred, and baby Araminta, soon would be sold in Cambridge. Tubman went to Baltimore, where her brother-in-law Tom Tubman hid her until the sale. Kessiah's husband, a free black man named John Bowley, made the winning bid for his wife. Then, while the auctioneer stepped away to have lunch, John, Kessiah and their children escaped to a nearby safe house. When night fell, Bowley sailed the family on a log canoe 60 miles (97 kilometres) to Baltimore, where they met with Tubman, who brought the family to Philadelphia.[58]

The next spring she returned to Maryland to help guide away other family members. During her second trip, she recovered her brother Moses and two unidentified men.[59] Tubman likely worked with abolitionist Thomas Garrett, a Quaker working in Wilmington, Delaware.[60] Word of her exploits had encouraged her family, and biographers agree that with each trip to Maryland, she became more confident.[59][61]

In the fall of 1851, Tubman returned to Dorchester County for the first time since her escape, this time to find her husband John. She saved money from various jobs, purchased a suit for him, and made her way south. Meanwhile, John had married another woman named Caroline. Tubman sent word that he should join her, but he insisted that he was happy where he was. Tubman at first prepared to storm their house and make a scene, but then decided he was not worth the trouble. Suppressing her anger, she found some slaves who wanted to escape and led them to Philadelphia.[62] John and Caroline raised a family together, until he was killed 16 years later in a roadside argument with a white man named Robert Vincent.[63]

Because the Fugitive Slave Law had made the northern United States a more dangerous place for escaped slaves to remain, many escaped slaves began migrating to Southern Ontario.

*Frederick Douglass, who worked for slavery's abolition alongside Tubman, praised her in print.*

In December 1851, Tubman guided an unidentified group of 11 fugitives, possibly including the Bowleys and several others she had helped rescue earlier, northward. There is evidence to suggest that Tubman and her group stopped at the home of abolitionist and former slave Frederick Douglass.[64] In his third autobiography, Douglass wrote: "On one occasion I had eleven fugitives at the same time under my roof, and it was necessary for them to remain with me until I could collect sufficient money to get them on to Canada. It was the largest number I ever had at any one time, and I had some difficulty in providing so many with food and shelter. . . ."[65] The number of travelers and the time of the visit make it likely that this was Tubman's group.[64]

Douglass and Tubman admired one another greatly as they both struggled against slavery. When an early biography of Tubman was being prepared in 1868, Douglass wrote a letter to honor her. He compared his own efforts with hers, writing:

> The difference between us is very marked. Most that I have done and suffered in the service of our cause has been in public, and I have received much encouragement at every step of the way. You, on the other hand, have labored in a private way. I have wrought in the day—you in the night. ... The midnight sky and the silent stars have been the witnesses of your devotion to freedom and of your heroism. Excepting John Brown—of sacred memory—I know of no one who has willingly encountered more perils and hardships to serve our enslaved people than you have.[66]

Over 11 years, Tubman returned repeatedly to the Eastern Shore of Maryland, rescuing some 70 slaves in about 13 expeditions,[2] including her other brothers, Henry, Ben, and Robert, their wives and some of their children. She also provided specific instructions to 50 to 60 additional fugitives who escaped to the north.[2] Because of her efforts, she was nicknamed "Moses," alluding to the prophet in the Book of Exodus who led the Hebrews to freedom from Egypt.[67] One of her last missions into Maryland was to retrieve her aging parents. Her father, Ben, had purchased Rit, her mother, in 1855 from Eliza Brodess for $20.[68] But even when they were both free, the area became hostile to their presence. Two years later, Tubman received word that her father was at risk of arrest for harboring a group of eight escaped slaves. She traveled to the Eastern Shore and led them north to St. Catharines, Ontario, where a community of former slaves (including Tubman's brothers, other relatives, and many friends) had gathered.[69]

## Routes and methods

Tubman's dangerous work required tremendous ingenuity; she usually worked during winter months, to minimize the likelihood that the group would be seen. One admirer of Tubman said: "She always came in the winter, when the nights are long and dark, and people who have homes stay in them."[70] Once she had made contact with escaping slaves, they left town on Saturday evenings, since newspapers would not print runaway notices until Monday morning.[71]

Her journeys into the land of slavery put her at tremendous risk, and she used a variety of subterfuges to avoid detection. Tubman once disguised herself with a bonnet and carried two live chickens to give the appearance of running errands. Suddenly finding herself walking toward a former owner in Dorchester County, she yanked the strings holding the birds' legs, and their agitation allowed her to avoid eye contact.[72] Later she recognized a fellow train passenger as another former master; she snatched a nearby newspaper and pretended to read. Since Tubman was known to be illiterate, the man ignored her.[73]

While being interviewed by author Wilbur Siebert in 1897, Tubman named some of the people who helped her and places that she stayed along the Underground Railroad. She stayed with Sam Green, a free black minister living in East New Market, Maryland; she also hid near her parents' home at Poplar Neck. She would travel from there northeast to Sandtown and Willow Grove, Delaware, and to the Camden area where free black agents, William and Nat Brinkley and Abraham Gibbs, guided her north past Dover, Smyrna, and Blackbird, where other agents would take her across the Chesapeake and Delaware Canal to New Castle and Wilmington. In Wilmington, Quaker Thomas Garrett would secure transportation to William Still's office or the homes of other Underground Railroad operators in the greater Philadelphia area. Still is credited with aiding hundreds of freedom seekers escape to safer places farther north in New York, New England, and present-day Southern Ontario.[74]

Tubman's religious faith was another important resource as she ventured repeatedly into Maryland. The visions from her childhood head injury continued, and she saw them as divine premonitions. She spoke of "consulting with God," and trusted that He would keep her safe.[75] Thomas Garrett once said of her, "I never met with any person of any color who had more confidence in the voice of God, as spoken direct to her soul."[76] Her faith in the divine also provided immediate assistance. She used spirituals as coded messages, warning fellow travelers of danger or to signal a clear path. She sang versions of "Go Down Moses" and changed the lyrics to indicate that it was either safe or too dangerous to proceed.[77] As she led fugitives across the border, she would call out, "Glory to God and Jesus, too. One more soul is safe!"[78]

Tubman also carried a revolver, and was not afraid to use it. The gun afforded some protection from the ever-present slave catchers and their dogs; however, she also purportedly threatened to shoot any escaped slave who tried to turn back on the journey since that would threaten the safety of the remaining group.[79] Tubman told the tale of one man who insisted he was going to go back to the plantation when morale got low among a group of fugitive slaves. She pointed the gun at his head and said, "You go on or die."[80] Several days later, he was with the group as they entered Canada.[75]

Slaveholders in the region, meanwhile, never knew that "Minty," the petite, five-foot-tall, disabled slave who had run away years before and never come back, was behind so many slave escapes in their community. By the late 1850s, they began to suspect a northern white abolitionist was secretly enticing their slaves away. While a popular legend persists about a reward of $40,000 for Tubman's capture, this is a manufactured figure. In 1868, in an effort to drum up support for Tubman's claim for a Civil War military pension, a former abolitionist named Salley Holley wrote an article claiming $40,000 "was not too great a reward for Maryland slaveholders to offer for her."[81] Such a high reward would have garnered national attention, especially at a time when a small farm could be purchased for a mere $400. No such reward has been found in period newspapers. (The federal government offered $25,000 for the capture of each of John Wilkes Booth's co-conspirators in President Lincoln's assassination.) A reward offering of $12,000 has also been claimed, though no documentation exists for that figure either. Catherine Clinton suggests that the $40,000 figure may have been a combined total of the various bounties offered around the region.[82]

Despite the best efforts of the slaveholders, Tubman was never captured, and neither were the fugitives she guided. Years later, she told an audience: "I was conductor of the Underground Railroad for eight years, and I can say what most conductors can't say—I never ran my train off the track and I never lost a passenger."[3]

## John Brown and Harpers Ferry

In April 1858, Tubman was introduced to the abolitionist John Brown, an insurgent who advocated the use of violence to destroy slavery in the United States. Although she never advocated violence against whites, she agreed with his course of direct action and supported his goals.[83] Like Tubman, he spoke of being called by God, and trusted the divine to protect him from the wrath of slaveholders. She, meanwhile, claimed to have had a prophetic vision of meeting Brown before their encounter.[84]

Thus, as he began recruiting supporters for an attack on slaveholders, Brown was joined by "General Tubman," as he called her.[83] Her knowledge of support networks

*Tubman helped John Brown plan and recruit for the raid at Harpers Ferry.*

and resources in the border states of Pennsylvania, Maryland and Delaware was invaluable to Brown and his planners. Although other abolitionists like Douglass did not endorse his tactics, Brown dreamed of fighting to create a new state for freed slaves, and made preparations for military action. He believed that after he began the first battle, slaves would rise up and carry out a rebellion across the slave states.[85] He asked Tubman to gather former slaves then living in present-day Southern Ontario who might be willing to join his fighting force, which she did.[86]

On May 8, 1858, Brown held a meeting in Chatham, Ontario, where he unveiled his plan for a raid on Harpers Ferry, Virginia.[87] When word of the plan was leaked to the government, Brown put the scheme on hold and began raising funds for its eventual resumption. Tubman aided him in this effort and with more detailed plans for the assault.[88]

Tubman was busy during this time, giving talks to abolitionist audiences and tending to her relatives. In the autumn of 1859, as Brown and his men prepared to launch the attack, Tubman could not be contacted.[89] When the raid on Harpers Ferry took place on October 16, Tubman was not present. Some historians believe she was in New York at the time, ill with fever related to her childhood head injury.[89] Others propose she may have been recruiting more escaped slaves in Ontario,[90] and Kate Clifford Larson suggests she may have been in Maryland, recruiting for Brown's raid or attempting to rescue more family members.[91] Larson also notes that Tubman may have begun sharing Frederick Douglass's doubts about the viability of the plan.[91]

The raid failed; Brown was convicted of treason and hanged in December. His actions were seen by abolitionists as a symbol of proud resistance, carried out by a noble martyr.[92] Tubman herself was effusive with praise. She later told a friend: "[H]e done more in dying, than 100 men would in living."[93]

## Auburn and Margaret

In early 1859, abolitionist Republican U.S. Senator William H. Seward sold Tubman a small piece of land on the outskirts of Auburn, New York, for $1,200.[94] The city was a hotbed of antislavery activism, and Tubman seized the opportunity to deliver her parents from the harsh Canadian winters.[95] Returning to the U.S. meant that escaped slaves were at risk of being returned to the south under the Fugitive Slave Law, and Tubman's siblings expressed reservations. Catherine Clinton suggests that anger over the 1857 Dred Scott decision may have prompted Tubman to return to the U.S.[95] Her land in Auburn became a haven for Tubman's family and friends. For years, she took in relatives and boarders, offering a safe place for black Americans seeking a better life in the north.[63]

Shortly after acquiring the Auburn property, Tubman went back to Maryland and returned with her "niece," an eight-year-old light-skinned black girl named Margaret. [95] There is great confusion about the identity of Margaret's parents, although Tubman indicated they were free blacks. The girl left behind a twin brother and both parents in Maryland.[95][96] Years later, Margaret's daughter Alice called Tubman's actions selfish, saying, "she had taken the child from a sheltered good home to a place where there was nobody to care for her."[97] Alice described it as a "kidnapping."[98]

However, both Clinton and Larson present the possibility that Margaret was in fact Tubman's daughter.[99][100] Larson points out that the two shared an unusually strong bond, and argues that Tubman—knowing the pain of a child separated from her mother—would never have intentionally caused a free family to be split apart.[101] Clinton presents evidence of strong physical similarities, which Alice herself acknowledged.[99] Both historians agree that no concrete evidence exists for such a possibility, and the mystery of Tubman's relationship with young Margaret remains to this day.[102]

In November 1860, Tubman conducted her last rescue mission. Throughout the 1850s, Tubman had been unable to effect the escape of her sister Rachel, and Rachel's two children Ben and Angerine. Upon returning to Dorchester County, Tubman discovered that Rachel had died, and the children could be rescued only if she could pay a $30 bribe. She had no money, so the children remained enslaved. Their fates remain unknown. Never one to waste a trip, Tubman gathered another group, including the Ennalls family, ready and willing to take the risks of the journey north. It took them weeks to safely get away because of slave catchers forcing them to hide out longer than expected. The weather was unseasonably cold and they had little food. The children were drugged with paregoric to keep them quiet while slave patrols rode by. They safely reached the home of David and Martha Wright in Auburn on December 28, 1860.[103]

## American Civil War

*Tubman in the late 1860s*

When the Civil War broke out in 1861, Tubman saw a Union victory as a key step toward the abolition of slavery. General Benjamin Butler, for instance, aided escaped slaves flooding into Fort Monroe in Virginia. [104] Butler had declared these fugitives to be "contraband"—property seized by northern forces—and put them to work, initially without pay, in the fort. [105] Tubman hoped to offer her own expertise and skills to the Union cause, too, and soon she joined a group of Boston and Philadelphia abolitionists heading to the Hilton Head district in South Carolina. She became a fixture in the camps, particularly in Port Royal, South Carolina, assisting fugitives.[106]

Tubman met with General David Hunter, a strong

supporter of abolition. He declared all of the "contrabands" in the Port Royal district free, and began gathering former slaves for a regiment of black soldiers.[107] U.S. President Abraham Lincoln, however, was not prepared to enforce emancipation on the southern states, and reprimanded Hunter for his actions.[107] Tubman condemned Lincoln's response and his general unwillingness to consider ending slavery in the U.S., for both moral and practical reasons. "God won't let master Lincoln beat the South till he does *the right thing*," she said.

> Master Lincoln, he's a great man, and I am a poor negro; but the negro can tell master Lincoln how to save the money and the young men. He can do it by setting the negro free. Suppose that was an awful big snake down there, on the floor. He bite you. Folks all scared, because you die. You send for a doctor to cut the bite; but the snake, he rolled up there, and while the doctor doing it, he bite you *again*. The doctor dug out *that* bite; but while the doctor doing it, the snake, he spring up and bite you again; so he *keep* doing it, till you kill *him*. That's what master Lincoln ought to know.[108]

Tubman served as a nurse in Port Royal, preparing remedies from local plants and aiding soldiers suffering from dysentery. She rendered assistance to men with smallpox; that she did not contract the disease herself started more rumors that she was blessed by God. [109] At first, she received government rations for her work, but newly freed blacks thought she was getting special treatment. To ease the tension, she gave up her right to these supplies and made money selling pies and root beer, which she made in the evenings.[110]

## Scouting and the Combahee River Raid

HARRIET TUBMAN.

*A woodcut of Tubman in her Civil War clothing*

When Lincoln finally issued the Emancipation Proclamation in January 1863, Tubman considered it an important step toward the goal of liberating all black people from slavery. [111] She renewed her support for a defeat of the Confederacy, and before long she was leading a band of scouts through the land around Port Royal.[112] The marshes and rivers in South Carolina were similar to those of the Eastern Shore of Maryland; thus her knowledge of covert travel and subterfuge among potential enemies was put to good use.[112] Her group, working under the orders of Secretary of War Edwin Stanton, mapped the unfamiliar terrain and reconnoitered its inhabitants. She later worked alongside Colonel James Montgomery, and provided him with key intelligence that aided the capture of Jacksonville, Florida.[113]

Later that year, Tubman became the first woman to lead an armed assault during the Civil War.[114] When Montgomery and his troops conducted an assault on a collection of plantations along the Combahee River, Tubman served as a key adviser and accompanied the raid. On the morning of June 2, 1863, Tubman guided three steamboats around Confederate mines in the waters leading to the shore.[115] Once ashore, the Union troops set fire to the plantations, destroying infrastructure and seizing thousands of dollars worth of food and supplies.[116] When the steamboats sounded their whistles, slaves throughout the area understood that it was being liberated. Tubman watched as slaves stampeded toward the boats. "I never saw such a sight," she said later,[117] describing a scene of chaos with women carrying still-steaming pots of rice, pigs squealing in bags slung over shoulders, and babies hanging around their parents' necks. Although their owners, armed with handguns and whips, tried to stop the mass escape, their efforts were nearly useless in the tumult.[116] As Confederate troops raced to the scene, steamboats packed full of slaves took off toward Beaufort.[118]

More than 750 slaves were rescued in the Combahee River Raid.[119][120] Newspapers heralded Tubman's "patriotism, sagacity, energy, [and] ability,"[121] and she was praised for her recruiting efforts—most of the newly liberated men went on to join the Union army. [122] Tubman later worked with Colonel Robert Gould Shaw at the assault on Fort Wagner, reportedly serving him his last meal.[123] She described the battle by saying: "And then we saw the lightning, and that was the guns; and then we heard the thunder, and that was the big guns; and then we heard the rain falling, and that was the drops of blood falling; and when we came to get the crops, it was dead men that we reaped."[124]

For two more years, Tubman worked for the Union forces, tending to newly liberated slaves, scouting into Confederate territory, and nursing wounded soldiers in Virginia. [125] She also made periodic trips back to Auburn to visit her family and care for her parents.[126] The Confederacy surrendered in April 1865; after donating several more months of service, Tubman headed home to Auburn.[127]

During a train ride to New York, the conductor told her to move into the smoking car. She refused, explaining her government service. He cursed at her and grabbed her, but she resisted and he summoned two other passengers for help. While she clutched at the railing, they muscled her away, breaking her arm in the process. They threw her into the smoking car, causing more injuries. As these events transpired, other white passengers cursed Tubman and shouted for the conductor to kick her off the train.[128]

## Later life

Despite her years of service, Tubman never received a regular salary and was for years denied compensation.[129][130] Her unofficial status and the unequal payments offered to black soldiers caused great difficulty in documenting her service, and the U.S. government was slow in recognizing its debt to her.[131] Her constant humanitarian work for her family and former slaves, meanwhile, kept her in a state of constant poverty, and her difficulties in obtaining a government pension were especially taxing for her.[132]

Tubman spent her remaining years in Auburn, tending to her family and other people in need. She worked various jobs to support her elderly parents, and took in boarders to help pay the bills.[63] One of the people Tubman took in was a 5-foot, 11-inch tall farmer

*Harriet Tubman after the Civil War*

named Nelson Charles Davis. Born in North Carolina, he had served as a private in the 8th United States Colored Infantry Regiment from September 1863 to November 1865.[133] He began working in Auburn as a bricklayer, and they soon fell in love. Though he was 22 years younger than she was, on March 18, 1869, they were married at the Central Presbyterian Church.[134][135] They adopted a baby girl named Gertie in 1874, and lived together as a family; Nelson died on October 14, 1888, of tuberculosis.[136][137]

Tubman's friends and supporters from the days of abolition, meanwhile, raised funds to support her. One admirer, Sarah Hopkins Bradford, wrote an authorized biography entitled *Scenes in the Life of Harriet Tubman*. The 132-page volume was published in 1869 and brought Tubman some $1,200 in income.[138] Criticized by modern biographers for its artistic license and highly subjective point of view,[139] the book nevertheless remains an important source of information and perspective on Tubman's life. In 1886 Bradford released another volume, also intended to help alleviate Tubman's poverty, called *Harriet, the Moses of her People*.[140]

*Tubman in 1887 (far left), with her husband Davis (seated, with cane), their adopted daughter Gertie (beside Tubman), Lee Cheney, John "Pop" Alexander, Walter Green, "Blind Aunty" Sarah Parker, and her great-niece Dora Stewart at Tubman's home in Auburn, New York*

As Tubman aged, the seizures, headaches, and suffering from her childhood head trauma continued to plague her. At some point in the late 1890s, she underwent brain surgery at Boston's Massachusetts General Hospital. Unable to sleep because of pains and "buzzing" in her head, she asked a doctor if he could operate. He agreed and, in her words, "sawed open my skull, and raised it up, and now it feels more comfortable."[165] She had received no anesthesia for the procedure and reportedly chose instead to bite down on a bullet, as she had seen Civil War soldiers do when their limbs were amputated.[166]

By 1911, Tubman's body was so frail that she was admitted into the rest home named in her honor. A New York newspaper described her as "ill and penniless," prompting supporters to offer a new round of donations.[167] Surrounded by friends and family members, she died of pneumonia in 1913.[167] Just before she died, she told those in the room: "I go to prepare a place for you."[168] Tubman was buried with semi-military honors at Fort Hill Cemetery in Auburn.[169]

# Elizabeth Van Lew

*Portrait of Elizabeth Van Lew*

**Elizabeth Van Lew** (October 12, 1818–September 25, 1900) was a Richmond, Virginia abolitionist and philanthropist who built and operated an extensive spy ring for the Union Army during the American Civil War.

## American Civil War

Upon the outbreak of the war, Van Lew began working on behalf of the Union with her mother, caring for wounded soldiers.[4] When Libby Prison was opened in Richmond, Van Lew was allowed to bring food, clothing, writing paper, and other things to the Union soldiers imprisoned there. She aided prisoners in escape attempts, passing them information about safe houses and getting a Union sympathizer appointed to the prison staff.[6] Recently captured prisoners gave Van Lew information on Confederate troop levels and movements, which she was able to pass on to Union commanders.[4] She even helped hide escaped Union prisoners and Confederate deserters in her own mansion.[7]

Van Lew also operated a spy ring during the war, called "Richmond Underground," including clerks in the War and Navy Departments of the Confederacy and a Richmond mayoral candidate. Van Lew reportedly convinced Varina Davis to hire Bowser as a household servant, enabling Bowser to spy in the White House of the Confederacy.[6] Varina Davis adamantly denied ever hiring Bowser, although it would be unlikely she would have known of Bowser's real identity or admitted hiring her after the fact.[8] Although Bowser used several pseudonyms during and after the war, making her contributions especially difficult to document, newly uncovered sources confirm her involvement in the Union espionage circle run by Van Lew.[9] Van Lew's spy network was so efficient that on several occasions she sent Lt. Gen. Ulysses S. Grant fresh flowers from her garden and a copy of the Richmond newspaper.[6] She developed a cipher system and often smuggled messages out of Richmond in hollow eggs.[6] Union commanders highly valued Van Lew's work; George H. Sharpe, intelligence officer for the Army of the Potomac, credited her with "the greater portion of our intelligence in 1864–65." Because of the merit of her work, General Grant appointed Van Lew Postmaster General of Richmond for the next eight years.[10]

In 1864, Van Lew risked her entire spy network to see that the corpse of Union Col. Ulric Dahlgren, who died trying to free Union prisoners in Richmond, was properly buried. Reports of disrespectful display of his corpse had outraged Northern public opinion, and Van Lew herself. Furthermore, during the long siege of Petersburg, Van Lew assisted civilians of both sides.[1]

## Postwar life

When Richmond fell to U.S. forces in April 1865, Van Lew was the first person to raise the United States flag in the city.[7]

On Grant's first visit to Richmond after the war, he had tea with Van Lew, and later appointed her postmaster of Richmond.[11] Grant said of her, "You have sent me the most valuable information received from Richmond during the war." Van Lew modernized the city's postal system and employed several African-Americans until new President Rutherford B. Hayes had her replaced in 1877.[12] She was allowed to return as a postal clerk in Richmond, where she served from 1883 to 1887.[1]

After the Reconstruction, Van Lew became increasingly ostracized in Richmond. "No one will walk with us on the street," she wrote, "no one will go with us anywhere; and it grows worse and worse as the years roll on."[7] She reportedly persuaded the United States Department of War to give her all of her records, so she could hide the true extent of her espionage from her neighbors. Having spent her family's fortune on intelligence activities during the war, she tried in vain to be reimbursed by the federal government. [11] When attempts to secure a government pension also failed, the elderly spinster turned to the family and friends of Union Col. Paul Joseph Revere, whom she had helped at the Henrico County Jail in 1862. These Bostonians gladly collected money for the woman who helped so many Union soldiers during the war.[13] However, neighborhood children, including future novelist Ellen Glasgow, were told to consider her a witch.[1]

## Death and legacy

Van Lew died on September 25, 1900, (aged 81), and was buried in Richmond's Shockoe Hill Cemetery. She was purportedly buried vertically, facing the north, and relatives of Union Colonel Paul J. Revere, whom she had aided during the war, donated the tombstone. Even into the twentieth century, however, many Southerners regarded Van Lew as a traitor.

In her will, Van Lew bequeathed her personal manuscripts, including her account of the war, to John P. Reynolds, Col. Revere's nephew. In 1911 Reynolds was able to convince the scholar William G. Beymer to publish the first biography of Van Lew in *Harper's Monthly*. The biography indicated that Van Lew had been so successful in her spying activities because she had feigned lunacy, and this idea won Van Lew the nickname "Crazy Bet." However, it is unlikely that Van Lew actually did pretend to be crazy. Instead, she probably would have relied on the Victorian custom of female charity to cover her espionage.[14]

The city of Richmond acquired and demolished the Van Lew mansion, her former home, in 1911, during a period of increasing racial polarization.[15] Bellevue Elementary School (which still remains) was erected on the site the following year. Historical plaques and a marker now memorialize her activities, and those of Bowser (a/k/a Mary Jane Richards).[16] Furthermore, the daughter of two of Van Lew's servants, Maggie Walker, became a prominent Christian entrepreneur in Richmond, founding the country's first African-American-woman owned bank.

Elizabeth Van Lew was inducted into the Military Intelligence Hall of Fame in 1993.

# Loreta Janeta Velázquez

*Loreta Janeta Velázquez as herself (right) and disguised as "Lieutenant Harry T. Buford" (left)*

**Loreta Janeta Velázquez** (June 26, 1842–1923), was a Cuban-born woman who masqueraded as a male Confederate soldier during the American Civil War. After her soldier husband's accidental death, she enlisted in the Confederate States Army in 1861. She then fought at Bull Run, Ball's Bluff, and Fort Donelson, but was discharged when her gender was discovered while in New Orleans. Undeterred, she reenlisted and fought at Shiloh, until unmasked once more. She then became a Confederate spy, working in both male and female guises, and as a double agent also reporting to the U.S. Secret Service. She remarried three more times, being widowed in each instance. According to William C. Davis, she died in January 1923 under the name Loretta J. Beard after many years away from the public eye in a public psychiatric facility, St. Elizabeths Hospital. She spied on the Union for about 5 years.

## The Woman in Battle

Velázquez recorded her adventures in her 600-page book, *The Woman in Battle: A Narrative of the Exploits, Adventures, and travels of Madame Loreta Janeta Velázquez, Otherwise Known as Lieutenant Harry T. Buford, Confederate States Army* (1876) to support her son.[1] The Confederate general Jubal Early refused to accept her memoirs as fact, but recent scholars have verified some of her claims on the basis of secondary documents, including stories in contemporary newspapers.[2]

## Birth and family

Loreta Janeta Velázquez was born in Havana, Cuba, on June 26, 1842, to a wealthy Cuban official and a mother of French and American ancestry. She also used the name Alice Williams. According to her own account, Velázquez was of Castilian descent and related to Cuban governor Diego Velázquez de Cuéllar and artist Diego Velázquez.

Her father was a Spanish government official who owned plantations in Mexico and Cuba. He felt a deep resentment towards the United States after losing an inherited ranch in the Mexican–American War at San Luis Potosi. This animosity perpetuated the estrangement between Velázquez and her father after her elopement with an American soldier.

Velázquez learned the English language at school in New Orleans in 1849, while living with an aunt. Her father's wealth as a plantation owner allowed her this opportunity to travel and continue her education.[3] While in New Orleans, Velázquez took to fairy tales and stories of heroism, citing Joan of Arc as a particular inspiration.[4]

Velázquez was engaged young to Raphael, a Spaniard, in what she referred to in her memoir as a "marriage of convenience." [4] At fourteen years old, she eloped with a Texas United States Army officer known only as William on April 5, 1856, despite the threats to be sent to a convent or back to Cuba from her family.[4] Her decision to elope was poorly received by her family, causing their estrangement.[4] She initially continued to live with her aunt, but after a quarrel with her she moved in with her husband and lived at various army posts, estranging herself further from her family by converting to Methodism.[5]

## American Civil War

At the outbreak of the American Civil War, Velázquez's husband resigned his U.S. commission and joined the Confederate Army. The couple became more interested in the Civil War after the early deaths of three of their children.[6] At first, William actually aided Velázquez in her endeavors to cross-dress and to enlist. He agreed to a night out together with Velázquez disguised as a man, assured that upon seeing the behavior of other men she would be dissuaded. Velázquez's desires to enlist, however, were only strengthened. [7] Velázquez failed to convince her husband to let her join him, so she acquired two uniforms, adopted the name Harry T. Buford and moved to Arkansas. There she recruited 236 men in four days, shipped them to Pensacola, Florida, and presented them to her husband as her command.[8] Her husband died soon after in an accident while he was demonstrating the use of weapons to his troops.[8] Velázquez turned her men over to a friend and began to search for more things to do.

Her first experience in combat was as an independent soldier in the First Battle of Bull Run. She eventually grew tired of camp life, however, and again donned female garb to go to Washington, D.C., where she spied for the Confederacy. She claimed to meet Abraham Lincoln and Secretary of War Simon Cameron on this excursion. When she returned to the South, she was assigned to the detective corps. She later left for Tennessee.

In Tennessee, she fought in the siege of Fort Donelson until the surrender. She was wounded in battle, but was not exposed. She fled to New Orleans, where she was arrested, suspected of being a female Union spy in disguise. After she was released, she enlisted to get away from the city.

At Shiloh, she found the battalion she had raised in Arkansas and fought in the battle. As she was burying the dead after a battle, a stray shell wounded her. When the army doctor who examined her discovered she was a woman, she again fled to New Orleans and saw Major General Benjamin F. Butler take command of the city. She gave up her uniform at that point.

Afterwards, in Richmond, Virginia, authorities again hired her as a spy and she began to travel all around the US. At that time, she married a Captain Thomas DeCaulp; he reportedly died soon after in a Chattanooga hospital. (An officer of that name is known to have survived the war.)

She then traveled north where officials hired her to search for herself. In Ohio and Indiana, she tried to organize a rebellion of Confederate prisoners of war.

## Travels

After the war, Velázquez traveled in Europe with her brother, as well as throughout South America and the southern United States.[9] She married Major Wasson and emigrated with him to Venezuela. When he died in Caracas, she returned to the United States. During her subsequent travels around the U.S., she gave birth to a baby boy and met Brigham Young in Utah. She arrived in Omaha, almost penniless, but charmed General W. S. Harney into giving her blankets and a revolver.[10] Two days after her arrival in the mining area of Nevada, she received a proposal of marriage from a sixty-year-old man,[10] which she refused. After eventually marrying a younger man, whose name is not known, Velázquez soon left Nevada, travelling with her baby.

## Reception of her book

Her book appeared in print in 1876. In the preface, Velázquez stated that she had written the book primarily for money so she could support her child, perhaps to combat the notion of her profiting from the war.[9] The veracity of the account was attacked almost immediately, and remains an issue with scholars. Some claim it is probably entirely fiction, others that the details in the text show a familiarity with the times that would be difficult to completely simulate.

Shortly after its appearance, former Confederate General Jubal Early denounced the book as an obvious fiction.[11]

In 2007, The History Channel aired *Full Metal Corset*, a program that presented details of Velázquez's story as genuine. However, the overall truthfulness of her account remains indeterminate and highly questionable.

## Career after the war

She became very active in public life and politics, and was particularly involved in grand speculative schemes around mining and railway building, as well as being involved in journalism and writing. Her biographer William C. Davis suggests that her actions were generally fraudulent, intending to raise money for herself and associates, although such schemes were typical business practices at that date. Some press accounts were impressed by her vitality and business acumen, such as in an 1891 account from the *New York Herald* reprinted in the *Saturday Evening Mail* Terre Haute. Here Velázquez was described as "a woman of business, a woman who can 'run things like a man.'"[12]

## Death

Loreta Janeta Velázquez is said to have died in 1897, but historian Richard Hall states that her death is unknown and the place and date of her death are also unknown. Hall, in *Patriots in Disguise*, takes a hard look at *The Woman in Battle* and analyzes whether its claims are accurate or fictionalized. Elizabeth Leonard, in *All the Daring of the Soldier,* assesses *The Woman in Battle* as largely fiction, but based on real experience. A newspaper report mentions a Lieutenant Bensford arrested when it was disclosed that "he" was actually a woman, and gives her name as Alice Williams, a name which Loreta Velázquez apparently also used.

# James Iredell Waddell

**James Iredell Waddell** (July 3, 1824–March 15, 1886) was an officer in the United States Navy and later in the Confederate States Navy.

During the American Civil War, Waddell took command of the CSS *Shenandoah*, which he used to sail around the globe and launch raids against the U.S. Navy. It was not until August 1865 that he learned the war had ended. He eventually surrendered his vessel to British authorities in Liverpool on November 6, marking the last official surrender of the Civil War.

## Early life and career

Waddell was born in Pittsboro, North Carolina. He joined the United States Navy as a Midshipman in September 1841, and later graduated from the United States Naval Academy. His nearly two decades in the U.S. Navy included early service in USS *Pennsylvania*, Mexican–American War operations off Veracruz aboard USS *Somers*, a tour off South America in USS *Germantown*, an assignment as a United States Naval Academy instructor, eastern Pacific duty in USS *Saginaw* and a cruise with the East Indies Squadron with USS *John Adams*. Lieutenant Waddell resigned his commission while returning home in the latter ship late in 1861 at the outbreak of the American Civil War and was dismissed from the U.S. Navy in January 1862.

## American Civil War

In March 1862, Waddell was appointed a Lieutenant in the Confederate States Navy. Sent to New Orleans, he was assigned to the incomplete ironclad CSS *Mississippi* until her destruction in late April. The next month, while serving as an artillery officer ashore, he participated in the battle between Confederate shore batteries and Federal ironclads at Drewry's Bluff, Virginia. He saw more shore-battery service at Charleston, South Carolina, during the rest of 1862 and into 1863. Sent abroad in March 1863, First Lieutenant Waddell was stationed in England awaiting the availability of a seagoing position.

That opportunity finally arrived in October 1864 at sea in the central Atlantic, where he converted the British steam/sailer *Sea King* to the Confederate cruiser CSS *Shenandoah*. As her commanding officer, Commander Waddell made a long and productive cruise through the south Atlantic, across the Indian Ocean and into the north Pacific. In the Arctic waters there, he devastated the United States-flagged whaling fleet during June 1865.

On June 27, 1865, he learned from a prize, the *Susan & Abigail*, that General Robert E. Lee had surrendered his Army of Northern Virginia. Her captain produced a San

Francisco newspaper reporting the flight from Richmond, Virginia, of the Confederate Government 10 weeks previously. However, the newspaper also contained Confederate President Jefferson Davis's proclamation that the "war would be carried on with re-newed vigor."[1] Waddell then captured 10 more whalers in the space of 7 hours just below the Arctic Circle.

On August 3, 1865, Waddell finally learned of the war's end when he met at sea the Liverpool barque *Barracouta*, which was bound for San Francisco.[2] He received the news of the surrender of General Joseph E. Johnston's army on April 26, Kirby Smith's army's surrender on May 26, and crucially the capture of President Davis and a part of his cabinet. Captain Waddell then knew that the war was over.[1]

Waddell lowered his Confederate flag, and the CSS *Shenandoah* underwent physical alteration. Her guns were dismounted and stored below deck, and her hull was painted to look like an ordinary merchant vessel.[3]

Captain Waddell presided over the last official lowering of the Confederate flag when he surrendered the CSS *Shenandoah* to Captain Paynter of HMS *Donegal* on November 6, 1865, in mid-river on the River Mersey at Liverpool. The banner was lowered in front of the crew and of a Royal Navy detachment who had boarded the vessel—this marked the last surrender of the American Civil War. The very last act of the Civil War involved Captain Waddell walking up the steps of Liverpool Town Hall with a letter to present to the Mayor of Liverpool surrendering his vessel to the British government.[4]

## Later life

Waddell did not return to the United States until 1870,[5] when he became captain of the commercial steamer *City of San Francisco*. He later was in charge of the State of Maryland's oyster regulation force.

He died at Annapolis, Maryland on March 15, 1886, and was buried at St. Anne's Cemetery in Annapolis.

# Mary Edwards Walker

*Walker with her Medal of Honor*

**Mary Edwards Walker, M.D.** (November 26, 1832–February 21, 1919), commonly referred to as **Dr. Mary Walker**, was an American abolitionist, prohibitionist, prisoner of war and surgeon.[1] She is the only woman to ever receive the Medal of Honor.[2]

In 1855, she earned her medical degree at Syracuse Medical College in New York,[3] married and started a medical practice. She volunteered with the Union Army at the outbreak of the American Civil War and served as a surgeon at a temporary hospital in Washington, D.C., even though at the time women and sectarian physicians were considered unfit for the Union Army Examining Board.[4] She was captured by Confederate forces[3] after crossing enemy lines to treat wounded civilians and arrested as a spy. She was sent as a prisoner of war to Richmond, Virginia until released in a prisoner exchange.

After the war, she was approved for the Medal of Honor, for her efforts to treat the wounded during the Civil War. Notably, the award was not expressly given for gallantry in action at that time, and in fact was the only military decoration during the Civil War. Walker is the only woman to receive the medal and one of only eight civilians to receive it. Her name was deleted from the Army Medal of Honor Roll in 1917 (along with over 900 other, male MOH recipients); however, it was restored in 1977.[3] After the war, she was a writer and lecturer supporting the women's suffrage movement until her death in 1919.

## American Civil War

Walker volunteered at the outbreak of American Civil War as a surgeon—first for the Army, but was rejected because she was a woman (despite having kept a private practice for many years). She was offered the role of a nurse but declined and chose to volunteer as a surgeon for the Union Army as a civilian. The U.S. Army had no female surgeons, and at first, she was allowed to practice only as a nurse.[3] During this period, she served at the First Battle of Bull Run (Manassas), July 21, 1861, and at the Patent Office Hospital in Washington, D.C. She worked as an unpaid field surgeon near the Union front lines, including at the Battle of Fredericksburg and in Chattanooga after the Battle of Chickamauga.[11] As a suffragist, she was happy to see women serving as soldiers, and alerted the press to the case of Frances Hook, in Ward 2 of the Chattanooga hospital, a woman who served in the Union forces disguised as a man.[12] Walker was the first female surgeon of the Union army.[11] She wore men's clothing during her work, claiming it to be easier for high demands of her work.[11]

In September 1862, Walker wrote to the War Department requesting employment as a spy, but her proposal was declined.[13] In September 1863, she was employed as a "Contract Acting Assistant Surgeon (civilian)" by the Army of the Cumberland, becoming the first female surgeon employed by the U.S. Army Surgeon.[14] Walker was later appointed assistant surgeon of the 52nd Ohio Infantry. During her service, she frequently crossed battle lines and treated civilians.

On April 10, 1864, she was captured by Confederate troops, and arrested as a spy, just after she finished helping a Confederate doctor perform an amputation. She was sent to Castle Thunder in Richmond, Virginia, and remained there until August 12, 1864, when she was released as part of a prisoner exchange.[15] While she was imprisoned, she refused to wear the clothes provided her, said to be more "becoming of her sex." Walker was exchanged for a Confederate surgeon from Tennessee on August 12, 1864.[4]

She went on to serve as supervisor of a female prison in Louisville, Kentucky, and as the head of an orphanage in Tennessee.[14]

## Later career

*Walker, c. 1870. She often wore masculine clothes.*

After the war, Walker was awarded a disability pension for partial muscular atrophy suffered while she was imprisoned by the enemy. She was given $8.50 a month, beginning June 13, 1865, but in 1899 that amount was raised to $20 per month.[16]

She became a writer and lecturer, supporting such issues as health care, temperance, women's rights, and dress reform for women. She was frequently arrested for wearing men's clothing, and insisted on her right to wear clothing that she thought appropriate.[17] She wrote two books that discussed women's rights and dress. She replied to criticism of her attire: "I don't wear men's clothes, I wear my own clothes."[18]

Walker was a member of the central woman's suffrage Bureau in Washington, and solicited funds to endow a chair for a female professor at Howard University medical school.[4] She attempted to register to vote in 1871, but was turned away. The initial stance of the movement, following her lead, was to claim that women already had the right to vote, and Congress needed only to enact enabling legislation. After a number of fruitless years advocating this position, the movement promoted the adoption of a constitutional amendment. This was diametrically opposed to her position, and she fell out of favor with the

movement. She continued to attend suffrage conventions and distribute her own literature, but was virtually ignored by the rest of the movement. Her penchant for wearing
masculine clothing, including a top hat, only exacerbated the situation.[14] She received a
more favorable reception in England than in the United States.[19]

In 1907, Walker published "Crowning Constitutional Argument," in which she argued
that some States, as well as the federal Constitution, had already granted women the
right to vote. She testified on women's suffrage before committees of the U.S. House of
Representatives in 1912 and 1914.

After a long illness, Walker died at home on February 21, 1919, at the age of eighty-six.
[20] She was buried at Rural Cemetery in Oswego, New York, in a plain funeral, with an
American flag draped over her casket, and wearing a black suit instead of a dress.[21] Her
death in 1919 came one year before the passage of the Nineteenth Amendment to the
United States Constitution, which guaranteed women the right to vote.[14]

## Honors and awards
### Medal of Honor

*Mary Edwards Walker, around 1911.*

After the war, Walker sought a retroactive
brevet or commission to validate her service.
President Johnson directed Secretary of War
Edwin Stanton to study the legality of the issue,
and he solicited an opinion from the Army's
Judge Advocate General, who determined that
there was no precedent for commissioning a
female, but that a "commendatory acknowledgment" could be issued in lieu of the commission. This led Johnson to personally award
the Medal of Honor as an alternative. Thus,
Walker was not formally recommended for the
Medal of Honor, and this unusual process may
also explain why authorities overlooked her
ineligibility, ironically on the grounds of lack-

ing a commission.[22]

In 1916, the U.S. Congress created a pension act for Medal of Honor recipients, and in
doing so created separate Army and Navy Medal of Honor Rolls. The Army was directed
to review eligibility of prior recipients in a separate bill not related to the pension rolls, but
which had been requested by the Army in order to retroactively police undesirable awards.
The undesirable awards resulted from the lack of regulations on the medal; the Army
had published no regulations until 1897, and the law had very few requirements, meaning
that recipients could earn a medal for virtually any reason, resulting in nearly 900 awards
for enlistment extensions not in combat. The Army's Medal of Honor Board deliberated from 1916 to 1917, and struck 911 names from the Army Medal of Honor Roll,

including those of Dr. Mary Edwards Walker and William F. "Buffalo Bill" Cody. Both were considered ineligible for the Army Medal of Honor because the 1862, 1863, and 1904 laws strictly required recipients to be officers or enlisted members. In Walker's case, she was a civilian contract surgeon, and was not a commissioned officer. Nevertheless, the Medal of Honor Board perhaps discriminated against Walker because it declined to revoke the Medal of at least two other contract surgeons who were equally ineligible. One of these was Major General Leonard Wood, a former Chief of Staff of the Army who was a civilian contract surgeon in the same status as Walker when he was recommended for the award. This was known to the Medal of Honor Board, as board president General Nelson Miles had twice recommended Wood's medal and knew that he was ineligible. The disenrolled recipients were not ordered to return their medals per a recommendation from the Army Judge Advocate General, who noted that Congress did not grant the Army the jurisdiction to enforce this provision of the statute, rendering both the repossession and criminal penalties inoperative.[23]

Although several sources attribute President Jimmy Carter with restoring Walker's medal posthumously in 1977, this is probably incorrect, since the action was taken well below the Secretary of the Army, at the level of the Army's Assistant Secretary for Manpower and Reserve Affairs, which was acting on a recommendation from the Board for Correction of Military Records. In fact, both the Ford and Carter Administrations opposed the restoration; the Carter White House reacted with confusion to the announcement of the Board's decision.[24] A recent historical work documented that the Board for Correction probably exceeded its authority in making a unilateral restoration of the medal, since the Board is merely a delegation of the authority of the Secretary of the Army, and thus cannot contradict a standing law much less a law that expressly required the revocation of Walker's medal. Therefore, the decision was controversial because it raised separation of powers issues; the Board's mandate was only to correct errors or injustices within its authority, not act against the authority of public law. This very point was illustrated by the awarding of Garlin Conner's Medal of Honor in early 2018, which also originated from the Board for Correction, but instead went through the President and required a statutory waiver from Congress—seen to be a requirement because the Board lacked the authority to contravene a public law and the associated statutes of limitations.[25]

Walker felt that she had been awarded the Medal of Honor because she had gone into enemy territory to care for the suffering inhabitants, when no man had the courage to do so, for fear of being imprisoned.[4]

## Attribution and citation

Rank and organization: Contract Acting Assistant Surgeon (civilian), U.S. Army. Places and dates: Battle of Bull Run, July 21, 1861; Patent Office Hospital, Washington, D.C., October 1861; Chattanooga, Tenn., following Battle of Chickamauga, September 1863; Prisoner of War, April 10, 1864–August 12, 1864, Richmond, Va.; Battle of Atlanta,

September 1864. Entered service at: Louisville, Ky. Born: 26 November 1832, Oswego County, N.Y.

## Citation:

Where as it appears from official reports that Dr. Mary E. Walker, a graduate of medicine, "has rendered valuable service to the Government, and her efforts have been earnest and untiring in a variety of ways," and that she was assigned to duty and served as an assistant surgeon in charge of female prisoners at Louisville, Ky., upon the recommendation of Major-Generals Sherman and Thomas, and faithfully served as contract surgeon in the service of the United States, and has devoted herself with much patriotic zeal to the sick and wounded soldiers, both in the field and hospitals, to the detriment of her own health, and has also endured hardships as a prisoner of war four months in a Southern prison while acting as contract surgeon; and Whereas by reason of her not being a commissioned officer in the military service, a brevet or honorary rank cannot, under existing laws, be conferred upon her; and Whereas in the opinion of the President an honorable recognition of her services and sufferings should be made.

It is ordered, That a testimonial thereof shall be hereby made and given to the said Dr. Mary E. Walker, and that the usual medal of honor for meritorious services be given her.[26]

# Alexander S. Webb

**Alexander Stewart Webb** (February 15, 1835–February 12, 1911)[1] was a career United States Army officer and a Union general in the American Civil War who received the Medal of Honor for gallantry at the Battle of Gettysburg. After the war, he was a prominent member of New York Society and served as president of the City College of New York for thirty-three years.

## Civil War

At the outbreak of the Civil War, Webb took part in the defense of Fort Pickens, Florida, was present at the First Battle of Bull Run, and was aide-de-camp to Brig. Gen. William F. Barry, the chief of artillery of the Army of the Potomac, from July 1861 to April 1862. During the Peninsula Campaign, he served as Gen. Barry's assistant inspector general and received recognition for his assembling an impregnable line of artillery defense during the Battle of Malvern Hill; Brig. Gen. Daniel Butterfield wrote that Webb saved the Union Army from destruction.[7]

During the Maryland Campaign and the Battle of Antietam, recently promoted to lieutenant colonel, he served as chief of staff in Maj. Gen. Fitz John Porter's V Corps. After Antietam, he was ordered to Washington, D.C., where he served as Inspector of Artillery. In January 1863 he was again assigned to the V Corps, now commanded by Maj. Gen. George G. Meade, and served again as chief of staff. During the Battle of Chancellorsville, Meade gave Webb temporary command of Brig. Gen. Erastus B. Tyler's brigade and thrust him into battle. He performed well and Meade in his report on the battle paid particular detail to Webb's "intelligence and zeal." On July 1, 1863, President Abraham Lincoln appointed Webb brigadier general, to rank from June 23, 1863.[8][9] Three days before the Battle of Gettysburg, Brig. Gen. John Gibbon arrested the Philadelphia Brigade's commander, Brig. Gen. Joshua T. Owen, and Webb was given command of the brigade (the 2nd Brigade, 2nd Division, II Corps). Initially, the brigade resented having the meticulously groomed and well-dressed Webb as their commanding officer, but he soon earned their respect through his attention to detail, his affability, and his discipline.[6]

## Gettysburg

When the Union Army repulsed the Confederates at Cemetery Hill, General Webb played a central role in the battle. Coddington[10] wrote about Webb's conduct during Pickett's Charge: "Refusing to give up, [Webb] set an example of bravery and undaunted leadership for his men to follow . . . ." Webb's brigade was posted on Cemetery Ridge with the rest of the II Corps on the morning of July 2, 1863. The brigade repulsed the assault of Brig.

Gen. Ambrose R. Wright's brigade of Georgians as it topped the ridge late in the afternoon, chasing the Confederates back as far as the Emmitsburg Road, where they captured about 300 men and reclaimed a Union battery. Soon after, Webb sent two regiments to assist in counterattacking the assault of Maj. Gen. Jubal A. Early's division on Cemetery Hill.[11]

On July 3, Webb's brigade happened to be in the center of the Union line to defend against Pickett's Charge, in front of the famous "Copse of Trees." As the Confederates launched a massive artillery barrage to prepare for their infantry assault, Webb made himself conspicuous to his men, many of whom were unfamiliar with their new commander. He stood in front of the line and leaned on his sword, puffing leisurely on a cigar while cannonballs whistled by and shells exploded all around. Although his men shouted at him to take shelter, he refused and impressed many with his personal bravery. As Maj. Gen. George Pickett's Virginia division approached to within a few yards, two companies of Webb's 71st Pennsylvania fell back, and Webb feared the personal disgrace and the results of a breakthrough in his line. He shouted to his neighboring 72nd Pennsylvania to charge, but they refused to budge. He attempted to grab their regimental colors and go forward with them himself, but apparently the standard bearer did not recognize him, because he fought Webb for the colors before he went down, shot numerous times. Webb ultimately gave up on the 72nd and strode directly in front of the chaos as Brig. Gen. Lewis Armistead's Confederate brigade breached the low stone wall, over to his 69th Pennsylvania regiment. Webb was wounded in his thigh and groin by a bullet, but kept going. With the help of two of Col. Norman J. Hall's New York regiments, and Brig. Gen. William Harrow's men, who ran over in a mass to get in their shots, Webb and his men brought the Confederate assault to a standstill, inflicting heavy casualties.[11]

Webb received the Medal of Honor on September 28, 1891, for "distinguished personal gallantry in leading his men forward at a critical period in the contest" at Gettysburg on July 3, 1863. President Lincoln nominated Webb for appointment to the brevet grade of major general of volunteers for his service at Gettysburg, to rank from August 1, 1864, and the U.S. Senate confirmed the appointment on February 14, 1865.[12]

### Later in the war

After Gettysburg, Webb received command of the division six weeks later and led it through the fall campaigns. His division played a prominent role in the Battle of Bristoe Station. When Gibbon returned to command in the spring of 1864, Webb went back to brigade command for the Overland Campaign. At the Battle of Spotsylvania Court House, in May, he was hit by a bullet that passed through the corner of his right eye and came out his ear, but did not impair his mental abilities. The wound resulted in a false report that he had been killed and his death was reported in the *New York Times* on May 9.[13]

He returned to the army on January 11, 1865, and was chief of staff of the Army of the Potomac from that date until June 28, 1865.[14] Webb was the assistant inspector general of the Military Division of the Atlantic between July 1, 1865, and February 21, 1866.[14] Webb was mustered out of the volunteer force on January 15, 1866.[14]

On April 10, 1866, President Andrew Johnson nominated Webb for appointment to the brevet grade of brigadier general, USA (regular army), to rank from March 13, 1865, and the U.S. Senate confirmed the appointment on May 4, 1866.[15] On December 11, 1866, President Andrew Johnson nominated Webb for appointment to the brevet grade of major general, USA (regular army), to rank from March 13, 1865, and the U.S. Senate confirmed the appointment February 23, 1867, recalled the confirmation on February 25, 1867, and reconfirmed it on March 2, 1867.[16]

## Postbellum life

General Webb stayed with the Army until 1870, assigned as a lieutenant colonel to the 44th U.S. Infantry Regiment, July 28, 1866, and the 5th U.S. Infantry Regiment, March 15, 1869.[14] He became unassigned, March 24, 1869.[14] During his final year, he served again as an instructor at West Point. He was discharged on December 5, 1870, with the final permanent rank of lieutenant colonel.[14]

From 1869 to 1902, General Webb served as the second president of the City College of New York, succeeding Horace Webster, also a West Point graduate.[1] The College's curriculum under Webster and Webb combined classical training in Latin and Greek with more practical subjects like chemistry, physics, and engineering.

General Webb was an early companion of the New York Commandery of the Military Order of the Loyal Legion of the United States, being elected on March 18, 1866. He was a founder and first Commander General of the Military Order of Foreign Wars in 1894. He was also an honorary member of the New York Society of the Cincinnati.[6]

Webb died in Riverdale, New York, on February 12, 1911.[1] He is buried in West Point National Cemetery.[36] A statue of General Webb was dedicated in the Gettysburg National Military Park in 1915.[37]

# Cathay Williams

**Cathay Williams** (September 1844–1893) was an American soldier who enlisted in the United States Army under the pseudonym William Cathay. She was the first African-American woman to enlist, and the only documented to serve in the United States Army posing as a man.[1]

## Early life

Williams was born in Independence, Missouri, to a free man and a woman in slavery, making her legal status also that of a slave. During her adolescence, Williams worked as a house slave on the Johnson plantation on the outskirts of Jefferson City, Missouri. In 1861 Union forces occupied Jefferson City in the early stages of the Civil War. At that time, captured slaves were officially designated by the Union as "contraband," and many were forced to serve in military support roles such as cooks, laundresses, or nurses.

*Painting of Cathay Williams by William Jennings from the U.S. Army Profiles of Bravery*

## American Civil War

For the next few years, it is alleged that Williams traveled with the army as a soldier on marches through Arkansas, Louisiana, and Georgia. It is possible that Cathay Williams was present at the Battle of Pea Ridge and the Red River Campaign. There is no evidence, however, that supports any claims to her service in the Civil War, although a soldier named "Finis Cathay" did enlist in the 32nd Missouri Infantry as early as 1862 and participated in most of the major campaigns in the west, including the siege of Vicksburg and Sherman's March to the Sea, before helping to force Joseph E. Johnston's last Confederate army into surrender in North Carolina. This unit's history parallels many of the wartime stories told of Cathay Williams, including its presence in Washington, D.C., at the final Grand Review on May 24, 1865. [2]

## U.S. Army service

Despite the prohibition against women serving in the military, Cathay Williams enlisted in the United States Regular Army under the false name of "William Cathay"[3] on November 15, 1866, at St. Louis, Missouri, for a three-year engagement, passing herself off as a man. She was assigned to the 38th United States Infantry Regiment after she passed a cursory medical examination.[3] Only two others are known to have been privy to the deception, her cousin and a friend, both of whom were fellow soldiers in her regiment.

Shortly after her enlistment, Williams contracted smallpox, was hospitalized and rejoined her unit, which by then was posted in New Mexico. Possibly due to the effects of smallpox, the New Mexico heat, or the cumulative effects of years of marching, her body began to show signs of strain. She was frequently hospitalized. The post surgeon finally discovered she was a woman, and informed the post commander. She was discharged from the Army by her commanding officer, Captain Charles E. Clarke, on October 14, 1868.

## Post-military service years

Cathay Williams went to work as a cook at Fort Union, New Mexico, and later moved to Pueblo, Colorado. Williams married, but it ended disastrously when her husband stole her money and a team of horses. Williams had him arrested. She next moved to Trinidad, Colorado, where she made her living as a seamstress. She may also have owned a boarding house. It was at this time that Williams' story first became public. A reporter from St. Louis heard rumors of an African-American woman who had served in the army, and came to interview her. Her life and military service narrative was published in *The St. Louis Daily Times* on January 2, 1876.

In late 1889 or early 1890, Cathay Williams entered a local hospital where she remained for some time, and in June 1891, applied for a disability pension based on her military service. The nature of her illness and disability are unknown. There was precedent for granting a pension to female soldiers. Deborah Sampson in 1816, Anna Maria Lane, and Mary Hayes McCauley (better known as Molly Pitcher) had been granted pensions for their service in the American Revolutionary War.

## Declining health and death

In September 1893, a doctor employed by the U.S. Pension Bureau examined Cathay Williams. Despite the fact that she suffered from neuralgia and diabetes, she had all her toes amputated, and could only walk with a crutch, the doctor decided she did not qualify for disability payments. Her application was rejected.[4][5]

The exact date of Williams' death is unknown, but it is assumed she died shortly after being denied a pension, probably sometime in 1893. Her simple grave marker would have been made of wood and deteriorated long ago. Thus her final resting place is now unknown.

# Wikipedia Credits—List of Article URLs

| | |
|---|---|
| William T Anderson | https://en.wikipedia.org/wiki/William_T._Anderson |
| Clara Barton | https://en.wikipedia.org/wiki/Clara_Barton |
| P.G.T. Beauregard | https://en.wikipedia.org/wiki/P._G._T._Beauregard |
| Judah P. Benjamin | https://en.wikipedia.org/wiki/Judah_P._Benjamin |
| Ambrose Bierce | https://en.wikipedia.org/wiki/Ambrose_Bierce |
| Malinda Blalock | https://en.wikipedia.org/wiki/Malinda_Blalock |
| John Wilkes Booth | https://en.wikipedia.org/wiki/John_Wilkes_Booth |
| Mary Bowser | https://en.wikipedia.org/wiki/Mary_Bowser |
| Belle Boyd | https://en.wikipedia.org/wiki/Belle_Boyd |
| Mathew Brady | https://en.wikipedia.org/wiki/Mathew_Brady |
| Braxton Bragg | https://en.wikipedia.org/wiki/Braxton_Bragg |
| John Brown | https://en.wikipedia.org/wiki/John_Brown_(abolitionist) |
| Ambrose Burnside | https://en.wikipedia.org/wiki/Ambrose_Burnside |
| William Harvey Carney | https://en.wikipedia.org/wiki/William_Harvey_Carney |
| Albert Cashier | https://en.wikipedia.org/wiki/Albert_Cashier |
| Joshua Chamberlain | https://en.wikipedia.org/wiki/Joshua_Chamberlain |
| Alonzo Cushing | https://en.wikipedia.org/wiki/Alonzo_Cushing |
| Pauline Cushman | https://en.wikipedia.org/wiki/Pauline_Cushman |
| Jefferson Davis | https://en.wikipedia.org/wiki/Jefferson_Davis |
| Martin Delany | https://en.wikipedia.org/wiki/Martin_Delany |
| Abner Doubleday | https://en.wikipedia.org/wiki/Abner_Doubleday |
| Frederick Douglass | https://en.wikipedia.org/wiki/Frederick_Douglass |
| Lewis Henry Douglass | https://en.wikipedia.org/wiki/Lewis_Henry_Douglass |
| Sarah Edmonds | https://en.wikipedia.org/wiki/Sarah_Emma_Edmonds |
| Anna Etheridge | https://en.wikipedia.org/wiki/Anna_Etheridge |
| David Farragut | https://en.wikipedia.org/wiki/David_Farragut |
| Nathan Bedford Forrest | https://en.wikipedia.org/wiki/Nathan_Bedford_Forrest |
| Ulysses S. Grant | https://en.wikipedia.org/wiki/Ulysses_S._Grant |
| Rose O'Neal Greenhow | https://en.wikipedia.org/wiki/Rose_O%27Neal_Greenhow |
| Winfield Scott Hancock | https://en.wikipedia.org/wiki/Winfield_Scott_Hancock |
| David Herold | https://en.wikipedia.org/wiki/David_Herold |
| A.P. Hill | https://en.wikipedia.org/wiki/A._P._Hill |
| John Bell Hood | https://en.wikipedia.org/wiki/John_Bell_Hood |
| Joseph Hooker | https://en.wikipedia.org/wiki/Joseph_Hooker |
| Stonewall Jackson | https://en.wikipedia.org/wiki/Stonewall_Jackson |
| Harriet Ann Jacobs | https://en.wikipedia.org/wiki/Harriet_Ann_Jacobs |
| Andrew Johnson | https://en.wikipedia.org/wiki/Andrew_Johnson |
| Joseph E. Johnston | https://en.wikipedia.org/wiki/Joseph_E._Johnston |
| Robert E. Lee | https://en.wikipedia.org/wiki/Robert_E._Lee |
| James Lewis | https://en.wikipedia.org/wiki/James_Lewis_(Louisiana_politician) |
| Maria Lewis | https://en.wikipedia.org/wiki/Maria_Lewis_(soldier) |
| Abraham Lincoln | https://en.wikipedia.org/wiki/Abraham_Lincoln |
| James Longstreet | https://en.wikipedia.org/wiki/James_Longstreet |

| | |
|---|---|
| George B. McClellan | https://en.wikipedia.org/wiki/George_B._McClellan |
| Ben McCulloch | https://en.wikipedia.org/wiki/Benjamin_McCulloch |
| Wilmer McLean | https://en.wikipedia.org/wiki/Wilmer_McLean |
| George Meade | https://en.wikipedia.org/wiki/George_Meade |
| John S. Mosby | https://en.wikipedia.org/wiki/John_S._Mosby |
| Samuel Mudd | https://en.wikipedia.org/wiki/Samuel_Mudd |
| John Frederick Parker | https://en.wikipedia.org/wiki/John_Frederick_Parker |
| J. Johnston Pettigrew | https://en.wikipedia.org/wiki/J._Johnston_Pettigrew |
| George Pickett | https://en.wikipedia.org/wiki/George_Pickett |
| Leonidas Polk | https://en.wikipedia.org/wiki/Leonidas_Polk |
| David Dixon Porter | https://en.wikipedia.org/wiki/David_Dixon_Porter |
| Lewis Powell | https://en.wikipedia.org/wiki/Lewis_Powell_(conspirator) |
| William Quantrill | https://en.wikipedia.org/wiki/William_Quantrill |
| Henry Rathbone | https://en.wikipedia.org/wiki/Henry_Rathbone |
| William H. Seward | https://en.wikipedia.org/wiki/William_H._Seward |
| Robert Gould Shaw | https://en.wikipedia.org/wiki/Robert_Gould_Shaw |
| Philip Sheridan | https://en.wikipedia.org/wiki/Philip_Sheridan |
| William Tecumseh Sherman | https://en.wikipedia.org/wiki/William_Tecumseh_Sherman |
| Robert Smalls | https://en.wikipedia.org/wiki/Robert_Smalls |
| Edwin Stanton | https://en.wikipedia.org/wiki/Edwin_Stanton |
| Harriet Beecher Stowe | https://en.wikipedia.org/wiki/Harriet_Beecher_Stowe |
| J .E. B. Stuart | https://en.wikipedia.org/wiki/J._E._B._Stuart |
| John Surratt | https://en.wikipedia.org/wiki/John_Surratt |
| Mary Surratt | https://en.wikipedia.org/wiki/Mary_Surratt |
| George Henry Thomas | https://en.wikipedia.org/wiki/George_Henry_Thomas |
| Harriet Tubman | https://en.wikipedia.org/wiki/Harriet_Tubman |
| Elizabeth Van Lew | https://en.wikipedia.org/wiki/Elizabeth_Van_Lew |
| Loreta Janeta Velázquez | https://en.wikipedia.org/wiki/Loreta_Janeta_Vel%C3%A1zquez |
| James Iredell Waddell | https://en.wikipedia.org/wiki/James_Iredell_Waddell |
| Mary Edwards Walker | https://en.wikipedia.org/wiki/Mary_Edwards_Walker |
| Alexander S. Webb | https://en.wikipedia.org/wiki/Alexander_S._Webb |
| Cathay Williams | https://en.wikipedia.org/wiki/Cathay_Williams |